Critics across America acclaim "A People's History"

"This People's History is a celebration."　　　—*The New York Times Book Review*

"Readers are sure to be rewarded. . . . Smith's multi-volume story of who we Americans are and how we came to be is an admirable project."
　　　　　　　　　　　　　　　　　　　　—*The Washington Post Book World*

"Engrossing narrative history . . . bound to invigorate and instruct . . . Amazing in its sweep and scope"　　　　　　　—*Chicago Sun-Times*

"Popular history set down with the candor of a maturing New Journalism"
　　　　　　　　　　　　　　　　　　　　　　　　—*Publishers Weekly*

"Smith's achievement is truly remarkable. No American historian since Charles Beard has produced anything comparable in length, scope, or readability. To find standards with which to judge this work we must go back to 19th-century masters like George Bancroft, Francis Parkman, and Henry Adams."　　　　　　　　　　　—*San Francisco Chronicle Book Review*

"A remarkable achievement in the writing of popular history"
　　　　　　　　　　　　　　　　　　　　　　—*Dallas Times Herald*

"The individual characters' lives Smith dramatizes truly live."　—*Miami Herald*

"Distinguished . . . Belongs on the shelves of anyone who wants to understand where we've been, so he can form a more educated opinion on where we're going."　　　　　　　　　　　　　　　　　—*Milwaukee Journal*

"Smith brings to his work not only a clear and thorough knowledge of his subject, but a literary elegance rarely found among today's scholars."
　　　　　　　　　　　　　　　　　　　　　—*The Boston Sunday Globe*

"The author's great gift lies in his unerring eye for the evocative or perceptive quotation that opens for the reader a view of the times as seen by the women and men living in them."　　　　　　　　—*The Philadelphia Inquirer*

"Smith writes as a lover loves—from the heart. . . . Not since the 19th century has an American historian written so extensively and passionately about his country."　　　　　　　　　　　—*Los Angeles Times Book Review*

For Samuel Eliot Morison,
Master of the art of narrative history

PENGUIN BOOKS

A NEW AGE NOW BEGINS

Page Smith was educated at the Gilman School in Baltimore, Dartmouth College, and Harvard University. He has served as research associate at the Institute of Early American History and Culture, and has taught at the University of California at Los Angeles and at Santa Cruz, where he makes his home. Dr. Smith is the author of numerous books, including the highly acclaimed two-volume biography *John Adams,* which was a Main Selection of the Book-of-the-Month Club, a National Book Award nominee, and a Bancroft winner; *The Historian and History; The Constitution: A Documentary and Narrative History; Daughters of the Promised Land: Women in American History;* and *Jefferson: A Revealing Biography.* His People's History series consists of the following volumes: *A New Age Now Begins: A People's History of the American Revolution* (two volumes); *The Shaping of America: A People's History of the Young Republic* (an American Book Award nominee); *The Nation Comes of Age: A People's History of the Ante-Bellum Years; Trial by Fire: A People's History of the Civil War and Reconstruction; The Rise of Industrial America: A People's History of the Post-Reconstruction Era; America Enters the World: A People's History of the Progressive Era and World War I;* and *Redeeming the Time: A People's History of the 1920s and The New Deal.* He is also coauthor, with Charles Daniel, of *The Chicken Book.*

A
PEOPLE'S
HISTORY
OF THE
AMERICAN
REVOLUTION

A NEW AGE NOW BEGINS

Page Smith

VOLUME ONE

PENGUIN BOOKS

PENGUIN BOOKS
Published by the Penguin Group
Viking Penguin, a division of Penguin Books USA Inc.,
40 West 23rd Street, New York, New York 10010, U.S.A.
Penguin Books Ltd, 27 Wrights Lane,
London W8 5TZ, England
Penguin Books Australia Ltd, Ringwood,
Victoria, Australia
Penguin Books Canada Ltd, 2801 John Street,
Markham, Ontario, Canada L3R 1B4
Penguin Books (N.Z.) Ltd, 182–190 Wairau Road,
Auckland 10, New Zealand

Penguin Books Ltd, Registered Offices:
Harmondsworth, Middlesex, England

First published in the United States of America by
McGraw-Hill Book Company 1976
Reprinted by arrangement with McGraw-Hill, Inc.
Published in Penguin Books 1989

10 9 8 7 6 5 4 3 2 1

Half-title page: Great Seal of the United States, reverse side.
Courtesy of the Library of Congress #44633/2784.

LIBRARY OF CONGRESS CATALOGING IN PUBLICATION DATA
Smith, Page.
A new age now begins: a people's history of the American
Revolution/ Page Smith.
p. cm.
Reprint. Originally published: New York: McGraw-Hill, c1976.
Bibliography:
Includes index.
ISBN 0 14 01.2253 2 (v. 1)
1. United States—History—Revolution, 1775-1783.   2. United
States—History—Revolution, 1775-1783—Campaigns.   I. Title.
E208.S67   1989
973.3—dc19   89–2910

Printed in the United States of America
Set in Baskerville

CONTENTS

VOLUME ONE

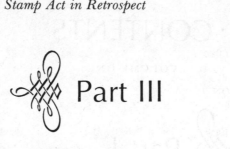

Part III

Part IV

Part V

Part VI

List of Maps

A

NEW

AGE

NOW

BEGINS

INTRODUCTION

THE American Revolution initiated what one historian has called "the Age of Democratic Revolutions," a series of episodes of vast historical moment that changed the world in profound ways. It had two progenitors: the English Civil War of 1640–60, in which the king, Charles I, was overthrown and beheaded, and Parliament ruled the country supported by Oliver Cromwell's Puritan legions; and the Glorious Revolution of 1688–89, which consolidated the legitimate gains of the Civil War. The Glorious Revolution was brief and virtually bloodless. James II was deposed for his Catholicism and his tendency toward arbitrary rule, and William and Mary, monarchs of the German principality of Orange, were brought in to succeed him. The price paid by the new monarchs was the so-called Revolution Settlement, in which the king accepted provisions guaranteeing the rights of Englishmen under the law (the Bill of Rights) and limiting his own powers to those of a constitutional monarch.

If the American Revolution traced its ancestry back to seventeenth-century England, it, in turn, may be said to have produced a lusty, indeed violent progeny: the French Revolution, which began in 1789 (the same year that saw the beginnings of a national government in the United States under the Federal Constitution) and continued intermittently for almost a hundred years; the Russian Revolution, which transformed a semifeudal empire into a modern nation; and the Chinese Revolution, a vast upheaval whose nature and consequences are only faintly perceived at present. In addition, dozens of lesser uprisings against injustice or tyrannical governments have invoked the American Revolution as their inspiration.

Toward the end of the Revolution, Congress prescribed for the reverse side of the Great Seal of the United States a phrase from the great Roman poet, Virgil: *Novus Ordo Seclorum* ("a new age now begins").

1

That was their ambition, not merely to free themselves from a situation of dependence and subordination that had become unsupportable to them, but to initiate "a new age" in which people in every part of the globe would be encouraged by the example of the American colonists to fight for freedom and independence and, in the process, to create agencies of government and forms of common social life that would give greater dignity and hope to masses of humanity that had for so long been suppressed and exploited.

The American Revolution culminated in a constitution that has proved a remarkably flexible and enduring document, the prototype for many other frames of government and presently the oldest of all written constitutions.

John Adams, one of the patriot leaders, wrote years afterward that the Revolution had started long before Lexington and Concord; that it had taken place in the hearts and minds of the American people, and only then, when it had taken its essential form, had it manifested itself in revolutionary action. This certainly is a basic assumption of this work. The chapters that follow are an effort to understand and trace, however imperfectly, the growth and development of those aspects of life in the English colonies of North America that produced that strange hybrid called, eventually, an American.

In distinction from most revolutions, the radical phase of the American variety came first, at that moment when the authority of Parliament was first called into serious question as a consequence of the passage of the Stamp Act. In that instant it was revealed for all who had wit to see (and many certainly did not) that the American colonists had in some mysterious way come of an age when they were no longer willing to have their affairs decided for them by a remote government some three thousand miles away. The fury of the colonists' reaction to the Stamp Act startled American patriot leaders almost as much as it did the British Ministry. In the face of the threat of rebellion and anarchy, the more responsible patriots undertook to temper the passions of their followers and educate them in the principles of government under law. Thus the "Revolution" grew more moderate as it approached its climax—the armed clash at Lexington and Concord.

What followed was a long and exhausting war, a war of attrition on the British side, an effort to wear down and finally exhaust the Americans by force of superior arms, better-trained, better-equipped, and better-led soldiers, more guns and gun powder, more money, more ships and sailors, more experience in warfare; by more guile at the council table; by the raids of Indian auxiliaries against an unprotected frontier; by the destruction of coastal towns; by all the vast resources at the command of the greatest imperial power in the world.

For the Americans, it was a matter of simple endurance. They had only to endure to be independent, and endure they did—but at the cost of infinite suffering and hardship, at the cost of many lives and much property, at the cost of much bitterness between patriot and Tory neighbors, between sons and fathers, friends and relatives. When a revolution becomes an item in a textbook, it is difficult to preserve a sense of its human reality: its terrors and alarms, the constant anxieties, the fear and despair that are the inevitable accompaniments of such upheavals.

We know the famous battles. We learned them in school by a kind of thoughtless rote, perhaps even resentfully. When was the Battle of Bunker Hill? Who commanded the British army at Yorktown? Who won the Battle of Brandywine? Where did Washington surprise and capture a Prussian force? The very questions intervene between us and the reality of these names—names describing battles in which men died, often painfully and horribly, or suffered desperate wounds, went hungry, sweated with fear. No historian can recapture the full reality of those events. Perhaps not even the participants could absorb or bear the reality. But it is the virtue of narrative history that it at least endeavors to carry the reader into the events themselves, so that he or she is, in however modest a degree, stirred by the same emotions, the same hopes and fears, as the long-dead actors in the particular historical drama in view.

Even the famous battles, when seen in the intimate perspective of the individual soldier, take on a new significance and power. In addition, the reader will here discover innumerable minor engagements that are often as full of human drama as the great set pieces of historical literature, and that, in sum, may well outweigh in importance the more spectacular clashes so familiar to readers; this because they reveal that the Revolution was less a story of contending armies than of ordinary citizens determined to be free.

It has been our ambition to open before the reader the remarkable and inexhaustible volume of history itself, a tale of extraordinary richness and variety, not the creation in any sense of the historian but merely the consequence of his desire to set down, as directly as possible, a narrative of the events—a narrative full of surprises, of dramatic adventures, defeats, victories; of words, speeches, newspapers, letters, diaries, journals, and public documents.

While armies maneuvered and scattered militia units rallied to defend their homes, while warships engaged each other and privateers went their stealthy ways, the delegates to the Continental Congress spent long, weary, and often fruitless hours debating how to supply the Continental forces with food, uniforms, guns, and munitions; how to effect alliances with France or Holland; how to deal with internal subversion or to discourage desertion. Inept as it often was, the Continental Congress managed to constitute a government of a kind and to function throughout most of the Revolution without a constitution to guide its steps. The deliberations of that body are an essential part of the story of the Revolution.

In a certain sense everything fell back on the states themselves. They had enormous problems to contend with: British armies, Tory irregulars, underpaid and usually unpaid militia forces, Continental levees (troop requisitions) to fill up, new constitutions to draft, and always and always, mouths to feed and refugees to provide for. Their crucial role must be acknowledged.

It is also a major thesis of this work that the Revolution cannot possibly be understood without attention to the British side, not simply the British army and its officers, but the British government—that obstinate king, George III; his pliant minister, Lord North, and North's Tory backers; the great Whigs, friends of the American cause who saw that cause as their own and called Washington's army "our army" and applauded its victories. And the English people themselves—from Lord Effingham, who resigned his cherished commission rather than help to extinguish liberty in America, to the merchants, divided in sentiment; to the respected Quaker, Dr. Frothingham, who tried to intercede with the king to persuade him to take a more moderate line with the Americans; to John Wesley, the founder of Methodism, who warned Lord North, in truly prophetic words, of the fatal results of his colonial policy; to the common man, the man at the bottom of the British heap, who often felt closer to the American colonists than to those Englishmen on top of him, pushing him down and holding him down like some enormous weight. He frequently refused to enlist when appealed to, and when conscripted and shipped off to America, he deserted at the first opportunity.

And then there were the Hessians, unwilling soldiers in a war that was of no concern to them. Perhaps of all those who fought in the Revolution, they are most to be pitied. Speaking a strange language, condescended to by the British, given the dirty military jobs, hated by the Americans as foreign mercenaries, they nonetheless fought with the pride of professional soldiers and often died for no better purpose than to make a few pounds for the German princes who had rented them out.

The military campaigns were, of course, the pivots around which the entire Revolution revolved. The rival armies were not just military units performing prescribed maneuvers ill or well; they were projections of the societies in whose names they fought, and the battles in which they engaged have thus to be read in a social and cultural dimension as well as a military one. Burgoyne's invasion from Canada was defeated less as the result of the superior strategy of the Americans than because the invaders drowned in a sea of New England militiamen—armed peasants, in modern parlance. These men might be reluctant to enlist in the Continental Army for the duration of the war, but they had no hesitation about defending their own hearths.

Because Washington was such a compelling figure, most accounts of the Revolution focus very largely on the campaigns in which he and his troops were involved. The result has been a considerable distortion of what one historian has called "the War of the Revolution." In practical fact, it could be argued that the far less well-known campaigns of the Southern Department were every bit as important as those engaged in by Washington's Continentals. Washington's army fought in no major battles from the Battle of Monmouth in June, 1778, to Yorktown in October, 1781, more than three years later. Meanwhile, a succession of American generals, starting with Robert Howe and running through Horatio Gates to Nathanael Greene, the most skilled of the American general officers, fought a series of protracted campaigns, primarily in the Carolinas. We have tried here to restore a proper balance between the campaigns in the South and the more familiar ones that took place north of Mason and Dixon's line.

Somewhat the same could be said of the war in the West, whose most spectacular figure was George Rogers Clark. This was, in a sense, almost a separate war. Yet it, too, was full of dramatic engagements, and its outcome had enormous importance for the future of the new United States. The frontier fighting is perhaps less important from the military point of view than for what it reveals about the temperament of the frontier settlers, who constituted such a colorful and consequential element in the evolving American character.

Like the frontier war, the naval warfare of the Revolution, except for the famous engagement between the *Serapis* and the *Bonhomme Richard*, is usually rather dimly perceived. In fact, it involved *in toto* as many men as the land battles, but these were scattered in thousands of ships and hundreds of armed encounters over all the western oceans, from the Caribbean to the Grand Bank of Newfoundland, and from the Strait of Gibraltar to the North Sea. Some were as modest as a few armed men in a fishing skiff; others were classic engagements between heavily armed frigates. Although most of them were in themselves insignificant, they again weighed heavily in the ultimate equation that sums up the Revolutionary struggle. Indeed, they had a special significance, for Americans from the first considered themselves a seagoing people, and while the naval warfare, conducted primarily by privateers, was largely a stand-off, a stand-off was no small achievement for Americans fighting against the ships of the greatest maritime power in the world.

It is, then, the aim of this work to be a narrative account of how the inhabitants of thirteen heterogeneous and diverse colonies, stretched out along a thousand miles of coastline, became a single people—Americans. And how they did this, first in the quiet growing of farms and towns and seacoast cities, and then, to everyone's astonishment, in the fiery crucible of war and revolution. In telling this story, I wish to restore to our general knowledge of the events of the Revolutionary War itself a better sense of proportion, an awareness of how disparate things related to each other and how, finally, a whole was created—the United States of America.

Because I believe that the past, present, and future are indissolubly joined together, I have, throughout the writing of this work, been very conscious of the present situation and the future prospects of this nation, born in the travail of an earlier revolution. That is not to say that I have consciously bent or warped my account of the Revolution to fit modern notions: it is rather that the events of my own time have opened my eyes to aspects of the American Revolution that I would otherwise have been unaware of. This is always true of the study of history. We search it for lessons to apply to the problems and dilemmas of an often precarious present; we look to it for instruction as to how we may create a better future, as those before us did for us and as we must do for our children, for, as the Founding Fathers liked to put it, "millions yet unborn."

We live today in a period of considerable doubt and uncertainty. I sense among many Americans a general confusion about the meaning of our past and the relevance of some of our most cherished traditions to the particular urgencies of the moment.

The times we live in are extraordinary times, "interesting times" in the true sense of the ancient Chinese curse: "May you live in interesting times." The times are more than interesting; they are perilous and profoundly instructive. We cannot turn to Clio, the muse of history, confident that she will infallibly instruct us in the meaning of our present troubles or reveal to us a proper course of action; her Delphic voice is clearly ambiguous. But turn to her we must, and the particular history we turn to here is that history a proper understanding of which is so crucial to our understanding of ourselves—the history of our Revolutionary origins; that history, indeed, which is the only common resource upon which we can and must all draw if we are to heal the divisions of our nation and have a reasonable prospect of creating a humane future, not only for Americans, but for all the people who inhabit this greatly diminished globe.

I am thus disposed to argue that there is a happy coincidence between the two-hundredth anniversary of the Declaration of Independence and our present need to review thoughtfully the events that led to our birth as a nation.

In addition to the particular significance of the events of the Revolutionary era for Americans today, there are, inextricably intertwined with these events, the lives of those men we denominate "the Founding Fathers." It is they, indeed, who in large part created and shaped the events. To the degree that their lives and thoughts are relevant today, they exist as much in our future as in our past. They may for a fact exert more influence on us than our own contemporaries. In a sense, it could be said that it is our obligation to create a future in which they will be at home. Put another way, they, through us, already exist in that future and beckon to us to join them there. Jacques Amyot, translator of Plutarch's great *Lives,* wrote in his introduction: "An history is an orderly register of notable things said, done, or happened in time past, to maintain the continual remembrance of them, and to serve for the instruction of them to come. . . ." The American Revolution, to a peculiar degree, furnishes us, in Amyot's words, "with examples of men of high courage and wisdom, [who] . . . have willingly yielded their lives to the service of the commonweal, spent their goods, sustained infinite pains both of body and mind in defence of the oppressed, in making common buildings, in stablishing of laws and governments, and in the finding out of arts and sciences necessary for the maintenance and ornament of man's life."

It could be said of history generally what Sir Thomas North said of Plutarch: "All other learning is private, fitter for universities than cities, fuller of contemplation than experience, more commendable in the students themselves than profitable unto others. Whereas stories are fit for every place, reach all persons, serve for all time, teach the living, revive the dead . . . as it is better to see learning in noble men's lives than to read it in philosopher's writings."

In a lyceum address given by Abraham Lincoln in 1838, the President-to-be spoke of the meaning of the American Revolution. Although he hoped that "the scenes of the Revolution . . . will be read of and recounted, as long as the Bible shall be read," they could not "be so universally known nor so vividly felt as they were by the generation just gone to rest." What that generation had known at first hand, it remained for future generations to retrieve. The heroes of the Revolution were "pillars of the temple of liberty; and now that they have crumbled away that temple must fall unless we, their descendants, supply their places with other pillars, hewn from the solid quarry of sober reason." The experiences of the Revolutionary generation must "be molded into general intelligence, sound morality, and, in particular, a reverence for the Constitution and laws," Lincoln declared. The events of our times pose new problems and questions for us. We thus turn to the past with different questions to ask of Clio, the muse of history, than those asked in Lincoln's day. By the same token, the events of our own time open our eyes to aspects of our past to which we were formerly blind. In order for the American Revolution to be once more a potent force in our thinking and in our lives, in creating our common future, that remarkable story must be retold in light of the urgencies and crises of the present.

The basic conclusions of these volumes may be summarized as follows: The American Revolution is still a potentially vital force in our national life and in our future and the future of the human race; the Revolution was not the work of a few middle-class radical intellectuals like Sam Adams and John Hancock; nor was it the consequence of a quarrel over the profits from the colonial trade. It was a profound popular movement of a people, or a substantial portion of those people, against the state of dependence and subordination in which they found themselves in relation to the mother country. In the long struggle that resulted from the effort of Americans to be masters of their own destinies, a new understanding of the relations between the governors and the governed developed, a new sense of the potentialities that lay in ordinary men and women, a new appreciation of possibilities of a better life for people in every continent and every nation.

I trust the reader will discover, as I have, innumerable interesting and absorbing details in this great story, and come away from it with a fresh sense of obligations that we lie under as the heirs of this remarkable event, which, as much as any other episode, began the transformation of the modern world. If we can understand our proper relation to the American Revolution, I believe we will be much better able to cope with the often demoralizing and confusing world in which we live today.

PART I

A New World

O<small>N</small> the nineteenth of April, 1775, a British expeditionary force under Sir Hugh Percy was fighting its way from Concord back to Boston, harassed at every step by New England militia and, indeed, by every farmer with a gun, who fired at them from the houses that lined the road and from behind the tree stumps and fences along the dusty road to the city. The British, as every schoolboy knows, were retreating from a raid, hot and weary and badly frightened. Every mile was paid for in British dead and wounded. The fire from the houses was especially galling to the retreating redcoats.

Flanking parties of British soldiers were dispatched to rout out their tormentors. In the words of one British officer, "They (the Americans) suffered for their temerity for all that were found in the houses were put to death." He might have added, "indiscriminately." At the Jason Russell house near the town of Arlington, eight American militiamen from another nearby settlement, Danvers, opened fire on the British. A flanking party commanded by Lieutenant Frederick Mackenzie of the Royal Welsh Fusiliers was sent to the house. Russell, the owner, who was crippled, was shot in the doorway as he tried to escape, and seven of the defenders were quickly shot or bayoneted. The eighth, cornered, "continued," in the words of another British officer, "to abuse them [the British soldiers] with all the rage of a true Cromwellian, and but a moment before he quitted this world applyd such epithets as I must leave unmentioned."

The hatred and the resolution that Mackenzie saw in the eyes of the cornered militiaman told their own somber story. Americans had once loved the mother country. It had been their greatest pride to call themselves Englishmen, citizens of the most powerful and enlightened empire in the world. And now this Englishman, transformed into an "American" and willing to die for what he considered his rights as an American, asked by his defiant death a mute and terrible question: How had a loyal British subject been changed into a furious rebel? The answer to that question is, in large measure, the theme of this work. And the search for that answer begins some hundred and seventy-five years before the battles of Lexington and Concord and the death of our nameless soldier whose fierceness so disconcerted Lieutenant Macken-zie. It begins with the first rather tentative efforts of British entrepre-neurs to establish trading ventures in the New World.

There were three or four such ventures that are little known to history because, for all the hopes and pounds sterling invested in them, they came to nothing—a few hardy souls who wintered on the frosty shores of later-day Maine or an island off the coast of what was to become Virginia, and who returned gratefully to England the following spring, or, as in the case of the Roanoke settlement, simply disappeared, leaving a tantalizing mystery behind them.

Jamestown, settled in 1607, was, of course, the first permanent English settlement in continental North America. (The Spanish had established a little colony at St. Augustine, Florida, in 1565, forty years earlier.) The promoters of the Jamestown venture were for the most part concerned with turning a profit for those who had invested in the undertaking, although they also took pleasure in the thought that they were playing a role in spreading the British Empire, in counterbalanc-ing the New World ventures of the Spanish (who had preceded them by more than a century), and in converting the heathen savages who roamed through the forests of North America. The Virginia Company of London was a joint stock company in which English men and women, from seamstresses and artisans to great lords and wealthy merchants, held stock. These were the "adventurers"—those who risked their money. Those who consented to venture across the vast and dangerous waters of the Atlantic were the "planters." They were both "planted" in the new land and were, in turn, to plant in it the crops that would hopefully return a profit to the backers of the enterprise. The shrewd and energetic men who conceived the undertaking (they were, incidentally, also known as "the undertakers"—a rather ironic term considering how many of the planters were to lose their lives at Jamestown) obtained a charter from the king that guaranteed the settlers, or planters, all the "priviledges, immunities and franchises of Englishmen" and a generous allotment of land between the thirty-fourth and forty-first parallels, stretching from the Atlantic Ocean to the Pacific (which, incidentally, was thought to be only a few hundred miles away).

The story of Jamestown is a familiar one and need not be retold here. It produced the first great American romance—the tale of Captain John Smith, the Indian princess Pocahontas, and her deceitful old father, Chief Powhatan. If John Smith's role was a somewhat ambiguous one—that of father-lover—it is clear that he was devoted to her. It was John Rolfe, however, a less free spirit than Smith, who married her, and their single frail child became in time the source of a vast progeny, all of whom would claim to be members of the very First Family of Virginia.

If Jamestown was a financial disaster—and indeed a human disaster, since hundreds of settlers died from starvation, Indian raids, and a terrible massacre—it did at least survive. Pride came to be more important than shillings and pounds. When an expedition for the relief of the little settlement was about to set out from London in 1613, William Crashaw, a prominent Puritan divine, gave a stirring sermon to the "Adventurers and Planters of the Virginia Company."

The colonists of Virginia were, Crashaw declared, to be, like David's four hundred, the seed of a great nation. Observers must not be misled by the colony's modest beginnings: all great leaders were at first children, "carried in the arms of sillie women." The planting was, in fact, an event of "such nature and consequence, as not only all nations stand gazing at, but even heaven and hell have taken notice of it, the holy Angels hoping, and the divvels fearing that will be the issue. Therefore let all nations see to their amazement that the English Christians will not undertake a publick action which they will not prosecute to perfection." Crashaw deplored the luxury of contemporary England. It had not always been so—"our forefathers were not such mecocks and milksops." Therefore he urged the "adventurers" to support the "planters" unstintingly, "to assist this noble action with countenance and counsell, with men and money, and with continual supplies, till we have made our colonies and plantation able to subsist of itself, until there be a Church of God established in Virginia, even there where Satan's throne is [a reference to the pagan Indians]." And to those waiting to sail for America, who undertook "the greatest ventures and bear the greatest burdens . . . you that desire to advance the gospell of Jesus Christ, though it be at the hazard of your lives, go forward in the name of the God of heaven and earth. . . . Cast away fears and let nothing daunt your spirits remembering whom you go unto, even to English men your brethren who have broke the ice before you. . . ."

Thirteen years after the establishment of Jamestown, a small group of Calvinists, whose leader, Robert Brown, insisted that the Church of England was corrupt beyond redemption and that true Christians must therefore separate from it, moved to Holland to be freer in the exercise of their faith. Called Brownists or Separatists (Brownists after their spiritual leader and Separatists because they wished to separate from the Anglican Church), they agreed or "covenanted" to remove to New England, in large part because they felt themselves in danger of becoming absorbed by the Dutch and their children in danger of being misled: ". . . of all the sorowes [suffered in Holland] most heavie to be borne, was that many of their children, by these occasions, and the great licentiousness of the youth in that countrie, and the manifold temptations of the place, were drawne away by evill examples into extravagant and dangerous courses, putting the raines off their neks and departing from their parents. . . ."

In the first chapter of an almost endlessly repeated story, these determined and independent people set out to establish a community where they could raise their children free of the contaminations of the larger society. The story of the perils and dangers encountered by the Pilgrims in establishing their little settlement at Plymouth is one of the best-known events in our history. William Bradford expressed the spirit of the enterprise most vividly in his history of the colony:

Here I cannot but pause and stand amazed, and so, too, I think will the reader when he considers this poor people and their present condition. For they had no dwelling places for their weatherbeaten bodies; no houses or much less towns to repair to, to seek for succor. And for the season it was winter, and they that know the winters of that country know them to be sharp and violent, and subject to cruel and fierce storms, dangerous to travel to known places, much more to search an unknown coast. Besides what could they see but a hideous and desolate wilderness, full of wild beasts and wild men—and what multitudes there might be of them they knew not. Neither could they, as it were, go to the top of Pisgah to view from this wilderness a more goodly country to feed their hopes; for which way soever they turned their eyes (save upward to the heavens) they would have little solace or content in respect of any outward objects. For summer being done, all things stand upon them with a weatherbeaten face, and the whole country, full of woods and thickets represented a wild and savage hue. . . . If they looked behind them, there was the mighty ocean over which they had passed and was now a main bar and gulf to separate them from all the civil parts of the world. . . . What could now sustain them but the spirit of God and His Grace?

When the Pilgrims landed at Plymouth they were in a most precarious situation. The year was late, and there was much sickness among the settlers. "All this while," Bradford wrote, "the Indians came skulking about those who were ashore and would sometimes show themselves aloof, at a distance, but when they approached them, they would run away. Once they stole the men's tools where they had been at work and were gone to dinner. About the 16th of March a certain Indian came among them, and spoke to them in broken English, which they could well understand but were astonished at." (It was almost as though astronauts landing on Mars were to be greeted in broken English.) The Indian was Samoset, and he introduced them to another English-speaking Indian, Squanto, who became the particular friend and counselor of the Pilgrims. Through Samoset, the Pilgrims made friends with Massasoit, the sachem of the Wampanoags, and a peace was concluded that remained unbroken for almost fifty years. The picture of the Indians attending the first Thanksgiving at Plymouth is one of the most familiar icons in American history. The tragedy was that these early and happy encounters—Pocahontas in Virginia and Samoset and Squanto at the Plymouth colony—were so soon succeeded by bloody and violent conflicts.

At the same time that the Pilgrims were negotiating so successfully with the Wampanoags, Thomas Weston with a little group of men was trying to establish a settlement near what was to become Boston. There the settlers were so poorly organized and so undisciplined, begging and stealing from the Indians and even going to live among them, that the Indians decided to exterminate the whites. Captain Miles Standish, at the head of a band of settlers, came to the rescue and gave a bloody rebuff to the hostile Indians.

It was not only the menace of Indian attacks that discomforted the leaders of the Plymouth colony; the free and, indeed, capricious life of the Indians had a sometimes irresistible attraction.

One of the principal thorns in the side of the Pilgrims was Thomas

Morton of Merry Mount, who had, in Bradford's words, become "Lord of Misrule, and maintained (as it were) a School of Atheism." To compare Bradford's indignant account of Morton's activities with Morton's own story demonstrates most vividly two perspectives on the Indians. According to Bradford, "After they [Morton and his followers] had got some goods into their hands, and got much by trading with the Indians, they spent it as vainly in quaffing and drinking both wine and strong waters in great excess. . . . They also set up a maypole, drinking and dancing about it many days together, inviting the Indian women for their consorts, dancing and frisking together like so many fairies, or furies, rather; and worse practices. As if they had anew revived and celebrated the feast of the Roman goddess Flora, or the beastly practices of the mad Bacchanalians." Most serious was the fact that Morton traded guns and powder and flints to the Indians and thus armed them against the white settlers.

Morton, on the other hand, plainly took a different view. He got his own version on record by writing a book sarcastically entitled *New England's Canaan*. After describing his harassment by the Plymouth colony, Morton wrote of the "salvages" of New England: "According to humane reason guided onely by the light of nature, these people leades the more happy and freer life, beying voyde of care, which torments the minds of so many Christians: They are not delighted in baubles, but in useful things. . . . I have observed that they will not be troubled with superfluous commodities. Such things as they finds, they are taught by necessity to make use of . . . that their life is so voyd of care, and they are so loving also that they make use of those things they enjoy (the wife onely excepted) as common goods, and are therein so compassionate that rather than one should starve through want, they would starve all, thus doe they passe away the time merrily, not regarding our pompe (which they see dayly before their faces) but are better content with their owne, which some men esteeme so meanely of."

Thus did Thomas Morton of Merry Mount express a view of the "more happy and freer life" of the Indians that many white settlers came to share. The attitude of the "planters" to the Indians was often compounded of envy (seldom, to be sure, as explicitedly expressed as by Morton) and fear: fear of losing one's scalp as one lay in one's bed, fear of the blood-chilling war whoop that announced the arrival of Indians on the warpath.

It was a decade after the Pilgrims established themselves at Plymouth under the leadership of Bradford that the most important English colony in New England was established—the Puritan settlement headed by John Winthrop. The Puritans, in contrast to the earlier Separatists (Pilgrims), who were for the most part simple farmers and artisans, included in their company a number of prosperous and educated Englishmen, among them a half-dozen popular and prominent preachers. In contrast to the Separatists, the Puritans insisted that they were still members of the Church of England, bent on reforming that institution rather than abandoning it. Moreover, the Puritan ranks in England contained enough powerful and important members to make reform of the established Church at least a practical possibility. What attracted some of the leaders of English Puritanism to the idea of a colony in the New World was the prospect of founding a Bible Commonwealth, a community or series of communities based on the principles of the Reformed faith. In New England, free of the hostility and opposition of Episcopal prelates and ministers of the Crown, not to mention more orthodox churchgoers, the Puritans thought it possible, for the first time, to "purify" the Christian faith. Their vision beheld communities of saints, those chosen by God as His "elect," those predestined for eternal salvation. They had in mind the flight of the children of Israel from the land of Egypt. England was Egypt; New England was the new Canaan, the promised land where God's new testament, or new covenant, might at last be fulfilled. This passion to reform and redeem Christendom spurred on the first wave of the great Puritan migration to America.

Many of the Puritans (certainly the leaders) sacrificed wealth and position to hew out their new home in the wilderness under conditions of great hardship and danger. John Winthrop, a graduate of Cambridge and a substantial country gentleman, was one of the leaders. On board the *Arbella,* headed for the New England coast, Winthrop wrote a sermon that became a guide for the colonists in their great venture. "A Modell of Christian Charity" is, I believe, one of the half-dozen most important documents in American history. In it Winthrop enunciates the spiritual character of New England and spells out for his followers and for posterity the basic principles that motivated him and his coadjutors to embark on such a perilous enterprise.

They were not fleeing persecution (harassment at worst, and they were perhaps as often the harassers as the harassed), nor were they seeking religious liberty in any real sense of that phrase, or even primarily the right to worship as they chose. What drove them on so zealously, so fanatically, was a passion for the redemption of the world for and through their Lord, Jesus Christ. This is clear enough in

Winthrop's tract. It was God's intention that "every man might have need of other, and from hence they might all be knit more nearly together in the bonds of brotherly affection." The Puritans were God's new chosen people ("He has taken us to be His after a most strict and peculiar manner"); they had entered into a covenant or contract with Him in which the Lord had permitted them to draw up the terms of the agreement. By allowing them to arrive at New England, He had indicated His acceptance of the covenant. However, one did not enter casually into contractual relations with the Lord. If the Puritans failed to live up to their agreement, "the Lord will surely break out in wrath against us; be revenged of such a perjured people and make us know the price of a breach of such a covenant." The only way, therefore, to avoid the Lord's wrath was to follow the counsel of Micah, "To do justly, to love mercy, to walk humbly with our God. For this end," Winthrop continued, "we must be knit together in this work as one man. . . . We must hold a familiar commerce together in all meekness, gentleness, patience, and liberality. We must delight in each other; make others' conditions our own, rejoice together, having always before our eyes our commission and community in the work, our community as members of the same bond. . . . We shall find that the God of Israel is among us. . . . When He shall make us a praise and glory that men shall say of succeeding plantations 'the Lord make it like that of NEW ENGLAND.' For we must consider that we shall be as a city upon a hill. The eyes of all people are upon us. . . ."

This was the spiritual charter of every community of Puritan New England, each one of which drew up and subscribed to its own particular covenant. That of Braintree, Massachusetts, was typical: With God's help the signers meant to "renounce the devil, the wicked world, a sinful flesh . . . and all our former evil ways . . . and we give up ourselves also to one and another by the will of God . . . and we also manifest our joint consent herein this day in presence of this assembly, by this present our public confession, and by giving one another the hand of fellowship."

It should be noted that the charter of the Massachusetts Bay Company was, like its predecessor the Virginia Company of London, that of a commercial stock company. The principal difference was that the investors in the Massachusetts Bay Company—the "adventurers"— were also the settlers or "planters." The charter of the Massachusetts Bay Company conferred those rights of self-government on the "Great and General Court" of stockholders as were commonly granted to all such commercial companies. Armed with these rights, the stockholder-settlers simply took the commercial charter with them to New England and there, under the more than dubious authority of a commercial charter, undertook to govern themselves in a civil way. The government of the officers, or magistrates, of the Massachusetts Bay Company was a hard one, too rigid and demanding for many of the religious enthusiasts who had joined the venture in hopes of finding a place where they could freely pursue their own private religious vision. Indeed, the Puritan leaders had hardly had time to assert their authority on the frosty shores of the bay before they were challenged by a fanatical and determined woman, Anne Hutchinson, who accused the Puritan ministers and magistrates of being more agents of the evil one than of the true Lord. The magistrates and leading preachers put too much faith in laws and ordinances to forward God's work, she charged. Only those individuals who were in direct contact with the Divine were truly saved. These happy few were, not surprisingly, Anne Hutchinson and her followers. Persons in a true state of grace were, moreover, outside of all worldly laws and statutes; they were responsible only to God himself, not to civil authorities. They were "outside the law," hence "antinomian"—antilaw. Such a doctrine was a kind of religious anarchy. By calling all authority into question, it seemed to Governor John Winthrop and the magistrates of the colony that Anne Hutchinson and her followers were imperiling the very existence of the new colony, threatened already by enemies in England as well as by the savages who lurked in the forests that pressed upon the little settlement. They argued and expostulated with her, and then, finding her obdurate, tried her for heresy and banished her and her supporters, who, rather surprisingly, included some of the most prominent settlers, among them William Coddington, one of the richest men in the colony. The exiles settled on the northern end of a large island—known as Aquidneck by the natives—that divides Narragansett Bay into two parts. They called their little settlement Portsmouth and there did "solemnly, in the presence of Jehovah, incorporate ourselves into a Bodie Politick . . . and will submit our persons lives and estates unto our Lord Jesus Christ. . . ." Thus was Rhode Island born of heresy and dissent, and in dissent it grew. First Coddington quarreled with his spiritual leader, Anne Hutchinson, and withdrew with his followers to the southern end of the island, where he established Newport. Anne Hutchinson was as restless as her followers, and when her long-suffering husband died in 1642, she removed with her family (all that was left of her more numerous band) across the sound to the western end of Long Island. There she, her children and grandchil-

dren, and the members of her household—some sixteen people in all—
were murdered by the Indians. The bitterness of feeling that she had
aroused in Massachusetts Bay by her bold challenge to its leaders was
indicated by John Winthrop's comment: "God's hand is the more apparently seen therein, to pick out this woful woman to make her and those
belonging to her, an unheard of heavy example of their [the Indians']
cruelty."

Rhode Island soon received another dissenter, a far more formidable figure than Anne Hutchinson. Roger Williams came to Boston in
1631, just at the beginning of a wave of settlers who, a little more than a
decade after Winthrop arrived in the *Arbella,* swelled the population of
Massachusetts Bay alone to sixteen thousand. Williams was, in a sense,
more Puritanical than the Puritans. His initial complaint was that the
leaders of the Bay colony had not followed the example of the Pilgrims
and declared themselves "separated" from the corrupt and godless
Church of England (when he was asked to take the place of an absent
minister, he declared that he "durst not officiate to an unseparated
people"). That was his more rigorous side. On his liberal side, he
denounced the leaders of the colony for requiring that everyone must
"go to the religious services provided by the state or be punished."

Unhappy in Boston, Williams moved to Plymouth, where he
worked as a laborer and volunteered his services as a minister. The
tolerant Bradford, noting that he had "many precious parts, but [was]
very unsettled in judgment," discouraged him, and soon Williams established himself in Salem. There he took an even more disconcerting line.
The colonists of New England were, he declared, "under a sin of
usurpation of others' possessions," namely the lands belonging properly
to the Indians. Since the leaders of both Plymouth and Massachusetts
had been at considerable pains to pay the Indians for the lands they
occupied, they felt that Williams was both unfair and reckless in his
charges. Williams was reprimanded by the magistrates, but he persisted
in his contentious way, and soon he was called before the magistrates
again for "teaching publicly against the king's patent, and our great sin
in claiming right thereby to this country, etc. and for usually terming the
churches of England anti-Christian." Williams was forced to surrender
his pulpit at Salem and resigned with a bitter letter, in which he referred
to the Massachusetts congregations as "ulcered and gangrened." When
he persisted in his attacks an effort was made to arrest him, but he
escaped and spent the winter with the Indians. From there he went to
Rhode Island, where he started a tiny settlement that he named Providence. Here at last he had a home, a territory, modest as it was, where

he could propound his heresies undisturbed. These were, most simply, that no man should be forced to attend church service, but that each individual should be allowed to follow his own conscience in matters of religion. It is this doctrine for which Roger Williams is, very properly, best known. He was far ahead of his time in his views of religious toleration. Much the same spirit prevailed in the civil affairs of Providence. That town and, finally, the colony, when Williams secured a charter in 1663, became a stronghold of the dissenting and democratic spirit, enjoying greater rights of self-government than any other colony.

The colony of Connecticut, again an amalgamation of several towns founded independently of each other—New Haven on the one hand and Wethersfield and Hartford on the other, the latter founded by Thomas Hooker, a Puritan minister who found the atmosphere of Boston somewhat constricting—received a very liberal charter in 1662. Thoroughly Puritan in principle and policy, Connecticut, along with Plymouth (which eventually was incorporated somewhat unwillingly into the Massachusetts Bay colony) and Rhode Island, formed the heart of New England Puritanism, where a prickly independence and stubborn self-reliance flourished.

New York had, of course, very different origins. Originally settled by the Dutch, New Netherlands was governed in its early years by the choleric and tyrannical Peter Stuyvesant, and then it was simply seized by Charles II following his restoration in 1660 and was granted to his brother, James. New York thus became a proprietary colony; that is to say, like Maryland, the Jerseys, the Carolinas, and Pennsylvania, it was given to a proprietor (an individual or a group of individuals) to be used for his own profit, if profit could be extracted, and to be governed in accordance with English law, which once more granted to the settlers all "the privileges, franchises and immunities" of Englishmen. The property of the original Dutch settlers was undisturbed, and some of the patroons—Dutch settlers who owned vast estates, with tenants under feudal laws—became leaders in the affairs of the new proprietary colony of the Duke of York.

New Jersey, initially divided into proprietary grants known as East and West Jersey, was united under one charter in 1702, but it was known as the Jerseys for another hundred years. There was a strong New England flavor to its theology and politics, since many of its early settlers had drifted south from Massachusetts and Connecticut, seeking their fortunes in alluvial farmlands, so much easier to cultivate than the stony soil of their home colonies.

We know Maryland as a refuge for persecuted English Catholics under the leadership of Cecilius Calvert, Lord Baltimore. While the second Baron of Baltimore did not live to visit the colony established as a result of his initiative, his brother Leonard Calvert, with some Jesuit priests and a handful of settlers, many of them Protestants, sailed in the *Ark* and the *Dove* and established a settlement at St. Marys near the mouth of the Potomac River in 1633. In return for some knives, axes, hoes, and cloth, Indians camped nearby turned over their huts to the newcomers, and the colony of Maryland, named so after Henrietta Maria, wife of Charles I, was founded. Maryland is perhaps best known in this early period for Calvert's "Act Concerning Religion," in which the proprietor granted to Protestants in Maryland those rights to freedom of worship that his Catholic coreligionists had been denied in the mother country. The act, drawn up by Lord Baltimore and ratified by the Maryland assembly in 1649, provided that no one "professing to believe in Jesus Christ shall, from henceforth, be any ways troubled, molested, or discountenanced for, or in respect of his or her religion, nor in the free exercise thereof. . . ."

More than humanitarian motives undoubtedly prompted Calvert— for one thing, Catholics were already outnumbered in the colony and thus apprehensive lest they suffer from restraints laid on them by the more numerous Protestants—but the results were salutary; the "Act Concerning Religion" helped to advance the principle of toleration in British America.

We have already described the earliest settlement of Virginia. After the desperate "starving" times and a devastating Indian massacre, that colony finally got on its feet with the introduction of tobacco as a crop, farmed first by white slaves (another term for indentured servants) and then by black slaves imported from Africa to work the large plantations that stretched inland along the James and York rivers. However, the Virginia Company of London failed to make a go of the colony financially, and by the end of the 1620's Virginia had passed into the hands of the king as a royal colony.

Farther south lay a vast area that attracted the attention of a group of great English lords, chief among them the learned and liberal Anthony Ashley Cooper, Earl of Shaftesbury. Shaftesbury had recruited the Lords Albemarle, Clarendon, Berkeley, Carteret, and Craven, and these powerful men secured a grant of this region from King Charles II in 1663, shortly before the king gave New Netherlands to his brother James. The terms of the Carolina charter confirming the grant of land were similar to those of Lord Baltimore's charter. The lords were liberally inclined, and, as in Maryland, toleration was granted to all dissenting settlers who were firm in their allegiance to the king. The rather involved history of the Carolina settlements lies beyond the scope of this work, but it is worth remarking one aspect of its history that reveals a good deal about the nature of proprietary colonies in general. Shaftesbury, one of the most striking figures in the history of seventeenth-century England, had virtually made a career of espousing liberal principles in religion and government. In addition, Shaftesbury had as his secretary a young man as liberal as and even more learned than he. John Locke was thirty-six years old and yet to win fame as a philosopher, psychologist, and political theorist. He had some skill as a surgeon and had even performed an operation on his patron. Shaftesbury enlisted Locke in framing a government for the new colony, which as yet had only a handful of prior settlers to be governed. The frame of government, "The Fundamental Constitutions of Carolina," was a curious combination of the old and the new, of the feudal spirit and the modern. The senior proprietor was to hold the title of Lord Palatine (indeed, everyone had a high-sounding title—Admiral, Chamberlain, Chancellor, etc.). The colony was to be divided into sections of twelve thousand acres; forty of these constituted a county. The counties, in turn, were divided into "seignories" for the proprietors themselves; "baronies" for an American nobility; and "colonies," to be settled by freeholders. The titles of the nobles were taken, engagingly enough, from the titles of German princes and Indian chieftains—landgraves and caciques. A single-house parliament was to be made up of the proprietors or their representative, the landgraves and caciques, and one freeholder out of every precinct. All laws were to come to an end a hundred years from the time of their passage, so that a fresh start could be made and no one need bear the burden of past mistakes.

The Fundamental Constitutions contained numerous other eccentric provisions. No matter. It was too impractical ever to be put into effect. The proprietors put up a substantial sum of money to underwrite the initial settlements, and they got very little of it back. Hostile Indians, poor communication, and lack of enterprise on the part of the settlers themselves resulted in a very slow growth for the Carolinas. The two areas—the settlements in the Albemarle region and those much further south, along the Cooper and Ashley rivers—came to be increasingly sharply differentiated and finally were formed into two separate colonies.

Aside from Georgia, the latest English colony to be founded (and the one that had the most spectacular growth once established) was the colony of William Penn. Like Maryland (and to some extent, Plymouth and Massachusetts), Pennsylvania was settled as a refuge for a persecuted religious group, in this instance the Quakers, a sect that by its violent attacks on the Church of England (and much of English society as well) brought down upon itself the wrath of the ecclesiastical establishment and with it that of the government. As a youth, William Penn, the son of Admiral Sir William Penn, was sent off to Oxford by his father, who had managed to serve Oliver Cromwell during the period of the Parliamentary government and then make the rather awkward transition to being a trusted servant of Charles II at the time of the Restoration. At Oxford, young Penn heard a Quaker minister preach and became an instant convert. The indignant authorities at Oxford sent him home, where the admiral beat him soundly, turned him out of the house, and then, thinking better of it, dispatched him to Paris, apparently hoping that the allurements of that city would deconvert him. Indeed Penn returned to England sans Quakerism, but there he again encountered the preacher who had so stirred him while expounding the text: "There is a faith which overcometh the world, and there is a faith which is overcome by the world."

The die was cast. Penn announced his Quakerism and was locked up in the Tower by the bishop of London. After being released he began preaching and was once more arrested for "being present at an unlawful and tumultuous assembly in Gracechurch Street and there addressing a great concourse and tumult of people. . . ."

In 1680 Penn petitioned the Crown for a grant of land in America as a settlement of "the debts due to him and his father from the Crown." His intention was to establish a colony where the Quakers might worship as they wished and govern themselves according to the dictates of their consciences. The result was, of course, the province of Pennsylvania, the most liberal of all the English colonies with regard to religious toleration, the most just and equitable in its dealings with the Indians, and soon the most flourishing in agriculture and commerce.

The frame of government drawn up by Penn provided, in conformity with the most advanced political thought of the day, for a single legislative body, the assembly. But the mild and temperate rule of the Quakers grew less benign as the years passed, and the Quakers in the colony were soon engaged in bitter conflicts with the proprietor. After Penn's descendants returned to the Church of England, the rift widened, and much of the subsequent history of Penn's colony, established as a peaceable kingdom in the wilderness, was marked by clashes between the proprietary party and the Quaker elite, a group that clung to its enlightened policy toward the Indians but became increasingly conservative in other matters.

In this hasty review of the founding of the principal colonies, I have tried to convey a sense of the remarkable diversity represented in these ventures. A number of human varieties and social forms, some as old as England itself, others as new as the new commercial and mercantile spirit of the age, were planted in the virgin soil of the New World. There they would grow luxuriantly, each in its particular way, in a vegetative mold made up of new ideas and opportunities. There religious enthusiasm and rigid orthodoxy would shape one colony, while tolerance and a vigorous commercial spirit would place an unmistakable stamp on another. In the South, the best traditions of the English landed gentry would grow on the incongruous foundation of black slavery. In the North, the democracy of the New England village would be nurtured by a spirit that seems to the modern consciousness to be marked by simple religious fanaticism. America was like some strange new garden where all kinds of transplanted vegetables and flowers lived together in vigorous incompatibility, growing with astonishing speed in that fertile ground and developing, in the process, new strains and varieties. The New Englanders indeed liked the image of a new land of Canaan, a refuge for a new Chosen People; other colonists spoke of a Garden of Eden, a world of innocence where humanity might start anew. Perhaps it was this vision of a new world and a new opportunity that ran as a common theme through all the colonies. North or south, all reverberated to that grand chord, a silken thread that tied them all together and that, in time, would become a mighty rope.

2

Who Came?

THE American colonists came from a variety of backgrounds, as we have seen. What united them was the wilderness to which they came, a vast land inhabited by two hundred thousand or so aborigines—native tribes of different languages and social customs to whom the settlers from the Old World gave the general and misleading name of "Indians." The land to which they came was, literally, incomprehensible; it reached beyond the mind's imagining, threatening and promising, larger than all of Europe: coastal shelf and then mountains and endless plains and more mountains and, finally, the Pacific. No one could measure its extent. The English settlers for their part clung to its eastern margins, to the seacoast strip that faced the ocean highway to the Old World. Even here there were terrains, climates, and topographies as dramatically different as one could imagine—from the rocky, frigid shores of New Hampshire to the sunny beaches of South Carolina.

There was a kind of mad presumption about the whole venture: a few thousand, and then a few hundred thousand, and finally a few million souls scattered along almost two thousand miles of coastline. And in truth it could be said that those who made this strange odyssey to the New World were as diverse as the land they inhabited. Those from England itself represented every class and condition of men. And then

there were the Swedes, who settled on the Delaware long before William
Penn and his followers arrived, and the stolid and intractable Dutch,
reputed to have bought Manhattan from the aborigines for a few strings
of beads—the most famous real estate deal in history. And the French
Huguenots, Protestants fleeing from persecution in a Catholic country;
the Catholics of Maryland, fleeing persecution in a Protestant cóuntry;
the Quakers, fleeing the harassments of the Anglican establishment, the
Church of England; and Germans from innumerable principalities,
fleeing military draft and the various exactions of petty princes.

Within the British Isles themselves—Ireland, Scotland, England,
and Wales—there was striking diversity among the New World emigrants. The Separatists—the Pilgrims under William Bradford—
wanted, in essence, to be separate; the Puritans wanted to found a Bible
Commonwealth and redeem a fallen world. When Cromwell and the
Puritans dominated England and beheaded Charles I, certain Royalists
found refuge in Virginia and New York. When the restoration of the
monarchy brought Charles II to the English throne and re-established
the Stuart line, the regicides—those involved in the execution of
Charles I—found refuge in Puritan New England. When the Scottish
Covenanters, or Presbyterians, so akin in spirit to the Puritans of New
England, rose against the highhanded and tyrannical actions of the re-
established monarchy, they were crushingly defeated by the Duke of
Monmouth at Bothwell Bridge in 1679 and cruelly repressed. Many, in
consequence, came to America. And they continued to come for a
hundred years.

When the Stuart dynasty was succeeded by the Hanoverian line,
beginning with the reign of George I in 1714, the Scottish Highlanders,
a very different breed from the Lowland Covenanters, took up the
cause of the Stuart claimants to the throne of England. Finally, in 1745,
the supporters of the so-called Young Pretender, Charles Edward,
rallied to his cause; but after three initial victories they were destroyed at
Culloden in April of 1746. In the aftermath of this disaster, many of the
Scottish Highlanders found refuge in America on the Carolina frontier.

And then there were the Irish. They were a special case. They fled
famine and rent-wracking landlords. They fled Cromwell and his
Roundheads; then they fled Charles II as they had earlier fled Cromwell. A Catholic people, they fled their Protestant masters. But above all
they fled poverty, the poverty of a ruthlessly exploited peasantry. Generation after generation, the Irish came to the American colonies,
primarily to Maryland and Pennsylvania, where they gravitated to the

frontier areas. In addition to the Catholic Irish, Scotch-Irish Presbyterians came in substantial numbers to the colonies throughout the eighteenth century. The Scotch-Irish were those Covenanters, or militant Presbyterians, who had been forced by the bitter divisions in Scotland itself to seek the protection of the English armies in Northern Ireland (hence Scotch-Irish). For many of them, Ireland was little more than a way station to the colonies, where they showed a marked preference for Pennsylvania and settled, typically, on the frontier.

Like the Scotch-Irish, the Welsh, many of them Quakers, made Penn's colony their common destination. There they founded prosperous communities and took a leading role in the affairs of the colony.

So the immigrants came in an ever-growing tide—the hungry, the oppressed, the contentious, the ambitious, those out of power and out of favor, the losers, whether in the realm of politics or of economics. And America could accommodate them all: Irish peasant and his land-poor master, Scottish Highlander and Lowlander, persecuted Protestant and persecuted Catholic, fortune-seeker and God-seeker, they found their places, their kinfolk, the familiar accents of their home shires or counties or countries.

But the essence of them all, of all that human congress, the bone and marrow, the unifying principle, the prevailing and pervasive spirit was English. Like the others who came, the English came, as we have already noted, for a number of reasons. Most of them shared some particular expectation, whether for spiritual or material betterment or, happily, both. Many of those who came later shared, of course, the hopes of the original settlers. Many more came because conditions were desperately hard in England and Ireland for poor people, even for those who had not yet sunk into the pit of abandoned hopelessness that was the lot of the most wretched.

It has been estimated that London in the eighteenth century had 6,000 adult and 9,300 child beggars. In the entire country of some 10,000,000 persons, there were estimated to be 50,000 beggars, 20,000 vagrants, 10,000 idlers, 100,000 prostitutes, 10,000 rogues and vagabonds, 80,000 criminals, 1,041,000 persons on parish relief. Indeed, over half the population was below what we would call today "the poverty line," and many, of course, were profoundly below it—below it to the point of starvation. An estimate of the different classes—and class lines were almost impassable—in 1688 suggests that nobility, gentry, merchants, professionals, freeholders (those who held land on their own), craftsmen, and public officials constituted 47 per cent of the population; while common sailors and soldiers (recruited, for the most part, from the lowest levels of British society and enduring desperately hard conditions of service), laborers, servants, paupers, and all those other remarkable subdivisions that we have listed above such as rogues and vagrants made up 53 per cent of the population. The colonies, for their part, had a virtually inexhaustible demand for labor. Anyone willing to work could be put to worthwhile labor, and might (and often did) in a few years establish himself as an independent farmer or artisan.

Yet it was one thing to be an undernourished London apprentice who hated his master and another to find a way to get to America. Some indication of the situation of the working class in the larger cities may be discerned from the condition of pauper children in London in the early eighteenth century. Orphaned, or more frequently illegitimate and abandoned at birth, they were sent to workhouses and to parish nurses. A Parliamentary study found that of all such infants born or received in London's workhouses in a three-year period, only seven in every hundred were alive at the end of that time. As part of the "surcharge of necessitous people," orphaned and impoverished children who were public charges were sporadically dispatched to the colonies as indentured servants. People worked, typically, from six in the morning until eight at night for a pittance that barely supported life. They had no holidays except at Christmas, Easter, and on hanging days, when everyone might be entertained and edified by watching wretches hanged for crimes that, in many instances, would be classed as misdemeanors today.

Despite the cruelty of punishments, London had a large criminal class and was infested with prostitutes. The working class drowned its miseries in bad gin and beer. There were some 7,000 ginshops in the suburbs of London and, by 1750, 16,000 in the city itself (only 1,050 of which were licensed); most of them were in the poorest sections of the city, whose horrors are vividly recorded in Hogarth's etchings of Gin Lane. The hard liquor consumed in one year (1733) in London alone amounted to 11,200,000 gallons, or some 56 gallons per adult male.

Next to public hangings, the principal entertainments available to the poor—and enjoyed by the rich as well—were cockfighting, bullbaiting, and badger baiting. In such circumstances there was ample incentive to emigrate almost anywhere. In the words of a seventeenth-century historian of Virginia: "Now let me turn back and look upon my poore spirited countrymen in England and examine first the meanest, that is the poore ploughman, day labourer and poore Artificer [it is doubtful, indeed, if they were "the meanest"] and I shall find them labouring and sweating all dayes of their lives; some for fourteen pence, others for sixteen, eighteen, twenty pence or two shillings a day; which is the highest of wages to such kind of people, and the most of them to end their dayes in sorrow, not having purchased so much by their lives labour as will scarce preserve them in their old days from beggery." But to the penniless, the question was: How? The growing need for labor in the colonies supplied the answer, and a system of indenture, based on the long-established apprenticeship, was devised. Agents paid for the ship's passage of improvident men and women who were willing to contract themselves in America to work off the cost of their transportation. By this means, tens of thousands of English and Irish workers of both sexes found their way across the ocean.

The system was easily and often abused. A class of men "of the lowest order," called spirits and crimps, arose, who spirited away unwilling lads and sold them into bondage. A contemporary wrote: " . . . there are always plenty of agents hovering like birds of prey on the banks of the Thames, eager in their search for such artisans, mechanics, husbandmen and labourers, as are inclinable to direct their course for America." Another man wrote, "Well may he be called a spirit, since his nature is like the devil's, to seduce any he meets withal, whom he can persuade with allurements and deluding falsities to his purpose." One spirit boasted that he had been spiriting persons for twelve years at a rate of five hundred persons a year. He would give twenty-five shillings to anyone who would bring him a likely prospect, and he could sell such a one to a merchant at once for forty shillings. Often spiriting was a profitable sideline for a brewer, hostler, carpenter, or tavern keeper. The tavern keeper was in an especially advantageous position, since a drunken patron was an easy victim. So dreaded were these dismal agents that mothers frightened their children into obedience by warning them that a spirit would carry them off if they were bad. It was no idle threat. In 1653 Robert Broome secured a warrant for the arrest of a ship's captain charged with carrying off his son, aged eleven, who had been spirited aboard. A few years later, a commission going aboard the *Conquer* found that eleven out of nineteen servants had been "taken by the spirits." Their average age was nineteen. Not all spirits were depraved men, however, and even the worst of them often performed a useful service in arranging transportation for a servant who wished to emigrate to the colonies against the wishes of parents or a master. In the words of the historian Abbott Smith: "A much larger proportion of our colonial population than is generally supposed found itself on American soil because of the wheedlings, deceptions, misrepresentations and other devices of the 'spirits'; a very small proportion indeed were carried away forcibly and entirely against their wills."

Hugh Jones, in *The Present State of Virginia,* published in 1724, put the matter succinctly: "What shoals of beggars are allowed in Great Britain to suffer their bodies to rust and consume with laziness and want?" England was "over-stocked . . . with vast numbers of people of all trades and professions." But few of them were ready to try their fortunes in America. These people were ideal material for the colonies, but they had a "home fondness" and a suspicion of foreign lands that made them reluctant to leave the mother country. This sentiment had "retarded the plantations from being stocked with such inhabitants as are skillful, industrious, and laborious. . . ." Instead, America had received, for the most part, "the servants and inferior sort of people, who have either been sent over to Virginia, or have transported themselves thither, have been, and are, the poorest, idlest, and worst of mankind, the refuse of Great Britain and Ireland, and the outcast of the people." It seemed ironic to Jones that "the vilest of mankind" must be utilized for the "noblest and most useful undertakings."

For a time it proved easier to get women servants than men servants (or as they were called earlier, before the word began to be associated with blacks in permanent servitude, "slaves"). Mathew Cradock, captain of the *Abraham,* sailing for Virginia, made elaborate preparations for carrying a shipload of servants, men and women alike, to Virginia on a four-year indenture. On his ship's arrival in various English ports, he "caused the drume to be Betten, and gave warning to all those that disposed to goe servants for Virginea. . . ." By such means, he rounded up forty-one men and twenty women, the latter "from 17 to 35 yeares and very lustye and strong Boddied which I will hopp," the captain wrote, "be meyns to sett them of to the best Advantiag . . . and for women they are now Reddear to goe then men, whereof we ar furnished with as many as we have rome."

Clothing, "peppar and Gingar," and three-and-a-half pounds of tobacco for the men were all purchased before the ship set sail, and a midwife was hired to make sure none of the women were pregnant. Soon after the ship sailed it was driven into the harbor of Cowes, and it was a month before it got favorable winds. By that time, three of the women were pregnant and were sent home; some who were put ashore to do the washing ran away and had to be tracked down at a cost of ten shillings; and another was found "not fette to be entertained havinge the frentche dizeas," and was sent packing.

If a female indentured servant became pregnant during her service, her misdeed represented a loss to her master, so that an indentured servant guilty of bastardy was required to pay the usual charges levied against unwed mothers as well as to indemnify her master for the loss of her services during the later stages of her pregnancy and her lying-in. Not infrequently, the master was the culprit. In Maryland, Jacob Lumbrozo, a Portuguese Jew, alias Dr. John, was charged with having made persistent overtures to his maid, Elisabeth Weales, and when rebuffed, "hee tooke her in his armes and threw her upon the bed she went to Cry out hee plucked out his handerchif of his pocket and stope her mouth and force her whether shee will or noe when hee know that she was with Child hee gave her fickes to distroy it and for anything shee know hee woold distroy her too. . . ." By the time the case came to court, Lumbrozo had married Elisabeth Weales, who became a prominent if contentious figure in the affairs of the county. In Virginia, a statute was passed to prevent a master who had impregnated his servant girl from claiming extra service from her beyond her indenture: "Late experiments shew that some dissolute masters have gotten their maides with child, and yet claime the benefitt of their service." However, the maid got off no better. After the end of her indenture she was to be sold by the church wardens for the use of the parish for two years.

One depot for the collection of servants to be sold in the colonies was at St. Katherine's, near the Tower of London. Here a kidnaper would bring his victim, who might be forcibly detained for a month before the master of a ship would carry him off. We have a contemporary account of such a dive. After the kidnaper asked his intended victim "many impertinent questions, he invited me to drink with him. . . . He brought into a Room where half a score were all taking Tobacco: the place was so narrow wherein they were, that they had no more space left, than what was for the standing of a small table. Methought their mouths together resembled a stack of chimneys, being in a manner totally obscured by the smoak that came from them; for there was little discernable but smoak, and the flowing coals of their pipes. . . . After I had been there awhile, the Cloud of their smoak was somewhat dissipated, so that I could discern two more in my own condemnation: but alas poor Sheep, they ne'er considered where they were going, it was enough for them to be freed from a seven years Apprenticeship, under the Tyranny of a rigid master . . . and not weighing . . . the slavery they must undergo for five years amongst Brutes in foreign parts, little inferior to that which they suffer who are *Gally-slaves*. There was little discourse amongst them, but of the pleasantness of the soyl of that Continent we were designed for, (out of design to make us swallow their gilded Pills of Ruine), & the temperature of the Air, the plentry of Fowl and Fish of all sorts; the little labour that is performed or expected having so little trouble in it, that it may be accounted a pastime than anything of punishment; and then to sweeten us the farther, they insisted on the pliant loving natures of the women there; all which they used to bait us silly Gudgeons. . . ."

In the words of the mayor of Bristol, "Among those who repair to Bristol from all parts to be transported to his majesty's Plantations beyond seas, some are husbands that have forsaken their wives, others wives who have abandoned their husbands, some are children and apprentices run away from their parents and masters, often times unwary and credulous persons have been tempted on board by men-stealers, and many that have been pursued by the hue-and-cry for robberies, burglaries or breaking prison, do thereby escape the prosecution of law and justice."

The terms of indenture required the master to provide food and clothing for his servants and, often in the case of German or Swiss servants, to take the responsibility for seeing that they learned English during the term of their indenture. At the end of their terms they were to be provided with a stated sum of money and a suit of presentable clothes so that they could make a proper start in life. South Carolina required that a female servant at the expiration of her service be given a waistcoast and petticoat, a new shift of white linen, shoes and stockings, a blue apron and two white linen caps. In some colonies, indentured servants received land at the end of their term of indenture. Thus in North Carolina during the proprietary period a servant's "freedom dues" were fifty acres of land and afterward three barrels of Indian corn and two new suits of a value of at least five pounds. Maryland made generous provision for "one good Cloth suite of Keirsy or broad cloth a Shift of white linen one new pair of stockings and Shoes two hoes one axe 3 barrels of Corne and fifty acres of land . . . women Servants a Years Provision of Corne and a like proportion of Cloth & Land."

It was also true, according to one John Hammond, writing in 1656, that some servants received these benefits before the end of their indenture. "Those servants that will be industrious," Hammond wrote, "may in their time of service gain a competent estate before their freedoms, which is usually done by many, and they gain esteem and assistance that appear so industrious. . . . He may have cattle, hogs, and tobacco of his own, and come to live gallantly; but this must be gained . . . by industry and affability, not by sloth nor churlish behavior."

That there was another side of the coin is indicated by a letter from an indentured servant to her father in 1756: "What we unfortunat English People suffer here is beyond the probability of you in England to Conceive, let it suffice that I am one of the unhappy Number, am toiling almost Day and Night, and very often in the Horses druggery, with only this comfort that you Bitch you do not halfe enough, and then tied up and whipp'd to that Degree that you'd not serve an Animal, scarce anything but Indian Corn and Salt to eat and that even begrudged nay many Negroes are better used, almost naked no shoes nor stockings to wear . . . what rest we can get is to rap ourselves up in a Blanket an ly upon the Ground."

Whether wickedly abused or treasured and rewarded—and certainly they experienced both cruelty and kindness—indentured servants made up more than half the immigrants to the middle and southern colonies. During the twenty-five-year period between 1750 and 1775, some 25,000 servants and convicts entered Maryland, and a comparable number arrived in Virginia. Abbott Smith estimates that during the same period at least twice as many servants and redemptioners entered Pennsylvania, of whom perhaps a third were German and the rest, in large part, Irish. The Irish, in addition to being contentious, dirty, and strongly inclined to drink, were Catholics. To Protestants, this fact made the Irish the least desirable of all immigrant groups. The more substantial class of immigrants, especially the Germans and the Swiss, came as redemptioners. Redemptioners were carried to America by a ship captain with the understanding that after they reached the colonies, they would undertake to sell themselves to the highest bidder and then pay the captain the cost of their passage. Most of the redemptioners were craftsmen whose skills were much in demand in the colonies and who could thus sell themselves on favorable terms to a master. If they could not sell themselves, it was the shipmaster's right to undertake to sell them, often at highly disadvantageous terms. Since a master could buy much cheaper from a ship captain, collusion between prospective buyers and the captain was not uncommon.

The story of indentured servants is one of the most dramatic in colonial America. While many of those who came under indenture were the "scum and offscourings of the earth"—convicts, paupers, runaway apprentices, prostitutes, and the like—many, particularly among the non-English, were respectable and decent people who had fallen on hard times or simply wished to improve their fortunes. We also know that in the rude conditions of colonial life, many of the dissolute were redeemed.

In seventeenth- and eighteenth-century England, crime was endemic. The alarm of the more prosperous classes was expressed in cries for law and order. The penalty of death was prescribed for all felonies. In seventeenth-century England, almost three hundred crimes were classed as felonies; a conviction for anything, indeed, from housebreaking and the theft of goods worth more than a shilling must result in the sentence of death by hanging, since the judge had no discretionary power in felony cases. The benefit of clergy and royal pardon were the only mitigations. A convicted felon could "call for the book," usually a Bible, and if he could read it, he was freed of the penalty of death, branded on the thumb, and released. The practice stemmed from medieval times, when generally speaking only those in holy orders were able to read, and they were subject to their own ecclesiastical courts. The benefit of clergy was undoubtedly a great incentive to the development of a literate criminal class, but in a time when the vast majority of the poor were illiterate, it had little else to recommend it. The simple fact was that if you were poor and illiterate you might be hanged for stealing a few shillings' worth of cloth, while a villainous cutpurse who could decipher a simple text would be branded and then would go free.

In 1705, Parliament, conscious of the absurdity as well as the injustice of the practice, came up with a typically English solution that permitted a felon to plead benefit of clergy even though he could not read, but at the same time set forth a list of some twenty-five felonies that were "nonclergyable," among them petty treason, arson, murder, burglary, stealing more than the value of a shilling, and highway robbery. Other offenses were added periodically until by 1769 there were 169 crimes classified as felonies for which there was no relief in pleading benefit of clergy.

The royal pardon was the only amelioration of a murderous system. Again in a typically English accommodation, judges who thought sentences too severe could send up a list of those convicted felons they considered worthy of mercy, and these would be pardoned by the king. For many years more than half of those sentenced to hang were pardoned, and increasingly it came to be the practice to issue such pardons on the condition that the culprit agreed to leave the country. From the middle of the seventeenth century until early in the eighteenth, thousands of convicts left England under this arrangement. Of these, a substantial majority found their way to the English colonies in the West Indies and in North America. In 1717, Parliament passed a law permitting the "transportation" out of the realm of certain classes of offenders "in clergy." From 1619 to 1640 all felons reprieved by royal pardon were transported to Virginia to help make up the toll of those settlers lost by disease, and between 1661 and 1700 more than 4,500 convicts were dispatched to the colonies. In the years from 1745 to 1775, 8,846 convicts, 9,035 servants, and 3,324 slaves landed at Annapolis, Maryland.

Convicts were certainly not ideal settlers. In one contingent, twenty-six had been convicted for stealing, one for violent robbery, and five for murder. Stephen Bumpstead stole a grey gelding worth forty-six shillings and was sentenced to death, Richard Enos stole a silver cup, Jacob Watkins removed a necktie from a victim in Thames Street at ten o'clock at night, and Charles Atley, a young child, stole twenty-eight shillings and eleven pence. The character of such settlers is indicated by the career of Jenny Voss, who was eventually hanged at Tyburn after having been transported to the colonies, where "she could not forget her old Pranks, but used not only to steal herself, but incited all others that were her fellow Servants to Pillfer and Cheat," so that her master was glad to be rid of her, the more so since "she had wheadled in a Son of the Planters, who used to Lye with her and supply her with Moneys. . . ."

Virginia and Maryland, which had been the principal outlets for transported felons, had passed laws forbidding their importation by the end of the seventeenth century. The Virginia House of Burgesses reported "the complaints of several of the council and others, gent. inhabitants . . . representing their apprehensions and fears lest the honor of his majesty and the peace of this colony be too much hazarded and endangered by the great numbers of felons and other desperate villains sent hither from the several prisons in England. . . ." But despite such protests, Parliament in 1717 passed a statute that overrode colonial efforts to stem the tide of undesirables. A total of thirty thousand convicted felons were shipped from England in the fifty-year period prior to the Revolution, of whom the greater number apparently went to Maryland and Virginia. Since convicts were bound into servitude for seven or fourteen years, which often proved to be a lifetime, the colonists usually bid actively for the most likely ones. The men sold for from eight to twenty pounds or, roughly, twenty-five to fifty dollars. Women brought slightly less, while the old and infirm were given away or, if no taker could be found, a subsidy was paid to anyone who would take them in.

It was not a humane or enlightened system, and the most that can be said for it is that the majority of the transported felons who were sold into white semislavery were slightly better off alive than dead. For those who escaped their masters, fled to other colonies, and established themselves as respectable citizens, it was a handsome bargain. Those willing to work, and fortunate enough to have a kind master, had a far better life than the one they had left behind in England. It is safe to surmise that a substantially higher proportion of women than men were redeemed to a decent life—from which it would presumably follow that a substantial number of Americans who trace their line of descent back to colonial times have an ancestress or two who arrived here as a convicted felon, a sneak thief, or a prostitute.

Three or four times a year, the convicts to be transported were marched in irons through the streets of London from Newgate Prison to Blackfriars. This procession provided, like hangings, a popular form of entertainment for mobs who would hoot at the convicts and, when the convicts replied with obscene epithets, sometimes pelt them with mud and stones. The more prosperous convicts could buy special privileges. Thus in 1736, four felons rode to the point of embarkation in two hackney coaches, and another, "a Gentleman of Fortune, and a Barrister at Law," convicted of stealing books from the Trinity College library, had a private coach to carry him in style. These men paid their own passage and shared a private cabin.

Besides the large number of convicted felons, there were many other Englishmen who fell in the rather commodious category of "rogues and vagabonds." Although they came from a very different economic stratum, these were the hippies and dropouts of seventeenth- and eighteenth-century English society, the men and women so alienated from the dominant culture that they had devised their own. They lived on the margins of the law, devoted to preying in a thousand ingenious ways on the public. A statute of Parliament defined them as "all persons calling themselves Schollers going about begging, all Seafaring men pretending losses of their Shippes or goods on the sea going about the Country begging, all idle persons going about in any Country eyther begging or using any subtile Crafts or unlawfull Games and Playes, or fayning themselves to have knowledge in Phislognomya Palmestry or other like crafty Scyence, or pretending that they can tell Destenyes Fortunes or such other like fantasticall imagynacons; all persons that be or utter themselves to be Proctors Procurers Patent Gatherers or Collectors for Gaoles Prisons or Hospitalls; all Fencers Bearewards comon Players of Enterludes and Minstrells wandring abroade . . . all Juglers Tynkers Pedlers and Petty Chapmen wandring abroade; all wandring persons and comon Labourers . . . loytering and refusing to worcke for such reasonable wages as . . . comonly given in such Parts where such persons do . . . dwell or abide . . . all such persons as shall wander abroade begging pretending losses by Fyre or otherwise; and all such persons not being Fellons wandering and pretending themselves to be Egipcyans, or wandering in the Habite Forme or Attyre of counterfayte Egipcians." What services "counterfayte Egipcians" might have offered that should have made them such a menace, the statute does not reveal, but it does summon up an extraordinary picture of life in the latter part of the sixteenth century, when England was beginning to feel most acutely the results of the rural enclosures. Punishments were meant to be exemplary and painful. All beggars were to be stripped to the waist and whipped until they were bloody, then sent home or to the grim confines of a house of correction. Moreover, any rogue who appeared to be a hardened and dangerous character would be sent to such places beyond the seas as the Privy Council might designate.

By these provisions, incorrigible lawbreakers could be shipped out of the mother country even more readily than convicts throughout the colonial period. How "manie Drunkards, Tossepottes, whoremoisters, Dauncers, Fidlers and Minstrels, Diceplaiers, & Maskers" were dispatched to the colonies is not revealed by British court records. On the other hand, we know of enough charlatans, fortunetellers, minstrels, jugglers, tinkers, and actors in the colonies to assume that a good many of these roguish varieties made their way to America and provided lively if not always discreet entertainment for the less sophisticated colonists. What seems remarkable is that the colonies (like Virginia and Maryland) receiving the largest numbers of indentured servants and convicted felons were not utterly submerged and demoralized by these successive waves of human flotsam. Vicious and depraved as many of them must have been, the great majority made the adjustment to colonial life with reasonable success. Otherwise it is hard to see how these colonies could have survived, let alone prospered in their material and spiritual endeavors.

The transatlantic voyage from England to America was a terrible ordeal for most of those who made the crossing. Indentured servants signed up by crimps and spirits embarked on small, poorly equipped, and often dirty sailing vessels that took from one to as much as five months, depending on prevailing winds, to make the crossing. The *Sea-Flower,* with 106 passengers aboard, took sixteen weeks; forty-six of her passengers died of starvation, and of these, six were eaten by the desperate survivors. The long crossing meant bad food; the water stank and grew slimy, meat spoiled, and butter turned rancid. If the captain or owner was a profiteer, the food was often rotten to begin with. In small boats tossed by heavy seas, seasickness was commonplace. One passenger on such a crossing wrote a crude verse describing the effects of a storm on his fellow voyagers: Soon after the storm began, "there was the odest scene betwixt decks that I ever heard or seed. There was some sleeping, some spewing . . . some damning, some Blasting their legs and thighs, some their liver, lungs, lights and eyes. And for to make the scene the odder, some curs'd Father, Mother, Sister, and Brother."

A French Protestant named Durand sailed for Virginia after the revocation of the Edict of Nantes and the resumption of active persecution of the Huguenots. There were fifteen prostitutes on board ship, headed, hopefully, for a new life in the New World. During the passage, they spent their time singing and dancing and making love with the sailors and the indentured servants aboard. Durand, kept awake by their revels, wrote: "Certainly their insolence wrought a change in my nature, for my acquaintances would no doubt impute to me, as my greatest failing, an exaggerated love of the fair sex, & to tell the truth I must admit that in my youth there was no injustice in this accusation. Not that I was ever low enough or coarse enough to feel an affection for prostitutes, but I am obliged to confess I did not abhor their debauchery as I should have. . . . But when I saw those wenches behave so shockingly with the sailors and and others, in addition to the distress caused by their songs and dances, it awakened within me so intense a hatred of such persons that I shall never overcome it." Durand's wife died at sea, the food ran out, and the captain proved to be a knave and a bully. Their voyage took nineteen miserable weeks, long enough for weakness and hunger to quiet the gaiety of the prostitutes.

In the German principalities, the counterparts of the English "spirits" were the Newlanders, agents who tried to persuade guileless coun-

tryfolk to set sail for America. Gottlieb Mittelberger, a German immigrant from Enzweiningen who arrived in Philadelphia in 1750, gave a
vivid account of his crossing of the Atlantic. He was bitter about the "sad
and miserable condition of those traveling from Germany to the New
World, and the irresponsible and merciless proceedings of the Dutch
traders in human beings and their man-stealing emissaries—I mean the
so-called Newlanders. For these at one and the same time steal German
people under all sorts of fine pretexts, and deliver them into the hands
of the great Dutch traffickers in human souls." The trip meant "for most
who undertake it the loss of all they possess, of freedom and peace, and
for some the loss of their very lives and, I can even go so far as to say, of
the salvation of their souls." Mittelberger's journey took six months, the
people "packed into the big boats as closely as herring. . . ." The water
distributed to thirsty passengers was often "very black, thick with dirt
and full of worms." Mittelberger's description of conditions on the ship
refers to "smells, fumes, horrors, vomiting . . . boils, scurvy, cancer,
mouthrot . . . caused by the age and the highly-salted state of the food,
especially of the meat. . . . Add to all that shortage of food, hunger,
thirst, frost, heat, dampness, fear, misery, vexation, and lamentation . . .
so many lice . . . that they have to be scraped off the bodies. All this
misery reaches its climax when in addition to everything else one must
suffer through two to three days and nights of storm . . . all the people
on board pray and cry pitifully together." Under such circumstances,
what little civility there might have been collapsed completely. People
grew so bitter "that one person begins to curse the other, or himself and
the day of his birth, and people sometimes come close to murdering one
another. Misery and malice are readily associated, so that people begin
to cheat and steal from one another." It is hardly surprising that
America, when the immigrants reached it, seemed a land of deliverance:
"When at last after the long and difficult voyage the ships finally
approach land," Mittelberger wrote, "for the sight of which the people
on board had longed so passionately, then everyone crawls from below
to the deck, in order to look at the land. . . . And the people cry for joy,
pray, and sing praises and thanks to God. The glimpse of land revives
the passengers, especially those who are half-dead of illness. Their
spirits, however weak they had become, leap up, triumph, and
rejoice. . . ."

As difficult as were the conditions under which indentured servants
and redemptioners crossed the Atlantic, the circumstances of the prisoners were, as might be imagined, substantially worse. They were

chained below decks in crowded, noisome ranks. One observer who went on board a convict ship to visit a prisoner wrote: "All the states of horror I ever had an idea of are much short of what I saw this poor man in; chained to a board in a hole not above sixteen feet long, more than fifty with him; a collar and padlock about his neck, and chained to five of the most dreadful creatures I ever looked on." Living conditions were little better than those obtaining on slave ships, and before the voyage was over it was not uncommon to lose a quarter of the human cargo, most frequently to the ravages of smallpox. (Only half as many women as men died on these hell ships, a fact attributed by merchants in the convict trade to their stronger constitutions.) Convicts so often arrived in the colonies more dead than alive that Parliamentary statutes finally set minimum allowances of bread, cheese, meat, oatmeal, and molasses per passenger—with two gills of gin issued on Saturdays.

The feelings of the colonists concerning the apparently endless stream of transported felons and vagabonds are indicated by a passage in the *Virginia Gazette* of May 24, 1751: "When we see our Papers fill'd continually with Accounts of the most audacious Robberies, the most cruel Murders, and infinite other Villanies perpetrated by Convicts transported from Europe," the correspondent wrote, "what melancholy, what terrible Reflections must it occasion! What will become of our Posterity? These are some of thy Favours, Britain! Thou are called our Mother Country; but what good Mother ever sent Thieves and Villains to accompany her children; to corrupt some with their infectious Vices and murder the rest? . . . In what can Britain show a more Sovereign contempt for us than by emptying their Jails into our Settlements. . . ." Whatever the colonists' feelings, the English were delighted with the practice of transporting their convicts to America. By such a procedure, the criminal was separated from evil companions and from the usually deplorable conditions that had induced him to take up a life of crime.

Not all convicts appreciated, by any means, the opportunity afforded them to start life over in the colonies. Not a few found their way back home (risking certain death, if caught) and declared that they would rather be hanged than return to America.

Servants and convicts who had served out their indentures often drifted to the frontier areas of the colonies, particularly to the southern frontier. Some took up cattle ranching in western Carolina, where the cattle were turned loose to graze, rounded up yearly into pens (hence Cowpens, South Carolina), and driven to the seacoast markets for meat and hides. Some, like the Hatfields and the McCoys, would in time feud with each other for decades; others lived lives of lawlessness and banditry, preying on staid planters in more settled areas and becoming, in some instances, the ancestors of the Southern mountain folk, who for successive generations resisted the incursions of tax collectors.

A number, of course, gathered in the seaport towns of Baltimore, Philadelphia, New York, Charles Town, and Boston, where they drank excessively, did occasional labor, committed petty crimes, rioted, and formed the nucleus of revolutionary mobs. The truth was that with few exceptions, they belonged to that class of people whose feelings lie very close to the surface. Violent and passionate by nature, they were peculiarly susceptible to both religious conversion and revolutionary ardor. Restless and rootless, they were readily swept up by any emotional storm. Many of them were converted at the time of the Great Awakening into pious Presbyterians, Methodists, and, somewhat later, Baptists. These denominations, with their emphasis on personal experience, were perfectly suited to the psychological needs of such individuals. Thus a substantial number of servants and ex-convicts accommodated themselves to the Protestant Ethic and became in time indistinguishable from their orthodox neighbors.

Less colorful, but equally important, were those settlers who came on their own initiative and at their own expense. By a process of natural selection, such individuals were usually aggressive, ambitious, and, as we would say today, highly motivated. Prominent among them were the Scotch-Irish, typically those Covenanters who had fled Scotland to escape the devastating and constant warfare with the Highland lairds supporting the cause of the Stuart Pretenders, and who had found Northern Ireland inhospitable. They sprang from the Lowland Scots— independent yeoman farmers who were stout Presbyterians, often shared a common Scottish aversion to the British, and were now removed in turn to the congenial atmosphere of the colonies, particularly Pennsylvania. Hardy, enterprising Calvinists, they made their way in large numbers westward, where land was plentiful and cheap. There, serving as "the guardians of the frontier," they were constantly embroiled with eastern land speculators or various Indian tribes over ownership of land.

There was a special affinity between native Lowland Scots and the inhabitants of the middle and eastern colonies. This led to a substantial immigration of Scotch-Irish in the middle years of the eighteenth century preceding the Revolutionary crisis. Never large in numbers, the Scots nonetheless, like the Jews and Huguenots, played a disproportionately important role in colonial affairs and were prominent in the patriot cause.

The Rhineland country in present-day Germany was in the eighteenth century divided into a number of principalities, including the Rheinpfalz or Rhenish Palatinate, Württemberg, Baden, and Brunswick. These petty states were constantly embroiled in European conflicts, and many German peasants, most of them pious Lutherans, fled from the exactions of their princes: from conscription, heavy taxes, and a condition of chronic insecurity. The majority came to Pennsylvania, with some in New York, Virginia, and the Carolinas. In Penn's colony, they established tight-knit, self-contained farming communities, where they clung to their language and their folk traditions. Travelers noted that they were stolid, hard-working, and usually more tidy than their English or Scotch-Irish neighbors. From *Deutsch,* they became Pennsylvania Dutch, developing their own patois and, by clinging stubbornly to their folk traditions, making their villages into small fortresses of cultural separatism. The most conspicuous and long-lived of the German immigrant groups that came to America were the Moravians, a pietist sect that traced its spiritual descent from John Huss. This group settled primarily in Salem, North Carolina, and Bethlehem, Pennsylvania, and to this day they preserve a rich tradition of church music, especially that of Johann Sebastian Bach. The Dunkers, who excelled in choral singing and bookmaking, and their close cousins the Mennonites also came largely to Pennsylvania. Today, forbidden by their religion to wear clothes with buttons, to drive cars, to use electricity, radios, or television, the Mennonite men with their chin hair, plain black clothes, and broad-brimmed black hats, and the women with their long skirts and bonnets, still farm the rich and carefully tended soil of central Pennsylvania and are frequently embroiled with the state over their determination not to send their children to public schools.

The Welsh, most of them Quakers, also came in substantial numbers to Pennsylvania, where they prospered strikingly. In France, under Henry V, Protestantism put down substantial roots in the mercantile middle class, but the French people remained overwhelmingly Catholic. As Protestant England had persecuted its Catholics, so Catholic France persecuted its Protestants (known as Huguenots). In consequence many Huguenots looked to the New World. Since they were denied entry into New France, a number were strung out from Boston to Charles Town, favoring the toleration and commercial opportunities offered by these port towns. Peter Faneuil, the rich merchant who built Faneuil Hall,

Boston's "Cradle of Liberty," and who was both a good patriot and a public benefactor, was of Huguenot ancestry, as were Paul Revere and—in South Carolina—the Rhetts, the Gadsdens, the Ravenels, the Laurenses, the Deveaux and the L'Enfants.

A handful of Jews came to the American colonies in the seventeenth and eighteenth centuries, with Pennsylvania and Rhode Island as the preferred locations. The first American synagogue was built in Providence, Rhode Island. Aaronsburg, Pennsylvania, was founded by Jewish settlers, and in Philadelphia the wealthy Gratz family contributed generously to the patriot cause. A Jewish scholar taught Hebrew at Harvard in the middle of the eighteenth century.

How this collection of astonishingly diverse individuals, from a dozen countries and twice as many religious sects and denominations, spread out over a vast territory and coalesced into a nation and eventually into a united people is the subject of this history.

3

Legacy of Liberty

THE story of colonial America is in large part the story of action in England and reaction in America; of periods of close attention by the British to the "plantations," followed by periods of "salutary neglect." Indeed, the colonists could not have chosen a better century in which to settle in America than the seventeenth. It was certainly one of the most turbulent in British history; whatever their intentions, the men or, more accurately, the factions that directed the affairs of England in those stormy decades had little time to devote to colonial affairs. The colonies, left largely to their own devices, flourished. But salutary neglect was not, of course, the whole story. A policy worked out laboriously by a succession of governments, primarily through the Lords and then by the Board of Trade and Plantations, defined the relationship between the mother country and her American colonies. Some able men concerned themselves with the colonies in the eighteenth century, among them the great diarist Samuel Pepys and the philosopher John Locke.

Beyond that, the colonies followed, as closely as they could from the other side of the Atlantic, the course of events in England. And those events exerted an enormous influence on the attitudes and aspirations of the colonists themselves. What they believed they were witnessing in the homeland was nothing less than a struggle to the death between

47

arbitrary power, in the persons of the Stuart kings, and constitutional government, represented by Parliament. The colonists were convinced that on the outcome of that struggle rested their own fate as free men under lawful authority. The great struggle of the kings against Parliament that took up almost the entire seventeenth century in England helped implant in the colonists their belief in their "rights as Englishmen"—rights that they were willing to fight to protect.

The Scottish ruling family, the Stuarts, succeeded to the English Crown on the death of childless Queen Elizabeth in 1603. First of the Stuarts was James VI of Scotland, who became James I of England. James was a hardheaded Scottish theoretician with little common sense. Indeed, he was so ignorant of the laws of England that on his way from Edinburgh to London in 1603 to be crowned king he ordered a thief to be hanged without trial, which was illegal in England. It was an inauspicious beginning to what was at best a difficult succession. It was James's fate to follow Elizabeth, one of the greatest and most loved monarchs in English history. For her remarkable political skills, he substituted the narrow dogmatism of his Scottish background.

Almost at once James found himself embroiled with his new subjects over the royal prerogatives. Underlying this issue was the rise of a new strain of Englishman. While avowing themselves members of the Church of England, they were, in fact, strongly influenced by the more radical religious notions spawned by the Protestant Reformation. John Calvin, the great theoretician of the Reformation, wished to reform the world by sweeping away the accumulated ecclesiastical practices of centuries, and with them much of the luxury and extravagance that characterized the lives of the European upper classes. Simplicity of spirit, austerity as regards material and worldy things, piety, and personal responsibility were all elements in Calvin's new creed. It was the wish of those who followed the teachings of Calvin of Geneva to be pure in mind and spirit, purer than the contaminated world around them. They were thus called "Puritans" in derision, and they took the name in pride. It was largely from this radical wing of the new Protestantism that a breed of politicians arose who undertook to defend what they conceived to be the traditional rights of Englishmen against usurpations by the new monarch. They made Parliament the stumbling block to James. Another critical issue that confronted James was whether he would grant a kind of legitimacy to those Englishmen who were, strictly speaking, somewhat heterodox in their religious views. To have done so would have been a wise and reconciling act. But that was not James's nature. The dissenters must accept the authority of their bishops like every proper Anglican. "No Bishop, No King!" he declared. And then he added, fatefully, "I shall make them conform themselves or I will harry them out of the land." A king, however exalted his power and mighty his name, is as surely a politician as any democratically elected president or small-town mayor. And irreconcilability is the antithesis of wise politics. Yet James proved as good as his word. He and his bishops proceeded to harry a substantial number of his dissenting subjects "out of the land."

If he did not thereby lay the foundations for English America (Virginia, after all, was founded without any direct reference to James's hostility to the Puritans), he for a certainty provided the colonies with a company of settlers who, by transplanting that Puritanism that so enraged the king to the New World, determined the character, temper, consciousness—call it what you will—of that New World more conclusively than any other body of people who came to the English colonies. James, of course, did more than that. He solidified parliamentary opposition to him, for the dissenters were strongly represented in Parliament, and such men as John Eliot and John Hampden proved to be as skilled in mustering parliamentary support as the king was clumsy in dissipating it. Men like Eliot and Hampden were assiduous in developing the latent powers in the House of Commons; they mastered all the intricacies of procedure and debate, and they transformed that body into a modern legislature that proved quite capable of defying a monarch who claimed excessive power as a divine right.

In one of its first addresses to the Stuart king, Parliament sounded themes that would reverberate for generations to come. The House of Commons was "the sole proper judge" of the actions of its members and of the terms under which they were elected. "The rights and liberties of the Commons of England consisteth chiefly in these three things," the petition continued; "first, that the shires, cities, and boroughs of England . . . have free choice of such persons as they shall put in trust to represent them," second, that such persons should be free from arrest or restraint during the sessions of Parliament, and "thirdly, that in parliament they may speak freely their consciences without check and controlment."

The manor houses of England in these years produced a number of responsible, politically astute country gentlemen to sit in the Houses of Parliament. These manor lords, as an English historian has said, were "antiquarians in learning, and devotees of law, custom and precedent, they persuaded themselves and their countrymen that they were only claiming ancient privileges, and carrying out the spirit and even the letter of the Magna Carta." The study of history was an enormously important part of this growth of self-conscious resistance to royal claims. History was the basis for all the claims put forth by those who opposed the Crown in the name of the ancient liberties of Greece and Rome.

In a series of bitter encounters with Parliament, James I called it up, fought with it, dissolved it, convened it when he needed money, again fought with it, and finally dissolved it. The nature of the conflict between James I and Parliament is well shown by an angry letter from the king to the House of Commons in 1621. "Mr. Speaker we have heard by divers reports, to our great grief, that our distance from the house of parliament, caused by our indisposition of health, hath emboldened some fiery and popular spirits of some of the House of Commons to argue and debate publicity of matters far above their reach and capacity, tending to our high dishonor and breach of prerogative royal. These messages are therefore to command you to make known in our name unto the House that none therein shall presume henceforth to meddle with anything concerning our government or deep matters of state. . . . we think ourselves very free and able to punish any man's misdemeanours in parliament, as well during their sitting as after; which we mean not to spare hereafter, upon any occasion of any man's insolent behaviour there that shall be ministered unto us."

In answer the House drew up and placed on record the famous Great Protestation: "The Commons now assembled in parliament, being justly [concerned about] . . . sundry liberties, franchises, and privileges of parliament . . . do make this protestation following: that the liberties, franchises, privileges, and jurisdictions of parliament are the ancient and undoubted birthright and inheritance of the subjects of England; and that the arduous and urgent affairs concerning the king, state, and defense of the realm and of the Church of England, and the maintenance and making of laws, and the redress of mischiefs and grievances which daily happen within this realm are proper subjects and matter of counsel and debate in parliament; and that . . . every member . . . hath and of right ought to have freedom of speech, to propound, treat, reason, and bring to conclusion the same; and that the Commons in parliament have like liberty and freedom to treat of these matters . . . as in their judgments shall seem fittest; and that every member of the said house hath like freedom from all impeachment, imprisonment, and molestation . . . for or concerning any speaking, reasoning, or declaring of any matter or matters touching the parliament or parliament business. . . ."

Contentious and inflexible at home, James was pacifistic and unwarlike in his dealings with England's rival states. He let the English navy, built up under his predecessor Elizabeth, deteriorate. Ancient enemy Spain flouted English power, but Holland committed the greater outrages, and England was powerless to strike back. On the Continent, the Catholic Counter Reformation was routing Protestantism—as well as devastating Europe in the Thirty Years' War. James's response to Spanish outrages was appeasement. He even offered to marry off his son Charles to the Spanish infanta, hoping thereby to bring peace to Europe. But the English were appalled at the prospect of a Catholic king of England, and the rift between the king and his subjects continued to widen.

James I died in 1625. By that time a group of dissenters who called themselves Separatists or Pilgrims had been harried out of the land, and a more important and powerful contingent was soon to leave for Massachusetts Bay.

Charles I, James's son, was if anything less liked and less successful than his father. He was, first of all, married to a French Catholic, the Princess Henrietta Maria. Further, with no real weapons to carry on wars, Charles followed a policy of militancy as disastrous as his father's pacificism. Expensive and bungled campaigns brought with them taxation without Parliament's approval and arbitrary imprisonment without due process of law.

Parliament showed at once that it was determined to resist what most of its members considered royal encroachments. The issue was, in effect, whether the English king would make good his claim to powers that would have drawn England in the direction of the medieval French monarchy, or whether Parliament would move the nation toward constitutional reforms resulting in representative government.

As Charles pressed for more money for his floundering military enterprises, Parliament presented to him in 1628 the Petition of Right, which they forced him to accept in order to get the taxes he needed. The petition started off by stating that in the time of Edward I, a statute had been passed saying that "no tallage or aid shall be laid or levied by the king or his heirs in this realm without the good will and assent of the archbishops, bishops, earls, barons, knights, burgesses, and the other freemen of the commonalty of this realm."

The petition continued, "And where also by the statute called The

Great Charter of the Liberties of England [Magna Charta] it is declared and enacted, that no freeman may be taken or imprisoned or be disseised [dispossessed] of his freehold or liberties or his free customs, or be outlawed or exiled or in any manner destroyed, but by the lawful judgment of his peers, or by the law of the land.

"They do therefore humbly pray your most excellent Majesty, that no man hereafter be compelled to make or yield any gift, benevolence, tax, or such like charge, without common consent by act of parliament. . . ." In addition, there was to be no forced quartering of soldiers and no martial law, and all things were to be done "according to the laws and statutes of this realm."

The parliamentary struggle with James and then with Charles had the effect of increasingly shifting the power in the House of Commons from the Anglican moderates to the Puritan radicals. This trend culminated in 1629, when members of Parliament held the speaker in his chair and, despite his tears and protests, passed a resolution against "Popery or Arminianism." Popery, of course, referred to Catholicism, and the resolution was thus a slap at the Catholic queen and, indirectly, at Charles. "Arminianism" was a reference to the doctrines of Jacobus Arminius, a Dutch theologian who had undertaken to refute the harsh doctrine of Calvin that all men and women were predestined for "election" or damnation, and that they could do nothing in their own lives, no matter how faithful and pious they might be, to alter that divinely predestined fate. The fact that Arminianism was coupled with popery showed that the radical Calvinist faction had gained control of the House of Commons. The king, when he heard of this calculated insult to the authority of the Church of England (the Anglican establishment was heavily Arminian) and of the state (in the insult to the queen), sent the sergeant at arms to dismiss Commons, but he was locked out. Thereupon Parliament was dissolved by the king and did not sit again for eleven years. Sir John Eliot, leader of the parliamentary forces, was imprisoned in the Tower of London and died there rather than recant his criticisms of the use of the royal prerogative.

Charles, determined to have his own way, dismissed those judges who persisted in interpreting the laws impartially. This, with the dismissal of Parliament, meant that all constitutional checks on the Crown were removed, and the king was free to do as he pleased. He pleased to use the executive courts of Star Chamber and High Commission, whose members were appointed by the king, to silence what remained of his parliamentary opposition, and in so doing he raised the great lawyers against him to protect the integrity of the common law. The Archbishop of Canterbury, William Laud, the chief prelate of the Anglican Church, made a bad situation worse by trying to force ministers of Puritan sentiments to perform church rituals and ceremonies that to them smacked of popery. The result of these royal attacks on the masters of the common law and on those Englishmen who refused to conform to the stipulated ecclesiastical forms was a formidable alliance between parliamentary lawyers and Puritan dissenters.

Meanwhile, Catholicism revived under the influence of Charles's French wife, thus increasing the fears and resentments of the people at large. The Scottish Revolt of 1638 marked the beginning of a Civil War that engulfed the whole country. When the Scots successfully defied the armies of Charles, he misjudged the temper of the country and summoned Parliament into session to seek ransom money to buy off the invaders. But the members of Parliament were in no mood to oblige the king. They began, instead of voting money, to discuss the abuse of the royal powers. Charles promptly prorogued Parliament, but it soon assembled again. The historian George Trevelyan calls the lengthy session that followed "the true turning-point in the political history of the English-speaking races. It not only prevented the English monarchy from hardening into an absolutism of the type then becoming general in Europe, but it made a great experiment in direct rule of the country and of the Empire by the House of Commons."

During the first two years of the new Parliament, the more moderate elements—Puritans, Roundheads, Church of England men, and constitutional cavaliers—joined forces to establish English rights and liberties on a firm rock that was never subsequently shaken. Then the religious issue broke Parliament wide open. The Puritans, who were unwilling to compromise, did not want religious toleration; they rejected the Book of Common Prayer and wished to reform the Church of England along Presbyterian lines. On the third of January, 1642, Charles ordered the impeachment of the leaders of the House of Commons, John Hampden among them, for treasonable correspondence with the Scots. When Commons refused to surrender the men, Charles himself, with several hundred soldiers, entered the House to make the arrests. The indicted members escaped and took refuge in the City of London, a stronghold of antimonarchial sentiment, until Charles himself withdrew to York. Then they returned in triumph to the House and helped to draw up nineteen propositions to present to the king. The propositions would, in effect, have stripped the king and the Church of most of their powers, and Charles not unnaturally refused to sign them. Parliament, now securely in the hands of the radicals, thereupon appointed a committee of public safety, an extralegal and thus revolutionary body, and placed in the field an army of 20,000 hastily mustered amateur soldiers with 4,000 cavalry. The king, joined by thirty-two peers and sixty-five of the more conservative members of Commons, prepared to oppose the parliamentary army by raising a force of his own at Nottingham.

Speaking very generally, the gentry, the peasantry, the Anglican clergy, and those members of the working class unaffected by the Puritan faith supported the king, while the parliamentary faction recruited its forces from a strange alliance of prosperous merchants, great aristocrats, and what might be described very loosely as the middle class, made up in large part of dissenters of various persuasions from the Church of England. The first battle at Edge Hill favored the Royalist forces, but a group of strongly Puritan counties raised a force that was placed under the leadership of Oliver Cromwell. Cromwell proved to be a military genius; in a remarkably short time, he welded his citizen army into a formidable body of fighting men under strict discipline. Cromwell's Ironsides, as his troops came to be called, decisively defeated the supporters of Charles at the Battle of Marston Moor on July 2, 1644. Another battle at Naseby a year later completed the destruction of the Royalist armies. Charles surrendered to a force of Scotch Presbyterians; they in turn "sold" him to Parliament for their back pay of some 400,000 pounds.

This unsavory bargain backfired by splitting Parliament from the army, and the Civil War entered a second phase, with Charles forming an alliance with the Scotch Presbyterians. In the fighting that followed, it was again the superior discipline and greater resources of Cromwell's Roundheads and Independents that carried the day against the Royalists and their new-found Scottish allies. Edward Hyde, Earl of Clarendon, the great historian of the rebellion and a supporter of Charles, wrote of the New Model Army of Cromwell that they had "great discipline, diligence and sobriety; which begat courage and resolution in them, and notable dexterity in achievements and enterprises." The Royalists, on the other hand fell into "license, disorder and impiety," so that "one side seemed to fight for monarchy with the weapons of confusion, and the other to destroy the King and government with all the principles and regularity of monarchy."

The Scots, invading England, were defeated by Cromwell at the

Battle of Preston in August of 1648. Charles was captured once more, tried before a high court of sixty-seven members appointed by an abbreviated Parliament, sentenced to death, and beheaded at Whitehall on January 30, 1649. For the next eleven years England lived under the Commonwealth, a nominally republican form of government that was actually largely under the control of Cromwell, who in 1653 took effective power as lord protector of the Commonwealth of England, Scotland, and Ireland under a written constitution called the "Instrument of Government," which gave Cromwell essentially dictatorial powers. He used these with restraint during a war with Spain and until his death in 1658. After a brief interval, during which Cromwell's inept son Richard, called Tumble-down Dick, succeeded him as lord protector, Parliament decided that it and the English people had endured enough civil war and disorder and voted to restore the Stuart monarchy by declaring Charles II king of England, Ireland, and Scotland.

The period of the Civil War was a period of enormous political and social ferment. Radical Christian social groups called Diggers, Levelers, and Fifth Monarchy Men expounded their doctrines. The leader of the Diggers, Gerrard Winstanley, challenged the parliamentary leaders and Roundheads with doctrines too radical for them to consider. "What stock," he asked, "is provided for the *poor, fatherless, widows*, and *impoverished people*? And what advancement of encouragement for the *laboring* and *industrious*, as to take off their burthens, is there?" Another Digger wrote, "*England* is not a Free People, till the Poor that have no Land, have a free allowance to dig and labour the Commons." John Lilburne wrote angry tracts against tyrannical kings and rapacious bishops. Social bitterness flamed out in many of the pamphlets that circulated through the army and among the restless farm tenants and city poor. "'Tis the rich men that oppresse you," one pamphleteer declared. Winstanley went so far as to argue that the earth should be made a *"common Treasury of livelihood to whole mankind, without respect of persons."* The *"Community of Mankind,"* the first community, was composed of all those joined in "the unity of the spirit of Love, which is called Christ in you, or the Law written in the heart, leading mankind into all truth, and to be of one heart and one mind." The second community was the *"Community of the Earth,* for the quiet livelihood in food and raiment without using force, or restraining one another: These two Communities . . . [contain] the true Levelling which Christ will work at his more glorious appearance; for Jesus Christ the Saviour of all men, is the greatest, first, and truest Leveller that ever was spoke of in the world."

Winstanley and four followers went to St. George's Hill in Surrey on Sunday, April 1, 1649, and started to dig up the earth and plant beans, carrots, and parsnips. In six months fifty "Diggers" had joined the original group. They dug and planted in common unclaimed land, but they nonetheless aroused the fury of their neighbors, who attacked and beat them, destroyed their tools, pulled up their crops, and burned their houses.

In John Lilburne the so-called Levelers had a more effective leader—one who waged warfare more by pamphlets than by symbolic actions such as those taken by the unfortunate Diggers. Where Winstanley envisioned a communistic society "without buying or selling, without money, without tithes, without hereditary titles, without inequality of income," and with its leaders elected by all men over twenty, Lilburne more modestly wished for a new constitution based on popular consent, and he published almost two hundred pamphlets in defense of his radical proposals.

More famous than either Lilburne or Winstanley, but sharing many of their radical doctrines, was the poet John Milton, whose *Areopagitica,* published in 1644, remains the great argument for a free press. It was written, as Milton expressed it, "in order to deliver the press from the restraints with which it was encumbered; that the power of determining what was true and what was false, what ought to be published and what to be suppressed, might no longer be entrusted to a few illiterate and illiberal individuals. . . ."

Inevitably, many of the Leveler pamphlets and the ideas they espoused found their way to America, where they fell like seeds in a welcoming soil. Milton's works, which relentlessly championed freedom in every area of man's social and political life, became as familiar as the Bible and John Bunyan to colonists of the Protestant persuasion—Congregationalists, Presbyterians, Quakers, and Baptists alike. It is difficult to convey the intensity of attention with which the colonists attempted to follow the bewildering course of events in the mother country. Their own fortunes hung on the outcome of events across the ocean, events so complex and tumultuous that historians still contend about them and still understand them imperfectly. Perhaps all we can say with certainty is that the ferment of radical religious, political, and social ideas that kept England in a turmoil for twenty years or more became a permanent legacy of the English colonists, especially those of "New" England. The connection is symbolized by the return of Massachusetts Governor Sir Henry Vane to Old England, where he became a leader of the Independents, that party that opposed a state church of any kind, Anglican or Presbyterian.

Charles II came back under the carefully stated conditions of the so-called Restoration Settlement. Charles's Declaration of Breda, which provided for a general amnesty and contained appropriate expressions of respect for Parliament, promised England religious toleration "because the passion and uncharitableness of the times have produced several opinions in religion, by which men are engaged in parties and animosities against each other . . . they shall hereafter unite in a freedom of conversation. . . ." Parliamentary control over taxation was clearly established. The executive courts of Star Chamber and High Commission were abolished and the rights of executive courts in general delimited.

With the Restoration, the British upper classes, hoping doubtless to forget the horrors of the Civil War, plunged into an orgy of hedonistic pleasures that made the era's name a synonym for bawdy and licentious behavior. The doctrines of the Levelers and the Diggers, the visions of democracy and equality, appeared as delusive as dreams, as, indeed, nightmares. Even during their brief lifetime the radical leaders had been denounced by all men of good judgment. Now they were quickly forgotten.

Moreover, with the Restoration a spirit developed in England quite hostile to the colonies. In the mother country Anglicanism and aristocracy once more suppressed Puritanism and incipient democracy. Correspondingly, the colonies, so far as they manifested a leveling and democratic temper, served to remind Englishmen of events they would have preferred to forget. There was widespread disquiet among dissenters in the colonies as well as in England over the severity of the Cavalier Parliament's Clarendon Code, four statutes directed against religious noncomformists.

Charles, pinched for funds by Parliament and surrounded by unscrupulous advisers, courted France and agreed with Louis XIV to attack Holland. A secret portion of the treaty committed the French monarch to supply Charles with money and French soldiers in order that he might become a Catholic, suppress the Protestants, and raise his fellow Catholics to positions of dominance in England.

Before Charles had an opportunity to put such a nefarious scheme into practice, he died and was succeeded, in 1685, by his Catholic brother, James. The Parliament that James II summoned was thoroughly royalist in sentiment. With James's encouragement the Whigs were hounded and suppressed, and a campaign of terror was instituted against those dissenters powerless to protect themselves. With the principal enemies of the royal power scattered and demoralized, James with some tact and discretion might have been able to carry the country a long way toward the ideal of kingship held by his grandfather, James I. But the new James was a zealot, determined to push Catholicism, and this was the one issue on which Parliament was unwilling to yield.

Indeed, James's efforts to protect his fellow Catholics from persecution united most of England against him. The birth of an heir to the throne brought matters to a head. The opponents of James invited William of Orange to save England from the imagined horrors of Catholicism. William landed at Torbay; James fled England; and the Revolution Settlement, guaranteeing the rights of Parliament and of individual citizens, was accepted by William as the condition of his accession to the throne of England.

The Declaration of Rights, the formal document in which William of Orange and his wife, Mary, accepted the limitations on the royal powers that Parliament had wrested from the Stuarts after almost a half-century of struggle, provided also that no Roman Catholic could ever be sovereign of England, and that the succession to the throne would pass through the heirs of Mary. The Bill of Rights, which accompanied the Declaration, reaffirmed the cherished rights that Englishmen felt had been trampled underfoot by the Stuarts. These included the right of trial by a jury of one's peers in the "vicinage" or neighborhood; freedom of speech and assembly; the right to just and equal laws; freedom from self-incrimination; and freedom of worship (except, of course, for Catholics). The so-called Glorious Revolution of 1689 was primarily glorious because it was virtually bloodless. From almost a century of fierce conflict it ultimately rescued certain classic principles of human freedom and parliamentary government, summarized in the Bill of Rights. It affirmed further that no Englishman would henceforth be taxed without his consent, as channeled through his elected representatives in the House of Commons. Englishmen, although often negligent, did not forget the lesson. Moderation, tolerance, restraint, a bone-deep conservatism that sought compromise and accommodation before confrontation, became conspicuous traits of the average Englishman. Fanaticism was to be avoided at all costs; eccentricity, quirkiness, a kind of intractable independence, became typical and indeed valued qualities.

The lesson that the Americans learned was rather different. They absorbed, to be sure, the lesson that fanaticism lets loose dangerous forces in society. But they certainly learned equally well another lesson—that the rights and liberties of a free people have to be fought for, and that in the mother country such a struggle had been crowned with success.

The Glorious Revolution had notable effects on the colonists both practically and intellectually. Political upheavals in New England, New York, and Maryland were related directly or indirectly to the overthrow of James. The reaffirmation of British liberties recalled the wild days of the Civil War. All the democratic ferment that seemed to fade so rapidly in England persisted in America and entered into the consciousness of many of those colonists who would have been called dissenters had they remained in England.

It was not surprising under the circumstances that the colonies were more frequently neglected during the course of the seventeenth century than attended to. What was rather to be wondered at was that a series of Parliaments, starting in the reign of Charles I, enacted a series of statutes, given effect through the Board of Trade and Plantations, that progressively defined the relationship between Great Britain and her American possessions and did so, on the whole, in a remarkably generous spirit. Perhaps it was because, at least in those times dominated by the Independents and Roundheads, there was a keen sense among the leaders in the House of Commons of religious and moral affinity with the colonies, especially those of New England. It was certainly no coincidence that the charter of Rhode Island, the most liberal granted any colony, was obtained by Roger Williams in 1643. Even the Restoration of Charles II could not immediately undo this bond. Moreover, the political instability of the mother country was a powerful incentive to emigration in the days when being out of power often meant losing one's head in the bargain. So the English colonies grew greatly in numbers during that tumultuous century, and they learned, perhaps better than the British themselves, whatever lessons the events of that era were capable of teaching to attentive students on the other side of the Atlantic.

4

New England and the Middle Colonies

A s important as the question of who came was the matter of how those who came lived in this strange new environment. Human beings form social groups; they adopt principles to guide their common life and call these principles laws and constitutions; men and women labor in order that they and their children may eat. The first settlers who came to English America joined together for mutual protection against the aborigines, worked to sustain themselves, and combined, in many instances, to promote their own visions of redeemed and purified communities. These firstcomers, or founders, established the pattern for those who followed them. It might be said that they formed a matrix or, since there were many different kinds of communities and social groups, a number of matrices into which those who came later had to fit themselves willy-nilly. In some instances, the newcomers would not or could not fit in and therefore formed new communities more to their liking. Historians once would have said that, responding to God's intentions for them, the firstcomers and their successors, diverse as they were, grew in inscrutable ways toward a common destiny. The modern student of colonial settlement may reject the argument of divine intention, but he has nonetheless to acknowledge that the processes by which these very different groups, races, classes, religious sects, and nationalities came to form first a people and then a nation are mysterious indeed. From New Hampshire to Georgia, what we would call today the life-styles of the settlers varied almost as widely as their origins, yet in the ways they lived and thought and worshiped there existed some essential common elements of what would in time constitute their peoplehood.

The firstcomers did not, of course, invent the social institutions and political forms that gave coherence and order to their lives. They brought these with them from England and adapted them to their new circumstances. The original settlers of "New" England were perhaps most enterprising in modifying old social forms and devising new ones. There the township, roughly six miles square, furnished the matrix that molded the Puritan community.

Adapted from the classic rural town of medieval England, the American township was thus the new wine of the Puritan consciousness, poured into the ancient bottles of the medieval commune. The village common in the center of the town was what the name implied, a common grazing ground for the cows of the householders whose town allotments fronted on the common. There were in addition, of course, the farming allotments, usually drawn by lot from the best farming land in the township, and a common wood lot where everyone could collect his own firewood. The institutions of the town that were most responsible for the forming of the character of rural New Englanders were the church or meeting house, which stood invariably in the most commanding spot on the common, the schoolhouse, and, in time, the militia-day drill.

The town church, with its unadorned simplicity, was a stark rebuke to the vain ostentation of those "popish structures" of the Old World, so filled with idolatrous statuary and lavish decoration. Here everything centered on the Word of God, as expressed in interminable sermons, delivered in the "plain style." There were two services on Sunday, one in the morning and one in the afternoon, each featuring sermons usually an hour or more in length. In addition, there was an evening of study and preparation, often a Thursday. The congregation was made up of the saints—originally those who had borne public witness to an experience of conversion—although those inhabitants of the community who were presumably in a more benighted state were required also to attend services. Such a division proved in time an embarrassment, and by means of the Half-Way Covenant, which admitted the children of the saints into full communion, and similar ameliorations, the congregations eventually encompassed the whole population of a town. Gathered as a secular body at the annual town meeting, the members of the community raised taxes, elected officers, and tried to resolve their common problems. In a community without elaborate machinery for law enforcement, the most sensible way to secure compliance with those modest laws deemed necessary for the common good was to include everyone in what we call today "the decision-making process." Someone who had had his say in town meeting was much more apt to abide by a statute he objected to than someone on whom such a statute had simply been imposed. Thus common sense and good policy dictated a wide practical democracy that went, in most instances, substantially beyond the letter of those voting laws based on property qualifications. Such laws were well and good for the Great and General Court to promulgate in Boston, but most towns went their own more democratic way and made no fuss about it.

Each community was charged with maintaining a school—certainly a dame school where young children were taught to read and write by means of the *New England Primer*. From their hornbooks, children began their quest of learning with that stern reminder of mankind's original sin, under "A": "In Adam's fall, we sinned all." A girl's education, typically, ended at the dame school, while boys continued through grammar school and the more able and ambitious prepared for college, often with the help of a tutor. In grammar school a student generally learned "little Greek and less Latin," but in the better schools, usually to be found in the larger towns, the education was often as rigorous as the theology that prompted it.

The militia usually had two "little trainings" a year when the soldiers drilled on the common. The officers were elected by their troops, which accounts for some looseness of discipline, but the men themselves were hardy farmers used to shooting deer or bear to supplement an often scanty larder. Once a year, there was a regimental muster when neighboring towns joined together for a collective drill and carnival. Each musketeer was required to present for inspection a flintlock musket, two spare flints, a priming wire, and a brush. While the inspectors were progressing with their work, the officers and privates were presented by the selectmen of their towns with money for a "military banquet" full of toasts and much tippling. Crowded around the edge of the town common were peddlers who sold "hats, jewelry, cutlery, patent medicines, books, pictures, etc." as well as "candy, gingerbread and other sweetmeats. . . ." Sometimes a trained bear or a live rattlesnake would be displayed. Invariably, there was a good deal of gambling, and sometimes wrestling matches and footraces.

Matthew Patten was a New England farmer, a native of New Hampshire, who in the 1750's kept a journal of his day-to-day affairs. Besides farming, he acted as judge along with two other lay judges, represented the towns of Bedford and Merrimack in the colony's legislature, and was a justice of the peace. Some entries from his "Day Book," or journal, written in a small, firm hand, give as vivid a picture of the life of a New England farmer in the period prior to the Revolution as one could find.

On October 1, Patten noted: "I got a steel Trap from Samuel Caldwells negroe of James Wallace which I am to have for my own on my likeing it for 2 Dollars with the Chain. . . . 21 sowed between 8 and 9 bushell of Rie & some Wheat at the back of the house. . . . I settled with James Patterson for my Expences with him and Lieut. Little at Amoskieg and I owe them above what fish I let them have. . . . and I finished sowing Rie I have sowed 9 bushell and about 26 Quarts yesterday. . . . I Carried a Web to my Cousen William Patten to be Wove and I proceeded to Boston and Rid all night."

In November Patten went with Colonel Goffe to view a township the colonel was about to buy in Maine. The trip was an arduous one, lasting more than a month. The little party, which included several other promoters of the project, built a log canoe and paddled up the Connecticut River. In addition to surveying the township site, the men spent a week hunting, and Patten recorded that "we catched 5 beaver and a Sapple (sable). . . . I sold my Traps to John Lahhe for a Gun and a pair of Silver Buckles and papuss Beaver skin which I got and took his note of hand for 12 saple skins on their face value in money to be paid on demand with interest at 10 pr Cent pr annum untill pd. . . ." In the days that followed his return, Patten drew up the papers relating to the township survey, helped his neighbor, David McClure, raise his barn, threshed and cleaned three bushels of rye, took it around to Blaisell's mill, got three bushels of potatoes on credit from a nearby farm, got "10 Tile from Deacon Walker and some broken Brick on Credit," laid the bottom of his oven, had two pots mended, had his mare shod, and "mended our Windows and set the Glass in a new frame & sashes for the back side bed Room."

Several things are notable about Matthew Patten's account of the daily routine of a New England farmer. One, of course, is the versatility of a man who farmed, fished, hunted, carpentered, and did a thousand tasks with reasonable competence. Another thing that strikes the reader is the absence of ready money, the freedom with which credit was given, and the trust in payment. There was, in addition, a remarkable degree of dependence of people upon one other. Much of the life of people in rural communities revolved around this constant trading and bartering: an ax for a gun, a gun for a beaver fur, a sable fur for so many pounds of fish or the shoeing of a horse or the performance of some needed service. Grain was taken to a mill to be ground, and some of it was swapped for rum or gin or beer at the tavern adjacent to the mill. Nails were traded for potatoes, or butter for molasses or coffee or tea. It was a pleasant business—part of the pleasure of course was driving a shrewd bargain, just as part of the pleasure was, on occasion, spontaneous generosity. Further, it was necessitous, since life ultimately might depend on it. It meant the constant considering of things, their weight and value, their quality, their texture, their nature, their desirability; how much one wanted a particular thing himself as opposed to how much a neighbor might desire it. In that attentiveness to the worth and quality of things, and to the relation between things and services (Patten fitted his neighbor's ax handle while the neighbor, using Patten's ax, chopped wood for him), was to be found the secret of the community that became an essential building block of the nation.

Of course, much more was involved in that apparently simple but actually intricate structure. The church bound the community together and answered all the basic questions about the meaning of life that have become such a distraction and anguish for modern man. At the same time, the church, or, more properly, the faith subscribed to by the congregation—for there was no institutional church—was full of intellectual problems and paradoxes. Thus a constant reflection on subtle points of doctrine produced even in the simplest farmer a precocious skill in dialectic that was as readily applied to political as to theological questions.

In proof of this point we have a remarkable essay written by a Massachusetts farmer named William Manning. While Manning's "Key to Liberty" was composed at the time of the Jay Treaty in 1795, it demonstrates so well the relationship between theological and political principles in the mind of an uneducated (or, more properly, self-educated) farmer that it is appropriate to introduce it here. Although

Manning's political awareness had unquestionably been sharpened by the events of the Revolutionary era, his basic assumptions might be said to have been those that brought on the Revolution rather than those that followed from it. He was not, Manning wrote, "a Man of Larning . . . for I neaver had the advantage of six months schooling in my life. I am no travelor for I neaver was 50 Miles from whare I was born in no direction, & I am no grate reader of antient history, for I always followed hard labour for a living. But I always thought it My duty to search into & see for my selfe in all maters that consansed me as a member of society. . . ." It was Manning's conviction that "to search into & know our selves is of the gratest importance, & the want of it is the cause of the gratest evils suffered in Society. If we know what alterations might be made in our Minds & Conduct by alterations in our Edication, age, Circumstances & Conditions in this Life, we should be vastly less sensorious on others for their conduct. . . ."

Men were born and grew up, according to Manning, "with a vast veriaty of capacityes, strength & abilityes both of Body & Mind, & have strongly implanted within them numerous pashons & lusts continually urging them to fraud violence & acts of injustis toards one another." Since man is by nature selfish and self-seeking, "the higher a Man is raised in stations of honour power and trust," the greater are his "temtations to do rong & gratify those selfeish prinsaples. Gie a man honour & he wants more. In short he is neaver easy, but the more he has the more he wants."

Manning's principal concern at the time he wrote his essay was what seemed to him to be the inclination of "the few" (the doctors, lawyers, professors, and merchants) to control the affairs of "the many" (that is, primarily, farmers, mechanics, and artisans), who made their living by manual labor and who often paid too little attention to government. Every free man, in order to preserve his freedom, must have "A Knowledge of Mankind—A Knowledge of the Prinsaples of the government & Constitution he lives under—A Knowledge of all the laws that immediately consarnes his conduct & interests. . . ."

Manning's disenchanted view of human nature was based solidly on his Calvinistic background and supported by his reading and interpretation of Scripture. Against sloth, selfishness, greed, and the desire for power, only good laws, wisely administered by men who took the teachings of Christ as their guide, could prevail. Or at least there was a chance that they might. This view of human nature as "fallen" or tainted by the original sin of Adam was held by all Americans who were more or less orthodox Calvinists and, in fact, by a good many who were of a more liberal theological persuasion.

In the Puritan community, the center of all life, social and otherwise, was the family. Children played the games that children have played for ages—ring-around-a-rosy, London Bridge Is Falling Down, jacks, marbles, hide-and-seek, cat's cradle games, games of ball, card games with homemade cards and counters. Indeed, everything was homemade or traded. The marbles were of fired clay, the balls of wood or tightly wound twine. Jonathan Fisher, a Harvard-trained minister, noted in his diary, "I made a little wagon for Jonathan [his son] today. I also made a hat for him." "This morning I made a squirrel cage for my children's pet squirrels." "This afternoon I fitted the handles to small axes for my various children." "Made a little sleigh, placed it on runners and painted it red for my seven children to take to school with them." "Today I made a wooden sword for my son Josiah." "Ground paints and made a little set of water-colors for each of my children."

Puritan parents were loving but strict, and children were given responsibilities at an early age. Young Jonathan Fisher, at the age of ten, drove the family grain to the mill in a wagon to have it ground. At thirteen he hired out as a hand to farmers in the neighborhood. His sister Sally, when she was eleven, wove "23½ yds. of woolen cloth." Often girls worked out at a neighbor's house, since it is the universal experience of parents that their children always work much better for someone else than for them. Fisher and his three young sons, the smallest only eight, dug potatoes, and their father carefully tallied their harvest: "My bushels 126, Jonathan's 50, Josiah's 19½, Willard's 12."

Cotton Mather, it seems safe to assume, was more persistent than most in his efforts to raise his children as pious Christians, but again, like William Manning, he was by no means atypical. Mather was at pains to entertain his children "with delightful Stories, especially *Scriptural* ones. And still conclude with some *Lesson* of Piety; bidding them to learn that *Lesson* from the *Story*. And thus, every Day at the *Table*, I have used myself to tell a *Story* before I rise. . . . When the Children at any time accidentally come in my way, that may be monitory and profitable to them. . . . Who can tell, what may be the Effect of a continual *Dropping?*"

In addition to leading the children in family prayer, Mather also instructed them in *"secret Prayer."* He tried to "form in the Children a Temper of *Benignity.* I putt them upon doing of Services and Kindnesses for one another, and for other Children. I applaud them, when I see them Delight in it. . . . I caution them exquisitely against all revenges of injuries. I instruct them to return good Offices for Evil Ones. . . . I would never come, to give a child a *Blow;* except in Case of *Obstinacy* or some gross Enormity, to be chased for a while out of *my Presence.* I would make to be looked upon, as the sorest Punishment in the Family. . . . The *slavish* way of Education, carried on with raving and kicking and scourging (in *Schools* as well as *Families*) tis abominable; and a dreadful judgment of God upon the World." Above all, as soon as the children were able to understand the import of the instruction, Mather lost no opportunity to impress on them the fact that "the *eye of God*" was always on them and that they were ultimately responsible to Him for their conduct.

To waste was as serious as to blaspheme. Everything had to be utilized to the fullest. The reasons were in part economic, of course, but far more important, they were doctrinal. Thrift pleased the Lord because it showed a proper stewardship of His things. The bones of slaughtered farm animals were made into buttons, filed and pierced and often dyed. Reeds and twigs were woven into baskets; feathers from chickens that went into the pot were kept to stuff pillows and comforters; scraps of meat were saved to make soup, hides of animals to make rawhide, shoe leather, gloves, mittens, belts, harnesses, and buckets. The Fishers enjoyed the beauty and fragrance of their roses, and then made them into rose conserve to sell or barter. They made butter molds and rolling pins and toothpaste of "pulverised hardwood coals, rendered savory by a few drops of oil of lavendar."

Then there were quilting bees and barn raisings and, as we have mentioned, muster days for the militia. But there were no saints' days, of course, no delightful festivals, no dancing, and little music besides the militia's fife and drum. The Puritans were ubiquitous writers of verse, but it was difficult for them to follow the psalmist's advice to make a joyful noise unto the Lord. Loud singing, exuberant laughter, convivial drinking were thought unseemly, even blasphemous. They drank enough, heaven knows, and not a few drank themselves to death, unable to cope with so austere an existence, unable to obey the stern injunctions of a demanding God. But it was usually bitter, solitary drinking, secretly at home, or sheepishly at a tavern. "Discreet," "sober," "modest," "humble" were the most praiseworthy qualities. New Englanders had no rustic bacchanalia to refresh their spirits and relieve their nerves. Even in relatively cosmopolitan Boston, dancing was frowned upon and for years the theater was forbidden.

Boston and nearby Cambridge were the center of the political and intellectual life of New England. Andrew Burnaby, a visiting English clergyman, found the buildings of Boston impressive in 1759. "The streets," he noted, "are open and spacious, and well-paved; and the whole has much of the air of some of our best country towns in England." From a "hill which stands close to the town, where there is a beacon to alarm the neighborhood in case of any surprise, is one of the finest prospects, the most beautifully variegated, and richly grouped, of any without exception that I have ever seen." Burnaby took note of the fact that "the Arts and Sciences . . . have made a greater progress here, than in any other part of America. Harvard College has been founded above a hundred years; and altho it is not upon a perfect plan, yet it has produced a very good effect. The arts are undeniably forwarder in Massachusetts Bay than either in Pennsylvania or New York. . . . The public buildings are more elegant; and there is a more general turn for music, painting, and the belles lettres."

Burnaby also observed that while the Congregational Church was the established church in Massachusetts, the Church of England was gaining ground in Boston and becoming "more fashionable every day." Christ Church had been recently built on the Cambridge Common across from Harvard, "which has greatly alarmed the Congregationalists, who consider it as the most fatal stroke that could possibly have been leveled at their religion."

Burnaby found "the character of the inhabitants of this province . . . much improved in comparison of what it was: but Puritanism and a spirit of persecution is not yet wholly extinguished." There was in the New Englanders generally and Bostonians specifically "more stiffness and reserve than in the other colonies." The women of Boston were "formed with symmetry, are handsome, and have fair and delicate complexions," he noted, "but are said universally and proverbially to have very indifferent teeth."

As for the common people, they were inquisitive and uppity. They plagued Burnaby with questions whenever he went into an "ordinary" (a tavern) to put up for the night. Benjamin Franklin, who observed the same inquisitiveness, had instructed Burnaby on how to gain some peace. Franklin informed him that in similar circumstances, he called for the master of the tavern, the mistress, the daughters, the menservants, and the maidservants (and presumably any fellow tipplers) and began in this manner: "Worthy people, I am B. F. of Philadelphia, by trade a printer, and a bachelor. I have some relatives at Boston to whom

I am going to make a visit; my stay here will be short, and I shall then return and follow my business as a prudent man ought to do. This is all I know of myself. . . . I beg therefore that you will have pity upon me and my horse and give us some refreshment."

But if Bostonians were curious about and full of questions for a stranger, they were traditionally reserved in giving answers themselves. When Dr. Alexander Hamilton, a Maryland doctor and no relation to the first secretary of the treasury, took a tour through the colonies, he found "the middling sort of people" in Boston "to a degree disingenuous and dissembling, which appears even in their common conversation in which their indirect and dubious answers to the plainest and fairest questions show their suspicions of one another." The better sort were "polite, mannerly, and hospitable to strangers, such strangers, I mean," Hamilton added, "as come not to trade among them (for they are jealous)." He found, indeed, "more hospitality and frankness shown . . . to strangers than either at New York or Philadelphia." Conversation was perhaps the greatest pleasure Boston offered, witty and learned and amiable conversation in any refined company on any topic. By the time of Hamilton's visit in the 1750's, fashionable Boston had relaxed its ban on balls and dances, and they were a prominent feature of the lively social life of the city. Hamilton was present on several such occasions "and saw as fine a ring of ladies, as good dancing, and heard music as elegant as I had been witness to anywhere."

Burnaby was plainly intrigued by one New England custom that has continued to fascinate students of New England history. This was the ancient country custom of "tarrying" or "bundling." As Burnaby described it: "When a man is enamoured of a young woman, and wishes to marry her, he proposes the affair to her parents; if they have no objection they allow him to tarry the night with her, in order to make his court to her. After the young ones have sat up as long as they think proper, they get into bed together, also without pulling off their undergarments in order to prevent scandal. If the parties agree, it is all very well; the banns are published and they are married without delay. If not they part, and possibly never see each other again; unless, which is an accident that seldom happens, the foresaken fair prove pregnant, and then the man is obliged to marry her."

Burnaby's observations on bundling raise the question of the sexual practices of the Puritans. There is abundant evidence that premarital sexual relations were common in New England. If a young man and woman intended to get married, they could exercise the right of Pre-

Contract, a custom surviving from medieval times. Under the Pre-Contract, the couple had only to announce their intention publicly, and subsequent sexual relations were viewed most indulgently. If a newly married couple had a child within six months of their marriage, it was assumed that the child had been conceived prior to wedlock, and they were required to confess publicly in church to the sin of fornication and to pay a small fine. The church records are full of such cases, and in some parishes between a quarter and a third of all couples getting married confessed to premarital sexual relations. Indeed, this particular failing was so common that at least one parish simply had a printed form that read: "We, the subscribers, trusting that by the Grace of God we have been brought to see the evil of sin in general and especially of the sins we have committed, do now humbly, we hope, and penitently confess the sin of fornication of which we have been guilty, and this we do from a conviction that it is reasonable to bear public and marked testimony against scandalous offenses whereby we have been instrumental in weakening the bonds of society and injuring the cause of religion. . . ."

Such an attitude reflected simply the practical common sense of rural life, where young blood ran hot and mismatings could have serious consequences. It was thus better to tolerate premarital sexual relations if they eventuated in marriage than to have incompatible partners whose unsatisfied sexual needs would be a constant threat to good order in the community. Seen in this light, bundling appears as a kind of trial marriage quite consistent with basic Puritan attitudes toward sexual matters.

We have earlier described the circumstances surrounding the establishment of Connecticut and Rhode Island. These colonies, with Massachusetts and New Hampshire, made up the area (and state of mind) called New England. In the century following the original settlements, the colonies of New England grew more and more like one another. There remained, of course, important differences. Massachusetts (and Harvard) was more liberal than Connecticut (and Yale). Boston was a far more enterprising and bustling town than Portsmouth, New Hampshire, or New Haven, for that matter. But the similarities far outweighed the differences. The exception might be Rhode Island. It had been born in contention—"a nest of vipers," Winthrop had called it—and it had preserved through a rather stormy history a stubborn tradition of democracy and dissent. The colony was the only one, with the exception of Connecticut, whose citizens elected their own governor.

Its only rival in toleration of religious irregularity was Pennsylvania. The Jewish synagogue at Newport was one of the first and the most flourishing in English America; there were a number of Catholics in Rhode Island; and Baptists, who often felt the effects of prejudice in other parts of New England, found a haven in Rhode Island, where, indeed, they had first put down roots in America.

Burnaby, on his tour of New England, visited Rhode Island, which he found "intirely democratical; every officer, except the collector of the customs, being appointed, I believe, either immediately by the people, or by the general assembly," which in turn was elected every half year. The consequences were not ones that the traveling Englishman applauded. "Arts and sciences are almost unknown," he wrote, "except to some few individuals; and there are no public seminaries of learning; nor do the Rhode Islanders in general seem to regret the want of them." He found the character of the inhabitants "by no means engaging, or amiable, a circumstance" principally owing, in his view, "to their form of government. Their men in power, from the highest to the lowest, are dependent upon the people, and frequently act without that strict regard to probity and honour which ought invariably to influence and direct mankind," he noted, with more than a touch of self-righteousness considering the state of politics in his home country. In Burnaby's judgment the "private people are cunning, deceitful, and selfish. They live almost entirely by unfair and illicit trading. Their magistrates are partial and corrupt. . . . If judges were to act impartially there, and to decide a cause to the prejudice or disadvantage of a popular leader, they would probably never be re-elected; indeed they are incapable of determining the merits of a suit, for they are exceedingly illiterate. . . ."

Dr. Alexander Hamilton also noted the "democratick" nature of the government, adding, "They have but little regard to the laws of England, their mother country, tho they pretend to take that constitution for a precedent." The customs officials and royal officers in Rhode Island were "cyphers." "They dare not exercise their office for fear of the fury and unruliness of the people. . . ." On the other hand they profited from generous bribes for looking the other way when illicit cargoes entered their ports.

Perhaps the most striking irony was that in this religiously tolerant and politically liberal colony, smuggling contraband cargoes and trading in slaves were perhaps more actively engaged in than anywhere else in the British colonies, indeed in the British Empire. Here was another paradox. In Rhode Island, the balance between individualism and community, between the desires on the one hand of the individual to pursue his own ambitions and the requirements of his neighbors on the other, was tipped as clearly to the side of the individual as, in the other New England colonies, it was weighted on the side of the community.

Before we leave New England it might be well to take some notice of the status of women in that region. The relationship between Protestant fathers and their daughters in the colonial era was an especially close one, and proved, eventually, to be the agency by which American women re-established their rights in the nineteenth century. Most Puritan fathers were directly concerned with the education of their daughters. Jonathan Edwards and his wife took special pains with their daughters' education, and they were bright and able girls. Most of them married ministers. In three generations of Edwards' female descendants, the emphasis on daughterhood persisted. Esther Burr, an intelligent and energetic woman, evidently passed on to her son Aaron a solicitude for the proper education of daughters. Burr's preoccupation with the training of his remarkable daughter, Theodosia, was almost an obsession. While she was still in her teens, she was known for her striking beauty and her intellectual attainments.

Ezra Stiles was keenly interested in the intellectual capacities of women and took special pains over the education of his five daughters. He also recorded in his diary the occasion on which he had examined Lucinda, the precocious twelve-year-old daughter of the Reverend John Foot, and had given her a certificate testifying to her learning. But for her sex she could have entered the freshman class at Yale. Stiles's own daughters displayed no marked intellectual gifts, but they were "accomplished and refin'd." The Otis family produced a number of talented daughters, the most famous being Mercy, daughter of James Otis and wife of James Warren. She was a delightful letter writer, a mediocre poet, and a skillful if contentious historian of the American Revolution.

Anne Bradstreet, perhaps the foremost poet of New England, was the daughter of Thomas Dudley, one of the leaders of the great Puritan emigration from England to New England, who took great pains with her education. She was married at sixteen to Simon Bradstreet and came with him and her father to Massachusetts Bay, settling eventually in North Andover and raising a large family. Between domestic tasks, faithfully performed, she wrote learned poems on the popular themes of her day—the seasons, the four monarchies, Divine love. These were published in England in 1650 under the title *The Tenth Muse Lately Sprung up in America, Or, Severall Poems, compiled with great variety of Wit and Learning, full of delight.* It is, however, in her lyrics that Anne Bradstreet speaks most vividly and touchingly—"Before the Birth of One of her Children," on the occasion of her house burning down, on her own reflections on her poems, and in her charming love lyrics to her husband:

> If ever two were one, then surely we,
> If ever man were loved by wife, than thee.
> If ever wife was happy in a man,
> Compare with me, ye women, if you can.
> I prize thy love more than whole mines of
>   gold,
> Or all the riches that the East doth hold.
> My love is such that rivers cannot quench,
> Nor ought but love from thee give
>   recompense.
> Thy love is such I can no way repay;
> The heavens reward thee manifold, I pray.
> Then while we will, in love let's so perserver,
> That when we live no more we may live ever.

In another poem she compares her absent husband to a sun gone from her sky: "My chilled limbs now numbed lie forlorn:/ Return, return, sweel sol, from Capricorn./ In this dead time, alas, what can I more/ Than view those fruits which through thy heat I bore?"

Her lyric poems were published posthumously in Boston in 1678 under the title, *Several Poems Compiled . . . By a Gentlewoman in New England.* That poems so sensuous and so intimate were considered suitable for publication was perhaps as significant as the fact that they were written at all. They were passionate love poems from a wife to her husband, a wife who bore nine children and, in all the terrible rigors of pioneer life, preserved inviolate her faith and good spirits.

It was not until the end of the colonial era that the idea of a "suitable" or "proper" sphere of feminine activities began to emerge. Women were thought of primarily as wives or mothers, and their functions were defined positively in terms of these basic roles. There were, in the early years, very few negative definitions—that this or that activity was unsuitable or inappropriate for a woman to engage in. In consequence, colonial women moved freely into most occupations in response to particular needs and opportunities, rather than to abstract theories of what was proper. Most frequently, they took over a dead husband's or father's business, and we find them acting as shopkeepers (in very considerable numbers), teachers, blacksmiths, hunters, lawyers, innkeepers, silversmiths, tinworkers, shoemakers, shipwrights, tanners, gunsmiths, barbers, and butchers. Eleven women ran printing presses, and ten printers' widows published newspapers in America before 1776.

Many women served as midwives. Rachel Bunker of Nantucket, who left 113 grandchildren and 98 great-grandchildren when she died in 1796, assisted at 2,994 births, among whom were 31 pairs of twins. Mrs. Lucretia Lester of Southold, Long Island, who practiced from 1745 to 1779, was described as "Justly respected as nurse and doctress to the pains and infirmities incident to her fellow mortals, especially to her own sex. . . . She was during thirty years, conspicuous as an angel of mercy; a woman whose price was above rubies. It is said that she attended at the birth of 1,300 children, and of that number, lost but two." Judith Corey advertised in the *New England Palladium* as late as 1808 that "she follows the Midwife and Doctress business; that she cures Burns, Salt Rheum, Canker, Scald-head, Fever Sores, Rheumatism, & the Piles."

When doctors began to crowd out midwives, the men were attacked as awkward and brutal practitioners. An indignant newspaper editor wrote that the familiarities taken by men in attending pregnant women and those in labor were "sufficient to taint the Purity and sully the Chastity of any Woman breathing."

A strict morality based on Christian piety; prudential economic and social behavior; a basically democratic polity in church and state; a passion to redeem the world—these were the guiding principles of the great majority of New Englanders of both sexes. These qualities found their focus in the family and in the community. Husband and wife, equal in the eyes of God, were partners in the great work of redemption, partners in the demanding economy of the farm, partners in the Christian nurture of those young Puritans who must be trained to carry on the Lord's work. And the family was imbedded in the community.

The community supported and sustained the family, verified and reinforced its values, provided the essential context in which this new breed, so strangely compounded of fanaticism (or perhaps, more gently, zeal) and democracy, grew and flourished. The Puritan made the town, and the town made the Puritan. The Puritan was, at one and the same time, the most sturdily independent of characters and the most profoundly oriented toward the community. There was no tyrant like the community, and yet, paradoxically (that word so necessary to the historian), the community, so demanding in its orthodoxy, produced that classic figure of independent individualism, the New England Yankee. Individual and community: community and individual—in that mysterious balance, that alternation, lay the answer to the riddle of the Puritan character.

Of all the human strands and strains woven into the complex fabric of America, none was to prove more potent than the New England Puritan, the very mention of whose name bespoke the quintessence of individualism, and who, at the same time, founded and maintained the most closely knit communities in modern history, communities whose explicit intention it was to reproduce the unity of the earliest Christian communities. These were the New Englanders' primary contributions to what was to become, in time, the American states united, or, more familiarly, the United States of America.

New York, along with Boston, Philadelphia, Baltimore, and Charles Town, was one of the five port cities of the colonies. In the 1750's, it was a clean, well-paved town of some twenty thousand people. When Burnaby visited there, King's College (later Columbia) was in the process of being built on the high ground north of the city. "The college when finished," Burnaby wrote, "will be exceedingly handsome, and will be the most beautifully situated, I believe, in the world." Only one wing, built of stone, had been finished. Every two students were to have an apartment consisting of a large sitting room with a study and bedroom. The inhabitants of New York were, in most respects, like those of Philadelphia. The population of New York was perhaps the most cosmopolitan of all the colonial cities, "being . . . of different nations, different languages and different religions"—which made it difficult to characterize, but Burnaby tried in any event. Most of the middle rank were merchants and "therefore, habitually frugal, industrious, and parsimonious." The ladies were handsome and their amusements much the same as those of the Philadelphia ladies, "viz. balls and sleighing expeditions in the winter; and in the summer going in parties upon the water and fishing or making excursions into the country." One of the most popular diversions of the social elite was turtle feasts, where thirty or forty young bachelors would meet with their ladies, have lunch, fish, dine together on their catch, and then return home in their fast Italian chaises, "a gentleman and a lady in each chaise." On the way home there was a bridge, some three miles from New York, "which you pass over as you return, called the Kissing Bridge; where it is the part of etiquette to salute the lady who has put herself under your protection."

Dr. Hamilton was more critical of New York. The water of the city was "hard and brackish." The best was to be bought in the streets from a large cask on a sledge. It was carried into the city from country springs and was sold primarily for the brewing of tea. Hamilton found the citizens of the city "seemingly civil and courteous," but acceptance seemed to rest largely on being well recommended or on being a good tippler, since drinking was a favorite diversion. "To drink stoutly with the Hungarian Club, who are bumper men," he wrote, "is the readiest way for a stranger to recommend himself, and a sett among them are very fond of making a stranger drunk. To talk bawdy and to have a knack att punning passes among some there for good sterling wit." The governor of the colony was a "jolly toaper," which gave him great prestige among the citizenry.

Hamilton visited the great patroonship of Rensselaerwyck and met the reigning patroon, "a young man of good mein and presence. He is a bachelor," Hamilton noted, "nor can his friends persuade him to marry." He had the common New York disposition to dissipation, and "by paying too much homage to Bacchus," Hamilton wrote, "he has acquired a hypochondriac habit." Rensselaerwyck had several thousand tenants, and the patroon, like a feudal baron, told Hamilton "he could muster 600 men fit to bear arms." The patroons had their own courts, in which they dispensed justice for minor infractions; they collected a series of feudal dues and rents from tenants who were more like medieval serfs than free men. The patroonships were an anomaly in eighteenth-century colonial America, where the citizens of Massachusetts and Rhode Island enjoyed more extensive political rights than any citizens in the world. The patroonship was certainly an anachronism in the colony of New York, with its enterprising merchant class that so well represented the commercial spirit of the new age. The tenants of the patroons had risen up in rebellion on several occasions, but without materially improving their situation.

The political divisions in New York were deep and of long standing. They went back, essentially, to the abortive uprising of Jacob Leisler, who in 1689, at the head of a small army had ousted the governor of the colony and his clique and had taken over the office himself. He and his followers were subdued, several were hanged, and their estates were confiscated, but the bitterness and the factionalism caused by the uprising and its suppression remained a bothersome legacy in the politics of the colony.

That women were active in business and in crafts in New York is suggested by a notice in a newspaper in 1733: "We, widows of this city, have had a meeting as our case is something deplorable, we beg you will give it place in your weekly Journal, that we may be relieved, it is as follows. We are house keepers, pay our taxes, carry on trade and most of us are she merchants, and as we in some measure contribute to the support of the government, we ought to be entitled to some of the sweets of it. . . ."

The *Independent Journal* of New York announced the arrival of a Mrs. Malcolm from Edinburgh, "where she studied and practised Midwifery for a considerable number of years, and had the honour of attending several Ladies of the first rank in that City. She has recommendations from most of the principal professors of that art in Scotland, with a Diploma from the late Dr. Thomas Young, Professor of Midwifery in the University of Edinburgh." The course of study at Edinburgh was evidently an arduous one. A Mrs. Monroe, coming to America in 1796, stated that she had studied Midwifery at the University for six years.

Philadelphians considered their city to be, unofficially, a kind of capital of colonial America. Although founded a half-century after its principal rivals, Boston and New York, it had become in the relatively brief span of some eighty years a flourishing and sophisticated metropolis. Reflecting on its brief history, Burnaby wrote of Philadelphia: " . . . if we consider that not eighty years ago the place where it now stands was a wild and uncultivated desert inhabited by nothing but ravenous beasts and savage people, [it] must certainly be the object of everyone's wonder and admiration."

The city had about three thousand houses and a population of some twenty thousand. It was handsomely laid out in a grid pattern, with wide streets named after trees—Locust, Laurel, Pine, etc. What was also notable was that rather than pedestrians having to contest the streets with horses, carriages, wagons, and, not infrequently, pigs and chickens, there were paved ways, or "pavements," on either side of the street, made of broad stones and reserved for "foot passengers." Moreover, the streets were well lighted with whale-oil lamps—a striking innovation for which Benjamin Franklin was primarily responsible— and were watched by a patrol that helped confirm Philadelphia's claim to be the most up-to-date and progressive city in the world.

The central area was dominated by the State House, a large, handsome building, although in Burnaby's opinion somewhat "heavy." One of the building's innovations was that it had "apartments for the accommodation of Indian chiefs or sachems" who came to the capitol to treat with the officers of the colony. There were likewise two libraries, one, The Library Company, founded by Franklin and open to the public, the other established by the association of carpenters of Philadelphia. Franklin had also been instrumental in starting the first volunteer fire department—made up of gentlemen armed with leather buckets and drilled in putting out fires—and the first fire-insurance company, the Hand-in-Hand. He had also started the American Philosophical Society for the Promotion of Useful Knowledge to be Held at Philadelphia, to give it its full name. The society had a modest collection of medals and medallions, as well as the skin of a rattlesnake twelve feet long, and several Northern Indian costumes made of furs and skins. Burnaby commented on "a noble hospital for lunatics, and other sick persons." A public market was held twice a week on Market Street, "almost equal to that of Leadenhall." To Burnaby, it was a singular pleasure to contemplate "this wonderful province . . . a rich and opulent state arising out of a small settlement." The soil was fertile, "the mountains . . . enriched with ore, and the rivers with fish." European visitors often agreed that Penn's sylvan retreat was well named.

What struck Peter Kalm, a visiting Swedish scientist, most forcefully about Pennsylvania was the thought that "it has not been necessary to force people to come and settle here; on the contrary foreigners of different languages have left their country, houses, property, and relations and ventured far and wide over stormy seas in order to come hither. Pennsylvania which was no better than a wilderness in the year 1681 . . . has received hosts of people which other countries, to their infinite loss, have either neglected, belittled or expelled."

Burnaby was convinced that while a number of the leading citizens of the city were conspicuous for their public spirit, yet the populace in general concerned themselves "with little except about getting money." Making money seemed indeed the major preoccupation of the inhabitants of all of the colonial cities.

In Philadelphia, as elsewhere, the women outshone the men. They were "exceedingly handsome and polite: they are naturally sprightly and fond of pleasure; and, upon the whole, are much more agreeable and accomplished than the men . . . and without flattery, many of them would not make bad figures even in the first assemblies in Europe." Again, like all American women, those of Philadelphia loved dancing, which was their chief amusement in the winter; in the summer, it was boating on the Schuylkill River. There was a society of sixteen young men and women called the "fishing company" that met every fortnight at a "very pleasant room erected in the romantic situation upon the banks of [that] river, where they generally dine and drink tea. . . . There are boats and fishing tackle of all sorts, and the company divert themselves with walking, fishing, going up the water, dancing, singing, conversing, or just as they please." The ladies wore a uniform, "and appear with great advantage from the neatness and simplicity of it."

The Pennsylvanians were, Burnaby observed, "a frugal and industrious people: not remarkably courteous and hospitable to strangers . . . but rather, like the denizens of most commercial cities, the reverse. They are great republicans, and have fallen into the same errors in their ideas of independency as most of the other colonies have." They seemed to him "by far the most enterprising people on the continent."

Hamilton noted that the Quakers were "the richest and the people of greatest interest in this government. . . . They have the character of an obstinate, stiff necked generation and a perpetuall plague to their governors." There was more than a little irony in the fact that the despised, abused, persecuted, and often impoverished Quakers, who had fled to their wilderness refuge two or three generations earlier, had now become the prosperous and powerful merchant leaders who opposed the Penn proprietor (who had now become Anglican) and his agent, the governor, at every turn. The proprietary interest was forced to form an alliance with the Presbyterian Scotch-Irish, the Irish, and those other factions who found the Quaker yoke onerous.

A particular bone of contention was the protection of the frontier against Indian raids. Until the outbreak of the French and Indian War, the province had lived in peace with its Indian neighbors. The Quaker-dominated assembly had no notion of sending arms or militia into the western counties to engage in warfare with their aborigine friends. The frontiersmen, who believed that the only good Indian was a dead one, took a different view of the matter. Frontiersmen believed that their families and farms were threatened with destruction from forays of Indians led on the warpath by French officers. In one especially distressing incident, a group of frontier bullies who called themselves Paxton's Boys slaughtered, in trumped-up revenge, a peaceful settlement of Christianized Indians.

The quality that most clearly characterized Pennsylvania was the heterogeneity of its population. Dr. Alexander Hamilton, traveling in Penn's colony, reported that he "dined at a *tavern* with a very mixed company of different nations and religions. There were Scots, English, Dutch, Germans, and Irish; there were Roman Catholics, Churchmen,

Presbyterians, Quakers, Newlightmen, Methodists, Seven Day men, Moravians, Anabaptists, and one Jew. The whole company consisted of 25 planted round an oblong table in a great hall well stocked with flies. The company divided into committees in conversation; the prevailing talk was politics and conjectures of a French war. A knot of Quakers talked only about selling of flower and the low price it bore."

Gottlieb Mittelberger gave a similar description of the variety of sects to be found in Pennsylvania, which suggested a kind of religious Babel. "We find there," he wrote, "Lutherans, Reformed, Catholics, Quakers, Menninists or Anabaptists, Herrnhuters or Moravian Brethren, Pietists, Seventh Day Baptists, Dunkers, Presbyterians, Newborn, Freemasons, Separatists, Freethinkers, Jews, Mohammedans, Pagans, Negroes, and Indians. . . . In one house and one family four, five, and even six sects may be found. . . ." Mittelberger indeed wondered if there was perhaps not too much freedom in Penn's colony. He reported a common saying: "Pennsylvania is the heaven of the farmers, the paradise of the mechanics, and the hell of the officials and preachers."

As Burnaby noted, the group that gave unity to this remarkable diversity were the Quakers. Starting as a poor, despised company of men and women, they seemed to be living proof of the adage that thrift, hard work, and piety brought the favor of the Lord in material possessions. By the middle of the eighteenth century, pious as they might be, they were also indubitably the wealthiest segment of the population, and their detractors said (what was also said of Boston Puritans) that they prayed for their neighbors on Sunday and preyed on them the rest of the week. But Americans have seldom accounted prosperity a sin. Even though it might be an impediment to grace, it seems to have been one that most Quakers felt confident they could surmount. And if some of the Friends dressed in costly though simple attire and rode in handsome carriages, there was no gainsaying that under their leadership the spirit of toleration manifested itself more vigorously in Penn's province than in any other English colony with the exception of Rhode Island.

Correspondingly, it could be said that if the Quakers took in their charge the keeping of the consciences of their fellow citizens, the keeper of the Quakers' conscience was John Woolman, born in "West Jersey" in 1720 and associated through most of his life with the colony of Pennsylvania. Piety came early to young Woolman. "Before I was seven years old," he wrote, "I began to be acquainted with the operations of divine love."

While John Woolman was still a little boy he threw a stone and killed a mother robin. The thoughtlessly cruel act, and the sense of guilt that he suffered as a consequence of it, taught him that "He, whose tender mercies are over all his works, hath placed a principle in the human mind, which incites to exercise goodness towards every living creature, and this being singly attended to, people become tender-hearted and sympathizing. . . ." Woolman's compassion and sympathy were directed toward the freeing of black men and women held as slaves by his fellow members of the Society of Friends. Conquering his coreligionists, he made many of them, in turn, advocates of the antislavery cause. In his journal, which breathes the generosity and goodness of this simple man, he tells of his long battle to free slaves and, later, his efforts to repair some of the wrongs done by the English settlers to the American aborigines. It was a weary labor, for, as Woolman wrote in his journal: "Deep-rooted customs, tho' wrong, are not easily altered." His business as a tailor and traveling merchant prospered so that it threatened to distract him from his primary mission, which was to purge the Society of Friends from the evil of slavery; so he gave up his business ventures and contented himself with the modest income of a tailor, reminding himself of the admonition of Jeremiah: "Seekest thou great things for thyself? Seek them not."

In all his preaching, he was sustained by the thought that he labored for God's black children. "I believe liberty is their right, and I see they are not only deprived of it, but treated in other respects with inhumanity in many places. . . ." The struggle might be a long one, but Woolman was confident that in the end, "He, who is a refuge for the oppressed, will, in his own time, plead their cause. . . ." The slaves were a people who had made "no agreement to serve us, and who have not forfeited their liberty that we know of: these are the souls for whom Christ died, and for our conduct towards them, we must answer before Him who is no respecter of persons."

Toward the end of his life, Woolman turned his attention to the plight of the Indians exploited by the greed of the settlers, and he made arduous and dangerous journeys to tribes that often slew a white man on sight. As in the case of black slaves, the Indians were the victims of the settlers' desire to turn an ungodly profit. To Woolman, the solution appeared to be a society in which "all our inhabitants lived according to sound wisdom, labouring to promote universal love and righteousness, and ceased from every inordinate desire after wealth. . . ." Then all might live comfortably "on honest employments, without having that temptation they are often under of being drawn into schemes to make settlements on lands which have not been honestly purchased of the Indians, or of applying to that wicked practice of selling rum to them."

John Woolman, it might be said, was in truth a voice crying in the wilderness. But as his accents reach us today, more than two hundred years later, and touch our consciences, so they touched thousands of his fellow Quakers and tens of thousands of Pennsylvanians of other religious persuasions. His teachings, more often ignored than taken to heart, nonetheless represented the spirit of toleration—indeed more than toleration, active compassion—at its best, and it can be safely said that some saving element of the devout and selfless spirit of John Woolman entered into the often crass, ambitious, greedy, heedless soul of young America.

5   The Southern Colonies

I N those colonies that stretched south of Mason and Dixon's Line, a way of life developed that was strikingly different from that of colonies in the North. Southern society centered around large farms or plantations using, to an ever-increasing degree, black slave labor. Except for Baltimore and Charles Town, the South lacked the busy seaports and thriving towns that were to be found in New England and the middle colonies. The South found its ideal in the English country gentleman. Of course the plantation owners, with their endless acres and hundreds of slaves, made up a very small portion of the total population, but they established the tone and style of life to which less prosperous farmers aspired, and they had firm control over the economic and political life of their colonies. The vast majority of the residents of the Southern colonies were farmers of modest means, who might own a slave or two. In some areas, such as Winston-Salem, where the German Moravians predominated, many families refused to own slaves on religious grounds.

    Maryland, Virginia, and North Carolina, the northernmost of the colonies of the South, had much in common. Maryland had a number of large slaveholding plantations that had been established in the early period of settlement. In addition, the colony had a thriving seaport,

Baltimore, and an active and prosperous merchant class. Maryland also had a substantial class of small, independent farmers who were well represented in the lower house of the legislature and were frequently at odds with the royal governor and his council, who supported the interests of the merchants and large planters. The colony thus enjoyed a modest measure of popular government, but it paid a stiff price in wrangles and contentions that often left the government virtually paralyzed.

Maryland, despite prosperous Baltimore and its few elegant plantations, had a reputation in colonial times for being slovenly and down-at-heel. That tireless traveler, Dr. Alexander Hamilton, although he was from Maryland, had little that was favorable to say about the common run of his fellow colonists. Traveling with some Pennsylvanians, Hamilton heard them dilate upon "the insufficiency of the neighbouring province of Maryland when compared to that of Pennsylvania" and "upon the immorality, drunkenness, rudeness and immoderate swearing so much practised in Maryland." Hamilton listened in silence "because I knew that the . . . proposition was pretty true." Maryland had about it a general air of dishevelment, a randy and run-down appearance, a shiftlessness quite evident among the poorer sort who were but little constrained by religion or enlightened policy. Yet Marylanders bred and raced fine horses, and the provincial aristocracy in their handsome estates affected a style of living similar to that of the great Virginia plantations.

Every Maryland county had a free public school where reading, writing, and making accounts were taught, but there was no academy or preparatory school and no college. In Burnaby's view, "the education of youth is little attended to." Parents who did not wish to expose their sons to the rather austere life and radical notions of Harvard sent them to Oxford or, less frequently, to Cambridge. Later, when the College of New Jersey was started, they sent their sons, generation after generation of them, to Princeton. There, if the ideas were scarcely less radical (at least in the eighteenth century), the social atmosphere was more congenial.

For some unknown reason, Maryland got the curious reputation of being a particularly happy hunting ground for women who wished to find husbands. George Alsop, an indentured servant who became a planter, declared, "The Women that go over into this Province as Servants, have the best luck as in any place of the world . . . for they are no sooner on shoar, but they are courted into a Copulative Matrimony."

Some of the women, Alsop observed, were so ill-favored that they would have had a hard time finding husbands anywhere else. As Alsop put it, rather tartly, "some of them (for aught I know) had they not come to such a Market with their virginity, might have kept it them untill it had been mouldy. . . ." Some years later Nicholas Cresswell, a British visitor, echoed Alsop's opinion. Maryland was "a paradise on Earth for women. . . . That great curiosity, an Old Maid is seldom seen in this country. They generally marry before they are twenty-two, often before they are sixteen." Widows were equally or perhaps even more in demand, as being proven out, so to speak. One colonial verse tells of a wife who is importuned at the moment her husband is expiring, and who replies modestly: "From this pledge I beg you' me excuse, /For I'm already promised to John Hughes."

Maryland's neighbor Virginia ran westward from the tidewater, the peninsulas that were divided by the Potomac, the Rappahannock, the York, and the James rivers. The nineteenth-century historian John Fiske called it a "sylvan Venice." Along these rivers stretched the great plantations of the Virginia aristocrats—the Harrisons, the Byrds, the Carters, the Pages, the Randolphs, the Lees—some of which are extant today. Carefully tended lawns ran down to the slow, broad waters of the river and to the plantation docks, where vessels tied up to deliver English goods ordered by the plantation owner and to take on loads of tobacco. From the tidewater, the land ran uphill through heavily wooded forests of pine and hardwood to the Blue Ridge, which marked the beginning of the Allegheny range. The land, where it was cleared and cultivated, was rich and deep and there virtually for the taking in what seemed endless acres.

Virginians have cherished the tradition that the younger sons of the British aristocracy came in substantial numbers to establish plantations and provide them with noble progenitors. In fact, few if any members of the British aristocracy came to Virginia or any other colony. Prosperous and ambitious tradesmen and craftsmen like the original William Byrd came, as did some substantial immigrants of the middle rank who wished to improve their situation in life or ape the manners of the upper classes. A few of the minor gentry also came, looking for greener pastures and cheap land. In order to encourage emigration, the pro-moters of the Virginia settlement offered land on attractive terms: fifty acres for the head of a household, and another headright of fifty acres for each member of his family that he brought with him and for each servant that he transported at his own cost. Thus John Page, who carried with him to the colony seventeen persons, including family and servants, received 850 acres of land.

Virginia was the anchor of the South, the center, as Boston was in the North, of the best talents and energies of its section. Starting out with a crude kind of democracy, the Old Dominion grew into the most aristocratic of the colonies, the one that most nearly reproduced the envied style of life of the English country gentleman. Virginians loved liberty but had little use for what the ancient philosophers called democracy. It was the opinion of Virginia planters that the wealthy and well-born should manage political matters, and Virginians of less-exalted rank seemed, by and large, to agree with them.

For decades, white indentured servants provided the principal labor that supported this gentlemanly way of life. Very slowly, the plantations replaced them with blacks, imported from Africa and the West Indies. As Durand, the French Huguenot who was so offended by the cavorting prostitutes on his voyage to America, put it: "A difference exists between the slaves that are bought, to wit: a Christian twenty years old or over, cannot be a slave for more than five years, whereas Negroes and other unbelievers are slaves all their lives."

It seemed to Durand that the land was so fertile "that when a man has fifty acres of ground, two men-servants, and a maid and some cattle, neither he nor his wife do anything but visit among their neighbors. "Most of them," he added, "do not even take the trouble to oversee the work of their slaves, for there is no house, however modest, where there is not what is called a lieutenant, generally a freedman, under whose commands the servants are placed." The ease with which tobacco was grown by white or black slaves and the ready market for it in England discouraged the thrift and practical ingenuity that were characteristic of colonists to the north. Durand, a frugal Frenchman, was most impressed with the unused opportunities so much in evidence. The Virginians engaged in no manufacturing of any kind, although raw materials were plentiful. All they did, Durand noted, was raise tobacco, and "as they can get anything they need for this commodity they become so lazy that they send to England for clothes, linen, hats, women's dresses, shoes, iron tools, nails, and even wooden furniture, (although their own wood is very fine to work on and they have loads of it) such as tables, chairs, bedsteads, chests, wardrobes."

The Virginians did, of course, grow their own food—but they even did that in a rather wasteful manner. One standard crop was Indian corn; it made a bread "as white as paper," which was delicious but,

Durand noted, lay "rather heavy on the stomach for those not used to it." The Virginians did not plant corn efficiently, however; ploughs were almost unknown, and the corn was planted by the wasteful Indian method of drilling holes in the ground.

The Virginians were obsessed with horses, with breeding and racing and hunting, and some planters had as many as thirty horses simply for riding, which impressed Durand as reckless extravagance.

The life of the planter class revolved around games and sports, visiting and being visited, parties, balls, birthdays, and weddings, all drawing in relatives (including uncounted cousins) and neighbors for miles about. As in most aristocratic societies, there was a great emphasis on kinship. First cousins not infrequently married, and the Reverend Jonathan Boucher, an Anglican minister in Surry County, noted that "family character both of body and mind may be traced thro' many generations; as for instance every Fitzhugh has bad eyes; every Thornton hears badly; Winslows and Lees talk well; Carters are proud and imperious; Taliferros mean and avaricious." A certain nose or a certain squint, a particular physique or a noble forehead, appeared generation after generation with a comforting predictability. In one generation, seven members of the large Nelson clan married seven members of the Page family. Durand attended a wedding where there were "at least a hundred guests, many of social standing, and handsome, well-dressed ladies." Although it was November, it was a perfect fall day, and lunch was served at two in the afternoon under the trees, with meats of all kind "provided so copiously . . ." Durand observed, "that I am sure there would have been enough for a regiment of five hundred soldiers." There was no wine, but the wedding party drank a potent punch, "prepared in a large bowl," and made of three jugs of brandy, three pounds of sugar, some nutmeg, and cinnamon. While "making away with the first, they prepare another bowl of it."

Most of the guests were expected to stay the night, but beds were provided only for the women, so that "about midnight, after much carousing, when some were already lying on the floor," Durand fell asleep in a chair by the fire. His host came and, collecting blankets, took him to the women's chamber and made a bed for him on the floor, saying "he would not put it in the hall for fear the drunken fellows would fall over me and keep me from sleeping." The carousing went on all night long, and in the morning Durand did not see a guest "who could stand straight."

He visited another planter, Colonel Fitzhugh, a few days later, and again there was "good wine and all kinds of beverages, so there was a great deal of carousing." The colonel sent for three fiddlers, a jester, a tightrope dancer, and "an acrobat who tumbled about," and the guests were royally entertained. Virginia ladies and gentlemen were "of genuine blood," Philip Fithian, a teacher and minister, observed. "They will dance or die." They clearly preferred the more active jigs—"vulgar Capers" an English visitor called them—to the minuet or the waltz. "Betwixt the Country dances," the same observer noted, "they have what I call everlasting jogs (to some Negro tune) others comes up and cuts them out, and these dances always last as long as the fiddler can play. This is sociable, but I think it looks more like a Bacchanalian dance than a polite assembly."

The life of a planter was a leisurely and pleasant one. That of William Byrd II might be taken as typical. The first of the Byrds born in America, William built Westover, the handsome family mansion on the James River. His father, a London silversmith, had come to Virginia and had prospered exceedingly as a planter; his son was an amateur writer, surveyor, member of the governor's council of state, and one of the richest men in the colony. He kept a meticulous record of his daily life. On a typical day he rose at six o'clock and read from the Psalms and "some Greek in Cassius." Then he said his prayers, did some calisthenics, and had a frugal breakfast of milk. Anaka, the Byrd family maid, was sick, and Byrd administered "a vomit" and then had her "sweated and bled"—which, strangely enough, seemed to improve her, "however her fever continued violently." Byrd then rode over to visit a neighbor, Colonel Hill, and there "played at cricket and I sprained my backside." After lunch the game was continued, and when he tried to depart, Byrd "was forced to get on my horse by a chair." After dinner he played piquet with his wife and then retired, "said my prayers, and had good health, good thoughts, and good humor, thanks be to God Almighty."

The next day was much the same, as indeed were most days. Instead of cricket, Byrd played the less strenuous game of billiards with a friend in his own billiard room, had rice and pork for lunch, and in the afternoon "we shot with bow and arrow and I hit the mark." After dinner Byrd took a walk with his friend, and when they returned they consumed two bottles of wine between them and "I was very merry. I said my prayers and good health, good thoughts, and good humor, thanks be to God Almighty. My maid Anaka was better thank God."

Conviviality, a gracious and active social life, eating and drinking (always well and often to excess), leisurely and sometimes learned

conversation, shooting and hunting, a kind of openhanded opulence—
these made up the life of a Virginia planter. They were coupled with a
sense of noblesse oblige and a scrupulous care for those dependent on
him, including his wife and children, improvident relatives, and slaves
both old and infirm as well as young and healthy. In comparison with his
Puritan neighbors of the "eastern" colonies, the Southern plantation
owner appeared extravagant with life's bounty, careless, charming,
profligate, and absorbed in satisfying his own creature comforts instead
of redeeming the world.

The Reverend Andrew Burnaby, traveling in Virginia one
hundred years after the Frenchman Durand, made many of the same
observations. Not a tenth of the land was cultivated, "and that which is
cultivated," he wrote, "is far from being so in the most advantageous
manner." But Virginia pork, the famous hams, were superior in flavor
to any in the world, and "the horses [were] fleet and beautiful." Virginia
breakfasts were famous, the lady of the house presiding at the head of
the table crowded with tea and coffee urns, and the sideboards "gar-
nished with roast fowls, ham, venison, game and other dainties."

A British traveler in America in the era of the Revolution, J. F. D.
Smyth, wrote a description of the life of a Southern planter that rivals
Byrd's diary. "The gentleman of fortune rises about nine o'clock; he
perhaps may make an excursion to walk as far as his stables to see his
horses, which is seldom more than fifty yards from his house; he returns
to breakfast between nine and ten, which is generally tea or coffee,
bread and butter, and very thin slices of venison-ham, or hung beef. He
then lies down on a pallet in the coolest room in the house, in his shirt
and trousers only, with a negro at his head, and another at his feet, to
fan him, and keep off the flies; between twelve and one he takes a
draught of bombo, or toddy, a liquor composed of water, sugar, rum
and nutmeg. . . . at dinner he drinks cyder, toddy, punch, port, claret,
and madeira, which is generally excellent here: having drank some few
glasses of wine after dinner, returns to his pallet, with his two blacks to
fan him, and continues to drink toddy or sangaree, all the afternoon. . . . between nine and ten in the evening, he eats a light supper of
milk and fruit, or wine, sugar, and fruit, etc. and almost immediately
retires to bed, for the night; in which, if it not be furnished with
musketoe curtains, he is generally so molested with the heat, and
harrassed and tormented with those pernicious insects the musketoes,
that he receives very little refreshment from sleep. This is his general
way of living in his family, when he has no company. No doubt many

differ from it, some in one respect, some in another; but more follow it than do not."

The lower and middling classes lived somewhat differently, Smyth noted, doing at least some work around their plantations. However, "the poor negro slaves alone work hard," Smyth wrote, "and fare still harder. It is astonishing and unaccountable to conceive what an amazing degree of fatigue these poor, but happy, wretches do undergo, and can support. He is called up in the morning at day break, and is seldom allowed time enough to swallow three mouthfuls of homminy, or hoe-cake, but is driven out immediately to the field to hard labour; at which he continues, without intermission, until noon. . . . About noon is the time he eats his dinner, and he is seldom allowed an hour for that purpose. His meal consists of homminy and salt, and if his master be a man of humanity, he has a little fat, skimmed milk, rusty bacon, or salt herring to relish his homminy or hoe-cake, which kind masters allow their slaves twice a week. . . . They then return to severe labour, which continues in the field until dusk in the evening."

Even after such labor he goes off to a dance "in which he performs with astonishing agility, and the most vigorous exertions, keeping time and cadence, most exactly, with the music of a banjor (a large hollow instrument with three strings), and a quaqua (somewhat resembling a drum), until he exhausts himself, and scarcely has time, or strength, to return home before the hour he is called forth to toil next morning. . . . Yet not withstanding this degrading situation, and rigid severity to which fate has subjected this wretched race, they are certainly devoid of care, and actually appear jovial, contented, and happy." This disposition, Smyth added, was fortunate, for otherwise they "must sink under the pressure of such complicated misery and wretchedness."

While the blacks did all the work, the plantation-owning whites continued to enjoy themselves. In addition to the numerous private pleasures of the plantation, there was a theater at Williamsburg, the capital of the colony, and itinerant performers of every kind who found in the planters an eager audience, always seeking some new diversions. Gambling was the besetting vice of the Virginia planters, and a measure of the boredom of a spoiled and wealthy class with more leisure than it knew how to employ. Every young man was cautioned against it, often to no avail. William Byrd III destroyed himself by gambling and drinking, as did his young companion John Landon, whose father wrote bitterly: "They play away and play it all away. . . . I hate such vulgarity."

For the simpler people there were fairs with a variety of attractions:

horse races ("four horses to run for a silver watch the hindmost to win the race"), cockfights, bearbaiting, four old women to grin for a plumb pudding (the most hideous to carry off the prize), "some curious fireworks," a "hoop-petticoat to be run for by two ladies," and a hat to be run for by two men in bags. Many of the diversions were rough in the extreme. Wrestling was a popular sport. It sometimes deterioriated into gouging matches in which opponents tried to gouge out each other's eyes—or perhaps, in a milder spirit, to bite off a nose, ear, or finger.

The small farmers of the interior of Virginia lived in a manner far removed from that of the plantation owners. William Byrd II, ubiquitous author of the diary, traveling in the interior of Virginia in 1728, gave an account of the residents of that region.

In the frontier settlements, the inhabitants did "not know Sunday from any other day, any more than Robinson Crusoe did; which would give them a great advantage were they given to be industrious. But they keep so many Sabbaths every week, that their disregard of the seventh day has no manner of cruelty in it, either to servants or cattle." Many of the farmers Byrd met had scurvy from lack of fruits, and a number had the yaws from eating too much pork. The men seemed good for nothing but breeding. "They made their wives rise out of their beds early in the morning, at the same time that they lie and snore, till the sun has run one-third of his course, and dispersed all the unwholesome damps. Then, after stretching and yawning for a half an hour, they light their pipes, and under the protection of a cloud of smoke venture out into the open air; though if it happens to be ever so little cold, they quickly return shivering into the chimney corner. When the weather is mild, they stand leaning with both their arms upon the cornfield fence, and gravely consider whether they had best go and take a small heat at the hoe, but generally find reasons to put it off till another time. Thus, they loiter away their lives, like Solomon's sluggard, with their arms across, and at the winding up of the year scarcely have bread to eat."

The poor and slovenly farmers of Virginia's interior were, however, in a minority. By far the greater proportion of Virginians worked good, fertile land, of which there was a seemingly inexhaustible supply. Further, many plantations bordered the Potomac or James rivers or their tributaries, thus enabling the plantation owner to ship his tobacco from his own wharf. This idyllic situation was summed up by Burnaby, who wrote that the land was "so plentiful that every person may procure a small plantation, can ship his tobacco from his own door, and live independent."

Perhaps the last phrase is the most important—"live independent."
To live independent had a special meaning for individuals emerging
from Old-World practices, where most people were bound in an explicitly dependent relationship; where one owed customary rents, certain
fees and services, a humble diffidence, a forelock-pulling obsequious-
ness to those who stood above. In the old country, a man's life and labor
were spent on land that was not his own, and therein lay the basis of all
his various dependences. He was dependent for his bread and for that
of his wife and children on the good will of the landlord. If he grew
restive or openly rebellious, if he stepped out of line, he was stigmatized
as "a rude, rough fellow" with ideas above his station, and the society
mustered all its agents and agencies to put him down again. If he
poached the lord's deer or pheasants, or snared his rabbits, though it
might be to feed hungry mouths, he might be hanged or transported. He
was engaged in a war for survival with an enemy who had the advantage
of the high ground and virtually all the available weapons, while the
tenant had only guile and subterfuge—the scanty, immemorial weapons
of the poor. So to "live independent" was to live transformed from an
underling to someone who could stand on his own two feet and insist on
a proper regard for his rights, who owned the land he farmed, made the
bread that fed his own, and owed no one for his livelihood. Secure in his
modest holdings, aware of his rights as an Englishman, hardy and self-
reliant, this independent farmer was the sort of citizen of which a free
and independent nation might in time be built.

Virginia was happy in its politics because the small, "yeoman"
farmer, as Jefferson persisted in calling him, made common cause with
the great plantation owner. They were both in fact "farmers." One was
richer and grander than the other, but very informal and friendly in his
ways, eager to solicit the good will and the vote of his less prosperous
neighbor. At election time Mr. Edmund Randolph or Mr. Patrick Henry
or Mr. Benjamin Harrison was the soul of affability, "swilling the
planters with bombo," laying on barbecues, and even on occasion, it was
rumored, spreading a few shillings about where they would do the most
good.

The Virginia legislature, the House of Burgesses, was the nursery
of politicians—or perhaps it might better be said that the parish vestry
was the nursery where promising young men were inducted into the
rudiments of politics and their capacities were measured by their elders.
The more promising young men then proceeded from being vestrymen
to election as burgesses, and they might in time be promoted to the

governor's council. The result of this winnowing was that very able men (indeed a substantial number of the ablest in American history) emerged from an indulgent and hedonistic society.

If a social scientist were to sit down to plot out some combination of environment and heredity designed to produce great men, he would not, one assumes, come up with anything remotely resembling colonial Virginia. Andrew Burnaby was a touring English parson, not a sociologist, but his analysis of Virginia society suggested that no significant potential lay concealed there. "The climate," he wrote, "and the external appearance of the country conspire to make them indolent, easy and good natured; extremely fond of society, and much given to convivial pleasures. In consequence of this, they seldom show any spirit of enterprise, or expose themselves willingly to fatigue."

Beyond this, there was another aspect of Virginia life that Burnaby (and other visitors) felt was thoroughly inhibiting to the development of any native genius—slavery. "Their authority over their slaves," Burnaby wrote, "renders them vain and imperious, and entire strangers to that elegance of sentiment which is so peculiarly characteristic of refined and polished nations. Their ignorance of mankind and of learning exposes them to many errors and prejudices, especially in regard to Indians and negroes, whom they scarcely consider as much of the human species; so that it is almost impossible in cases of violence, or even murder, committed upon those unhappy people by any of the planters, to have the delinquents brought to justice." It seemed natural to Burnaby that people so circumstanced would be inclined to "acts of extravagance, ostentation, and disregard for economy." It thus followed that they were often in debt. "The public or political character of the Virginians corresponds," he wrote, "with their private one; they are haughty and jealous of their liberties, impatient of restraint, and *can scarcely bear the thought of being controlled by any superior power* [italics mine]. Many of them consider the colonies as independent states, not connected with Great Britain, otherwise than by having the same common king, and being bound to her by natural affection." The Virginians had little need for business, and indeed thought it common and beneath the attention of a gentleman. "In the matter of commerce they are ignorant of the necessary principles that must prevail between a colony and the mother country," Burnaby noted.

The collective portrait of Virginians skillfully drawn by Burnaby is a confusing and paradoxical one: arrogance and indolence, generosity and cruelty, lavishness and improvidence. But this society produced a

Thomas Jefferson, a James Madison, a John Marshall, a George Mason—energetic and intelligent men if there ever were any. The question remains to haunt historians: What was there about life in colonial Virginia, so casual and so self-indulgent, that produced so many outstanding individuals? The answer, if unpalatable to devoted democrats, seems simple enough. Aristocracy, whether in ancient Greece or Renaissance Florence, England or Virginia, seems to be the form of social organization that is most fecund for men of unusual gifts. Along with a large number of amiable fools and effete snobs, an aristocracy can also produce a significant proportion of men of the highest capacity; equally important, it is quick to patronize the unusually gifted in lower social orders and give them scope and encouragement for the exercise of their special talents. The democratic spirit, on the other hand, is commonly, as Alexis de Tocqueville and others have noticed, jealous of excellence and assiduous in trying to reduce everyone to a common level. Indeed, John Adams declared that his fellow New Englanders were so envious of superiority that he felt sure they would curtail the omnipotence of the Almighty if it were in their power. It may be one of those indigestible facts of history that a social system that subordinates a large majority of the population for the benefit of a privileged few is apt, at the same time, to be richest in the production of the superior individuals. This, in any event, was the case with Virginia.

North Carolina was as different from neighboring Virginia as two colonies could be. North Carolina received its greatest influx of settlers not directly from England, but rather from down the Great Wagon Road, the most traveled of all colonial highways, which ran from a point on the Schuylkill River near Philadelphia down the Shenandoah Valley, along the Blue Ridge Mountains, and ultimately to the Yadkin River in North Carolina, 435 miles away. From the frontier counties of the more settled colonies—Pennsylvania, Maryland, and Virginia—families moved south looking for cheaper land and more fertile soil. Those who were restless, discontented, dissenting, or simply adventurous made their way in substantial numbers to North Carolina, where the absence of a great landed aristocracy or an established commercial class produced a liberal and democratic atmosphere much to these restless settlers' taste.

North Carolina, while it had its great plantations worked by slaves, was primarily a colony of small, fiercely independent farmers; they contested the leadership of the tidewater planters, whose centers were Edenton and Wilmington on the coast. The three western counties of

North Carolina increased tenfold in population between 1746 and 1756; the newcomers were for the most part Irish Protestants and Germans. Under the threat of Indian attack, Virginians from the Piedmont area moved south in such numbers as to "appear almost incredible." Five thousand crossed the James River at one ferry. "Many of these," the Reverend James Maury, a Virginia divine, wrote, "are not the idler and the vagrant pests of society . . . but honest and industrious, men of worth and property, whom it is an evil to a community to lose." The governor of North Carolina, William Tryon, wrote in 1766, "I am of the opinion this province is settling faster than any on the continent, last autumn and winter, upwards of one thousand wagons passed thro' Salisbury with families from the northward, to settle in this province chiefly. . . ." In the Rocky Mount area, a traveler found people crowded together, "thick as in England." They were, those frontier voyagers moving down the Shenandoah, a hardy and independent lot. Some would express that independence by remaining loyal to the British Crown; other "over the mountain men" would fill the frontier regiments of Daniel Morgan and fend off the bloody attacks of British Indians during the Revolution.

Life was far from elegant on the frontier; the rough life bred a rough people. A traveler observed on a trip to the frontier in 1753 that the settlements swarmed with children, but that their parents did not "bestow the least education on them, they take so much care in raising a Litter of Piggs, their Children are equally naked and full as Nasty. The Parents in the back Woods come together without any previous Ceremony, and it is not much to be wondered at that the Offspring of such loose Embraces should be little looked after."

North Carolina is hard to characterize. Yet it was by no means a nonentity. Without great figures or brilliant leaders, it represented, better in fact than Virginia, the ideal of the yeoman farmer: the small, independent landowner who tended his acres and was jealous of his rights. North Carolinians would have doubtless been more at home in New England than sandwiched between Virginia and South Carolina.

The life and culture of the latter colony centered in the port city of Charles Town. This circumstance of being city-dominated, more than anything else, distinguished South Carolina from its older rival, Virginia. South Carolina combined the characteristics of a bustling commercial center with the plantation life of the great estates that stretched back from the coast along the moss-hung banks of the Santee and Ashley rivers. The economic base of the colony rested primarily on the crops of rice and indigo; Charles Town, where these products were shipped, was the largest and most prosperous colonial city south of Philadelphia. In the years prior to the Revolutionary crisis, the colony underwent an expansion only slightly less spectacular than its northern neighbor, accompanied by an economic boom that brought large fortunes to many South Carolinians. Joseph Allston at the age of forty had five slaves and a modest farm; in a comparatively few years he acquired five plantations and between 500 and 600 slaves. Henry Laurens, who was the son of a saddler, became one of the wealthiest men in the province. Thomas Elfe was a cabinetmaker who by shrewd investments left an estate of 17,000 pounds, probably the equivalent of half a million dollars today. Henry Middleton owned 50,000 acres and 600 slaves. The efforts of the older aristocracy to maintain their domination of the colony were thwarted by the spectacular rise of the new rich. By 1770 the population of Charles Town was more than 12,000, half white and half black, but in the plantations along the rivers there were approximately 100,000 inhabitants, of whom only 26,000 were white, the rest Negro slaves.

Charles Town gloried in the hectic social life of a community that is making money hand over fist and is determined to enjoy it. A visitor noted that "the people of Charles Town live rapidly, not willingly letting go untasted any of the pleasures of life. Few therefore reach a great age." But it was also true that "no city of America exhibits, in proportion to its size, so much splendor and style." When Josiah Quincy of Boston went to dine with Miles Brewton, one of the nabobs of Charles Town, he was awed by "the grandest hall I ever beheld, azure blue, with gilt, mashee borders, most elegant pictures, excessive grand and costly looking-glasses," and a wine better than any served in Boston.

Although there were tutors for the sons and daughters of the rich, South Carolina, like Virginia, had virtually no public schooling. Lieutenant Governor William Bull admitted that "we have not one good Grammar School. . . . All our Gentlemen, who have anything of a learned education, have acquired it in England, and it is to be lamented that they are not more numerous." There were, however, for those who could afford them, "teachers of Mathematics, Arithmetic, Fencing, French, Drawing, Dancing, Music, and Needlework, to fit men for the busy work and ladies for the domestic social duties of life."

Calliope was the muse who flourished most conspicuously in Charles Town. The St. Cecilia Society consisted of 120 gentlemen who paid twenty-five pounds a year for the privilege of attending concerts and bringing as many ladies as they wished. These events were held for years at Robert Dillon's hostelry. The theater was also popular. In 1763 the American Company of Comedians played for almost five months in Charles Town, opening with *The Mourning Bride* and closing with *King Lear.*

In South Carolina, where the taking of black concubines by upper-class white men was openly acknowledged, the Charles Town *Gazette* printed a debate on the comparative sexual accomplishments of slave women and white strumpets. In a letter to the editor purporting to be written by some ladies newly arrived from Bermuda, the young bachelors and widowers of the city were advised that "if they were in a Strait for Women, to wait for the next Shipping from the Coast of Guinny. Those African Ladies are of a strong, robust Constitution: not easily jaded out, able to serve them by Night as well as Day . . . the cheapness of a Commodity becomes more taking when it fully Answers the end, or T—l."

The next week the correspondent was answered by a champion of the Charles Town bawds: "In my Opinion, our Country Women are full as capable for Service either day or night as any African Ladies whatsoever. . . . In all Companies wheresoever I have been, my Countrywomen have always the praise for their Activity of Hipps and . . . in what Posture soever their Partners may fancy, which makes me still hope that they'll have the Preference before the black Ladies in the esteem of the Widowers and Batchelors at C—town."

The South Carolina frontier filled up with a hotchpotch of Scotch-Irish, runaway servants, and common criminals. Between the port of Charles Town and the great lowland plantations on the one side, and the backcountry on the other, lay not only the pine barrens, a broad belt of sandy, arid soil, sparsely populated, but also the greatest extremes of wealth and poverty. The seacoast aristocrats and *nouveaux riches* were more indifferent to the poor farmers and renegade whites of the interior than they were to their own slaves, and they were indifferent enough to the latter, leaving them to the mercies of overseers, who were often coarse and brutal men, while they enjoyed the glittering balls and lavish parties of the metropolis. As contrasted with their Virginia counterparts, the Carolina aristocrats gave little evidence of what we would call today social conscience. This was partly the fault of geography—the physical separation of the eastern and western parts of the state—and partly a result of the distractions of new wealth. In the backcountry, alienated white settlers had the same grievances against the colonial rulers as the residents of Charles Town had, in turn, against Great Britain: taxation without representation, manipulation of the law, self-ishness, and callous disregard of the rights and needs of the frontier. The Revolution, when it came, seemed less a fight for freedom than an effort of the seacoast aristocracy to protect its own narrow interests, interests that frequently were quite at odds with the interests of the inhabitants of the interior country.

Conditions of life on the Southern frontier are indeed a separate story. The settlers of the New England frontier shared the same ideals and aspirations as the Boston merchant. Although there were clearly strains and tensions, no open schism marked the relations between the backcountry and the coastal cities. In Virginia, it was not uncommon for planters' sons to seek their fortunes farther west. This fact, plus the attention of the planter class generally to the interests of the small farmers and their skill in political matters, preserved a substantial degree of unity in the Old Dominion.

From Virginia south, however, the frontier was comparatively iso-lated, and the conditions of life were crude indeed. We are fortunate to have a graphic account of the Carolina frontier from the pen of an Anglican missionary, the Reverend Charles Woodmason, who traveled through the backcountry trying to convert the settlers, keeping a diary, and reporting to the bishop of London about the hazards of his minis-try.

The problem with the South Carolina frontier, Woodmason noted, was the absence of any law enforcement at all. The worst elements on the frontier gathered to rob and pilage. "Here vile and impudent fellows, would come to a planter's house, and Tye him, lie with his wife before his face, ravish virgins before the eyes of their parents, a dozen fellows in succession," Woodmason wrote to the bishop. Robbers would "place irons in the fire and burn the flesh of persons to make them confess where they concealed their money. All merchant stores were broke up. No pedlars with goods dared to travel. No women ventured abroad. . . ."

The backcountry folk were poor because of their indolence, in Woodmason's opinion, "for they possess the finest Country in America, and could raise but ev'ry thing." However, instead of bestirring them-selves, "they delight in their present low, lazy, sluttish, heathenish, hellish Life, and seem not desirous of changing it. Both Men and Women will do any thing to come at Liquor, Cloaths, furniture, etc. etc. rather than work for it—Hence their many vices—their gross Licen-

tiousness, Wantonness, Lasciviousness, Rudeness, Lewdness, and Profil-
gacy they will commit the grossest Enormities, before my face, and
laugh at all Admonition."

The young women in their state of virtual nakedness were a particular distraction to Woodmason. Burdened by his wig and clerical robes,
he watched them with disapproval in which there was plainly more than
a touch of envy and desire. "They draw their Shift as tight as possible to
the Body," he noted in his journal, "and pin it close to their Hips to shew
the fineness of their Limbs—so that they might as well be in Puris
Naturalibus—indeed Nakedness is not censurable or indecent here, and
they expose themselves often quite Naked, without Ceremony—Rub-
bing themselves and their Hair with Bears Oil and tying it up behind in
a Bunch like the Indians—being hardly one degree removed from
them." After Woodmason had conducted a service, they often "went to
Reveling Drinking Singing Dancing and Whoring—and most of the
Company were drunk before I quitted the Spot. . . ."

In one community Woodmason was urged to settle as minister. It
was even proposed that a certain handsome young woman would make
him an excellent wife. Woodmason was apparently tempted until he
inadvertantly discovered that the lady in question was the local light of
love. Quite evidently the townspeople hoped to kill two birds with one
stone: acquire a minister and decommission, so to speak, the local
whore.

Although Woodmason often went hungry and usually ate the
simplest fare—"fat rusty Bacon, and fair water with Indian Corn
Bread" was a typical frontier meal—he persisted in his efforts to bring
the true doctine to the inhabitants of the region. In one rude settlement
after another, he found "Not a Bible or Prayer Book—Not the least
Rudiments of Religion, Learning, Manners or Knowledge (Save of Vice)
among them." Devoured by mosquitoes, drenched by rain, fed thin fare,
and full of self-pity, he persevered and developed in time a genuine
affection and concern for his benighted charges, who, as he described
them, were "without Laws or Government Churches Schools or Ministers—No police established—and all Property quite insecure." Woodmason himself drew up a remonstrance to present to the South Carolina
Assembly, listing the grievances of the backcountry inhabitants. The sad
fact was that the assembly was indignant at the charges. And, as Woodmason noted, "finding that they were only amus'd and trifled with, all
the confidence of the poor in the great is destroyed and I believe will
never exist again."

But all Woodmason's troubles were not with the South Carolina Assembly. When he tried to celebrate Holy Communion at Little Lynch's Creek, the Presbyterians "gave away 2 barrels of Whisky to the Populace to make drink, and for to disturb the Service. . . . The company got drunk by 10 o'th Clock and we could hear them firing, hooping, and hallowing liked Indians." At Granny Quarter Creek, he tried to preach to "the lowest Pack of Wretches my Eyes ever saw, or that I have met with in these woods—as wild as the very Deer—No making of them sit still during services—but they will be in and out—forward and backward the whole Time (Women especially) as Bees to and fro to their Hives—All this must be born with at the beginning of Things— Nor can be mended till Churches are built, and the Country reduc'd to some Form." In many places the inhabitants had "nought but a Gourd to drink out off Not a Plate Knife or Spoon, a Glass, Cup, or any thing— it is well if they have some Body Linen, and some have not even that."

Woodmason's encounters with shouting Baptists and cunning Presbyterians were frequent. In one community, a man entered his room when he was asleep, stole his "gown," and then visited "a Woman in Bed, and getting to Bed to her, and making her give out next day, that the Parson [Woodmason] went to Bed with her." This was a scheme cooked up by the Baptists, according to Woodmason. On another occasion, Presbyterians let loose a pack of barking dogs in the spot where Woodmason was trying to conduct a service. After the service was over, Woodmason caught one of the dogs, took it to the house of a Presbyterian elder, "and told Him that I had 57 Presbyterians came that Day to Service, and that I had converted one of them, and brought Him home—I left the Dog with Him."

At the end of two years of missionary activity on the frontier, Woodmason summed up his accomplishments. He had ridden "near Six thousand Miles. . . . Wore my Self to a Skeleton and endured all the Extremities of Hunger, Thirst, Cold, and Heat." He had baptized some 1,200 children, given more than 200 sermons, started some 30 congregations, and, perhaps most important of all, "distributed Books, Medicines, Garden Seed, Turnip, Clover, Timothy Burnet, and other Grass Seeds—with Fish Hooks—Small working tools and variety of implements to set the Poor at work, and promote industry. . . . Roads are making—Boats building—bridges framing, and other useful Works begun thro' my Means, as will not only be of public Utility, but make the Country side wear a new face, and the People become New Creatures."

Beyond all this, he had helped to arouse the inhabitants of the backcountry to a sense of their grievances against the colonial assembly and a concern with trying to redress them. Standing on the principle of no taxation without representation, the more substantial settlers formed themselves into companies of Regulators to take law into their own hands and hunt down the thieves and bandits who had terrorized the interior country for years; from this they went on to openly defy the authorities, the courts of law, the tax collectors, and even, on several occasions, the colony's militia. This feeling of alienation persisted, and when the war broke out many frontier families who had looked in vain to the Carolina legislatures for relief put their hopes for justice in the British Crown and became Tories.

Woodmason's vivid account of the Carolina backwoods gives us a picture of frontier life much at variance with the usual romantic perspectives and, in doing so, serves to remind us of the rawness and crudeness of much of life in America. The contrast between the luxurious ways of the tidewater aristocracy and the rough vulgarity of the settlers in the interior country dramatizes the range and diversity of eighteenth-century colonial life-styles. Moreover, the conflicts between seaboard and interior were to have profoundly important consequences in the military campaigns of the Revolution.

Of course the overriding reality in those parts of the South that we are most concerned with—primarily the seacoast regions—was Negro slavery. The servitude of black men and women affected every aspect of Southern life, including the sexual relations between the two races. The first shipment of Negroes arrived in Virginia in 1619. In John Rolfe's words, "About the last of August came in a dutch man of warre that sold us twenty Negars." It is not clear that these were sold as perpetual servants, but in the years that followed the evidence, however scanty, makes clear that a distinction was made between white Christian indentured servants (slaves for a stated term) and black slaves who, increasingly, are referred to as slaves for a lifetime. In the middle of the seventeenth century, when both common practice and law were poorly defined, some black slaves were released by their masters after a period of service; and at least one free Negro owned a slave himself. Sexual relations and even marriage apparently took place between whites and blacks, although from the earliest times there seems to have been considerable uneasiness about such alliances. By 1662, a Virginia statute declared that "if any christian shall committ Fornication with a negro man or woman, hee or shee soe offending" must pay twice the usual fine. In 1664 Maryland forbade interracial marriages, and a subsequent act, passed almost twenty years later (which suggested that the practice was still not uncommon), spoke of such marriages as "always to the Satisfaction of theire Lascivious and Lustfull desires." In Maryland, a husband advertised in 1759 that he would not pay his wife's debts because *"Mary Skinner,* my wife, has, after all the Love and Tenderness which could possibly be shown by Man to a Woman, polluted my Bed, by taking to her in my Stead, her own Negro Slave, by whom she hath a Child, which hath occasioned so much Disgrace to me and my Family, that I have thought proper to forbid her my Sight any more."

Reading the record of the slow hardening of white sentiment against the black slave, several things become apparent. From the beginning, few Negroes had any way of coping with the white world. Those who had served for a time in the West Indies might have acquired the rudiments of English; the great majority, however, came from a variety of African tribes and spoke a variety of tongues. Torn out of the context of their tribes, which contained the totality of their experience and their only identity, and of whose collective consciousness they were a part, slaves were indeed less than human. They had no consciousness of themselves as individuals in the sense in which that word was understood in the Post-Reformation West.

If this assumption is granted, it is easier to understand the gradual process by which, although no one clearly wished or planned it, the Africans who were captured and brought to the colonies initially as a supplementary labor force became "slaves for life." The vast majority, by their tribal antecedents and the conditions of their servitude, were rendered incapable of existing outside the plantation system. Such blacks were entirely dependent on their masters. For one thing, they were limited in their means of communication by having to learn an unfamiliar language that, once learned in an imperfect and rudimentary way, was of little help in relating their former life to their present one. These blacks could not, during any reasonable term of servitude, become prepared to make their own way in colonial America. If transported convicts and indentured servants had great difficulty in adjusting to the circumstances under which they found themselves and in subsequently establishing themselves as substantial citizens, how vastly more difficult was the case of blacks who had, in addition to every other kind of obstacle, a *different consciousness.* It thus followed that many white masters of black "slaves" kept them on without reference to a specific term of service. The fact was that it was impractical to free them when, in most cases, they were clearly unable to fend for themselves. Had blacks been able to assume freedom, it is logical to believe that, with the experience of white indentured servants as a guide, their masters would, at least in the beginning, have given them their freedom at the end of a stated period of years, and that they in turn would have become in time integrated with the more numerous white community. That this latter did not happen is the clearest indication that it could not happen.

At the same time that the colonists were gradually evolving a relationship with the Negroes being imported into English America, the Southern plantation owners began to discover the practical advantages of black slaves "for life" over white indentured servants with a limited term of servitude. The white slaves were very close to constituting a criminal class, and of course in the cases of transported convicts they were exactly that. They were far from docile; they ran away with comparative ease and often took a good portion of their master's goods with them. The "refuse and off-scourings" of the London streets, they were an actively demoralizing element in every colony where they were found in substantial numbers. Only greed and a desperate need for field hands could have reconciled the colonists to accepting them at all. So it gradually became apparent that black slaves were much preferable to white. Precisely those qualities that made it virtually impossible for the black slave to accommodate himself to white society made him most valuable doing the simple if arduous work of a field hand. His distinctive appearance made him easy to identify; his inability to shift for himself in the world beyond the plantation bound him to his master, who provided food, clothing, and even, in a degree, protection. Moreover, the black slave had the vast advantage that he reproduced himself. If a black father and mother could not be freed, it followed that it would be improper to free their children, even less able in their years of child-hood dependence to fend for themselves. Thus what began as a practi-cal expedient—retaining black slaves in at first an indefinite and then a permanent condition of bondage—gradually hardened into a system that was cruelly exploitative. It would not be inaccurate to say that the colonists drifted into black servitude without termination—drifted into slavery. It is necessary to stress how slowly this transformation to a slave society took place. It was not a matter of decades but of generations before white field labor was entirely replaced by blacks, and the full-blown plantation system emerged.

Throughout all this time, many white Southerners publicly and privately deplored the growth of black slavery, and some of the most eloquent indictments of the institution came from Southern slave owners, men like Jefferson, George Mason, James Madison, and George Washington. If there was ever a classic case of economic determinism, it was demonstrated in the growth of the slave system in the South. Humanity, common sense, and long-term self-interest all condemned it as morally wrong and socially disastrous, and yet it spread its cancerous cells throughout the whole of that gracious culture on which the South so prided itself.

The class of Southerners represented by men like Thomas Jefferson felt themselves trapped in a system that they loathed; and since they were, virtually without exception, believers in the workings of natural law—that is to say, that there was a structure of divine justice, and that individuals and nations were punished for their sins—they spoke constantly of the retributive justice that hung over all of them. "Indeed I tremble for my country," Jefferson wrote, "when I reflect that God is just: that his justice cannot sleep for ever: that considering numbers, nature and natural means only, a revolution of the wheel of fortune, an exchange of situation, is among possible events: that it may become probable by supernatural interference! The Almighty has no attribute which can take sides with us in such a contest."

It is easy to condemn Jefferson for tolerating an institution about whose evils he felt so strongly. True, he could have freed his own slaves, but it would, on balance, have been a quixotic and cruel gesture. It might have given him a feeling of rectitide and self-righteousness, but it would have turned the slaves out into a world that most of them could not cope with. Moreover, Jefferson would have destroyed his own political influence, and with it whatever good he might have effected, without at the same time making the slightest breach in the system itself.

What is most striking, of course, is Jefferson's perception of the evils of slavery. The fact that he and his compatriots felt as they did made it possible for them to be genuine spokesmen of freedom and equality. While Thomas Paine was a native-born Englishman, his comments on slavery may be taken to represent the attitudes of most of the leading political figures in his adopted country: "With what consistency, or decency they complain so loudly of attempts to enslave them," Paine wrote, "while they hold so many thousands in slavery; and annually enslave many thousands more, without any pretence of authority, or claim upon them? How just, how suitable to our crime is the punishment with which Providence threatens us? We have enslaved multitudes, and shed much innocent blood in doing it; and now are threatened with the same. And while other evils are confessed and bewailed, why not this especially and publicly; than which no other vice, if all others, has brought so much guilt on the land?"

The story of slavery in the English colonies of North America in the period before the American Revolution is a tragedy much too vast and complex to treat adequately here. A modern Gibbon or a Parkman will be needed to do it full justice. But as a profoundly important aspect of pre-Revolutionary America, slavery must be thoughtfully considered. For a people who were engaged in a struggle not only for their own liberties and rights as Englishmen but for, as they so often said, the universal rights of man, the anomaly of black servitude in their own household was a grim reminder of the compromised nature of all human aspirations.

Considering the major geographical and social divisions of the colonies—New England, middle, and Southern—it is as though various tendencies and impulses in English life, which in the mother country were inhibited by often bitter internal divisions, had an opportunity to develop in America according to their own inner logic, free of the constraints and conflicts of the homeland. Thus in New England the extraordinary energies released by English and Continental Puritanism flowered in the classic form of the New England township. In the town was forged that overriding force of will that would erupt into what, for better or worse (and often clearly for worse), was to be described as American individualship, or "rugged individualism." There, too, was created the archetypal community, what we today call an "intentional community," a community made up of people bound together by a common need, dream, or vision.

In the middle colonies, and especially in Pennsylvania, there developed the spirit of what we might call "positive toleration," and in addition that impulse to civic reforms, to philanthropic works and enlightened discourse, found so abundantly in Benjamin Franklin's Philadelphia. Franklin himself was, after all, born in Boston and transplanted to the City of Brotherly Love, where he might be taken to stand for a secularized Puritanism typified by his *Do-Good Papers*.

The South was perhaps the oddest case of all. Whatever there was that was politically and socially creative in the ideal of the English country gentleman was emulated in those colonies that lay south of Mason and Dixon's Line. Even the curse of slavery could not outweigh or obliterate the ideal of the politically astute gentleman, well read in ancient history, a student of the classics, a lover of freedom; hospitable, courteous, aware of his responsibilities to those dependent upon him, black or white; determined to do his duty and determined to be master of his own affairs.

Small wonder, then, that foreign travelers were far more impressed by the differences among the colonists than by their similarities. They seemed as unlikely to mix as oil and water. What, indeed, did the Virginia planter with his lavish style of life, his vast acres and degraded slaves, have in common with a Boston merchant or a New Hampshire farmer? Or for that matter with a pious Quaker or a ranting Baptist?

Events were to show that they shared a world of ideas. Or perhaps we might say they were, quite unwittingly, part of a new kind of consciousness.

6

Indians and Settlers

THE encounter between the English colonists and the American aborigines, to whom the English gave the general name of "Indians" because of the darkness of their skin, was one of the most dramatic meetings between different cultures in all history. The Indians were divided into innumerable tribes that spoke some five hundred different tongues and dialects. (This was one of the facts about the native Americans that led to the speculation of the colonists that the Indians might be the Lost Tribes of Israel—once a single people, but now cursed by God for their presumption in seeking to build the Tower of Babel and condemned to be divided and to speak in a multitude of strange tongues.) Many of these tribes were constantly at war with each other. With few exceptions, the culture of those Indians encountered by settlers from the Old World was based upon a perpetual state of war. Fierce courage in battle and stoic endurance under horrible tortures were the highest ideals of tribal life. In almost every respect, colonists and the Indians represented radically different patterns of culture. In the eastern part of the North American continent most of the aborigines were warrior-hunters, people of extraordinary physical hardihood and stamina. Roaming over vast territories, they had no notion of landed property and no idea of abstract justice. Cruelty, violence, and constant warfare were the facts of

107

daily life. Yet the European mind was captivated by the idea of the noble savage as it has been by few ideas in its history. Both Voltaire and Rousseau, philosophers who nurtured the Enlightenment, saw society as corrupt and decadent, far removed from the wholesomeness and simplicity of the natural man. They romanticized the savage man, whom they saw as being close to nature, his intelligence unclouded by priestly superstition, by social conventions, fashion, greed, and ambition. Voltaire wrote a novel called *L'Huron*, about an Indian who came to France and everywhere encountered and saw through the superficiality and falseness of French life. Religion, government, philosophy, the *haut monde*—all were revealed as empty and meretricious.

This was an eighteenth-century phenomenon. The planters or original settlers in the preceding century had a somewhat different perception of the Indian. For them he was alternately a poor heathen soul to be saved for the greater glory of God, or a figure of startling exoticism and terrible menace. Most of the English adventurers and planters in the New World were entirely sincere in their desire to bring to the savages of America the benefits of European Christianity. The task simply proved inordinately difficult.

Quite typically, Captain John Smith, who had his hands full contending with the deceitful Powhatan, was constantly exhorted by the officers of the Virginia Company to make more progress in converting the Indians to Christianity. To one such admonition, the captain replied testily that he needed some soldiers to force the Indians to pay attention to the preachers. It was difficult to convert an Indian who was shooting arrows at you or was plainly intent on trying to scalp you. If the settler's Christian faith had not inclined them to try to make peace with the various tribes of aborigines they encountered, simple prudence would have. Outnumbered and untrained, with a few exceptions, in the art of warfare—and certainly unfamiliar with the Indian guerrilla tactics of stealth and cunning—they did their best to avoid conflict. But the problem of maintaining peace was complicated by the constant state of warfare among the various tribes, conflicts that the settlers could only with the greatest difficulty avoid. In addition, the prolonged cold war between France and England for possession of North America, which smoldered for one hundred years before it burst into open flames in the French and Indian War or the Seven Years' War starting in 1754, was profoundly demoralizing to Indians and settlers alike. Neither the French nor the English could forbear using the tribes as pawns in their struggle for the dominance of the continent. The French repeatedly

encouraged their Indian allies to make forays against English settlements, while the English played the same unscrupulous game.

In Virginia, where the first meeting of planters and aborigines took
place, we had the inexhaustibly romantic encounter of Captain John
Smith with the Indian chief Powhatan and his daughter Pocahontas.
People will believe or disbelieve according to their own disposition the
story of Pocahontas saving John Smith's life when her bad-tempered
and wily old father was about to have Smith's brains bashed out. We
have only the captain's word for it, and some historians have said he was
a notorious liar (though others, as is the way with historians, have
defended him very resourcefully). What is quite clear is that there was a
close and affectionate relationship between the grizzled English captain,
half-suitor, half-father, and the Indian princess. And she must have
been a charming girl, running naked through the square at Jamestown
with her bacchanalian troop of Indian girls. The problems of Indian
diplomacy were pointed up by the fact that as soon as John Smith left
the colony, Powhatan began to harass the settlers. The response of the
colonists was to seize Pocahontas and hold her as hostage for her father's
good behavior. While she was being held at Jamestown, John Rolfe, who
perhaps first observed her turning cartwheels in the square, fell in love
with her and went through a profound struggle with his conscience to
decide whether or not to marry her. He wished to be sure that he was
"called hereunto by the spirit of God." And he protested that he was not
led, as he put it, "with the unbridled desire of carnall affection: but for
the good of this plantation for the honour of our countries, for the glory
of God, for my own salvation and for converting to the true knowledge
of God and Jesus Christ, an unbeleeving creature." That combination
proved, as might have been expected, irresistible. Rolfe married Pocahontas and took his Indian princess, now called Rebecca Rolfe and
dressed in English finery, to England to be introduced to the queen and
stared at as a seven-day wonder.

Rebecca Rolfe died on the voyage back to Virginia. She left an
infant son from whom—the romantics say—many present-day inhabitants of Virginia descend. The story symbolizes the romance and the
tragedy of the white-Indian relationship, which started out so promis-
ingly in the marriage of John Rolfe and Pocahontas and came at last,
after innumerable colorful and often bloody episodes, to such a dismal
end.

In 1620, several years after the death of Pocahontas, the Virginia
Indians turned on the whites and massacred almost the entire colony.

Those who survived did so only because of a warning from an Indian woman. And this fact points up one of the most striking aspects of the relations between the whites and the Indians: Time and again, groups of settlers were saved from surprise attack and extermination by an Indian woman who, at the risk of her own life, warned them of an impending raid.

John Lawson, a gentleman and a surveyor, who was well acquainted with the Indians of North Carolina, was particularly charmed by the Indian women, who were in his opinion "as fine shaped Creatures, (take them generally) as any in the Universe. They are of a tawny Complexion, their eyes very brisk and amorous, their Smiles afford the finest Composure a Face can possess, their Hands are of the finest Make, with small, long Fingers, and as soft as their Cheeks, and their whole Bodies of a smooth Nature. They are not so uncouth or unlikely as we suppose them, nor are they . . . not Proficients in the soft Passion." The "trading girls" were young unmarried women who would sleep with white traders for a price if their families and the sachem agreed on the arrangement and the sachem got a portion of the price (frequently a bottle of brandy). Such women, without any stigma attaching to them, usually married Indian warriors after a time and made good wives. Those white men who traded with the Indians "commonly have their Indian Wives," Lawson noted, "whereby they soon learn the Indian Tongue, keep a friendship with the Savages; and, besides the Satisfaction of a She-Bed-Fellow, they find these Indian girls very serviceable to them, on account of dressing their Victuals, and instructing them in the Affairs and Customs of the Country."

One of the unhappy consequences of these relationships, at least from Lawson's point of view, was that the children of such unions grew up as Indians. "Nevertheless," he added, "we often find, that English Men, and other Europeans that have been accustomed to the Conversation of these Savage Women and their Way of Living, have been so allured with that careless sort of Life, as to be constant to their Indian Wife, and her Relations, so long as they lived, without ever desiring to return again amongst the English. . . ." By the same token, it was Lawson's observation that "the Indian Men are not so vigorous and Impatient in their Love as we are." The Indian girls were thoroughly independent, and "those . . . that have conversed with the English and other European, never care for the Conversation of their own Countrymen afterwards."

The word "conversation" or "conversing" as used by Lawson means living with, including sexual relations. The hint of a particularly close relationship between Indian women and white men is a fascinating one, borne out by numerous other bits of evidence, equally fragmentary. It seems apparent that one of the aspects of Indian life that appealed most to the white man was the Indian woman. This was probably the result, in part, of the easy accessibility of Indian women, and of the simplicity and naturalness of the relationship. Moreover, Indian women were strong-minded and independent, but gentle, loving, and loyal to their white "husbands." To the Indian woman, the white man evinced the power, the complexity, and the exoticism that women of all races and ages seem to have found attractive in man. A special poignancy in the relationship between the settlers and the Indians was this evident tie between the white men and the Indian woman, a tie that was often the means of saving a frontier settlement from extermination.

Unfortunately, few colonists followed the example of John Rolfe. William Byrd, in *A History of the Dividing Line,* lamented the fact; "for after all," he wrote, with more facetiousness than wisdom, ". . . a sprightly lover is the most prevailing missionary that can be sent among these, or any other infidels. . . . Nor would the shade of skin have been reproached at this day; for if a Moor may be washed white in three generations, surely an Indian might have been blanched in two." Byrd was of the opinion that the Indian women "would have made altogether as honest wives for the first planters, as the damsels they used to purchase from aboard ships. . . . It is strange, therefore, that any good Christian should have refused a wholesome, straight bedfellow, when he might have had so fair a portion with her a claim to some of the Indian lands, as [well] as the merit of saving her soul."

If the colonists did not marry Indians in any substantial numbers, they nevertheless extended hospitality to them. When Durand attended a Virginia wedding in the 1690's, a company of Indians came to visit. Durand described the women as wearing "some kind of petticoats, others wore some piece of shabby blue cloth from which were made the blankets they had traded on some ships in exchange for deer skins. They had made a hole in the center to put their heads through and fastened it around their body with deer-thongs." They mixed freely with the guests and added a colorful note to the ceremonies.

Members of tribes who were on friendly terms with a particular colony did not hesitate to visit individuals or to claim to be guests of the colony itself, as in the case of Pennsylvania, which maintained apartments in the State House for the use of visiting sachems. In Virginia, the tradition of hospitality to passing Indians lingered on as the residue of the days when reciprocal hospitality was quite common. Jefferson recalled that they came often, and in considerable numbers, to Williamsburg. The Virginian spent much time with them and was a friend of the great Cherokee warrior and orator Outacity, who always stayed with Jefferson's father on his trips to and from the colonial capital. John Adams likewise recalled from his childhood frequent visits by the priest and the king of the Punkapog and Neponset tribes, named, respectively, Aaron and Moses, "the tallest and stoutest Indians I have ever seen." In turn, Adams on his rambles would often stop at the wigwam of an Indian family who lived nearby, where, he wrote, "I never failed to be treated with Whortle Berries, Blackberries, Strawberries, or Apples, Plumbs, Peaches, etc., for they had planted a variety of fruit trees about them."

Unfortunately, to befriend one tribe was to make inveterate enemies of *their* enemies. The Indian ethic allowed of no compromise on this score. If you were the friend of a particular tribe, you were of necessity an ally against its enemies. Anything else was the darkest treachery. Weak tribes or tributary tribes often tried to form an alliance with settlers in the hope of defeating a tribe to whom they had been tributary. The French in Canada, by forming an alliance with the Hurons, incurred the enmity of the Iroquois, the most powerful and warlike tribe in the northeast. Thus the traditional opponents of the Hurons became English allies when the great European powers brought their war to America. In Connecticut, settlers were invited to establish themselves on Indian lands, apparently in hopes that they would strengthen a particular tribe against its enemies. When Connecticut settlers under John Mason and John Underhill exterminated the Pequot tribe in 1637, they were assisted by the Narragansets and the Mohegans, the two most powerful tribes in the area, with whom the Connecticut settlers managed, on the whole, to maintain friendly relations.

Later, when the Massachusetts Bay colony was founded, John Eliot translated the Bible into the Indian tongue. But Eliot was only the most famous of a number of missionaries who labored to improve the lot of the Indians and to convert them to Christianity. Harvard built a building especially for the instruction of Indians, and Caleb Cheeshateaumuck, an Indian, obtained an early bachelor's degree. When the College of William and Mary was founded at Williamsburg in 1694, it included an Indian school, as, of course, did Dartmouth. The Dartmouth school produced Samson Occom, the noted Indian preacher and scholar.

All such efforts were ultimately unavailing. The white man's perception of the Indian was too limited. He wanted in effect to turn the Indian into a "white Protestant"—to which project the Indian was stubbornly resistant. The problem was vastly complicated by the fact that in a real sense there was no such thing as an Indian. There were members of tribes of frequently very different speech, customs, and manners, whose consciousness was a tribal consciousness. These did not and could not fully exist outside of the tribe of which they were members. The white man's ways and culture were as unfathomably strange to the so-called Indian as his ways were to the white man.

In any event, despite all efforts by enlightened spirits on both sides, the white settlers and the Indians were periodically involved in bitter warfare. The warfare was invariably, after the early years, to the Indians' disadvantage, because it provided opportunities for whites to take possession of Indian lands secured by treaties that could not be readily broken.

Through all the contacts between the Indian and the white man there runs a fascinating doubleness or ambiguity. There was much that was attractive in Indian life to the bearer of the Protestant ethic. White society was organized around the notion of contractual relationship, around predictable behavior. The Indian would have understood a medieval knight better than a sober Puritan, and vice versa. The Reformation, which made its adherents into "individuals," also made them hopelessly alien to a people who still lived in a tribal consciousness. And yet, to the white settler with his psychological burdens, the most basic of which was the sense that he must always behave as he was expected to behave, the free and, indeed, capricious life of the Indians had a sometimes irresistible attraction.

Observing the Indians, who "have few but natural wants and those easily supplied," Benjamin Franklin was inclined to propose a whole new theory of human development. If man could be so content in a state of nature, he asked himself, how had civilization ever arisen? It must have been as a consequence of a condition of scarcity, where some peoples, driven from lands that afforded an easy living, were forced to create a more complex and varied economic and social life. Franklin wrote to a friend: "They are not deficient in natural understanding and yet they have never shown any inclination to change their manner of life for ours, or to learn any of our Arts." Even when an Indian child had been brought up among whites, "taught our language and habituated to our Customs," if "he goes to see his relations and makes one Indian Ramble with them there is no persuading him ever to return. . . ." Indeed, when whites of either sex who had been taken prisoner at a tender age and had lived for a time among the Indians were returned to white society, "in a Short time they become disgusted with our manner of life . . . and take the first good Opportunity of escaping again into the woods, from whence there is no reclaiming them."

William Penn gave a vivid account of his initial meeting with the Indians of Pennsylvania, and a close account of their appearance and customs:

> For their persons, they are generally tall, straight, well-built and of singular proportion. They tread strong, and clever, and mostly walk with a lofty chin. Of complexion black, but by design as the gypsies in England. They grease themselves with bears-fat clarified, and using no defence against sun or weather, their skins must need be swarthy. Their eye is little and black, not unlike a straight-look't Jew. The thick lip and flat nose so frequent with East-Indians and blacks are not common among them; for I have seen as comley European-like faces among them of both sexes, as on your side the sea. . . ."
>
> Their language is lofty, yet narrow, but like the Hebrew . . . one word serves in the place of three. . . . I must say that I know not a language spoken in Europe that hath words of more sweetness or greatness, in accent and emphasis than theirs; for instance Octorockon, Rancoros, Ozicton, Shakamacon . . . all of which are names of places and have grandeur in them.

As soon as Indian children were born, they were washed and plunged into cold water to harden them.

> Having wrapped them in a clout they lay them on a straight thin board, a little more than the length and breadth of the child and swadle it fast upon the board; wherefore all Indians have flat heads; and thus they carry them on their backs. . . . When the young women are fit for marriage, they wear something upon their heads for an advertisement, but so as their faces are hardly to be seen but when they please. The age they marry at, if women, is about thirteen and fourteen, if men seventeen and eighteen; they are rearely elder.
>
> Their diet is maze, or Indian corn, divers ways prepared; sometimes roasted in the ashes, sometimes beaten and boiled with water which they call homine; they also make cakes not unpleasant to eat.

They have likewise several sorts of beans and pease that are good nourishment and the woods and rivers are their larder. . . . They are great concealers of their own resentments, brought to it, I believe, by the revenge that hath been practised among them; in either of these, they are not exceeded by the Italians.

But in liberality they excell, nothing is too good for their friend: give them a fine gun, coat, or other thing, it may pass twenty hands, before it sticks; light of heart, strong affections, but soon spent; the most merry creatures that live, feast, and dance perpetually; they never have much; nor want much. Wealth circulateth like the blood, all parts partake . . . If they are ignorant of our pleasures, they are also free from our pains. They are not disquieted with bills of lading and exchange, nor perplexed with chancery-suits and exchequer-reckonings. We sweat and toil to live; their pleasure feeds them; I mean their hunting, fishing and fowling. . . . They eat twice a day, morning and evening; their seats and table are on the ground. Since the European came into these parts, they are grown great lovers of strong liquors, rum especially. If they are heated with liquors, they are restless till they have enough to sleep, that is their cry—some more and I will go to sleep; but when drunk, one of the most wretchedst spectacles in the world.

The justice they have is pecuniary: In case of any wrong or evil fact, be it murder itself, they attone by feasts and presents of their wampum, which is proportion to the quality of the offense or person injured, or of the sex they are of: For in case they kill a woman, they pay double, and the reason they give is, "That she breedeth children which men cannot do."

Penn's formula for Indian negotiations was simple. "Don't abuse them, but let them have justice, and you win them. The worst is that they are the worse for the Christians who have propagated their vices and yielded them tradition for ill, and not for good things. . . . I beseech God to incline the hearts of all that come into these parts, to out-live the knowledge of the natives by a fixt obedience to their greater Knowledge of the will of God, for it were miserable indeed for us to fall under the just censure of the poor Indian conscience, while we make profession of things so far transcending."

The Reverend John Heckewelder, a Moravian missionary, expressed the same admiration for Indian life. "They think," he wrote, "that [God] made the earth and all it contains for the common good of mankind . . . it was not for the benefit of a few, but of all. Every thing was given in common to the sons of man. Whatever liveth on the land, whatsoever groweth out of the earth, and all that is in the rivers and waters flowing through the same, was given jointly to all, and every one is entitled to his share. From this principle, hospitality flows as from its source. . . . They give and are hospitable to all, without exception, and will always share with each other and often with a stranger, even to their last morsel."

"Yours" and "mine," "ours," "his," "hers," were not the determinative words for the Indians that they were for the white man. The Indian did not think that the land was "his" in the sense that the white man insisted that it was his property. The whole notion of buying and selling land was so alien to the Indian that while he could understand driving an enemy off a hunting range or general territory, he had no notion of marking off a specific area as belonging in perpetuity to some individual tribe, and certainly not to an individual Indian. Thus he often "sold" the same land to several English purchasers, thereby causing vast confusion and misunderstanding, if not bloody skirmishes.

Franklin's classic account of the effort to interest the Indians in the white man's education suggests some of the difficulties involved in trying to reconcile the two cultures. According to Franklin, in a treaty meeting between the Six Nations and the authorities of one of the colonies, the Indian commissioners told the Indians that as a special gesture of friendship and good will, "a particular foundation in favour of the Indians" would "defray the expense of the Education of any of their sons who should desire to take the benefit of it." If the Indians were agreeable, the English would take half-a-dozen of their brightest young men "and bring them up in the Best manner." The response of the Indians was, in effect, that a college education was impractical. "Some of their Youths had formerly been educated in that College, but it had been observed that for a long time after they returned to their Friends, they were absolutely good for nothing being neither acquainted with the true methods of killing deer, catching beaver or surprizing an enemy." However, the chiefs, impressed by the evident kindness in the proposal, offered in return "if the English Gentlemen would send a dozen or two of their Children to [the Indian settlement at] Onondago," they would undertake to bring them up in what really was the best manner and make men of them. The story is probably apocryphal—just the kind of moral-making yarn Franklin was forever spinning—but it does make the point, and the fact is that the purported answer of the Indians was typical of their sense of humor. Much of the conflict between white and Indian revolved around the Protestant "work ethic" of the settlers, especially those of New England. For the whites, a man who was not working or who would not work was, as a matter of course, a weak and foolish, if not a wicked, man. Not to work, and to drink as well, was vagabondage and a certain damnation. The Indian did both—he was resistant to work and drank himself into insensibility whenever he had the chance. Josiah Cotton's *Vocabulary of the Massachusetts (or Natick) Indians,* which was written for the Christianized "praying Indians" who lived at Natick as wards of the colony, reveals white attitudes quite clearly. The most striking phrases in the dictionary have to do with work and drink: "Why don't you work hard?" *(Kah tohawal mat menukanakausean.)*; "So I would with all my heart, but I am sickly." "But it might be work will cure you, if you would leave off drinking too." And again, "Idleness is the root of much evil."

The numerous treaty meetings with the Indians were always colorful and dramatic affairs. There the Indians appeared at their noblest and most striking. Merciless and cruel in warfare, they were magnanimous in peace. When a site for the powwow had been agreed upon, the Indian tribe or tribes would begin to assemble. With none of the white man's preoccupation with being "on time," they were often maddeningly slow to appear, days or weeks late by English time. They came in full panoply, in a bizarre combination of English and Indian finery, a beaded buckskin shirt set off by a plumed beaver hat festooned with shells, or a headdress with a blue broadcloth coat with tarnished silver buckles. The Indian orations were lengthy and extraordinarily eloquent, woven with rich metaphorical figures and conceits. Agreements were bound by smoking the calumet, or pipe of peace.

The colonists were clearly much impressed by Indian oratory, and some historians have suggested that the "stem-winding," "spread-eagle" oratory much favored by American politicians of the nineteenth century had its origin in the treaty speeches of Indian chiefs. Treaty meetings were usually accompanied by much drinking and revelry, especially after a treaty had been agreed upon, since a keg of rum was not infrequently part of the treaty settlement, and the Indians might linger on for days of celebration.

A typical treaty meeting was one that took place at Albany in 1754 between the governor of the province of New York and the Onondagas and Cayugas. "Brother: You are a mighty sachem and we but a small people. When the English first came to New York, to Virginia and Maryland, they were but a small people and we a large nation, and we finding they were good people gave them land and dealt civilly with them. Now that you are grown numerous and we decreased you must protect us from the French, which if you don't we shall lose all our hunting and beavers. The French want all the beavers and are angry that we bring any to the English. We have put all our land and our persons under the protection of the Great Duke of York, brother to your mighty sachem. The Susquehanna River which we won by our sweat, we have given to this government. And we desire that it may be a branch of that great tree which is planted here, whose top reaches to the sun and under whose branches we shelter ourselves from the French or any other enemy. Our fire burns in your houses. Your fire in our houses and we desire it may ever so continue. . . . We have submitted ourselves to the Great Sachem Charles who liveth on the other side of the Great Lake and now we give you in token thereof two white buckskins to be sent to him." Then came the presentation of wampum and skins by the Indians and of presents by the white men—needles, cloth, lace, shirts, beads, mirrors, guns, etc.

Jefferson, who, like Franklin and indeed most American intellectuals, was fascinated by Indian life, was present in the camp of Outacity, a chief of the Cherokees, when he made his farewell oration to his people on the evening of his departure for England. As Jefferson recalled the scene many years later: "The moon was in full splendor, and to her he seemed to address himself in his prayers for his own safety on the voyage, and that of his people during his absence. His sounding voice, distinct articulation, animated action, and the solemn silence of his people at their several fires, filled me with awe and veneration, altho' I did not understand a word he uttered."

As Wilcomb Washburn has put it: "The white man as officeholder is, in many ways, a more perplexing and perverse figure to the Indian than the individual conqueror, or fur trapper, or explorer. Under the panoply of European formality the government representative communicated with the Indian leaders, but too often the form and spirit were not in close juxtaposition. The Indian, valuing the spirit rather than the recorded form, which in his letterless society was, for the most part, superfluous, could not cope with the legalisms of the white man. Nor could an alien government sympathize with, let alone understand, the plight of a race organized into categories that had no parallels in the white bureaucratic machinery."

This was certainly the case in those constant negotiations between the white man and the Indian that began when John Smith seized Powhatan by the hair of his head and quite literally wrung concessions from him. A famous instance of hard bargaining by whites at Indian expense was the so-called Walking Purchase of Indian lands in Pennsylvania. The Indians sold, at a reasonable price, that area of land that a man could walk around in one day, from sunup to sunset. This was for a moderately fast walker, let us say, some twenty square miles. However, the white purchasers arranged for relays of runners to cover a vastly larger territory and thus claim several times the extent of land the Indians intended to sell. To the Indians this was simple deceit and chicanery. To the whites, it was a clever ruse. It is small wonder that to Pocahontas it was a plain truth that Englishmen "lied much," or that later generations of Indians took it for granted that the white man spoke with a forked tongue. The irony of the situation was that the society of nascent capitalism that was developing out of the Protestant passion was based on contractual relationships and, above all, on a man's word being as good as his bond. Thus "English honor" came to be a synonym for fair dealing. However, in time the burden of personal honesty was shifted to the contract. Whatever could be negotiated into the contract (or treaty) was fair enough. Deviousness was part of the game. People who live without or outside of conventional bureaucratic structures are inevitably thrown back on the requirement of personal integrity and oftentimes appear naive to sophisticated negotiators.

Whether the aborigines of North America were "squalid savages" or nature's noblemen; whether the English settlers were ruthless exploiters or pious Christians anxious to save heathen souls, it is hard to imagine how the two cultures could have coexisted on the same continent without the bitter conflicts that marked their historic encounters.

The so-called Indians taught the colonists how to plant corn and tobacco, peas, beans, pumpkins and squash, melons, and cucumbers; how to harvest maple sugar; how to use fish for fertilizer; how to hunt and trap; how to make canoes. They supplied them with innumerable place names and, finally, with the ubiquitous barbecue. But of far greater importance, they stirred the deepest levels of the white imagination. Did they represent a freer and more spontaneous life, a new vista of human possibilities? Or did they by their cruelties and violence awaken in the souls of "civilized" men the savage passions that they had struggled to repress? However one might approach that unanswerable question, the fact was that white man and red man were locked in a strange and terrible embrace that degraded the white and ultimately destroyed the Indian's tribal life.

7

Common Grievances and Common Dangers

DIVERSITY in unity is one of the major themes in American history; certainly it is the essence of the idea of a federal union. The diversity is simple enough to state and to understand. It lay in the variousness of the original settlements—from feudal Maryland to democratic Rhode Island—and in the extraordinary variety of immigrants—from members of the English gentry to convicted felons. The unity is more difficult to explain, although two key factors were a common allegiance to the British Crown and, if we except small settlements scattered here and there where Germans or Swiss or Dutch clung to their native tongues, a common English language. Among the other common denominators was the fact that the charter of each colony guaranteed its inhabitants "all the rights, privileges and immunities of Englishmen" and that the colonists were, if anything, more aware of these rights and more determined to protect them than their cousins across the Atlantic.

If England in the seventeenth century had flamed with a zeal for "rights" that had produced the classic immunities of the famous English Bill of Rights, the dedication to those principles had cooled considerably by the middle of the next century. Those Englishmen who determined, in large part, the mood and temper of the country were too prosperous, too complacent, and too arrogant to be concerned about the miserable conditions in which the mass of the poorer people lived. They continued, however, to congratulate themselves on the glories of the British constitution and its superiority to any other form of government in the world. This is not to say, of course, that the constitution was without substantial virtues, or that the middle ranks of Englishmen as well as the aristocracy did not enjoy broader rights than those enjoyed by the citizens of other European countries. But a self-congratulatory spirit can be dangerous for a country as for an individual, for it blinds those possessed of it to a proper sense of their own shortcomings and of the mutability of all earthly enterprises.

The colonists, on the other hand, interpreted "the rights of Englishmen" much more practically and directly. They still lived in the "glorious" spirit of the Revolution of 1689. They did not have to view those splendid rights through intervening layers of exceptions and exemptions. Where the Englishman, challenged on some glaring inequity quite at odds with the sacred principles of English justice, would doubtless have replied haughtily, "But my dear fellow, that is the way we have always done it," considering that quite a sufficient answer, the English colonist, confronted with a similar discrepancy between principle and fact, would have been at some pains to effect a reconciliation. Even in the case of slavery, many Southern slaveholders were profoundly troubled by the moral implications of the institution.

The colonists were continuously reminded of their rights by what they considered abuses of them—abuses that led to constant minor friction between the colonial legislative assemblies and the agencies of the Crown in England—the Board of Trade and Plantations and the Privy Council—and, in the colonies, between the Americans and the royal governors (where the colony was a royal one), and the customs officials. Parliament and the ministry thus became increasingly bored with the continual clamor of the colonists over their precious "rights as Englishmen." "Ask a colonist for some money to help protect his borders against the French and Indians," said one exasperated official, "and he will deliver you a lengthy lecture on his rights."

Nothing is as apt to unite a heterogeneous collection of people as common grievances. But there were, of course, a number of other relatively simple and obvious events that forced the various colonies to support each other and forge at least some tentative links of common action. If common grievances were one bond, common danger was another. The constant menace of the French and their Indian allies to the north forced the colonies to devise measures for mutual defense.

The first of a series of so-called intercolonial wars broke out following devastating Indian raids on the New England frontier. The details of these interminable campaigns lie, fortunately, outside the scope of this work. It is sufficient to review them briefly.

King William's War, as it was called in America, was the colonial phase of a European campaign (the War of the League of Augsburg) against Louis XIV. It lasted some eight years (1689 to 1697), but the active fighting was largely confined to New England.

Four and a half years after the Treaty of Ryswick, which ended King William's War, Queen Anne's War (the War of the Spanish Succession) broke out. Like the preceding conflict, it began with an Indian massacre of settlers and again, in its colonial phase, was fought primarily in New England and Canada. It was ended in 1713 by the Treaty of Utrecht. While the American campaigns of these "wars" were modest, they represented major expenditures of men and money for the American colonies.

Spain was the enemy in the War of Jenkins' Ear (1739 to 1742), which grew out of rough treatment by the Spaniards of English seamen, and which involved an unsuccessful attack by troops from Virginia, Carolina, and Georgia, under General James Oglethorpe, the founder of Georgia, against the Spanish city of St. Augustine in Florida. Between 1744 and 1748, colonial troops fought in King George's War, the American accompaniment to the War of the Austrian Succession. King George's War marked the most notable success of colonial arms in the series of protracted conflicts that characterized the first half of the eighteenth century: A well-supplied and well-organized attack against the French fort at Louisburg, one of the strongest fortresses in the New World, by Sir William Pepperell, leading volunteers from Massachusetts, Connecticut, and New Hampshire, forced the surrender of the fort. Encouraged by this triumph, New England militia attempted an abortive invasion of Canada; the French and Indians counterattacked against the New York and Pennsylvania frontiers.

In 1748 the Treaty of Aix-la-Chapelle put an official end to King George's War. Once again the interlude of peace was brief, for however often officials in Europe might call off the fighting, the causes of conflict remained in America; treaties were merely recesses that gave the antagonists time to plan new strategies.

By 1752 an aggressive new French governor of Canada, the Marquis Duquesne, was dispatching French parties down the Ohio Valley in an effort to outflank the British colonies. A force of some one thousand men occupied Presque Isle on the southern shore of Lake Erie, uncomfortably close to the English settlements in the Mohawk Valley. From Presque Isle, the soldiers hacked their way laboriously to Riviera aux Boeufs (the River of the Cattle) and built a fort—Fort Le Boeuf. Three hundred men were left to man the two isolated posts; the remaining force made its way back to the French settlements on the St. Lawrence.

News of the French expedition caused concern in the English colonies. The land along the Ohio occupied by the French forts was claimed by Virginia, part of the almost immeasurable expanse granted in that colony's original charter. The lieutenant governor of Virginia was Robert Dinwiddie, a resolute Scotsman, who fancied himself a man of action. He decided to send an emissary to the French, with a letter warning them that they were encroaching on territory claimed by a colony of Great Britain and instructing them to withdraw or suffer the consequences. George Washington, a young favorite of Dinwiddie's, was chosen for the mission. Accompanied by the experienced guide and Indian fighter Christopher Gist and six companions, Washington headed west from Williamsburg and fetched up eight days later at Venango, an English trading post at the confluence of French Creek and the Allegheny.

Washington and his men quickly discovered that Venango had been taken over by the French and named Fort Machault. Chabert Joucaire, the French officer in command, received Washington as one gentleman would receive another, whether in a European salon or in the remote forest of America. They bowed; they exchanged courtesies. The Frenchman was *charmé* to encounter Monsieur Washington *et ses amis*. Washington was as correct and formal as he would have been at a fancy-dress ball. When the Dinwiddie letter was delivered, however, Joucaire politely but firmly rejected its demands. The Americans thanked their amiable host and returned to report to Dinwiddie that the French were agreeable enough but showed no inclination to budge.

Dinwiddie, to prove to the French the seriousness of his intentions, sent a party of Virginia militia to the forks of the Ohio with instructions to build a fort there. The French countered by interrupting the work of construction and forcing the Virginia militia to withdraw. As in a chess game, move followed move. The French, having taken possession of the forks, built a more elaborate fortification of their own, Fort Duquesne. Not a man to be easily checkmated, Dinwiddie rounded up another small force under Colonels Joshua Fry and George Washington with orders to go to the Ohio by way of Wills Creek and drive off any venturesome Frenchmen they might encounter.

Action was not long in coming. At Great Meadows on the western slope of the Alleghenies in May, 1754, a group of Virginians under the command of Washington came upon a party of Frenchmen. It was doubtless Washington's thoroughness and attention to detail that assured his scouts of a few moments' advantage in spotting the enemy. Washington, without hesitating, ordered his men to open fire. The leader of the French force, Ensign Joseph Coulon Sieur de Jumonville, and a dozen of his men were killed; some twenty were captured.

This minor incident was the *casus belli,* the first overt act of what was known in America as the French and Indian War and in Europe as the Seven Years' War—a global conflict that was to cost France its vast New World empire, draw the colonies closer together than ever before, and launch the career of the young Virginia militia officer who had reacted with such speed and confidence to this chance encounter.

The next significant battle on the American front was triggered by Washington. Returning to Great Meadows, Washington built a simple fortification, which, with sardonic humor, he named Fort Necessity— perhaps it is characteristic of Americans to make a virtue of necessity, or perhaps it was only characteristic of George Washington. At any rate, Washington and his men had hardly completed their makeshift fort when a French force under Captain Louis Coulon de Villiers, brother of the slain Jumonville, surrounded it and forced the Virginians to surrender. Had Villiers been a vindictive man, the career of George Washington might have ended prematurely at Great Meadows, but Washington and most of his men were set free; a few Americans were sent to Quebec as prisoners. The French were more interested in territory than in captives.

The threat posed by the French was the incentive for the Albany Congress, called at the behest of the Lords of Trade in England to discuss the conduct of Indian affairs. In 1754 commissioners from all the colonies except New Jersey, Virginia, Rhode Island, and Connecticut met with representatives of the Iroquois Confederacy at Albany, New York. Benjamin Franklin, one of the commissioners, came armed with a "Plan of Union" that looked well beyond the Indian alliance to a colonial union for security and defense. While Franklin's plan received the principal attention of the commissioners, at least three other plans were drafted. Franklin's proposal, which the commissioners adopted with minor modifications, called for a "general government" of all the colonies, a government that, while reserving to each colony "its present constitution," provided for a President-General appointed by the Crown and a "Grand Council, to be chosen by the representatives of the people of the several colonies met in their respective assemblies." The colonies were to be proportionally represented: Massachusetts and Virginia, as the largest colonies, would have seven delegates each; New Hampshire and Rhode Island, the smallest, each would have two. The President-General, "with the advice of the Grand Council," would have the power "to hold or direct all Indian treaties in which the general interest of the colonies may be concerned; and make peace or declare war against Indian nations." The President-General and Grand Council would make all purchases from the Indians "of lands not within the bounds of particular colonies," or (and this was an alarming phrase to some colonies) "that shall not be within their bounds when some of them are reduced to more convenient dimensions." (Virginia, for instance, claimed a great pie-shaped piece of the continent reaching to the Pacific Ocean.) The President-General and Grand Council were also to have jurisdiction over any new settlements formed on lands purchased from the Indians "until the crown shall think it fit to form them into particular governments." Most disturbing of all, the President-General and Grand Council had the power to raise and pay soldiers and take other necessary measures for the defense of the colonies, and could, in addition, "make laws, and lay and levy such general duties, imposts, or taxes as shall appear to them most equal and just . . . rather discouraging luxury than loading industry with unnecessary burdens."

The Albany Plan of Union went much further than the colonial legislatures were prepared to go. It spoke of taxes—always a tender subject—and also infringed directly on one of the most sensitive of all areas, the speculation in western lands by many colonial leaders. This issue was, of course, tied directly to negotiations with the Indians. To have yielded up such powers would at once have curtailed the ambitious schemes of land speculators who were well represented in most colonial assemblies. The fact was that Franklin's plan went much too far for either the English government or the colonies—all of them jealous of their own prerogatives and suspicious of one another. It would perhaps not be putting it too strongly to say that each colony wished to be free to swindle the Indians without interference from its neighbors.

While the commissioners were engaged in their largely futile deliberations in Albany, England and France were girding for what one historian has called The Great War for Empire, a colossal struggle carried on over a large part of the globe that was to settle once and for all the fate of the French domain in North America.

The British did not wish a full-scale war with France, but they were determined, on the other hand, to oust the French from the Ohio Valley. To accomplish this they dispatched an amiable bumbler, General Edward Braddock, to head a joint British-colonial expedition. Braddock took leave of his mistress in London in a gloomy mood, convinced that his mission was destined to failure and that he himself would never live to return to England. He proved a better prophet than a soldier. His disastrous defeat near Fort Duquesne in July, 1755, became a byword. The only positive consequence of the campaign was that it provided Washington with another opportunity to display his qualities as a leader.

It was Washington who regrouped the survivors and led them back to Fort Cumberland, at the juncture of Wills Creek and the Potomac. He wrote of the engagement, "We have been beaten, most shamefully beaten by a handful of men." But for Washington the campaign had been instructive. In his first major engagement he had learned the bitterest lesson that war can teach—a humiliating defeat—and he had rallied from it, showing the remarkable leadership that he would some-day exhibit on a larger stage. He was the kind of rare officer who from the first held both the respect and the affection of the officers and men who served under him. At the end of the French and Indian War, when Washington announced his intention of resigning his command, his officers framed a protest that tells very well the qualities of their leader.

"The happiness we have enjoyed, and the honour we have acquired together," they wrote, "with the mutual regard that has always subsisted between you and your officers, have implanted so sensible an affection in the minds of us all, that we cannot be silent on this critical occasion. . . . Your steady adherence to impartial justice, your quick discernment, and invariable regard to merit, wisely intended to inculcate those genuine sentiments of true honor and passion for glory . . . first heightening our natural emulation and our desire to excell. . . . Judge, then, how sensibly we must be affected with the loss of such an excellent commander, such a sincere friend, and so affable a companion. How rare it is to find those amiable qualifications blended together in one man! How great the loss of such a man!" If Washington would consent to remain, his presence, the petition concluded, would "cause a steady firmness and vigour to actuate in every breast, despising the greatest dangers, and thinking light of toils and hardships, while led on by the man we know and love."

Ten months after Braddock's defeat, Great Britain declared war on France. What followed at first was a series of disasters for British arms. It took the genius of William Pitt to reverse the fortunes of war and launch the British navy and the armies on a series of victories that forced France to sue for peace on terms highly favorable to Britain. Pitt found himself a brilliant general in young James Wolfe, whose defeat of General Louis Joseph de Montcalm in the classic encounter on the Plains of Abraham outside Quebec in September, 1759, marked, for all practical purposes, the end of French power in North America.

A word might be said here about eighteenth-century warfare. The fighting was done by small professional armies that were expensive to train and maintain and were thus, for the most part, used sparingly. Wars were fought in as restrained and gentlemanly a manner as possible. The ideal was a decisive naval engagement, in large part because it was fought on the water and thus involved no devastation of the lands of the combatants. In both land and naval warfare the object was not so much to seize and occupy territory as to bring about a decisive battle in which the enemy, being outmaneuvered and surrounded, might be persuaded to surrender after having fought boldly enough to preserve his honor and without excessive loss of life on either side. In winter, armies and navies usually retired to quarters or, if possible, transferred their operations to a more agreeable climate, say the Mediterranean or the Caribbean. Officers commonly bought their commissions, and for a younger son of the aristocracy who had little hope of inheriting his family title or estate, being an officer was a reasonable alternative to being an Anglican priest.

Eighteenth-century generals believed, for the most part, that he who fights until it is no longer practical to continue the struggle and then surrenders, lives to fight another day. Thus when General John Burgoyne surrendered at Saratoga in 1777, the terms of surrender called for his army to be disarmed and returned to Britain, not greatly the worse for wear and ready to fight elsewhere. War was so far from being total that both partners were constantly making careful audits of profit and loss. Was it advisable or expedient to continue the campaigns? Had enough been won, or lost, to make peace desirable? And if so, how desirable?

Peace treaties were thus more like chess games than the imposition of harsh terms by ruthless victors on a crushed foe. Unconditional surrender is, by and large, a modern invention. Canada was weighed as a prize against Guadeloupe, Florida against Cuba. Everyone should get something agreeable, and no one must suffer too much. After all, the monarch of the defeated country might be the cousin of the monarch of the victorious country; there was no profit in vindictiveness. What one wished for, in most instances, was a slight or substantial tipping of the balance of power in one's direction: a few more colonies (since empire, i.e., colonies, equaled power) with consequent advantages in trade, the return of some territory illegally seized, or perhaps the disavowal of a dynastic marriage intended to double a rival's power at one stroke. Especially desirable was the destruction of enemy fleets. Armies could be more rapidly rebuilt; a navy was not so easily replaced. Moreover, a nation without an effective navy was at a considerable disadvantage in the competition for commerce and colonies, since maritime vessels were subject to constant harassment in peace as well as in war (as we have seen in the case of the English colonies) and had to conform to elaborate rules and regulations.

In terms of the future relationship of the British government to its colonial charges, the American phase of the Seven Years' War left a mixed legacy.

The colonists believed that they had loyally borne at least their fair share of the burdens of the war. They gloried in the fact that colonial soldiers and officers had been involved in most of the fighting, at least as auxiliaries of the British regulars; they took great pride in the success of British arms and in the fact that they had learned the hard lesson of military campaigning by observing their seasoned British counterparts.

One of the clearest gains for the colonists was a cadre of excellent junior officers who would, in time, lead their own troops against the British. The colonists had an opportunity to observe the problems of organizing and supplying troops in the field, and of constructing and besieging forts and fortified positions. They also got to know and respect the abilities of soldiers from other colonies, and to a practical knowledge of contemporary warfare they therefore added an enlarged consciousness of what it meant to be an American.

The Americans also shone in the reflected glory of the brilliant and romantic young General Wolfe. Wolfe was almost deified as the savior of Protestant America from the Catholic French. The circumstances of his death, especially his own presentiment of his end, took on mythic qualities. The poignant details were avidly read. The fatalistic song that he was reported to have sung the night before the battle (from Gray's "Elegy," containing the line, "The paths of glory lead but to the grave") was sung in a thousand colonial taverns. Forty-five years later, Alexander Hamilton, on the eve of his fatal duel with Aaron Burr, sang the same song.

The British, however, did not look back upon the war in so rosy a light. From their point of view, the colonial contributions to the war had been niggardly in the extreme. Moreover, the help that was reluctantly granted was frequently hedged about with reservations and demands for political concessions, and it was usually too little and too late.

At the end of the Seven Years' War, the English negotiators had to decide what territories to demand from the French as the cost of defeat. A key question for the British was whether to hold on to the captured French sugar islands and perhaps return Canada to France, or to retain Canada and give up some of the Caribbean Islands taken during the war. The Duke of Bedford, a leader in the Newcastle government, was for returning Canada to the French on the grounds that a French Canada would be the greatest security for the dependence of the colonists on the mother country. The French minister at the Treaty of Paris peace conference, the Duc de Choiseul, naturally anxious to encourage this notion, declared that a Canada in the hands of the French would keep the colonies "in that dependence which they will not fail to shake off the moment Canada should be ceded to Britain." But in the end Canada was kept by the British, and most of the Caribbean islands were returned to France.

Some historians have agreed with Bedford and Choiseul that the British retention of Canada was the key factor in bringing on the American Revolution. In the absence of the threat from the French and their Indian allies, so the argument goes, the colonies were emboldened to resist unpopular measures of the British ministry. Thomas Hutchinson, governor of Massachusetts in the turbulent pre-Revolutionary era, had no doubts. Ten years after the treaty, he wrote: "Before the peace of 1763 I thought nothing so much to be desired as the cession of Canada. I am now convinced that if it had remained to the French none of the spirit of opposition to the Mother Country would have yet appeared & I think the effects of it worse than all we had to fear from the French or Indians."

It is certainly true that there was an enormous sense of relief in the colonies. The perpetual menace of Catholic New France was removed. For frontiersmen, the Indian problem was reduced to manageable proportions. And once the common dangers were removed, common grievances could assert their primacy. Further, the colonists, as a consequence of their contributions to the victory, modest as these were in British eyes, felt a greatly increased boldness and self-confidence. But at the same time, the British conquest of French Canada stimulated a great outpouring of patriotic fervor among the colonials, who exulted in their Englishness. So there was the irony: A heightened sense on the part of the colonists of the glory of being Englishmen was coupled with greater determination to stand on their own feet and to defend their rights. Even before the war was over, some colonists had begun to think and talk about the glorious future of America in terms that were only vaguely related to their status as British subjects.

One colonist, for instance, rejoiced over the "Security of our Civil Liberty, a Happiness we justly glory in; for the Britons have preserv'd it pure and uncorrupted thro' all the Struggles of Ambition and the most dangerous Attacks of Power: They have set the World a fair Example that the highest Ambition of Princes shoul'd be to govern a free People, and that no People can be great or happy but such as are so. . . . Oh Liberty! Thou art the Author of every good and perfect Gift, the inexhaustible Fountain from whence all Blessings flow."

This was hardly the lesson that the British would have wished the colonists to draw from the outcome of the Seven Years' War.

Nathaniel Ames, a Massachusetts doctor and a staunch patriot, was moved to even grander speculations "Upon the Past, Present, and Future State of North America." Some people, Ames suggested, had begun to wonder if it made entire sense for the interests of an ambitious and industrious people occupying a territory considerably larger than that of the British Isles and containing above two million inhabitants to be entirely subordinate to the mother country. "The Curious have observ'd," Ames wrote in an exuberant flight of fancy, "that the Progress of Humane Literature (like the Sun) is from East to West: thus has it travelled thro' *Asia* and *Europe* and now is arrived at the Eastern Shore of *America*. As the Coelestial Light of the Gospel was directed here by the finger of G O D, it will doubtless, finally drive the long! long! Night of Heathenish Darkness from *America:*—So Arts and Sciences will change the Face of Nature in their Tour from Hence over the Appalachian Mountains to the Western Ocean." In the place of wild beasts, "the Stones and Trees will dance together at the Music of *Orpheus*,—the

Rocks will disclose their hidden gems"; and huge mountains of ore will provide the people with inestimable riches and employ "Millions of Hands" to make "an Infinity of Utensils" for the benefit of man; the stones of inexhaustible quarries will be "piled into great Cities"; "O! Ye unborn Inhabitants of America!" he concluded, "Should this Page escape its destin'd Conflagration at the Year's End, and these Alphabetical Letters remain legible,—when your Eyes behold the Sun after he has rolled the Seasons round for two or three Centuries more, you will know that in Anno Domini 1758, we dream'd of your Times." Such talk would have seemed to an Englishman, and doubtless to many colonists, as the maddest bombast, yet an increasing number of colonists began to think that way, and some to talk it.

In a soberer mood John Adams, a restless young schoolmaster in Worcester, Massachusetts, wrote to a friend in 1756 reflecting on the rise and fall of civilizations. History recorded a number of nations that had risen "from contemptible beginnings" to spread their influence "till the whole globe is subjected to their sway." "When," he continued, "they have reached the summit of grandeur, some minute and unsuspected cause commonly effects their ruin, and the empire of the world is transferred to some other place." So it had been with Rome, and so in time it might well be with England, presently "the greatest nation upon the globe." Some years back England had lost a small and, for the most part, inconspicuous number of its citizens, for reasons of conscience, to an untamed wilderness. "This apparently trivial incident," Adams wrote, "may transfer the great seat of [power] into America." With the threat of French Canada removed, the colonies within one hundred years would have a greater population than the mother country, Adams pointed out. The only way for Great Britain "to keep us from setting up for ourselves is to disunite us. *Divide et impera.* Keep us in distinct colonies, and then, some great men in each colony, desiring the monarchy of the whole, they will destroy each other's influence and keep the country in *equilibrio.*"

It may seem paradoxical that at the moment when the colonists felt most keenly the special distinction of being English, many of them began to feel also the somewhat different and rather contradictory emotion of pride in being American. But life is paradoxical, not logical (as R. H. Tawney has put it, "contradictions live in the heart of man in vigorous incompatability"). The colonists loved what they *imagined* England to be: Powerful (which she was), wise, benign, and just, with a scrupulous regard for the rights of all her citizens (these latter attributes she possessed to a far more modest degree, but most conspicuously in contrast to her notably unenlightened rivals, France and Spain).

Between 1700 and 1763 the colonists had been involved in five "intercolonial" wars, culminating in the dramatic struggle with the French for Canada. There can be no doubt that these wars, taxing as they were to colonial resources, did serve in a notable way to draw the colonies closer together—or to prevent them from flying apart, split a dozen ways by petty feuds and jealousies. The wars were, in short, an essential training ground, a primary element in the slowly emerging consciousness of Americans. Like their common grievances against the mother country, their common French enemy was a compelling force for unity.

In addition to the intercolonial wars, the colonies were increasingly bound together by economic ties. The merchants of Boston and Newport traded with those of New York and Philadelphia. New England ships carried Virginia tobacco. Letters of credit from prominent merchants circulated like money. Agents of commercial houses in New York traveled to Baltimore and Charles Town to solicit business, to purchase hides or indigo. Less apparent, but ultimately as important, the children of leading families in the various colonies intermarried. There were numerous family ties between Virginia and Maryland, Maryland and Pennsylvania (or, more specifically, Baltimore and Philadelphia), Virginia and Pennsylvania, and of course between Pennsylvania and Delaware and the Jerseys, and between New York and Philadelphia. Only Boston remained aloof from this network of familial relationships, doggedly provincial, separated by both geographical and social distance from its southerly neighbors.

Measured against a multitude of things that divided the colonies, these were precarious ties at best, but they grew stronger as the colonies expanded.

8

Mercantilism

BESIDES engaging the French in a shooting war, the government of England was involved in an almost equally intense and protracted trade war—with consequences for the colonies that were just as great. The weapons in this conflict were raw materials and various products; any product that merchants of one country had to purchase from another was thought to weaken the purchaser in relation to the seller. This was especially the case with the purchase of strategic materials. It was considered harmful, for example, if England, which was deficient in the raw materials required for building warships, had to pay out good English coin to buy naval supplies from Scandinavian countries. Moreover, it was downright dangerous, since such supplies might be cut off entirely, either by the country involved in the trade or by a power hostile to the interests of Great Britain.

In 1697, at the end of the first intercolonial war, one British trade official, John Pollexfen, said of the French: "They have made war on us with much of our own money got by trade. As matters now stand, nothing can be more dangerous than to permit them, so far as we can help it, to obtain anything that may tend to increase their naval strength or diminish ours."

One result of this continual rivalry between nations was the theory of mercantilism. In essence, mercantilist theory held that the interests of any colony should be entirely subordinated to those of the mother country. Colonies were weapons in the continuing trade warfare between nations. As England applied the principles of mercantilism to her colonies, they were designed to give her a favorable balance of trade (thus insuring an inflow of gold), and to develop her merchant marine as the primary means of commercial supremacy and as the foundation of a strengthened navy.

The ideal mercantilist relationship between a mother country and her colony can be described in the following terms: A colony produces raw materials that are shipped to the mother country in vessels belonging to the latter's merchants; then these materials are manufactured into finished products, some of which at least are sold to the colonies— earning, in the process, another profit for the owners of the vessels that transport them. England was inclined to value its colonies to the degree that they conformed to this model. Virginia was highly valued because it produced tobacco (but nothing that might compete with products of the mother country), which was carried in English ships to England (and nowhere else), and there marketed or transshipped. English merchants made a profit on each transaction. In addition, Virginians ordered many articles of domestic use from England, were constantly in debt to their agents or bankers in London, and paid substantial interest in consequence.

New England was far less satisfactory from the mercantilist point of view. The northern colonies did indeed furnish the raw materials for naval supplies, especially masts. But otherwise the New Englanders were entirely too enterprising for the taste of the merchants of the mother country. They built and sailed their own vessels in competition with their English counterparts, they provided craft work that could be favorably compared with that of English craftsmen, and they were constantly pushing into other areas that threatened competition with English manufacturers.

The first mercantilist legislation was passed by Parliament as early as 1621, the year Virginia was ordered to bring its tobacco only to English ports (Parliament, in return, ruthlessly stamped out tobacco growing in England itself). In 1660–61, Parliament began to spell out in more detail the restrictions on colonial trade. Captains and vessels and three-fourths of the crews carrying freight to and from the colonies must be English or colonial. In addition, certain specified articles could be shipped only to England or to other British colonies. That effectively prevented the Dutch, for example, from carrying Virginia tobacco to Europe, and the French from bringing to Paris English sugar from the West Indies. In the words of the statute, "no sugars, tobacco, cotton-wool, Indigoes, ginger, fustic, or other dyeing wood . . . shall be shipped, carried, conveyed, or transported from any of the said English plantations to any land, island, territory, dominion, port or place what-soever, other than to such other English plantations as do belong to his Majesty."

In 1704, molasses was added to the list of enumerated articles. The intention was to keep English plantation molasses from the Indies out of the hands of the Dutch and the French, and also to prevent Dutch and French molasses from being imported into England. A secondary object was to persuade Englishmen to drink rum, rather than to bolster the French economy by buying French brandy.

Three years after the Navigation Act of 1660 sharply restricted the export trade of the colonies, Parliament took over the import business. It enacted another law declaring that, with a few exceptions, "no commodity of the growth, production or manufacture of Europe" could be imported into any land under the British Crown unless the goods had been first landed in England, then reloaded and carried to the colonies in English shipping.

In short, whenever the colonies began to develop a profitable trade, either export or import, the British merchants pre-empted it. The colonists naturally resisted, as is indicated by the periodic efforts of Parliament to plug loopholes in the Navigation Acts discovered by ingenious colonials. The act of 1696 began with the complaint that "great abuses are daily committed to the prejudice of the English navigation, and the loss of a great part of the plantation trade to this kingdom, by the artifice and cunning of ill-disposed persons. . . ." The ill-disposed persons were colonial merchants who resented the curtailment of their freedom to trade with whomever they wished and wherever the better profit was to be made. To colonial complaints, English merchants responded by reminding the colonists that they existed primarily to insure a profitable trade for the mother country, of which they, the merchants of England, were the agents. They went further and pointed out to those who grumbled that it was no small benefit to be included within the protected system of the most active trading nation in Europe. The colonial merchants were accused of taking for granted the advantages of having access to British markets and British credit, while being reluctant to play their assigned role in a generally beneficent system.

The colonials remained unimpressed. They saw plainly enough that their interests were invariably subordinated to those of English merchants who, from the American perspective, seemed greedy and rapacious. Little was done, however, to protest the Acts of Trade and Navigation because of two facts. First, the colonial merchants who found Parliament's restraints on their trade onerous made up a very small portion—no more, perhaps, than one or two per cent—of the population of the English colonies. The great majority of colonists, being farmers, were affected indirectly, if at all. Consequently, the aggrieved handful of colonial entrepreneurs, while they exercised a disproportionate influence in the assemblies of their colonies, had little hope of rallying behind them any substantial number of ordinary Americans. But equally important, colonial merchants generally found it easier to live with the laws than to protest them. The mercantilist system did offer some advantages. Parliament paid special bounties for essential items such as indigo and naval supplies, and these bounties were a substantial stimulus to colonial enterprise. And the most objectionable restrictions on trade were simply ignored or evaded.

Smuggling was endemic—and quite easy, because law enforcement was lax. Parliament wished to squeeze maximum profit from colonial trade but did not bother to see that its statutes were obeyed. Since trade profits went largely into private hands and the return to the royal exchequer was relatively modest, it seemed dubious policy to expend large sums to employ sufficient customs officials to prevent smuggling and other infractions of the Navigation Acts.

The climax of the Acts of Trade and Navigation was the Molasses Act of 1733, which made illegal a profitable method devised earlier for evading the restrictions on molasses commerce. The colonies had developed a flourishing sugar and molasses trade with the French islands in the West Indies. For the French materials they exchanged a number of products, from salt fish and livestock to precut lumber ready to be fashioned into the eighteenth-century version of prefabricated houses. Ship captains could sail from Boston or Newport to the West Indies with a cargo of horses (which were much in demand), lumber, or salt fish. There they could collect bills of exchange and West Indian products to carry to England, then return to the Indies with a shipment of English goods to be sold there, and then carry back to New England hogsheads of West Indian molasses, which was in heavy demand as a sweetener, as a medicine, and as the raw material for New England rum.

The Molasses Act of 1733 interrupted this profitable "triangular trade" by levying a prohibitive tariff on French sugar products. To the colonists, the Molasses Act seemed typically designed for the benefit of someone else, in this instance the planters or, as one colonist called them, "the nabobs" of the West Indies. The act's preamble was explicit enough: "whereas the planters of said sugar colonies have of late years fallen under such great discouragements that they are unable to . . . carry on the sugar trade upon an equal footing with the foreign sugar colonies without some . . . relief be given them from Great Britain: for remedy. . . ." The remedy was a series of import duties: nine pence on every gallon of French West Indian rum, six pence on every gallon of foreign molasses, and five shillings on every hundredweight of foreign sugar.

The tax was meant to bail out the plantation owners in the English Sugar Islands at the expense of the colonists. But its effect was to increase the profits for those colonial merchants willing to engage in smuggling—and a substantial number, it turned out, were. However, a precedent was established: colonial trade might be manipulated for the benefit of particular Englishmen.

Mercantilist policy often bumbled—setting up restrictions that alienated the colonists yet were so easily evaded they failed to help the mother country—partly because of the way colonial America was governed. The British agencies for administration evolved slowly in response to the growth of the colonies and to their increasing commercial importance. During the seventeenth century, a succession of councils and commissions were set up to direct colonial affairs. Then, in 1696, Parliament established the Board of Trade and Plantations, a professional body that presided over Britain's colonies down to the Revolution. Among the eight commisioners appointed by William III was John Locke, who was a very active and important member. The board met three or four times a week and became the clearing-house for colonial affairs. It had no Power of action—that remained the province of the Privy Council—but it had wide if poorly defined duties. Its original charge was to encourage manufacturers, supervise the administration of the colonies through the royal governors, determine obstacles to trade, send out investigating committees or inspectors, and most important, make recommendations to the Privy Council.

The Board of Trade had its ups and downs, but generally speaking its importance declined steadily until it was largely a clerical body. At one time it had only two members who made any pretense of attending to business. One was called, facetiously, "Board" and the other, "Trade."

The administrative confusion was compounded by the fact that the Board of Trade was dependent, for the most part, on the reports and correspondence of the colonial governors. The colonial legislatures were required to send copies of their journals and related materials to the Board of Trade, but these documents piled up faster than the members could read them. One historian describes the results in these words: "Upon the rough and unsubdued country, the free and easy way of the colonists, the looseness which prevailed in business relations, the narrow and local views, the parsimony of legislative bodies, the financial vagaries of communities which were permanently in debt, and upon much besides, the royal officials looked with the prejudice born of admiration for the maturer European conditions from which they had come."

The board was so inefficient and so clogged with work through much of its existence that important correspondence sometimes lay unread for a year or so; it might take several years for a colonial governor or assembly to receive an answer to a query or a request. As a result of this inefficiency, the board's existence encouraged the growth of an independent spirit in the colonies.

The colonial legislatures occasionally passed laws of their own that favored their merchants and manufacturers. These laws could be vetoed by the royal governor even before the measures were sent to England for approval by the British Privy Council. The colonial legislatures, however, soon found ways of bringing heavy pressure to bear on governors to withhold their vetoes.

The governor, as the man-in-the-middle, often had to decide whether to persevere in the face of constant harassment from the assembly or risk the remoter and later indignation of his English masters. In those instances where his instructions allowed him any leeway at all, a pliant governor often gave way. It was certainly tempting to let the government in England bear the onus of nullifying legislation close to the colonists' hearts and pocketbooks. Sometimes assemblies were able to buy a governor's concurrence to a statute that would almost inevitably be revoked in England. But since official notice of the veto might take a year or two to reach the colony, the law was often worth enacting; when it was finally declared void, another similar law could be passed, and a similar interval would follow during which the law would accomplish its intended purpose. In 1705, Queen Anne vetoed fifty-three laws of Pennsylvania. One law was repealed three years after its passage and two years after it had expired. This legal treadmill operated smoothly because of a clause in the Pennsylvania charter requiring that all laws passed in the colony be reviewed by the king within five years. Pennsylvania thus often enacted laws that were good for four years, and then passed them again for another four-year period.

And so it went. Move and countermove. Small wonder that those in England responsible for administering the affairs of the colonists took them for a singularly stubborn and deceitful lot, determined to disobey the lawful enactments of Parliament and the orders of the king's ministers. The colonial leaders, for their part, came to be masters of parliamentary maneuver.

In the practical concerns of their daily lives, from religion to commerce, the colonists had to find ways to do as they wished—whatever was desirable, convenient, profitable, or, in their view, simply necessary—within the increasingly restrictive framework of laws and regulations promulgated by a body of men, indifferent, for the most part, to colonial needs and desires, whose notion was that the colonies existed and should exist, primarily if not exclusively, for the benefit of the mother country. The British, for their part, persisted in seeing the American colonies less as a collection of people whose needs should be attended to, than as the means by which the wealth and power of England could be enhanced. Colonial interests were, above all, subordinate to those of Englishmen in England. This attitude was not odd, because the interests of a great many Englishmen, primarily those too poor and debased to make their wishes known in any other way but through desperate riots, were similarly subordinated to the interests of their betters.

This arrogant and unsympathetic approach to colonial affairs was exacerbated by the quality and character of the royal governors. They were appointed by the Crown and were drawn largely from three classes: from British military men; from those to whom the Crown owed favors; and, in a few instances, from among the colonists themselves. The governors were often men of inferior abilities, who received their appointments as political patronage and who undertook the governorships with the hope of making money. Some were petty and venal; some stayed in England and sent lieutenants out to govern for them; a few were able and intelligent men, with genuine sympathy for the colonists, who tried to do their job intelligently and conscientiously. These latter were, not surprisingly, very much in minority.

The colonial governors were beset with problems, and one of the most difficult of these was factionalism within the colonies. From the moment a governor arrived on the scene, conflicting groups tried to gain his ear, seeking to make him an ally in their cause. Few governors were able to remain entirely above partisan politics; the most unfortunate were those who chose the wrong side.

The governor was further handicapped by the fact that he could not, in most cases, appoint his own subordinates. In the elaborate system of political patronage, these offices were also filled by the Crown, and like the governorship itself they usually went to individuals with influence. Such a system made for administrative inefficiency and irresponsibility—weaknesses the colonists quickly learned to exploit. If they could not inveigle a governor into doing what they wanted, they could often buy off his subordinates.

The governors did gain considerable personal power through their control of the courts. They commonly appointed judges to serve during "good behavior," which was taken by some governors to mean as long as the judges returned verdicts favorable to the Crown. If, in a governor's opinion, a judge was too partial to the colonists, he was, by definition, no longer well behaved and thus was removable. This potential for friction between governor and citizens was particularly serious in the admiralty courts. These courts were a sore point, since it was to them that alleged violations of the Navigation Acts were usually brought; and the colonists were convinced that evenhanded justice was impossible there, because the salaries of the judges as well as their tenure were dependent on the number of convictions handed down. Admiralty courts had no jury, that ancient guardian of English justice, and as smuggling grew, more and more colonists experienced the rigor of a politically appointed judge who had little sympathy for the defendants.

Mercantilist policy can be summed up as a patchwork of restrictive laws conceived in a spirit of arrogance and administered with an inefficiency that invited evasion. One example perhaps best indicates the effect of this highhanded bungling: the chaotic state of the currency. All trade in the colonies was hampered by the lack of a reliable medium of exchange. In the absence of minted coins of established value, the estimation of the worth of the jumble of currencies that circulated was an art in itself, and one that added a good deal to the economic instability of the colonies.

The basic colonial coin was not British but foreign—the Spanish dollar or piece of eight—a fact that in itself tells a good deal about the state of the currency. But coins from France, Portugal, and Holland were also legal tender in America, all valued in terms of the Spanish dollar. The English pound, always in short supply, was the equivalent of one dollar. Among other Spanish coins in use, the silver pistareen was worth about twenty-five cents, the gold escudo two dollars, and the gold pistole or doblon about four dollars. The Portuguese dobra or double johannes, called in America a "joe," was widely used and had a value of about sixteen dollars.

So confused was the currency that some colonies issued their own money. As early as the 1650's, Massachusetts produced the pine-tree shilling, intended only for use in the colony. When Massachusetts lost its charter in 1684, it had also to suspend its mint. Thereafter the most acute need for money was met by bills of credit, which were issued by many assemblies and approved by the governors. While bills of credit circulated as currency in the larger towns and cities, they gave little relief to the average colonist. The most popular scheme was that of a land bank that would issue currency upon land as security. But seacoast merchants and Crown officials were generally united in opposition to all land-bank proposals, and the currency problem persisted as a symbol of British indifference to colonial needs and a constant if minor source of irritation to most Americans.

From the perspective of the administration of the colonies, it could be argued the British government performed so badly, and with such entire disregard of the principles of proper administration, that the wonder was not that the colonies finally revolted but that they endured such blunders and inequities as long as they did. The answer is, of course, that the inefficiency of the British administration of the colonies provided the colonists with innumerable opportunities to alleviate or evade the most burdensome aspects of British policy. Had the colonies been more efficiently administered, the Revolution might indeed have come much sooner.

9

The Delights of the Homeland

IF we are to understand colonial Americans, especially those of the upper class, from which, by and large, the leaders of the Revolution were drawn, we must understand the "Englishness" of these Americans, and the particular fascination that England held for them. The mother country drew them like a magnet and was always present in their imaginations. They dreamed of visiting that "storied isle," and whenever the opportunity and their finances made such a journey possible, they cheerfully faced the very real discomforts and dangers of an Atlantic crossing to immerse themselves in the delights of the homeland.

One of the earliest and most persistent visitors to London was Henry Sewall, father of the famous diarist Samuel Sewall, who made several crossings in the 1650's. William Byrd of Virginia made five voyages to England, which should have entitled him to a place at the captain's table, and Benjamin Franklin crossed the Atlantic three times. The colonists who traveled to England found a kind of American community there, centering on several coffee houses in London that provided lodgings for those who did not have friends or relatives to take them in. Visitors from each colony usually had a favorite meeting ground. When the New England Puritan divine Increase Mather was in London in 1689, he wrote of spending pleasant hours with fellow

Harvard graduates at the New England Coffee House. Thomas Parke, a young Philadelphian studying medicine in Scotland, met with friends at the London Coffee House when he visited the city. His companions on one occasion included Jacob Rush, who was studying law at the Middle Temple; Thomas Combs, in England to take Anglican orders; a friend from Lancaster, Pennsylvania; and two Pennsylvania sea captains. William Shippen, who was from Philadelphia and who was also studying medicine, noted in his diary in 1759 that he had dined with the governor of his colony, the provost of the College of Philadelphia, and a Long Islander who was studying law at the Inner Temple.

An association of colonists, under the name of the American Club, gathered regularly at the New England Coffee House to exchange news from home and compare the pleasures of life in London. Always accessible to these colonists were the agents of this or that colonial legislature, who were in England as lobbyists, working to advance some cause favorable to their client colonies or, most typically, to prevent the Privy Council from vetoing some piece of legislation much needed at home but opposed by vested interests in the mother country. Such agents could be counted on to be friendly and helpful to compatriots in need of guidance and advice. Benjamin Franklin, who served as a colonial agent for fifteen years, befriended a succession of his fellow colonists in that time, dispensing his famous wisdom at no charge—though it is doubtful that many of his young auditors took his advice to heart, for the pleasures and distractions of London, from its plays to its whores, were notoriously seductive.

The traffic to London was fostered in part by distinguished Englishmen whose special interest was sponsoring their ruder cousins from over the ocean. Many young men were encouraged to undertake the study of medicine in England by Doctor John Fothergill, one of the leading physicians of his day. Harvard graduates, arriving in London, could count on the sympathy and support of Thomas Hollis, the great Whig eccentric, who sent a constant supply of the most up-to-date Whig literature to the Harvard library (many of the volumes may still be found in the Harvard stacks) to strengthen the love of liberty among the students and faculty.

Many of the colonists visited England on fund-raising missions, soliciting pounds and shillings to found or to carry on various educational or religious undertakings. The British were especially responsive to plans for educating and improving the Indians. When the Reverend Nathaniel Whitaker went to England to raise money for John Wheelock's Indian school—which later became Dartmouth—he took with him Samson Occom, a Christian Indian, who was to become a famous preacher and missionary in his own right. Together, Wheelock and Occom collected substantial sums for the New England college.

Moreover, as the eighteenth century wore on, Americans in increasing numbers were sent to England and Scotland for at least a portion of their education. Many of these young scholars were from the South, where adequate schooling was absent on both the secondary and college levels. At least thirty Southerners went to Eton, several hundred went to the Inns of Court to study law, and more than one hundred attended Oxford. The University of Edinburgh was favored by parents of students from the middle and "eastern" (New England) colonies, especially for its training in medicine and theology. The Scottish university was less expensive than Oxford, less fashionable, more in sympathy with American ideas and ideals, and, even more important, more practical and up-to-date than the English universities. As the center of a Scottish renaissance, Edinburgh had a faculty that, in the opinion of Benjamin Franklin, was "a set of as truly great Professors of the several branches of knowledge, as have ever appeared in any age or Country." The acidulous English clergyman and writer Sydney Smith recalled that at Edinburgh he encountered "odious smells, barbarous sounds, bad suppers, excellent hearts and most enlightened and cultivated understandings."

The sentimental ties between the middle and eastern colonies and Scotland were even closer than those between the colonies and England itself. As Presbyterianism grew stronger in the colonies, Scotland came to be regarded by many colonists as their true homeland. When the College of New Jersey needed a president, the trustees sent Benjamin Rush to Scotland to persuade the prominent Scottish divine, John Witherspoon, to come to America to assume the office. Indeed, in Pennsylvania higher education was almost a Scottish monopoly. By the same token, the colonists had a special taste for the writings of Scottish moral and political philosophers such as Francis Hutcheson; Thomas Reid, founder of the so-called common sense school of philosophy; and James Burgh, whose *Political Disquisitions* were widely read in the colonies. Since Scotland, with its strong Covenanter or Presbyterian background, was treated very much like a rough colonial outpost by the English, it was not surprising to find Scottish and American hearts vibrating to the same chords.

Even so, London was the city that most impressed the American visitors, and it afforded an endless variety of attractions. Samuel Sewall recorded during a visit that he had attended a "Consort" of music at Covent Garden, drank currant and raspberry wine in Mile End, played ninepins at a tavern called Dog and Partridge, attended the Goose Green Fair, and swam in the Thames. Visits to the British Museum were popular with colonials, as were trips to the Garden of Medical Plants at Chelsea, the Gresham College scientific collection, and Rackstraw's famous anatomical exhibition. The stage was much in vogue by the 1750's, when the actor David Garrick was at the height of his fame, transforming the British theater from something not much better than cheap vaudeville into art.

The newly arrived colonists were dazzled by the wealth and lavish display of London, with its famous shops; the ancient grandeur of the English universities; the nobility and vastness of England's country houses, with their priceless art treasures passed on from generation to generation; and the brilliance of a society that had brought wit and conversation to the level of remarkable if sometimes brittle sophistication. There was another, less attractive, side to London. Beneath the urbanity, the charming ostentation, the wealth and elegance of British society, lay much that was callous, complacent, and decadent. This same London, so full of delights for the prosperous young colonial visitor, was infested with prostitutes and criminals. Tens of thousands of desperate and embittered poor groveled for the most meager living. Bridewell was a pestilential madhouse, and Newgate Prison was synonymous with debauchery and abysmal neglect, as well as with corruption and cruelty. Public offices and army commissions were bought and sold to the highest bidders. The king kept thousands of placemen as his compliant tools. The "rotten boroughs" returned members to Parliament although such boroughs no longer contained any voters, and "pocket boroughs"—boroughs that were said to be in the pocket of powerful members of Parliament—were cynically traded off for political favors.

Decadence reached into the highest places. Sir Francis Dashwood, a wealthy aristocrat and a member of Parliament, was a symbol of the depravity of the upper classes. Dashwood entertained himself and his friends of the Hell-fire Club by arranging orgies and black masses at his country estate. His gardens were laid out so that from a tower of the manor house one could see a naked woman traced out in the planting of the shrubbery, with fountains at strategic points. At an abbey built on the ruins of a medieval monastery near his own estate, Sir Francis, who called his evil order the Friars of St. Francis, would play the role of Christ, with his friends enacting the apostles in an obscene parody of the Holy Communion. The stained-glass windows of the abbey bore indecent pictures of the twelve apostles; there was a pornographic fresco on the ceiling, and adjacent to the abbey was the greatest collection of pornographic books in England. Prostitutes were imported from London and dressed as nuns to join the black masses, and these women of the streets mingled, it was rumored, with the masked wives and mothers of the titled celebrants. Many distinguished Englishmen visited the abbey and were involved in the orgiastic goings on at one time or another, among them the First Lord of the Admiralty and the Earl of Bute, prime minister of England in the early 1760's and principal adviser to George III. George Potter, son of the Archbishop of Canterbury and a member of the Hell-fire Club, boasted, "I poison all my friends' morals," and in the opinion of the Earl of Sandwich, "No man ever carried the art of seduction to so enormous a height" as Dashwood. (It is only fair to note that public scandal drove Dashwood and his friends from the scenes of their revels.)

The degree of sexual license in London was startling to young (or old) colonials, bred in a very different tradition. The wealthy Virginia planter William Byrd was not, presumably, the only visitor to succumb, but he happens to have left the most complete record of his liaisons. In April, 1719, Byrd, then forty-five, noted in his dairy on the twenty-ninth: "About 6 o'clock I went to Will's Coffeehouse, and from thence to Lady Guise's and then I went to Will's where Margaret G-t-n called on me and I went with her to the bagnio where I rogered her three times with vigor, twice at night and once in the morning. I neglected my prayers." A few days later, he visited his mistress and then went back to Will's Coffee House: "About ten came Betty S-t-r-d and I went with her to the bagnio and lay with her all night. . . . It threatened rain." Byrd divided his constant sexual activities between his mistress, the courtesans from the bagnio, and the whores and casual girls he picked up in the street, with occasional attentions to his maid.

But while William Byrd was busy neglecting his prayers, other, more proper colonists were determined to shun the dangerous temptations of English life. The young Pennsylvanian John Dickinson resolved that "virtuous company is the strongest guard to a person's morals," and made up his mind to associate only with those of his compatriots in whose virtue he had complete confidence. He would thus be "defended from attacks on his innocence; and hope to return to his parents not only pure in my morals, but improved in everything you desire, especially in my business." But his frequent mention in his letters of the dangerous temptations of London makes clear that if he avoided them, they were as much on his mind as they were clearly on the minds of his parents, who needed and got constant reassurance.

Dickinson, on arriving in London, wrote to his mother that he found himself "in a social wilderness, as much at a loss amongst houses and men as in the strangest forest, and in a much more disagreeable situation, for instead of peace and quietness, I was surrounded with noise, dirt, and business and equally inconvenient. . . ." Though "tir'd with the vast extent of the city, and puzzled with the winding of the street," so different from the wide, geometrically laid-out avenues of his native Philadelphia, he visited London Bridge, Westminster Bridge, and Buckingham and St. James's palaces, attended service at St. Paul's Cathedral, and went to the theater and saw the great Garrick, who, with Mrs. Pritchard, much celebrated for her Lady Macbeth, were "exact pictures of life, and easily persuade you that they are the very persons they represent." An educated young colonial was so familiar at second hand with the splendors of London that Dickinson could write his mother that since he "had heard or seen particular descriptions of everything, nothing excited my admiration, but only confirmed or lessened, as it frequently happens, my former notions, though there certainly are many grand and noble works."

Dickinson's reception in London was typical of that accorded to most young Americans who came with proper introductions. He wrote his mother, "[I] never was treated with more tenderness and kindness by my nearest friends than I have been by perfect strangers to me. Professions of friendship seem made here with sincerity, and kept with truth." John Hanbury, a merchant in the American trade and a partner in colonial land speculations, was especially hospitable. "I drop in at dinner, tea, or supper," young Dickinson wrote his mother, "and pass away two or three hours with the greatest happiness." The Hanburys treated him like a son. Mrs. William Anderson, born in Somerset County, Maryland, and married to a wealthy London merchant, was a friend of the Dickinson family and received young John "with the greatest signs of joy and regard." All in all, within a few weeks he had numerous friends and acquaintanceships "with persons of fashion and politeness, from whose conversation I hope for the greatest advantages."

Dickinson was in London to study law, and in a letter to his father, he wrote ecstatically about his studies. "I dayly behold objects which call me to my duty," he noted. "I tread the walks frequented by the ancient sages of the law; perhaps I study where a Coke or Plowden has meditated. I am struck with veneration . . . when I read their works, by these familiarising reflections I almost seem to converse with them." Visiting Parliament, he was "filled with awe and reverence" by the "Hall where the most important questions have been debated, where a Hampden and a Holt have opposed encroaching power and supported declining Justice. In short, upon whose Judgements the happiness of a nation has depended. . . ." His ambition was fired when he thought of these famous champions of liberty who had advanced by their own efforts, rather than by hereditary right, "to the highest honours of their country." They had become men of renown by their own diligence. "The same means," he reflected, "are in my power . . . my breast beats for fame!"

Despite the attractions of London, John Dickinson was resolute in affirming his preference and his affection for his native land. "America," he wrote his father, "is, to be sure, a wilderness, and yet that wilderness to me is more pleasing than this charming garden. I don't know how, but I don't seem to have any connection with this country; I think myself only a traveller, and this the inn. But when I think of America, that word produces a thousand pleasing images; it is endeared by my past pleasures there, by my future prospects. . . . I cant bear a comparison between it and any other place. 'Tis rude, but it's innocent. 'Tis wild, but it's private. There life is a stream pure and unruffled, here an ocean briny and tempestuous. There we enjoy life, here we spend it."

Many of the more thoughtful and responsible of the colonial visitors, however much they might relish the diversions of English life, clearly perceived the bitter inequities of the British social system, so generous to some, so niggardly to others. These observers were often deeply troubled by what they saw. They were children of this homeland; in a real sense it held the power of life and death over them. They were proud of its power and wealth, but more particularly of its tradition of liberty, of Parliamentary government, of uncowed dissent. Yet could a people so insensitive to the sufferings of their own poor, so arrogant in their strength, and so preoccupied with the pursuit of wealth and pleasure, govern wisely and well their distant cousins? Clearly they felt toward Americans at best a patronizing, more than slightly condescending sympathy, and at worst an interest limited to the determination to render them docile and profitable. These American observers were especially troubled by the more conspicuous signs of decadence eating at the heart of the ruling class.

Especially dismayed by the gap between England's rich and poor was William Samuel Johnson, a young Connecticut lawyer. He mentioned it in a letter to a friend, Benjamin Gale, who himself knew something of conditions in the mother country. "The Common people of England," Gale replied, "are a very different sett of Men from the people of America, otherwise they never would submitt to be taxed in the Manner they are, that a few may be loaded with palaces and Pensions and riot in Luxury and Excess, while they themselves cannot support themselves and their needy offspring with Bread. I thank God we are not such Jack Asses in America, and I hope in God we never shall be brought to submit to it."

By 1755 English political life seemed in disarray to Dickinson. The House of Commons was leaderlesss, and there was much jockeying for place and power—"restless ambition harrasses all the great." "Bribery is so common," Dickinson noted, "that it is thot there is not a borough in England where it is not practised, and it is certain that many flourishing ones are ruind, their manufactories decayd and their trade gone by their dependance on what they get by their votes." In one midcentury Parliamentary election it was said that a million pounds had been drawn out of London as bribes (a sum that would be the equivalent today of perhaps some ten million dollars). Dickinson was told that in one small borough in the north of England each voter was paid two hundred guineas, or again, roughly, something in excess of two thousand dollars, and this in a day when a young man might live quite well on an income of two hundred pounds a year, and the fortunate poor made twenty pounds annually. "It is astonishing," Dickinson wrote, "to think what impudence and villainy are practizd on this occasion. If a man cannot be brought to vote as he is desird, he is made dead drunk and kept in that state, never heard of by his family or friends till all is over and he can do no harm." The solemn oath that voters were required to take attesting that they had not accepted bribes was "so little regarded that few people can refrain from laughing while they take it."

An interesting sidelight on British elections was provided for John Dickinson by his patron, John Hanbury. Robert Earl Nugent, a sometime poet who made his way chiefly by marrying a succession of wealthy women, had political ambitions. Hanbury, with extensive business interests in Bristol, hearing of Nugent's interest in running for Parliament, promised to bear all expenses of his campaign up to ten thousand pounds if he would run for the seat from that city. Encouraged by the Duke of Newcastle, the foremost political manager in England, and by the king himself, Nugent ran for the seat and won "chiefly by Mr. Hanbury's interest." It was a great convenience for a prominent merchant to have a member of the House obliged to him for his seat in Commons.

Despite this close look at the rotten side of British political life, Dickinson hated the thought of returning home. As the time of his return approached, Dickinson's resolution began to fail him. "It would be impossible to enumerate all the benefits to be acquired in London," he wrote his father, "but it cannot be disputed that more is learnt of mankind here in a month than can be in a year in any other part of the world. Here a person sees and converses with people of all ranks, of all tempers. He acquires an ease and freedom of behaviour with his superiors, complaisance and civility to his inferiors. The wise are his patterns to imitate. The weak shew him, as in a glass, the faults and follies he ought to avoid. Here a man learns from the example of others what in another place nothing but his own sufferings and experience could teach him. London takes off the rawness, the prejudice of youth and ignorance. He finds here that he has been frequently deceived; he ceases to gaze and stare, and finds at last that nothing is really admirable but virtue." The appeal was an astute one. Young Dickinson insisted, perhaps not entirely candidly, that his desire to prolong his stay in England in no way "proceeds from any liking I have taken to this place," but only from the advantages that would accrue to him as a practicing lawyer upon his return home. In addition, another two years in England should greatly improve his health, so great were the benefits of the salubrious London climate (which he had earlier indicted for its killing smog).

It is clear that the colonists who visited England felt a profound ambiguity about the mother country. In the crossing and recrossing of the ocean, a new kind of self-consciousness blossomed. As alluring as the pleasures of a city like London might be, the American visitor could not cast off the sense of being a provincial, of coming from a cruel, raw land. The American artist John Singleton Copley spoke for most colonial visitors when he wrote, " . . . really in comparison with the people of this country, we Americans are not half removed from a state of nature." But at the same time, the visiting colonists could not forget that their homeland possessed something that even the wealthiest and most privileged of Englishmen lacked: a strange essence of Americanism.

The colonists who had made the trip to England were much in demand on their return. One sardonic observer noted that no guest was so sought after in the colonies as a recent arrival from the mother country, who "can move a minuet after the newest fashion in England; can quiver like a butterfly; is a perfect connoisseur in dress; and has been author to all the new cock't hats and scratches in town; has learnt the art of address from the gentility of Covent Garden, which, by Jove, he declares has ruined his constitution. Amongst the accomplished beaux, he has learned those elegant expressions, Split me, Madam; By God, Dam me; and fails not to use them on all ocasions."

But there was something more important than minuets and elegant expressions that the visiting colonists had learned in England. As the Revolutionary crisis mounted, they were to be found in the ranks of those who urged caution and moderation. Far more deeply than most Americans, they were conscious of the profits and pleasures of being Englishmen. At the same time, as outsiders in that opulent and sensual world, they were troubled by the sense that this luxurious life was supported by masses of people living often in desperate poverty. And having witnessed the corruption of the English government at first hand, they were determined to preserve America from exploitation and repression.

10

"What Then Is the American, This New Man?"

How did a new way of looking at the world grow up in America, a vision that made Americans different even from their English cousins? If there is such a thing as a uniquely American consciousness, from whence was it derived? Certainly not from any unity of interest, as can be seen from the diverse motives of those who established the first colonies. Some, like Lord Baltimore, wished to perpetuate in the new world forms of feudalism that were rapidly disappearing in the old. The Puritans wished to redeem a fallen world. The Virginia settlers wished to emulate the landed aristocracy of England. The Quakers sought to establish freedom of worship for themselves and to create a haven where others could enjoy this same freedom. How was it possible for that new sort of being, the American, to emerge from such disparate backgrounds?

Societies take their shape from any number of forming elements, some roughly identifiable, some obscure and mysterious. There is a strange interplay between ideas and geography, between thought and the landscape that thought encounters; between inherited ideas and acquired environment. We have talked thus far about origins and aspirations, about political and economic forces, but insufficiently about those ultimate views of the meaning of the universe and our relationship to it that are perhaps best comprehended under the word "religion"—and religion was the key. Of all those forces—physical or mental—that gave shape to the American consciousness, that created, so far as there was one, a new man, the reformed faith of Protestant Christianity was pre-eminent.

The beginning of the new man, therefore, may literally be traced to the beginning of the Protestant Reformation itself in 1517, when Martin Luther nailed his ninety-five theses to the church door at Wittenberg, Germany. These ninety-five theological propositions attacked a whole string of abuses that Luther felt had grown up in the Roman Catholic Church, like weeds in a garden. But Luther was not content simply to attack the grossest abuses of the Roman Church and a decadent Papacy. He struck at some of the basic dogmas of the church. He insisted that a man could find salvation not through charitable deeds, not through dearly bought indulgences, not through priestly intermediaries or formal rituals, but only through faith in God. And—perhaps most significant in its later effect on the New World—Luther held that the individual was wholly responsible for his own salvation.

If Luther was the originator and bold activist of the Reformation, John Calvin, the studious theologian of Geneva, was the Reformation's most formidable theoretician. In his mammoth *Institutes of the Christian Religion,* Calvin presented the doctrinal basis of that branch of Protestantism that, as Calvinism, became the foundation of American Puritanism. In the *Institutes* Calvin put forth the charter for a new kind of consciousness, and new way of looking at the world and at one's fellows, as well as a new way of understanding the relationship of the individual to the Divine—to God and to His Son, Jesus Christ. Before the Reformation, people had belonged to immutable social groups or orders. They had been members of clearly delineated social classes—aristocrat, bourgeois, priest, scholar, land-holding farmer, or landless peasant. Each person was located in the world not only by class, but also by family, church diocese, community, guild, or other corporate order of some kind.

Customary law, reinforced by the universal church, set the obligation of each class and order to the others. No one had to live in doubt or uncertainty about his position in the world, his duties, or his prospects of future rewards or punishments, since everyone was somehow incorporated, belonging to a group or a community that defined his role in the wider society. Medieval man did not think of himself as "an individual"; he thought of himself as a member of one or more of society's orders.

These traditional orders did not so much submerse him as define and protect him. But above all, they contained him.

Luther and Calvin, by postulating a single person entirely responsible for the state of his own soul, plucked a new human type out of this traditional protective context, and put him down naked, a reformed man in a reformed world.

Both Luther and Calvin insisted that the most crucial aspect of the individual was his responsibility for his own spiritual state. This doctrine of the "priesthood of all believers"—each man his own priest—meant of course new burdens for the individual psyche, but it also meant remarkable new opportunities as well. Reformed congregations were genuinely reformed, drawing people out of their traditional positions and functions into a new relationship to one another and to the outside world. These congregations established their own churches, managed their own affairs, chose their own ministers. There were no popes or bishops—no church hierarchy. The importance of this transformation was that it produced not only an individual, but a highly introspective, aggressive individual, who was able to function remarkably well outside those older structures that had defined people's roles and given them whatever power they possessed. To put it another way, Luther and Calvin invented the individual, and it was just such individuals—secure in their relationship to God and confident of their own powers—who dared to stand up for their rights as Americans when they felt that the mother country was infringing on those rights. Further, this new individual in turn could establish not only new religious sects and new congregations, but also new businesses, new financial enterprises, entire new communities, and even new ways of conceiving of the relation of individuals to one another—new ways, that is, of designing political and constitutional arrangements. One of the obvious by-products was the notion of a contract entered into by two people or by the members of a community among themselves that needed no local sanctions to make it binding. This concept of the Reformers made possible the formation of contractual or, as the Puritans called them, "covenanted" groups, formed by individuals who signed a covenant or agreement to found a community. The most famous of these covenants was the Mayflower Compact, a document signed by almost all the male Pilgrims before they landed at Plymouth. In it they formed a "civil body politic" and promised to obey the laws their own government might pass. In short, the individual Pilgrims invented on the spot a new community, one that would be ruled by laws of its making.

The Reformers, having rejected the notion of priestly hierarchy, returned to what they understood to be the practice of the early church. Each congregation of the faithful elected its own leaders, teachers and preachers alike. The power to create new congregations and erect new churches (or "meetinghouses") lay with the company of the faithful. All were equal in the eyes of God, and in the simple, practical democracy that resulted, all exercised an equal voice in congregational affairs.

The Reformers maintained that the Roman Catholic Church, by reserving to itself—to its priests and functionaries—all the doctrines and teachings of the Church, had kept people locked up in rituals and ceremonies, which, as Calvin put it, condemned "the miserable multitude" of believers to "the grossest ignorance." "Faith," Calvin went on, "consists not in ignorance, but in knowledge. . . ." The faithful must know at first hand the word of God. The only infallible way of knowing God's word was to read and study it as it appeared in Holy Scripture. Thus it followed that knowledge rather than authority was essential to an enlightened faith. The importance of the Reformers' emphasis on the literacy of all the faithful was recognized by Massachusetts lawyer-patriot John Adams. "They were convinced from history and their own experience," he wrote, "that nothing could preserve their posterity from encroachments of the two systems of tyranny, the Roman Church and the English monarch . . . but knowledge diffused generally through the whole body of the people. Their civil and religious principles, therefore, conspired to prompt them to use every measure and take every precaution in their power to propagate and perpetuate knowledge. For this purpose they laid very early the foundations of colleges . . . and it is remarkable that they have left among their posterity so universal an affection and veneration for those seminaries, and for liberal education, that the meanest of the people contribute cheerfully to the support and maintenance of them every year. . . . So that the education of all ranks of people was made the care and expense of the public in a manner that I believe has been unknown to any other people ancient or modern."

One of the most fundamental changes wrought by the Reformation was to give the family unit an importance that it had never enjoyed before. In the new, reformed family the father assumed the priestly duties once performed by the church. He usually led family prayers, read the Bible aloud in the vernacular, and even assumed certain teaching responsibilities. The family, as the essential unit and center of Christian life, took on a new dignity and power; it was as though the power of the institutional church had been divided up among the reconstituted families of the Protesting faith.

This change in the family also promoted the freedom of the

individual. In doing so it served to release new energies in society, to create new enterprises and new wealth. In traditional European societies, sons characteristically expressed their loyalty to their fathers by following the same trade or calling. However, since the son in the new family learned the most crucial truths—those necessary for the salvation of his soul—from his father, he was relieved of the need for loyalty in other spheres, becoming free to go beyond his father in terms of his own worldly ambition. If his father was a carpenter or a farmer, the son might aspire to be a lawyer or a merchant without feeling that he was rejecting his father. On the contrary, the son might best express his gratitude for his father's guidance by going beyond what his father had achieved. The result was a great increase in what we have come to call social mobility.

The impetus to get ahead in the world grew out of the new faith. Calvin placed great emphasis on the work a man did as a way of serving and pleasing God. Work was not a sure road to salvation, for Calvin was a strict predestinarian—that is, he believed salvation was bestowed by God according to His inscrutable plan and could not be earned by either faith or works. But to work conscientiously and well at any task, however menial, was to praise and bear witness to the goodness of the Lord. The consequences are familiar. Protestant countries, and perhaps most characteristically America as the most Protestant of all countries, have been work-oriented. Work has been the major American preoccupation or indeed obsession, an avenue to salvation, a vindication of the individual and of individualism itself.

Closely related to the ethic of work was Calvin's view of time. Time was seen as an arena in which one worked out, as far as possible, one's own salvation. All time was impregnated with the Divine Spirit. Everything done in time and with time came under God's scrutiny. None of it was private, or neutral, or unobserved. Time must, therefore, be used carefully, prudently, profitably, devoutly, every hour and every minute of it accounted for and none wasted. Benjamin Franklin produced dozens of aphorisms exalting this concept: "Early to bed and early to rise"; "The Devil makes work for idle hands." Indeed, Americans like Franklin often seemed to feel that work (and its hoped-for concomitant, money) was a surer path to salvation than piety. This typically American attitude toward time had important ramifications and consequences.

Austerity, reserve, and self-denial were also demanded by Calvin. The Reformer took thought for the morrow; he laid something by to care for himself and his less fortunate fellows. He enjoyed the good gifts of God, but with restraint. In Calvin's words, good Christians "should indulge themselves as little as possible . . . they should perpetually and resolutely exert themselves to retrench all superfluities and to restrain luxury; and they should diligently beware lest they pervert into impediments things which were given for their assistance." Calvin did not require excessive austerity; this would have been a denial of the bounty and generosity of the Maker. But license was a sinful perversion of means into ends.

Such preoccupations led, quite naturally, to an extreme degree of self-consciousness and introspection. Those present-day Americans who are constantly examining the state of their psyches are, in this respect at least, descendants of the Puritans. The faithful Reformer spent an inordinate amount of time in a painstaking audit of his state of grace or gracelessness. He frequently kept a diary or journal in which he recorded every step forward and every dismal backsliding, a ledger of moral debits and credits, often written in cipher to preserve its secrets from prying mortal eyes. Even Cotton Mather, one of the greatest of the late Puritan leaders, confessed to his diary that he was tempted to "self-pollution," suicide, and blasphemy, was full of doubts, and was on occasion uncertain of the existence of God and of his own salvation.

We might thus say that the Reformer set out on the lonely and difficult task of learning and doing God's will. "Not my will, but Thy will, O Lord, be done," he prayed. If he did not always understand God's will or was not able to conform to it, he learned to live, to a remarkable and perhaps unprecedented degree, by his own will. This self-willed struggle proved to be an unusually demanding, endlessly challenging, and often exciting enterprise.

The Reformation left its mark on every aspect of the personal and social life of the faithful. In the family, in education, in business activity, in work, in the community, and ultimately in politics, the consequences of the Reformation were determinative for American history.

Today we are perhaps most conscious of the negative aspects of the consciousness or character type that we understand to be our heritage from the Reformation. It is depicted as sour, austere, repressive, materialistic, competitive, anxious, arrogant, authoritarian, both defensive and aggressive, inhibited, excessively individualistic. And it may well be that the creative potentialities in that consciousness have been mined out, that what we presently experience in such a negative way are the unattractive residues that remained when the Puritans' zealous faith and passionate desire to redeem the world for the glory of God had dwindled away.

Remote or repugnant as Puritanism may be to us today, it is

essential that we understand that the Reformation in its full power was one of the great emancipations of history. Those who drew together under the new revelation unquestionably felt themselves filled with the grace of God and experienced the joy of creation in its deepest sense. Those who embraced the Reformed faith were, or at least felt themselves to be, truly liberated; they entered into a genuinely new world of the spirit and received in consequence the power to establish a geographically new world. The Reformers were not simply men and women who subscribed to a set of theological propositions, most of which seem thoroughly uncongenial or obscure to us today. They were men and women, individuals in a quite new sense, with a transcendent vision and the passionate determination to transform the world in accordance with that vision. For better or worse, we are their children, and our country, different as it is from their vision, is the fruit of that vision.

The fact that colonial America produced a different kind of consciousness—a new man—is not simply a modern perception. The colonists themselves were never reluctant to boast that they were in the process of establishing a distinctive society, a new human order. Even the usually cautious John Adams envisioned America as the great power that would arise as Britain declined, the future seat of the arts and sciences. It was, however, a French immigrant who gave the most captivating picture of the new society emerging in the wilderness. Michel Guillaume Jean de Crèvecoeur came to America during the French and Indian War and fought in the French army against the British and the colonists. After the Treaty of Paris in 1763, Crèvecoeur left the French army, settled in New York State, married an American girl, and became a successful farmer. In his *Letters from an American Farmer,* he assumed the role of a second-generation English immigrant whose father had come to the colonies penniless and, by hard work, had acquired a modest competence that he had passed on to his son. Letter number three is devoted to the famous question: "What then is the American, this new man?"

Crèvecoeur saw "this new man" as distinguished by the society he had created. "It is not composed, as in Europe, of great lords who possess every thing, and a herd of people who have nothing. Here are no aristocratical families, no courts, no kings, no bishops, no socialistical dominion, no invisible power giving to a few a very visible one; no great manufacturers employing thousands, no great refinement of luxury.

The rich and the poor are not so far removed from each other as they are in Europe. . . . We are a people of cultivators, scattered over an immense territory . . . united by silken cords of mild government, all respecting the laws, without dreading their power, because they are equitable. We are all animated with the spirit of an industry which is unfettered and unrestrained because each person works for himself."

If a visitor travels through the rural districts, Crèvecoeur continued, "he views not the hostile castle, and the haughty mansion, contrasted with the clay-built hut and miserable cabin, where castle and men help to keep each other warm. . . . A pleasing uniformity of decent competence appears throughout our habitations. . . . Lawyer and merchant are the fairest titles our towns afford; that of farmer is the only appelation of the rural inhabitants of our country. . . . We have no princes, for whom we toil, starve, and bleed: we are the most perfect society now existing in the world. Here man is free as he ought to be . . . . In this great American asylum," he went on, "the poor of Europe have by some means met together. . . . In Europe they were as so many useless plants, wanting vegetative mould, and refreshing showers; they withered, and were mowed down by want, hunger, and war; but now by the power of transplantation, like all other plants they have taken root and flourished. . . ."

Summing up, Crèvecoeur again confronted the question, "What then is the American, this new man?" and provided this answer:

"He is an American, who leaving behind him all his ancient prejudices and manners, receives new ones from the new mode of life he has embraced, the new government he obeys, and the new rank he holds. He becomes an American by being received in the broad lap of our great Alma Mater. Here the individuals of all nations are melted into a new race of men, whose labours and posterity will one day cause great changes in the world. . . . The American is a new man, who acts upon new principles; he must therefore entertain new ideas, and form new opinions. From involuntary idleness, servile dependence, penury, and useless labour, he has passed to toils of a very different sort, rewarded by ample subsistence. This is an American."

There was enough truth in Crèvecoeur's idealized dream of an egalitarian America based on just law to disguise its shortcomings and to charm subsequent generations of Americans, who have been delighted to see themselves and their country through the eyes of the rhapsodic Frenchman. The rough equality of colonial society, the remarkable mixture of nations, peoples, and sects (Crèvecoeur's letter was perhaps the first celebration of the American melting pot), the absence of an oppressive governmental bureaucracy—all these were true.

But of course America was never the new Eden, the paradise on earth, that Crèvecoeur described. He ignored what were perhaps the most conspicuous characteristics of "the American." He ignored the state of almost feudal dependence in which the tenant farmers of the great patroons of his own colony of New York lived. He said nothing of the bitter wrangles between the colonial assemblies and the British authorities. Of the Puritan fanaticism, the crudeness and the simple vulgarity of the lower orders of colonial society, the ruthless pursuit of fortunes by colonial entrepreneurs, the systematic despoiling of Indian lands by speculators, the callousness of the Southern tidewater aristocracy to the desperate needs of the inhabitants of the backcountry—of all this, little was recorded by Crèvecoeur. Nor was there any mention of the petty feuds and jealous contentions among the colonies over land. The fact was that Maryland, Virginia, and Pennsylvania were engaged in a constant wrangle over their western boundaries. Pennsylvania officials arrested Virginia settlers for trespass. Connecticut, blocked by New York from western expansion, claimed a strip of northern Pennsylvania called the Wyoming Valley, where Connecticut families had settled, and there were armed skirmishes between Pennsylvanians and the Connecticut intruders. New York was several times on the verge of open hostilities with New Hampshire over the so-called Grants, an area that was to become Vermont. Massachusetts and New Hampshire were similarly embroiled in struggles over land. Strangest of all, Crèvecoeur made no mention of the Revolutionary crisis, which as he wrote was wracking the country and from which he, as a staunch Loyalist, fled in 1780 to France.

If Crèvecoeur failed to answer very honestly or fully the question that he posed so boldly, he had the wit at least to ask it. Since the *Letters* were not published until 1782, the answer came too late to be a vital part of the new consciousness that he was attempting to describe, the consciousness of being an American. But in time the third letter became a classic touchstone to that strange riddle of how a new man appeared— and how a new nation emerged from thirteen heterogeneous societies planted in a remote wilderness. Crèvecoeur's romantic American continues to haunt and beguile us. His evocation of what we wished we were, and then, looking back, believed we had been and yearned to be once more, plays so skillfully upon cherished fantasies that it will not lose its attraction as long as we dare to hope for a future worthy of our past. However flawed the American past may in fact have been, it contained and indeed still contains elements vital to the future of mankind. The people living in pre-Revolutionary America *were* different men and women from their cousins on the other side of the Atlantic. Indeed, the American experience up to 1775 was unlike any past colonialism and different from any consciousness that existed at that time, or had existed before, or would exist in the future. What Crèvecoeur missed entirely was that his new man, this American, was, in fact, being created under his very nose by the crisis he did not deign to mention, a circumstance that had no place in his gallery of romantic pictures.

PART II

PART II

1

The Revenue Act

BY the end of the French and Indian War, developments had taken place in England that had important consequences for the colonies. George III had acceded to the throne in 1760, determined to restore some of the powers of the Crown and check the arrogance of the great Whig families. Rather than enter into contention over the royal prerogative, he chose to use court influence, pensions, bribery, ties of personal allegiance, and the arts of political management, which he employed with considerable skill. His aim was not entirely an unworthy one: he wished to destroy party or factional government and to be a monarch above faction, uniting the country under his beneficent rule, much on the model of Henry St. John, Viscount Bolingbroke's "Patriot King." Lord Bolingbroke, writing in 1749, had assured his readers that he esteemed "monarchy above any other form of government, and hereditary monarch above elective. I reverence kings, their office, their rights, their persons," he wrote. "The character and government of a Patriot King can be established on no other, if their right and office are not always held divine and their persons always sacred." He then went on to state that it was the duty of such a king "to espouse no party, but to govern like the common father of his people. . . ." Those princes who yield to the temptation to govern by party "must always end in the government of a faction." According to Bolingbroke, in a constitution-ally limited monarchy such a "Patriot King" was the best defender of the liberties of his subjects.

The profoundest irony was to be found in the fact that George III's determination to free his government and himself from the predomi-nating influence of the Whigs led him into the most inveterate partisan-ship. As Lord Bute, who served briefly as prime minister, wrote to the Duke of Bedford, the king was determined "never upon any account to suffer the ministers of the late reign [the Whigs] who have attempted to fetter and enslave him, ever to come into his service while he lives to hold the sceptre."

The other development that had great significance for the Ameri-cans was the growing movement for reform of the imperial administra-tion. Whereas the colonists felt, at the conclusion of the French and Indian War, a surge of pride and affection for the mother country, England saw a heterogeneous collection of contentious and uncoopera-tive provincials who needed to be brought under far stricter supervision and control. The officers of the Crown, many English leaders felt, had been far too permissive in their treatment of the colonies. Disobedience had gone unpunished; imprudence masked itself as laudable ambition.

One of the first measures that heralded the new era was the so-called Proclamation Line of 1763. In the words of the Proclamation: "whereas great frauds and abuses have been committed in purchasing lands of the Indians, to the great prejudice of our interests, and to the great dissatisfaction of the said Indians . . . ," and in order to convince the Indians "of our justice and determined resolution to remove all reasonable cause of discontent [we] do . . . strictly enjoin and require, that no private person do presume to make any purchase from the said Indians within the limits of our colonies. . . ." Any land purchases must be made through officials of the British government, and no trading could be conducted with the Indians without a license issued in the name of the governor of the province.

In May of 1763 Pontiac's frontier uprising had led to a series of bloody skirmishes. An English officer, Colonel Henry Bouquet, broke the back of the rebellion, but a number of northern tribes were intermit-tently on the warpath until 1766. The Proclamation Line was an effort to bring some kind of order and system into Indian affairs by setting a policy and prescribing certain rules to govern the acquisition of Indian lands. The Proclamation established four "distinct and separate govern-ments" over the land ceded by France and Spain under the provision of the Treaty of 1763. These were Quebec, East Florida, West Florida, and Grenada. All the land outside these jurisdictions was to be reserved for the Indians, who were not to "be molested or disturbed in the possession of such parts of our dominions and territories as, not having been purchased by us, are reserved to them ... as their hunting grounds. ..."

However the Indians may have viewed the Proclamation Line, to the colonists it seemed another example of the readiness of the British ministry to subordinate their interests to the interests of others, in this case to the Indians, so often their rod of affliction. The fact was that, as in so many other instances, the government was not ready to supply the funds for the systematic enforcement of the enlightened principles put forth in the Proclamation. Superintendents of Indian Affairs of the Southern and Northern departments tried to protect the Indians and restrain western settlement, but the odds were against them. Their efforts to prevent western settlement were like trying to dam a stream with a sieve. Settlers, encouraged by speculators, continued to filter into the interior and establish themselves well beyond the line indicated in the Proclamation.

George Washington's comments on the Proclamation Line are revealing. He wrote to a fellow land speculator, William Crawford: "I can never look upon that Proclamation in any other light (but this I say between ourselves) than as a temporary expedient to quiet the Minds of the Indians and must fail of course in a few years especially when those Indians are consenting to our Occupying the Lands. Any person who therefore neglects the present oppertunity of hunting out good Lands and in some measure marking and distinguishing them for his own ... will never regain it. ..."

The Proclamation of 1763 was followed by the "Plan of 1764," which fixed tariffs for trade and terms for licensing, established regulations for traders, and repealed all conflicting colonial laws involving Indian affairs. Undoubtedly an additional motive of the ministers was to try to confine settlement as much as possible to a narrow strip along the Atlantic coastline. As the Board of Trade and Plantations reported to the Privy Council, English policy had been "to improve and extend the commerce, navigation, and manufactures of this Kingdom, upon which its strength and security depend: (1) by promoting the advantageous fishery carried on upon the northern coast; (2) by encouraging the growth and culture of naval stores, and of raw materials ... for perfect manufacture and other merchandize. ... In order to answer these salutary purposes it has been the policy of this Kingdom to confine her settlements as much as possible to the sea coast and not to extend them to places inaccessible to shipping and consequently more out of the reach of commerce. . . ."

Nevertheless, a number of great land ventures were undertaken in the years prior to the outbreak of the Revolution; not a few men of wealth and substance on both sides of the Atlantic were engaged in American land speculation.

In England, Benjamin Franklin enlisted the support of such men as Charles Pratt, Earl Camden; Francis Seymour-Conway, Earl of Hertford; and the Walpoles, all of whom became stockholders in the proposed colony of Vandalia, west of Virginia. Wells Hill, Earl of Hillsborough, who became secretary of state of the American Department in 1768, was also a friend of the enterprise; but Viscount William Barrington, the secretary at war, and Thomas Gage, commander in chief of British forces in North America, were strongly opposed on the grounds that such an undertaking would be sure to stir up the Indian tribes on the frontier, and a charter was never granted.

In Virginia, however, Royal Governor Lord Dunmore freely granted Crown lands beyond the line of 1763 to veterans of the French and Indian War. And two young Virginians, James Robertson and John Sevier, settled with some followers in what is now eastern Tennessee, at the headwaters of the Watauga River, in 1769. They had no title to the land, but they recruited other settlers and organized what was, in effect, an independent state, the Watauga government, making a treaty with the Cherokee Indians.

On the eve of the Revolution, thousands of Americans were pressing into the areas of the frontier, especially from the forks of the Ohio southward. An irresistible tide, they moved westward like some force of nature. To the British, it appeared that a major source of disturbance in the colonies was this constant pressure of land speculators and settlers on the western lands claimed by the Indians. Speculators (including Washington) formed companies to buy tracts of land numbering in the millions of acres, undertaking at the same time to extinguish the Indians' claims by treaty purchase. The results were usually unfortunate. The Indians were extremely volatile. Often they could not resist the attractive trinkets offered by the speculators for vast areas of land. Once having "sold" it—a concept in any event alien to the Indian's way of thinking about land—they not unnaturally felt pangs of regret, especially when the speculators were able to prevail on settlers to buy up the land, often on credit, and establish wilderness communities that intruded into traditional hunting grounds of the tribe. Such regrets turned readily to bitterness and hostility. To the pressure of western settlers the Indians occasionally responded with armed forays, which invariably brought calls for assistance that were hard to ignore and sometimes brought reprisals from the whites that led to more bitter feelings and threatened to set the whole frontier aflame.

More pressing to the British than the matter of the Indians was the issue of the debt incurred during the protracted campaigns of the French and Indian War. This debt was calculated at some 140 million pounds, an enormous sum for the time. The country gentry who controlled Parliament felt themselves already overburdened with taxes. Windowpanes were taxed, along with beer, cider, salt—indeed, almost everything in common use bore a tax. It seemed to the ministers of the Crown that England had come close to exhausting its taxing ability.

George Grenville, who became prime minister in 1763, was the agent of the business interests and believed in sound finance and a balanced budget. Economy was his blind passion—a contemporary described him as someone who considered "a national saving of two inches of candle as a greater triumph than all Pitt's victories." The historian William Lecky spoke of him as a man who "possessed ordinary qualities to an extraordinary degree." In Lecky's words, "He was a conspicuous example of a class of men very common in public life, who combine considerable administrative powers with an almost complete absence of political sense—who have mastered the details of public business with an admirable competence and skill but who have scarcely anything of the tact, the judgment, or the persuasion that are essential for the government of men." More important, Grenville had the kind of moral obtuseness in matters of public concern so characteristic of his type of politician. As head of the government, Grenville personally filled both the office of first lord of the treasury and the post of chancellor of the exchequer.

Among England's financial burdens was the cost of maintaining the ten thousand British troops stationed in America. The ministers and their allies among the members of Parliament made much of the fact that the debt borne by the colonies, largely as a consequence of the war, was calculated at eight shillings per person, while the corresponding debt in England was eighteen pounds. This, they claimed, was manifestly unfair. In addition the government had in a single year paid eight thousand pounds to customs agents, who themselves collected only two thousand. So on every side there seemed to be ample arguments for bringing system into the administration of the colonies and, hopefully, collecting a substantial revenue in the process.

Many colonists considered such measures inevitable. As early as 1754, Governor William Shirley, the enlightened and popular governor of Massachusetts, believed that since "the several assemblies within the colonies will not agree among themselves upon such fund [to help defray the costs of the French and Indian War]; that consequently it must be done in England, and that the only effectual way of doing it there will be by an act of Parliament, in which I have great reason to think the people will readily acquiesce, and that the success of any other method will be doubtful."

In retrospect, it may well have been that under the special stresses of an exhausting and protracted war the colonists would indeed have accepted some form of internal taxation with little protest. If so, the British ministry clearly missed a golden opportunity. Pitt, who headed the government at the time, was a brilliant strategist but a lackadaisical financier. More concerned with winning campaigns than raising revenues, he seems to have felt, perhaps correctly, that nothing should be done that would lessen the most crucial colonial support: manpower in the form of colonial militia who, if they were not the most accomplished of soldiers, were courageous and willing enough.

Governor Shirley was not the only one who believed it was proper and indeed inevitable for Parliament to tax the colonies. When Benjamin Franklin was maneuvering to have Pennsylvania changed from a proprietary to a royal colony, he noted that the "bugbear raised to terrify us from endeavouring to obtain a king's government" was the prospect of having to maintain a standing army. Franklin was not alarmed at the idea; it seemed to him "very possible that the Crown may think it necessary to keep troops in America henceforth, to maintain its conquests and defend the colonies, and that Parliament may establish some revenue arising out of the American trade. . . . It is possible too that we may, after a few years' experience, be generally very well satisfied with that measure, from the steady protection it will afford us against foreign enemies and the security of internal peace among ourselves without the expense and trouble of a militia."

One of Grenville's first measures regarding the colonies was an attempt to strengthen the enforcement of the Navigation Acts through an extension of the jurisdiction of the admiralty court; the common law courts and their juries had persistently freed colonists charged with smuggling and other infractions of the rules governing trade.

Another step that aroused colonial apprehension and indignation was passage of the Revenue Act (or, as it was called in the colonies, The Sugar Act) of 1764. This act was intended to stop the smuggling of molasses and sugar. It lowered the high but seldom-collected duties imposed by the Molasses Act of 1733 and spelled out the means of stricter enforcement. Under the provisions of the act, a "seizer" or informer could choose to take the case to a new vice-admiralty court to be established at Halifax, Nova Scotia. Customs officers were made immune to civil suits for damages in colonial courts (one of the most effective discouragements to customs officials formerly had been countersuits against them for improper action, tried before sympathetic juries). In addition, a variety of irritating new forms, permits, and procedures were required for all goods shipped in and out of the colonies.

Duties were imposed or levied on a list of goods ranging from "foreign white or clayed sugars" to silks and calicoes from Persia, China, or East India; a duty of seven pounds was exacted for every ton of Madeira or other wine. A number of colonial articles for trade—among them coffee, whale fins, raw silk, hides, skins, and potash—were added to the list of enumerated articles. As one colonial editor saw it: "Americans are apt to see their property seized by a numerous swarm of horseleeches, who never cease crying 'Give, give!' to be thrown into a prerogative court[a court of Admiralty] and there judged forfeited and condemned. . . ."

Typical of the trials and tribulations of a customs official was the experience of John Robinson with the sloop *Polly*, out of Taunton. When *Polly* sailed into Newport Harbor, her owner, Job Smith, reported sixty-three casks of molasses and paid the three-penny-a-gallon tax required under the Sugar Act. After the *Polly* had left port it occurred to Robinson that it carried a very small cargo for a vessel of its size. With a Captain Antrobus of a British man-of-war and a minor customs officer, Robinson set off in a boat, overtook the *Polly* at Dighton, and made a thorough inspection. The search confirmed Robinson's suspicions: the *Polly* carried twice the cargo its owner had declared. A triumphant Robinson seized the *Polly* and that part of her cargo on which duties had not been paid. He was, however, unable to find a crew at Dighton to sail the *Polly* back to Newport for condemnation proceedings, so he left the vessel in charge of an assistant and went to hunt up a crew in Newport.

While he was gone, some forty men with blackened faces rowed out to the sloop and took off the cargo and everything else that could be carried away. When Robinson later applied for assistance to the local justice of the peace, the latter suggested that the customs officials were in as much danger as their prize. He had, he told them, intercepted forty men, disguised and armed with guns and cutlasses. When Robinson and Captain Antrobus, who were accompanied by thirty marines and forty armed sailors, asked for writs of assistance, the justice replied that only the superior court could issue them. At Dighton the party found the *Polly* aground, her sails, rigging, cables, anchors, and cargo carried off and her hull full of holes. Robinson retrieved the sloop, but a sheriff appeared with a warrant for his arrest, issued at the behest of Job Smith. Smith claimed three thousand pounds in damages for the ship and cargo. Robinson spent three days in jail before he was bailed out by the surveyor general of customs.

The incident is an instructive one. Even this far from the event it is not difficult to imagine the outrage felt by both parties. Job Smith had doubtless been importing illicit Dutch molasses for years, in a trade that had been winked at by the authorities, and in which many of his neighbors were similarly involved. Far from believing himself to be a criminal, he considered himself a solid and respectable citizen, a pious Christian, a fair man with the sailors who manned his sloop. To obey the provisions of the Sugar Act would, he was convinced, ruin him. So he compromised. He paid what he thought was a reasonable portion of the full tax; and for that he had his ship and half his cargo seized and was threatened with ruin.

To Robinson and Antrobus (of whom it could be said that they were most conscientious in the performance of their duties and the kind of servants any state is fortunate to have in its employ), Smith appeared a thoroughly wicked and deceitful character, a cheat and a liar. What was worse, Smith was a man prepared to act in defiance of the authority of the Crown, to employ a mob, to commit violence against property and perhaps against persons as well, indeed a man whose actions fell but little short of treason.

Such episodes happened frequently in the colonial port cities, and at each instance the colonists grew bolder in their resistance to royal officials and unpopular statutes. Any customs official, simply doing his duty, might find himself surrounded by an angry, jeering mob. Beleaguered customs men, failing to get cooperation from local officials, were often forced to call on British naval officers stationed in the area to come to their aid. Since the officers and the marines or armed sailors who accompanied them were usually arrogant and highhanded, such incidents served to rouse the ire of any colonists involved. In addition, press gangs dispatched from British naval vessels were often ruthless in their pursuit of deserters and sometimes careless in taking up those suspected of being English sailors. Nor, again, was fault by any means all on the British side. When officers of the *Cygnet* and the *Jamaica* boarded a packet running between Newfoundland and Boston, one of the officers was attacked with a broad ax and several of the boarding party were thrown overboard. In defending himself, the officer ran his sword through a passenger's stomach. It was only this last part of the episode that was reported in the colonial press. On another occasion, when a ship's captain sent a party ashore to capture an impressed seaman who had escaped, a mob assembled, intercepted the longboat, seized the officer in charge, and rained rocks and bricks on the sailors until they retreated.

To Grenville and the British ministers, the Revenue Act seemed an entirely reasonable measure designed to stop wholesale cheating. To the colonists, it seemed a highhanded and arbitrary act that treated every colonist engaged in commerce as a thief, that encouraged informers and protected them against the consequences of making false accusations. A colonist might be charged, on inadequate evidence, with a violation of some article of the Acts of Trade and Navigation and be required, at considerable time and expense, to journey to Halifax and there appear before hostile judge and accuser—both of whom stood to profit, often substantially, from his conviction. Informing is not, of itself, a very desirable activity to sponsor. The honest merchant engaged in legitimate trade found himself surrounded by a thicket of restrictions and wound in a maze of red tape.

The colonial reaction was strong and immediate. One Bostonian complained bitterly: "A colonist cannot make a button, horse-shoe, nor a hob-nail, but some sooty ironmonger or respectable buttonmaker of Britain shall bawl and squal that his honors worship is most egregiously maltreated, injured, cheated and robb'd by the rascally American republicans." "Water is not permitted to flow, or the earth to produce," another colonial lamented, "for the same beneficial purposes to the American as for Briton."

For Rhode Island, considered a nest of smugglers by the British, the Sugar Act was especially severe. A resident of Providence pointed out the implications for that colony. Rhode Island imported well over a million gallons of molasses a year. A duty of three pence a gallon would produce a revenue in excess of fourteen thousand pounds a year. This was more hard money, one pamphleteer wrote, "than was ever in [the colony] at one time: this money is to be sent away, and never to return; yet the payment is to be repeated every year. . . . Can this possibly be done? . . . There is surely no man in his right mind believes this possible." And no one could blame the colony for protesting vigorously. While it was doubtless true that "when liberty is in danger, the liberty of complaining is dangerous; yet, a man on a wreck was never denied the liberty of roaring as loud as he could. . . ." The pamphleteer was perhaps not totally correct in claiming that "not one colony has been disaffected to this day; but all have honestly obeyed every royal command, and cheerfully submitted to every constitutional law . . . have risqued their lives as they have been ordered, and furnished their money as it has been called for; have never been troublesome or expensive to the mother country; have kept due order, and supported a regular government; have maintained peace, and practiced christianity. . . ."

When a new comptroller of customs reported to Rhode Island early in 1765, the governor, on instructions from the assembly, refused to administer the oath of office. When the comptroller went to Providence he discovered an illicit cargo from the Dutch island of Surinam being unloaded without regard for the customs official. He ordered that the ship be seized, but during the night a gang with blackened faces boarded the vessel and loaded her, and she put to sea before dawn. The ship, it turned out, belonged to a judge of the Rhode Island superior court.

When John Robinson, the zealous customs officer, seized a vessel charged with smuggling and attempted to have it condemned in the admiralty court of Rhode Island, he discovered that both the judge and the prosecuting attorney in the court were more sympathetic to the culprit than to the laws they were pledged to uphold. The judge would call cases before him when Robinson was away and then dismiss them because of lack of evidence, or the prosecuting attorney would fail to appear to state the charges and present evidence. When it was impossible to avoid convicting a smuggler, the court undertook to sell the ship, often to the owner himself, at a fraction of its true value. Subsequently Robinson was, in effect, offered a bribe of seventy thousand pounds per annum, in colonial currency, to disregard the merchants' violations of the Sugar Act.

In later life, John Adams declared that the Revolution had taken place in the hearts and minds of his countrymen long before warfare had broken out, and there is ample evidence to support his thesis. *The Pennsylvania Journal and Weekly Advertiser* in January of 1765 printed a lengthy essay from a correspondent in Rhode Island attacking the Sugar Act. The writer stated what was common opinion in the colonies: that "beyond doubt . . . the *British* subjects in *America,* have equal rights with those in *Britain;* that they do not hold those rights as a privilege granted them, nor enjoy them as a grace and favor bestowed; but possess them as an inherent indefeasible right; as they and their ancestors were free-born subjects, justly and naturally entitled to all the rights and advantages of the *British* constitution." Moreover Parliament and the Crown, in the opinion of the correspondent, had "always considered the colonies as possessed of these rights, and have always heretofore, in the most tender and parental manner, treated them as their dependant, though free, condition required." But all this was now changing. Even though the colonies had promptly and dutifully raised "both men and money . . . at all times when called for, with as much alacrity and in as large proportions as hath been done in Great Britain [an argument the British ministers would most certainly not have conceded] . . . the *British* ministry, whether induced by a jealousy of the colony, by false informations, or by some alteration in the system of government, we have no information; whatever hath been the motive," was now determined to "limit, restrict and burden" the trade of the colonies and, it was rumored, even impose internal taxation in the form of a duty on stamps.

In addition to colonial protesters, in England there were a number of advocates of more enlightened policy. One editorial in the London *Public Ledger,* widely reprinted in the colonies, urged that before efforts were made to raise a revenue in America, the British "must take off every restriction which has been laid upon their commerce; we must grant them an open, uninterrupted trade; and, instead of treating them as rivals or enemies in traffic, encourage them as Brothers and friends. . . ."

The colonies were not without champions also among the merchants with whom they did business. A series of letters appeared in English newspapers, many of them purporting to be from London merchants and a number doubtless stimulated by colonial customers or friends, urging a more liberal policy with regard to colonial trade in the name of self-interest. One letter, ostensibly from a London merchant to "a Noble Lord" soliciting his support in repeal of the Revenue Act of 1764, declared: "The goods I export to America yearly employ 2,000 men, women and children." If it could reasonably be assumed that there were thirty merchants in the city who exported a similar quantity of goods, and some much more, it seemed reasonable to calculate that some 60,000 poor were employed in support of trade with the mainland colonies. To these must be added the exports of Bristol and Liverpool, making in total somewhat more than 100,000 poor people, most of whom, if trade with America declined sharply, would be thrown out of work and left to go to the poorhouse, to prey upon the estates of the wealthy, or to depart for the colonies. "Is such a commerce," the writer asked, "to be trifled with and endangered? . . . Laying any difficulties and burthens on the Continent and Islands of America is giving the cramp if not the dead Palsy to their commerce and Navigation, and the dead Palsy in a limb must inevitably affect the whole body."

The volatile Charles Townshend, who succeeded Grenville as chancellor of the exchequer, annoyed with the inadequate response of the colonies to requests for troops and supplies during the French and Indian War, wrote: "It is a well-known fact that the provinces have been for many years engaged in a skillful design of drawing to themselves the ancient and established prerogative, wisely preserved in the crown as the only means of continuing the superintendency of the mother country, and the colonies' manner of doing this has been by their annual bills of supply in which they have appointed all the officers of the crown by name to be employed in the exchequer, substituted warrants for drawing out public money in place of the governor's orders, and in one word dispossessed the crown of almost every degree of executive power lodged in it." In support of his argument, Townshend pointed to "the history of America for the last fifty years where New York has gone for several years without force or legal administration of justice and exposed itself to a powerful enemy rather than relinquish the usurpations she began upon the crown in regard to public supply."

The words were portentous ones. Not only did Townshend speak for most Englishmen of his class and virtually all those charged with the management of colonial affairs; he was also, before long, to have an opportunity of putting his philosophy into practice and attempting to make the colonists bear, in his view at least, a fairer share of the considerable cost of governing them.

In addition to passage of the Revenue Act, one event in England that had major repercussions in America was the notorious Wilkes affair. John Wilkes was an unsavory character who married a woman much older than himself for her money, which was, to be sure, a perfectly respectable expedient for depleted fortunes in those days. He treated her abominably, however. He was a notorious rake and gambler, a member of Sir Frances Dashwood's circle of ingenious libertines, a quick wit and an entertaining companion. Wilkes, who had been a supporter of Pitt and a member of Parliament from Aylesworth since 1757, was also editor of the *North Briton*, a rancorous political journal much given to attacking Lord Bute and his fellow Scots. The so-called "King's Speech" that opened each session of Parliament was not prepared by the king but by his ministers. However, it enjoyed, by virtue of its title, immunity from criticism, since criticism might seem by inference to be directed at the king. On April 23, 1763, in the forty-fifth issue of the *North Briton*, Wilkes broke this tradition by subjecting the King's Speech to scathing criticism. He denounced the treaty concluding the French and Indian War, the Cider Act, and the promotion of Scotsmen by the government, and he stated, rather gratuitously, that "the King is only the first magistrate of this country . . . responsible to his people for the due exercise of the royal functions. . . ."

The speech was, Wilkes charged, "the most abandoned instance of ministerial effrontery ever attempted to be imposed upon mankind. . . . Every friend of his country must lament that a prince of so many great and amiable qualities, whom England truly reveres, can be brought to give the sanction of his sacred name to the most odious measures, and to the most unjustifiable public declarations. . . ."

The king and ministers were furious at Wilkes's insolence, and the king himself gave orders that he should be prosecuted for libel. Wilkes was seized and confined in the Tower of London, his house was searched and his papers confiscated. A week later he won his release on the grounds of Parliamentary privilege, whereupon he sued and obtained a judgment of one thousand pounds for the improper taking of his papers. As a result of the government's highhanded action, general warrants were declared by the courts to be illegal. Freed and vindicated, Wilkes attacked the government in Number 46 of the *North Briton*, reprinted the now famous Number 45, and wrote "an obscene and impious parody" of Pope's *Essay on Man,* entitled *Essay on Woman.* Lord North carried the motion in the House of Lords to have Number 45 declared seditious libel. Wilkes was summoned by the House to appear before it in answer to the charges against him, and when he failed to show up, the House expelled him in January, 1764. The persecution of Wilkes by the ministers of the Crown and, as it seemed to many, by Parliament, made him an idol to all those who believed that English liberty—particularly of the press—was at stake. Wilkes thus became a hero to the patriots of America, most of whom, it may be presumed, would hardly have approved of his profligate style of life. "Wilkes and 45" later became a slogan for the Sons of Liberty. The number forty-five turned out to have many convenient combinations for patriots. The *Boston Gazette* carried an account of a celebration in London on the fourteenth of February, 1766, when on "the 45th day of the year, a society of Gentlemen consisting of forty-five" met at the Mitre Tavern to mark the triumph of freedom over arbitrary government and drank forty-five toasts, including "to all staunch revolutionists, and friends to Liberty," "to our wives and sweethearts, and may we ever love and cherish them;—but no petticoat government," and finally, "health and prosperity to Mr. Wilkes, and may the year 1700 and 45 [the year of the defeat of the Stuart Pretender] and this 45th day of the year, and the Number 45 never be forgotten. Amen. Huzza! Huzza! Huzza!"

2

James Otis and the
Beginnings of Resistance

SAMUEL Adams and James Otis saw the Sugar Act for what it was: a revenue measure, the thin edge of a wedge of general taxation for revenue.

Otis, like Adams, had long been wary of British intentions. Four years earlier he had actively opposed an attempt by a Salem customs official named James Cockle to obtain writs of assistance from the justices of the superior court at Essex. Parliament had provided for the issuance of such writs in connection with the Acts of Trade and Navigation; they entitled customs officers to break into ships, homes, warehouses, or shops believed to contain smuggled goods without a specific warrant. In other words, they were general search warrants, the bane of every friend to English constitutional liberties.

James Otis and his friends had been determined to nip the viper of arbitrary search in the egg. Otis resigned his office as advocate general for the province of Massachusetts rather than argue Cockle's case for the Crown. Instead he appeared before the Court—presided over by Thomas Hutchinson, the newly appointed lieutenant governor of the colony, who was also judge of probate and a member of the Governor's Council—to argue on behalf of the merchants of Boston against the issuance of the writs.

As John Adams, who was among the many lawyers attending the case, listened to Otis's argument, it appeared to him that what was really at issue was "the views of the English government towards the colonies and the views of the colonies towards the British government"; these two views, he wrote, were "directly in opposition to each other," a fact about to be revealed because of the imprudence of the ministry that had deliberately "brought about a collision." It seemed evident to Adams that England "would never give up its pretensions" to having complete authority over the colonies, and that they, in turn, "would never submit, at least without an entire devastation of the country and a general destruction of their lives." James Otis had opposed the request for the writ on the highest grounds. It was, he told the court, "against the fundamental principles of laws. . . . A man who is quiet and orderly is as secure in his house as a prince in his castle." The statutes of Parliament had been cited, Otis declared, in support of writs of assistance, but the acts of Parliment were void if they conflicted with the clear intent of the British constitution. That constitution, although not written, embodied the historic concepts of English liberty. An act against natural justice and equity was therefore without effect. The argument was a bold and striking one, but the case was lost, and writs of assistance were added to the grievances of the colonists against the mother country. In later years John Adams recalled, perhaps a bit too hyperbolically, that at the conclusion of Otis's speech "every man . . . appeared to me to go away, as I did, ready to take arms against writs of assistance."

Thus when word of the Sugar Act reached the colonies, Otis was already armed with legal and constitutional arguments against it. A town meeting was called in Boston, and there James Otis presented his *Rights of the British Colonies Asserted and Proved.* His speech was an extension of his earlier objections to the writs of assistance, but here Otis mustered most of the arguments that were to be used by colonial publicists and pamphleteers in the decade prior to the outbreak of the Revolution. He asked his audience, first, on what basis government rested. "Harrington," he declared, "has most abundantly demonstrated in his *Oceana* . . . that Empire [power] follows the balance of property." But it did not follow from this that government was founded in property alone, nor on force, or compact, but rather "in the unchangeable will of God, the author of nature, whose laws never vary." The "same omniscient, omnipotent, infinitely good and gracious Creator of the universe" who made matter to gravitate and "the celestial bodies to roll around their axes", made also families and communities, "as naturally, mechanically, and necessarily combined, as the dew of Heaven and the soft distilling rain is collected by all the enliv'ning heat of the sun." Government was therefore not an arbitrary contrivance of men, dependent, as Locke had suggested, upon "compact" or human will for its existence, but a divinely appointed order, part of the natural harmony of the universe, "most evidently founded on the necessities of our nature."

From this it followed that all human laws in order to be valid, must conform to those natural laws ordained by God for the governance of man. The unwritten British constitution, a splendid accumulation of rights and liberties, embodied, to a remarkable degree, the natural laws established by the Almighty for human societies. Thus if Parliament, misled by the passions and selfish interests of the moment, passed legislation that was contrary to natural law and equity, to common justice and the principles of the constitution, such laws would, as Otis had pointed out in the case of the writs of assistance, be null and void. Once the mistake was called to Parliament's attention, the legislators could be counted on to remedy it. But if Parliament, through some mischance, proved hesitant to redress such an error, the Crown or executive courts would declare "the Act 'of a whole Parliament void.'" "See the wisdom of our ancestors," Otis rhapsodized. "The supreme legislative, and the supreme executive, are a perpetual check and balance to each other. If the supreme executive errs, it is informed by the supreme legislative in Parliament: If the supreme legislative errs, it is informed by the supreme executive in the King's courts of law. Here the King appears as represented by his judges, in the highest lustre and majesty, as supreme executor of the Commonwealth. . . . This is government! This is a constitution! to preserve which, either from foreign or domestic foes, has cost oceans of blood and treasure in every age; and the blood and treasure have upon the whole been well spent." Otis quoted in support of his argument an obscure ruling, the so-called Calvin's Case, from the sixteenth century. But it is not hard to imagine the hubbub that would have ensued if, in 1764, an executive court had pronounced an enactment of Parliament unconstitutional.

To many an Englishman, Otis's doctrine seemed wild ranting; and it must have struck even many of his listeners, despite their enthusiasm for his principles, as both novel and chimerical. But it is a fact of history that what is today unthinkable is tomorrow quite routine. The principle that Otis enunciated was so powerful an idea that it came, eventually, to be embodied in the Supreme Court of the United States, which was specifically charged with checking Congress when that body should pass legislation that contravened, primarily, the natural law as incorporated in the first ten amendments to the Federal Constitution.

Having stated so boldly the principles of natural law on which a great part of the colonial resistance to the authority of Great Britain was to be based, Otis conceded that "the power of Parliament [was] uncontrollable, but by themselves, and we must obey." To act otherwise would be to bring all government and order into disrepute, indeed, to commit high treason. It must be assumed that the "wisdom and justice of that august assembly, always will afford us relief by repealing such Acts, as through mistake, or other human infirmities, have been suffered to pass, if they can be convinced that their proceedings are not constitutional or not for the common good. . . ."

Some colonists, anxious to draw a line beyond which Parliament might be persuaded not to go in imposing taxes, had made a distinction between "external" and "internal" taxation. They were willing to concede that England had the right to regulate colonial trade and to impose "external" taxes for that purpose, while rejecting the notion that Parliament had the right to levy "internal" taxes for the sole or primary purpose of raising a revenue. The first order of taxes were necessary if any control was to be maintained over British commerce, at home or abroad. The second, internal taxes were plainly taking money out of one's pocket without one's consent, given through one's proper representatives. But Otis was unwilling to make any such concession, and he warned his listeners of its dangers. "There is no foundation," he declared, "for the distinction some make in England, between an internal and external tax on the colonies . . . a tax on trade is either a tax of every man in the province, or 'tis not."

Otis ended his speech by rejecting the notion, put forth on occasion by British advocates of colonial taxation, that the colonies were like British corporations, which no one questioned the right of Parliament to tax, rather than, as the colonists insisted, "subordinate states" with their own rights and lawful jurisdictions. "The sum of my argument," he reminded his audience, "is that civil government is of God," and that the British constitution "is the most free one, and by far the best, now existing on earth: that by this constitution, every man in the dominions is a free man: that no parts of His Majesty's dominions can be taxed without consent: that every part has a right to be represented in the supreme or some subordinate legislature. . . ."

Finally, Otis concluded, it was time to consider whether the colonies had not grown to an importance and weight where they "should be represented in some proportion to their number and estates, in the grand legislature of the nation: that this would firmly unite all parts of the British empire, in the greatest peace and prosperity; and render it invulnerable and perpetual."

In Otis's *Rights* lay not only the embryo of the Revolution itself and the essence of those arguments advanced in greater detail by a series of patriot pamphleteers, but also the foreshadowing of the Federal Constitution as well. Thus in the first moment of resistance to Great Britain there was contained, like the oak in the acorn, all that remarkable drama that would unfold in the years ahead.

A cynic would have said, and some doubtless did, that the system of checks and balances between the legislative and executive branches that Otis described so eloquently as the glory of the British constitution existed nowhere except in his own head. And this was certainly true; the British constitution, whatever it was, did not, in simple fact, function as Otis stated that it did. But far more important was the fact that Otis's illusion became in time a very substantial reality.

Perhaps the most striking thing about Otis's speech was the fact that he rejected all forms of Parliamentary taxation of the colonies at the very moment that Grenville was planning a new, comprehensive internal tax, a tax on stamps. Whatever he might have thought of its logic or the validity of its constitutional principles, any thoughtful Englishman reading Otis's speech could hardly have helped being struck by the temper of mind that it revealed. It would have been clear enough that if Otis spoke for any substantial body of colonists, Englishmen in America and Englishmen in England had a radically different view of a number of things; that they indeed had differences so profound that only unusual tact and wisdom on both sides could avoid a series of increasingly bitter confrontations.

The American Revolution cannot be understood unless it is possible to see each party to the dispute through the eyes of its opponent. We often speak rather glibly today of the tensions and hostilities between groups in our society as being caused by "lack of communication." On closer examination this loose phrase seems to mean that each faction must make a special effort to understand the needs, fears, ambitions, and apprehensions of the other. Certain words may, for instance, have quite a different meaning to people with different backgrounds, who have undergone quite different processes of "socialization." It is evident that the colonists saw several Englands, none of which corresponded very closely to the real England. This is, of course, not surprising, because a poll of Englishmen themselves would doubtless have turned up as many different Englands as there were classes and traditional orders.

Many colonists still saw England as it was in the seventeenth century, the England of the Civil War, of Parliament's revolt against the prerogatives of the Crown, the England of the Glorious Revolution of 1689 that secured to all Englishmen their sacred rights. Those few colonists who had been to England saw it as a country that was rich, powerful, and corrupt, where the upper classes, distracted by material prosperity, gave no more than lip service to the great principles of English justice and freedom and were callously indifferent to the condition of the urban and rural poor.

The average colonist, in the middle years of the eighteenth century, was conscious of contemporary England through its emissaries and functionaries in the various colonies. If he was one of a comparatively small number of Americans engaged in ocean-going commerce, he was aware of Britain primarily as the source of a set of prohibitions enforced, often quite sporadically and even capriciously, by a place-man—either a grasping, avaricious political appointee who was often dependent on fines and fees for his livelihood, or a colonial appointed because of his allegiance to the royal interest.

The common view of royal officials is suggested in a letter from an American living in England, who, in 1758, wrote: "For many years past ... most of the places in the gift of the Crown have been filled with broken Members of Parliament [men who had been turned out], of bad if any principles, pimps, valets de chambre, electioneering scoundrels, and even livery servants. In one word, America has been for many years made the hospital of Great Britain for her decayed courtiers, and abandoned, worn-out dependents. I can point out to you a chief justice of a province appointed from home for no other reason than publicly prostituting his honour and conscience in an election; a livery servant that is secretary of a province, appointed from hence; a pimp, collector of a whole province, who got this place of the man in power for prostituting his handsome wife to his embraces and procuring him other means of gratifying his lust." A member of the House of Commons,

Captain Phipps, charged that "individuals have been taken from gaols to preside in the seat of justice; offices have been given to men who had never seen America."

These contemporary contacts and historic memories were hardly an adequate representation of the mother country. At the same time it must be said that the colonists' picture of the homeland (specifically, their consciousness of England) was undoubtedly more accurate, or at least more extensive, than British notions of the colonies. This was true because the colonists in a sense existed at the pleasure of the mother country; they were the beneficiary of its triumphs and material accomplishments and the victims of its whims and what appeared, at least to the colonists, to be its greed. At every point—in warfare and commerce, in intellectual, cultural, and political life, in the enjoyment of those luxuries that enhanced even the simplest life—they were involved with, if not dependent upon, their homeland three thousand miles and many weeks away.

For the British the matter was quite different. The Englishman's perception of the colonies was, at best, peripheral. The colonies hardly existed in the consciousness of most Englishmen. Their attention was taken up with those great matters that stood at the center of world history: the prolonged and bitter contests for European hegemony waged between the great powers of the time—Holland, Russia, Spain, the Prussia of Frederick the Great, and most particularly, of course, France and England.

That is not to say there was not substantial interest in the American colonies among a number of Englishmen. A considerable portion of the mercantile class was involved in colonial trade, but their interest was, for the most part, limited to making a profit from the colonies. The interest of those men who directed the affairs of state was to use the colonies partly to increase the revenues of the Crown, but primarily as pawns in the protracted struggle with the other European powers for commercial and military dominance. They wished for colonies to be, above all, docile, tractable, grateful (for the power and protection afforded by the mother country), and cooperative; to willingly supply men and money when called upon to do so; in short, to do what they were told.

Such expectations were not unreasonable from the British point of view. That was what colonies were for. There were those who ruled and those who were ruled; those who were dominant and those who were subordinate; those who arranged things to suit their best interests and those who were dependent upon them for whatever might come their way, largely as a consequence or by-product of the prosperity of those who dominated. Only a few radicals and ranters had any different notion; and these were ignored or thrown into prison for showing disrespect to the king if they became too persistent.

Indeed, one is tempted to say that the colonists existed in the consciousness of Englishmen somewhat as blacks in America have existed, until very recently, in white consciousness; that is, as people who were there but who were basically unimportant and irrelevant to the serious (and profitable) concerns of life, and of whose particular world the dominant whites had little idea or concern.

It thus followed that what the colonists saw as a perfectly natural concern for their rights and liberties was seen by the British as the noisy contention of a group of spoiled children who, instead of being grateful for being included in the comfortable, capacious household of an indulgent mother, refused to do the simplest chores and were unwilling to share common tasks or to contribute their bit to the upkeep of the premises. To some Englishmen the Americans were "scum or off scourings of all the nations," a "hotch potch medley of foreign enthusiastic madmen," "a mongrel breed of Irish, Scotch and Germans leavened with convicts and outcasts."

The proposal that Americans be represented in Parliament prompted some revealing comments by English politicians. James Otis suggested that the colonists be represented in Parliament so that they would not be taxed without representation. Although the idea was soon rejected by most colonial spokesmen, it seemed to many Englishmen on both sides of the ocean such a simple solution to the problem that the idea of colonial representation in Parliament was constantly revived, only to be just as constantly abandoned. An English lawyer, Frances Masères, proposed admitting eighty representatives from the North American colonies and the West Indies to Parliament. The principal virtue of such a scheme, in Masères' opinion, was that it would smoke out the colonists and determine whether they were sincere in their cry of "no taxation without representation." If they refused representation, Britain could, in good conscience, proceed to force compliance with Parliamentary taxation.

There were other weighty advocates of Parliamentary representation or imperial union. Adam Smith in his *Wealth of Nations* argued that only Irish and colonial representation could preserve the empire. But by 1776 the scheme had few supporters in Parliament. Edmund Burke, generally a friend of the colonies, spoke of the idea as a "visionary union." The colonists, with their own different notion of representation, might spread a dangerous political virus in the mother country. Indeed, by attaching themselves to the Crown through bribery or the desire to avail themselves of the king's influence in Parliament, they might, Burke warned, strengthen the king at the cost of the Commons. The English professed to fear corruption from the colonial legislators.

One cynic declared that he knew a sea captain who would transport the American members of Parliament to England "for half what they would sell for when they arrived there," and another predicted that election to Parliament would merely give American members a chance to "riot seven years in the pleasures of England."

Above all, many Englishmen believed that the colonials were a rough, untutored lot, not fit for the company of gentlemen. New Englanders, in particular, were "a crabbed race not very unlike their half-brothers, the Indians, for unsociable principles, and an unrelenting cruelty." "Would our morals be safe under Virginia legislators," another Englishman asked, "or would our church be in no danger from pump-kin senators [Puritans]." The New Englanders would doubtless prepare "scaffolds for witches and quakers."

The colonies were clearly a source of anxiety as well as profits to Englishmen. They saw them as "now extremely populous, and extremely rich . . . every day rising in Numbers, and wealth. . . ." They must, "in the nature of things, aspire at a total independence, unless we are beforehand with them, and wisely take the power out of their hands." At the rate the colonies were growing they might come in time to rival the mother country, and it was therefore important "to stop those provinces in their career to opulence and importance" before it was too late. Otherwise, "the Seat of Royal Residence may be transferred from St. James to Faneuil Hall and this devoted Island made a pitiful Province to its Provinces!" If the colonists were confined to the seaboard, colonial cities would grow disproportionately, and these would attract skilled workers from England who would establish manufactures that would compete with England for labor, for raw materials, and for markets. On the other hand, if colonists were allowed to push westward along the frontier, they would cease to be consumers of English goods, would cause incidents with the Indians, escape from the jurisdiction of British courts and officials, and doubtless grow more lawless and republican than ever. There were many Englishmen who felt that the only sensible course of action was the cautious and skillful suppression of colonial growth and prosperity.

Anxiety over the practical economic effects of colonial growth was augmented by anxiety over "the Gangrene of *American* Republicanism," and this concern grew with each passing year of the revolutionary crisis. The "Leaven of Republican Principles," must not, above all, be allowed to infect "the *Canaille*" of England, the poor and depressed classes of the mother country. Particularly in New England there existed "a levelling, republican spirit, which would never be rooted out" except by British redcoats.

3

The Stamp Act

As early as the summer of 1764 the rumor of a tax on stamps began to circulate in the colonies. Writing to a friend in England, Jared Ingersoll, a colonial lawyer, observed that the minds of the people "are filled with the most dreadful apprehensions from such a Step's taking place, from whence I leave you to guess how Easily a tax of that kind would be Collected; 'tis difficult to say how many ways could be invented to avoid the payment of a tax laid upon a Country without the Consent of the Legislature of that Country and in the opinion of most of the people Contrary to the foundation principles of their natural and Constitutional rights and Liberties." Ingersoll told his friend that he had heard men of "the greatest property" in neighboring colonies say, "seemingly very Cooly, that should such a Step take place they would immediately remove themselves with their families and fortunes into some foreign Kingdom."

At the end of the session of Parliament of 1764, the agents of the various colonies went to Grenville to ask if he still intended to go ahead with his proposal for stamp duties. According to one of the agents present at the meeting, Grenville declared that "the late war had found us 70 millions and left us more than 140 millions in debt. He knew that all men wished not to be taxed, but in these unhappy circumstances it was his duty as a steward for the public to make use of every just means of improving the public revenue." Moreover, the cost of maintaining troops and royal officials in the colonies had increased from 70,000 pounds per annum at the time of the Treaty of Aix-la-Chapelle in 1748 to 350,000 after the Treaty of 1763, or by five times in the space of fifteen years.

Grenville was eloquent in his defense of the stamp duties. They would be easy to collect and equitable, falling on all colonists and not bearing heavily on any individual or group. "I am not," he concluded, "set upon this tax. If the Americans dislike it, and prefer any other method of raising the money themselves, I shall be content. Write therefore to your several colonies, and if they choose any other mode I shall be satisfied, provided the money be raised."

One of the odd aspects of Grenville's invitation to the colonial assemblies, issued through the colonial agents, to propose some alternate form of taxation if they did not like the idea of a tax on stamps was that he did not send this suggestion "through channels," that is, to the assemblies themselves, but simply left it to those colonial agents present to pass along the word—a most irregular procedure. Indeed, there was some truth to the *Boston Gazette*'s complaint after the passage of the act: "It has been said that the Stamp Act was put off a year, that the colonies might have notice to object and give their reasons against it. What notice the other colonies had, I know not." The Massachusetts assembly, however, never "had a line about it from one of the public offices. Mr. Jasper M-ud-t indeed told them that his brother Israel told him, that Mr. Gr-v-il haughtily told him, to tell his brother to tell his constituents, that if they did not stamp themselves, he would have them stamped, or very nearly to that effect."

Grenville was certainly disingenuous with the agents. Knowing very well that the colonies were able to agree on very little, he can hardly have supposed they would find agreement on so controversial an issue. The proposed tax was in fact discussed in most of the colonial assemblies, and Virginia undoubtedly spoke for her sisters when she protested that the stamp duties, if passed, "would establish the melancholy truth that the inhabitants of the colonies are the slaves of the Britons from whom they are descended." Pennsylvania replied most ambiguously that the colonies had a duty "to grant aid to the Crown, according to their abilities, whenever required of them in the usual constitutional manner," but it did nothing further. Other colonial assemblies, confused by the manner in which word of the proposed tax had reached them, limited their response to statements declaring such a tax to be, in their opinion, unconstitutional, since it plainly meant taxation without representation. Thomas Hutchinson believed that the petitions from most of the colonial assemblies, denying the right of Parliament to tax the colonies for any purpose, cut the ground out from under America's friends in Parliament, who were opposed to the Stamp Act but were unwilling to accept the argument that Parliament was not the "Supreme Legislative," with power to tax the colonies if it chose to do so. If, in the face of petitions denying the ultimate authority of Parliament in the matter of taxation, Parliament failed to pass the Stamp Act, this would inevitably be interpreted by most colonists as tacit acceptance of the colonial argument. Using this argument very persuasively, Hutchinson prevailed on the usually militant Massachusetts assembly to present an uncharacteristically meek and mild petition to Parliament instead of a fiery statement drafted by Oxenbridge Thacher.

In February, 1765, the agents of several of the colonies, among them Franklin, who had just arrived from America, made a final effort to dissuade Grenville from introducing the bill into Parliament. Much the same arguments were reviewed that had been discussed at the earlier interview. Again Grenville challenged his visitors to propose a better plan for raising revenue. Franklin, presenting the resolution of the Pennsylvania assembly, suggested the traditional form of a requisition addressed to each colony. "Can you agree," Grenville asked, "on the proportions each colony should raise?" Clearly the agents could not, and the interview was terminated.

Several days later Grenville introduced the Stamp Act into a House of Commons "very lightly attended." Under the provisions of the act, all newspapers had to be printed on stamped paper that was taxed one shilling (roughly twenty-five cents) a sheet. A three-shilling stamp was required on virtually all legal documents. School and college diplomas were taxed two pounds. The stamp on a lawyer's license cost ten pounds, while appointments to public office had to be written on paper that was taxed four pounds. Liquor licenses cost as much as four pounds, and playing cards were taxed a shilling a pack. The proceeds of the tax were to be used exclusively for the protection of the colonies. One of the most objectionable aspects of the bill in colonial eyes was that all violations were to be tried in courts of admiralty without juries.

While the House of Commons was in general apathetic, only a few opponents of the measure spoke against it. Charles Townshend, as an officer of the government, had asked: "And now, will these Americans,

Children planted by our care, nourished up by our indulgence until they are grown to a degree of strength and opulence and protected by our arms, will they grudge to contribute their mite to relieve us from the heavy burdens which we lie under?"

Colonel Isaac Barré was a veteran of the French and Indian War who had fought under General Wolfe and had been with him at the time of his death on the Plains of Abraham. He carried a disfiguring wound in his cheek that gave him, his enemies said, "a savage glare." Barré was a fearless and effective spokesman for the colonial cause and a *bête noire* to George III. He immediately rose to challenge Townshend's description of the colonies: "They planted by your care?" he said scornfully. "No, your oppressions planted them in America. They fled from your tyranny to a then incultivated and unhospitable country— where they exposed themselves to almost all the hardships of which human nature is liable, and among others to the cruelty of a savage foe. . . . And yet actuated by principles of true English liberty, they met all hardships with pleasure, compared with those they suffered in their own country, from the hands of those who should have been their friends.

"They nourished by *your* indulgence? They grew by your neglect of em: as soon as you began to care about em, that care was exercised in sending persons to rule over em, in one department and another, who were perhaps the deputies of deputies to some member of this House— sent to spy out their liberty, to misrepresent their actions, and to prey upon em; men whose behavior on many occasions has caused the blood of those sons of liberty to recoil within them. . . .

"They protected by *your* arms? They have nobly taken up arms in your defence, have exerted a valor amidst their constant and laborious industry for the defence of a country whose frontier was drenched in blood. Its interior parts have yielded all its little savings to your emolument. And believe me, remember I this day told you so, that same spirit of freedom which actuated that people at first will accompany them still—But prudence forbids me to explain myself further. God knows I do not at this time speak from motives of party heat; what I deliver are the genuine sentiments of my heart."

If Barré's words, as transcribed by the agent of Connecticut and shipped off posthaste to America, failed to move his colleagues, they thrilled the colonists when they read them. The Boston patriots promptly called themselves "the Sons of Liberty," and a small town in what was to become Vermont proudly took the name of Barré. Posterity owes the enterprising agent a vote of thanks. Barré's words were among the most eloquent and prophetic spoken in the entire controversy over the rights of the colonies. That they were spoken by an Englishman is especially striking. No colonial could have delivered such an address without having it written off as special pleading. It was particularly appropriate coming from Colonel Barré, who had fought alongside of colonial troops in the campaign against Quebec and had attracted the attention of his superior officers by his valor.

But Parliament remained adamant; it refused even to hear the petitions from the colonial assemblies. General H. Seymour Conway, a Whig leader, reminded the House that it had postponed action on the Stamp Act for a year in order to allow time for the colonies to respond to the proposal. "This time has been given," he declared. "The Representations are come from the Colonies, and shall we shut our Ears against that Information, which, with an Affectation of Candour, we allotted sufficient Time to reach us? . . . from whom, unless from themselves, are we to learn the Circumstances of the Colonies, and the fatal Consequences that may attend the imposing of this Tax?"

Barré, Conway, and a handful of advocates of the colonial cause could do nothing to deflect the members of the House who supported the government. There was little debate and little interest. Certainly there was no indication that the House took Barré's and Conway's warnings seriously.

In the hope of moderating opposition to the act, Grenville told the colonial agents that the sale of the stamps would be placed in the hands of collectors chosen from among the colonials, rather than officials dispatched from England. He requested nominations of those they thought best qualified in their respective colonies. Several prominent patriots, opposed in principle to the tax but believing its passage inevitable, had applied for positions as stamp distributors, and Franklin named one of his close friends for an appointment. Indeed, so little anticipated was the strength of popular reaction to the Stamp Act that William Samuel Johnson of Connecticut wrote to Jared Ingersoll, offering to be distributor for his home town. "Since we are doomed to Stamps and Slavery," he noted, "and must submit, we hear with pleasure that your gentle hand will fit on our Chains and Shackles, who I know will make them set as easie as possible."

When news of the Stamp Act reached the colonies the reaction was spontaneous and virtually unanimous. Never again would the colonists respond so single-mindedly to an act of the British government.

A typical reaction was expressed by William Smith, Jr., who had helped frame the New York petition to Parliament that had, with the others, been rejected—or that Parliament, more accurately, had refused even to consider. Writing to a friend in England, Smith observed: "When the Americans reflect upon the Parliament's refusal to hear their Representations—when they read abstracts of the speeches within door [inside of Parliament], and the ministerial pamphlets without, and find themselves tantalized and condemned, advantages taken of their silence heretofore, and Remonstrances forbidden in time to come; and above all, when they see the prospects of innumerable loads arising from this connection with an overburdened nation interested in shaking the weight off their own shoulders, and commanding silence in the oppressed Beast on which it is cast; what can be expected but discontent for a while, and in the end open opposition. The boldness of the Minister amazes our people. This single stroke has lost Great Britain the affection of all her Colonies."

The *Pennsylvania Journal* contained an account of the colonial reaction to the news of the passage of the Stamp Act that was accurate if somewhat florid. As soon as word of "this shocking Act was known, it filled all British America from one End to the other, with Astonishment and Grief. . . . We saw that we, and our Posterity were sold for Slaves. . . . A considerable time we lay in silent Consternation, and knew not what to do!—We seemed to be in a frightful Dream; we could hardly be convinced of the dreadful Reality—We knew not what to say or write—even our Presses almost ceased to utter the Language of Liberty—At last by degree we became to recollect our scattered Thoughts. The Spirit of Liberty informed the Press.—One or two well judged Pieces set our Privileges in a clear and striking Light. . . . As soon as the latent Spark of Patriotism began to kindle, it flew like Lightening from Breast to Breast—it flowed from every Tongue, and Pen, and Press, 'till it had diffused itself through every Part of the British Dominions in America; it united us all, we seem'd to be animated by one Spirit, and that was the Spirit of Liberty."

While petitions and remonstrances were framed for presentation to Parliament, most colonists were determined to take such resolute action that it should never again be thought by Parliament and the ministers of the Crown "that the Enjoyment of [their rights by the colonists] depended merely upon the Success of these Representations, or the Courtesy of those to whom they were made." The colonists wished to make it clear that they would use whatever measures were necessary to resist unconstitutional enactments of Parliament.

In the northern colonies, where most of the clothing of ordinary people was homemade, many colonists resolved not to wear black clothes to funerals and for mourning, since black cloth was almost exclusively of English importation. But for a large number of colonists, more direct forms of action seemed called for. In Boston, the Sons of Liberty (formerly the Loyal Nine) began to lay plans for organized protest. The group was originally made up of substantial craftsmen, artisans, and small businessmen. So far as it is possible to tell, it grew up quite spontaneously, and there is no evidence that it was a tool of radical patriots like James Otis and Samuel Adams, or, conversely, of merchants still smarting from the Sugar Act and alarmed by a measure with dangerous implications for all colonial trade. In fact it is worth repeating that the opposition to the Stamp Act was almost universal in the colonies. It was not so much a matter of who was for or against as it was a question of what remedies were to be employed to effect repeal of the offensive statute.

When word of the passage of the Stamp Act reached Williamsburg, Virginia, near the end of April, the House of Burgesses (the Virginia assembly) was approaching the close of its session. The initial reaction was simply that the inevitable had happened, but when further word made clear the manner in which the act had been passed—that is, with little debate and without even listening to the colonial petitions—feelings were exacerbated. Even so, a number of members had already departed when Patrick Henry, a new member who had only been seated in the House nine days earlier, got up to present a set of resolutions against the Stamp Act. The resolutions were preceded by the famous speech in which, as reported in John Burk's *History of Virginia,* the bold young delegate declared that "Caesar had his Brutus, Charles his Cromwell and (pausing) George the Third (here a cry of treason, treason was heard, supposed to issue from the chair, but with admirable presence of mind he proceeded) may profit by their examples. Sir, if this be treason," continued he, "make the most of it."

This account, which used to be familiar to every schoolboy, turns out to have been somewhat inflated. A visiting Frenchman who was present in the House reported that a member named Henry "stood up and said he had read that in former times Tarquin and Julius had their Brutus, Charles had his Cromwell, and he did not doubt but some good

American would stand up in favour of his Country; but (says he) in a more moderate manner, and was going to continue when the Speaker of the House rose and, said he, the last that stood up had spoke traison, and was sorey to see that not one of the members of the House was loyal enough to stop him before he had gone so far." To which rebuke Henry replied quite meekly (and quite wisely, considering he was the junior member of the House) "that if he had afronted the Speaker or the House, he was ready to ask pardon, and he would show his loyalty to His Majesty King George the third at the expence of the last drop of his blood; but what he had said must be attributed to the interest of his country's dying liberty which he had at heart, and the heat of passion might have lead him to say something more than he intended; but, again, if he had said any thing wrong, he begged the Speaker and the House's pardon." Some of the other radical delegates rose to defend Henry, and the matter was dropped. But the resolutions that Henry proposed were as militant as his oratory.

The first resolve declared that the "adventurers and settlers . . . brought with them, and transmitted to their posterity . . . all the liberties, privileges, franchises, and immunities, that have at any times been held, enjoyed and possessed, by the people of Great Britain." Taxation, the resolves continued, must always be "of the people by themselves, or by persons chosen by themselves to represent them." Only in this way can taxes be fairly laid by those who know "what taxes the people are able to bear, or the easiest method of raising them, and must themselves be affected by every tax laid on the people. . . ." This, in fact, was "the distinguishing characteristick of British freedom, without which the ancient constitution cannot exist." From this it followed in the fifth resolve that the "General Assembly" of Virginia had "the only and sole exclusive right and power to lay taxes . . . upon the inhabitants of this Colony." Any attempt "to vest such power in any person or persons whatsoever other than the General Assembly aforesaid," the resolves continued, "has a manifest tendency to destroy British as well as American freedom." This was a crucial point with the colonists: they were, in defending their own rights, defending those of every Englishman.

It followed from these propositions that no one in Virginia was bound to obey any law "designed to impose any taxation whatsoever upon them" (the sixth resolve), except those passed by the General Assembly. Finally, the boldest thought of all was put forward in the seventh resolve: "That any person or persons who shall, by speaking or writing, assert or maintain that any person or persons other than the

General Assembly of this Colony, have any right or power to impose or lay any taxation on the people here, shall be deemed an enemy to His Majesty's Colony." What, in fact, did such a bizarre statement mean? It seemed to say that anyone who upheld the authority of Parliament and the English Crown in matters of taxation was a traitor to the colony of Virginia. But Virginia and Virginians professed to be loyal subjects of England. How by being loyal to England could one be disloyal to the Crown colony of Virginia? Or, conversely, if you were loyal to Virginia, under the terms of the resolutions proposed, how could you help but be disloyal to the Crown?

The debate on the resolutions was a warm one. The fifth resolution gave rise to a "most bloody" oratorical exchange, passing by a single vote, 20 to 19. (Out of 116 members, only thirty-nine were left when the debate began on the Stamp Act resolves. Jefferson remembered hearing Peyton Randolph declare, as the members were leaving the House after voting on the fifth resolve, "by God, I would have given 500 guineas for a single vote." One more vote would have produced a tie, giving the Speaker of the House the right to cast the deciding vote that would have defeated the motion.)

The sixth and seventh resolves were much more defiant than the fifth. As Governor Fauquier put it: "The initiators of the resolutions had two more in their pocket, but finding the difficulty they had in carrying the 5th which was by a single voice, and knowing them to be more virulent and inflammatory; they did not produce them." Apparently they were produced and debated, but they were never passed.

The moderate group of burgesses, among them Jefferson's law teacher George Wythe, were outraged by Henry's challenge to their control of the House and their standing as the senior political leaders of the Old Dominion. The next day, in the absence of Patrick Henry, who had started for home, they devised a parliamentary maneuver to get the resolves expunged from the journal of the House. The strategy succeeded only with the fifth resolve; but although the fifth was erased from the records of the assembly, it was included in the reprintings in newspapers throughout the colonies and thus made Virginia appear even bolder than she was. The *Newport Mercury* was the first to print the resolves on June 24. The radical strategy, if it was that, was to publish the additional resolutions, the sixth in the *Mercury* and the seventh when the resolutions appeared in the *Maryland Gazette*. By this time Virginia appeared to be urging open rebellion.

When word of the Stamp Act reached Rhode Island the assembly of that colony was in session; but it adjourned without taking action, and it was not until September, after the publication of the Virginia resolves and the instructions from the Providence town meeting to its delegates, that the legislature adopted resolutions modeled after those of Virginia. Following the lead of Virginia and Rhode Island, all the colonies—except Georgia, North Carolina, Delaware, and New Hampshire—passed resolutions rejecting the right of Parliament to tax the colonies.

The Maryland Lower House of Assembly "resolved unanimously" that "it was granted by *Magna Charta,* and other good Laws and Statutes of *England,* and confirmed by the Petition and Bill of Rights, that the Subject should not be compelled to contribute to any Tax, Tallage, Aid, or other like Charge, not set by common Consent of Parliament."

During the regime of the notorious Lord Cornbury as Governor of New York in the reign of Queen Anne, the general assembly of that colony had appointed a committee to draw up charges against the governor. In addition to a detailed recounting of Cornbury's malfeasance, the committee presented a series of resolves to be forwarded to the Queen's ministers, beginning, "It is the opinion of this committee, that the *imposing* and levying of any monies upon her Majesty's subjects of this colony, under any pretence or colour whatever, without consent in General Assembly, is a grievance and a violation of the people's property." The colonists interpreted the fact that Cornbury, although a cousin of the Queen, was relieved of his commission as governor and called home as confirmation of the validity of their claim that they could not be taxed without their consent as expressed in their own legislature. They now revived this incident and argued from it that Parliament was acting unconstitutionally.

When word of Virginia's purported action reached Boston, Oxenbridge Thacher, the revered dean of the colony's bar, was on his deathbed, but according to John Adams he raised his venerable head and cried: "They are men!" The memory of the modest and respectful petition to Parliament that, under the influence of Hutchinson, had been substituted for Thacher's more militant draft still rankled. Thacher and some friends wrote a response to the news from Virginia in which they contrasted the "sensible" tone of the Virginia resolves with the "tame, pusillanimous, daub'd insipid Thing, delicately touched up and call'd an address; which was lately sent from this Side the Water, to please the Taste of the Tools of Corruption on the other. . . ."

The Virginia resolves had been called treasonous by "the frozen Politicians of a more northern Government," a not very thinly veiled reference to the Hutchinson faction. "Pray Gentlemen," the writers asked, "is it Treason for the Deputies of the People to assert their Liberties, or to give them away? . . . We have been told with an Insolence the more intolerable, because disguis'd with a Veil of public Care, that it is not prudence for us to assert our Rights in plain and manly Terms: Nay, we have been told that the word RIGHTS must not be once named among us! Curs'd Prudence of interested designing Politicians."

4

The Riots

It is ironic that Boston was the focus of popular resistance to the Stamp Act, the city's people staging the most violent, colorful (and subsequently famous) Stamp Act riots. The Massachusetts colony's royal governor, Francis Bernard, was as dismayed by the Stamp Act as his radical opponents, fearing it might cause considerable friction. He had ordered his second-in-command, Lieutenant Governor Thomas Hutchinson, to consult with the Massachusetts Great and General Court—which, despite its name, was the colony's legislative body—and help with the drafting of a protest to Parliament. But his efforts were all to no avail. The act was approved by Parliament, and Bernard, as a loyal officer of the Crown, had to attempt to enforce it.

His first step after news arrived in Boston telling of the act's passage was to go before the Great and General Court and plead for patience. The act, he said, was only a part of a general revamping of the colonial administration. As such, the Stamp Act would at first appear to be a disagreeable novelty. "But," he added, "I am convinced, and doubt not experience will confirm it, that they will operate, as they are designed, for the benefit and advantage of the colonies." In the meantime, "respectful submission" to Parliamentary decrees was in the best interests of the colonies as well as their duty. "The right of the Parliament of

Great Britain to make laws for the American colonies," he told the members of the General Court, "however it has been controverted in America, remains indisputable in Westminster."

The members of the Great and General Court did not wholly agree. It was not up to them, the delegates admitted, "to presume to adjust the boundaries of the power of Parliament." However, boundaries there undoubtedly were. Parliament, they said, "has a right to make all laws within the limits of their own constitution; they claim no more. Your Excellency will acknowledge that there are certain original inherent rights belonging to the people which the Parliament itself cannot divest them of, consistent with their own constitution. . . ." Prominent among these was the right of representation in any body that imposed taxation. Since it was, on the face of it, impractical for the colonists to be represented in Parliament, Parliament had no right to tax the colonies. The proposition was as simple and logical as ABC. Either there were limits to the powers of Parliament, limits imposed by the very idea of English rights, or there were not.

What was quite plain, and even more galling than the Stamp Act itself, was the fact that Parliament had paid no attention to the Great and General Court's protest. The colony's only recourse was another form of protest—or so thought the Sons of Liberty, who were determined to resist Parliamentary encroachments on colonial liberties. If peaceful remonstrances had no effect, perhaps other sorts would have better results.

In Boston the Sons of Liberty were well provided with publicity. Benjamin Edes, the editor of the *Boston Gazette,* was an active member of the Sons. The Boston patriots also took pains to enlist the support of Ebenezer McIntosh, a shoemaker and leader of the South End mob, which periodically engaged in exuberant street brawls with the rival North End gang. McIntosh is generally described as a common street brawler, manipulated by such radical leaders as Sam Adams and James Otis, but there is no reason to believe that he and his followers were less sincere in their opposition to the British than Adams or Otis. For it was from their class that press gangs, searching for sailors to man British warships, drew their victims, and men such as McIntosh were far more apt to have felt the rough side of a British officer's tongue or the flat side of his sword than the patriot leaders who were protected by their rank and position from open affronts.

McIntosh himself was a colorful, impressive figure, given to wearing a blue and gold uniform, strutting about with a cane, and using a speaking trumpet to bark forth his orders. His revolutionary ardor is perhaps best attested by the fact that he named his son Pasquale after Pasquale di Paoli, the famous Corsican revolutionary who freed his native island from the domination of Genoa in 1755.

When Ebenezer McIntosh and his legions took to the streets, even the highest royal officials were not safe. In response to the Stamp Act's passage, McIntosh joined his South End brawlers with their traditional North End rivals to burn royal officials in effigy, lay waste their houses, and create such havoc that the royal governor himself fled the city in despair.

On August 14, 1765, some patriots hung an effigy of Andrew Oliver from a tree on Newbury Street near Deacon Elliott's house. Oliver had been newly appointed stamp distributor for Massachusetts, and he had another strike against him because he was the brother-in-law of Lieutenant Governor Hutchinson, who had become for many Boston patriots a symbol of colonial acquiscence to British tyranny. Hanging beside Oliver's effigy was a boot with a devil crawling out of it, meant to represent Lord Bute, former minister to George III, who was believed to be one of the instigators of the Stamp Act. Greatly alarmed by news of the effigy hanging, Hutchinson called together the members of the Great and General Court and the sheriff to remove the offensive objects. The sheriff soon reported back that a defiant mob had gathered before the effigy, and the sheriff and his deputies did not even try to remove the effigy.

At nightfall the effigy of Oliver was taken down from the tree by the mob and carried past the house where the governor and his council were meeting. Then, led by "forty or fifty tradesmen, decently dressed," the mob filed down to a dock near which Oliver had recently erected a brick building that, rumor had it, was to be used for a stamp office. This structure was leveled by the mob, which then proceeded to Oliver's house.

Oliver and his family had fled, leaving the house barricaded and defended by friends. The rioters then enacted a bit of what today might be called guerrilla theater, beheading and abusing the effigy and then breaking the windows of the house. Finally the throng dragged the effigy to Fort Hill, a short distance away, where they stomped on it and burned it in a bonfire.

At this point, part of the crowd drifted away, but McIntosh led some men back to the Oliver house, where they ripped up fence palings, beat down the doors, and smashed a looking glass that was reputed to be the largest in North America.

On hearing of the havoc wrought by the mob, Governor Bernard gave orders to the colonel of the colonial militia to beat an alarm. But the colonel in command replied that any drummer who attempted to sound the alarm would have his drum smashed—if indeed a drummer could be found who was not helping to smash Oliver's house. Events had clearly passed beyond Bernard's control.

Thoroughly alarmed, the governor now took refuge in Castle William, a fortress in Boston Harbor, under the protection of British troops. Lieutenant Governor Hutchinson, however, showing more courage than caution, went with the sheriff to Oliver's house to try to persuade the mob to disperse. They were pelted with stones and driven off into the night.

The next day a delegation of respected citizens called on Oliver to urge him to resign his post as stamp distributor in the hope that such a step would calm the mob. Although Oliver had not even received his commission and had no stamps, he consented to write to England and request permission to resign.

This easy victory only fired the ardor of the mob. On the evening of August 26, news circulated through the city that the patriots were preparing another spree directed against officers of the customs and of the admiralty courts, as well as against Hutchinson himself. That night a crowd collected about a bonfire on King Street. Before going after Hutchinson, the mob divided into two contingents, one of which headed for the home of William Story, deputy register of the admiralty court and a prominent Boston Tory. The rioters damaged Story's house and destroyed most of this public and private papers. The other group descended on the handsome home of Benjamin Hallowell, comptroller of customs and a member of one of the dominant families in the colony. Hallowell was absent, but the mob smashed his windows, shutters, and doors, broke up the furniture, carried away books and papers, and pillaged the well-stocked wine cellar.

Ebenezer McIntosh, who was in charge of the evening's activities, then led the two contingents, now united, to Hutchinson's empty house. There the violence reached new heights. Handsome paintings were slashed, the wainscoting was ripped off the walls, and the walls themselves were battered with axes. Windows and doors were torn from their frames, furniture was burned, and the trees in the yard were cut down.

Nine hundred pounds in cash, personal belongings, and silverware were stolen, and the house was left a total wreck. The next day Hutchinson appeared before the Great and General Court; it was obvious that he had not slept, and his soiled and untidy garments spoke more eloquently than words of his ordeal. Lawyer Josiah Quincy, a member of the legislature, who counted himself one of "the warmest Lovers of Liberty," later reported that he was distressed to see "Such a Man, in such a Station, thus habited with Tears starting from his Eyes, and a Countenance which strongly told the inward Anguish of his Soul." The assembly debated the events of the night before. Hutchinson proclaimed his own personal opposition to the Stamp Act but added some strong words about the dangers of inciting the populace. Quincy, much moved, wrote in his notebook: "O ye Sons of Popularity: beware lest a Thirst of *Applause* move you groundlessly to inflame the Minds of the People. . . . Who, that sees the *Fury and Instability* of the Populace, but would seek Protection under the ARM OF POWER? . . . who that beholds the *Tyranny and Opression* of arbitrary Power, but would lose his life in Defence of his LIBERTY?"

Josiah Quincy was not the only patriot who was appalled by the "fury and instability of the populace." John Adams was profoundly disturbed by the mob's reckless contempt for law and order. In his diary, Adams made a careful audit of all that could be said with certainty against Oliver, concluding that there was no substantial evidence that he was a deliberate and malicious enemy of the liberties of the people. "Is it known," Adams asked, "that he ever advised the . . . [British] to lay internal Taxes upon Us? That he ever solicited the office of Distributor of Stamps? Or that he has ever done any Thing to injure the People? . . . If there is no Proof at all of any such injury done to the People by that Gentleman, has not the blind, undistinguishing Rage of the Rabble done him irreparable injustice?" To be treated as Oliver had been treated was, in Adam's judgment, "a very attrocious violation of the Peace and of dangerous Tendency and Consequence."

It was a sobering experience for a man like John Adams, with his respect for law and order, to see the evidence of the destructive power of the "lower classes." Still, as a radical leader, Adams could sympathize with the motives of the mob that had destroyed Hutchinson's house. The ambiguity of his feelings tells a good deal about the emotions of his fellow patriots. Deploring the deed, he could not refrain from reflecting on those actions and attitudes that had provoked it. Had the lieutenant governor not "discovered to the People in innumerable instances, a very ambitious and avaricious Disposition? Has he not grasped four of the most important offices in the Province into his own Hands? Has not his Brother in Law Oliver another of the greatest Places in Government?" Adams then went on to list the relatives of Hutchinson who held important offices in the colony through the lieutenant governor's patronage.

In spite of these misgivings about Hutchinson, the events of the night of August 26 made Adams and other upper-class Bostonians shiver with apprehension.

After the attack on Hutchinson's house, a town meeting was held in Boston and the rioting was condemned. Three companies of militia were ordered to patrol the town, and an uneasy peace settled over Boston. A warrant was issued for the arrest of Ebenezer McIntosh, and he was taken into custody—whereupon word was sent round by the patriots that unless he was released, the customhouse would be demolished. Under this threat the sheriff released McIntosh and so reported to Lieutenant Governor Hutchinson and the Governor's Council, who mildly rebuked the sheriff and wisely let the matter rest.

The virus of Stamp Act rioting quickly spread to other colonial cities. One of the most destructive demonstrations took place in Newport, Rhode Island, where the radical patriots, inspired by the news from Boston, launched a campaign to harass the town's conservative faction. The day before the demonstration was to take place, a leading conservative, Martin Howard, Jr., who had previously advocated that the government of the colony be placed under direct control of the Crown, took an advertisement in the *Newport Mercury* defending his royalist convictions. It was strange, he said, that certain men, "under a pretence of serving the Cause of Liberty, would take away the Right of private judgment, and stop the Avenues to Truth, by instigating the Populace, and endeavouring to point their Fury against the Person and Interest of a Man, meerly because he happens to differ in Opinion from his Countrymen."

Howard's newspaper ad served only to inflame the Rhode Island patriots. The morning after it appeared, a crowd carried three effigies with ropes about their necks through the streets of Newport and hung them from a gallows in front of the courthouse. The effigies were identified as Howard, Augustus Johnston, rumored to be the distributor of stamps for Rhode Island, and Dr. Thomas Moffat, who had joined Howard in advocating royal control of Rhode Island.

Moffat retired to his farm across the bay from Newport, while Howard and Johnston took refuge on a British man-of-war in the harbor. Meanwhile, the promoters of the mock lynching offered the assembled patriots (as reported by the *Newport Gazette*) "strong drink in plenty with Cheshire cheese and other provocations to intemperance and riot." The three effigies were burned in a bonfire, and the crowd scattered.

Howard, Johnston, and Moffat returned to Newport the next morning, satisfied that the storm had blown over. But that evening trouble broke out again. The three men were out walking with John Robinson, the unpopular customs officer, when a townsman accompanied by a group of friends came up and grabbed Robinson by the coat. Howard remonstrated with the group for their rude behavior, and a crowd gathered. Egged on by their leaders, the crowd took off for Howard's house and attacked it with clubs and broadaxes.

From there the crowd proceeded to Dr. Moffat's house. Moffat was a collector of paintings and of what were then called philosophical—that is, scientific—instruments. His house was full of telescopes, microscopes, barometers, compasses, and hydrometers, along with handsome china, valuable paintings, and books. The pictures were slashed and the china was smashed. Many of Dr. Moffat's books were thrown down a well, and others were carried off by the raiders, who had blackened their faces to escape detection.

In the confusion of the evening, Robinson, managed to slip away. When the patriots had finished gutting Dr. Moffat's house, they went looking for Robinson and the colony's comptroller, John Nicoll. These gentlemen were nowhere to be found, so the crowd set out for stamp distributor Johnston's house. Johnston was not there, and even though some friends of his told the mob that he intended to resign as stamp distributor the next morning, the rioters sacked his house anyway, tearing up hearths, floors, and chimneypieces; they left the building a shell. Johnston later resigned his office, although he had never actually received his commission. Moffatt and Howard sailed for England on the next ship and never returned to Rhode Island. Robinson retained his post as customs officer for a while by ignoring the enforcement provisions of the Stamp Act. Ultimately, he also returned to England.

In Connecticut the demonstrations against the Stamp Act assumed a theatrical form. Pageants were held in a number of towns, featuring mock trials of newly appointed stamp distributors. An account of one such affair in Lebanon, Connecticut, reported that the "Criminal" appeared "In person of his VIRTUAL representative"—that is, as a straw-filled dummy. The dummy was tried, placed in a cart with a rope around its neck, and dragged through the streets. To the right of the "prisoner" stood a man impersonating the devil, hissing "Accept this office [of stamp distributor] and inslave your country." On the other side of the prisoner stood a chained woman dressed as the villain's mother and representing "his injured country." She pleaded with her "unnatural child," as she termed him, to take pity on her and remember her past tenderness. To which, according to the account, "her ungrateful, degenerate son replied, 'Perish my country, so that I get that reward'"—that is, the yearly four-hundred-pound salary for distributing stamps. The mother, speechless with grief and wrath, displayed her response on her bosom:

> Heaven crush those vipers,
> Who, singled out by a community,
> To guard her rights, shall for a grasp of ore,
> Or paltry office, sell them to the foe.

The Lebanon pageant came to its lurid climax when the effigy of the "ungrateful, degenerate" son was hanged and delivered to the devil who threw the body on a bonfire.

In New York, the patriot faction was stirred to action by the heavyhanded tactics of royal officials. First the lieutenant governor, Cadwallader Colden, aroused indignation by ostentatiously arming New York City's Fort George in anticipation of trouble. The fort was already manned by a sizable British garrison, but the governor ordered reinforcements of mortars, guns, and ammunition, and "all the necessaries for the regular attack of the enemy." Then the British commander, Major James, made things much worse by announcing that he was determined to cram the stamps down the throats of the people of New York and he would not hesitate to fire upon the town if he judged it necessary.

Incensed, the New York chapter of the Sons of Liberty staged its own guerrilla theater. The Sons placed an effigy of Colden on top of a carriage and then defiantly wheeled the carriage under the guns of the fort, where soldiers could be seen at the ports with their muskets at the ready and artillerymen were standing by their pieces. For a while it seemed as though the crowd, led by some 400 or 500 seamen, might attack the fort, but the demonstrators decided instead to set fire to the carriage and effigy.

Most of the crowd then dispersed, but a number went on to the house of the hated Major James, an elegant mansion with handsome gardens and summerhouses. The crowd burst open the doors and destroyed or carried off every single article in the house. As one observer described it, "The Beds they cut open, and threw the Feathers abroad, broke all the Glasses, China, Tables, Chairs, Desks, Trunks, Chests." The mob then built a fire and threw everything in it, "drank or destroyed all the Liquor," tore out the partitions and windows, and reduced the house to a gutted shell. Finally, the men pulled down the summerhouses and left the garden in ruins.

In all of the colonies, a particular resentment was directed against those Americans, who, like Andrew Oliver in Boston and Augustus Johnston in Newport, had been appointed or were rumored to have been appointed as stamp distributors. Some of the new appointees, like Pennsylvania's Ben Franklin and Virginia's Henry Lee, were good patriots and enemies of Parliamentary taxation. They had opposed the Stamp Act, but when its passage appeared inevitable they had applied for distributorships, doubtless on the ground that if profits were to be made from the sale of the stamps, it was better for them to be made by good patriots.

Franklin and Lee quickly resigned their posts when the displeasure of their fellow colonists became apparent, and other newly designated stamp distributors followed suit. In New York, James McEvers, a prosperous merchant who had been named distributor, resigned without urging, explaining to a friend in England that he was quitting because "I have a large store of Goods and Seldom Less than Twenty thousand Pounds Currency value in it with which the Populace would make sad Havok." McEvers went on to suggest that it should be easy enough "to have Some Other Person Appointed in my place, as there are many who are not in so good a way of Business and not so large a Store at Risque."

The stamp distributor for New Hampshire, George Meserve, was in England at the time of the passage of the act, and although he was a friend to colonial liberty, he applied for and received a distributorship. As Meserve's ship entered Boston Harbor, the pilot brought him a letter demanding that he relinquish his office before heading for New Hampshire. When Meserve realized that the Boston patriots would not permit his ship to dock until they could determine that there were no stamps on board, he announced his resignation; he was thereupon hailed as a hero and feted at the Exchange Tavern. Even so, many of the citizens of his home colony were not impressed. Their animosity remained so evident that Meserve slept with a loaded pistol by his bedside and refrained from doing business for fear, he said, of having his "interests destroyed by a mob."

Some of the newly appointed stamp distributors required more persuading than McEvers or Meserve before they gave up their commissions. In New Haven, Connecticut, when a town meeting resolution called for Jared Ingersoll's resignation, Ingersoll rose to his feet and declared that he had no intention of quitting his post until he was instructed to do so by Connecticut's general assembly. Word of Ingersoll's recalcitrance spread, and several days later a large group of mounted men gathered at Hartford with the avowed purpose of seeking out Ingersoll and persuading him to resign. Acting on the rumor that Ingersoll was on his way to Hartford to place himself under the protection of the assembly, the riders, their numbers now considerably augmented, set off and came upon Ingersoll near Weathersfield.

Ingersoll was a stubborn and independent man who refused at first to yield to the crowd, but finally their threats overbore him and he agreed to resign his commission. He was thereupon forced to sign a statement to that effect, read his resignation aloud, and pronounce the words, "liberty and property" three times. The crowd replied with three cheers, and Ingersoll then went off to a local tavern in congenial enough spirits. After dinner some five hundred of his new friends accompanied him to Hartford, where he was persuaded to read his resignation again in public and where once more he received three cheers—which doubtless rang a little hollow in his ears. Then, as a local newspaper reported a bit ingenuously, the whole company immediately dispersed without the least disturbance.

An equally dramatic incident took place in Charles Town, where it was rumored that a leading South Carolinian, Henry Laurens, was to be distributor of stamps. By Laurens' own account, he and his family were awakened in the middle of the night by "a most violent thumping & confused noise" at his doors and windows, and then by cries of "Liberty, Liberty & Stamp'd Paper. Open your doors & let us search your House & Cellars." Laurens raised his window and saw a crowd of men, most of them disguised. He assured them that there were no stamps in his house. The men refused to be appeased, and when they began an assault on the doors, Laurens angrily accused them of cruelty to "a poor sick Woman far gone with Child & produced Mrs. Laurens shrieking & wringing her hands." Laurens then challenged any man in the crowd to a duel.

At this boldness, Laurens later wrote, "they replyed in general that they Loved & respected me—would not hurt me nor my property but that they were sent even by some of my seemingly best friends to search for Stamp'd Papers which they were certain were in my custody [and] advised me to open the door to prevent worse consequences." Laurens hesitated. But the inflamed mood of the crowd and his wife's cries of alarm convinced him to open up. While two intruders held cutlasses at his throat, the rest, crying "Lights Lights & Search," dashed through the house. Laurens recognized several of them under their "thickest disguise of Soot, Sailors habits, Slouch hats, etc. & to their great surprise called no less than nine of them by name."

The crowd, doubtless disconcerted at having some of their number identified, made a hasty and superficial search of Laurens' home, cellar, and stable, and of the nearby counting house where he carried on his business as a merchant. They then attempted to make Laurens take "a Bible Oath" that he had no knowledge of the stamps. When he refused profanely, they threatened to carry him off and beat him. Very well, Laurens said, if they would, they had the numbers to do so, but he dared any single man to try it alone. A "softer Oath" was proposed: "May God disinherit me from the Kingdom of Heaven if I knew where the Stamped Papers were." Laurens again refused; he would not have "one word extorted from my mouth." He had given his word of honor voluntarily, and that was to him a trust. The mob, he declared defiantly, "might Stamp me to Powder but should not make me betray it." At that, one of the men, throwing his arm around Laurens' shoulders, assured him that they loved him and would love him the more if he would agree to have no further relationship with the governor Sir James Grant. "This provoked me not a little," Laurens later wrote a friend. He indignantly rejected the notion that he should shun his friends. "In one word for all, Gentlemen, I am in your power; you are very strong & may if you please Barbicue me—I can but die—but you shall not by any force or means whatsoever compel me to renounce my friendship or to speak ill of Men that I think well of or to say or do a mean thing."

This speech won the crowd. There were shouts of approval and three cheers and the crowd withdrew, one man calling, "God bless your honour. Good night Colonel. We hope the poor Lady will do well. . . ." Laurens had, indeed, faced down the crowd. On the other hand, it must be noted that, in addition to his bravery, he had a number of other assets—he had recognized a number of the company, he was a well-known patriot, he held no office and had no stamps (the invasion had been based on the vaguest rumors), and he had a sick and pregnant wife. Thus, though he escaped unscathed, Laurens doubtless would not have been so fortunate had he been commissioned as a stamp distributor.

Zachariah Hood, the new stamp distributor for Maryland, met a more ignominious fate. Hoping that England would take a strong line and enforce the Stamp Act, he resolutely refused to resign, even after his house was pulled down. As a result, he was forced to flee for his life with nothing but the clothes on his back.

One of the striking facts about the so-called Stamp Act riots is that resistance to the Stamp Act was spontaneous in virtually all the colonies. Moreover, the resistance included quite different social groups; it was evident in all segments of colonial society and reached from longshoremen and artisans to rich merchants and, in the South, great plantation owners. In New York John Morin Scott, who was a graduate of Yale and the son of a wealthy merchant, led the Sons of Liberty. In South Carolina it was Christopher Gadsden, one of the wealthiest planters in the province. In North Carolina, the governor found the merchants "as assiduous in obstructing the reception of the Stamps as any of the Inhabitants." Likewise in Virginia there were leading men among the forces of resistance. Governor Fauquier declared, "This Concourse of People, I should call a Mob, did I not know that it was chiefly if not altogether Composed of Gentlemen of Property in the Colony—some of them at the Head of their respective Counties, and the Merchants of the Country whether English, Scotch or Virginians, for few absented themselves."

The situation nevertheless was somewhat different in the South than it was in the North. In the South, with few exceptions, the great families were aligned against the Stamp Act, although there was considerable difference of opinion between a Henry Laurens and a Christopher Gadsden as to how the resistance to the Stamp Act was best to be expressed. Gadsden supported open defiance, while Laurens counseled a more moderate course. In the "Eastern" or New England colonies, a major portion of the richest and most prominent families remained allied with the Crown, and the leadership passed into the hands of the "second rank"—specifically, members of a rising bourgeois class, like

John Adams. By November of 1765 there was a kind of informal popular government in Boston. A letter from Thomas Hutchinson to Thomas Pownall, a former governor of Massachusetts, makes clear that the mob was anything but a "headless beast." It was controlled by "a superior set consisting of master-masons, carpenters, etc. of the town"— who were in turn controlled by a committee of merchants. "All affairs of a general nature" having to do with opening the law courts required a meeting of all the inhabitants of Boston. There the town would first determine "what is necessary to be done and then apply either to the Governor and council or resolve that it is necessary that the general court should meet. . . ." From Hutchinson's description it is clear that what had evolved was a remarkably democratic procedure in which most of the concerned inhabitants of the city participated.

In New York, Robert Livingston stated that he was unfamiliar with the "secret party" that had sparked the demonstrations. Cadwallader Colden, on the other hand, was convinced that "the Lawyers of this Place are the Authors, Promoters, and Leaders" of the resistance to the Stamp Act. General Gage blamed the lawyers in every colony for instigating the trouble and added, "The whole Body of Merchants in general, Assembly Men, Magistrates, etc. have been united in this Plan of Riots, and without the Influence and Instigation of these the inferior People would have been quiet. Very great Pains was taken to rouse them before they Stirred."

But this was wisdom after the event. Gage was no better equipped to understand the nature of the popular reaction to the Stamp Act than most colonial leaders, and his account is substantially in contradiction to that of Hutchinson, who paints a picture of a popular "shadow government" in Boston. "It is the opinion of the better sort of people," General Gage wrote, "that if the provinces were left much longer in the situation they are now in, the Inhabitants would rise and attack each other." Zachariah Hood, the Maryland stamp distributor, taking refuge in New York, observed that the better sort were much alarmed by the "plebian phrenzy" and have "begunn to dred the Consequences." To some, the patriots seemed more concerned with "commiting riots, breaking city lamps, violently assaulting the peace officers, cutting off their noses, rescuing criminals; or marching away to fall upon a parcel of his Majesty's subjects," than with securing the repeal of the Stamp Act.

The attitude of the more respectable members of the Sons of Liberty—the merchants and lawyers—toward the general membership of artisans, sailors, carpenters, manufacturers, and workers was a profoundly ambivalent one. Some, like James Otis, were discomfited and alarmed at the intensity of popular feeling and especially its tendency to manifest itself in violence. If it is clear that from the beginning some leading citizens joined in with the mass of demonstrators, most often they were the voices of moderation who interceded at some critical moment to try to prevent the more destructive acts of the mob. It may well have been that on occasion they tried to direct the anger of the demonstrators toward targets that were of special interest to them. It seems clear that, on the whole, their influence was on the side of discouraging the worst sorts of violence whenever possible, and it may have been due largely to their presence and periodic intervention that no royal official, however abused and reviled, lost his life.

The *Boston Gazette* in May, 1766, carried a revealing article. The charge had been made by some that the Sons of Liberty had encouraged or condoned acts of violence, and that with the repeal of the Stamp Act further violence would be practiced against the act's supporters. The editor, Benjamin Edes, himself a Son of Liberty, indignantly refuted the charge that the Sons were given to violence as a tactic. "The Sons of Liberty," he wrote, "have all along born Testimony against the Violences at first committed by a Rabble, and have distinguished themselves in maintaining Order and a due and regular Execution of the Laws of the Land."

Nevertheless, the colonial riots that may be said to have begun with the Stamp Act marked a new era in this familiar form of social protest. They were, at least retrospectively, revolutionary and ideological. They were more often planned than spontaneous; they were, to be sure, directed to the redress of particular grievances, but they frequently looked beyond that to a radical alteration in the relationship between the mother country and her colonies. If the change seemed to the colonists simply a matter of preserving existing liberties from encroachment, to the British it seemed genuinely revolutionary. The relationship that the colonists wished was, to most Englishmen, unimaginable, unconstitutional, and, in that fine, eighteenth-century word, chimerical.

While the mobs rampaged through the streets and stamp distributors quit their jobs, a war of words raged back and forth across the Atlantic. In its way, that contest was as important as the shooting war that followed, because it served to inspire the colonial patriots and to establish the intellectual underpinnings of the Revolution.

On the American side of the ocean, colonial essayists and orators inveighed against taxation without representation, while in Britain Parliamentary spokesmen countered this argument by maintaining that the colonists were not unrepresented there. It was a good example of two groups of people talking about the same thing and meaning something entirely different. To the Americans, "representation" meant the presence in Parliament of delegates who were duly elected by the areas they represented. But for Englishmen, the word had a different meaning. Voting rights were limited in England, and it was not necessary that every area of the British Empire pick its own delegates. As the Englishmen saw it, a delegate from one part of the empire could readily represent people from another area. As a matter of fact, this was actually the case. Cities such as Manchester and Liverpool were not actually represented in Parliament. They were considered to be "virtually" represented in the House, and so were the colonies—or so the British argument went—since it could be assumed that any laws passed by Parliament were good for all of England and her colonies as well. This English point of view was set forth most cogently in an essay published by Soame Jenyns, a minor poet, member of Parliament, and a member of the Board of Trade and Plantations. "The right of the Legislature of Great Britain to impose taxes on her American colonies" seemed to Jenyns so "indisputably clear" that he should have thought it unnecessary to argue the point had not "many arguments been lately flung out which with insolence equal to their absurdity" deny that right. Jenyns felt that it was enough to remind his readers that not one Englishmen in twenty was directly represented in Parliament. Tenants (those who leased rather than owned property) had no vote, and neither had the residents of "our richest and most flourishing trading towns." Yet these people were required to pay taxes.

The colonists' situation, Jenyns said, was similar. He cited the example of virtual representatives, and said: "I will ask one question, and on that I will rest the whole merits of the cause. Why does not this . . . representation extend to America as well as over the whole island of Great Britain? If it can travel three hundred miles, why not three thousand? If it can jump over rivers and mountains, why cannot it sail over the ocean?" The colonists, said Jenyns, only claimed to be Englishmen when they desired the protection of the mother country, "but not Englishmen when taxes are required to enable this country to protect them." Then he added scornfully, "The liberty of an Englishman is a phrase of so various a signification, having within these few years been used as a synonymous term for blasphemy, bawdy, treason, libels, strong

beer, and cyder, that I shall not here presume to define its meaning."
Whatever it might mean, Jenyns concluded, it certainly could not be
interpreted to mean exemption from those taxes that every Englishman
had to pay.

The most effective rebuttal to Jenyns' argument was made by a
Maryland planter and lawyer, Daniel Dulany, who had been educated in
England—at Eton, at Cambridge, and at the Inns of Court, where he
had been called to the bar. Dulany was a member of the Maryland
Governor's Council and secretary of the colony, and he was referred to
as "a man of great parts, of general knowledge, indisputably the best
lawyer on this continent [and] a very entertaining companion when he
pleases." In an essay called "Considerations on the Propriety of imposing Taxes in the British Colonies, for the Purpose of Raising a Revenue," Dulany attacked the concept of virtual representation as "a mere
cobweb, spread to catch the unwary, and intangle the weak." For one
thing, there was not "that intimate and inseparable relation between the
electors of Great Britain and the inhabitants of the colonies which must
inevitably involve both in the same taxation." Englishmen could not
properly represent the colonies in tax matters, because not a single
actual elector in England was directly affected by taxes imposed on the
colonies. Finally, acts "oppressive and injurious to the colonies in an
extreme degree might become popular in England, from the promise or
expectation that the very measures which depressed the colonies, would
give ease to the inhabitants of Great Britain."

Dulany also grasped the crux of the issue between England and the
colonies. It lay in the British notion of superior and inferior. England
was superior; the colonies, inferior. The power of Parliament was
absolute, and the colonies were dependent. And here there was a
supreme irony. For this was what the English Civil War of the seventeenth century was all about. At the heart of that protracted and bloody
conflict was Parliament's effort to limit the power of the Stuart kings.
The king could not act arbitrarily, said Parliament. There were limits to
his powers, and he must be willing to act within these.

The situation was now reversed, according to Dulany. Parliament
was attempting to exercise a despotic, absolute power over the colonies,
robbing the colonists of their "liberties as Englishmen." Having clipped
the wings of the king, Parliament now assumed that it had inherited his
absolute power. As Dulany saw it, this conflicted with both natural law
and settled constitutional practice.

In effect, Dulany and other colonial writers were saying to Parliament: "Having placed limits on the powers of the Crown in order to free yourselves, and by proxy every Englishman, from the exercise of arbitrary power, you must now do the same for us. You must voluntarily forego some of those absolute powers that you hold, and agree to limit yourselves to actions consistent with the tradition of English rights and liberties, of which you have been, in better times, the champions and defenders. We must know where we stand. What is intolerable to us is just this feeling that was once intolerable to you; a feeling that there is no check or limit on the actions that you can take that will affect our lives and property." Dulany's essay was published in the fall of 1765, part of a torrent of words poured forth by the colonists.

Erudite essays by lawyers like Dulany were not the only effective written attacks on the Stamp Act. From the first word of the act's passage, newspaper columns were filled with assaults on the revenue measure and its perpetrators. Some were lengthy, running essays extending over a number of issues of a particular paper. Others were brief satires, fugitive pieces, exercises in invective directed at royal officials and unpopular administrators.

The *New York Gazette* declared: "It is enough to melt a stone, or even the harder heart of a villain, when he views this wretched land, sinking under the merciless and ill-timed persecutions of those who should have been its upholders and protectors." The *Gazette* editorial went on to say that "every good patriot's heart should be broken by the spectacle of his country, fainting and despairing, hourly expecting to be utterly crushed by the cruel rod of power." The argument against colonial oppression was set forth in Boston's *American Chronicle,* which offered an allegorical play about "Lady North American Liberty," who was depicted as dying on the seventh of February, 1765, "of a cruel *Stamp* on her Vitals." According to the allegory, her father was John Bull, who married her off to "a Gentleman of noble blood, tho' of no large fortune, whose name was TOLERATION. . . ." The lady went to live with her husband on "a certain Tract of uncultivated Land" and there flourished until her mother "conceived an irreconcileable jealousy against her, on Account of a foreign Gentleman, who called himself COMMERCE." The mother, after forbidding her daughter to have any correspondence with Mr. Commerce, then set out utterly to destroy her, "disavow her Son-in-Law, make Slaves of all her Children and Servants, and take the Estate into her own Hands." She thereupon issued orders that her servants take Lady North American Liberty and stamp her to death. "Thus died the most amiable of Women." Happily, she "left one

Son, who was the child of her Bosom and her only Hope; him she often said she prophetically named i-d-p—d—ce, and on him the Hopes of all her disconsolate Servants are placed for Relief under their Afflictions, when he shall come of Age."

One argument that recurred repeatedly in colonial essays, tracts, and editorials was that the Stamp Act was only "an entering wedge," an "introduction to future oppressions and impositions," a "Trojan Horse, this engine big with exorbitant mischiefs." If Americans accepted the Stamp Act, it would soon be cited "as precedent for imposing still greater hardships and wrongs upon America. . . ."

A correspondent of the Providence, Rhode Island, *Gazette* amplified this theory by arguing that should the Stamp Act "be put in Execution in the Colonies, adieu Liberty, and every Privilege which our brave Ancestors, when driven from their Mother Country, fought, found, and 'till of late fully enjoyed. I hope the Administration will not be so mad as to think of compelling the King's most dutiful Subjects here to take stamped Paper against their Wills." However, if the British sent troops to enforce the Stamp Act, they would, the writer predicted, soon be seduced by liberty: "As the Army is composed of the lower Class of the People, most of whom are Manufacturers or Husbandmen, an introduction of Ten or Twelve Thousand Men, would be very useful in this new Country, where we have land enough for them, and might afford to supply them with Provisions until they could procure it for themselves."

The points made in these newspaper articles were accessible to every colonist, however unrefined his intelligence. The simplest farmer or the roughest sailor could grasp the main issue—that he would become, in effect, a slave if taxes were imposed upon him by a distant Parliament in which he had no voice. He could grasp the main issue perhaps more readily than a learned graduate of Harvard College, for he did not feel the same intricate web of ties to Great Britain—cultural, financial, intellectual, historical, and, above all, emotional. To a James Otis or a Daniel Dulany, England was a second home, the most powerful and enlightened nation in the world, enhanced by fond memories of their visits. But to a Philadelphia wheelwright or cordwainer, Great Britain undoubtedly seemed an infinitely dim and remote reality to which it was difficult to relate.

A number of historians have maintained that the mobs that rioted against the Stamp Act and later Parliamentary acts were manipulated and egged on by colonial leaders such as Dulany, Samuel Adams, and

James Otis. There is little evidence to support this view and a good deal of evidence to the contrary.

Studies of the nature of political protest have by now made clear what thoughtful observers of history have known for a long time—that public opinion cannot be manipulated unless it exists. And this is as true of the Revolution as of any other event in American history. The notion that in thirteen colonies, stretching from Georgia to New Hampshire, radical middle-class leaders were able to whistle up furious crowds to act at their behest is certainly naive.

The Stamp Act proved unenforceable because "the people"—the mass of ordinary colonists—were determined that the stamps should not be distributed or used. Without their intractability, all the humble petitions, loyal protests, closely reasoned articles, and newspaper polemics would have weighed as a feather on the Parliamentary scale. This simple fact is crucial to an understanding of the American Revolution. In the decisive moments of the Stamp Act crisis the future relations between the mother country and her colonists were determined by a firmness and unanimity on the part of the people that no one had anticipated and hardly anyone understood.

5

The Stamp Act Congress

WHILE demonstrators throughout the colonies were asserting their determination that the Stamp Act should not be enforced, a plan went forward to call a meeting or congress of the colonies to take common action in regard to the odious statute. The Great and General Court of Massachusetts was the instigator, sending a circular letter in June, 1765, to its counterparts in the other colonies, inviting them to dispatch representatives to New York in October "to consider of a general and united, dutiful, loyal and humble Representation of their Condition to His Majesty and the Parliament; and to implore Relief."

The convening of the Stamp Act Congress was certainly one of the most significant episodes in the history of the colonial resistance to the authority of Parliament and the Crown. That fact, in turn, makes the Congress one of the most important bodies in the development of modern political institutions. Earlier efforts at collective colonial action in America, starting with the Albany Congress, had not been notably successful. The Massachusetts assembly's call in 1764 for a convention to resist the Sugar Act had fallen on indifferent ears. As a result of these discouragements, it was by no means certain, prior to the calling of the Stamp Act Congress, that a common will to oppose Parliamentary taxation existed throughout the colonies. Mutual jealousies and suspicions had been more characteristic of the relations between colonies than intelligent cooperation. Thus, the Stamp Act Congress provided the first convincing evidence of the determination and capacity of the colonies to act together when they conceived their common rights to be imperiled.

When the congress convened in New York in October, 1765, twenty-seven delegates from nine colonies were present. Virginia, North Carolina, and Georgia were unable to send delegates because the governors of those colonies refused to convene their legislative assemblies for the purpose of electing representatives. New Hampshire also failed to attend. But when the governors of Delaware and New Jersey rejected requests for meetings of their respective assemblies to choose delegates, those colonies held rump sessions and appointed representatives to attend the Congress.

The Stamp Act ⤛Congress attracted a glittering array of talent. Caesar Rodney, one of the delegates from Delaware, declared, a bit immodestly perhaps, that the men who gathered in New York constituted "an Assembly of the greatest Ability I ever Yet saw." Included in the gathering was a solid core of unshakable patriots—at least half of whom were to be leading figures in the Revolution itself and in the tedious years of agitation that preceded the actual fighting. The delegation from Delaware included not only Caesar Rodney, but also Thomas McKean; both were to have distinguished careers as Revolutionary statesmen. Thomas Lynch, Christopher Gadsden, and John Rutledge from the Carolinas were likewise to be prominent throughout the Revolutionary era. From Connecticut came Eliphalet Dyer and William Samuel Johnson, both able men and patriot leaders who were to continue active in the colonial cause. The New York delegation was made up of the brothers Philip and Robert Livingston. Wealthy and aristocratic landowners, the Livingstons were basically conservative and suspicious of the rabble-rousing New Englanders, but they were nevertheless determined to resist the encroachments of Parliamentary power, and they remained staunch patriots through the entire Revolutionary era. The political coloration of the Pennsylvania delegation was mixed: John Dickinson, who was closely allied with the Quakers of Philadelphia, represented the conservative wing of that colony's patriot party, while George Bryan, a Philadelphia merchant and leader of the Scotch-Irish of the city, stood with the more radical farmers of the interior. Both of these men, however, were confirmed opponents of the Stamp Act.

Ironically, the Massachusetts delegation was one of the most conservative. The Bay colony's Governor Bernard had used his influence to secure the appointment of Oliver Partridge and Timothy Ruggles, described by the governor himself as two "prudent and discreet men such as I am assured, . . . will never consent to any undutiful or improper application to the Government of Great Britain." Moreover, James Otis, the third Massachusetts delegate, had recently undergone a remarkable change of heart. Always somewhat unstable and given to the wide swings of emotion and opinion, the fiery comet of the early resistance to Parliamentary encroachments had now inexplicably burned out. Governor Bernard reported that Otis "now repents in Sackcloth and ashes" for publishing his *Rights of the British Colonies* and, indeed, had publicly recanted. Otis was reported to have called the Virginia resolves treasonable and to have declared: "If the government at home [England] don't very soon send forces to keep the peace of this province they will be cutting one another's throats from one End to the other of it." In a letter to an English friend, Henry Shelburne, Otis expressed his anxiety over the course of events. The colonists, he said, should cease their clamors and dispatch "dutiful and loyal addresses to his Majesty and his Parliament, who alone under God can extricate the Colonies from the painful scenes of Tumult, Confusion and Distress."

After an unsuccessful effort to secure the position of chairman of the Congress, Otis lapsed into silence and took only a modest part in the subsequent proceedings. We can only speculate on the reasons for Otis's change of heart, but it is hard not to believe that, like a good many of the more radical leaders, he had come to have serious doubts about the actions of the common people of Boston and Newport. It was one thing to use inflammatory language; actions that produced real flames were another matter. There is a good deal of evidence that most patriot leaders—almost all substantial members of the upper and middle classes—were dismayed at the destructiveness of the populace or, more plainly, the lower classes.

The Stamp Act Congress got off to a promising start for the conservatives when Timothy Ruggles of Massachusetts, one of Governor Bernard's "men," was elected chairman of the assembly. The conservatives were hoping that the delegates might be prevailed upon simply to request that Parliament repeal the Stamp Act because of its adverse effect on trade between the colonies and the mother country. But the delegates were of a different temper. As General Gage, commander of the British troops in America, wrote, "They are of various Characters and opinions, but it's to be feared in general, that the Spirit of Democracy, is strong amongst them." Instead of basing their argument on "the inexpediency of the Stamp Act," as Gage had hoped, the delegates insisted on taking the line "that it is unconstitutional, and contrary to their Rights, Supporting the Independency of the Provinces, and not subject to the Legislative Power of Great Britain." In the relatively brief period of twelve days (they were working against the deadline of November 1 as the day when the act was supposed to go into effect), the delegates produced thirteen resolves that summarized quite effectively the colonial case against unlimited taxation by Parliament.

The resolves began with the avowal that "the members of this Congress" were "sincerely devoted, with the warmest Sentiments of Affection and Duty to his Majesty's Person and Government." Nevertheless they felt it their "indispensable Duty, to make the following Declarations of our humble Opinion, respecting the most Essential rights and Liberties of the Colonists, and of the Grievances under which they labour. . . ."

The first three resolves reviewed the now familiar arguments about the rights of Englishmen, specifically the right not to be taxed without representation. Resolve III stated that freedom from taxation "is inseparably essential to the Freedom of a People," in addition to being the right of all Englishmen. This clause brought the argument back to James Otis's invocation of natural law as the ultimate ground on which all human rights, those of non-English as well as of English, rested.

Resolve IV was important for its rejection of the idea that the colonists could be effectively represented in Parliament; Americans had come to realize that representation there would simply give away the argument of no taxation without representation. Even a delegation of thirteen or twenty-six colonial members drawn from all of the colonies could not prevent the passage of objectionable legislation. So Resolve IV stated that the colonies "from their local Circumstances cannot be represented in the House of Commons in *Great Britain.*"

Resolves V and VI claimed for the colonial assemblies the exclusive right of taxation, while VII stated that trial by jury was "the inherent and invaluable Right of every *British* subject in these Colonies." (This was a swipe at the increasing use of the admiralty courts, which were firmly under the control of officials loyal to the Crown and were able to act without the embarrassment of juries.) With Resolve VIII the delegates came to the central issue, which was that the Stamp Act, "by extending the Jurisdiction of the Courts of Admiralty beyond its ancient Limits," had "a manifest Tendency to subvert the Rights and Liberties of the Colonists"; that the duties imposed were "extremely Burthensome and Grievous"; and that since the trade of the colonies "ultimately centered in Great Britain," which had a monopoly of their commerce, the colonies in fact already contributed "very largely" to the prosperity of the mother country. The eleventh and twelfth resolves urged the repeal of the Stamp Act and, by implication, the Sugar Act, on the grounds of their crippling effects on trade and their contravention of "the Rights and Liberties" of the colonies. Resolve XIII affirmed the rights of *British* Subjects . . . to Petition the King, or either House of Parliament," and the resolves ended with another plea for repeal of the Stamp Act.

On these principles most of the delegates were agreed. But the effort to set forth the specific rights of Parliament—to define in other words the limits of Parliamentary power with respect to the colonies— proved impossible. Some delegates favored denying Parliament's right to impose any taxes, including import-export duties, on the colonies. As one delegate wrote: "What gave us most trouble was whether we should insist on a Repeal of all acts laying Duties on Trade as well as the Stamp Act." Most delegates, however, were in general agreement that Parliament had the right to regulate colonial trade, since that power lay beyond the competence of any individual colony. But then the delegates split once more over whether or not it was wise to include a statement to that effect in their resolves. Robert Livingston of New York wanted an explicit statement acknowledging Parliament's right to control colonial trade, adding, "I find all sensible people in town to agree with me in this but we had some who were much too warm [or extreme] to do any good." Other delegates drew back from making such an explicit admission. The problem as they saw it was this: if such a right were conceded, it would be very difficult to prevent Parliament from levying duties with the avowed purpose of regulating trade but with the actual purpose of raising a revenue.

Christopher Gadsden of South Carolina spoke for those delegates who wished to stand on general principles and not get enmeshed in particulars. "I have ever been of the opinion," he wrote, "that we should all endeavor to stand upon the broad and common ground of those natural and inherent rights that we all feel and know, as men and as descendants of Englishmen, we have a right to. . . . There ought to be no New England men, no New York, etc., known on the Continent, but all of us Americans. . . ."

In summarizing the achievements of the Stamp Act Congress, one point should be emphasized. The statements and actions of the patriot leaders in 1765 can best be understood as an effort to catch up with, and then establish control over, popular reactions to the Stamp Act.

While the Congress was in session, the colonists received some encouragement from England's liberals. Word was circulated in America, based largely, it seems, on Barré's brilliant speech, that the colonies had numerous warm friends in the House of Commons. This encouraging news was confirmed by *The Pennsylvania Journal and Weekly Advertiser,* which announced that during the Parliamentary debate over the Stamp Act, "the speakers in favour of the colonies were more numerous than their opposers, much better speakers, and incomparably superior in point of argument." Report had it that the ministerial majority was small, and that outside Parliament "every person who was at all qualified for any judgment of the matter seem'd unanimous in favour of the colonies."

Only nine colonies had been mustered for this congress, but the tone of its proceedings and the reaction in England settled one point. The colonies, despite their many differences, were as one in rejecting Parliament's right to levy internal taxes, and the Stamp Act Congress had taught them how to meet and cooperate to further their common aims. Thereafter, the colonies would be working together toward the same end—defiance of Parliament's claim to unlimited powers over British America.

6

America in Rebellion

As the month of November approached, apprehension mounted in the colonies. The tone of newspaper editorials, letters, and occasional pamphlets bordered on the hysterical. Arms were collected and quasi-military preparations made in many quarters. The upper social strata, among whom could be counted a number of Sons of Liberty and many sympathizers, increased their efforts to prevent incidents that might escalate into armed conflict and open rebellion. Popular fears centered on the question of how the royal officials might attempt to enforce the use of the stamps. The impotence of the officials was not as evident to the people as it was to those individuals themselves.

In this atmosphere of confusion and uncertainty, attention focused on the stamps themselves. To the patriots, it seemed essential that the stamps be seized and destroyed, or at least placed under patriot lock and key until they could be returned to England, for destroying the property of the Crown was a most serious offense. The fact that the stamp distributors had been forced to resign and that, in the absence of substantial numbers of armed soldiers, royal officials were powerless to insure their use did not impress the people who were obsessed by a deep if irrational fear of the stamps.

In Boston, Lieutenant Governor Hutchinson, who, in the absence of Bernard, was acting governor, conferred nervously with General Gage about the best place to keep the stamps; for the moment they were in Castle William, guarded by some hundred and thirty British soldiers with artillery. Rumors circulated that the people of the city were arming, had procured artillery of their own, and were preparing to assault the fort and seize the stamps. Hutchinson had agreed to put the stamps on board a British man-of-war but had then reneged on this proposal. Gage urged him to return to his earlier intention. If the fort was attacked, it was almost inevitable that the soldiers would be ordered to fire. Moreover, "the King's military Stores and magazines, as well as many others," would be open to the people if the fort was seized. The agreement not to take stamps had brought many businesses to a standstill and left many men unemployed. In Gage's opinion, "the people, idle and exasperated," would "immediately fly to arms and a rebellion begun without any preparation against it, or any means to withstand it." Great numbers of sailors (led by the captains of privateers and other ships), the inhabitants of the town of Boston, and many farmers who had come into the city from the countryside would make a formidable force, amounting to "some thousands," Gage believed. It was even said that "many people of substance" were among those pouring into the city. Gage had sent messages to the nearest posts containing British troops ordering them to gather at Albany and to be prepared to march, weather permitting, to Boston. But the troops Gage could muster would be inadequate to deal with the aroused populace.

Gage reported to H. Seymour Conway, the secretary of state, that the fury of the populace against Hutchinson had reached such a height that "the people of property having no more influence over them began to be filled with terrors for their own safety." The elected officials of the city of Boston were driven to the expedient of offering to take charge of the stamps themselves. Hutchinson, blowing hot and cold, at first accepted the offer and then procrastinated. The Boston city officials "in the greatest confusion and terror" then came to Gage to beg him to intercede with the lieutenant governor, "to save their families from ruin and their city from destruction which must inevitably follow from an assault upon the Fort. . . ." Hutchinson used the anxiety of the council and the City Corporation to force the council to be "answerable" for the stamps as the condition of turning them over. "You will perceive," Gage wrote, "that this insurrection has not been that of a common mob. It is certain that many of the country people came in with arms. . . ." There was no question in Gage's mind that if the stamps had not been deposited in the city hall the fort would have been attacked, and the attackers, when turned back, would have ravaged the city—"an open rebellion began, and the city in great part have been destroyed, and the remainder become a receptacle for all the rabble and heated enthusiasts of this and other Provinces."

On the last day before the Stamp Act was to go into effect, although it was by this time quite evident that no stamps could be distributed, a number of newspapers printed skulls and crossbones on their mastheads and officially went out of business. William Bradford, editor of the *Pennsylvania Journal,* one of the most militant patriot papers, ran a head that bore the inscription: "Expiring: In Hopes of a Resurrection to Life again." He was suspending publication, he informed his subscribers, "in order to deliberate, whether any Methods can be found to elude the Chains forged for us, and escape the insupportable Slavery. . . ." But the *Journal* expired with a bang rather than a whimper, carrying an item from the *Boston Gazette* that called for coercive measures against anyone who tried to enforce the Stamp Act. "Rouse, then my countrymen, and let them know coercive measures shall be used!" If the "Stamp Man . . . now bid you kiss his a—e? . . . Shall he do it and live? The first of November is very nigh, let not your courage cool, nor your resentment fail . . . let not a few hectoring bullies . . . scare you. . . . Indeed fear nothing but Slavery. Love your LIBERTY, and fight for it like men who know the value of it. If you once lose it, it never will be regain'd, and children yet unborn will be eternally cursing your memory."

Although the *Pennsylvania Journal* suspended publication, it was soon back in business. A number of other editors who tried to shut down their newspapers rather than pay the tax were forced, by threats against their property and their persons, to continue publication at the risk of official prosecution. The printer of the *North Carolina Gazette* closed up shop on November 1, was forced to resume publication on the sixteenth, and was suspended two weeks later by the governor and the council for printing too radical a letter in his paper.

Since there were no stamp distributors left to pass out stamps, and no stamps in fact to pass out, the efforts made after November 1 to enforce the Stamp Act were of necessity desultory and unsuccessful. The problem was that the Stamp Act stipulated that ships whose papers had not been stamped were engaged in illegal trade and subject to heavy fines. Ships whose papers did not carry the required stamps might sail from America, but they could not land and be unloaded in England.

Thus an immediate consequence of colonial resistance was that merchants' ships sat idle at the dock or rode at anchor without cargoes. Many merchants had been able to load and dispatch their vessels before the November first deadline. But ships terminating their voyages in colonial harbors could not legally be unloaded or dispatched again without the stamps.

In Georgia the problem was solved at least temporarily by the governor and the council, who simply certified that no stamps were available. In Pennsylvania, merchants had their ships partly loaded, got port clearance papers for them dated prior to November 1, and finished the loading after that date had passed. Virginia took the same course as Georgia, dispatching vessels with a statement by the governor and the surveyor general attesting to the unavailability of stamps, and most of the other colonies followed the same procedure. With the approach of winter, there was the danger that vessels in the northern ports might be frozen in, "which will occasion great distress and perhaps Ruin, to many of his Majesty's subjects," as one customs collector wrote, "and at the same time be a means of lessening the Revenue of Customs." Moreover, prolonged delay would undoubtedly bring a fresh outbreak of violence, since "People will not sit quiet, and see their interests suffer, and perhaps ruin brought upon themselves and Families, when they have it in their power to redress themselves." Thus, with evident misgivings and anxieties, many customs officials began to clear vessels with unstamped papers.

The collector of customs in Philadelphia pointed out to his superiors in England, in justification of clearing vessels from that port, that with some hundred and fifty ships confined in the harbor over the winter, "Numbers of Seamen shut up for that Time in a Town destitute of all Protection to the Inhabitants [and more especially of course to customs officials] . . . would commit some terrible Mischief." The New York customs official, who opened that port on December 4, wrote, "This step we thought the more advisable as we understood the Mob (which are daily increasing and gathering Strength, from the arrival of Seamen, and none going out, and who are the people that are most dangerous on these occasions . . .) were soon to have a Meeting."

In North Carolina, Governor Tryon tried to stall off colonists demanding that the ports of Wilmington and Brunswick be opened. It was in fact the end of February, 1766, before North Carolinians seized the port of Brunswick and the customs officials therein and forced them to abandon their efforts to enforce the act. Getting their vessels cleared was, of course, only part of the problem. The real question was what ports the ships should sail to. If they were dispatched to England or the West Indies, the chances were good that they would be seized for defying the law. Thus the merchants had a difficult decision to make: to let their ships lie idle, or to risk seizure at their destination. Antigua, it was said, was "Miserably off for want of Lumber and Northward Provisions," and other Caribbean islands suffered similarly.

The Stamp Act also required stamps on all legal documents, and with none available many courts were, in effect, closed down. The courts were not as vulnerable as the ships. Judges and lawyers, many of whom though they deplored the Stamp Act could not bring themselves to do anything illegal, in most instances simply stayed home. Moreover, criminal courts did not need stamps, and as for the admiralty courts, which did, their operation was a common grievance and many colonists were, of course, delighted to have them closed. In addition, all debtors, of whom there were a very considerable number, in part because of the shortage of money, were glad to have the courts closed, as were those merchants who had debts in England that might be recovered in the courts.

William Samuel Johnson of Connecticut wrote to Eliphalet Dyer that "our colony being so excessively in debt to the Neighbouring Governments seems to be a Reason peculiar to us why we sho'd be less hasty than others in opening the Courts of Law, but I am not fully determined what is best in this matter." On the other hand, there were many creditors and many who were both debtors and creditors; a Philadelphia merchant expressed a characteristic dilemma when he wrote of his misgivings about "the many Mischiefs that will attend us in that we shall not be able to commence Actions against Persons who are indebted to us nor proceed legally in many other Respects, until it [the Stamp Act crisis] is in some Way Settled. In Short we know not whose Lot it may be to be ruin'd." Another merchant observed, "No writs are issued. No land can be Conveyed, No Bonds can be taken; Some take the Opportunity to walk off without paying their debts, others dont pay knowing they can't be sued, thus we are in the utmost confusion."

In New York, where many tenants on the great landed estates had smoldering resentments against their landlords, some farmers took advantage of the closing of the courts to refuse to pay their rents, and a New Yorker reported that "a large Majority of the Inhabitants of the Colony where I live, esteem the present Cessation of Business as a Kind of Jubilee." When the courts in the Hudson River Valley were opened in the spring of 1766 after the repeal of the Stamp Act and actions were brought against tenants for nonpayment of rent, there were riots, and troops had to be called out to put down the rioters.

Of all the colonies, Rhode Island was the only one whose courts remained open throughout the time the Stamp Act was in effect. Since the assembly had promised to reimburse anyone who lost money as a consequence of doing legal business without stamps, the principal inhibition to keeping the courts open was removed. Rhode Island, moreover, had no royal governor to threaten the use of the prerogative. When Augustus Johnston, the deposed stamp distributor and the king's attorney, failed to perform the duties of his office, he was replaced by Silas Downer, the corresponding secretary of the Sons of Liberty.

The fact that the courts in most of the colonies remained closed (those in New Hampshire, Maryland, and Delaware, although initially closed, were opened before the repeal of the Stamp Act) was due in large part to the indifference of the average colonist. There was thus never enough popular sentiment to force the opening of the courts. The situation was further complicated by the fact that many of the lawyers and a number of the judges were ardent Sons of Liberty. They were thus, to a degree, immune from popular pressure. If Parliament and the Crown had decided to take punitive action against all those who defied the Stamp Act, judges and lawyers could have been much more readily identified than the members of the New York mob who had forced the resignation of the stamp distributor.

The period from November 1, 1765, to April of the following year was a time of great stress and anxiety for all Americans. The royal officials were on an especially excruciating rack, as their letters to their superiors both in the colonies and in England make crystal clear. On the one hand they were pledged to uphold the authority of Parliament and the Crown—but without having the means to do so. (In some instances they were literally under bond to enforce the Stamp Act.) On the other hand they were beset by the Sons of Liberty, including in some instances personal friends and even relatives, and were subject to constant threats and harassment. They saw their edicts ignored, their authority and that of the Crown itself daily flouted. They made, of necessity, numerous minor and some major compromises simply to preserve a semblance of civil order. They did so with no assurance that they would not thereby incur the severe displeasure of British officialdom, from the king on down. Their letters are thus full of elaborate explanations, of apologies, of self-justification. Writing home, they were inclined to paint things in the darkest colors in order to excuse their own actions or, more often, inactions. But the colors certainly were dark enough; they needed little augmentation.

The emotions of the royal officials were shared in greater or lesser degree by all those colonists who were alarmed on practical grounds by, or opposed on theoretical grounds to, resistance to Parliament. While these were, initially, a relatively small number (they grew larger in the years after the repeal of the Stamp Act), they included some of the leading figures in every colony, and they felt the full weight of their fellow colonists' displeasure. They were forced to publicly recant (often against their settled convictions), lie low, and suppress their feelings and beliefs, or endure continual calumny and virtual ostracization. Certainly it took far more fortitude, if one believed in the supreme authority of Parliament over the colonies, to say so than it did to state the opposite. Revolutions are not usually remarkable for their tolerance of dissent, and the American Revolution was, in this regard, no different from others.

In New York, for instance, two merchants who had signed a customs bond on stamped paper were called on promptly by the Sons of Liberty to give an account of their action. In the words of John Holt, printer of the *New York Gazette,* "the matter was to be done privately, but it got wind, and by ten o Clock I suppose 2000 people attended at the Coffee House, among them most of the principal men in Town—The Culprits apologies did not satisfy the people, they were highly blamed and the Sons of Liberty found it necessary to use their Influence to moderate the Resentments of the People." The crowd grew to some five thousand, in an angry and troublesome mood. Even the burning of stamps by the accused merchants did not satisfy the company. "Toward the Evening . . . tho' the Sons of Liberty exerted themselves to the utmost, they could not prevent the gathering of the Multitude, who went to Mr. Williams [one of the merchants in question] house, broke open the Door and destroyed some of the Furniture, but thro' the Influence of the Sons of Liberty and on his most earnest Entreaty . . . they were prevail'd on to leave the House, and then went to the Merchants [the other gentleman] where, after huzzaing for some time, they were prevail'd upon to forbear any mischief—on Consideration that both the men were well beloved in Town, and bore fair Characters, that the Merchants Wife was not in good Health, and very near her Time. . . ."

Even in Connecticut it was reported that "the principal Men are obliged to throw cold water, and to use the utmost address to extinguish and prevent the Flames breaking out. . . . Men of Eighty are ready to gird the sword . . . the very Boys as well as the hardy Rustics are full of fire and at half a Word ready to fight."

Governor Bernard, in a series of letters to General Conway, painted a very vivid picture of "the power of intimidation" and the "popular despotism" that did not hesitate to bully the governor's councillors or members of the General Court who failed to vote as the people wished. Bernard himself hoped for the repeal of the Stamp Act; "for really," he wrote, "the enforcing the execution of the Act affords a very frightful prospect." From every colony Bernard reports "of the most shocking instances of the madness and desperation of the common people. They talk of revolting from Great Britain in the most familiar manner, and declare that tho' the British Forces should possess themselves of the Coast & Maritime Towns, they never will subdue the inland." Bernard heard of a veteran of the French and Indian War who went from town to town "to see what number of men may be depended upon; and he gives out he can command 10,000 men."

On the other hand, those who had defied royal authority had certainly done so at a substantial risk, especially patriots prominent enough to be readily identified. These individuals had marked themselves out for punitive action if the struggle against the Stamp Act were to fail. If Great Britain had followed the perfectly possible course of armed suppression, many of these men would have been liable to charges of treason, to the loss of their estates and perhaps of their lives, while the "mobs" were protected by collective anonymity. In addition, those merchants whose ships, without stamps, lay idle in port, or sailed with unstamped cargoes on uncertain voyages, stood to lose large sums, or indeed their entire fortunes; the greater part of their wealth, in the absence of banks of deposit, was tied up in ships and cargoes, so that even very rich merchants had little liquid capital except that which floated or the molasses or rum that lay in the holds of their vessels.

With English goods boycotted, small storekeepers felt a severe pinch, and the manufacturers of goods for export found business sharply curtailed. Sailors, artisans, and workers of all kinds were largely unemployed. The only ones who profited were the farmers whose produce, in the restricted market, brought inflated prices. Thus it would be a grave error to assume that resistance to the Stamp Act was based primarily on economic considerations. The colonists themselves of course encouraged such a notion by proclaiming constantly that the

Stamp Act would bankrupt them. Some of them doubtless believed it would, but for most of them opposition to the act proved far more costly than compliance possibly could have. What the Stamp Act doubtless would have done was, by draining off a good part of the precious specie or hard money that circulated in the colonies, to make trade and commerce even more difficult and awkward than it had been prior to the act, but it is hard to believe that colonial ingenuity would not have found a way to cope with this problem, as it had with all others that imposed constraints on colonial commercial activity.

Lawyers would not have been seriously affected, since the tax was to be paid, typically, by their clients rather than by themselves. And certainly the tax had little economic effect on those whose opposition was most vociferous and determined—the great mass of colonists of the lower and middling ranks.

In addition to the general demoralization produced by uncertainty about all business and commercial transactions, there hung over the heads of all colonists, patriot and Tory alike, the deadly specter of war and revolution. No one could be sure that the next day would not bring a British man-of-war sailing into the harbor of Boston or New York or Charles Town, bristling with guns and carrying British troops to carry the stamp tax into effect by force of arms. And however some colonists might boast and bluster about their determination to resist the tax to the last drop of their blood, they were perfectly well aware of the hazard of taking up arms against the foremost military and naval power in the world. Many of them knew at first hand the fighting qualities of the redcoat, the skill and courage of his officers, and the awesome machinery of war at the command of Great Britain. Any colonist in his right mind must have felt his hot blood run cold at the thought of armed conflict with the legionnaires of the mother country.

John Dickinson saw, as many of his countrymen did, that the determination of the British to enforce the Stamp Act could only produce war and ultimately independence. Writing to Pitt, he assured him that colonial squabbles and jealousies had all been submerged by a common concern for their constitutional freedoms. Americans would not seek for independence "unless excited by the Treatment they receive from Great Britain," but once such an issue was joined, "the Strength of the Colonies, their Distance, the wealth that would pour into them on opening their Ports to all Nations, the Jealousy entertained of Great Britain by some European Powers, and the peculiar Circumstances of that Kingdom, would insure success." This was a prospect that

Dickinson could not view without dismay. What must follow would be "a multitude of Commonwealths, Crimes & Calamities, Centuries of mutual Jealousies, Hatreds, Wars of Devestation; till at last the exhausted Provinces shall sink into Slavery under the yoke of some fortunate Conqueror."

The activities of the Sons of Liberty are difficult to separate from the general actions, and historians have, in the absence of much concrete evidence, expended considerable ingenuity imagining who the Sons of Liberty were and exactly what they did. The problem is that at least initially, in the absence of any organization, rules, bylaws, minutes, or formal membership, anyone who was opposed to the Stamp Act might, and usually did, call himself a "Son of Liberty." The name has thus been used both to describe a general popular movement and, just as commonly, to designate a particular set of leaders in the various colonies, who are often spoken of as Sons of Liberty as though, from the first, a formal organization existed. The Sons of Liberty in its first stage seems to have consisted of all those colonists who met to formulate plans for resistance to the Stamp Act. These were, as we have seen, men from all strata of colonial life, from all pursuits and professions, with the predominant weight among the artisans, craftsmen, mechanics, and small businessmen.

In the next phase, a number of those patriots who, like Samuel Adams and James Otis, had made themselves conspicuous in many instances by their opposition to British authority prior to the Stamp Act, shared or gained control over such organization as had emerged.

In the third phase, essentially the period between the first of November and the time that word reached the colonies that Parliament had repealed the Stamp Act, the upper-class patriot leaders—the lawyers and merchants in the North, the plantation owners in the South—took over the detailed organizational work of knitting the various loose collections of Sons in the different colonies together into some kind of coherent political association, looking at worst to armed resistance against the mother country.

The Sons of Liberty in Providence, Rhode Island, sent out circular letters to their counterparts in other colonies suggesting that an active correspondence be initiated, and adding: "We shall be ready at all Times not only to vindicate ourselves and the People under our more immediate Inspection, from lawless Might, but as Occasion may require to give aid to the other Colonies, for the rescuing them from every Attempt against their Liberties." Delegates from the New York Sons met

December 25, 1765, with Connecticut Sons of Liberty to form a kind of mutual defense pact, promising "to match with the utmost dispatch, at their own proper costs and expence, on the first proper notice . . . with their whole force if required, and it can be spared, to the relief of those that shall, are, or may be in danger from the *stamp act,* or its promoters and abettors, or any thing relative to it. . . ."

So, for almost six months the American colonies of Great Britain existed in an excruciating limbo. To be sure, they had things to occupy them. They went on periodic hunts for new shipments of stamps rumored to have arrived in this or that port. They filled the newspapers with lengthy editorials that repeated, in an endless litany, the rightness of the colonial cause and the iniquity of Parliament, as though by simple incantation the Stamp Act could be rendered null and void; the same papers weekly exhorted their readers to stand firm, and were plainly obsessed with the fear that the strain of the prolonged delay would weaken the resolution of many patriots. Guerrilla theater groups enacted pageants depicting the death of Liberty or, conversely and more hopefully, of arbitrary government. Where the courts were open, efforts were made to close them; and where they were closed, efforts were made to open them. As we have seen, Sons of Liberty made plans for intercolonial cooperation on the battlefield in the event that Parliament decided the Stamp Act must be enforced. But the cloud of anxiety, dark and ominous as a thunderhead, lay over everyone.

The general state of tension was increased, especially in the period from February to April, by a stream of rumors concerning the intentions of Parliament. One ship would bring news that a resolution favorable to the colonies was anticipated; the next, word of growing opposition to repeal. With the laborious means of communication that then existed, these rumors chased each other around the colonies in a thoroughly confusing and alarming fashion.

Finally, in the middle of April, authoritative word reached America: the Stamp Act had been repealed! It had been voted against in the House by 275 to 167 on February 22, and then carried up to the Lords the first week in March. The most important bit of news ever to reach the American colonies had taken almost eight weeks to cross the Atlantic. For two months after the repeal of the hated tax, the colonists had continued to live in doubt and fear of the outcome.

7

Parliament's Battle over Repeal

WORD of American resistance to the Stamp Act had reached Britain promptly. A heated debate over the wisdom of the act ensued, first in the press and among the people and then, starting in December, 1765, in Parliament itself.

The first bad news came from colonial merchants, who wrote their English counterparts lamenting the disastrous effects the act would have on commerce. The letters often had a strong impact because of the affectionate regard that existed between many colonials and their associates in Britain. These letters were followed by reports from royal officials—from the lowliest customs officers, from the governors of colonies, from military commanders like General Gage, and from naval officers on station in American waters. These reports, on the whole, gave a vivid and accurate picture of the colonies as being in a state close to open rebellion.

At first, the rising flood of letters and petitions from merchants who anticipated—or had already begun to experience—heavy losses, created a disposition to repeal the obnoxious act. However, as evidence accumulated of colonial defiance, the destruction of property, the persecution of Crown officers, and the increasingly bold claims for colonial rights, the attitude of the British government and of many members of Parliament hardened. At first, the news of violent demonstrations against the Stamp Act caused little concern. The English were used to riots; they were common occurrences. But when the May, 1765, resolutions passed by the Virginia assembly reached England, asserting the colonies' right to tax themselves, official Britain took notice, proclaiming the resolutions "a daring attack upon the constitution of the country" and "a matter of utmost importance to the kingdom and the Legislature of Great Britain."

There were also numerous public expressions of indignation, especially in the conservative Tory press. "An American rioter and rebel," one correspondent wrote, "thinks he has a right to defraud the customs, to perjure himself at the Custom-house, to tar and feather Custom-house Officers. . . . But the laws of nature, that give such surprising rights to the American traitors, give no rights of retaliation to the King's Officers."

Another correspondent wrote that England would run "the risque of ruin, by transferring too much of its own freedom to its remote colonies," and pictured the Sons of Liberty as drunken louts who "roared against oppression and tyranny . . . and staggered home with impunity, swearing they were in danger of slavery, while every one they met, who did not join in their cry, was in danger of a broken head." The famous literary figure Dr. Samuel Johnson was equally contemptuous of those "incendaries" who, wearing the cloak of liberty, "hope to rob in the tumults of a conflagration, and toss brands among a rabble passively combustible." If the "fractious demagogues" who lead the mob were caught and hanged, Johnson wrote, "all would be well." To most Englishmen, the colonists were a contentious rabble who enjoyed every privilege of being Englishmen but resisted every duty. (Ironically, while the British saw James Otis as a "red-hot Provincialist" who had only to blow a whistle to summon up "their High Mightinesses, the Mob," Otis was in fact doing his best to cool the mob's hasty ardor.)

In July, 1765, George III had called on Charles Watson-Wentworth, the young Lord Rockingham, to form a new government. Thus it was the inexperienced and rather indecisive Rockingham who had to face the colonial uproar over the Stamp Act.

The new Rockingham ministry faced a host of nagging problems. The curtailment of American trade had already had a deadening impact on Britain's economy. In Manchester, Leeds, Nottingham, and other industrial towns, thousands of workmen were already unemployed. To force the colonists to capitulate would, it was increasingly clear, require a major military and naval effort, and that at the very moment when the country was still heavily burdened by the enormous costs of the French and Indian War. It would be self-defeating to pay out vast sums to collect the relatively modest revenue anticipated by the Stamp Act. Nonetheless the conservatives breathed fire and destruction. The colonists, they said quite accurately, were in rebellion, and the rebellion with all its "clamorous bawlings" must be suppressed. It would be fatal to Great Britain "to talk big at the Courts of Madrid and Paris and be Timid and Pusillanimous at Boston and Rhode Island." There was a general view that Boston was the source of infection. A good cannonading might cure Boston of its distemper and bring the other colonies to their senses.

When Parliament met on December 17, 1765, lines were clearly drawn between those who wished to use force to put down the colonists and those who were determined to repeal the Stamp Act. The champions of force were those who, in the words of the British historian W. E. H. Lecky, believed that "it was the right and duty of the Imperial Legislature to determine in what proportions the different parts of the Empire should contribute to the defence of the whole, and to see that no one part evaded its obligations and unjustly transferred its share to the others. The conduct of the colonies, in the eyes of these politicians, admitted of no excuse or palliation. The disputed right of taxation was established by a long series of legal authorities, and there was no real distinction between internal and external taxation. . . . It was a simple truth that England governed her colonies more liberally than any other country in the world. They were the only existing colonies which enjoyed real political liberty." The colonies had grown in size and prosperity at an astonishing rate under the benign protection of the mother country. Yet Britain's reward for these benefactions was a refusal on the colonies' part to pull their share of the load, a refusal accompanied by violent and treasonable actions. If Parliament now gave way, it could never hope to re-establish its legislative authority over its insolent subjects across the ocean. Moreover, the bad example of the North American colonies could infect Great Britain's other possessions in the Indies, East and West.

Such were the arguments from principle. But the supporters of Rockingham, who included virtually all the followers of Pitt, relied for much of their support on the merchant and manufacturing class. They were determined to be realistic in their approach. A statute designed to produce a revenue had produced instead trouble. It was only practical common sense to remedy the matter as promptly as possible. It was foolish to make too much of a few distant disturbances when riots were a fact of everyday life. They were best understood as an "effervescence of liberty," a "favourable crisis by which nature throws off the peccant humors in the body politic." When the debates over the repeal of the Stamp Act began, William Pitt, now Lord Chatham, rose from his sickbed to defend the rights of the colonists.

William Pitt, the Elder, is one of the most striking figures in English history. He was perhaps the greatest of all Parliamentary orators and leaders—mercurial, flamboyant, of enormous personal magnetism, a charismatic statesman of the highest order. It was above all as an orator that he had exerted his influence and worked his will. As the historian Lecky, in his ornate nineteenth-century style, says of Pitt: "He possessed every personal advantage that an orator could desire—a singularly graceful and imposing form, a voice of wonderful compass and melody . . . an eye of such piercing brightness and such commanding power that it gave an air of inspiration to his speaking, and added a particular terror to his invective." Pitt depended in debate on inspiration, speaking extemporaneously or from brief notes. In Horace Walpole's words, "Though no man knew so well how to say what he pleased, no man ever knew so little what he was going to say"; and Lord Lyttleton recalled: "His words have sometimes frozen my blood into stagnation and some-times made it pace in such a hurry through my veins that I could scarce support it."

For Pitt to undertake to speak in behalf of the American colonies was in itself an act of great drama, heightened by his retirement from politics, his illness, and the rumor of periodic madness or aggravated eccentricity. Pitt at first spoke, as was his custom, in a voice so low that it was difficult to hear him, and it was not clear to his auditors whether he had strength to continue. But he gathered energy, and soon he could be heard in every part of the House. He had been too ill at the time of the passage of the Stamp Act, he said, to speak against it, though he would have willingly been carried to the House on his bed, "so great was the agitation of my mind for the consequences!" The question of American taxation was "a subject of greater importance than ever engaged the attention of this house!" The only possible exception was the debate, "near a century ago," that produced the Revolution Settlement and confirmed the Bill of Rights.

Honor was a false guide, he declared. It was his opinion that since the colonies were not represented in Parliament, "this kingdom has no right to lay a tax upon the colonies. . . . They are the subjects of this kingdom, equally entitled with yourselves to all the natural rights of mankind and the peculiar privileges of Englishmen. . . . The Americans are the sons, not the bastards of England. Taxation is no part of the governing or legislative power. . . . The distinction between legislation and taxation is essentially necessary to liberty. . . ." "Some have the idea," Pitt continued, "that the colonies are virtually represented in this house. I would fain to know by whom an American is represented here?" Certainly the peers in the House of Lords did not represent him, nor did any member of Parliament. "The idea of a virtual representation of America in this house, is the most contemptible idea that ever entered into the head of a man—it does not deserve a serious refutation." The various legislative assemblies of America have, Pitt declared, "ever been in possession of the exercise of this, their constitutional right, of giving and granting their own money. They would have been slaves if they had not enjoyed it. At the same time, this kingdom, as the supreme governing and legislative power, has always bound the colonies by her laws, by her regulations, and restrictions in trade, in navigation, in manufactures—in every thing, except that of taking their money out of their pockets without their consent.

"Here I draw the line."

After a long pause, Secretary of State Conway rose. Having waited to see if anyone else wished to answer the honorable gentleman, he could only say that he entirely agreed with him, but he wished to correct a false impression left by Lord Chatham's remarks. The implication was that the members of Parliament had not been kept informed of the extent and seriousness of colonial resistance. "I can assure the House," he declared, "the first accounts were too vague and imperfect to be worth the notice of parliament."

Grenville rose to give the rebuttal. "Great Britain protects America," Grenville said, "and America is bound to obedience." It was captious to talk as though there were any valid legal distinction between legislation and taxation. The colonies had, in effect, been asked by Parliament to make a modest contribution toward "an expence arising from themselves"—the French and Indian War—and in return "they renounce your authority, insult your officers, and break out, I might almost say, into open rebellion." The seditious spirit of the colonies,

Grenville continued, "owes its birth to the factions in this house." In the very warning of members like Barré and Conway against taxing the colonies, there was contained an incentive to colonial resistance.

When Grenville finished speaking, several members got up to reply, Pitt among them. The cries of "Mr. Pitt, Mr. Pitt" were so prolonged that the speaker was forced to call the House to order. After a debate over whether it was protocol for Pitt to speak again on the same topic, Pitt was allowed to continue. "The gentleman [Grenville] tells us America is obstinate; America is almost in open rebellion. I rejoice that America has resisted. Three million of people so dead to all the feelings of liberty, as voluntarily to submit to be slaves, would have been fit instruments to make slaves of the rest." He had not, Pitt told the House, come "with a statute book doubled down in dog-ears to defend the cause of liberty." He would leave the finer points of the law to Grenville. "But, for the defence of liberty upon a general principle, upon a constitutional principle, it is a ground on which I stand firm; on which I dare meet any men. . . ."

Grenville had made much, Pitt said, of the debt the colonies owed the mother country as a consequence of the late war. Pitt suggested that a fairer way of looking at the matter would be to compute "the profits to Great Britain from the trade of the colonies, through all its branches" at two million pounds a year. This was the sum that carried England successfully through the war. "You owe this to America. This is the price that America pays you for her protection." England had the power, Pitt continued, to "Crush America to atoms," but she would pay a heavy price if she tried it. "America, if she fell, would fall like the strong man. She would embrace the pillars of the state, and pull down the constitution with her. Is this your boasted peace? Not to sheath the sword in its scabbard, but to sheath it in the bowels of your countrymen. . . . The Americans have not acted in all things with prudence and temper. They have been wronged. They have been driven to madness by injustice. Will you punish them for the madness you have occasioned? Rather let prudence and temper come first from this side. I will undertake for America, that she will follow the example. . . . Upon the whole, I will beg leave to tell the house what is really my opinion. It is, that the Stamp Act be REPEALED ABSOLUTELY, TOTALLY, and IMMEDIATELY. . . ."

The speech was Pitt in his great style, biting, brilliant, impassioned. It thrilled his listeners, or those favorable to the government, and of course delighted Americans. That the greatest statesman of his time, already a hero to the colonists, should have espoused their cause, using their own arguments, embellished and exalted by his rhetorical powers, was enchanting. It renewed their pride once more in being Englishmen; it strengthened their resolve and filled them with confidence in their own fortitude and devotion to liberty.

Pitt was supported by Lord Camden, the greatest legal figure of the day, who insisted that taxation was not among the general rights of legislation and that taxation and representation were, indeed, inseparable. "This position," he declared, "is founded on the laws of nature; nay, more, it is itself an eternal law of nature. For whatever is a man's own is absolutely his own. No man has a right to take it from him without his consent, either expressed by himself or [his] representative. Whoever attempts to do it attempts an injury. Whoever does it commits a robbery."

There clearly seemed to be a preponderance of Englishmen in favor of repeal, and this was equally clearly the disposition of the majority of the Rockingham ministry. However, Rockingham had been forced to include in his cabinet Charles Townshend and several other persons allied more with Grenville than with the new government. These men were strong supporters of the taxation of the colonies. Robert Henley, Earl of Northington, spoke for this faction, delivering a tirade against the colonies. Lord Northington declared, "if they withdraw allegiance, you must withdraw protection, and then the little State of Genoa or the kingdom of Sweden may soon overrun them."

In these circumstances, the policy of Rockinghamites was to appease the opponents of repeal by the so-called Declaratory Act, which stated that the Parliament of Great Britain clearly "had, hath and of right ought to have full power and authority to make laws and statutes of sufficient force and validity to bind the colonies and the people of America in all cases whatsoever." Parliament went on to condemn as unlawful the resolutions of colonial assemblies that denied the authority of Commons to tax them.

Despite the Declaratory Act—and the fact that the only alternative to repealing the Stamp Act seemed to be armed conflict—the debate in Parliament was long and bitter. The members of Parliament who had received royal patronage upheld King George's opinion that repeal— giving in to the colonies—would demean Great Britain. Finally, Rockingham went to the king and persuaded him to withdraw his objection to repeal. The king reluctantly wrote that he thought "the Repealing infinitely more eligible than Enforcing, which could only tend to widen the breach between this Country & America"; it was a move the king came to regret as the worst mistake of his reign.

With this final barrier removed, repeal, accompanied by the Declaratory Act, was finally passed by a majority of two hundred votes. There was general approval in England, and Edmund Burke, the great spokesman for the Whigs, described repeal as "an event that caused more universal joy throughout the British dominions than perhaps any other that can be remembered."

Little was said about the Declaratory Act. Lord George Sackville, a member of the Rockingham party, writing to American friends, put the matter bluntly: "You should know that the great obstacle in the way of the ministers has been unhappily thrown in by yourselves—I mean the intemperate proceedings of various ranks of people on your side of the water—and that the difficulties of the repeal would have been nothing if you had not by your violence in word and action awakened the honour of Parliament, and thereby involved every friend of the repeal in the imputation of betraying the dignity of Parliament. This is so true that the Act would certainly not have been repealed if men's minds had been not in some measure satisfied with the Declaration of Right."

The Declaratory Act, then, was the price required for the repeal of the Stamp Act. The Duke of Richmond, a leading member of the Rockingham ministry, put the issue simply. The only reason he had supported the Declaratory Act "was to obtain repeal of the Stamp Act. Many people of high principles would never . . . have been brought to repeal the Stamp Act without it; the number of those who opposed that repeal, even as it was, was very numerous."

When Benjamin Franklin was asked by a committee of the House of Commons whether his fellow Americans would be satisfied with repeal of the Stamp Act even if accompanied by the Declaratory Act stating the right of Parliament to tax the colonies, he replied: "I think the resolutions of right will give them very little concern, if they are never attempted to be carried into practice."

News of the repeal of the Stamp Act was greeted with jubilant celebrations in America. Church bells rang wildly, guns were fired, bands played, and subscriptions were circulated in several colonies to erect statues of Pitt. Everywhere there was a profound sense of relief that expressed itself in exuberant mirthmaking and carousing.

The fact was that many colonists, perhaps most, although they had been carried along on the emotional currents of the resistance to the Stamp Act, had been badly frightened at finding themselves, quite suddenly, in virtual revolt against the mother country. The vast majority certainly did not intend to have it happen again. They had come to the brink, and the view of the abyss had not been attractive. It could be argued that it took the colonists ten years to get their nerve back (and many never did).

Mixed in with the fervent expressions of loyalty and devotion, "of the warmest Sentiments of Duty and Affection to your Majesty's sacred Person and Government," was a touch of the triumphant, a hint of arrogance, or at least self-congratulation. The colonists had, after all, refused to obey a statute of Parliament, had defied the mother country, and had forced that proud parent to capitulate. One indignant Tory wrote, "Every dirty fellow, just risen from his kennel, congratulated his neighbour on their glorious *victory over England.*" This victorious spirit was expressed in a popular song:

> In spite of each parasite, each cringing slave,
> Each cautious dastard, each oppressive knave,
> Each gibing ass, that reptile of an hour,
> The supercilious pimp of abject slaves in power.
> We are met to celebrate in festive mirth,
> The day that give our freedom second birth.
> That tell us, British Grenville never more
> Shall dare usurp unjust, illegal power,
> Or threaten America's free sons with chains,
> While the least spark of ancient fire remains.

In Boston, joyful patriots gathered at the Liberty Tree and fired a salute with two fieldpieces. At night all good patriots put candles in their windows to express their delight at news of the repeal, and some of those who failed to do so had rocks crash through the windows. It was appropriate that Boston, a leader in the fight against the stamps, should produce the most spectacular celebration. In addition to the usual cannons, guns, bells, flags, and illuminations, the Sons of Liberty built on the Boston Common "a magnificent pyramid, illuminated with 280 Lamps." The four upper stories were ornamented with figures of the king and queen and fourteen "of the worthy Patriots who have distinguished themselves by their Love of Liberty." On the top of the pyramid was a round box of fireworks, and a hundred yards away was another stage from which fireworks were discharged. The next tier, supported by Doric columns, bore a poem written for the occasion:

> O thou whom next to Heav'n we most revere,
> Fair LIBERTY: thou lovely Goddess hear:
> Have we not woo'd thee, won thee, held thee long,
> Lain in thy Lap and melted on thy Tongue;
> Thro' Death and Dangers rugged Paths persu'd,
> And led thee sailing to this SOLITUDE:
> Hid thee within our Hearts most golden Cell,
> And brav'd the Powers of Earth and Powers of Hell.
> GODDESS: we cannot part, thou must not fly,
> Be SLAVES: we dare to scorn—dare to die.
> Our FAITH approv'd, our LIBERTY restor'd,
> Our Hearts bend grateful to our sov'r'gn Lord,
> Hail darling Monarch, by this act endear'd.
> Our firm Affections are thy best Reward. . . .

The poem went on to say that if George III ever found himself menaced by enemies, he could be confident that he might "To this Asylum stretch thine happy Wing,/ And we'll contend who best shall love our KING." These sentiments would doubtless have startled that monarch had he read them.

During the day, the houses displayed colors and pennants, flags and banners, and many trees were festooned with ribbons and bright cloths. John Hancock, the richest merchant in Boston, who had been frequently at odds with the customs officials and royal authorities of the province, had the most grandly illuminated house of all, with his own display of fireworks and a large keg of Madeira wine set out for public refreshment.

At dusk the displays began with the firing of twelve rockets in a marvelous shower of sparks that made the onlookers gasp. And then came more and more in inexhaustible profusion: "The Air was filled with Rockets—the Ground with bee-hives and Serpents," and pinwheels scattered showers of sparks in every direction. James Otis and other gentlemen whose houses were adjacent to the Common kept open house, and the ladies and gentlemen strolled from one handsome establishment to another, drinking innumerable toasts to liberty. At eleven o'clock sharp, the horizontal wheel of fireworks on the top of the pyramid was set off, ending in "the discharge of sixteen dozen serpents that twisted and writhed in the air." Thus the celebration, conducted "with the utmost Decency and good Order, not a reflection cast on any Character," came to a happy end, marred only by the fact that the pyramid caught fire from one of the candles that illuminated it and burned to the ground with the portraits of the king and queen, an event in which the more apprehensive might have seen an omen.

In Philadelphia, the long-awaited official word was brought by Captain Wise of the *Minerva*. The "glorious tidings" were read to an enthusiastic crowd at the London Coffee House; a deputation waited on Captain Wise, gave a present to the ship's company for bringing such welcome news, and conducted the captain, with colors flying, to the London Coffee House, where a large punch bowl was ready. The captain drank "prosperity to America" and was presented with a gold lace hat in honor of the occasion. A special "extraordinary" supplement to the *Pennsylvania Journal and Weekly Advertiser* was printed bearing the good news in a handsome broadside. The next night the town was splendidly illuminated, a grand bonfire was built, and "many barrels of beer [were given] to the populace." The "principal inhabitants" of Philadelphia threw an elegant entertainment at the State House, presided over by the mayor, and after dinner twenty-one toasts were drunk, starting with one to the king, and including the present ministers, the Houses of Parliament, "the glorious and immortal Mr. Pitt," "America's friends in Great Britain," "the Virginia Assembly," "Daniel Dulany," and, finally, "The Liberty of the Press in America." Seven guns were fired after each toast, the bells of the city were rung, free beer was again distributed to the populace, and the gentlemen present resolved to buy handsome new suits "of the manufacture of England" and give the homespun ones they had been wearing as protest against the Stamp Act to the poor. There is no record of the response of the poor to this magnanimous gesture.

In Charles Town, South Carolina, Henry Laurens was away when the Sons of Liberty ordered the houses of the town illuminated. In his absence Mrs. Laurens, as her husband wrote a friend, "was as brilliant as anybody—& saved her Bacon." Laurens himself, as with many who had defended the right of Parliament to tax the colonies, was uncertain as to the motives that lay behind repeal, and not confident about "the durability of our present state of happiness."

And so it went from colony to colony, an enraptured orgy of celebration and delight. It was a revealing display; in this release from long months of fear and tension, the colonists turned, in a touching desire to affirm their Englishness, to the figure of the king. They did not know or did not care to know that he favored their suppression by whatever means necessary. Of all those in England who were unmoved by the appeal for colonial liberties, there were few, ironically, less sympathetic than the king. All the autocratic tendencies of this ambitious and headstrong monarch, frustrated by the protections surrounding Parliament, came to focus on the colonies. These he wished, so far as Parliament might allow him, to bring to heel. But the colonists were determined to see him as a symbol of all that they loved and honored in the motherland, their generous and considerate master, the champion of their rights. Such misunderstandings are never helpful. Perhaps it would have made little difference if the colonists had possessed a more accurate grasp of the facts of the matter. That they so grossly misread them was certainly no help in the conflicts and frictions that were, inevitably, to follow the brief honeymoon of the Stamp Act repeal.

For the moment, though, everything was happiness and serenity. John Adams noted in his diary, "The repeal of the Stamp Act has hushed into silence almost every popular clamor, and composed every wave of popular disorder into a smooth and peaceful calm." And that was the way the Sons of Liberty wished it to be. They were determined to develop the means of guiding and controlling the activities of "the populace." The memory of two frightening nights of rioting and violence remained with them quite vividly.

Moreover, many of them read the provisions of the Declaratory Act more carefully and thoughtfully than their fellow citizens, and while they participated cheerfully in the festivities marking the demise of the Stamp Act, they had few illusions about its significance. George Mason, the Virginia planter-lawyer, spoke for these when he parodied the British attitude: "We have, with infinite Difficulty and Fatigue got you excused this one Time; pray be a good boy for the future; do what your Papa and Mamma bid you, & hasten to return to them your most grateful Acknowledgements for condescending to let you keep what is your own; and then all your Acquaintances will love you, & praise you, & give you pretty things. . . ." Mason then continued, "Is not this a little ridiculous, when applyed to three Millions of as loyal & useful Subjects as any in the British Dominions, who have been only contending for their Birth-right, and have now only gained, or rather kept, what cou'd not, with common Justice, or even Policy, be denied them?" The Virginia House of Burgesses recognized that the matter was a powder keg and proposed that the Declaratory Act be laid upon the table. The members of the assembly could then "without mentioning anything of the Proceedings of Parliament . . . enter upon their journals, as strong Declarations of their own Rights as Words can express. Thus one Declaration of Rights will stand against another, and Matters will remain in *Status quo.*"

There the matter rested for the time being. The colonies were grateful for what turned out to be, in a sense, only a stay of execution. Those responsible for the direction of British policy were somewhat chafed at having had to concede for practical reasons what they firmly adhered to on theoretical grounds: the supreme authority of Parliament over the colonies *in all cases whatsoever.* The two parties to the dispute, England and her American colonies, were at the end as far apart as they had been at the beginning. Appearances, as it turned out, were deceiving. What had happened was that a full-blown revolution had been interrupted by a truce; neither party had budged an inch. One party (Great Britain) had reluctantly yielded to the argument of expediency. The other had interpreted this as they wished, that is to say, as capitulation.

The immediate reaction was of gratitude and loyalty, but things were never to be as they had been before. Royal governors found that the king's subjects, while constantly affirming their devotion to the Crown, were more fractious and intractable than ever. Not only were the colonists strengthened in the conviction that they could wrest concessions from Parliament when they deemed it necessary to do so, but also many of those colonists and royal officials who had supported the powers of Parliament and the Crown at great risk to their lives and fortunes felt undermined by repeal. "The Great Witless Vulgar," the Tory *Boston Post* declared, were "following, huzzaing, and adoring" their leaders, who, in turn, were "indefatigably stabbing the most distinguished virtuous characters—poisoning the minds of the people— sapping and assaulting the whole structure of our government." In Massachusetts the new customs commissioner was called "an infamous pimp" by the patriot press, and of the thirty-two supporters of the Stamp Act in the Massachusetts Great and General Court, most were voted out of office in the next election.

The Acts of Trade and Navigation, which the colonists had borne with relatively good spirit, now seemed more oppressive than before; and of course there had been no repeal of the Sugar Act, or more accurately the Revenue Act, which was quite clearly a form of taxation—external as opposed to internal, but still a tax for all that. The colonists were faced with that old nagging dilemma again—what to do about acts ostensibly to regulate trade but actually to produce a revenue. When was regulation of trade de facto taxation? This problem proved, in the end, to be insoluble.

8

The Stamp Act in Retrospect

Davıd Ramsay, one of the first historians of the Revolution (who was also an actor in the remarkable drama of which he wrote), called the Stamp Act "the hinge of the Revolution," and so it certainly was. Everything that followed after the Stamp Act and its repeal was an extended re-enactment of the turbulent events surrounding that fateful statute. When John Adams stated that the Revolution had taken place in the hearts and minds of Americans before the actual military struggle itself took place, he was assuredly thinking, in large part, of the effects of the Stamp Act.

In retrospect, it is clear that the colonists reacted to the Stamp Act in a way that virtually no one had foreseen. Moreover that reaction, far from being a carefully manipulated response, was one of the most striking popular movements in modern history. There is abundant evidence, if one chooses to look at it, that the reaction to the Stamp Act was a response primarily of the people, that is to say the ordinary citizens of the various colonies. Members of the colonial aristocracy were neither the creators nor the directors of the so-called mobs. It would be naive to believe that a few dozen such individuals in each colony could, in the space of a few weeks, have produced such a unanimous sentiment in opposition to the Stamp Act. It was they, for the most part, who feared the fury of the mob and did their best, albeit intermittently, to dampen that fury. This class of patriots turned out the essays and pamphlets that argued the colonial case in learned fashion. Direct action was not, with a few exceptions, their style. Many of them certainly joined the crowds who coerced stamp distributors into resigning their commissions, and more of them gave moral support, but there is little evidence that they formed or led such demonstrations.

The passage of the Stamp Act brought home to Americans of every colony and of every rank and condition their state of powerlessness and their dependence on the Parliament of Great Britain. This intolerable sense of subordination welded the people together, revealing that a remarkably heterogeneous collection of persons spread out over a vast extent of territory—and with, in many cases, very different origins, traditions, customs, and ideals—had become a people or, more properly, were capable of being almost instantly transformed into "a people." The evidence is in the rhetoric. In the space of a few weeks the colonists stopped talking of "our colony," or "our province" and began speaking of "our poor degraded country," and of themselves as "Americans" rather than as New Hampshire men or Virginians or Marylanders. They were still provincials, of course, and very conscious of being so, but they were suddenly conscious of belonging, in a profound sense, to the larger category of Americans, and they found this an intoxicating experience. For the first time a current of sympathy and mutual affection flowed from colony to colony. Ideas and actions spawned in one province were quickly and enthusiastically adopted in another. Massachusetts praised the boldness and energy of the Virginia resolves, and Virginia acclaimed the courage and enterprise of the patriots of Rhode Island.

These people might have accepted a limited, defined, "constitutional" subordination, at least for some years to come. But a vague, indefinite, and, in plain terms, an absolute dependence they could not and would not accept. It was utterly inconsistent with that sense of their own worth and dignity that had grown up as a consequence of their impressive achievements in making civilized life flourish where only savages and wild beasts had been before. The whole course of history indicates that one of the most potent bases of common action is a common sense of unjust subordination. The constitutional arguments were, for the great majority of Americans, secondary.

Something more must also be said about the "mobs" who made the Stamp Act impossible to enforce. The large assemblies of the citizens who gathered in Boston or Providence or New York were not mobs in the ordinary sense of collections of volatile and alienated individuals, committing out of rage and frustration acts of wanton violence. Everv· one who commented on the composition of the mobs noted that they contained many of "the better sort," and were not to be confused with the rabble of apprentices, drunken sailors, and city riffraff who made up the typical waterfront brawl. It might be more realistic to call them "guerrilla armies," or "civilian irregulars." Their actions were not spontaneous or casual but carefully planned and organized, often days in advance. Word was systematically spread through the city and neighboring countryside. Entertainment in the form of patriotic pageants was planned, and refreshments often were served. Destruction was almost never random: rather it was directed at a few carefully chosen targets, typically the houses of individuals who had been chosen as stamp distributors, or of customs officials whose actions had aroused popular resentment.

This reflection brings us to a final fact about the anti-Stamp Act demonstrations. In dozens of forays in which the lives of stamp distributors and Crown officers were often threatened and considerable property destroyed, no life was lost. No rioter was shot by British soldiers, and no supporter of the Stamp Act or royal official was killed. This fact should tell us a good deal about the nature of the colonial resistance.

The final question that should be asked is this: Could the colonists have prevented the Stamp Act from taking effect by lawful means? Was the violence against persons and property necessary? It seems clear that only coercion could have prevented the Stamp Act from taking effect on the first of November, 1765. All the indignant essays, editorials, and pamphlets in the world could not have accomplished that. If rendering the Stamp Act null and void was the *desideratum,* it could not have been accomplished without a course of violence dramatic enough to attract universal attention.

The point is that the Stamp Act crisis was, in effect, a bloodless revolution in which Americans made clear that they were unwilling, regardless of the consequences, to obey a noxious law passed by Parliament. They made this fact clear by behavior that, strictly speaking, was treasonous: they rejected the authority of Great Britain. The fact that they did so in the name of the rights of Englishmen, or from the most exalted motives, cannot obscure the fact that their actions constituted a rebellion.

But this was clear only later. The great mass of colonists were not, in any event, rising up to defeat a particular Parliamentary statute so much as to make it dramatically clear that they were unwilling to accept the position of unlimited dependence and subordination, which was symbolized for them by the Stamp Act. They gave the mother country a warning so unmistakably clear that only a king and ministers of particular shortsightedness and obduracy could have failed to get the message. Perhaps it would be fairer to say that they got the message but were determined nevertheless, when the opportunity next presented itself, "to reduce the colonies to that proper state of subordination which ought to exist between the mother country and her colonies."

If there is one immutable law of history, it is this: when the response is out of all proportion to the provocation, look further for the causes than the apparent facts of the matter. The response of the colonists to the Stamp Act was out of all proportion to the provocation—or so it certainly seemed to virtually all Englishmen, and to many startled colonists as well. The Stamp Act was, therefore, not so much the cause as the occasion of the riots. The cause was to be found in the fact that the colonists were no longer willing to accept a completely subordinate and dependent relationship to the mother country. That was the issue and nothing else. What was of the greatest importance, of course, was how the issue was conceived, what ideological and theoretical garments it was clothed in, what rationalizations were advanced in its defense or explanation—in the name of what new visions of social and political order were people rallied to its standard.

Perhaps the most dramatic effect of the Stamp Act crisis on the patriot leaders was to impel them to sharpen and refine their own notions about the nature of constitutional government. In the decade between the Stamp Act and the outbreak of the Revolutionary War, the patriot leaders went to school with the greatest ancient and modern philosophers who considered the nature of the universe and the proper forms of government. They ransacked all the leading authorities on natural law, constitutional government, and individual rights. They read vast amounts of history and pondered its lessons. The hiatus that followed the repeal of the Stamp Act provided the patriot leaders with an opportunity to make themselves the most learned politicians in history.

The lawyers who were the theoreticians of the Revolution ranged first of all through English common law—Sir Edward Coke, Camden himself, Sir Matthew Hale, Sir Thomas Littleton, and a dozen others. Already familiar with classical authors, especially Cicero and Vergil, the American theorists read the great historians of the ancient world— Herodotus, Xenophon, Thucydides, Polybius, Tacitus, and Livy. Nurtured on John Locke, they practically committed him to memory. They read "the incomparable Harrington," particularly his *Oceana,* and "the divine Hooker," Locke's master. They read Algernon Sidney, the English martyr, whose works Jefferson judged "a rich treasure of republican principles, supported by copious and cogent arguments and adorned with the finest flowers of science . . . probably the best elementary book of principles of government, as founded in natural right, which has ever been published in any language."

It was Sidney, beheaded for his alleged part in a plot against the Crown and for his subversive writings, who had written: "That power is originally in the people; that the king is subject to the law of God, as he is a man; and to the people who make him, as he is a king; that the king ought to submit his interest to theirs since he is not superior to them in any other respect than that he is, by the consent of all of them, raised above any other. . . . The people may change or take away kings without breaking any yoke . . . the people must be judges of what happens between them and the king whom they did constitute." Sidney seemed to speak just as directly to the colonial cause when he wrote, "That which is not just, is not law; and that which is not law ought not to be obeyed. . . . The sanction that deserves the name of law, which derives not its excellency from antiquity, or from the dignity of the legislators, but from intrinsic equity and justice, ought to be made in pursuance of that universal reason to which all nations at all times owe an equal veneration and obedience."

Among the most important influences on the American theorists were the Scottish philosophers, who in the middle decade of the eighteenth century had made the University of Edinburgh the greatest center of scholarship in the world. Chief among these was Frances Hutcheson, whose *Moral Philosophy* had this to say about the relations between the colonies and Great Britain: "If the plan of the mother country is changed by force or degeneration by degree from a safe, mild, and gentle limited power to a severe and absolute one . . . or if any colony is so increased in numbers and strength that they are sufficient by themselves for all good ends of a political union; they are not bound to continue in their subjection when it is grown so much more burdensome than was expected. . . . There is something . . . immaterial in supposing a large society sufficient for all the good purposes of an independent union, remaining subject to the direction and government of a distant body of men who know not sufficiently the circumstances and exigencies of this society. . . ."

And no less a personage than Lord Camden agreed that England must sooner or later give up her colonies. "It is impossible," he wrote, "that this petty island can continue in dependence that mighty continent, increasing daily in numbers and strength. . . . To protract the time of separation to a distant day is all that can be hoped." Meantime, Camden said, England should so manage the affairs of the colonies that when the time of departure came it would take place in a spirit of mutual good will and affection.

The colonists found the Scottish theorists particularly sympathetic because they, like the colonists, stood in a dependent relationship to England, and, again like the colonists, their dominant spirit was that of the radical Protestantism of the founder of Presbyterianism, John Knox. Hutcheson was the forerunner of what came to be called the Scottish Common Sense School of Philosophy. The notion that common sense was grounded in morality was much admired by both Americans and Scotsmen, and it was encouraging to have it elevated to the status of a "philosophy." Another important Scot was Henry Home, Lord Kames, who held that there was nothing in the nature of man "that subjects him to the power of any, his Creator and his parents excepted. . . . Hence it is a principle embraced by the most solid writers that all men are born free and independent of one another."

Adam Ferguson and James Burgh were two other Scottish theorists who were widely read in the colonies. In his *Essay on the History of Civil Society* Ferguson stated, "The influence of laws, where they have any real effect on the preservation of liberty is not in any magic power descending from shelves that are loaded with books, but it is, in reality, the influence of men resolved to be free." James Burgh's *Political Disquisitions* were subscribed to by a distinguished group of Americans when they appeared in 1774. Burgh, after relating in great detail the venality and corruption of Parliament and the Court party of Great Britain, added, "I have exposed to your view some of the capital abuses and grievances which are sinking you into slavery and destruction. I have shown that as things go on, there will soon be very little left of the *British* constitution besides the name and the outward form." Whenever the executive or legislative power "endeavor to take away and destroy the property of the people or reduce them to slavery under arbitrary power, they put themselves into a state of war with the people, who are thereby absolved from any further obedience, and left to the common refuge which God hath provided for all men against force and violence."

It was not simply their reading—law, history, political and moral philosophy—that made the colonial lawyers the most learned men of their age, the most scholarly statesmen in the history of this or any other republic; it was the context in which their reading took place. The generation of revolutionary lawyers read with a special intensity; they searched through all the wisdom of the past to find a formula in the name of which the liberties of all Englishmen might be preserved. That transformation of consciousness, whose seeds lay in the slow unfolding of a new social order, and which had come to sudden flowering in the emotional hothouse of the Stamp Act crisis, opened them to an exhilarating new world of ideas, an unexplored intellectual empire that stretched as far as the mind could reach. Like schoolboys cramming for an examination, they devoured every book they could get their hands on that seemed to speak to their own peculiar situation. They gained, thereby, a vast access of power; they stepped forward, often quite self-consciously, to take a place in that same history of which they were such assiduous students, and in doing so they shed, almost casually, the limitations and inhibitions of provincials, of haphazardly trained and indifferently schooled colonials, and appeared as men able to hold their own intellectually in any company. The great Pitt was glad to be instructed by them, and Camden espoused their principles.

If lawyers represented this new power in its most evident and dramatic form, they were by no means alone. Americans, stirred to a new consciousness of their place and their role in the world as a consequence of the conflict with the mother country, were transformed from provincials to individuals aware of new creative energies in themselves and in their society.

David Ramsay in his history has a striking description of the capacities drawn forth by the Revolution. It "gave occasion for the display of abilities which, but for that event, would have been lost to the world. When the war began, the Americans were a mass of husbandmen [farmers], merchants, mechanics, and fishermen; but the necessities of the country gave a spring to the active powers of the inhabitants and set them on thinking, speaking, and acting in a line far beyond that to which they had been accustomed. While the Americans were guided by the leading strings of the mother country, they had no scope or encouragement to exertion. All the departments of government were established and executed for them, but not by them." The events of the Revolutionary era created new needs and opportunities. In Ramsay's words, "As they severally pursued their objects with ardour, a vast expansion of the human mind speedily followed."

Had Britain failed to repeal the Stamp Act, the military phase of the American Revolution would have started in 1766, with efforts by Parliament and the Crown to enforce the act with British troops met in turn by armed resistance on the part of the colonists. It is fortunate that this did not take place. Enormous strides were taken during the ten-year truce between the repeal of the Stamp Act and the skirmishes at Lexington and Concord.

The outcome of the revolutionary struggle would have been very different had the conflict between the colonies and the mother country reached its climax in 1765 instead of 1775. The ten intervening years provided time for the creation of a remarkably well-articulated set of political principles, and for the emergence and the training of an unusually gifted group of leaders, men of a profoundly conservative frame of mind who, when armed conflict came at last, were able to guide the first great democratic revolution of modern times through the troubled waters of revolutionary anarchism into the harbor of orderly, constitutional government. The American Revolution began in 1765 with resistance to the Stamp Act. It was then in its most radical phase; in the years that followed it became more and more moderate, more and more carefully tuned and modulated, more and more sophisticated in its ideology, and in its strategies as well as its tactics. The American Revolution thus is distinguished from other revolutions in that its most radical popular phase came first, its moderate phase last. The reverse has been true of most other revolutions. The English Civil War began with the Parliamentary independents and proceeded to the beheading of King Charles I. The French Revolution began with the Girondists and grew more radical each year. The Russian Revolution began with the Mensheviks and ended with the Bolsheviks. The American Revolution began with the riots occasioned by the Stamp Act and proceeded to the cautious resolves of the First Continental Congress.

The Sons of Liberty, from having been a radical underground organization of informal if not secret membership, developed into an organization with a large and respectable membership that included all levels of colonial society. Control of it was firmly in the hands of upper-class patriot leaders like James Otis, Sam and John Adams, John Dickinson, Joseph Galloway, Christopher Gadsden, and Henry Laurens. And the emphasis was as much social as political. Frequent patriotic rallies and gatherings were held in most of the colonies. Typical was a meeting of 350 Sons of Liberty at the Sign of the Liberty Tree Tavern in Dorchester, Massachusetts. The company overflowed the tavern, and two long tables were set for some 400 guests in an open field by Robinson's barn, under a sailcloth awning. John Dickinson's brother was an honored guest, and after the meal forty-five toasts were drunk in honor of John Wilkes. Then Mr. Balch, a famous local mimic, did several of his popular turns—"the lawyer's head" and "the Hunting of a Bitch fox." The company then joined in singing John Dickinson's "Liberty Song," written by the Pennsylvania patriot, and adjourned in high spirits. John Adams, who was present, noted in his diary, "This is cultivating the Sensations of Freedom. . . . Otis and [Samuel] Adams are politick, in promoting these Festivals, for they tinge the Minds of the People, they impregnate them with the sentiments of Liberty. They render the People fond of their Leaders in the Cause, and averse and bitter against all opposers."

But parties and festivals were not enough. There was, in addition, a vast amount of laborious and undramatic work to be done in organizing cadres of patriots. In later years John Adams wrote his son John Quincy a letter describing the techniques of political organization and control that he had learned during the revolutionary crisis from such mentors as his cousin Samuel Adams and James Otis. The revolutionary politician needed to know "1. The State of Parties in Religion, Government, Manners, Fashion. 2. The Leading Characters in Church and State. 3. The Machine, Arts and Channels by which Intelligence and Reports are circulated through the Town. 4. The Makers and Spreaders of Characters [in other words, the individuals whose support helped to establish aspiring politicians in the community]. 5. The State of the various Tradesmen and Mechanicks their Views designs and Projects. . . . The Characters of all the Clergymen of all denominations, Physicians, Surgeons, Apothecaries, Lawyers and Merchants of Eminence & shopkeepers. . . . 13. The State of Diversified Amusement Spectacles etc. 14. The various clubs. . . . 15. The Buffoons, the Merry Andrews, the story tellers, the Song Singers, Mimicks." All these were the "wheels Springs bags or Pins some of them dirty ones" that made the great machine of politics run. It was only by careful attention to detail that the patriot leaders could organize and direct public sentiment. Only by mastering such rudiments of political life could they sustain and control that enthusiasm for liberty so essential to a free people. Only by such means could they be sure that the next encroachment by Parliament on colonial liberties would be met with both unflinching resolution and moderation—a difficult combination.

Popular sentiment is notoriously volatile. The task of the patriot leaders in the years following the Stamp Act crisis was twofold. On the one hand they needed to establish control over popular sentiment so that it would never again manifest itself in such a tumultuous and dangerous outpouring as it had at the time of the Stamp Act, when the whole structure of colonial society was threatened with anarchy. Equally important, they had to sustain and organize popular sentiment in such a way as to turn the passionate protest of 1765 into a disciplined will to resist all assaults on colonial "liberties." Both tasks were vitally important. The latter was, if anything, the more difficult. Popular sentiment against Great Britain was never again to be as strong and as widespread as it had been at the time of the Stamp Act. The inevitable price paid by the patriot leaders for organization and control was a lowering of the political temperature and a loss of interest and support for the cause of colonial liberty among many colonists.

The people did not need to be taught revolutionary principles— they had given evidence enough of these—they needed to be instructed in the principles of free government. It must be said, therefore, that there were four stages of colonial resistance: theoretical formulation (James Otis, Daniel Dulany, et al.); passionate reaction (coercion, violence, mobbing); political organization; and, continuing on to the outbreak of war itself, popular education.

PART III

1

The British Blunder Again

WHILE patriot leaders worried about the best means of sustaining a proper zeal for colonial liberties in the face of détente, the British ministry was busy preparing another inflammatory issue. It decided to invoke a regulation, long on the books but seldom enforced, requiring the colonists to provide quarters and certain supplies for British troops stationed in their midst. As though this impolitic action were not enough, a new set of taxes were proposed, this time on specific articles imported into the colonies. The British ministry professed to believe that the opposition to the Stamp Act was based on the principle that Parliament had no right to impose *internal* taxes on the colonies, conceding thereby the right of Parliament to impose *external* taxes, those on trade. That this was a complete misreading of the position of the vast majority of those colonists who had so resolutely opposed the Stamp Act was soon to become evident.

What was perhaps most notable about the colonial reaction to both these ill-considered decisions on the part of the British government was that resistance was to be conducted this time with far greater restraint than had been shown at the time of the Stamp Act crisis. But with equal determination.

The fateful first moves that led to these events took place in the summer of 1766, only months after the repeal of the Stamp Act. The Rockingham ministry, never strong, fell apart, partly because of exhaustion from the Stamp Act debates. The government that succeeded Rockingham's was led by Augustus Henry Fitzroy, the Duke of Grafton, who had the special confidence of the king, and by the pro-American Pitt. Among the members of the cabinet were General Conway, who had made the original movement for the repeal of the Stamp Act, and William Petty, the Earl of Shelburne, who had been a friend to the Americans. The chancellor of the exchequer was Charles Townshend—known facetiously as "Champagne Charlie" because of his addiction to the bubbly—an able man when not in his cups. In a gesture designed to appease the Tories and the king, Sir Frederick North, a staunch defender of royal power, was included in the government. The colonists, it seemed, could hardly have asked for an administration more favorable to them.

But then trouble set in. Pitt's health took a turn for the worse, and he was forced to withdraw from active political life. In his absence, Townshend, the minister most hostile to the colonists and, as chancellor of the exchequer, the one best situated to harm their interests, became the strongest figure in the government.

Soon a vexing question surfaced—how to pay for the upkeep of the army, especially the troops stationed in America. There were those in the ministry (Charles Townshend was one) as well as in the colonies who believed that the scattering of soldiers about the colonies served little or no purpose in terms of defense against the Indians. Indeed, Lord Barrington, the secretary at war, had serious misgivings about a policy whose principal effect seemed to be the demoralization of the troops themselves in isolated posts where boredom and relaxed discipline had a bad effect on morale. Barrington, described by a fellow politician as a "frivolous, little-minded man" who had "no regard for the truth," had, however, no suggestions as to how the expenses of the army in North America should be defrayed.

While the debate was going on, word reached the British ministry that the New York legislature had refused to comply with that portion of the Mutiny Act, passed in 1765 to improve discipline in the British army, that directed that British troops in America be quartered at the expense of local citizens. This was the so-called Quartering Act, which stipulated that colonial authorities must provide the king's troops with barracks or billets and furnish them with "candles, firing, bedding, cooking utensils, salt and vinegar, and five pints of small beer or cider, or a gill of rum per man, per diem." In the spring of 1766, General Gage had begun to press the New York assembly for the supplies required under the Quartering Act. After some procrastination, that body provided five thousand pounds for quartering expenses. New Jersey followed suit, although protesting that the Quartering Act was "as much an Act for laying taxes on the inhabitants as the Stamp Act." Pennsylvania also complied.

While misgivings were voiced by a number of colonists about the constitutionality of the Quartering Act, there was a general disposition to provide the support stipulated by the act. Even Samuel Adams, although he too protested in a letter to Christopher Gadsden that the Quartering Act was as much a tax as the Stamp Act and should be resisted, added, "If a number[of soldiers] should happen to come into a Province through necessity and stand in Need of Supplys, as is the case at present here, is it not a Disgrace to us to suppose we should be so wanting in humanity, or in regard to our Sovereign as to refuse him the aid with our free Consent." The "free consent" was, for most colonists, the crucial issue.

The next year the New York assembly had second thoughts. The greater portion of British troops stationed in America were in New York. Thus the colony of New York was·being asked to bear an unfair burden. Having, as they saw it, complied with the Quartering Act in a spirit of generosity (rather than as an obligation) in 1766, they felt overburdened and declined to provide the required 1767 ration of "salt, vinegar and liquor."

Pitt himself, pro-American as he was, felt indignant over the action of the New Yorkers. From his sickbed he wrote Lord Shelburne, the minister in charge of colonial affairs, that a "spirit of infatuation has taken possession of New York. Their disobedience to the Mutiny Act will justly create a ferment here, open a fair field to the arraigners of America, and leave no room to any to say a word in their defence." "I foresee confusion will ensue," Pitt continued, "the merchants of New York . . . are doing the work of their worst enemies themselves. The torrent of indignation in Parliament will, I apprehend, become irresistible." A few days later, he wrote again of New York as having "drunk the deepest of the baneful cup of infatuation, but none [of the colonies] seem to be quite sober and in full possession of reason. It is a literal truth to say that the Stamp Act of most unhappy memory has frightened those irritable and umbrageous people quite out of their senses."

In Shelburne's report to the ailing Pitt, he wrote, "Though every-body is strongly for enforcing [the Quartering Act] nobody chooses to suggest the mode." A suggestion was shortly forthcoming, however from George Grenville, an advocate of strong measures to keep the colonies in line. Grenville urged in Parliament that a test oath be re-quired of every colonial official before he could undertake the duties of his office, stating that he admitted the right of Parliament to tax Amer-ica. Even Shelburne himself recommended Draconian measures, suggesting that a military officer be sent to govern New York with power "to act with force or gentleness as circumstances might make necessary," and authority to quarter troops in private houses if the assembly was uncooperative. In another letter to Pitt, Shelburne also suggested that the Quartering Act and the Declaratory Act be joined with a proviso that all past acts of resistance to British authority be pardoned, but that any such acts in the future would be punished. Anyone who spoke or wrote against the Quartering Act would be guilty of high treason and subject to trial in Great Britain if it seemed impossible to secure convictions in America.

Shelburne's ill-considered advice did not prevail, but the fact that one of the most influential members of the cabinet, generally considered an advocate of America, could seriously have proposed such stern measures is an indication of how badly the British ministers misjudged the temper of the colonists. Finally, Charles Townshend's proposal that all enactments of the New York assembly be suspended until they complied with the terms of the Quartering Act was adopted by the cabinet and cast in the form of a Parliamentary statute.

The determination of the ministry to enforce the Quartering Act in New York by such means was bad policy. There was in it clearly a measure of the punitive, and policies that are in part punitive are invariably bad policies. Enforcement of the Quartering Act was a wholly inadequate solution to the real problem of how to finance the army. The returns could not possibly be proportionate to the friction and irritation it would cause in the colonies where soldiers were already quartered (as in New York)—where, in fact, they performed no useful function and simply served to remind the colonists of the essentially arbitrary nature of British authority.

To many Americans, as to the great majority of Englishmen, the whole matter seemed simple enough: "The great Object," as an Ameri-can merchant in London wrote, "is the Reduction of the public Debt and the Encouragement of every Branch of Commerce, upon which the national Credit wholly depends." In the face of this practical problem, the continual prating of colonial agitators and malcontents about their precious liberties seemed captious. "It is, in some measure," William Strahan, a London merchant wrote his friend and associate, David Hall, "the unavoidable Consequence of our Liberty, which every now and then run into Licentiousness. But still, take for all in all, we are the happiest Nation this World ever contained. . . . I hope, before matters come to Extremity, the Nation will come to their senses, and not suffer a Fabric, the work of Ages, and the Envy of the rest of the World, to be materially injured. . . ."

When the Boston patriots heard about the suspension of the New York assembly for refusing to comply with the Quartering Act, they requested Bernard to call a special meeting of that colony's legislature, the Great and General Court, to consider what action might be taken in support of their sister colony. Bernard refused, whereupon the patriot leaders called a town meeting on October 28, 1767. Out of that meeting came a resolution encouraging local manufacture and proposing a "nonconsumption" agreement whereby the supporters of colonial liberty would refuse to purchase English goods. An extensive campaign to "buy American" was organized. Women were called on to sacrifice English finery, and it was recommended that whiskey, "a real American drink, by God," be substituted for rum. Americans would then be "a more hardy and manly race of people when our constitutions are no longer jaundiced nor our juices vitiated by abominable West Indian distillations." Tea made out of pine needles was recommended in place of imported tea. Pine needle tea was declared to "far surpass the teas of India, whether in fragrance, color or virtue." Since Americans depended primarily on England for homeopathic remedies, which had been consumed in large quantities since the earliest days of settlement, receipts for homemade drugs and medicines appeared in all the papers. "The dry bellyache or nervous colick" was a peculiarly American ailment (then as today), caused by the demanding pace of colonial life, the fierce competition, and nervous strain. It could be cured or moderated by that era's version of Tums—a compound containing fine-ground chalk and peppermint in water. The homespuns, so recently discarded, were donned once more, though whether they were retrieved from the poor is not recorded.

During the same 1766–67 session of Parliament that suspended the New York assembly, the problem of revenues that the Stamp Act had been designed to alleviate came again to the fore. The cost of the military establishment continued to rise, and in the view of some members of Parliament, America's recent mutinous behavior made a large army more necessary than ever. At the same time, the country members of Parliament, gentlemen of landed estates, had long complained about the burden of taxation and were certainly in no mood to see their load increased. And a recent tax on cider had produced riots in England and had helped to bring down the government that had proposed it.

In this atmosphere, Townshend undertook to attack the colonies for their miserly and intransigent spirit, deploring the repeal of the Stamp Act and ridiculing the notion that there was any real difference between internal and external taxes. Taunted by Grenville that despite his bold words he dared not tax the colonies, Townshend stamped his foot peevishly and cried, "I will, I will."

Charles Townshend's attitude of petulant irritation with the colonies was characteristic of the Tory British reaction to the repeal of the Stamp Act. The politicians closest to the king lost no opportunity to declare that it had been a cowardly accommodation that, instead of reconciling the colonists, had left them bolder and more intractable than ever. Thus, besides the perfectly apparent need for revenue, there was a growing feeling of vindictiveness on the part of many Englishmen toward the Americans.

Townshend had made his pledge to tax the colonies in January, 1767, less than a year after the repeal of the Stamp Act. In May he brought in his proposed legislation. In the meantime, the news from the colonies had served to stiffen the determination of many members of the House of Commons to put the colonists firmly in their place. In Massachusetts, the legislature—the Great and General Court—had proved most dilatory in compensating those royal officials who had suffered heavy property losses in the Stamp Act riots. The hectoring tone that Governor Bernard had taken with the delegates to the legislature was ill-designed to induce them to comply. The "respectable inhabitants [of this Town]" Bernard reminded them, "have already suffered much, in the Opinion of the world, for having been tame Spectators of the Violence committed in it." The governor urged them to "remove this Disgrace, without the least Delay, by ordering the Indemnification immediately to be made. . . ." The delegates replied that no formal application had been made to them for indemnification, but they would appoint a committee to look into the whole affair and make a report.

Bernard and other colonial governors sent a stream of letters to the secretary of state for the colonies and to other members of the government in London, all to much the same effect: The colonists, far from being humbly grateful for Parliament's repeal of the Stamp Act, were as difficult and contentious as ever. Reports of the abuse and harassment of customs officials and of defiance of the statutes of Parliament arrived in every mailbag from America.

Townshend's pledge to raise revenue by taxing the colonies was in direct defiance of the policy of the administration of which he was a part. It had been neither discussed nor authorized by the cabinet; it was his own unhappy inspiration. As the Duke of Grafton later wrote, no one, in the absence of Pitt himself, had enough power to force Townshend's dismissal. Under the circumstances, his dismissal might have brought down the government that had just been painstakingly patched together.

What followed had overtones of Greek tragedy: *Hubris,* or over-reaching pride, on the part of the mother country; obduracy on the part of her colonies; the same mistakes repeated as though nothing had been learned by all the recent turmoil. It is easy to imagine Greek divinities looking down on the scene with a certain cynical amusement. That nothing could be stopped or deflected was not owing to a want of time or consideration; to a proper understanding, by some people at least, of the realities of the situation; to lack of ample evidence of the consequences; to a knowledge of the means of effecting a sensible reconciliation; or on the other hand, to a spirit of tyranny, wickedness, or deliberate oppression. The fault was simply human perversity; the determination with which people cling to obsolete ideas, their willingness to sacrifice almost everything, including life itself, before surrendering some fatal prejudice, the adherence to which must inevitably bring their ruin.

The colonies were certainly not without fault; they were rude, contentious, devious, and ungrateful. But all their shortcomings were outweighed by the fact that they were contending for control of their own affairs, struggling to throw off a subordinate and dependent status for a position of dignity and consequence in the world. In the words of twentieth-century thinker Paul Goodman, "The excluded or repressed are always right in their rebellion, for they stand for our future wholeness."

It was small wonder that the British ministry misjudged the will and the capacity of the colonists to fight for their rights. Their experience with "the people" had been in the form of embittered mobs, of unemployed weavers, and of the desperate poor of the cities who were the principal victims of England's burgeoning industrialism. In addition, there were the desperate rural poor, men who burned hay ricks to express their rage and poached rabbits and fallow deer to keep from starving to death. That there might be a new kind of common man, or "peasant," or "lower order," hardly occurred to those upper-class Englishmen who controlled the machinery of government.

Thus when the farmers and mechanics of British America began to assert their determination to be "independent," hopefully within the British Empire, but independent in any case, the English had no frame of reference in which to place such an occurrence. Nothing in their experience prepared them to understand this phenomenon. The fact was that nothing like it had happened before in modern history—the movement of *a whole people*, or enough of them to make a revolution, to assert themselves on the stage of world history.

Beyond this, the members of Parliament knew that government was an intricate and demanding science that had been better mastered by the ruling class of Great Britain than by any other nation in modern history. In that great school of politics a Pitt, a Camden, a Burke had been nourished. Government was the business of gentlemen. It required, among other things, a proper sense of subordination among the rank and file of the population. To believe for a moment that contentious provincials and rural bumpkins could create the complex agencies of self-government was ridiculous on the face of it; as absurd as to believe that they could produce an army capable of standing against the finest soldiers in the world.

The British can hardly be blamed for their incomprehension. They could not have been expected to have penetrated a transformation in the nature of society and politics so profound that it is even today not fully comprehended. The new kind of consciousness produced by the Protestant Reformation and planted in the fertile soil of America had resulted in an individual who drew his strength from his membership in a faithful community, and whose values were so internalized that he moved, however modest his condition of life and his antecedents, with confidence and a sense of assurance into quite novel situations. Such individuals were able to form, in an astonishingly brief time, fresh combinations, communities, or organizations.

What was happening in brief was that, perhaps for the first time in history, the people were emerging. It was this rising of the people in what their British masters were disposed to refer to as "a Democratical phrenzy" that was probably the most striking fact of the American Revolution. This fact overshadowed all the immediate and specific issues and also, of course, confused them. The colonists were doing something so new in human experience that they could only explain it in terms of something old: a "fight to preserve their constitutional rights as Englishmen." They understood very little better than the British what they were up to. In a certain sense, it could be argued that the British understood better what the colonists were up to than the colonists did themselves. They perceived that the colonists wished independence, which the colonists themselves constantly denied. The British mistake was to vastly underestimate the depth and strength of this feeling, and to constantly console themselves with the notion that such sentiments were confined to a few ambitious demagogues who must capitulate to any resolute show of force.

That England should have repeatedly emphasized the ingratitude of the colonies is significant. The call for gratitude is the unmistakable signal that all moral authority has been dissipated; nothing is left but a generally fruitless appeal to gratitude. It is the cry of all parents who have lost, usually through their own obtuseness, the obedience of their children. And so Mother England mourned her ungrateful children, and was determined to punish them. Charles Townshend saw himself as the instrument of that chastisement. In the words of Edmund Burke: "The whole body of courtiers drove him onwards. They always talked as if the King stood in a sort of humiliated state until something of the kind should be done." Townshend was determined to vindicate his king.

The proposal that Townshend placed before Parliament was that the British forces in America should be reduced by half and the cost of maintaining them shifted to the colonists. In addition, since it was apparent that the dependence of most colonial officials on the assemblies of the respective colonies for their salaries seriously undermined their efficiency, Townshend wished to establish a colonial civil list of officers paid directly by the Crown. To finance these measures, special taxes were to be placed on a few English manufactured goods much in demand in the colonies—paper, painter's colors, glass, and tea; it was a modest enough proposal on the face of it.

Two acts that accompanied it and that were intended to facilitate its enforcement made it far more odious to the colonists. One bill provided for a Board of Commissioners of the Customs, with extensive powers to oversee the implementation of all laws regarding trade. In addition, to assist in enforcing these laws, the so-called "writs of assistance"—or in other words, general search warrants—were made legal.

The Townshend Duties were the swan song and only conspicous achievement of that politician. He died suddenly in September, 1767, a few months after the passage of the statute that insured him a dubious immortality. Certainly he was not without striking gifts. He was judged by many of his contemporaries to be one of the greatest orators in the House in an age of brilliant speakers. But all Townshend's gifts were frittered away because of his frivolousness of character and his moral obtuseness. His principal accomplishment was to revive colonial fears and animosities and thereby further disturb the already tense relationship between the colonies and the mother country.

Townshend's death created a new government crisis. Lord North, who had been brought into the Grafton ministry to please the king, now became, in the absence of Pitt, and with the support of the king, the most powerful figure in the government. Conway, Shelburne, and Pitt resigned, and a new cabinet was formed by North. The colonists were thereby left without powerful friends in the government. If there was in England a decisive moment, a turning point in the relations between the colonies and the mother country, it came with the collapse of the Pitt-Grafton ministry, friendly in the main to the colonists, and its replacement by Lord North. The new cabinet was made up almost exclusively of hard-liners who believed that the only way to handle the contentious colonists was to coerce them into obedience. To make matters worse, Wills Hill, the Earl of Hillsborough, a reactionary politician, became secretary of state for the colonies. To the new government fell the not uncongenial task of imposing the Townshend Duties.

The reaction in the colonies in 1767 to the Townsend Duties was a revealing one. Two years earlier the colonies had been on the brink of armed revolt over the Stamp Act. They had emphatically rejected the right of Parliament to tax them for purposes of raising a revenue, and they had hailed the repeal of the Stamp Act as a sign that Parliament accepted the validity of their arguments. Then, scarcely a year later, came new and more extensive taxes with the same object in view— raising a revenue. The colonial response was immediate and bitter, but in one striking respect different from the reaction to the Stamp Act: It was notably restrained. James Otis was quick to urge moderation, and in every colony, patriot leaders worked to direct popular feeling into channels of orderly protest. The patriot strategy was nonimportation agreements, rather than clubs and axes.

While the threat of violence was ever present, the exercise of it was notably infrequent. Colonial rhetoric was, to be sure, frequently violent, and Governor Bernard was the particular object of patriot hatred in Massachusetts. One of the Boston papers wrote of his "obstinate malice, diabolical thirst for mischief, effrontery, guileful treachery, and wickedness." The attorney general of the colony brought the editor before the Great and General Court under the charge of seditious libel, but the assembly refused to take any action. For a time there was talk of not allowing the Board of Commissioners of the Customs to sit, but Otis and other patriot leaders urged a more moderate line. Sporadic and scattered acts of violence were committed by infuriated colonists against Crown officials, but the mass assaults on persons and property that had characterized the demonstrations against the Stamp Act were notably missing. Economic pressure rather than direct coercion became the order of the day. Revolutionary agitation had passed from the populace to those whose principal concern was that resistance be orderly and dignified and supported at every stage by closely reasoned arguments. To arouse the people to action against injustice was simple enough; indeed the difficulty was in preventing the people from taking matters entirely into their own hands. The creation of an atmosphere in which organized and disciplined resistance was possible was far more complicated, but that was clearly the task that was required.

When the Great and General Court met in Boston in the fall of 1767, the delegates at once took up the matter of the Townshend Duties and prepared a letter to be circulated among the other colonies and sent on to the agent of the province in England, Dennis DeBerdt. The letter reiterated the colonial contention that "as the supreme legislative [Parliament] derives its power and authority from the constitution," and that the constitution in turn "ascertains and limits both sovereignty and allegiance," Parliament could not act in opposition to the constitution "without destroying its own foundation."

Further, it was "an essential unalterable right in nature, ingrafted into the British constitution, as a fundamental law, and ever held sacred and irrevocable by the subjects within the realm, that what man hath honestly acquired is absolutely his own, which he may freely give, but cannot be taken from him without his consent." The colonists were, therefore, determined "with a decent firmness" to "assert this natural, constitutional right."

Governor Bernard's immediate response to the letter was typical of beleaguered bureaucrats in every age. He denounced the "extraordinary and indecent Observations" it contained and declared, "Time and Experience will soon pull the Masks off those false Patriots, who are sacrificing their Country to the Gratification of their own Passions."

The same session of the Massachusetts legislature that framed the Circular Letter refused to adopt a colony-wide nonconsumption agreement put forth by the Boston members. Impatient with the legislature, Boston patriots then met with some of the more liberally inclined merchants and adopted an agreement to halt the importation of English commodities except for salt, coal, fishing supplies, lead, and shot for a period of one year. The agreement was not to go into effect unless New York and Philadelphia followed suit. A group of New York merchants passed a similar motion in April, to go into effect when supported by Boston and Philadelphia. But the conservative Philadelphia merchants refused to join in the agreements.

The more resolute Bostonians were not to be deterred by Philadelphia's languid attitude, and at a Boston town meeting in August, 1768, a call was issued for the nonimportation of all British goods for the following year; and systematic efforts were to be made to persuade or, if that failed, to force compliance by Boston merchants. Taking into account, the resolution read, "the deplorable situation of the trade" due to "the large sums collected by the officers of the customs for duties on goods imported . . . [and] the embarrassments and restrictions laid on our trade by the several late acts of the Parliament . . . We, the subscribers, in order to relieve the trade under those discouragements, to promote industry, frugality and economy, and to discourage luxury and every kind of extravagance do promise and engage with each other as follows. . . ." Included specifically were all the items taxed by the Townshend Duties.

The patriot merchants of Boston, actively supported by the Sons of Liberty, thereupon began a vigorous campaign to win adherents to their call for nonimportation. The merchants who did not agree voluntarily received some rather rough treatment. Many soon received threats against their lives as well as their property. At night their "Signs, Doors and Windows were daub'd over . . . with every kind of Filth, and one of them particularly had his Person treated in the same manner."

In New York, the Sons of Liberty began a campaign to induce the merchants of that city to accept the principle of nonimportation. New York adopted nonimportation unconditionally in the same month,

August, 1768, that Boston acted, and the retailers and tradesmen of the city agreed not to purchase goods in defiance of the nonimportation policy.

In Philadelphia the merchants again refused to join with their northern colleagues, this time on the grounds that the Pennsylvania legislature had submitted a petition to Parliament requesting relief. The Philadelphians did agree, however, to join nonimportation if the petition had no effect. When Parliament failed to respond, Philadelphia adopted nonimportation in March of 1769.

To the south, where commerce was less important, the colonies were slower to adopt nonimportation agreements, but when they did, the agreements often were more comprehensive than the earlier ones. Virginia adopted an agreement in May, 1769, and Maryland followed suit in June. In South Carolina, the merchants held back on the issue of nonimportation, but the South Carolina legislature took a strong position nonetheless on the repeal of the Townshend Duties and gave its formal support to the Massachusetts Circular Letter. The South Carolina resolution of nonimportation began: "We, his Majesty's dutiful and loving subjects . . ." and went on to declare that until "the colonies be restored to their former freedom" by the repeal of the said acts, the signers would "encourage and promote the use of North American manufacturers" and refuse to import "any of the manufactures of Great Britain, or any other European or East Indian goods." The Carolinians pledged themselves to practice the "utmost economy in our persons, houses, and furniture, particularly that we will give no mourning, or gloves, or scarves at funerals." Perhaps most sacrificial of all, they promised to buy no wines.

By the early months of 1769, nonimportation agreements were in force in all the colonies. The most notable consequence of the agreements was the degree of intercolonial cooperation that they represented. The observance of the agreements was spotty and uneven, but the contacts between patriot leaders in various colonies, the "ripening of counsels," the opening of lines of communication or the strengthening of lines already established during the Stamp Act crisis, were all-important steps in the development of colonial solidarity and the capacity for concerted action. In addition, the nonimportation agreements provided for an effective if primitive form of organization within particular colonies and thereby strengthened the "invisible government" whose existence so distressed Governor Bernard and other officials of the Crown. They also bound patriot leaders, ordinary citizens, and wealthy merchants in an alliance that, if informal and precarious, was nonetheless successful in moderating class antagonisms.

The Townshend Duties also brought forth, as had the Stamp Act, a barrage of newspaper editorials, diatribes, pamphlets, and other miscellaneous political writing. Some of it was downright inflammatory. In April, 1768, the *New York Gazette* printed an essay apparently from the pen of William Livingston, a member of the powerful and aristocratic Livingston clan, that looked forward to the day "in which the foundation of this mighty empire is to be laid, by the establishment of a *regular American Constitution*. All that has hitherto been done, seem to be little besides the colection of materials for the construction of this glorious fabrick. 'Tis time to put them together." "Our growth is so vast," Livingston wrote, "that before seven years roll over our heads the first stone must be laid—Peace or war: famine or plenty; poverty or affluence; in a word, no circumstance, whether prosperous or adverse, can happen to our parent; no, nay, no conduct of her, whether wise or imprudent, no possible temper on her part, whether kind or cross-grained, will put a stop to this building. . . . What an era is this to America; and how loud the call to violence and activity! As we conduct, so will it fare with us and our children." While few New Yorkers were ready to express or approve such radical doctrines, such essays worked a subtle transformation in people's thinking.

Less radical noises came from Philadelphia, including perhaps the most closely reasoned, widely read, and influential writings of this part of the pre-Revolutionary era. The author was John Dickinson, the young Philadelphian who, while studying law in London, had been both charmed by the pleasures of English life and dismayed at the signs of decadence and corruption so apparent in the mother country. Dickinson had returned to Pennsylvania to marry an heiress whose family was part of the conservative Quaker oligarchy. Dickinson's own sentiments were firmly on the side of colonial rights. Like James Otis, John Adams, Benjamin Franklin, Henry Laurens, and other patriot leaders, Dickinson had been dismayed by the violent eruption of popular feeling triggered by the Stamp Act. Yet, again in common with his counterparts in other colonies, he was determined to try to sustain the spirit of resistance to Parliamentary enactments unfavorable to the liberty of Americans.

He thus sat down in 1767 to write a series of "Letters," purporting to be from "a Farmer in Pennsylvania to the Inhabitants of the British Colonies." The character that Dickinson chose for himself is most revealing. Actually he was a prosperous lawyer married to a wealthy and prominent Quaker lady. He was, quite secondarily, and like most colonial lawyers, a gentleman farmer. But it was as a simple farmer that he presented himself to his readers—"I am a farmer, settled after a variety of fortunes near the banks of the river Delaware; in the province of Pennsylvania."

The "farmer" explained that his farm was small, his servants few; he had a "little money at interest" and wished for no more. Not only did Dickinson pretend to be in modest circumstances, he also posed as far older than he actually was. "With a contented, grateful mind, undisturbed by worldly goods or fears relating to myself, I am completing the number of days allotted to me by divine goodness." Dickinson was thirty-five. But the picture was of an elderly farmer withdrawn from the active affairs of life, educated, thoughtful, a wide reader, and a wise counselor. Through reading in his library and discussion "with two or three gentlemen of abilities and learning who honour me with their friendship," he had acquired "a greater knowledge in history and the laws and constitution of my country, than is generally attained by men of my class."

Dickinson did not intend to be deliberately deceitful. Eighteenth-century essayists characteristically adopted fictitious personalities and pseudonyms. The names they chose usually revealed a good deal about the way in which they conceived of themselves. Their tracts were often signed Rationales, Americanus, Cato, Vergil, Cicero, or Thersites. The names chosen also make clear the colonists' preoccupation with Republican Rome. Thus for Dickinson to write under a pseudonym or, more accurately, in a persona quite different from the real John Dickinson was part of the style of political disputation. What is significant is the persona he chose—a small farmer, informed, sensible, practical, experienced, and above all "independent." This was the character who would be listened to with the most respectful attention. Even more important, this was the character in which the vast majority of colonists wished to see themselves; this was the character with which, as we say today, they could most readily "identify."

"From my infancy," Dickinson continued, "I was taught to love humanity and liberty. Enquiry and experience have since confirmed my reverence for the lessons then given me, by convincing me more fully of their truth and excellence. Benevolence towards mankind excites wishes for their welfare, and such wishes endear the means of fulfilling them. These can be found in liberty only, and therefore her sacred cause ought to be espoused by every man on every occasion, to the utmost of his power."

"Parliament unquestionably possesses a legal authority," Dickinson conceded, "to regulate the trade of Great Britain and all her colonies. . . . Such an authority is . . . necessary for the common good of all. . . . Never did the British Parliament [until recently] think of imposing duties in America *for the purpose of raising a revenue*. . . . This I call an innovation; and a most dangerous innovation."

"If you ONCE admit that Great Britain may lay duties upon her exportations to us, *for the purpose of levying money on us only* she will have nothing to do but to lay those duties on the articles which she prohibits us to manufacture—and the tragedy of American liberty is finished."

Lest such sentiments might seem to some inflammatory, Dickinson began his third "letter" with an admonition to his readers to avoid any violent or unlawful action; "The cause of liberty," he wrote, "is a cause of too much dignity to be sulied by turbulence and tumult. It ought to be maintained in a manner suitable to her nature. Those who engage in it should breathe a sedate, yet fervent spirit, animating them to actions of prudence, justice, modesty, bravery, humanity, and magnaminity." No more riots and wanton destruction; no more threats and intimidation. In just such a spirit, Plutarch reminds us, the ancient Spartans, "as brave and free a people as ever existed," defended their liberties. The passage is a classic expression of the anxiety of the patriotic leaders over the disorderly and indeed terrifying outbursts that marked the resistance to the Stamp Act. Those who had stirred up the populace "under pretences of patriotism" were put on notice to mend their ways. On the other hand, the letters as a whole, with their frequently militant tone, their references to Carthage and to the Spartans, the most warlike of the ancients, reflected the ambiguity of the patriot leaders. Bold defiance was dressed in humble and modest garb. Veiled allusions to forceful resistance were followed by warning against "turbulence and tumult." If the colonists hastily and intemperately "separated from our mother country what new form of government shall we adopt," Dickinson asked, "or where shall we find another Britain to supply our loss? Torn from the body, to which we are united by religion, liberty, laws, affections, language and commerce, we must bleed at every vein." The prosperity and happiness of the colonies rested on their dependence on Great Britain. And she must soon return to her "'old good humor, and her old good nature' as Lord Clarendon expresses it. . . . We cannot act with too much caution in our disputes."

Finally, in the twelfth and last letter, Dickinson summed up his position: "let these truths be indelibly impressed on our minds—that we cannot be happy without being free—that we cannot be free without being secure in our property—that we cannot be secure in our property if without our consent others may as by right take it away—that taxes imposed on us by Parliament do thus take it away—that duties laid for the sole purpose of raising money are taxes—that attempts to lay such duties should be instantly and firmly opposed—that this opposition can never be effectual unless it is the united effort of these Provinces—that therefore benevolence of temper towards each other and unanimity of councils are essential to the welfare of the whole—and lastly, that for this reason, every man amongst us who in any manner would encourage either dissension, diffidence, or indifference between these colonies is an enemy to himself and to his country."

The last words were, once again, words of caution. By proceeding moderately, the colonists would demonstrate to the world that they could "resent injuries without falling into rage," and thus "all mankind must, with unceasing applause, confess that you indeed deserve liberty, who so well understand it, as passionately love it, so temperately enjoy it, and so wisely, bravely and virtuously assert, maintain and defend it."

The response to "The Farmer's Letters" showed that Dickinson had touched exactly the right note. The Letters were widely reprinted, read, and quoted. In England they were studied by those merchants and politicians particularly concerned with colonial affairs. They were translated into French, and the French translator "bestowed a number of encomiums upon Mr. Dickinson," among them that "the Pennsylvania Farmer" was more eloquent than Cicero. Indeed, the translator was so impressed by the Letters that he expressed the determination to travel to America "in order to pay his homage in person to Dickinson, Otis and all the illustrious advocates for *American Liberty.*"

Governor Bernard was among those who praised the letters. He sent a copy to Lord Barrington with a perceptive analysis of the colonial position. "My Lord," he added, "this is not a fictitious argument but a real one," pressed not captiously but sincerely by many of the most loyal and intelligent of the colonists. "What then shall be done?" he asked. "Shall the Parliament make a new declaratory Act?. . . Shall they take no notice of these American Pretensions? they then will be confirmed in the minds of the Americans. . . ."

The letters promptly established Dickinson as one of the leading patriots in America. Having published his letters with so many admonitions to moderation, John Dickinson composed a thoroughly militant song for patriots to sing. Sending it to that dean of patriots, James Otis, Dickinson wrote: "I enclose you a song for American freedom. I have long since renounced poetry, but as indifferent songs are very powerful on certain occasions, I venture to invoke the deserted muses. . . . My worthy friend, Dr. Arthur Lee, a gentleman of distinguished family, abilities and patriotism in Virginia, composed eight lines of it."

It was intended to stimulate patriotic zeal by being sung on those "certain occasions" when the Sons of Liberty and their adherents gathered together to strengthen their resolve. It was set to a familiar English drinking tune and ran as follows:

> Come join hand in hand, brave Americans all.
> And rouse your bold hearts at fair Liberty's call;
> No tyrannous acts, shall suppress your Just
> claim.
> Or stain with dishonor America's name.

Then followed the chorus:

> In freedom we're born and in freedom we'll live;
> Our purses are ready,
> Steady, Friends, steady.
> Not as *slaves,* but as *freemen* our money we'll give.

Then followed some eight stanzas, including the lines:

> Then join hand in hand brave Americans all,
> By uniting we stand, by dividing we fall.
> To die we can bear, but to serve we disdain.
> For shame is to freemen more dreadful than pain.

2

The Case of the *Liberty*

THE period of the Townshend Duties was not marked by the large-scale public demonstrations that greeted the Stamp Act. Nevertheless, the years between 1766 and 1770, when the bulk of the Townshend Duties were repealed, were far from quiet. There were numerous "incidents," characteristically between customs officials and merchants who were trying one way or another (often by smuggling) to by-pass the new and onerous duties on tea, painter's colors, and other commodities. Small crowds would gather at the wharves of Boston or other ports to support beleaguered merchants by pouring invective on the unpopular officers of the customs.

The most notable and violent of these clashes involved the patriot leader John Hancock and his sloop *Liberty*. It was also a clash that had many repercussions, embittering Parliament against the colonists and the colonists against all royal officials. It led to a famous long trial, and it involved the first use of British armed might against the colonies.

Hancock, only thirty-one years old in 1768, was already one of the most prosperous merchants in Boston. It was often Hancock who paid the bill when the Sons of Liberty bought banners, or needed handbills printed, or provided free rum for those gathered around the Liberty Tree. He was a marked man, a dangerous one in British eyes, and the customs officers kept a close watch to see if they could catch him violating any of the regulations governing imports and exports.

The customs officers' suspicions were aroused in May of 1768, when Hancock's *Liberty* tied up at a Boston pier and the captain claimed that his entire cargo consisted of only twenty-five pipes of Madeira wine—some 3,150 gallons. This was far below the *Liberty's* capacity. There was strong ground to suspect smuggling. Joseph Harrison, the chief collector of customs in Boston, decided to act. The suspected failure of the *Liberty's* captain to declare his full cargo, if proved, would have made the vessel liable to seizure, condemnation, and sale.

So far there was nothing unusual in the matter—except that the ship belonged to Hancock. Dozens of American vessels had been seized by British officials with only minor repercussions. But before Harrison could act, two British warships. H.M.S. *Romney* and the schooner *St. Lawrence,* sailed into Boston Harbor and triggered off a series of malign incidents that stirred the populace of Boston to violence and almost cost Harrison his life.

The *Romney,* it seems, was short-handed. The normal, if inhuman, method employed by British warships when they lacked a full crew was to impress sailors from merchant ships, or simply to send ashore a "press gang," composed of members of the ship's crew, to round up the required men from waterfront saloons. The impressed men had to serve or die—to refuse was tantamount to treason. So Captain Corner of the *Romney* sent his ship's longboat "man'd & arm'd with an officer" to find some sailors in Boston. They quickly had luck, coming upon an American seaman named Furlong. But when they went with their victim to collect his belongings from his regular ship, the *Boston Packet,* a crowd collected, showered the officers and men of the *Romney* with stones and invective, and rescued Furlong. Witnessing the furor from the deck of the *Romney,* which was moored not far from shore, Captain Corner issued a call to arms with the implied threat of firing on the crowd.

All of this put the people of Boston in a thoroughly ugly mood. Impressing seamen in American waters was, first of all, against the law, according to a Parliamentary statute passed one hundred years before in the time of Queen Anne. Further, American sailors hated service in the Royal Navy; it was impossible to attempt to impress one from an American ship without rousing bitter resistance. And now British naval power, for the first time in the conflict with the mother country, had openly employed a threat of gunfire to intimidate a group of colonists.

In this explosive atmosphere, customs officer Harrison decided on

June 10 to seize the *Liberty*. A tidewaiter—a minor customs official who boarded vessels entering port to ascertain the nature of their cargo— had told Harrison that he had been bullied into silence by the captain of the *Liberty*. He had been offered a bribe, and when he refused, he had been locked in a cabin for some three hours, while outside he heard the unmistakable sounds of a ship being unloaded—"a noise as of many people upon Deck at work hoisting out Goods." Acting on this information, Harrison not only decided to seize the *Liberty* but also arranged to have a boatload of armed sailors from the *Romney* meet him where the *Liberty* was docked, to assist in the seizure. Then the *Liberty* was to be towed off and moored under the *Romney's* guns.

This was a good deal too much for the Boston crowd. Harrison and his son and the customs comptroller, Benjamin Hallowell, got through the paperwork involved peacefully enough—"went thro' the necessary forms of seizing the vessel and met with no interruption." However, the appearance of the *Romney's* longboat full of armed sailors provoked a hail of stones and bricks from a crowd that had assembled on the wharf. The sailors nevertheless secured the *Liberty* and towed her off.

With the sailors out of range, the mob turned on the Harrisons and Hallowell. They were beaten with clubs and showered with rocks. The elder Harrison, badly battered, managed to escape through an alley. Hallowell was knocked to the ground and left there, bloody and half-conscious. Young Harrison was knocked down and dragged through the street by his hair. The mob then moved on to Hallowell's house, surrounded it, and smashed the windows. When they found that Hallowell himself was not there, they gave a similar treatment to Harrison's quarters and then marched on the home of John Williams, the inspector general of customs, whose house had been spared—but only just— during a recent and rather rowdy celebration commemorating the repeal of the Stamp Act. This time there were no patriot leaders to deflect the crowd, and they smashed one hundred windowpanes before Williams's wife could persuade them that her husband was not at home.

Now in full cry, the crowd roamed the waterfront looking for one of the longboats from the *Romney*. The captain had kept his sailors aboard, however, so the rioters had to be satisfied with Harrison's own boat, a pleasure craft "built by himself in a particular & elegant manner." This they took from the water and dragged about the streets, finally burning it on the Boston Common.

At this point the patriot leaders of the town made a determined effort to establish control over the mob. It was a delicate operation.

Heated by liquor and the excitement of the chase, the crowd showed a strong disposition to further mischief. The question of whether to disperse or not was warmly debated, with one loud and authoritative voice crying out, "to your tents, O Israel." Finally there was a vote, and the mob broke up reluctantly.

The events of June 10 were the sort of uncontrolled, dangerous outpouring that characterized the Stamp Act agitation and that the Boston patriot leaders were determined to avoid. As for the customs commissioners, they were not disposed to put to the test the capacity of the patriot leaders to control the more volatile elements of the town. "Being apprehensive of danger from the Outrageous Behaviour of the populace," they "apply'd for Boats to bring them on Board" the *Romney*. "At 6 P.M.," the ship's log noted, "sent three Boats man'd and arm'd—at 7 the Boats Return'd with Commissioners, their families, Clerks, Tidewaiters etc. to the Numr. of 67 persons."

While the customs officials enjoyed the *Romney's* rather crowded hospitality, Samuel Adams and James Otis took steps to try to force the withdrawal of the *Romney* and its recently acquired passengers. The Sons of Liberty were called upon to assemble under the Liberty Tree. From there, "vast numbers of the populace and others" proceeded in a misty rain to Faneuil Hall and then adjourned in order that a "Regular" town meeting might be officially called. When the company convened in the afternoon of June 11, it was under the guidance of James Otis as moderator. Faneuil Hall was so crowded that it was promptly resolved to adjourn to the somewhat more commodious Old South Meetinghouse. There the citizens approved a petition to the governor that complained of "an armed force, seizing, impressing, and imprisoning the persons of our fellow subjects," and they selected a committee of twenty-one prominent citizens of various ranks to present it to Bernard. The governor was enjoined to "issue your immediate order to the commander of his majesty's ship *Romney*, to remove from this harbour." The petition also referred, rather slyly, to the fact that since the customs commissioners had taken refuge in Captain Corner's man-of-war, they had thus voluntarily resigned their posts.

Bernard received the committee, listened "very cordially" to their spokesman, James Otis, and responded "very sensibly to some parts of the Speech & Petition & promised an answer in the morning." The committee was refreshed with wine and departed. Bernard, in his reply, promised to do his best to stop impressment, and a few days later

Captain Corner publicly consented not to impress any more Massachusetts seamen.

Harrison and Hallowell meanwhile contacted the patriot leaders in an effort to settle on some course that would allow public feeling to cool while permitting the customs officers to at least give the appearance of performing their duties. Harrison agreed to release the *Liberty* on Hancock's own security. But the patriot strategists had no intention of letting Harrison off the hook so easily. He had acted in an arrogant and high-handed manner and in doing so had played into the hands of his enemies. Now he must extricate himself and his fellow officials as best he could. Harrison found that "Mr. Hancock had taken the Advice of his Council & Friends & wou'd have nothing to do with the Business but wou'd let it take its course." The intimidated customs officials and their families made their home on Castle William, the island fortress in Boston Harbor, where they remained in self-imposed exile while one of their number went to England to present the whole matter to officials in London.

The court case involving Hancock and the *Liberty* dragged on into the fall and winter. John Adams and James Otis acted as defense attorneys for Hancock, and Jonathan Sewall as advocate general was the prosecutor for the Crown. It was not exactly an unbiased trial. Prosecutor Sewall shared the indignation of most of his townsmen over the way in which Harrison had proceeded against Hancock, and he believed, in addition, that the prosecution's case was a weak one simply in terms of evidence. After months of maneuvers and countermaneuvers, the Crown attorneys in March, 1769, abandoned the case: "The Advocate General prays leave to retract this information and says Our Sovereign Lord the King will prosecute no further theron." The case of the *Liberty* was thus another setback for the British ministry..

As for the mob, efforts to bring its leaders, if it had any, to justice were equally unavailing. Jurors were elected at the town meeting. Since the patriots controlled the meetings, it was futile to expect that jurors chosen under such circumstances would return verdicts unfavorable to the rioters. "There had been 2 or 300 hundred people who paraded and did the great part of the mischief in the public streets in the Daytime," the baffled Governor Bernard wrote to Lord Hillsborough, "and yet no man could be found who dares to charge any of them."

The riot set off by Collector Harrison's brazen seizure of the *Liberty* showed that in a certain sense things had changed very little in the two years following the repeal of the Stamp Act. The resistance of the colonists to Parliamentary taxation was still adamant. The inclination of the British was still to behave in an arrogant and arbitrary manner. A ship of the British navy had been used for the first time in support of the civil authority. The more militant citizens had made evident, at least in Boston, that they were not to be intimidated by this new instrument of coercion. The patriot leaders, after a brief flare-up of violence, had quickly re-established their control of the situation.

The episode of the *Liberty* seems, quite clearly, to have forced the hands of the patriot leaders. According to Bernard's information, which was usually reliable, they wished to give the British government an opportunity to respond to their request that the Townshend Duties be repealed and the customs commissioners called home. But the public excitement over the *Liberty* brought matters to a head prematurely. In any case, the affair of the *Liberty* and its aftermath continued to embitter relations between the royal officials and the patriots. Both sides, as we would say today, overreacted, and events spiraled closer and closer toward a showdown.

When General Gage in New York heard of the *Liberty* affair, he wrote to Lord Barrington that the British government "can not Act with too much Vigour" if it ever wished to force "a due submission" on the offending colony of Massachusetts. "Quash this Spirit at a Blow," he advised, "without too much regard to the Expence and it will prove economy in the End."

To make matters still more explosive, Hillsborough in London instructed Bernard to order the so-called Circular Letter rescinded by the Massachusetts Great and General Court under threat of dissolution. The Circular Letter was not that radical a document. It reviewed arguments that had been covered hundreds of times before by both colonial assemblies and countless individual essayists. It was the fact that it was circulated among the other colonies with a view to some common declaration of colonial rights that made it particularly offensive to the king's ministers. The Earl of Hillsborough was a man of principle, and his principles were offended by this new instance of Massachusetts' intractability. Moreover, the appeal to other colonies smacked of a treasonable cabal, a blatant effort to foment rebellion. Hillsborough's reply stated that "His Majesty considers this Step as inevitably tending to create unwarrantable Combinations, to excite an unjustifiable Opposition to the constitutional Authority of Parliament, and to revive those unhappy Divisions and Distractions which have operated so prejudicially to the true interests of Great-Britain and the Colonies." It was, therefore, "the King's Pleasure" that the Massachusetts Great and General Court should rescind the objectionable resolution by which the letter was approved "and declare their Disapprobation of, and Dissent to that rash and hasty Proceeding."

It was a blow to Bernard to be forced to pass on Hillsborough's letter to the assembly; he had won a "little popularity" by interceding with the captain of the *Romney* on the matter of impressment, and now he was required to squander it. He felt obliged, he confessed ruefully to Barrington, to behave rather like the captain of a fireship by providing "for my retreat before I light the fuse."

The Great and General Court delayed and procrastinated while Bernard importuned them for a prompt reply. The members would, they told Bernard, like a recess in order to consult with their constituents as to their wishes in the matter of rescinding. Their Circular Letter was composed, they said, in "Terms not only prudent and moderate in themselves, but respectful to the Authority of that truly august Body the Parliament of *Great-Britain,* and very dutiful and loyal in Regard to his Majesty's sacred Person, Crown and Dignity; of all of which we entertain Sentiments of the highest Reverence and most ardent Affection." "Should we ever depart from these sentiments," the reply continued, "we must stand self-condemned, as unworthy the name of British Subjects, descended from British Ancestors." They could not, indeed, understand how a letter "in all Respects so *innocent,* in most respects so virtuous and laudable, and . . . so truly patriotic" could have been so misinterpreted by the king's minister. Unless, of course, its intent had been deliberately and maliciously misrepresented by someone—which was to say by Bernard himself.

Bernard rejected the notion of a recess for the representatives to consult their constituents, which he discerned, quite rightly, as a plan to stir up popular support for the legislators; he insisted that a vote be taken immediately on the resolution to rescind. Finally on the thirtieth of June, 1769, the Great and General Court voted, 92 to 17, "not to rescind." The vote, accompanied by a long letter of explanation and justification that was filled with expressions of undying loyalty and devotion to the king and the mother country, was sent on to Bernard, who immediately dissolved the assembly. Whereupon John Hancock, Samuel Adams, and James Otis and his father were appointed to a committee to "prepare a humble, dutiful and loyal Petition to the King," praying that "his Majesty would be graciously pleased to remove his

Excellency *Francis Bernard,* Esq; from the Government of this Province."
The committee brought in a long list of charges against the governor.

The news of the overwhelming vote not to rescind the Circular
Letter was greeted with rejoicing and celebration by all patriots. The
Liberty Song was sung at numerous gatherings, and toasts were drunk
everywhere to "the Glorious 92"—those who had voted "nay." Paul
Revere fashioned a handsome punch bowl to be used at patriot head-
quarters, the Bunch of Grapes Tavern; it was engraved to the memory
of the "NINETY-TWO who, undaunted by the insolent Menaces of
Villains in Power, from a strict regard to Conscience and the LIBER-
TIES of their Constituents, on the 30th day of June, 1768, voted NOT
TO RESCIND." An insignia on the bowl bore the inscription, "No. 45,
Wilkes & Liberty," referring to the famous forty-fifth issue of the *North
Briton.* Two pennants carried the words "Magna Charta" and "Bill of
Rights." A piece of paper inscribed "General Warrants" was depicted as
torn in pieces; a liberty cap crowned the insignia.

The pattern set in Boston was soon evident in other colonies.
Following the dissolution of the Massachusetts legislature, the Virginia
assembly was dissolved in retribution for a series of resolutions condemning British policy. The assemblies of Maryland, Georgia, and
North Carolina were likewise dissolved, joining thereby the New York
assembly that had earlier been dissolved for refusing to comply with all
the provisions of the Quartering Act.

Bernard, meanwhile, did his best to prevent his own recall as
governor, which had been requested by the assembly, promising, it was
said, "to employ his great interest with the People for the Service of the
Crown." Reflecting on the news that the governor was determined to
cling to his post, Samuel Cooper, minister of the Brattle Street Church,
could not forebear to observe to Thomas Pownall, the former governor
of Massachusetts, that it was strange Bernard "should seem so loth to
leave a country He has so grossly injur'd and abus'd." The ironic fact
was that Bernard, in Cooper's opinion, had served the colony, or at least
the patriot cause, far better than he knew or intended. "Had he been
wise and smooth and known how to have establish'd himself upon a
broad Bottom, our Liberties might have been lost without a struggle."
But Bernard's constant deviousness and, at least from the colonists'
point of view, persistent misrepresentation of their attitudes and actions
served actually to undermine the more conservative elements in the Bay
colony and to unite the populace behind the patriot leaders. As Cooper
put it, the Governor's Council, usually the stronghold of pro-Parliamen-

tary sentiment, was "more than ever united with the House and the People—For this we are greatly indebted to the Governor."

It was clear to Bernard "that it is the intention of the Faction here to cause an Insurrection against the Crown Officers, at least of the Custom house, as soon as any Kind of Refusal of their extravagant Demands against Great Britain shall furnish a Pretense for so extraordinary a Step; & that they depend upon being join'd & supported in this by some of the other Colonies." In his view, "The Distemper contracted by the Stamp-Act seems to be too deeply rooted to be cured without physick; none of which has been applied as yet, unless what has encreased the Disease may be called so." The "physick" was plainly not, in Bernard's view, further concessions, but a resolute enforcing of the edicts of Parliament.

A further blow to Bernard's credibility was the publication of reports that the governor had made to Hillsborough. When a Parliamentary committee requested the papers, one of the Massachusetts agents in England secured copies through a friendly member of the House. The reports were quietly sent to the Boston patriots and promptly published. "In the Mean time," Bernard wrote, "they have been read by the whole Town at the Printers," creating, as one patriot put it, "great noise & censure." Bernard later maintained that the letters were no more than the factual reports of a colonial officer of the Crown to his superior, and that they were distorted and misrepresented for political purposes. The fact is that Bernard was inclined to put the worst face on things, and his fear of, and dislike for, the patriot leaders of Boston was plainly evident in his correspondence, as were his thinly veiled hints that the only way to bring the colonists into line was with a strong show of force. Such comments were bound to further embitter the patriot faction. Thus, the episode fanned a mutual paranoia.

Bernard's main faults were lack of candor coupled with indecisiveness. Together, they further complicated the aftermath of the *Liberty* affair, deepening colonial distrust and bitterness. A dramatic example of Bernard's indecisiveness was his handling of the matter of calling upon General Gage to send British troops to Boston to maintain order. Under pressure from the Tory supporters of the prerogatives of the Crown, but well aware of the dangers involved in such a course of action, Bernard decided to ask for two companies of British regulars from New York. But he hesitated to act without the support of the council, and he tried to persuade the council to agree to call for troops, first pledging them to secrecy. The members of the council would, of course, have no part of the proposal and promptly leaked the news that Bernard had made the proposition. This, naturally enough, further embittered the citizens of Boston against Bernard in particular and the British in general.

The fact was that Bernard himself was very much of two minds about the utility of the soldiers, as he had made clear to Hillsborough in a letter. Thus the course he actually followed was the worst possible one. Attracted, against his better judgment, by the prospect of military backing, he vacillated in such a manner as to make an already difficult situation worse and destroy what little influence he had left. Yet Bernard's letters were also full of hints that troops were needed in Boston and in fact should have been sent two years before. "If it had, there would have been no opposition to Parliament now, & above all no such Combination as threatens . . . the Overthrow of the British Empire." Instead, Boston "has been left under the uninterrupted Dominion of a Faction supported by a trained mob. . . ."

The governor's other salient weakness was lack of candor. He alternated between a hostile and supercilious attitude toward the patriot leaders and, on those occasions when he was maneuvering for political advantage, a surface affability that was often at odds with his real feelings. Certainly he was under constant pressure; harassed and denounced in the patriot press, he was constantly exhorted to defy his own instructions as an officer of the Crown. It is not surprising that he became increasingly devious and secretive, indeed almost paranoid, and that his letters to Hillsborough put the worst possible face on the actions and motives of his opponents. His task was an extremely arduous one that would have tested the restraint of a politician far more tactful and wise than Bernard.

The governor's primary anxiety was not directed to spontaneous outbreaks of mob action. He apparently felt these could and would be contained by the civil authorities, in cooperation with the responsible patriot leaders themselves. But that was just the point that troubled Bernard. It was clear that order in Boston, and to a lesser degree throughout the province, depended on the efforts of the patriot caucus. What was in effect an invisible government had grown up within the official, visible government of which he was the nominal head. The king's principal minister in the Massachusetts Bay colony was almost entirely dependent on the tolerance and restraint of his avowed and unrelenting enemies.

The consciousness of his own powerlessness, of the fact that he was a prisoner in his office—even, to a degree, in his own home—made Bernard strident and indecisive by turns. Better than most other officials, he realized that the issue was a genuinely revolutionary one. To call in troops to keep public order would not get to the heart of the problem; his real need was, of course, to depose his rivals, to destroy their invisible government, to break their power and free himself from his state of dependence upon them. To bring the troops for any other purpose would be simply to inflame public sentiment further and to substantially strengthen his opponents. To bring troops for the real purpose for which they were needed would be, in effect, to declare war upon the Massachusetts colony. Bernard was not yet ready to take that responsibility.

As things turned out, Bernard need not have agonized over calling for troops. The question had been decided for him. When the account of the *Liberty* riot reached England, Hillsborough, with North's support, promptly ordered that the Sixty-fourth and Sixty-Fifth regiments, then in Ireland, "should be immediately sent thither." The soldiers and the naval vessels stationed in American waters were to give whatever aid was necessary to the civil officers and especially to those charged with collecting revenue, and to enforce "a due Obedience to the Laws of this Kingdom, the Execution of which has, in several instances, been unwarrantable resisted, and their Authority denied."

Hillsborough's letter to Bernard implied that the governor had been vacillating and weak-kneed in failing to protect the commissioners. Henceforth "no Remissness of Duty will be excused on pretence of Terror and Danger in Execution of Office." Hillsborough charged Bernard to conduct a full investigation into the recent disturbances with a view to discovering and punishing the culprits. If the guilty ones could not be convicted in the colonies, Bernard should consider sending them to England to stand trial under a statute dating from the time of Henry VIII. The next meeting of the legislature should be moved from Boston, where the mob could too easily warp its counsels. Moreover, if the impressment issue arose again, it was the view of the government that impressment in America was legal. To support his argument, Hillsborough included two opinions by attorneys general of Great Britain, one dating from 1716 and one from 1740, that the statute of Queen Anne's time forbidding impressment in American waters was no longer in effect.

The ultimate effect, then, of the *Liberty* incident—in itself neither very important nor unusual—was the dispatch of armed force in the form of two regiments of redcoats that would (the British cabinet hoped) cow the people of Boston into submission. A simple matter of a customs inspection had escalated into a confrontation between the determined and fractious people of Boston and the might—and pride—of the British Empire. It also occasioned a resumption of impressment, a tyrannical practice loathed by the colonists. In the process the royal governor of Massachusetts had further disgraced himself in patriot eyes and further embittered the populace against the Parliament and England itself.

3

The Repeal of the Townshend Duties

THE British government slowly realized that the Townshend Duties were not working much better than had the Stamp Act. The nonimportation agreements drawn up by colonial merchants were working—not perfectly, but well enough to harm British manufacturers and the export trade. Further, the Townshend Duties themselves were bringing in only a paltry revenue. In the first year after the passage of the duties, American customs agents realized a revenue of only 295 pounds—in the neighborhood of one thousand dollars. Sending regiments of British troops from Ireland to Boston—where they were supposed to back up Governor Bernard and his customs officials and then help in collecting the tax—had cost the British government the whopping sum of 170,000 pounds. The British ledger sheet was, to say the least, unbalanced.

This state of affairs faced the Parliament when it met for its 1768–69 session. Yet there was no unanimous urge to repeal the Townshend Duties. Instead many members of Parliament were angry at the American colonies, especially Boston, for defying their edict, and wanted to force their will on the fractious colonials. And there was a good deal of pointless backbiting. Grenville blamed the state of affairs on the permissiveness of Pitt and other ministers sympathetic to colonial grievances.

293

By espousing the American cause, they had encouraged the colonials in their insolence and obduracy. To prove his point, Grenville brandished a copy of John Dickinson's *Letters from a Farmer in Pennsylvania,* read from it, and pronounced it "libelous throughout." Edmund Burke and Colonel Isaac Barré, both long-time champions of the American cause, replied by again asserting that the Parliament had had no right to tax the colonies in the first place. They were joined by Lord Cornwallis, the same Charles Cornwallis who, fifteen years later, would surrender the British army at Yorktown. Cornwallis took the lead in criticizing Lord Hillsborough, the cabinet minister responsible for colonial affairs, for his clumsy attempt to get the Massachusetts Great and General Court to disavow its Circular Letter.

Lord North, the new prime minister, was one of that class of politicians whose personal integrity and amiability, combined with conservative principles, formed the essential basis of their success in the political area. He was a large, awkward man, a poor speaker and an inept debater, but Lecky speaks of his "almost unfailing tact, his singularly quick and happy wit, and his great knowledge of business." He had been a vigorous supporter of all ministerial and parlimentary measures that the colonists had seen as assaults upon their freedoms. He had voted for the Stamp Act and had resisted its repeal. He had likewise been a strong advocate of the writs of assistance, the Quartering Act, and the Townshend Duties. He was to be the principal minister of the British government and the dutiful servant of the king for the next thirteen fateful years. George III could not have picked a man more suitable to his purposes, nor one who by temperament and principle was better equipped to be the king's coadjutor in severing the American colonies from the mother country.

Lord North promptly indicated the mood of the new government by declaring that even if "Prudence or Policy" might call for repeal of the ill-conceived Townshend Duties, they should not be repealed "till we saw America prostrate at our Feet." Yet as North perfectly well realized, the duties were not working and would not work. In short, the new ministry was both confused and demoralized.

In the colonies, Parliamentary inaction was interpreted by many as a sign of weakness and of an intention to capitulate. The effect was to encourage colonial hostility. Actually, while none of the king's ministers wished to take the responsibility for grasping the colonial nettle firmly, there continued to be little disposition in England to grant any validity to the arguments of the colonies. Parliamentary frustration and indignation with the colonies was expressed in resolutions condemning Massachusetts and the nonimportation agreement.

But behind the belligerent rhetoric lay the simple facts of dollars and cents, or rather pounds and shillings. The Townshend Duties were turning out to be difficult to enforce and were not producing anything like a substantial revenue. Meanwhile the nonimportation agreements were so successful that English exports to America, which had come to 2,378,000 pounds in 1768, dropped to 1,634,000 pounds in 1769.

The British ministry, however much it wished to hold firm, had little choice. If it persisted in maintaining the duties, they would effectively destroy colonial trade and negate the whole purpose of the Townshend Acts, which was to raise revenue. On the other hand, repeal of the Townshend Act would represent a second retreat by Parliament and the ministers; it would be taken as a victory by the colonial radicals (or patriot leaders, as one preferred). As such it would encourage further intransigence; it would demoralize all those charged with maintaining the authority of the Crown in America; and finally it would make it impossible for Parliament in fact, if not in law, to impose a tax upon the colonies in the future.

The cabinet itself was divided, and the issue was warmly debated. Finally the best solution seemed to them to be a compromise. The duties on glass, paper, and painter's colors would be repealed. However, the tax on tea would be maintained to preserve the principle that Parliament had the right to tax the colonies, thus preventing a complete rout. The tax on tea had produced the proverbial drop in the bucket, no more than three hundred pounds in revenue, but the king and North himself were determined to hold on to it. Thus the Townshend Duties died with the exception of the tea tax. Perhaps the most ingenuous aspect of the repeal of the Townshend Acts was that, while maintaining the duty on tea, the cabinet reduced the duty from twelve pence a pound to three pence.

Whatever moral satisfaction this may have given the gentlemen of North's cabinet, it was very bad politics. If one is forced to admit an error, it is the best policy as well as the best manners to do so openly and generously; to admit that a mistake has been made, and to accompany the rectification with all reasonable consolations and assurances so that a happy reconciliation may be the more readily effected. The repeal of the Townshend Acts meant, in practical fact, that Parliament could not tax the colonies without the armed occupation of the colonies, and doubtfully even then. Hillsborough even went so far as to notify the colonial governors not only that it was the intention of the ministry to repeal the Townshend Duties, but also to assure them that the cabinet "entertained no design to . . . lay any further taxes on America for the purpose of raising a revenue." To have faced this simple fact and admitted it, however hard it might have been to swallow—to admit that the policy of colonial taxation was wrong, divisive, and, above all, unworkable—would have been the enlightened response and the only response that could have preserved, for some years to come, the unity of the mother country and her colonies.

To admit a mistake is, unfortunately, a most difficult step for most human beings. And it seems even more difficult when they are in power as a government. Their own private vanities and ambitions compound an already difficult task. They seem to prefer any other course, including complete defeat and, on occasion, the destruction of the nation whose best interests they sincerely intend to serve. At the bottom of all this lies that strange human emotion that we call pride. The king (and in this sense he was the villain of the piece) and his ministers—the leaders of the most powerful, liberal, and enlightened nation in the world— could not bring themselves to accept the notion that their will could be frustrated by this "child of our loins, the bubble of our breath," the American colonies, full of contentiousness and disloyalty. As a result they kept one last meaningless and unprofitable tax, the one on tea. It was to prove a far sharper thorn in England's side than that of the colonies.

Even at that, wiser heads almost prevailed. The motion to retain the tax on tea passed in the cabinet by a single vote. North, who had worked hard to keep the tea tax, proving in his view that Parliament still possessed the right to tax the colonies, was pleased with his own strategy. The retention of the tax on tea would, he felt sure, "pit the well-disposed against the seditious" and bring about the collapse of the nonimportation agreements.

In retrospect it seems clear enough that the moment of truth for the British ministry came with the repeal of all the Townshend Duties except that on tea. The passage of the Stamp Act four years earlier, if imperceptive and heavy-handed, was an understandable error, the consequences of which took everyone by surprise, patriot leaders and British politicians alike. The Townshend Acts, coming so soon after the retreat on the Stamp Act, were a stupid blunder. With the repeal of the Townshend Duties, Parliament and the North government tacitly admitted that they could not tax the colonies for the purpose of raising a revenue. But they would not take the one additional step that would have made reconciliation possible. They spoiled the effect of their concession by making it grudgingly and ungraciously, accompanying it with threats and bullying and leaving one last useless tax.

The merchant William Strahan put the matter succinctly in a letter to his friend David Hall: The decision to leave a tax on tea while repealing the other Townshend Duties was a classic instance of "doing things by Halves, of all others, in my Mind, the worst Method." David Ramsay in his *History of the American Revolution,* published a few years after the end of the war, gave a succinct analysis of the problem. "Great and flourishing colonies . . . already grown to the magnitude of a nation, planted at an immense distance, and governed by constitutions resembling that of the country from which they sprung, were novelties in the history of the world. To combine Colonies so circumstanced, in one uniform system of government with the Parent State, required a great knowledge of mankind, and an extensive comprehension of things. It was an arduous business, far beyond the grasp of ordinary . . . [men], whose minds were narrowed by the formalities of laws, or the trammels of office. An original genius, unfettered with precedents, and exalted with just ideas of the rights of human nature, and the obligations of universal benevolence, might have struck out a middle line, which would have secured as much liberty to the Colonies, and as great a degree of supremacy to the Parent State, as their common good required: But the helm of Great Britain was not in such hands."

At the time of the repeal of the Townshend Duties the helm was in the hands of Lord North. Pitt, the "original genius" who might have "struck out a middle line," sulked in his tent like the great Achilles. Only Pitt had the largeness of vision and generosity of spirit to effect a genuine reconciliation with the colonies. North was the last man to accomplish such a task. The master of ingenious stratagems, of sly maneuvers and clever expedients, North had all the qualities that are the stock in trade of successful politicians. Such men keep the complex machinery of politics oiled and running in ordinary times. But in times of crisis, when moral leadership is required, they are calamitous. Skilled as they are in the small arts of politics, they possess a moral opaqueness that is fatally inadequate when profound issues must be faced and solved, when "just ideas of the rights of human nature and the obligations of universal benevolence" are called for.

So North was pleased with his strategy. At North's direction, Hillsborough wrote to the colonies informing them that Parliament was in

298 / A NEW AGE NOW BEGINS

the process of repealing the Townshend Duties and that the North administration "is well disposed to relieve the colonies from all 'real' grievances arising from the late acts of revenue." Although "the present ministers have concurred in the opinion of the whole legislature, that no means ought to be taken which can derogate from legislative authority of Great Britain over the colonies," they were willing to assure the colonies that they had "at no time entertained a design to propose any further taxes upon America for the purpose of a revenue." The ministry intended in the coming session of Parliament to take off the duties on glass, paper, and colors, believing them to be "contrary to the true principles of commerce," leaving only the tax on tea to maintain the principle of Parliament's right.

When word of Hillsborough's letter got around, the patriot leaders were more offended than appeased. It was clear enough to them that North hoped, by appealing to the self-interest of the merchants, to split them from the more radical elements in the colonies. By rejecting the argument about the "rights" of the colonists and repealing the duties on the grounds that they were "contrary to the true principles of commerce," the ministry hoped to salvage something from the debacle. As Massachusetts' Lieutenant Governor Thomas Hutchinson later wrote, the patriot leaders reasoned that "the fear of trouble" had brought the ministry to make a partial repeal; thus "a vigorous enforcement" of the nonimportation agreements "will increase the fear, and we shall certainly carry the point we contend for, and obtain the repeal of the whole"—that is to say, of the tax on tea as well.

In Boston a meeting was promptly called by the patriot leaders on receipt of Hillsborough's letter. The purpose was a proper response to the advance notice of repeal. The meeting, although well attended by merchants and traders, was firmly in the hands of these patriots determined to uphold nonimportation. Thus it was hardly surprising that the meeting resolved to continue the nonimportation boycott. A committee was appointed to remind Boston residents not to buy British goods imported into Massachusetts. Another committee was to examine the manifests of all vessels entering the port and to publish the names of merchants who imported goods unless they agreed to deliver such goods into the hands of "a committee appointed to receive them."

When word of the actual repeal reached Boston, the patriots there stood firmly behind nonimportation. Samuel Adams rounded up the patriot merchants and persuaded them that if nonimportation were continued for another year, the tax on tea would also be repealed—that grievances would be "redress'd or it would raise such a disturbance at home as would endanger the heads and necks of those great men who were the promoters of them." The merchants thereupon constituted themselves "the Board of Trade" and made plans to inspect cargoes of all vessels entering Boston Harbor. They also planned a campaign of harassment and intimidation of any backsliders to insure compliance. In doing so they kept Boston in a state of continual tension that ultimately would bear bitter fruit.

When word of the actual repeal reached New York, the patriot party there also tried to keep up nonimportation. The city's merchants, however, conducted a kind of poll, going from house to house to determine the public reaction, and reported that a substantial majority of the citizens of the city favored dropping nonimportation. The New York merchants were only too ready to bow to the public will and quickly resumed trade with great Britain. By August of 1770, William Strahan was able to write David Hall that "the New York Merchants here [in London] ... are shipping large Quantities of all Sorts of Manufactures; those for Woolen Goods, in particular, are so extensive that there are not enough in the Market ... to supply them. Thus the Ice being now broke, the other Colonies must soon follow their Example." One colonial center that did was Philadelphia, whose merchants, in the eyes of Boston Yankees, were a mercenary and unprincipled lot anyway. Soon after New York and Philadelphia capitulated, other major port cities also gave in and resumed trade with Britain. Except in intransigent Boston, the embargo was effectively broken.

The lull that followed was deceptive. The repeal of the Townshend Duties was not accompanied by any change of heart on the part of North and his followers. The collapse of colonial oppositon did not mean a decline in the resolution of the majority of patriots to continue to defend what they conceived to be their rights when those rights appeared in danger. Moreover, each party to the dispute—Tories in England, Whigs or patriots in America—interpreted the other's response to suit their own wishes. The great delusion thus persisted. None of the real points at issue were, in practical fact, any nearer to resolution.

4

Redcoats in Boston

THE dispatch of redcoats to Boston at the very moment when feelings had been inflamed by the Townshend Duties was perhaps the most ill-advised of all the unwise moves made by the British government during the period from 1765 to 1770. Passage of the Stamp Act and the Townshend Duties had been blunders; the repeal of the latter while still maintaining a meaningless but insulting tax on tea was probably a worse one. Sending troops was inviting catastrophe.

In Boston the feelings roused by the Townshend Acts and the *Liberty* affair were exacerbated by Lord North's determination to make Boston feel the weight of Britain's armed might. The dispatch of redcoats, however, was consistent with the confusion and error that characterized England's policy (or lack of policy) toward the colonies. Preoccupied with their own domestic political affairs, the British were reduced to reacting to the colonists' provocations. A hastily drafted and poorly conceived statute would provoke a bitter colonial response. Parliament might, in turn, pass an equally ill-advised measure expressing in essence its irritation at colonial impudence or insolence. Then, faced with what was, in effect, mutiny or even rebellion, Parliament would back down, and again accompany that retreat with another gesture or two designed to reduce the colonies to "a proper state of subordination."

Parliament always answered with half-measures, which are the worst kind of measures. Thus the ministry dispatched a thousand troops to overawe some fifteen thousand Bostonians. In any real showdown the British troops, unless heavily reinforced, could be little more than hostages to the colonists. On the other hand, their presence would certainly be a constant irritant that must, almost inevitably, provoke incidents between the soldiers and citizens.

The dispatching of troops, on the surface such an obvious response to the riotings and disorders, not only revealed the flimsiness of English policy—or, as has been said, the lack of it—but also demonstrated quite vividly the basic British misunderstanding of the problem of colonial resistance. If that resistance was the work of a few agitators and mobbers concentrated in the seaport towns, as the letters of most of the royal governors and customs commissioners suggested or, more commonly, stated to be a fact, then it was not unreasonable to dispatch a few thousand soldiers to assist the civil authorities in maintaining order. But if the "riots" were a crude expression of the sentiments of a substantial number of the most respectable and loyal English colonists wherever they might be found, the quartering of soldiers in the colonies was a measure that could only have disastrous results.

News that British troops were on their way not to protect colonists against the French or Indians but to overawe the inhabitants caused great alarm in the Massachusetts colony. That the British had decided to quarter a standing army upon a civilian population in time of peace summoned up the darkest apprehensions. The common ranks of professional armies in the eighteenth century were not notable for an elevated moral character. They were subject, moreover, to a brutal and brutalizing regimen, characterized by cruel beatings for minor infractions of the military code. Whether Connecticut Governor Jonathan Trumbull's misgivings were fair ones or not, they were generally held. In his view, "The Mischief, Rapine & Villainy commonly prevalent among Troops, who are kept up in idleness, are such as will be intolerable in the Colonies, & has a tendency to destroy the Morals of the people, and raise a Distrust of the good intentions of the Governors in the better sort, and stir up Strife and Contention among the whole. . . ."

James Otis and his Boston colleagues assembled a convention in defiance of the Massachusetts governor to discuss the coming of the troops, citing as precedent for their action the calling by Parliament of a convention at the beginning of the English Civil War. The convention, which condemned the decision to send troops to Boston and the Townshend Duties as well, proposed a day of fasting as a form of nonviolent protest. Further, it urged the people of the colony "to exercise themselves in the Use of their Arms." The excuse of this obvious gesture of belligerence was that England might go to war again with France. But no one was deceived by this bit of sophistry, nor, of course, was it intended that they should be.

The convention was designed, as Samuel Cooper wrote to Thomas Pownall, "to calm the People, to prevent Tumults, to recognize the Authority of Government by humble Remonstrances and Petitions, and to lead the People to seek Redress only in a Constitutional Way." The very publicity given the meeting, Cooper noted, was the best testimony to the good intentions of those who called it—"the surest Pledge of the Prudence and good Temper of their Proceedings." If the purpose had been seditious, secrecy would have been the only sensible course.

Yet the convention had issued a statement that sounded much like a call to arms. It seriously alarmed Governor Bernard, who proceeded, as was his habit, to write letters to his superiors in England that made the situation sound more serious than it was. Among Bernard's papers was an excited indictment of the convention, apparently intended for the eyes of Lord Barrington. The convention was, Bernard insisted, a "wild attempt to create a Revolt & take the Government of this Province out of the Kings and in their own Hands." There had been a "Plan to seize the Governor & Lieut Govr. and take Possession of the Treasury and then set up their Standard." It thus provided a perfect opportunity for "the Supreme Power to reform the Constitution of this subordinate Government [the Massachusetts Charter]." Should "so open & notorious an Attempt to raise a Rebellion remain unpunished because it was unsuccessful? . . . Some Punishment is surely due," Bernard wrote. The governor's suggestion was that the principal persons concerned with calling and running the meeting should be "disqualified by an Act of Parliament from sitting in the Assembly or holding any Place of Office during his Majesty's Pleasure." Included in such a group would be James Otis, John Hancock, Thomas Cushing, and Samuel Adams, some of the most prominent patriots of the colony.

Bernard also went to the trouble of securing from one Richard Silvester a sworn affidavit declaring that Samuel Adams, Thomas Chase, and Dr. Benjamin Church had all denounced the sending of British troops to the colony, had abused the king and Parliament, and had declared that they were determined to resist the soldiers by force of arms. It is, of course, impossible to establish the veracity of Silvester, but the document is highly suspect because each of the patriot leaders charged with treasonable utterance is quoted as having spoken almost exactly the same words and phrases, to wit: "that he [the particular speaker of treason] would take up arms & oppose the Soldiers in landing; that the King had no right to send them here to invade the country and that he looked upon them as foreign enemies." What is perhaps most interesting about the document is that Bernard took the trouble to procure it and send it to England, where its effect could only be to arouse further suspicion of the motives of the Massachusetts patriots.

Even while Bernard was urging that Otis, Adams, and others be disqualified from holding any public office, Parliament was proposing to the king that the most notorious colonial agitators and incendiaries be apprehended, under the terms of a long-unused law dating from the time of Henry VIII, and brought to England to be tried for treason. Undoubtedly, the Duke of Bedford had Samuel Adams in mind, among others, when he put forth the suggestion. Adams, perhaps even more than James Otis, had emerged as, in English eyes, the most infamous of all the colonial radicals. It was clearly Massachusetts, and more specifically Boston, that nurtured the egg of sedition, and it was Samuel Adams who seemed determined to hatch that egg into full-fledged revolution.

There was indeed, among the more militant, open discussion of revolution and independence. A Boston Tory named George Mason reported to a friend that "the Conversation I have lately had with the Sons of Liberty, leaves me under no doubt but that they are actually ripe for Rebellion, and they don't scruple to declare their wishes for a Revolt at Home [in England]." A deacon of the Medford church had stated that "the Revolution Principles were gaining ground daily and that by and bye" he did not doubt but "we should have a blessed form of Government in which no Tyrants would be allowed to oppress the People."

While Mason was scandalized by such remarks, they were not surprising. The colonists had been in a rebellious mood since the Stamp Act. Many of them had been determined since that time to resist, by any means necessary, acts of Parliament that seemed to them a violation of their rights and consequently were unconstitutional. While the grudging accommodation of the British government in repealing the Stamp Act and most of the Townshend Duties had averted an outright break between the colonies and the mother country, these repeals gave little or no assurance that those in charge of the affairs of state in Great Britain had any real understanding for or sympathy with the colonial position.

When word of the Boston convention reached England, there were many in and out of government who wished to see Bostonians tried for "high Crimes & Misdemeanors," if not for treason. It was the opinion of Lord Barrington that James Otis, "together with the Selectmen of Boston who signed the Letters convoking the Convention, should be impeach'd. This would convey terror to the wicked & factious Spirits all over the Continent, & shew that the Subjects of Great Britain must not rebel with impunity anywhere. Five or Six Examples are sufficient; And it is right they should be made in Boston the Only place where there had been actual Crime."

While such punishments were being debated, the troops arrived. At the end of September, 1768, transports carrying soldiers of the Fourteenth, Twenty-ninth, and Fifty-ninth regiments sailed into Boston Harbor accompanied by men-of-war that anchored so that their broadsides commanded the city. However distasteful in principle the arrival of the troops might be, they made a colorful and stirring sight as they formed into companies and marched up King Street with "Drums beating, Fifes playing and Colours flying." Preceding each regiment were two large and splendid silk banners on poles ten feet high—the king's colors and the regimental colors, with the regiment's number on a red field encircled by roses and thistles. The bright red coats of the soldiers, with their cross straps freshly whitened with pipe clay, were vivid spots of color, complimented by the drummers, a number of them black men, in yellow uniforms. The infantry wore black, tricornered hats trimmed with white lace. The grenadiers, special troops chosen for their size and strength, wore miter-shaped bearskin caps with red fronts, bearing the white horse badge of the House of Hanover and the inscription: *Nec aspera terrent* ("They fear no difficulty"). The officers of the grenadiers wore hats embroidered in gold and silver gorgets. Crimson sashes, swords, and spontoons (which were half-baton, half-pike) completed the officers' uniforms. There was no resistance to the soldiers as they marched through the city. Many of the citizens came to their windows to watch. The sight was especially pleasing to Tories and to the families of British officials. The feeling was mutual in at least one case. Captain Ponsonby Molesworth of the Twenty-ninth stepped out of ranks to observe his company pass by. As he did so, Susanna "Sukey" Shaeffe, the fifteen-year-old daughter of customs collector William Shaeffe, stepped out on the balcony of her father's house across the street. Dazzled by the girl's beauty, Molesworth turned to a fellow officer and declared, "That girl seals my fate."

The Twenty-ninth encamped on the Common, with the Four-teenth housed temporarily in the Court House and Faneuil Hall. Lieutenant Colonel William Dalrymple, officer in command, applied for quarters under the provision of the Quartering Act, but the council refused on the ground that the colony was not obliged to furnish quarters until all regular barracks were filled. Castle William, in the harbor, had plenty of barrack space available. Dalrymple was furious, but he had no choice except to rent buildings in the town.

Governor Bernard, with the support of the council, offered the Manufactory House, a large building owned by the town and presently occupied by a motley collection of tenants—"the outcasts of the Work-house and the scum of the Town." These "outcasts" had asserted a kind of squatters' rights, paid a nominal rent, and now, threatened with eviction, refused to budge. When the sheriff, with the support of some soldiers, managed to make an entrance through an unlocked window and demanded that they vacate, the tenants instead locked him up. And when his signals from a window alerted the soldiers to his predicament and they surrounded the house, they found themselves in turn besieged by a growing crowd of townspeople. Although the soldiers were denounced and abused verbally, they continued to blockade the building. After two days, with the tenants still obdurate and the council rejecting the use of force to dislodge them, the soldiers were withdrawn.

General Gage was naturally disgusted with what he judged to be the weakness of the governor and the council, and he declared that Boston was "under a kind of Democratical Despotism," with the powers of government "in Truth very little at present." But nothing could be done to empty Manufactory House of its determined squatters. So a large sugar warehouse was rented from James Murray, a recent arrival from South Carolina, along with another warehouse and several stores. Soldiers were scattered all over town, wherever other empty buildings, manufactories, or storehouses could be rented. The arrangement was obviously highly unsatisfactory from the point of view of any military order or discipline.

The officers themselves had little difficulty finding comfortable quarters. There were enough Tory sympathizers in Boston to offer ample hospitality to these "gentlemen," if not to their troops. Some of the officers joined in the town's social life. Captain Molesworth, who had been so smitten by Sukey Shaeffe, and Captain Jeremiah French, both

members of the Masonic order, were elected officers in the Grand
Lodge of Boston, where they joined in the order's ceremonies with such
patriot leaders as Dr. Joseph Warren, Thomas Crafts, and Paul Revere.

Predictably, there was friction between soldiers and civilians from
the first. A few weeks after the arrival of the troops, Captain John
Wilson of the Fifty-ninth Regiment, deep in his cups, encountered a
group of black slaves and began to harangue them. "Go home," he said,
in a voice that was plainly audible to several curious observers of the
meeting, "and cut your Masters Throats; I'll treat your masters, & come
to me to the parade; & I will make you free, & if any person opposeth
you, I will run my Sword thro' their Hearts." The fiery exhortation was
promptly reported to the authorities, and Judge Richard Dana placed
Wilson under bond to appear at the March session of the superior court.

A major part of the trouble was rum. Rum was cheap in Boston,
and the soldiers, seeking desperately for some relief from boredom and
loneliness, consumed large quantities of it. Under its influence they
fought bloody brawls with unemployed sailors in the numerous taverns
along the waterfront. They stole to support their taste for rum, and
Boston's rate of petty theft and robbery rose dramatically.

So did the prevalence of prostitution; wherever there are soldiers
there are usually whores. Boston was, as a seaport town, notorious for its
prostitutes, despite its Puritan morality. The soldiers attracted more,
and, emboldened by the soldiers' patronage, they were much in evidence, an offense to all decent people. The soldiers of course spent
money in Boston. Some estimates were that they squandered 250
pounds a week, and that sweetened the dose a bit, at least for those
tradesmen and tavern keepers who profited. But the greater part was
spent on rum and women. James Bowdoin, a member of the Governor's
Council and one of the patriots proscribed by Bernard for his treasonable actions, told Thomas Pownall that the currency shortage was less
acute because "the new guardians of our liberty and rights scatter with
the pox some of their loose money."

Within two weeks of the occupation of Boston, seventy soldiers had
deserted and taken refuge in the interior of the colony. To stop the
desertions, Colonel Dalrymple was forced to post guards around the
town, particularly at the principal access roads. It was a situation full of
irony. British troops had been sent to establish order in Boston. They
had hardly arrived before the attractions of colonial life proved so
compelling that they began to join the ranks of the colonists they had
been sent to police. There was a further irony. When sentinels posted to

prevent desertion ordered Bostonians to stand forth and identify themselves, they got silence, or streams of abuse, or, on more than one occasion, rocks and brickbats. The rules were relaxed; soldiers at most posts were told to make no challenge. And one soldier under such an injunction watched, it must be presumed with some malice, while a thief robbed a nearby house unchallenged. Why, he was asked by the court, had he not sounded a warning? "Because," the soldier answered, "he had orders to do nothing which might deprive any man of his liberty!" Doubtless apocryphal, the story was circulated among the Tories of Boston.

The desertions continued, and the encounters between soldiers and townspeople continued. General Gage, who had come to Boston to take command of the troops stationed there, tried to check it by court-martialing a deserter named Ames. Ames was sentenced to death, conducted to the Common dressed in white, and, after an extended ceremony, executed by a firing squad. The rest of the garrison then filed by the body. It is not hard to imagine the effect of this scene on the townspeople of Boston. Those with strong prejudices against the military had their prejudices confirmed; those who were favorably disposed had second thoughts.

The sentinels, despite constant friction with the inhabitants of the city, managed to keep desertion in check until winter, when the rivers froze over and deserters could escape across the ice. Gage even went so far as to send soldiers dressed as civilians into the countryside to try to capture deserters, but such parties encountered only hostility among the colonists, who, appalled by the fate of Ames, were glad to harbor any soldiers who had escaped. In several instances, deserters captured by parties of soldiers were freed by enraged citizens. "How far we can ever retake them or get them back but by voluntary surrendering is more than I can say," one British officer wrote.

The Bostonians were also appalled by the severity of army discipline. Soldiers were brutally whipped for minor offenses such as swearing, and for more serious breaches of regulations they were lashed until half-dead. Indeed, a medical officer stood by at all whippings to be sure that, while the culprit might be whipped almost to the point of death, he was not whipped beyond it. Such punishment was often meted out on the Boston Common, with soldiers on parade to witness the floggings and learn by example. It was sickening to hear the groans and cries of the tortured man and see his back whipped to a bloody pulp. Less agonizing, although annoying, were the fifes and drums of the soldiers on parade, which shattered the sacred calm of Boston Sundays and were "very displeasing" to the pious. The commander of the troops was requested to change the drill schedule so that "there might be no disturbance to the religious assemblies, during publick worship."

Despite the strict discipline under which the troops lived and the generally accommodating temper of Dalrymple, there were the inevitable incidents that accompany the presence of troops in any civilian center. These were carefully collected by the authors of a weekly sheet entitled *The Journal of the Times;* and since to publish such a paper in Boston would have exposed the editor to charges of seditious libel, the material so collected was sent to New York "to be published there, Journal-wise, with glosses, exaggerations, and additional circumstances." The items could then be copied with impunity by the Boston papers. According to Lieutenant Governor Hutchinson, "Many false reports, which had been confuted, were mixed with true reports, and some pretended facts of an enormous nature were published. . . . This paper had a very great effect. A story of a fictitious quarrel incensed the lower part of the people, and brought on a real quarrel." Such lies "in the cause of liberty" seemed to the lieutenant governor "a scurvy trick at best."

In their hostility toward the troops, citizens who were challenged by sentries and treated in what seemed to them a belligerent or threatening manner would bring the soldier before a patriot judge like Richard Dana or Timothy Ruddock—who would then give the soldier a standard lecture: *"What brought you here, who sent for you, and by what authority do you mount Guard,* it is contrary to the laws of the *Province,* and you should be taken up for so offending." Then the judge imposed a heavy fine.

On the other hand, soldiers charged with serious offenses were turned over to the superior court, where, it seemed to many Bostonians, their crimes were treated quite casually. The response of the patriot justices of the lower courts was to raise the fines of soldiers for minor offenses so high that the regimental funds out of which the fines were paid were soon exhausted. Thereupon the justices began to bind over soldiers who could not pay their fines as servants under indenture, to work the fines off. When word of this strategy reached General Gage, he was furious. "I can hardly write with Patience of this infamous Affair," he wrote. The soldiers themselves were understandably embittered, and their officers found it increasingly difficult to restrain them.

In spite of all the friction between soldiers and citizens, the Bostonians were, in regard to the troops, the beneficiaries of English experience and tradition. One of the strongest of those traditions held that there should be civilian control over military forces, most especially in time of peace. So deep lay the aversion to using soldiers to intimidate civilians that no British minister wished to have such a charge laid against him.

This particular English sensitivity went back to the bitter struggles with the Stuart kings in the preceding century. When the ministry authorized the stationing of troops in Boston, it was with the reminder that they could never be called out against the mob except on the authority of civilian officials. It followed as a corollary that no soldier could fire on a civilian, however severe the provocation. Thus the British soldiers, who in a sense occupied the city of Boston, were under strict orders never to fire upon or injure a citizen of the city except on the order of an officer. The officer in turn could not call out the soldiers against civilians without the written order of the civil authority, or order them to take any violent action except, quite literally, in defense of their lives.

As the townspeople became more aware of these restrictions, their harassment of the soldiers became bolder. From fearing the soldiers, they came to pity and despise them. The rougher elements in the city carried on a kind of guerrilla war of verbal and physical abuse that stopped just short of putting their lives in peril. The temptation to torment a bound giant is usually irresistible. The chained dog is a magnet for the bully or for the incipient sadist in all of us. The British troops were just such a bound giant or, perhaps better, chained bulldog, snarling and growling but unable to chew up his tormentors. It soon became clear that throwing a rock of appropriate caliber to bruise and wound but not to endanger life was a reasonably safe form of entertainment, as were blows by clubs and staves, although here the risks were plainly greater.

The patriot leaders most feared and resented the soldiers' presence because, by inciting numerous incidents that threatened to flame into major riots, they undermined the control of these leaders over the more volatile elements in the population. Men like James Otis and Samuel Adams were thus faced with the specter of the Stamp Act riots, with mobs of enraged townspeople bent on destruction, this time perhaps of lives rather than property. At every point at which some incident seemed about to grow into a dangerous encounter, leading Sons were on hand to try to cool the temper of the crowd. Thus, while Sam Adams and his coadjutors skillfully used every outrage or depredation committed by a soldier as propaganda, hoping thereby to create pressure for their withdrawal and, even more important, to win the sympathy and support of patriots in other colonies, he and the other patriots dreaded their presence and prayed for their removal.

So here again, British policy (or British expediency) was the worst possible. Nobody really wished British troops in Boston. Of those British ministers and officers with the most knowledge of the situation in Boston and the greatest responsibility, only Governor Bernard might be called an advocate of stationing troops in Massachusetts. Yet even he in his calmer moments had a clear understanding of the dangers and difficulties involved. No one, in fact, really wanted the troops around save the beleaguered customs officials, and when the redcoats arrived they proved of little value even to the customs men, since neither the council of the colony nor any public official dared call the troops out.

And yet, once there, it turned out to be impossible to extricate the troops. The same ministerial bungling and indecisiveness, confusion of counsel, and fear of being charged with weakness and cowardice kept the soldiers in Boston when every observer of the colonial scene—from the infantry private through his commander on up to the more sensible cabinet officers in the North government—knew that they were worse than useless.

Of course, it could equally well be said that sending troops to Boston—and keeping them there long after there was ample evidence that they served no rational purpose—made, in the long run, no substantial difference. The colonists in every province made abundantly clear at the time of the Stamp Act that they would not obey any statutes of Parliament that infringed on their liberties. From this point on, the only question of any consequence was what action Parliament and the king's ministers would take to force colonial compliance. In this context the stationing of soldiers, ostensibly to preserve order, was just the kind of tentative measure that might be expected of a government unable or unwilling to face hard realities. Sending troops to Boston did not modify in any substantial way the determination of Massachusetts' inhabitants to resist Parliamentary taxation. What it did do was to substantially lessen the chances that the British ministry might find some sensible way to extricate itself from the morass into which it had blundered. The chances, slim at best, were virtually foreclosed by—one could not really call it a decision — the ill-considered act of dispatching the troops. British policy thereafter was seriously cramped by the fact that it had in a sense placed hostages in the hands of its enemies.

Thus, there were three or four decisive stages in the train of events that led to the American Revolution. First, the Stamp Act fiasco might have been retrieved had the Declaratory Act not been tacked onto the Stamp Act repeal—or, having been tacked on, had it been allowed to become a dead letter. Where the Stamp Act was an understandable error, the Townshend Acts were plain folly, and many people understood them to be such when they were passed. If their repeal had been accompanied by the tacit abandonment of colonial taxation along with other generous and conciliatory gestures, the situation again could probably have been retrieved and harmony restored between the colonies and the mother country. Instead the effect of the repeal of the Townshend Duties was largely nullified by preserving the tax on tea. This niggling assertion of "principle," designed to save a few ministerial faces, by keeping alive colonial fear and suspicion largely nullified any possibility of genuine reconciliation.

Finally, sending troops to Boston deprived the British government of any real flexibility in attempting to develop a policy that might close wounds that, however deep, yearned for the healing touch of a skilled surgeon. The actual outbreak of armed conflict between England and her colonies did not wait, as historians have been inclined to suggest, upon the gradual hardening of colonial resolve, but upon the time and manner in which Great Britain should decide to maintain principles that she had never surrendered and that the colonists had never accepted. Stationing troops in Boston brought England, against her wishes and her better instincts, a long step closer to open warfare with her American subjects.

Despite numerous unpleasant incidents between the soldiers and citizens in Boston, all reported in great detail by *The Journal of the Times,* both parties established a kind of armed truce that eventually took on some elements of amiability. The British commander, General Gage, took great pains to assure Bostonians that his troops were not there to suppress colonial liberties; and if these assurances rang hollow in the ears of most Bostonians, there was no question of the general's good intentions and tact.

From the British perspective, it was equally evident that the patriot leaders, however much they might use the presence of the troops to play upon the apprehensions of the populace, had no intention of encouraging an open confrontation between citizens and soldiers.

When the Massachusetts Great and General Court met early in 1769, Governor Bernard was confident that at least for the moment, things promised to run smoothly. He assured Lord Barrington in a letter that it was clear a royal governor, firm and resolute and "supported from home," could "withstand a popular Clamour."

The Massachusetts assembly had sat a month without showing any disposition to stir up trouble, "so that it is probable that America may become apparently quiet notwithstanding their present pretensions." However, the real causes of trouble remained unchanged. "Wounds may be skinned over without healing; and a Calm may be more dangerous than a Storm." It was Bernard's conviction that "Great Britain will never be safe until the Wounds are probed to the Bottom and a Remedy applied that will prevent the Return of the Disorder. This must be the work of Parliament. . . ." Many Britons, including members of Parliament, consoled themselves with the notion "that America, if left alone, will come to herself and return to the same sense of Duty and Obedience to Great Britain which she professed before." But Bernard was under no such illusion. In the same letter to Lord Barrington, he noted that the animosity of the colonists was not "Bottomed" on the Stamp Act or any other particular statute or edict, but upon "Principles equally applicable to other Transactions which may arise in the Course of Government." Such an animosity would immediately revive "whenever the Parliament shall make Ordinances, which the Americans shall not choose to obey."

On the other hand there was, in many quarters in England, a growing irritation with the colonies. William Samuel Johnson, the Connecticut patriot, visiting in England in the summer of 1768, experienced much hostility to America. There was much talk of English pride and imperial power. "Many here," he wrote Jonathan Trumbull, "seem to be Infatuated, & Influenced by vain Ideas of Superiority & Imperial Dignity, seem determined to pull down destruction upon their own heads and ours, regardless of Consequences, to plunge the two unfortunate Countries into the deepest distress. . . ." Johnson, like so many other patriot leaders, urged that colonial resistance be without those "ill-judged Tumults and Violencies" that had characterized the Stamp Act crisis. These acts played into the hands of the most repressive enemies of America, men only too ready to find an excuse to suppress dissidents and troublemakers.

5

The Battle of Golden Hill

I⊤ was not just in Boston that clashes took place between soldiers and the civilian population. New York City also had its garrison of redcoats, and their presence, although of long standing, was also a constant irritant to its people. This irritation was exacerbated by the wrangle over the Quartering Act. This act required each colony to pay the expenses of the troops garrisoned there. New York had at first refused to pay the sums demanded, but then the New York assembly and the colony's lieutenant governor, Cadwallader Colden, had given in to Parliamentary pressure. This capitulation enraged New York's patriots, especially the Sons of Liberty. The resulting strife escalated swiftly and led eventually to the first major confrontation between British soldiers and citizens-patriots. The conflict took place in a section of old New York called Golden Hill, and is known as the Battle of Golden Hill.

The first act in the drama involved one Alexander MacDougall, a successful merchant and self-made man. One of the most outspoken of New York's Sons of Liberty, MacDougall wrote a powerful, insulting broadside attacking the assembly, Lieutenant Governor Colden, and the city's number one Tory family, the DeLanceys, for giving in on the Quartering Act. MacDougall was as inventive in distributing the broadside about the city as he had been in fabricating its rhetoric. He got hold of a sturdy Son of Liberty and a small boy. The Son carried about an object like a magic lantern box on a pole. Inside was the small boy. While the man leaned his box up against a convenient wall "as though to rest himself, the boy drew back the slide, pasted on the paper, and shutting himself up again, the man took the proper occasion [when no one was looking] to walk off to another resting place."

MacDougall's broadside was certainly an inflammatory one. "My dear Fellow Citizens and Countrymen," he began, "In a Day when the Minions of Tyranny and Despotism in the Mother Country, and the Colonies, are indefatigable in laying every Snare that their malevolent and corrupt Hearts can suggest, to enslave a free People; when this unfortunate Country has been striving under many Disadvantages for three Years past, to preserve their Freedom; which to an Englishman is as dear as his Life . . . It might justly be expected, that in this Day of Constitutional·Light, the Representatives of this Colony, would not be . . . so lost to all sense of Duty to their Constituents . . . as to betray the Trust committed to them."

The assembly had done this in complying with the Quartering Act, by which act the members had "implicitly" acknowledged "the Authority that enacted the Revenue-Acts, and their being obligatory upon us." The assembly by "so pusillanimous a Conduct" had, in effect, deserted the "American Cause." The broadside ended with an exhortation: "My Countrymen, Rouse! . . . Will you suffer your Liberties to be torn from you by your own Representatives? Tell it not in Boston; publish it not in the Streets of Charleston!" The remedy was to besiege the assembly and demand that they reverse their vote. If they did not, the New York patriots should make known to "the whole World" the true sentiments of the people of the colony as opposed to the action of a cowardly and servile legislature. The broadside, which was plastered all over New York on the seventeenth and eighteenth of December, 1769, roused the storm that its author intended, and served to further polarize feelings in the city and outside it.

The conservative members of the New York assembly were naturally furious at the broadside and, informed that MacDougall was the author by the man who had set it in type, charged the offending author with "a false, vile, and scandalous Libel" and clapped him in jail. The words of the indictment were similar to the charge leveled against John Wilkes for publishing the forty-fifth issue of the *North Briton*. Mac-Dougall at once became a hero to the New York Sons of Liberty, who hailed him as a new Wilkes. And the number 45 again became a talisman. A deputation of 45 Sons of Liberty visited him in jail, where, it was reported, they dined on 45 steaks cut from 45 steers, all 45 months old. This occasion was followed, according to the newspapers, by a visit from 45 patriotic virgins who sang MacDougall 45 patriotic songs. To which item one Tory paper observed that he must be quite a man to entertain 45 virgins, while another paper announced that the maidens were all 45 years old. MacDougall also was visited by 45 tradesmen and received 45 bottles of Madeira wine from a supporter, as well as 45 bottles of ale and from two Presbyterian ministers, 45 candles.

The Sons of Liberty stimulated a barrage of articles and essays in the newspapers attacking Colden and the assembly for trying to silence the patriots. The assembly was, they charged, no assembly; "all power was lodged in the people," who had the right to disband it and elect in its place one that better reflected popular feeling. The patriots (or "republicans," as the Tories began to call them) did their best to get a grand jury sworn in that would free MacDougall, and John Morin Scott, a prominent lawyer and ardent patriot, undertook to defend him. The sheriff, however, chose only "the most impartial, reputable, opulent, and substantial gentlemen in the city" to be on the grand jury, and MacDougall was, not surprisingly, indicted. He was brought from the jail to the court to enter his plea, escorted by, in the words of a Tory historian, "two or three hundred of the rabble of the town, headed by some of the most zealous partizans of the republican faction."

The trial itself did not go well for the prosecution. The printer who had informed on MacDougall and was to be the prosecution's star witness was hounded out of the city by the Sons of Liberty and forced finally to take refuge with the British army in Boston, from whence he fled to England. James Parker, owner of the shop that printed the broadside, was a stout patriot and most reluctant to testify against MacDougall. The trial was delayed in consequence, and Parker's death a few months later left the government without a witness. MacDougall was freed, having meanwhile provided much valuable propaganda for the Sons of Liberty.

It is impossible to tell exactly how much MacDougall's broadside had to do with the clashes between soldiers and townspeople that subsequently broke out. There is little doubt, however, that the broadside and the jailing of MacDougall raised the political temperature toward the boiling point. In New York, as in Boston, the Sons of Liberty entertained bitter feelings toward the governor and his supporters and the more conservative merchants. But the hostility was most intense between the city's sailors and artisans on the one hand and the British soldiers on the other. One source of friction was the fact that the troops, to supplement their miserable wages, were hiring out as cut-rate laborers, thus taking jobs away from members of the city's labor force. The soldiers added fuel to the fire by making repeated efforts to cut down the city's liberty pole. For four successive days, beginning on the thirteenth of January, 1770, they made forays, only to be beaten off by a crowd of townspeople guarding the pole. On the sixteenth, however, the troops succeeded, and not only cut down the pole but also sawed it into sections and piled these in front of the headquarters of the Sons of Liberty.

This was naturally resented by the patriotic citizens of New York. The next day three thousand Sons of Liberty and their supporters assembled at the stump of the liberty pole to erect another, meanwhile insisting that the soldiers remain in their barracks and that the inhabitants of the city agree not to employ them any more. The crowd thereupon dispersed peacefully.

The reply of the soldiers was a "scurrillous" handbill signed the "Sixteenth Regiment," which was posted throughout the city, "An uncommon and riotious disturbance prevails throughout this city," the handbill declared. And this condition was the work of "some of its inhabitants, who stile themselves the S———s of L———y, but rather may be more properly called real enemies to Society." Their liberty pole now destroyed, "we have reason to laugh at them. . . . these great heroes [who] thought their freedom depended in a piece of wood." The pamphlet compared the "Liberty Boys" to "Murderers, robbers, traitors . . . who have nothing to boast of but flippancy of tongue." The handbill ended with the soldiers challenging the people of New York—if they wanted a fight, the soldiers would give them one.

This handbill further aroused the already angry people of the city. Mobs roamed the street looking for trouble. Then, on January 19, a minor incident ignited the whole explosive situation. Several Sons of Liberty, led by Isaac Sears, a leading patriot, found three soldiers hard at work posting their hated handbill. The Sons seized the soldiers and carried them, after a struggle, to the mayor's office. Soon Sears and the Sons were besieged by British soldiers bent on rescuing their companions. Armed with clubs and staves, the Sons kept the soldiers at bay until twenty redcoats with cutlasses and bayonets joined the fray. The colonists wrenched up fences and tore pieces of wood from carts and sleighs nearby, and a free-for-all seemed imminent.

The intervention of the mayor, who ordered the soldiers back to their barracks, averted bloodshed for the moment. However, the retiring soldiers encountered reinforcements, apparently headed by an officer in disguise, and the redcoats turned on the crowd that had been following and taunting them and scattered it, pursuing those who fled. As word of the fray spread and more and more patriots hurried to the scene, the soldiers found themselves in turn pursued. Young Michael Smith, a chairmaker's apprentice, arrived at the height of the melee armed, appropriately enough, with a chair leg, and, catching a soldier off guard, he attacked him so fiercely that the battered grenadier quickly surrendered. Smith stripped him of his musket, bayonet, belts, and cartridge box, which he carried off triumphantly—and which through successive generations of Smiths remained treasured trophies of young Michael's valor.

Other patriots did not fare as well. Francis Field, a peaceful Quaker, was slashed on the check as he stood in his own doorway watching the battle. Three New Yorkers were wounded by swords or bayonets, and one was killed. Some of the soldiers were, like Smith's victim, badly beaten and disarmed. At the moment when the arrival of more soldiers seemed to threaten a general conflict, British officers appeared to direct the soldiers back to their barracks.

So ended the Battle of Golden Hill, so called because the major fighting took place on a promontory near the center of the city. It had been ferocious, a measure of the hatred that had been sown between the people and those symbols of British power, the redcoats. Most important, a man had been killed—the first colonial killed by British soldiers.

For days, like the aftershocks of an earthquake, there were further clashes between soldiers and Sons. On January 20, the day after the battle, a party of sailors clashed with soldiers, and one of the sailors was run through and killed by a bayonet—the second colonial victim. When the mayor ordered the troops to disperse, they refused. Once more, as word of the fighting spread, the Sons hurried toward the sounds of combat. This time the soldiers, outnumbered, withdrew, as they did again that same afternoon when a group of citizens rallied on the Common opposite the jail. Sailors, out to avenge the death of their fellow in the morning's fray, chased the redcoats away.

In two days of bitter fighting, two New Yorkers had been killed by British soldiers. The soldiers of New York were far more culpable than those who would, six weeks later, "massacre" four Bostonians. Yet the Battle of Golden Hill is virtually forgotten, while the "Boston Massacre" is familiar to every American. Why? The answer lies primarily in the nature of the patriot movement in New York. The movement was neither as active nor as well coordinated and well led as it was in Boston. New York's upper-class patriots were far more suspicious and fearful of their "mob" than were, say, Samuel Adams and James Otis of the people who made up the "mob" in Boston. The New York patriot intelligentsia did not lead and control the populace. As a result, the New York mob was, in fact, much more of a riotous and ill-disciplined rabble than the people who poured into Boston's streets to protest. Nor did the New Yorkers have any long-term object in view, such as the repeal of the Townshend Duties or the removal of all troops from the colony. They rioted primarily just to show their hatred for the redcoats, with no serious object or reform in view. The Battle of Golden Hill, then, despite the two deaths, was not as politically important as, for example, the Stamp Act riot in Boston. It was far nearer a waterfront brawl than a closely disciplined political protest. Thus it has been half-forgotten, despite the fact that it was the first bloodshed of the entire revolutionary movement.

6

More Trouble in Boston

DESPITE the furor in New York, the British ministry perceived the citizens of Massachusetts Bay, and more especially Boston, as their particular cross. By the summer of 1769 it had become evident to virtually everyone concerned that British troops in that city served no good purpose. As General Gage himself expressed it: "The people were as Lawless and Licentious after the Troops arrived, as they were before. The Troops could not act by Military Authority, and no Persons in Civil Authority would ask their aid. They were there contrary to the wishes of the Council, Assembly, Magistrates and People, and seemed only offered to abuse and Ruin. And the Soldiers were either to suffer ill usage and even assaults upon their Persons till their Lives were in Danger, or by resisting and defending themselves, to run almost a Certainty of suffering by the Law."

Hillsborough had already sent word to Gage that he could remove the troops if Governor Bernard concurred. Some were badly needed in Ireland, where the Irish were in a state approaching rebellion. Gage, to cover his own hand, sent a messenger to get Bernard's consent in writing for the withdrawal of the troops, but the governor, hoping daily for permission to return to England, was reluctant to accede. For almost a year, his request to leave had been delayed by the agitated state of

319

affairs in the Bay colony. Now that things had quieted down a bit, his hopes of being allowed to go home had revived, and he was unwilling to do anything that might, at the last moment, imperil his leave. He was equally unwilling to bear publicly the odium of having refused to approve the withdrawal of the British soldiers, so he procrastinated. It was decided to send two regiments away and keep two in Boston. Like the decision at a higher level to repeal the Townshend Duties with the niggling exception of tea, it was the kind of faint-hearted, halfway measure that disfigured English policy through the whole Revolutionary era.

Finally Bernard's leave came through and that weary gentleman departed, leaving the government of Massachusetts in the hands of his lieutenant governor, Thomas Hutchinson. At the same time, Bernard gave permission for the removal of the two regiments. This was a signal for public rejoicing in Boston. Bells rang, guns were fired from John Hancock's wharf, the Liberty Tree—where resistance to the Stamp Act had first been kindled—was festooned with flags, and a great bonfire was built on Fort Hill, where it was visible to Bernard, whose ship lay in the harbor awaiting a favorable wind. Bernard's departure was officially described as a leave, but in fact that worthy never returned to Massachusetts. Once in England, he applied for a pension and for a number of the gratuities available to loyal servants of the Crown.

As soon as the rumor spread that some of the troops might be removed, Sam Adams, as full of wily devices as Odysseus, maneuvered a set of resolves through the Great and General Court declaring (among other things) that no laws except those passed by the representatives of the people of the colony were of effect and need be obeyed. When the resolves were published, Colonel Mackay, commanding the troops, and Rear Admiral Samuel Hood, sharing with him responsibility for the decision to withdraw the troops, let it be known that they were having second thoughts about the advisability of embarking the troops. Adams replied that the publication of the resolves had been perhaps ill-advised and that if the troops were withdrawn, the assembly would doubtless rescind them; with this rather tenuous reassurance, Hood and Mackay, after conferring with Hutchinson, continued the embarkation. A week or so later the Great and General Court, under Adams' guidance, did indeed modify its claims. Parliament was conceded the right to legislate in all matters, including port duties—with the signal exception of taxes.

Bostonians were, of course, delighted when the Sixty-fourth and Sixty-fifth regiments sailed away. Not unnaturally, they assumed that the remaining soldiers were to follow. But the remaining troops did not leave. Hutchinson, acting in Bernard's absence, had no more confidence in the efficacy of their presence than Bernard had had, but he had no more resolution in terminating it, which is hardly surprising. The decision should have been made by Hillsborough or Gage. To place the responsibility on the governor or, in this case, the lieutenant governor (since Hutchinson was not to be named as Bernard's successor until the spring of 1770) was manifestly unfair. The customs commissioners were still convinced that they could not carry out their duties without the moral support provided by the presence of the troops. Again, buck-passing and vacillation took the place of intelligent policy.

When it became clear to the citizens of Boston that all the troops were not to be withdrawn, the mood of the town became increasingly hostile. Everyone's nerves were on edge waiting for what appeared to be the inevitable explosive encounter between the populace and the remaining regiments. Into this tense atmosphere a small bomb was dropped, in the form of another sheaf of letters written home by Bernard that had been stolen by friendly agents in Britain and shipped to a correspondent in Boston, plus some official correspondence from the Boston customs commissioners to the Board of Trade in London.

The always irascible—and sometimes unbalanced—James Otis, reading the letters, became convinced that two of the commissioners had defamed him, calling him a person "inimical to the rights of the Crown, and disaffected to his Majesty." The principal culprit, in Otis's view, was John Robinson, the unpopular commissioner of customs, who had been a central figure in the affair of the *Liberty*. Otis and Samuel Adams met with Robinson to try to get a retraction from him, and then just Otis and Robinson met. Getting no satisfaction, Otis attacked Robinson and the other commissioners in the pages of the *Gazette,* calling them "Superlative blockheads" who "have not learnt law enough to know they have no right to scandalize their neighbours." If Robinson "'*officially*' or in any other way, misrepresents me," Otis concluded, "I have a natural right if I can get no other satisfaction to break his head."

The same day this tirade appeared, John Adams found Otis in one of his strange, half-mad moods—"no Politeness or Delicacy, no Learning or Ingenuity, no Taste or Sense in this Kind of Conversation," Adams noted, dismayed and distressed at the state of mind of his idol. A day later, Otis, hearing that Robinson had purchased a heavy walking stick, bought a similar one and searched out Robinson in the British Coffee House, a gathering place for British officers and Tory sympathizers. Robinson came in soon after Otis. Since Otis was not carrying a sword, Robinson removed his and turned to face Otis. Otis demanded "a gentleman's satisfaction"—that is, that the issue be settled by a fist fight, since dueling was outlawed.

"I am ready to do it," Robinson replied.

"Then come along with me," Otis said, heading for the door. At that point, Robinson reached up as though to seize Otis by the nose, a particularly insulting gesture. Otis, in turn, warded Robinson off with his cane. The commissioner responded by striking at Otis's head with his own walking stick until the two men were disarmed by the bystanders, whereupon they began to belabor each other with their fists, the bystanders joining the brawl on Robinson's behalf. While several men pinioned Otis's arms, another landed a blow on his head. The blood gushed while Otis struggled to free himself. Young John Gridley, passing by on King Street, heard the melee and came to Otis's aid, grabbing at Robinson and ripping his coat to the pockets. Gridley, in turn, was struck on the head and half-blinded by his own blood. As he lashed out, someone brought a cane down on his wrist with such force that his arm was broken. Retreating, he heard behind him cries of "Kill him! Kill him!" Another passer-by, attempting to intercede, saw Otis being held by two or three men while Robinson punched him in the face. Finally Benjamin Hallowell, another of the customs commissioners, managed to extricate Otis from the room. Otis's wounds were painful but not, apparently, serious. He was up and about the next day, bruised and sore, but as much in command of his faculties as he ever was—that is, uncertainly and unpredictably.

The patriots of Boston were understandably incensed by the beating that Otis had received. The fact that he had brought his troubles on himself by his aggressiveness and belligerence counted less with them than the fact that he had been badly beaten in an unfair fight by men widely considered to be the agents of British tyranny and the enemies of colonial liberties. Otis added fuel to the fire by speaking of the encounter as "a premeditated, cowardly and villainous attempt . . . to assassinate me." John Rowe noted that the "Inhabitants [were] greatly alarmed at the Usage Mr. Otis met with—tis generally thought he was very Rascally treated." Even Colonel Dalrymple, writing to General Gage, admitted that "Mr. Robinson beat the other most excessively."

The British officers who had been present at the British Coffee House when Otis was beaten were beyond the reach of popular wrath.

So patriot anger focused on one William Browne of Salem. Browne was already suspected of being a Tory, because as a member of the Great and General Court he had voted in favor of rescinding the Circular Letter that the Massachusetts assembly had sent around to all the other colonies. Rumor had it that it was Browne who had broken Gridley's arm with his cane. So an angry crowd went to the Coffee House, routed Browne out from a hiding place, and took him to Faneuil Hall for a preliminary hearing before the justices of the peace.

But the crowd was not easily appeased. Although Browne was bound over to answer at the next court of general sessions to the charge of "assaulting, beating, and wounding" Gridley, James Murray, a justice of the peace, was hissed and abused, and someone snatched the wig off his head while others pushed him and tried to trip him. Finally, in the face of the warning, "No violence, or you'll hurt the cause," Murray and Browne were allowed to depart.

The Otis incident had hardly cooled when another serious incident disturbed the precarious peace of Boston. The cause was a tiny publisher & bookseller named John Mein. Mein and his newspaper, the *Chronicle* were the principal thorns in the side of The Sons of Liberty. Mein had embarrassed the patriots by publishing in his newspaper, during the period of the nonimportation agreements, customhouse lists of everyone who was importing goods from England. Among the names were those of a number of merchants who had signed the agreement. It was evident that they were cheating on the sly. Not only was the revelation damaging to the reputation of some Boston patriots, but also, by disseminating the information to other colonies, Mein endeavored to sow suspicion and distrust in patriot ranks in every colony.

When Otis, writing in the *Gazette* under the pen name "Americus," attacked Mein as "stained with the blackest Infamy," the editor tried to find out the name of his assailant from the editors of the *Gazette*. Failing to do so, Mein attacked one of them, John Gill, and beat him severely with his cane.

Mein now felt the full force of patriot indignation. When he received threatening letters and warnings from both friends and enemies that his life was in danger, Mein took to carrying a loaded pistol and appealed to Hutchinson for protection. As he pointed out to Hutchinson, in an incident provoked by his enemies he might, in defense of his life, wound or kill one of his assailants; and this might make him the unwilling cause of a major upheaval in the city. But

Hutchinson, like every public official before and since with responsibilities for law enforcement, replied that he could do nothing until an actual attack had been made upon Mein or his friends.

Failing to get satisfaction from the lieutenant governor, Mein satirized his opponents in the *Chronicle,* apparently on the theory that the best defense is an attack. The patriot Thomas Cushing was characterized as "Tommy Trifle, Esq.," Otis as "Muddlehead," and Hancock as "Johnny Dupe, Esq., alias the Milch-Cow," the simple-minded tool of the radical patriots who depended on his money to finance the cause. Hancock was described as "a good-natured young man with long ears— a silly conceited grin on his countenance—a fool's cap on his head—a bandage tied over his eyes—richly dressed and surrounded with a crowd of people, some of whom are stroaking his ears, other tickling his nose with straws, while the rest are employed rifling his pockets."

This lampoon was a bit too much for a number of patriots, and in February John Mein was attacked on King Street by ten or twelve persons, some, it was reported, of "considerable Rank." One of his assailants struck at Mein with a cane, leaving a "bloody contusion," upon which Mein drew his pistol and held off the crowd amid cries of "kill him," "knock him down." Mein eventually made his way to a guard post manned by British soldiers. As he was mounting the steps to the guardroom, one of his attackers rushed up behind him with a large shovel and aimed a blow at the back of his head. The blow missed Mein's head but split his coat, waistcoat, and shirt. A friend, attempting to defend Mein, discharged his pistol. It was quickly reported through the crowd that Mein had fired at a citizen of the town.

Soon more than a thousand men had collected in upper King Street, and the trouble spread. Someone apprehended a customs official who was reported to have informed on Hancock's sloop *Liberty.* The crowd stripped him naked, tarred and feathered the wretched man, and then dragged him in a cart to the Liberty Tree, calling out to the residents of houses along the way to illuminate their windows for the cause of liberty. The crowd then gathered around Mein's printing shop, which was barricaded in anticipation of their visit. There rocks were thrown and windows smashed. An apprentice of Mein's, apparently intending to frighten off the marauders, made the mistake of firing a blank charge at the crowd, which resulted in the doors of the printing shop being smashed and a search being made through the premises for Mein. "Some mischief" was done to his books and two guns were carried off by members of the mob, but the presses and the type fonts were, oddly enough, left undisturbed. By this time Mein, doubtless fearing that still worse treatment might be in store, made good his escape dressed as a soldier and took refuge on a British frigate in the harbor.

Mein was convinced that he had been the object of a deliberate and cold-blooded attempt at murder planned by some of the leading figures in the patriot faction. Mein also expressed himself bitterly to Hutchinson about the lieutenant governor's failure to protect him. Hutchinson readily acknowledged that he had not dared to act in a way that would have further inflamed the inhabitants of the city. To have called for help from the soldiers would have led to a major confrontation, and this Hutchinson was unwilling to have happen. As he wrote Hillsborough, while such a course might work in Ireland where there was a tradition of soldiers being summoned in support of the civil authority, it could only have precipitated a grave crisis in Boston. "In the present state of the colonies," he wrote, "I could not think it [advisable]." He was doubtless indignant with Mein for his deliberate baiting of the Sons of Liberty. With Hutchinson and Dalrymple doing their best to prevent an explosion, Mein seemed determined to provoke one.

Both Hutchinson and Dalrymple had the gloomiest forebodings. The British commander declared: "Authority here is at a very low ebb, indeed it is rather a shadow than a Substance. . . . The Crisis I have long expected comes on very fast, and the temper of the times is such that if something does not happen of the most disagreeable Kind, I shall with pleasure give up my foresight."

If the unhappy plight of Mein pointed up the powerlessness of the Crown officials in the Bay colony, the increasingly bitter dispute over nonimportation disclosed dangerous rifts in patriot ranks. Despite the effort of the more militant leaders to preserve the nonimportation agreements, there were daily signs of waning zeal in their ranks. The issue came to a head in the case of William Jackson, who had openly defied the agreements. Jackson remained obdurate, and on the eighth of February—market day, with the town filled with farmers and schoolboys out of school—a board was stuck up on the town pump with a hand painted on it pointing to Jackson's shop. Printed on the board was the word IMPORTER. The sign attracted the attention of "the boys, and Country people, who flock'd about it in great Number: the Boys insulting Every body who went in, or out of the shop, by Hissing and pelting them with Dirt." Jackson's efforts to take down the sign were rebuffed by "a Number of Idle people who were standing by with Clubs and

Sticks in their Hands." Just when it seemed that things might get out of hand, the board was taken away by those who had put it up and the crowd dispersed, after first plastering Jackson's windows and storefront with mud and dirt.

All week the importers felt popular hostility in numerous ways— their signs were defaced and they themselves were hooted at and jeered. Effigies of the importers, Boston's customs commissioners, and British ministers considered hostile to the American cause were paraded through the town and hung on the Liberty Tree. When four soldiers of the Fourteenth Regiment tried to cut the figures down, they were beaten off by the crowd and "one of them much Hurt."

On February 22, 1770, the sign of the hand again went up outside the shops of William Jackson and Theophilus Lillie, another merchant who was thought to have imported British goods. At Lillie's shop Ebenezer Richardson, an informer for the customs who was denounced by the patriots as "the most abandoned wretch in America," tried to prevail upon a countryman with a horse and cart to run over the sign and knock it down. When the countryman refused, Richardson turned next to a charcoal carter with the same suggestion. Again rebuffed, he seized a wagon himself and tried to level the offending sign. The crowd around Lillie's, made up largely of schoolboys, now turned their attention to Richardson and began pelting him with dirt clods, sticks, and stones. Under the barrage Richardson retreated to his house, which was nearby, calling out on the way to two Sons of Liberty: "By the eternal God, I'll make it too hot for you before night."

The Sons, taking up Richardson's challenge, followed him to the door of his house. "Come out, you damn son of a bitch" one of them shouted. "I'll have your heart out; your liver out." Richardson reappeared at this and exchanged abuse and threats with his tormentors. Gradually the youths who had been pelting Lillie's store drifted over and began throwing objects at Richardson's house. Richardson opened the door, shook a stick at the crowd, and swore that if they did not disperse he would "make a lane" through them. Apparently someone in the house threw out a brickbat. An older man picked it up and hurled it through a window. At this the boys, who had been throwing rotten fruits, eggs, and handfuls of dirt, unlimbered a heavier artillery of stones and rocks. Other windows were broken, and a stone struck Richardson's wife.

Richardson found a supporter in George Wilmot, who had commanded a company of Rangers in the French and Indian War. Wilmot slipped inside the house and assured Richardson that he would stand with him against the mob. He asked for a gun. Meantime the barrage continued. Some adults in the crowd tried to discourage the boys, but others laughed and egged them on.

Richardson appeared at a window with an unloaded musket and snapped the lock. In response the mob knocked in the front door, but no one entered. Richardson and Wilmot were then visible at the window handling their muskets, and Richardson must have loaded his, for soon after he placed the gun on the windowsill, knelt down, took aim, and while the crowd watched incredulously, fired the piece. The main pattern of slugs struck eleven-year-old Christopher Seider, just bending over to pick up a stone. Young Seider was carried into a house nearby and a doctor was sent for. Two slugs hit a nineteen-year-old youth, injuring two fingers and penetrating his thigh. Another stone was thrown, and Richardson aimed his musket once more. "Damn ye," he shouted, "come here. I'm ready for you." Wilmot, aiming his musket, called out, "Stand off or I'll fire." Alerted by the tolling of the bell in the New Brick Church, a large crowd now gathered around Richardson's house and forced an entrance. Wilmot's musket was seized and he gave himself up, while Richardson, defending himself with a cutlass, refused to surrender except to a proper officer of the town. At last, after a fierce struggle, Richardson was taken and carried out of the house, where the cry was immediately raised to lynch him. Someone produced a noose. It was swung over a signpost, and it appeared that summary justice would be meted out on the spot.

At this juncture the patriot leader Will Molineux appeared and deflected the crowd from its purpose. Dissuaded from hanging Wilmot and Richardson, the crowd hauled them through the streets to Justice Timothy Ruddock. Ruddock directed that a hearing be held at Faneuil Hall. There he was joined by Judges Richard Dana, Edmund Quincy, and Samuel Pemberton. Witnesses gave testimony, and the two men were charged with "firing off and discharging a gun loaded with gun powder and swan shot at one Christopher Seider thereby giving him a very dangerous wound." As they were being taken off to jail, there were cries of "hang them, hang them," and the crowd seized the two men. Ropes were quickly placed around their necks, and for a moment it once more appeared that they might be the victims of the mob's wrath. But "some of the leading men of the popular side" intervened, removed the nooses, and returned the terrified men to the custody of the constables.

At the time of the original hearing Christopher Seider was still alive, but at nine o'clock the same evening he died. Dr. Joseph Warren performed the autopsy, and the coroner's jury examined the body, declaring that the boy had died as a result of having been "wilfully and feloniously shott by Ebenezer Richardson." The Indictment was changed to murder.

Hutchinson, fearful that the general turmoil in the city might lead to some conclusive encounter between the crowds of aroused townspeople and the soldiers, pleaded with the council for "some measures to put a stop to these tumultuous assemblies, but to no purpose," which was hardly surprising. Only British soldiers could put a "stop to these tumultuous assemblies"—a remedy, in the opinion of the councilors, far worse than the disease. Meantime, Samuel Adams made preparations for Christopher Seider's funeral. The city lay under a deep pall of snow when the funeral procession, "the largest perhaps ever known in America," began at five o'clock on a cold grey afternoon, from the Liberty Tree. There a sign had been erected, painted with Biblical passages: "Thou shalt take no satisfaction for the life of a MURDERER—he shall surely be put to death," and "Though Hand join in Hand, the Wicked shall not pass unpunished." Some four hundred schoolboys walked two-by-two in front of the coffin, on which were inscribed Latin quotations relating to murdered innocence. The coffin itself was carried by six boys, and two thousand mourners followed. Thirty carriages and chaises brought up the rear of the procession, which extended for more than half a mile. John Adams, riding into town as the procession was forming, stopped at John Rowe's house to warm himself from the numbing cold and then joined the funeral. "My Eyes never beheld such a funeral," he noted in his diary, adding, "This Shewes there are many more Lives to spend if wanted in the Service of their Country. It Shews, too that the Faction is not yet expiring—that the Ardor of the People is not to be quelled by the Slaughter of one Child and the Wounding of another."

John Adams' curious comments on the death of the Seider boy are revealing. The shooting, so clearly the work of a furious and probably unbalanced man, had little or nothing to do with British tyranny, and could hardly be described as the death of a martyr to colonial liberty. John Adams was a sensible and rational man, if a hot-tempered one, with a profound suspicion of mobs. If he could transpose the incident in the privacy of his own diary into a demonstration of patriotic courage and sacrifice, it was not surprising that the great mass of Bostonians saw it in such a light. Historians have been inclined to treat the event simply as an example of Samuel Adams' skill in manipulating popular feeling. Whosoever's emotions Samuel Adams might play upon, he surely could not play upon his cousin John's, as events were to prove.

To realize how deeply and genuinely outraged the citizens of Boston felt at the shooting of young Seider, the reader would have to imagine himself in a similar situation, with all the distortions of reality that extreme emotions produce. The simple fact of the matter was that one of the most hated men in the city, a paid informer and an avowed enemy of everything that his fellow citizens believed themselves to be struggling for, had fired a weapon loaded with a lethal charge at a street full of riotous boys, had killed one who was little more than a child and wounded another. The funeral was a quite genuine outpouring of mass grief and indignation. No one who participated in it, however, was unaware of the political implications.

Least of all Thomas Hutchinson, who, noting the "inconceivable impression" it produced, speculated somewhat cynically that if the Sons of Liberty could have resurrected young Seider, they "would not have done it, but would have chosen the grand funeral." Hutchinson's reaction told a great deal about the limitations of those charged with the exercise of power under the authority of the Crown. Understandably paranoid, they saw behind every incident a plot by traitors to hold up to ridicule British authority, the Crown, and the king's agents. Since the arguments and "so-called principles" of the patriots seemed to men like Bernard and Hutchinson merely captious—clever subterfuges for ambitious and self-seeking men—they could never bring themselves to believe that these despised principles were sincerely held convictions for which men might be willing to give their lives. Thus they misunderstood and misjudged every situation, and the advice they gave their superiors was, inevitably, bad. If they were dealing with a few unscrupulous schemers who were misleading the simple-minded mass of people, then it made some sense to talk of shipping these troublemakers to England to be tried for treason, to advocate the use of troops to keep order, and to attempt to suppress popular gatherings. But of course this is not what Hutchinson faced at all.

The patriots had, to be sure, their own array of paranoias. It was as difficult for them to imagine that Bernard and Hutchinson might be decent and well-intentioned men, motivated with a real loyalty to the Crown and a firm belief in Parliamentary supremacy, as it was for those gentlemen to grant any probity or true idealism to the patriot leaders. In the eyes of Otis and the Adamses, Bernard and Hutchinson and their

330 / A NEW AGE NOW BEGINS

supporters were greedy sycophants, devious plotters against the liberties of the people they were paid to serve. Each side was devoted to its own particular conspiracy theory, seeing a plot in every chance happening, a design in the most coincidental combination of events. So it is in all times of revolution. That indeed is why they are revolutionary. Attitudes and beliefs become so polarized that words cease to bear the same meaning for those on different sides of a widening abyss. The revolutionaries must use old words in such a way as to illuminate new realities; the representatives of the existing order are equally insistent on using old words to obscure the existence of those same new realities. Hence, suspicion and distrust—and eventually violence—became inevitable.

7

The Boston Massacre

ALTHOUGH two regiments of the troops that had garrisoned Boston had been removed in the fall of 1769–70, two regiments still remained. And baiting these remaining "lobsterbacks" continued to be a favored occupation of the town's rougher elements. Both sides hurled violent and obscene epithets; the townies frequently sent rocks flying after their insults. The troops replied by threatening the townspeople with their bayonets. But all they could do was threaten; they were on strict orders not to harm their tormenters, let alone fire on an inhabitant. It was an explosive situation, rather like the prelude to New York's Battle of Golden Hill. In the early days of March, 1770, it built up more and more pressure until finally, on the fifth, it exploded. The result was one of the most famous and fateful incidents of the entire pre-Revolutionary period.

The two regiments still in Boston were the Fourteenth and the Twenty-ninth. The Fourteenth had temporary barracks in Murray's sugar house, off Dock Square. The Twenty-ninth, scattered among a number of buildings along Water Lane and Atkinson Street, was more spread out and vulnerable, and suffered as a result a double dose of harassment. The soldiers of the Twenty-ninth were considered an especially tough lot. Lieutenant Governor Hutchinson himself described them as "in general such bad fellows that it seems impossible to restrain them from firing upon an insult or provocation."

On Friday, March 2, a Boston ropemaker named William Green, busy with his fellows braiding fibers on an outdoor "ropewalk" or ropemaking machine, called to Patrick Walker, a soldier of the Twenty-ninth who was passing by, and asked if he wanted work. "Yes," Walker replied. "Then go and clean my shithouse," was Green's response. The soldier answered in similar terms, and when Green threatened him, he departed, swearing to return with some of his regimental mates. Return he did with no less than forty soldiers, led by a big Negro drummer.

Justice of the Peace John Hill had been watching the whole exchange from a nearby house. He now appeared and tried to prevent a brawl, ordering the ropemakers and the soldiers, in his capacity as justice, to keep the peace. His intervention was unavailing. The soldiers armed with clubs and the workers with the sticks they used in making rope battled furiously until, more workingmen having joined the fray, the increasingly outnumbered soldiers beat a retreat. Hill did manage to prevent pursuit by the victorious ropemakers and their supporters, and the soldiers were confined to barracks by their corporal. On the next day, however, there was another clash between the ropemakers and the soldiers, in which a private of the Twenty-ninth ended up with a fractured skull and a broken arm. That night, a ropemaker lodging with Benjamin Burdick complained to his landlord that several soldiers were "dogging" him. When Burdick asked a soldier lurking in the street outside what he was doing, the soldier replied, "I'm pumping shit." "March off," Burdick ordered. The soldier damned him, and Burdick beat him with a stick until he fled.

Rumors circulated through the town all weekend that the soldiers planned to take revenge, and a number of townspeople swore to give a good account of themselves in any fray. Lieutenant Colonel Maurice Carr, commanding the Twenty-ninth, was so alarmed that he wrote to Hutchinson expressing his deep concern about the escalation of the frequency and violence of the encounters between townspeople and soldiers.

The night of March 5 was clear and cold. Snow lay on the ground to the depth of almost a foot; where it had melted during the day, it soon froze hard. The center of old Boston was dominated by the Town House, where the council and governor met; it corresponded to a city hall. Near it stood the Custom House, the headquarters of the commissioners, where their official records were kept. Just south of the Town

House stood the Main Guard, the headquarters of the British forces in Boston. Two small brass fieldpieces stood on either side of the entrance door, and two soldiers occupied guard boxes in the same manner that British soldiers still mount guard at Buckingham Palace. Thirty or forty yards away at the corner of King Street and Royal Exchange Lane, near the Custom House, was another sentry box where Private Hugh White had his post. The captain of the day was Thomas Preston, an Irishman forty years of age who was generally acknowledged to be "a sober honest man and a good officer." Young Lieutenant James Basset, just turned twenty, was the officer of the guard. He had been commissioned, through family influence, at the age of twelve, but he had had little actual experience and was bored and resentful at his assignment to the Twenty-ninth Regiment.

There was a feeling of tension, almost of expectancy in the air, a sense that events were moving to some desperate conclusion. Parties of townspeople roved the streets armed with staves and clubs. "Parties of soldiers were also driving about the streets," one bystander reported, "as if the one, and the other had something more than ordinary upon their minds." At Private White's sentry post beside the Custom House, several wigmaker's apprentices baited the soldier. One, Edward Garrick, was particularly insulting. He declared that Captain-Lieutenant John Goldfinch was a stingy, shifty fellow who had refused to pay Garrick's master for a wig. The captain was a gentleman, the sentry replied, "and would pay every body." Garrick said scornfully that there were no gentlemen in the regiment. Peering into the darkness, the sentry dared Garrick to show his face. When the boy did, White struck him with the butt of his gun. Dazed and crying out with pain, young Garrick fled, pursued by another member of the guard, a sergeant, with a bare bayonet. As Garrick ducked into the doorway of a shop, the sergeant slashed at him with the bayonet and stuck it into a shutter. The sentry, Private White, joined the sergeant and struck the cowering, weeping lad once more as he cried out for help. A fellow apprentice and "a young man came up to the Sentinel and called him Bloody back." Attracted by the noise, other dim figures could be seen running down King Street toward the Custom House.

Somewhere a bell began tolling, and the cry of "fire" was heard. Private White was soon surrounded by a half-a-dozen boys shouting at the soldier—"Lousy rascal! Lobster son of a bitch! Damned rascally scoundrel lobster son of a bitch!" The crowd swelled rapidly, and word, exaggerated in the telling was passed among them of White's attack on

Garrick. White, mercilessly denounced, was now thoroughly frightened. He stationed himself on the Custom House steps, loaded his musket, and amid hoots and jeers, pointed it with its clumsy bayonet at the crowd. Henry Knox, a Boston bookseller and an amateur expert on military matters, warned White that if he fired his musket he would certainly "die for it." "Damn them," the alarmed and nervous soldier replied, "If they molest me I will fire."

The mood of the crowd around White was increasingly hostile. When Jonathan W. Austin, a law student of John Adams', came up and observed the scene, he urged the crowd to "come away, and not molest the sentry," but only a handful paid any attention. Snowballs began to spatter against the facade of the Custom House, with an occasional one finding its mark on White's head or body. They were soon supplemented by jagged chunks of ice. White tried to get into the Custom House, but the door was locked, and there was no response to his hammering. The barrage of shouts and snowballs continued: "Kill him, kill him, knock him down." White was repeatedly challenged to fire: "Fire, damn you, fire, you dare not fire." The town watchman, Edward Langford, who was observing the fray, attempted to bolster White's morale. His tormentors were only boys; they could do him no harm. In an agony of indecision, the sentry aimed his musket at the crowd, then pulled it up and bawled for reinforcement from the Main Guard.

Meantime, one of the members of the crowd in front of the Custom House dashed off through the streets calling out a curious rallying cry: "Town born, turn out! Town born, turn out!" A small crowd of civilians armed with clubs "and one thing and another" quickly collected in front of the principal barracks, Murray's converted sugar house. There a man yelled to four or five officers standing in front of the barracks, "why don't you keep your soldiers in the barracks?" The officers answered that they were doing their best. "Are the inhabitants to be knocked down in the streets? Are they to be murdered in this manner? You know the country has been used ill. You know the town has been used ill. We did not send for you. We will not have you here." The officers continued to try to pacify their interlocutor and the increasingly noisy group gathered around him. Finally, drawn by the sounds of conflict on King Street, this small crowd broke away, taking up the cry "the Main Guard!"

The British soldiers had watched the scene from the barracks windows. As people began to converge on the area around the Custom House from every part of town, the officers suddenly found themselves faced with a near-mutiny. One furious soldier rushed out of the barrack gate, knelt in the street, and aimed his musket at Boylston's Alley, where people were still congregated. "God damn your bloods," he shouted, "I'll make a lane through you all." Two of the British officers knocked the soldier down, took his musket away, and drove him back into the barracks. They had hardly done so when another soldier dashed out cursing the Bostonians and pointed his weapon at a knot of people who remained near the barracks. An officer interceded again, knocked the soldier down with the flat of his sword, and disarmed him. At Cornhill Street a group of soldiers held off townspeople with a fire shovel. When Captain John Goldfinch came on the scene, some townspeople pressed him to order the soldiers back to their quarters before someone was killed. Goldfinch, ducking snowballs, led the soldiers back to their barracks.

Everywhere that leaders of the Sons of Liberty mixed with the crowds, they did their best to persuade the people to return to their homes and clear the streets. Richard Palmes, a Boston merchant and a supporter of nonimportation, was bold enough to upbraid the officers for permitting their men to be out of quarters in light of the explosive atmosphere. "Pray, do you mean to teach us our duty," an officer asked. "I do not," Palmes replied, "only to remind you of it." "You see that the soldiers are all in their barracks, why do you not go to your homes?" Palmes, braving the snowballs, added his own injunctions: "Gentlemen, you hear what the officers say, and you had better go home." A number straggled off.

Andrew Cazneau, a moderate patriot, seeing men throwing lumps of ice at the windows of Tory merchant William Jackson's house, exhorted them not to "meddle with Mr. Jackson. Let him alone. Do not break his windows." Abashed, the throwers dispersed. Dr. Thomas Young, usually one of the more fiery patriots of the city, stationed himself at Royal Exchange Lane and tried to head off people pouring toward the Custom House. The soldiers had "made a rumpus and were now gone to their barracks, and now it was best for everyone to go home."

But his words had little effect. By now there were hundreds of Bostonians roaming the streets, most of them drawn, like filings to a magnet, toward the Custom House, ripping palings out of fences and legs off produce stalls along Market Street to arm themselves. An angry murmur like the noise of swarming bees rose from the streets, mingled with the ringing of bells and cries of "Fire! Fire!" and "To the Main

Guard." In the confusion, many citizens, hearing the frightening cry, turned out to fight an actual fire, carrying leather water buckets or helping to push the pump engines placed at strategic spots around the city for just such an emergency. Gradually the word got around that the trouble was not a fire but perhaps a more serious affair. One citizen, Benjamin Davis, seeing an acquaintance, Sam Gray, pass by equipped for fire fighting, called out, "There is no fire. It is the soldiers fighting." "Damn it," Gray replied, turning his steps toward King Street, "I'm glad of it. I will knock some of them on the head."

While all of this was transpiring in the space of a few minutes in various parts of the town, the beleaguered Private White was still surrounded by a growing crowd. He renewed his call for support from the Main Guard. Word was brought to Captain Preston as officer of the day that the Custom House post was in peril. Preston buckled on his sword, clapped his hat on his head, and stepped into the guardroom. A cool and cautious man with a reputation for personal bravery, Preston took his time deciding on a proper course of action. On the one hand, a terrified soldier of his command was in genuine danger. On the other, Preston was well aware that in the combustible atmosphere of the town, the appearance of a squad of armed soldiers would be seen as a serious provocation. A squad of soldiers could hardly be counted on to quell an angry mob of several hundred citizens, many of them armed with one kind of makeshift weapon or another. Moreover, Preston was painfully aware that "he had no right to defend the Custom House unless legally called upon" to do so, and that he could not be so called upon except by a civil official. With White's life perhaps in peril, Preston could hardly start out at nine o'clock at night to find a civilian authority willing to make such a request. Yet if he could muster up a force sufficiently large to rescue White from his post, he would leave the Custom House with all its crucial records exposed to invasion by the crowd. Indeed, there was no guarantee that a rescue party might not have to fight its way through the constantly growing crowd.

Preston's cruel dilemma on the night of March 5 was the simple and inevitable consequence of the folly of having troops in Boston to begin with. After the events of that night, Preston said what was undoubtedly true and would have been true for any responsible officer: that his primary concern was for the safety of White himself.

Finally, Preston ordered young Lieutenant Basset to turn out the guard. When it had formed, Basset reported it to Preston. What were his orders? "Take but six or seven of the men and let them go down to the assistance of the sentry." Preston had no sooner given the order than he decided he could not place such a crucial assignment in the hands of a young and inexperienced officer. He took command himself. The relief party consisted of Corporal William Wemms and Privates John Carroll, Matthew Killroy, William Warren, Hugh Montgomery, James Hartegan, and William McCauley. With the exception of the corporal, all were grenadiers. The squad moved off briskly, in a column of twos, with bayonets fixed but muskets unloaded.

Their first encounter was with a Bostonian named Nathaniel Fosdick, who was watching the proceedings from up the street. Fosdick was pushed by Corporal Wemms, at the head of the little column. He spun around angrily. "Why are you pushing me?" "Damn your blood," replied Wemms, "stand out of our way." "I will not. I am doing no harm to any man, and I will not stand aside for anyone." Fosdick replied. The column gave way to right and left and marched around him.

Seeing Preston and his soldiers approaching, Henry Knox, who had been doing "everything in his power to prevent mischief," ran up to Preston, seized him by the coat and cried, "For God's sake, take care of your men. If they fire, they die." "I am sensible of it," Preston replied, moving off to catch up with his men. At the sentry box, the soldiers stopped and began to load their muskets, charging the firing pans and ramming the cartridges home.

Preston's first act was to tell White to fall in with the squad from the Main Guard. He then attempted to march the guard back to the guard house, but the crowd pressed so thickly that the soldiers were unable to force their way through. So there was an impasse: the soldiers could not withdraw, and the crowd clearly had no intention of doing so. As though to speed the dénouement, individuals in the crowd began to bait the soldiers once more: "Damn you, you sons of bitches, fire. You can't kill us all." The soldiers, unable to penetrate the crowd, formed an arc extending from a hitching post at the corner of the Custom House to the sentry box.

Though a writer must, almost of necessity, impose some order on the scene simply by describing it, the scene itself was, in essence, indescribable. The noise, the shouting and clatter, the ringing of bells, the throbbing movement of the crowd as those in back pressed forward and those in front tried to prevent themselves from being pressed against the points of the soldiers' bayonets, the efforts of bolder spirits to gain a place in the front ranks and of the more prudent to withdraw— all this presented a picture of hopeless confusion. It must also be remembered that this took place with no more illumination than the moon and such fitful light as might be provided by torches and lamps. None of those present were later able to give a very coherent picture of what had happened, and among the many different versions there were innumerable discrepancies or outright contradictions.

But dozens and indeed hundreds of minor encounters took place that often stuck in people's memories as the most significant incidents in the whole tumultuous and frightening night. Private White, the terrified focus of the wild evening, saw Jane Whitehouse, who lived near his quarters in Royal Exchange Lane, in the front rank of townspeople and pushed her aside, saying "Go home or you'll be killed." One person was most deeply impressed by the constant ringing of bells. For another the most vivid memory was the large brass knocker on the Custom House door. Or the meeting of a friend or neighbor and the words exchanged. Young Joseph Hinkley, scared half out of his wits, felt a reassuring hand on his back. It was Sam Gray, slightly tipsy, who said, "Do not run, my lad, they dare not fire."

Captain Preston, meanwhile, stood in front of the soldiers trying to persuade the crowd to disperse. They should return to their homes. The soldiers were simply doing their duty. But the yells and catcalls and curses continued, and the captain could hardly be heard above the din. Amid the confusion, Justice of the Peace James Murray appeared to read the Riot Act, but he was driven off with a barrage of snowballs. By now some 300 to 400 men were pressed into the area in front of the Custom House. In a kind of suicidal litany, the mob dared the soldiers to shoot. "Why do you not fire? Fire and be damned . . . You dare not fire." Separate encounters took place between individual soldiers and members of the mob, as here and there a bold citizen armed with a club or stick fenced with a soldier and tried to strike down his bayonet. The hotheaded Nathaniel Fosdick, who had gotten a stick and was threatening a soldier with it, was jabbed in the chest and arm sharply enough to draw blood.

Theodore Bliss made his way laboriously through the crowd to Preston. "Are your men loaded?" he asked. "Yes." "Are they loaded with ball? . . . Are they going to fire?" "They cannot fire," Preston replied, "without my orders." Richard Palmes, who had helped to calm the crowd at the Murray's sugar house barracks, joined the two men and repeated the questions. "Sir," he said to Preston, "I hope you don't intend the soldiers shall fire on the inhabitants." "By no means, by no means," the captain replied. He was standing in front of the muskets and "must fall a sacrifice" if they fired. "My giving the word 'fire' under those circumstances, would prove me no officer."

At this point a club, thrown by someone in the crowd, struck the soldier named Montgomery and knocked him off his feet. The furious and frightened man rose, fully cocked his firing piece, and shouting "Damn you, fire!" pulled the trigger. Palmes, standing near the soldier, struck his arm with his club and then aimed a vicious blow at Preston's head. He slipped as he swung and hit Preston's arm, and Montgomery stabbed at Palmes with his bayonet, forcing him off.

After Montgomery's shot, which struck no one, the crowd fell back, leaving an open space in front of the soldiers. Another soldier, the one named Killroy, raised his piece and pointed it, without aiming, in the general direction of Edward Langford and Sam Gray. "God damn you, don't fire," Langford shouted at him, but the soldier fired, and Gray fell with a gaping hole in his head. Still there had been no order to fire from Preston. Another musket, apparently double-loaded, was fired, and two bullets struck Crispus Attucks' chest. Attucks, who was also known as Michael Johnson, was a large black man in his late forties, reputed to have come to Boston from New Providence in the Bahamas. There is some evidence that suggests he was part Indian and may have belonged to the nearby Natick tribe at Framingham. He had been in the thick of things since early in the evening.

Someone called out to charge the redcoats before they could reload, and a few started forward. There were more shots. One bullet passed through the body of a sailor standing in the middle of the street and another struck his shoulder. Robert Patterson was struck in the wrist of his right hand. Patrick Carr, an Irish immigrant and an apprentice to a breeches maker, was retreating toward a barber shop in Quaker Lane when a ball struck him and "went through his right hip & tore away part of the backbone & greatly injured the hip bone." Seventeen-year-old Samuel Maverick, apprentice to Jonathan Cary, a kegmaker, had started to run for home soon after the first shot was fired. As he ran a bullet ricocheted and struck him in the chest, killing him instantly. Edward Payne, a merchant of Boston, standing in his own doorway watching the wild scene before him, was struck in the right arm. Another seventeen-year-old, Christopher or Kit Monk, armed with a catstick for batting a ball, was standing with his friend James Brewer, a young mechanic, ten or fifteen feet from the soldiers. Monk staggered, and Brewer asked: "Are you wounded?" When Monk replied that he was, Brewer assured him it was only fright.

When the shots rang out, the crowd's reaction was that the muskets were loaded with blank charges and that the soldiers had simply fired to frighten them off. Even the sight of bodies lying on the street could not at first penetrate their consciousness. "I thought," one testified later, the people "had been scared and run away, and left their greatcoats behind them." Shock and incredulity paralyzed many people as the full realization struck them that their fellow townspeople lay dead or dying or seriously injured around them.

Meanwhile the soldiers reloaded and cocked their muskets. At this point Preston was finally able to assert his control over the men. He angrily challenged them for having fired without his orders. They protested that they had heard him give the command "Fire!" While he was upbraiding them, the crowd began to press forward, this time to retrieve the bodies of the dead and wounded. The soldiers, afraid they were about to be attacked, raised their muskets to the firing position, but Preston pushed up the barrels, shouting "Stop firing! Do not fire!"

Benjamin Burdick stepped up to the line of soldiers and peered at them in the dim light. "I want to see some faces that I may swear to another day." Preston turned at Burdick's words. The two men looked at each other for a long moment, and Preston said quietly, "Perhaps, sir, you may."

The casualties were carried off. Patrick Carr was taken to a house in Fitch's Alley while someone went for a doctor. The body of Crispus Attucks was carried with some difficulty to the Royal Exchange Tavern across from the Custom House. Gray's corpse was taken to Dr. Loring's house; the door was locked and no one responded to knocking, so the body was left on the steps. Samuel Maverick, coughing blood, was helped to his mother's boarding house, where he died a few hours later. Three of the crowd had been killed on the spot, two mortally wounded.

Preston marched the soldiers back to the Main Guard, turned out the whole guard, and placed them in "street firings," a formation intended to enable soldiers to deal with rioters. Rumors had reached him that four or five thousand enraged citizens of the city were preparing to attack the soldiers; the crowd in King Street, after initially scattering, had in fact swelled from a few hundred to more than a thousand. Preston could hear the town drums beating, calling out the militia, and the cry "To arms," summoning the inhabitants of the city to action. The bells of all the churches began a doleful tolling. Preston, thoroughly alarmed, had his own drummer beat "To arms," alerting the whole Boston garrison.

British officers, responding to the call "To arms," had difficulty reaching their units. Lieutenant Ross, an officer in the Fourteenth Regiment, was hit by a stick; two ensigns were beaten and knocked down. Captain Goldfinch was waylaid, struck in the face, and had his sword taken from him.

A number of citizens went to see Lieutenant Governor Hutchinson to tell him, in essence, that "unless [he] went out immediately, the whole town would be in arms and the most bloody scene would follow that had ever been known in America." Hutchinson, with some courage, set out immediately for the Town House accompanied by friends. They found it difficult going, however. At Dock Square "a great body of men, many of them armed with clubs and some few of them with cutlasses and all calling for fire arms" intercepted them, and when Hutchinson identified himself as the lieutenant governor and urged them to return to their homes, they cursed and threatened him. Hutchinson had to beat a hasty and undignified retreat, circling around through Pierce's Alley, past blood-spattered snow, to where the soldiers of the Twenty-ninth stood in their "street firings," their muskets at the ready. Joseph Belknap, a loyal supporter of the Crown, who had accompanied Hutchinson, called out to the soldiers:: "Here is his Honour, the Lieutenant Governor, come to talk with you. Where is your officer?" "Stand off, stand off," came the reply from the soldiers. Isaac Pierce, another member of Hutchinson's party, went over to Preston. "There is His Honor, the Commander in Chief." "Where?" "There, and you are presenting your firelocks at him." Hutchinson and Belknap came up as he spoke, and Hutchinson began to upbraid the unhappy captain. "How came you to fire without orders from a civil magistrate?"

"I was obliged to, to save my sentry," Preston replied.

"Then you have murdered three of four men to save your sentry," Pierce interjected.

"These soldiers ought not to be here," Hutchinson declared.

"It is not in my power to order them away," Preston replied. "Pray, sir, do you go up to the Guard House." There they could discuss what action might be called for. But Hutchinson was understandably wary. "I don't think it prudent for me to go to the Guard House," he told the captain.

Belknap, fearing for the lieutenant governor's safety, and seeing that nothing was to be accomplished by conversation carried on in front of the crowd and the soldiers, pressed him to "go into the Council Chamber, and speak to the people." Some of the nearby crowd, catching

Belknap's words, raised the cry: "The Town House, the Town House," and Hutchinson found himself hurried off willy-nilly to the building. There he found several of the patriot leaders, among them Will Molineux, who urged him to order the troops back to their barracks. Hutchinson chose instead to speak to the crowd from the balcony opening onto King Street. He spoke of his own distress at the tragic events of the night, and promised that a full investigation would be made and the guilty parties punished. Meantime they should return to their homes. "The law shall have its course," he declared; "I will live and die by the law." Some of the crowd responded with derisive shouts and curses, but a substantial number drifted off.

Hutchinson had hardly left the balcony when someone pushed his way out and urged the crowd, lingering indecisively, not to leave until the soldiers did. Molineux renewed his appeal to Hutchinson to order the soldiers off the streets; Hutchinson in turn suggested to Lieutenant Colonel Carr, the senior British officer present, that the soldiers be sent back to their barracks. It was advice, not an order, but Carr acted upon it. The soldiers were formed up and marched off, and the crowd straggled off to their homes to reflect upon the events of the evening.

Hutchinson at once summoned the justices of the peace and the commanding officer of the British forces, Colonel Dalrymple, and began on the spot to assemble evidence. Witnesses were hastily rounded up and testimony taken. Preston could not at first be located. The sheriff was sent off, armed with a warrant, and at two o'clock in the morning the exhausted captain was brought before the justices. Several witnesses swore they had heard him give the order to fire, and Preston was placed in jail by order of the justices at about 3:00 A.M. The next morning the eight soldiers appeared and were also imprisoned.

So ended the confused, tension-filled, and finally bloody encounter that is known as the Boston Massacre. That it was no worse is a tribute to British military discipline and the coolness of Captain Preston. It is also a tribute to the patriot leaders, who kept the mob from exploding into greater violence. Finally, it is a tribute to Thomas Hutchinson, who acted with great decision and courage. But last of all, it is a testament to the folly of the English government in adopting policies that could make the colonists so hate the mother country that such violence was inevitable.

8

The Aftermath of the Massacre and the Trial

LIEUTENANT Governor Thomas Hutchinson's forthright and courageous action on the night of the massacre doubtless saved Boston from a holocaust. His vow to put his trust in the law and see justice done took the heat out of an aroused and belligerent populace. His role as tactful intermediary between Will Molineux, as representative of the people, and Lieutenant Colonel Maurice Carr led to a withdrawal of the British soldiers and a quieting of the crowd. He might well have stopped there, believing he had done a night's work in defusing the crisis. Instead he immediately put into motion the legal machinery that he had pledged to support. Justices of the Peace Richard Dana and John Tudor were summoned to the council chamber, evidence was heard from witnesses, and warrants were issued for the arrest of Preston, Basset, and the soldiers. When Hutchinson left the Town House not long before dawn, he had performed his most notable service for the city of Boston, for the colony over which he presided so uneasily, and perhaps for the American cause as well.

On the morning of March 6, the day after the massacre, the selectmen of Boston met with Hutchinson at the Town House. The first order of business from the patriot point of view was to have the troops removed from the city to Castle William, the fort on an island in the harbor. To keep the soldiers in the city, the selectmen said, could only have disastrous consequences. Meanwhile, a meeting of citizens held at Faneuil Hall appointed a committee composed of Sam Adams, John Hancock, Will Molineux, and Deacon Phillips to take the lieutenant governor essentially the same message: "Nothing can rationally be expected to restore the peace of the town and prevent blood and carnage but the immediate removal of the troops." The committee proceeded to the Town House, delivered its message, and sat down to await the lieutenant governor's reply.

Hutchinson found himself in an uncomfortable position. It was one thing for his council of selectmen to urge the removal of the troops. The council was a legal governmental body. But the meeting at Faneuil Hall was unauthorized and extralegal. Could Hutchinson accede to its demands without recognizing the meeting as legitimate and thus betraying his duty to the Crown? It was a cruel dilemma, and Hutchinson could not decide what to do. So he adjourned the council meeting, agreeing to discuss the matter further that afternoon.

The meeting at Faneuil Hall also reconvened in the afternoon. This time the crowd was so large that it overflowed the hall, and the meeting adjourned to the Old South Church, which, with its ample balconies, had a larger capacity. Again the crowd rejected out of hand a suggested compromise that one regiment leave for Castle William and one stay in Boston. Again the Adams-Hancock committee was appointed to take this message to Hutchinson. Meanwhile his council had met again. One of its members. Royall Tyler, urged Hutchinson to comply. The men who were urging that the troops be removed, Tyler said, were "not such people as had formerly pulled down the lieutenant-governor's house," but people "of the best character among us—men of estates and men of religion." Tyler added a warning: if the soldiers were not removed, ten thousand men would be mustered to drive them out, even "should it be called rebellion." Several of the other council members backed up Tyler, stating that unless it was agreed to remove the troops, "they were sure the night which was coming on would be the most terrible that had ever been seen in America." Still Hutchinson balked. All that he had saved the night before, he now seemed determined to squander. But turn and twist as he might, he could not rally any support. The council was firmly and unanimously against him. Finally he gave in. "What else could you do?" Colonel Dalrymple asked to solace him.

The committee that had waited outside for Hutchinson's decision returned to the Old South Church and announced the good news, which "gave Great Joy to the inhabitants . . . and a General Satisfaction, so that they went from the Meeting very Peaceably to their Habitations." And well they might. By the threat of open rebellion, they had forced another capitulation. Quite plainly they were ready to revolt or, more strictly, were in a state of revolt, if revolt means determined and systematic rejection of the established authority.

Colonel Dalrymple was understandably uneasy about embarking the troops for Castle William without permission from his senior officer, General Gage. So Dalrymple rushed off a dispatch to Gage, who was with the British troops in New York. Gage wisely ratified the decision, and on March 10 the Twenty-ninth Regiment, accompanied by Molineux to protect the troops "from the indignation of the people," marched to the wharves to be carried by barge and longboat to Castle William. Four days later, the Fourteenth followed.

The funeral of the slain men took place on March 8. The patriots arranged a solemn procession that took the four coffins (Patrick Carr died six days later) around the Liberty Tree and to the Old Granary Burial Ground. An enormous crowd of some twelve thousand men and women marched in the cortege. Watching with contempt, the Reverend Mather Byles turned to an acquaintance and said, "They call me a brainless Tory. But tell me, my young friend, which is better—to be ruled by one tyrant three thousand miles away, or by three thousand tyrants not one mile away." It was a witty comment, but it suggested a serious truth. Many of those colonists who aligned themselves with the Tories did so less out of love for their distant monarch than out of distaste for "popular government" or, as they would have put it, mob rule.

With the two regiments in Castle William, the attention of the Bostonians turned to Captain Preston and the soldiers who had been arrested with him for causing the massacre. It was now up to the city to demonstrate that justice could be done even when passions were at their height. The first act of this drama took place in John Adams' office, when on the sixth of March a Boston merchant named James Forest arrived with tears streaming down his face. A Tory and a friend of Captain Preston's, Forest pleaded with Adams to act as counsel for the officer. Preston could find no lawyer willing to run the risk of popular displeasure by taking his case. Forest had gone first to Adams' friend young Josiah Quincy, and Quincy had declared that he would defend

Preston if Adams would join with him, but "without it positively he will not." Adams assured Forest that he would defend Preston, adding with a touch of that self-righteousness common to his nature, "Counsel ought to be the very last thing that an accused Person should want in a free Country." Further, "this would be as important a Cause as ever was tryed in any Court or Country of the World; and that every Lawyer must hold himself responsible not only to his Country, but to the highest and most infallible of all Trybunals [God Himself] for the Part he should Act." If Preston was convinced that he could not have a fair trial without Adams' assistance, he should certainly have it. The bargain was sealed with a one-guinea fee.

It took considerable courage for Adams to take on such an unpopular case in the charged emotional atmosphere of Boston. He felt he was risking, so he wrote in his diary, "a Popularity very general and very hardly earned" as a prominent patriot, and was incurring a "Clamour and popular Suspicions and prejudices" that would dog him the rest of his life. As it turned out, though, he somewhat overdramatized the case—as he was inclined to do. Sam Adams and the other most zealous patriots assiduously exploited the massacre for propaganda, but there is every indication that they wanted the British soldiers to have a fair trial.

While James Forest was engaging John Adams to defend Captain Preston, Samuel Adams and other patriot leaders were collecting testimony from witnesses, much of it to the effect that the soldiers had shot down their victims in cold blood. The painter John Singleton Copley stated to an investigating committee that after the shots had been fired, he had heard a soldier say that "the Devil might give [the inhabitants] quarter; he should give them none." Henry Pelham, Copley's half brother, also an artist, prepared a crude but dramatic drawing of the scene of the massacre, from which Paul Revere made an engraving. Without bothering to ask Pelham's permission, he turned out hundreds of prints, hand colored, that showed Preston, his sword raised, ordering the soldiers to fire on the defenseless citizenry. Inscribed on Revere's scene of the massacre were the lines:

> Shoulde venal courts, the scandal of the land ,
>   Snatch the relentless villain from her hand,
> Keen execrations, on this plate inscribed,
> Shall reach a judge who never can be bribed.

Rough as the engraving was, it helped to fix in the public mind the patriot's own version of what had happened.

Meanwhile Captain Preston, in jail with the eight soldiers, was made the target of public wrath. The Reverend John Lathrop preached a sermon in the Old North Church taking as his text the passage in Genesis: "The voice of thy brother's blood crieth unto me from the ground." The murdered men had fallen victims "to the merciless rage of wicked men." The man who "really intended to kill, unless in defence of his own life under absolute necessity, *he shall surely be put to death*," he intoned. There were threats to carry Preston off from prison and lynch him. Doctor Benjamin Church described the soldiers as "brutal banditti," "grinning furies gloating o'er their carnage." They deserved to "have had their Bones piled up in the Common as a Monument to Massachusetts Bravery." On the other hand, there were those who, like Adams, were anxious to see justice done and clearly felt sympathy for the captain's plight. Indeed, Preston wrote a touching letter, printed in the *Gazette,* thanking "the inhabitants in general of this Town—who throwing aside *all Party* and Prejudice, have with the utmost Humanity and Freedom stept forth Advocates for Truth in Defense of my injured Innocence. . . ."

When the superior court session began on March 13, a grand jury was impaneled, and Jonathan Sewall, attorney general of the colony, presented to it the indictments against Preston and the soldiers: "Not having the Fear of God before their eyes, but being moved and seduced by the instigation of the devil and their own wicked Hearts . . . did with force and arms feloniously, wilfully and of malice aforethought assault one Crispus Attucks, then and there being in the peace of God and of the said Lord the King." So read the ornate formal language of each indictment.

Jonathan Sewall, although the official prosecutor, was suspected of Loyalist sympathies and clearly did not have his heart in pressing the case again Preston and the soldiers. He discovered "petty Concerns" in Charlestown and Ipswich to occupy his attention. Samuel Quincy, also of doubtful firmness, was appointed special prosecutor in the case, and the patriots, alarmed at the prospect of an indifferently presented case against the soldiers, engaged Robert Treat Paine, a firm patriot, to help prepare the case for the prosecution. Bob Paine was a friend of John Adams from Harvard days and although Adams thought him crude and uncultivated, with a rough tongue, he respected his very considerable abilities as a lawyer.

Josiah Quincy, John Adams' fellow defense lawyer for Preston (and later the other soldiers), was a lively, warm-tempered young man whose nickname of "Wilkes" was a reference to his radicalism and to the fact that, like Wilkes himself, Quincy was cross-eyed. When Josiah Quincy's father wrote to upbraid him for "becoming an advocate for those criminals who are charged with the murder of their fellow citizens," the son replied that every man charged with a crime was entitled to legal counsel. Moreover, he assured his father, he had taken the case only after being "advised and urged to undertake it, by an Adams, a Hancock, a Molineux, a Cushing, a Henshaw, a Pemberton, a Warren, a Cooper, and a Phillips"—in effect the general staff of the patriot party in Boston.

It has been suggested that John Adams was similarly encouraged by the patriot leaders, on the grounds that they were confident the soldiers would be found guilty of murder and were therefore willing to see them defended by two of the ablest lawyers in the province. It seems more plausible to suppose that the patriots' general staff was willing to leave the issue to the working of the law, anxious only that the contest be an equal one.

The initial legal skirmish was over the issue of when the trial was to take place. Sam Adams pressed Hutchinson almost daily to order the trial held at once, even if it meant replacing two sick judges, John Cushing and Edmund Trowbridge. Hutchinson, for his part, did all he could to delay. The matter was complicated by the fact that informers Ebenezer Richardson and George Wilmot—the men who had defended Richardson's house on the night of February 22 and had fired on the crowd—were on the court docket ahead of Preston and the soldiers. Feeling against Richardson was, if anything, more bitter than against the soldiers. To postpone his trial until the next session in June would inflame popular feeling. Sam Adams, Hancock, Warren, Molineux, and Cooper descended on the court, followed by "a vast concourse of people," to warn against any delay. There is little reason to doubt that one factor in their pressing for speed was their genuine concern that if Richardson was not brought to trial, the rougher element in the city might try to lynch him, and the patriot leaders might be powerless to stop them. Indeed, Judge Peter Oliver believed that "had the trial been refused it was a more than equal chance that the Prisoners would have been murdered by the Rabble; and the Judges exposed to Assassinations."

The judges thus gave in and set Richardson's trial for March 23; but Richardson, arguing that he could not find a lawyer to defend him or witnesses who dared to testify in his behalf, was given a continuance until April 6, and a reluctant lawyer was appointed to defend him. A series of misadventures, including the illness of the court-appointed attorney, who was replaced by Josiah Quincy, delayed the formal opening of the trial until April 20.

When the trial began, Josiah Quincy, pulling no punches, made a brilliant defense of Richardson, based on the proposition that "a man's home is his castle." A mob had no right to force him from it; "a man is not obliged to fly from his own House." Robert Treat Paine made an able argument for the prosecution, and the case passed to the judges, who were in accord on the point that, since Richardson had acted in self-defense, he could properly be charged with no more than manslaughter. But Judge Oliver went further; he could not forebear to harangue the court and the spectators who were crowded into every corner. Richardson, he said, was not even guilty of manslaughter. The real culprits were those who had raised the signs and thereby encouraged mob action, and the magistrates, the sheriff, and the justices of peace who had failed to keep order.

There could hardly have been a more inappropriate or ill-timed outburst. A spectator shouted at him: "Damn that Judge, if I was nigh him, I would give it to him." As the jury started to file out of the courtroom, someone called out, "Remember jury, you are upon oath." "Damn him," called another, "don't bring in manslaughter!!" "Hang the dog! Hang him!" "Damn him, hang him! Murder, no manslaughter."

While the jury deliberated far into the night, the courtroom remained crowded with restless and impatient citizens. It was morning before the jurors appeared and the clerk asked the foreman for his verdict. Richardson was guilty of murder, Wilmot, not guilty. "A universal clap ensued," which was hushed when one of the patriot leaders called, "For shame, for shame, Gentlemen."

The judges, unwilling to accept the verdict of the jury, and not daring to refuse it, adjourned until May 29 without passing sentence. By that time Judge Oliver had fallen from his horse and incapacitated himself, and Judge Trowbridge was having a siege of nerves that made it impossible for him to sentence Richardson. It was also impossible to begin the trial of Captain Preston and the soldiers. Many patriots as well as Loyalists welcomed the delay. The Reverend Andrew Eliot, a good patriot, noted: "People complain of the delay of justice. Perhaps it was best to delay the trial at the first. The minds of men were too much enflamed to have given [Preston] a common chance."

The pending trial of Preston and the accused soldiers nevertheless became a focus for popular passions. A rumor, which turned out to be true, circulated that Hutchinson had received a letter from Hillsborough directing him, under the authority of the Crown, should Preston and his men be convicted of murder, to suspend the execution of the sentence until the matter had passed under royal review. Preston felt that the rumor prejudiced his case, since jurors might feel freer to convict him if they felt confident that he would be pardoned. Rumors of plots to remove Preston and the soldiers from jail and hang them circulated constantly. On the occasion of one such rumor, Hutchinson was sufficiently alarmed to instruct the sheriff to take charge of the jailkeeper's keys, so that "the Keeper himself if they should be demanded will not have the power to deliver them."

As the date of the long-postponed trial arrived, one particularly awkward problem presented itself. Preston's best hope for a favorable verdict lay in convincing the jury that he had not given the order to fire. Conversely, the soldiers' case must rest on the grounds that they were ordered to fire by the captain and were, as good soldiers, simply carrying out orders. While Preston's trial preceded that of the soldiers on the docket, they, aware of the hazard to them of a verdict that would, in effect, accept Preston's insistence that he had not given the order to fire, petitioned to be tried at the same time, "for we did our Captains orders and if we don't Obey his Command we should have been Confine'd and shott for not doing of it . . . we only desire to Open the truth before our Captains face for it is very hard he being a Gentleman should have more chance for to save his life than we poor men that is Oblidged to Obey his command."

When it came to impaneling a jury to try Preston, the prosecution was remarkably casual about exercising its right to challenge prospective jurors. One juror allowed to sit had been reported as saying that he "believed Captain Preston to be as innocent as the Child unborn," and if he were on a jury he "would never convict him if he sat to all eternity." It was not surprising that Samuel Quincy, suspected of Loyalist sympathies, was not relentless in trying to exclude from the jury anyone with a settled conviction of the innocence of the accused. But Robert Treat Paine was, after all, the representative of the patriot faction. He had been added to the staff of prosecution lawyers presumably to keep them honest and see that the Crown put forth the best case possible. The prosecution's lack of vigilance in the selection of a jury suggests that it (and the patriot leaders as well) were resigned to, if not actually desirous of, having Preston and later the soldiers acquitted, or at least not convicted of murder. They were surely aware that a verdict of murder, followed by a royal pardon, would have an inflammatory effect on *"the Fury and Instability of the Populace,"* which they wished to moderate. There were additional factors: the patriot leaders wished to vindicate the city of Boston before the bar of public opinion; their friends in England had already warned them of the unfavorable reaction they might expect, even among their allies on the other side of the ocean, if there was any indication that Preston and the soldiers had been sacrificed to popular prejudices and the law abused. There was also the fact that the whole colonial case against the authority of Parliament rested, after all, on legal and constitutional grounds. The generation of men who fashioned the revolution had a veneration for the law that in most ages has been reserved for the deity. From all this, it followed that defense and prosecution had a common interest in a trial that would manifestly result in a fair verdict.

During the course of the trial itself, a great part of the more substantial testimony contained in the depositions was repeated, with the important addition of cross-examination. Perhaps most helpful to Preston's case was the testimony of the merchant Richard Palmes, who was standing beside Preston when the firing began and had not heard him give an order to fire. Also of importance was the testimony of three black men: Andrew, "Servant to Oliver Wendell" (actually a slave), Jack, and Newton Prince, a freeman and a pastry cook from the West Indies. Andrew's testimony, the most extensive, helped to establish clearly the threatening mood of the crowd and the mistreatment of the soldiers. An officer of the Fourteenth Regiment, Captain James Gifford, also gave telling evidence in Preston's behalf. Had a command been given, the soldiers "would all have fired together, or most of them." And Thomas Handasyd Peck told of encountering Preston after the firing and asking, "What have you done?" To which the captain had replied, "It was none of my doings, the soldiers fired of their own accord, I was in the street and might have been shot."

To patriots of the persuasion of John Adams and his fellow defense lawyer Josiah Quincy, the trials of Preston and subsequently of the soldiers were splendid opportunities to act out before an audience made up of the citizens of Boston the function and meaning of law as opposed to mob rule. In Adams' own words: "It appeared to me, that the greatest Service which could be rendered to the People of the Town, was to lay before them, the Law as it stood, that they might be fully apprized of the Dangers of various kinds, which must arise from intemperate heats and irregular commotions."

John Adams' argument for the defense was a classic of logical exposition. "It is better," he read the jury from Hale's *Pleas of the Crown*, "five guilty persons should escape unpunished, than one innocent person should die." Adams then went on to demolish, bit by bit, the testimony unfavorable to Preston. When he had finished, Robert Auchmuty, former vice-admiralty commissioner, spoke briefly and heavily. Robert Treat Paine then concluded for the prosecution, and the judges charged the jury. The jury, after some three hours of deliberation, brought in a verdict of not guilty. There was some grumbling in the town, but on the whole the judgment of the court was accepted calmly if unenthusiastically. Perhaps this was in part because popular feeling against the soldiers ran much higher than it did against Preston himself. It was, after all, with the soldiers, not their officers, that the townspeople were constantly engaged in angry brawls.

Three weeks intervened between the end of Preston's trial on October 29 and the opening of the trial of the soldiers on November 20. The defense of the soldiers rested on grounds far different from those on which their captain had been indicted. There was no question that they had actually fired their muskets. It was now legally established that they had done so without a command from their officer. It thus remained to be argued only (1) that they had in fact heard an order to fire, which they had not unreasonably assumed to have come from Captain Preston, or (2) that in the absence of any clear order, they fired simply out of fear for their lives and in self-defense.

For the trial of the soldiers, John Adams again was senior counsel, aided by Josiah Quincy. When the court convened, Samuel Quincy, Josiah's brother, opened the case for the prosecution, calling the killings "the most melancholy event that has yet taken place on the continent of America." The Crown would support its case with the testimony of "credible witnesses." Six of these witnesses, three of whom had testified at the trial of Preston, were called on the first day. The town watchman, Edward Langford, gave an account of how Private Killroy's shot had struck and killed Sam Gray. In the testimony of most of the prosecution witnesses, the wild events of March 5 assumed the character of a peaceful gathering of mannerly citizens. Few had any recollections of rocks, snowballs, swords, clubs, or even sticks. The soldiers had been quite unprovoked, firing simply out of malice. But several of the Crown witnesses on cross-examination admitted the soldiers had been hard-pressed and "showered with pieces of ice . . . hard and large enough to hurt any man; as big as one's fist." James Bailey, a sailor, had seen Crispus Attucks carrying "a large cord-wood stick" and leading a "huz-zaing, whistling" bunch of sailors, many of them armed with stout sticks and clubs.

The most damaging evidence against the defense was the story that Killroy had been heard to declare sometime prior to March 5 that "he would never miss an opportunity, when he had one, to fire on the inhabitants, and that he had wanted to have an opportunity ever since he landed." Accounts of the behavior of British soldiers in the months before the massacre itself painted a vivid picture of hostility and aggression. Concluding his argument, Samuel Quincy said that "on the evidence as it now stands, the facts, as far as we have gone, against the prisoners at the bar, are fully proved, and until something turns up to remove from our minds the force of that evidence, you must pronounce them guilty."

Josiah Quincy followed his brother. "The eyes of all are upon you," he told the jurors. "Patience in hearing this cause is an essential requisite; candor and caution are no less essential. Nay, it is of high importance to your country, that nothing should appear on this trial to impeach our justice or stain our humanity." It was not up to the jurors to concern themselves with the question of whether the troops had been properly sent to Boston. Their natural resentment at that act must not affect their attitude toward the defendants: "We are to consider the troops, not as instruments for advancing our cause but as fellow citizens who, being tried by a law extending to every individual, claim a part in its benefits, its privileges, its mercy." The jurors themselves would have "a reflective hour . . . when the pulse will no longer beat with the tumults of the day—when the conscious pang of having betrayed truth, justice and integrity shall bite like a serpent and sting like an adder." If they had already made up their minds, there was nothing more to be said; but if they were "zealous inquirers after truth," if, Quincy added, "you are willing to hear with impartiality, to examine and judge for yourselves—enough has been said to apprise you of those avenues at which the enemies of truth and justice are most likely to enter."

At the end of an eloquent opening, Quincy called some fifteen witnesses who testified as to the hostile and provocative actions of the townspeople against the soldiers. After the court recessed for the day, John Adams conferred with his fellow defense lawyers and argued that it was futile and unnecessary to press further the line that the people of the town had persistently harassed and tormented the troops. Adams was quite as anxious as his cousin, Josiah Quincy, to see the soldiers acquitted, but he had not undertaken the defense of the soldiers to indict the city of Boston. In short, he would not continue as attorney for the defense if Quincy and a third lawyer, Sampson Salter Blowers, "would go on with such Witnesses who only served to set the Town in a bad light." Adams was, of course, right. The real issue was the precise situation at the moment on the night of March 5 when the soldiers fired their muskets. Thereafter Josiah Quincy's questioning of witnesses focused on the events of the night of March 5, rather than on a recital of the assaults and harassments by Bostonians against the soldiers. Here Quincy built a convincing case to show that the soldiers had been under merciless pressure from armed and aggressive citizens. Patrick Keaton, for example, told the court how Crispus Attucks had picked up two four-foot logs from a woodpile and had handed him one. And Jonathan W. Austin, Adams' own law clerk, stated that he expected to see White carried off bodily by the crowd, adding, "I thought if he came off with his life he would be doing very well." Andrew, Oliver Wendell's slave, testified again, describing Attucks' encounter with a soldier, the soldier parrying Attucks' blows with his musket.

One of the most telling witnesses for the defense was a young doctor, John Jeffries, a friend of Samuel Adams' and a strong patriot. Jeffries had attended the fatally wounded Patrick Carr, and he repeated a conversation with the Irishman. "I asked him," Jeffries said, "whether he thought the soldiers would fire. He told me he thought the soldiers would have fired long before. I asked him whether he thought the soldiers were abused a great deal, after they went down there. He said, he thought they were. I asked him whether he thought the soldiers would have been hurt, if they had not fired. He said he really thought they would, for he heard many voices cry out kill them. I asked him then, meaning to close all, whether he thought they fired in self-defense, or on purpose to destroy the people. He said he really thought they did fire to defend themselves; that he did not blame the man, whoever he was, that shot him."

And so the evidence of the danger to the soldiers' lives gradually accumulated until it made an impressive weight. It is important to emphasize that while some witnesses who were ardent Sons of Liberty clearly had very faulty memories or deliberately suppressed all recollections favorable to the soldiers, a number of others gave testimony that, although damaging to the prosecution and helpful to the defense, was, above all, the truth. On the whole the nature of the testimony indicates that those witnesses whose standing in the community was related to their reputation for integrity told the truth as best they could recall it. Others whose credibility was unrelated to their social or economic position did not hesitate, on occasion, to seriously misstate the facts.

When the testimony of witnesses for the prosecution and the defense was finished, the court adjourned to give counsel time to prepare their concluding statement and the judges to write their summations.

When the court reconvened, Josiah Quincy spoke first for the defense in an able argument in which he stated, "Upon the right of self-defence and self-preservation we rely for our aquittal." He finished his summary of the evidence by quoting the speech of Portia in the *Merchant of Venice:* "The quality of mercy is not strained, but falleth as the gentle rain from heaven."

Adams spoke next. Here was ideal opportunity for him to place the massacre and the tangled congeries of events and emotions that preceded and surrounded it in the larger framework of history, and in doing so, to instruct the people of Boston about the nature of revolutionary upheavals and the dangers they posed to the fabric of society, to humane and civil existence. "In the continual vicissitudes of human things," he declared, "amidst the shocks of fortune and the whirls of passion that take place at certain critical seasons, even in the mildest governments, the people are liable to run into riots and tumults. There are church quakes and state quakes in the moral and political world, as well as earthquakes, storms and tempests in the physical. . . . We have been entertained with a great variety of names to avoid calling the persons who gathered at the custom-house a mob. Some have called them shavers, some call them geniuses. The plain English is, gentlemen, a motley rabble of saucy boys, Negroes and mulattoes, Irish teagues and outlandish jack tars. And why should we scruple to call such a set of people a mob? I cannot conceive unless the name is too respectable for them. The sun is not about to stand still or go out, nor the river to dry up, because there was a mob in Boston on the fifth of March that attacked a party of soldiers. Such things are not new in the world, nor in the British dominions, though they are, comparatively, rarities and novelties in this town."

What of the particular events themselves? It was clear enough that Montgomery had been attacked and knocked down before he fired.

How much did the prosecution believe he was supposed to endure before retaliating? "When the multitude was shouting and hazzaing, and threatening life, the bells ringing, the mob whistling, screaming and rending an Indian yell; the people from all quarters throwing every species of rubbish they could pick up in the street . . . Montgomery in particular smote with a club and knocked down, and as soon as he could rise and take up his firelock, another club from afar struck his breast or shoulder . . . what could he do? You expect he should behave like a stoic philosopher, lost in apathy? Patient as Epictetus while his master was breaking his legs with a cudgel? It is impossible you should find him guilty of murder. You must suppose him devoid of all human passions, if you don't think him at least provoked, thrown off his guard, and into the furor brevis, by such treatment as this."

Having painted a vivid word picture of the circumstance under which the soldiers fired, and having stripped away the protective covering of their tormentors by assigning them the stark name of a mob, Adams ended by reminding the jurors of their responsibility. "Facts are stubborn things; and whatever may be our wishes, our inclinations, or the dictates of our passions, they cannot alter the state of facts and evidence. . . . To your candor and justice I submit the prisoners and their causes."

And then Adams directed a special word at the citizens of Boston, represented by the twelve jurors who sat listening to the small, florid man who was addressing them. "The law, in all vicissitudes of government, fluctations of the passions, or flights of enthusiasm, will preserve a steady undeviating course; it will not bend to the uncertain wishes, imaginations and wanton tempers of men. . . . It does not enjoin that which pleases a weak, frail man, but without any regard to persons, commands that which is good and punishes evil in all, whether rich or poor, high or low—'tis deaf, inexorable, inflexible.' On the one hand it is inexorable to the cries and lamentations of the prisoners; on the other it is deaf, deaf as an adder, to the clamors of the populace." A modern sociologist would not perhaps recognize in Adams' fervent words an accurate description of the functioning of the law in human societies. Adams was, nonetheless, articulating a view that was common to the patriot leaders of his generation. If God had once revealed Himself in revelation, He now very largely relied on law and on lawyers, who were not, after all, very far removed in spirit and in function from ministers of the gospel.

As in the case of Preston, Adams with consummate skill had

touched all the right chords. The court and the jury lay quite under his spell. Even Hutchinson, no admirer of either Adams, noted that he had "closed extremely well & with great fidelity to his Clients." Paine, who had the task of replying to Adams, was ill and convinced that he had "the severe side of the question to Conduct." He spoke at length but without fire and conviction. The summations of the judges added little to what had already been said. The case went to the jury at 1:30 P.M. Two and a half hours later the jurors were back. The clerk of the court then asked the foreman of the jury in the name of each defendant: "Gentlemen of the Jury, look upon the prisoner. How say you, is William Wemms guilty of all or either of felonies or murders whereof he stands indicted, or not guilty." "Not guilty," came the reply. "You upon your oaths do say, that William Wemms is not guilty, and so say you all."

So it was with each defendant except for Killroy and Montgomery, who were found guilty of manslaughter and taken off to be sentenced. Both pleaded benefit of clergy—a technicality to avoid the death sentence for manslaughter—were branded on the thumbs and discharged. The other six soldiers went free, making "their way thro' the Streets with little, if any, notice." Among those patriots pleased by the outcome of the trials was Samuel Cooper, who wrote to Thomas Pownall that the trials "must one w'd think wipe off the Imputation of our being so violent and Blood Thirsty a People as not to permit law and justice to take place on the side of unpopular Men." "I hope," Cooper added, "our Friends on your side of the Water will make this kind improvem't of them—administration has a very favorable opportunity of adopting gentle Methods respecting the colonies."

In the eighteenth century, physicians prescribed bloodletting for a variety of ailments, especially for "fevers." Someone fond of metaphor might have likened the Boston Massacre to a bloodletting (with the patient in this instance the populace of Boston) that reduced, if it did not cure, the revolutionary fever in that town. In another metaphor, it was as though the citizens of the Massachusetts Bay colony had come to the edge of the abyss and drawn back appalled at what they saw, which was the livid face of revolution.

Whatever metaphor one might prefer, the fact was that the aftermath of the massacre was a period of relative calm. The nonimportation agreements, which had been eroded in the other colonies, began to collapse in Boston. It was asking too much sacrifice of the merchants, and of their customers as well, to expect them to adhere to such a self-denying ordinance. Tea was foresworn by all good patriots, at least officially. But to keep up nonimportation in the hope of forcing the British government to renounce publicly the principle of Parliamentary taxation was a delusion and was soon seen to be such by the great majority of colonial patriots. Thus the efforts of the more doctrinaire colonists to maintain the nonimportation agreements failed. Though nothing in fact had changed, both parties to the dispute—the British ministers and the colonists—chose to assume that the other side must be having serious second thoughts and should be prepared in consequence for serious modifications of their positions.

The day after the trial of the soldiers ended was, ironically, the Queen's Birthday. It was celebrated by patriot and Tory alike. All day long the guns of the Boston militia were fired at intervals, and in the evening there was a "very Grand Assembly" at the Concert Hall attended by all the military officers from Castle William, by the customs commissioners, by the lieutenant governor himself, and, indeed, by "all the Best People in town." It was, in the enthusiastic words of one good patriot, "A General Coalition so that Harmony Peace & Friendship will once more be Established in Boston—Very Good Dancing & Good Musick but very Bad Wine & Punch."

But the people of Boston did not forget the massacre. Each year on March 5, Boston observed a day of mourning for those killed in the massacre. An orator inveighed against British tyranny and rehearsed the principles of American liberty, and the day was marked by the tolling of bells, illuminated pictures, and memorial services. Extravagant and naive as many of the speeches delivered by patriot orators on these occasions may seem to the modern consciousness, they did nonetheless give voice to emotions that lay very deep in patriot hearts. Some modern historians have spoken condescendingly of these yearly observances, seeing them more as examples of skillful propaganda on the part of Samuel Adams and Joseph Warren than sincere expressions of grief for the victims. This is to misunderstand and distort the memorials. To the great majority of Bostonians, the events of March 5, whomever the courts might have legally blamed or exonerated, were a dark and bloody tragedy. To remember them was far more an appropriate act of piety than a cynical manipulation of popular feeling. Christopher Monk, whose wounds left him permanently crippled, was always much in evidence on March 5, and John Hancock, in one memorial oration, drew his audience's attention to the "miserable Monk" with his "tottering knees, which scarce sustain his wasted body; look on his haggard eyes; mark well the death-like paleness on his fallen cheeks." A Tory, listening contemptuously to Hancock's lurid phrases, noted "the greasy rebellious Rogues swelling themselves up."

Samuel Adams came to his cousin John in December of 1772 to ask him, on behalf of the committee appointed to make arrangements for observing the massacre, if he, John, would give the principal oration of the day. It was the unanimous wish of the committee. John Adams refused on the grounds that the public were not able to make a proper distinction between a sincere observance of the day and a belief in the innocence of the soldiers; he would thus expose himself to the charge of hypocrisy. Historians have had the same difficulty. But Adams had a clear perception of the significance of the event itself. "On that night," he later wrote a friend, "the foundation of American independence was laid." Presumably Adams meant that the foundations were laid in the determination of the colonists of Massachusetts Bay that the British troops should be removed or driven out of Boston by whatever means necessary, and the demonstration to the British ministry that "order" could not be maintained in the colonies by a handful of soldiers; that nothing short of a full-scale army of occupation could henceforth compel obedience to any Parliamentary statutes to which Americans had strong objections.

While the occasions of the marking of March 5 may have witnessed much perfervid oratory, they were also opportunities to educate the populace in the proper principles of constitutional government. The speeches invariably resounded with classical allusions and a multitude of historical references. For knowledge and erudition they compare very favorably indeed with present-day political addresses. When John Adams refused in 1772, the choice fell on young Doctor Joseph Warren, who began by reminding his listeners of the great upheavals of the past; "When," he declared, "we turn over the historic page and trace the rise and fall of states and empires, the mighty revolutions which have so often varied the face of the world strike our minds with solemn surprise, and we are naturally led to endeavor to search out the causes of such astonishing changes."

The key to human freedom and happiness (whether in ancient Rome or more modern times), Warren told his audience, was "a noble attachment to a free constitution." From this point he reviewed the principal forms of government—monarchy, aristocracy, and democracy—and pointed out how the British constitution was a splendid combination of all three, a truly mixed government. The crucial question was whether, in fact, "the late Acts of the British Parliament for taxing America . . . are constitutionally laid upon us. First," he continued, "I would ask whether the members of the British House of Commons are the democracy of this province? If they are, they are either the people of this province, or are elected by the people of this province to represent them." Since they were clearly neither, it followed inevitably that "nothing done by them can be said to be done by the democratic branch of our constitution." Since the power to tax lay by tradition with the democratic branch of government, it followed that efforts by Parliament to tax the colonies were unconstitutional and must be resisted with the utmost determination.

Warren came eventually to the massacre itself. It was the inevitable outcome of mistaken policy. When it was "found that . . . taxation could not be supported by reason and argument, it seemed necessary that one act of oppression should be enforced by another, and therefore, contrary to our just rights as possessing, or at least having a just title to possess, all the liberties and immunities of British subjects, a standing army was established among us in time of peace; and evidently for the purpose of effecting *that,* which it was one principal design of the founders of the constitution to prevent (when they declared a standing army in a time of peace to be *against law*), namely, for the enforcement of obedience to acts which, upon fair examination, appeared to be unjust and unconstitutional." Soldiers were "ever to be dreaded as the ready engines of tyranny and oppression. . . . And this will be more especially the case when the troops are informed that the intention of their being stationed in any city is to overawe the inhabitants. That this was the avowed design of stationing an armed force in this town is sufficiently known; and we, my fellow citizens, have seen, we have felt the tragical effects! The fatal fifth of March, 1770, can never be forgotten. The horrors of that dreadful night are but too deeply impressed on our hearts. Language is too feeble to point the emotion of our souls, when our streets were stained with the blood of our brethren—when our ears were wounded by the groans of the dying, and our eyes were tormented with the sight of the mangled bodies of the dead."

Joseph Warren was careful to disclaim any view as to the guilt or innocence of the soldiers who had fired the shots. That issue had been decided by the courts. The real crime lay with those who had sent the soldiers. That fateful decision was like so many others affecting the colonies. "The infatuation," Warren continued, "which hath seemed, for a number of years, to prevail in the British councils, with regard to us, is truly astonishing! What can be purposed by the repeated attacks made upon our freedom, I really cannot surmise; even leaving justice and humanity out of the question. I do not know one single advantage which can arise to the British nation from our being enslaved."

This truth must in time penetrate even the consciousness of "a capricious ministry . . . they will in a short time," Warren assured his audience, "open their eyes to their true interest. They nourish in their breasts a noble love of liberty. . . . They are also sensible that Britain is so deeply interested in the prosperity of the colonies that one must eventually feel every wound given to their freedom. . . . I doubt not but that they will, ere long, exert themselves effectually, to redress your grievances."

Warren ended by congratulating the people of Boston for their "unanimity and fortitude." "It was your union and determined spirit," he declared, "which expelled those troops who polluted your streets with innocent blood. You have appointed this anniversary as a standard memorial of the bloody consequences of placing an armed force in a populous city, and of your deliverance of the dangers which then seemed to hang over your heads; and I am confident that you never will betray the least want of spirit when called upon to guard your freedom. None but they who set a just value upon the blessings of liberty are worthy to enjoy her. . . . May our land be a land of liberty, the seat of virtue, the asylum of the oppressed, a name and a praise in the whole earth, until the last shock of the time shall bury the empires of the world in one common undistinguished ruin!"

The period of deceptive calm that followed the massacre obscured the fact that both sides had emerged from the tragic event chastened and with a clearer view of the realities of conflict. To put the matter bluntly: the threat of armed insurrection had forced two regiments of British regulars to abandon their post. Even the British ministry could hardly fail to see the implications of that simple fact. On the other hand, the apparent readiness of the countryside to take up arms in defense of Boston had given evidence of a reassuring degree of solidarity in the colony. The trial of the soldiers had, at the same time, provided a perfect opportunity to demonstrate to the populace the fact that the law would not condone illegal and riotous behavior.

Thus, while the Boston Massacre was a genuine tragedy and was quite sincerely perceived to be such by the people of Boston, it was also—its so-called propaganda value aside—a great benefit to the patriot cause. It accomplished five things: (1) it helped the moderate patriots recapture control of Boston from "the populace," or from that part of the populace that, because of its taste for direct action, had come increasingly to affect the course of events and to threaten the city with anarchy; (2) it forced the withdrawal of the troops from Boston; (3) it gave dramatic evidence of solidarity within the colony; (4) it gave the British ministry a painful lesson in the nature of colonial resistance and the limitations of British power; (5) by inflicting a severe setback on the British government, it made its ministers for a time at least more cautious in their dealings with the colonies and thus provided the patriot leaders with another invaluable increment of time in which to consolidate their leadership and forge the bonds of intercolonial unity.

Recent generations of historians have been inclined to treat the Boston Massacre as a kind of hoax, the inevitable consequence of the tireless efforts of "agitators" and "radicals" to stir up popular resentment against what was, in effect, an army of occupation. But the truth is that the "populace" of Boston no more needed to be stirred up on the matter of the British troops than they did in the Stamp Act riots. To the natural independence, and one might even say combativeness, of the average Bostonian, one need only add that the soldiers *were* a daily affront to most Bostonians; they *did* have criminal propensities; they *did* engage in a kind of perpetual guerrilla warfare with their civilian counterparts among the sailors, mechanics, and apprentices of Boston who were simply giving more vigorous and uninhibited expression to emotions shared by their "betters."

Calling a riot that resulted in the death of "only" five persons a massacre has been pointed to by some historians as an example of the ingenuity of the patriot leaders in converting a rather minor and disreputable episode into highly effective propaganda. Again, the assumption is that the death of five Bostonians could not have been a genuinely shocking and distressing event for the people of that city. The implication is that the outrage was somehow feigned and used in a quite cold-blooded spirit to achieve certain political ends. But an inevitable question is: What number of deaths *would* constitute a proper "massacre"? When we speak scornfully of Bostonians calling the death of five unimportant people of the "lower Class" a "massacre" we perhaps reveal more about our own attitudes and values than about those of the Bostonians in 1770. Bostonians in general were deeply outraged and quite sincere in calling the bloody culmination of the events of March 5 a massacre.

One important by-product of the massacre was that the control of affairs passed more securely than ever into the hands of the patriots. Hutchinson reported to General Gage, as Bernard had done before him, that "government is at an end and in the hands of the people." Hutchinson was "absolutely alone, no single person of my Council or any other person in authority affording me the least support," he wrote. And Dalrymple confirmed the analysis: "if the people are disposed to any measure nothing more is necessary than for the multitude to assemble, for nobody dares oppose them or call them to account."

The Board of Commissioners of the Customs, thoroughly unnerved by the massacre and the decision to remove the troops, held a final furtive meeting on March 9 and then scattered. One left for England, two others took refuge in New Hampshire, and thereafter all pretense of doing business was abandoned. The facts of the matter seemed to be that a board of customs commissioners would never be allowed to sit in Boston except under the threat of troops stationed in the city; but troops could never again be stationed in the city without causing an armed insurrection; therefore customs officers could never perform their duties in Boston. From which it might not unreasonably be concluded, as many Tory sympathizers did indeed conclude, that Boston was in a state of more or less continuous rebellion against the authority of Great Britain.

9

The *Gaspee* Affair

In the months after the Boston Massacre and the trial that followed it, there was a period of calm in the colonies. No serious incident took place between soldiers and townsmen, no mobs arose to pillage customs officers' houses. Not even Samuel Adams' fertile brain could come up with a new cause out of which to make propaganda. But this unnatural calm was shattered in June, 1772, by that contentious little colony, Rhode Island. The Rhode Island uproar, which has come to be known as the *Gaspee* affair, involved an attack on a British navy vessel and had elements of piracy and clandestine guerrilla warfare. Its aftermath was also dramatic and important, helping the patriot leaders to consolidate their hold over the movement.

Rhode Island is split into two parts by a large, protected body of water, Narrangansett Bay, which has many coves and inlets. It was ideal for smuggling, and the Rhode Islanders became adept at avoiding paying duty on the goods they imported—so adept that the British took special steps to close off this leak in their maritime system. They sent a special schooner, the *Gaspee,* to hound the Narragansett Bay smugglers. In command was one Lieutenant William Dudingston, who was entirely too energetic and efficient in chasing smugglers to please the Rhode Islanders.

The contest between the citizens of Rhode Island and Lieutenant Dudingston began in March, 1772, when Admiral Montagu dispatched him and the *Gaspee* to patrol Narrangansett Bay. Montagu was a rigidly efficient naval officer compared to his predecessor as top commander in American waters, Admiral Wood. Montagu wanted results; Dudingston was to stop the smuggling and enforce the Acts of Trade and Navigation. This suited Dudingston very well. An arrogant and overbearing man, he would teach the colonists a lesson.

The first skirmish involved Dudingston and the governor of Rhode Island. Dudingston's highhanded methods and his contempt for the local authorities resulted in a firm rebuke and even a threat to arrest him from Governor Joseph Wanton. Dudingston wrote at once to Admiral Montagu, whose headquarters were in Boston, complaining of his treatment at the hands of Rhode Island officials. Montagu, in turn, wrote to Governor Wanton that he was "ashamed" to read such letters "from one of his Majesty's governors." Dudingston had been sent to "protect your province from pirates . . . to give trade all the assistance he can . . . to protect the revenue officer and to prevent (if possible) the illicit trade that is carrying on at Rhode Island." Rumor had reached him, the admiral said, that the people of Newport were talking of fitting out "an armed vessel to rescue any vessel the king's schooner may take carrying on an illicit trade. Let them be cautious what they do," Montagu warned, "for sure as they attempt it and any of them are taken, I will hang them as pirates." As for the governor's "insolent letters," they would be forwarded to the secretary of state.

Governor Wanton in turn wrote an equally sharp note to Montagu. Dudingston had been both imperious and devious. He had refused to state the basis of his authority, so that the governor could not tell "whether he has come hither to protect us from pirates, or was a pirate himself. . . . As to your attempt to point out what was my duty as governor, please be informed that I do not receive instructions for the administration of my government from the king's admiral stationed in America. . . . I shall also transmit your letter to the secretary of state, and leave it to the king and his ministers to determine on which side the charge of insolence lies. As to your advice, not to send the sheriff on board any of your squadron, please to know that I will send the sheriff of the colony at any time, and to any place, within the body of it, as I shall think fit."

It is not surprising that Dudingston soon aroused bitter resentment among Rhode Islanders. He was widely quoted as saying that he would be pleased to see Newport burn and that "he would be damn'd" if he or his crew would raise a hand to arrest such a fire. He was charged by the colonists with being "haughty, insolent, and intolerant, personally ill treating every Master and Merchant of the Vessels he boarded, stealing Sheep, Hogs, Poultry, etc. from the Farmers round the Bay, and cutting down their Fruit and other Trees for Fire-Wood; in a Word, his Behaviour was so *piratical* and provoking that Englishmen could not patiently bear it." He behaved in a manner "more imperious and haughty than the Grand Turk himself." Most offensive of all, he sharply curtailed smuggling.

In addition to having bad manners, Dudingston proved a bad sailor; on June 9, while chasing an American vessel, he ran the schooner *Gaspee* onto a sandbar a few miles from Providence. It was a happy accident. The schooner could not get off the sandbar until high tide. A drummer went about calling out that the *Gaspee* was aground and that interested citizens should meet at the home of James Sabin.

Arms were collected, and in the middle of the night a small flotilla of boats carried a boarding party of Sons of Liberty toward the stranded vessel. Dudingston, not insensible to such a possibility, had posted a sentinel, but the patriots' boats were within hailing distance of the *Gaspee* before the sentinel discerned them and gave the alarm. Dudingston hurried on deck to find the *Gaspee* virtually surrounded by the dim, silent shapes of the little fleet.

Dudingston: "Who comes there?"

Abraham Whipple: "I am the sheriff of the County of Kent, God damn you, I have got a warrant to apprehend you, God damn you; so surrender, God damn you."

"I will admit no sheriff at this hour of the night," Dudingston replied.

As though the lieutenant's words were a signal for action, a shout rose from the boats and they closed in on the *Gaspee,* approaching from the bow so as to avoid the schooner's guns. Dudingston ordered the ship's crew to repel boarders with small-arms fire. The crew, tumbling out of their berths half-asleep and confused by the shouts, put up a feeble resistance. Most remained below, and the few who found their way to the deck were immediately overwhelmed. Dudingston, aiming a blow with his sword at one of the attackers, had his arm smashed by a club and was struck in the groin by a bullet. Crying out, "I am mortally wounded," he struggled to his feet only to be knocked flat again.

"Damn it, you're not wounded," one of the boarders declared, standing over Dudingston. "If you are, your own people done it." "Beg for your life, you dog," called another. "Surrender the ship." Only if the invaders would promise that the crew should not be hurt. This condition was readily agreed to. They would all be put ashore. Dudingston gave the order; the men were brought up from below—their hands bound behind their backs—and were placed in boats. When Dudingston, in severe pain from his wounds and bleeding badly, begged either that he be killed or that his wounds be attended to, his servant was untied and ordered to get dressings. Then the wounded officer was carried below to his cabin, where two surgeons patched him up as best they could while his captors rifled through his papers. His wounds dressed, he was placed half-clothed in a large longboat with other members of the crew of the *Gaspee* and rowed to the point of Pawtucket, where, since Dudingston could not walk, five members of the crew were untied and given a blanket to use as an improvised stretcher.

Before the longboat reached the point, flames mounted from the marooned *Gaspee* illuminating the water for hundreds of yards around. The schooner soon burned to the waterline and was a total loss. The culprits disappeared as quickly and silently as they had appeared.

The next question was what the British government would do in response to such an audacious assault on its authority. Abraham Whipple and his commandos had committed an act of war. Seizing and burning a ship of His Majesty's Royal Navy was as bold and calculated an insult as could be conceived. The response of the ministry was to appoint a Commission of Inquiry made up of the chiefs of the supreme courts of Massachusetts, New York, and New Jersey, the judge of the vice-admiralty court of Boston, and Joseph Wanton, governor of Rhode Island. A recently passed statute permitted persons suspected of crimes against the naval establishment to be brought to England for trial. The task of the commission was to determine against which colonists there was sufficient evidence to warrant their being tried in Great Britain.

The appointment of the commissioners brought bitter complaints. An American called before such a court, one colonist charged, was in a situation "infinitely worse than that of a subject of France, Spain, Portugal or any other of the most despotic power on earth." The commissioners themselves were "a pack of Egyptian tyrants."

It is not to be wondered that the commissioners found it singularly difficult to collect evidence. Despite a five-hundred-pound reward, no Newporters were willing to come forward to testify against their fellow townspeople in what had been in effect a community venture led by

368 / a new age now begins

"Men of Estate and Property." The commissioners thus had no choice except to declare their inability to deal with the case. The collector of customs in Rhode Island described the situation accurately when he wrote that the commission's failure indicated an end "to security to government servants . . . an end to collecting a revenue and enforcing the acts of trade." By virtue of the *Gaspee* episode, Rhode Island joined Massachusetts as being, in practical fact, in open revolt against the authority of the mother country. Although Whipple's amphibians were described as a "water-borne mob" and their actions as a riot, it would have been much more accurate to call the disciplined men who carried out their raid so swiftly and efficiently, under the command of an experienced former officer, a guerrilla navy.

The repercussions of the *Gaspee* affair were wide-ranging. The British government's announced intention of bringing the accused men to trial in England threatened the most basic of English liberties: every man's right to trial by a jury of his peers, that is to say, men of his own community. The patriot leaders instantly recognized that this, in effect, put a noose around their own necks. If the British had decided to bring the men involved in the *Gaspee* affair to trial in Britain—supposing they could apprehend any of the nautical pirate-patriots involved—then surely the British might decide to try the patriot leaders there, should they ever round up such men.

This clear threat gave impetus to the formation of the committees of correspondence—an intercolonial information network. The idea for such a network had first been announced by Samuel Adams in a Boston town meeting. Each colony should have such a committee, which would pass on news of interest to all the other colonies. The committees could also concert measures in defense of colonial liberty.

The Massachusetts Committee of Correspondence, with its head-quarters in Boston and operating under the direction of Adams, became a model of revolutionary organization, circulating a stream of information to Sons of Liberty in every community, and binding leaders together with ties of unusual strength and durability. The Boston town meeting that formally established the committee directed that it be made up of twenty-one persons with the task of stating "the rights of the colonists, and of this province in particular, as men, as Christians, and as subjects; to communicate and publish the same to the several towns in this province and to the world as the sense of this town . . . also requesting of each town a free communication of their sentiments on this subject. . . ."

The British threat to try the *Gaspee* affair's perpetrators in England stimulated other colonies to join Adams' information network, most notably Virginia, the Southern focus of resistance to Parliament. Early in 1772, the Virginia House of Burgesses set up a Committee of Correspondence; among the members were Richard Bland, Richard Henry Lee, Patrick Henry, and Thomas Jefferson. They were instructed "to keep up and maintain correspondence and communication with our sister colonies" and "to obtain the most early and authentic intelligence of all . . . Acts and resolutions of the Parliament, or proceedings of administration, as may relate to or affect the British colonies in America. . . ."

In May, 1772, the Massachusetts Great and General Court, offering a handsome bouquet of praise to the Virginia assembly "for the vigilance firmness and wisdom, which they have discovered, at all times, in support of the rights and liberties of the American colonies," heartily concurred "with their spirited and judicious resolves"—the Virginia resolves—and officially appointed a similar committee to succeed the town meeting's unofficial committee. When other colonial legislatures soon followed suit, another step was taken toward the intercolonial unity essential to any successful resistance movement.

In addition to the *Gaspee* affair, another episode served to further embitter the relationship between the royal officials and the patriot faction. Benjamin Franklin, who had made a second career as an agent in England for various colonies—Pennsylvania originally, then New Jersey and Georgia and finally, in 1770, Massachusetts—had long been the object of suspicion on the part of the warmer patriots, especially in Massachusetts. Doubts about his orthodoxy dated from the days of the Stamp Act, when he had been assiduous in soliciting jobs as stamp distributors for his friends. He was rumored to be at least mildly heretical in his religious notions, and his constant admonitions to the patriots to avoid all violent opposition to British authority grated on patriot sensibilities. Franklin's prominence in English literary and social circles and his evident enjoyment of the pleasures of English life also caused some grumbling among the Sons of Liberty in Boston.

Whether to strengthen his standing with the Massachusetts patriots or for some more obscure and complex reason, Franklin got his hands on some letters written by Thomas Hutchinson to Thomas Whately, formerly private secretary to George Grenville, and shipped them off to Thomas Cushing, speaker of the Massachusetts assembly and one of the leading patriots in the colony. They were to be shown only to a few leading men and were not to be printed or copied, Franklin wrote; their source should not be disclosed, and the letters themselves should eventually be returned. At first Franklin's injunctions were respected. For a time the letters were passed from hand to hand where they would best serve the cause. In the most damaging letter, Hutchinson had written to Whately that he never thought "of the measures necessary for the peace and good order of the colonies without pain. There must be an abridgment of what are called English liberties. . . . I wish the good of the colony when I wish to see some further restraint of liberty rather than the connection with the parent State should be broken, for I am sure such a breach must prove the ruin of the colony."

The fact that Hutchinson felt his proposals were in the best interests of the colony failed to impress the patriots who read the stolen letters. The sentence, "There must be an abridgment of what are called English liberties," said it all. The patriots already had the settled conviction that Hutchinson was plotting against their rights as Englishmen. Until now they had lacked proof. The letters were placed before the assembly in secret session and severely censured as designed to "sow discord and encourage oppressive acts of the British Government, to introduce arbitrary power into the province and subvert its constitution." The assembly petitioned the king to remove both Hutchinson and Andrew Oliver, secretary of the province, from their offices.

Inevitably the letters were eventually reproduced and found their way into newspapers and thus back to England, where there was general indignation at the theft of the letters, an indignation increased by the fact that Whately's brother and executor of his estate accused a man named Temple of purloining the letters. Temple challenged Whately to a duel, and Whately was wounded. Franklin then confessed his part in the transaction in order to exculpate both Whately, who had been suspected by some, and Temple as well. Franklin defended himself by arguing that the letters "were written by public officers to persons in public stations, on public affairs, and intended to procure public measures." As agent for Massachusetts it was his duty to forward them to his constituents. He was, he stated, motivated by a desire to promote peace and harmony between England and her colonies. Like many patriots, he had assumed that the conspiracy against American liberty had been hatched in Britain, but the Hutchinson letters showed that the colonists had an enemy in their midst whose distorted views of American affairs had exerted a baneful influence on the minds of the British ministers.

The petition from the Massachusetts assembly for the removal of Hutchinson and Oliver resulted in a curious scene. The petition was referred to a committee of the Privy Council for adjudication, and representatives of both sides were permitted counsel. The interest in London was so great that thirty-five Privy Councilors attended the hearing, more members than were normally present at the regular business sessions of the council. A number of visitors crowded the chambers, including Joseph Priestley (the well-known English radical minister and a staunch friend of the colonies), Edmund Burke, and Jeremy Bentham, among others. Alexander Wedderburn, solicitor general in the North government, a brilliant and vindictive man with a mordant wit, turned the full fire of his scorn on Franklin—"a most severe Phillipic on the celebrated American philosopher," as a witness described it, "in which he loaded him with all the licensed scurrility of the bar, and decked his harangue with the choicest flowers of Billingsgate."

Referring to Franklin's own account of the affair, Wedderburn declared that it was impossible to read it without horror: "Amid these tragical events, of one person nearly murdered [a reference to Whately's duel] of another answerable for the issue, of a worthy Governor hurt in his dearest interests, the fate of America in suspence—here is a man who, with the utmost insensibility of remorse, stands up and avows himself the author of it all. . . . Men will watch him with a jealous eye," Wedderburn went on, "they will hide their papers from him, and lock up their escritoires. Having hitherto aspired after fame by his writings, he will henceforth esteem it a libel to be called a *man of letters*. . . . I ask, my Lords," Wedderburn said, turning to the Councilors, "whether the revengeful temper, attributed by poetic fiction only to the bloody-minded African, is not surpassed by the coolness and apathy of the wily New Englander?"

Franklin's own feelings were indicated by the fact that he later wrote a pamphlet describing the errors in British policy that had led to the Revolution, entitling it "Hints on How to Make a Great Empire into a Smaller One," and dedicating it to Wedderburn.

The Privy Councilors, on the other hand, were delighted by the solicitor general's performance. They laughed and applauded at each piercing phrase. "The indecency of their behaviour," Lord Shelburne wrote after the session, "exceeded, as is agreed on all hands, that of any committee of elections" [notoriously rude and rowdy hearings on disputed elections]. Charles James Fox, one of the great Whig parliamentarians, years later recalled how "all men tossed up their hats and clapped their hands in boundless delight at Mr. Wedderburn's speech." The committee voted that the Massachusetts petition was "false, groundless, and scandalous, and calculated only for the seditious purpose of keeping up a spirit of clamour and discontent in the province."

Franklin was attacked in the British press as "a viper . . . festering in the bosom of Government"; he was an American Wilkes, "with a brand lighted from the clouds" to set fire to the empire. "The old Dotard thought he saw himself the Founder of Empires and the Father of Kings." But he was, in truth, "a skunk or American Pole Cat."

The striking thing about the episode was not so much Wedderburn's invective but the pleasure of the members of the Privy Council in hearing Franklin, as representative of the American colonies, so brutally abused. Their reaction revealed a surprising depth of hostility and contempt for Americans in general, as indeed did the subsequent newspaper denunciations of the Pennsylvanian. Clearly, resentment toward the colonists was deep and wide and nowhere more evident than in the highest levels of government. The affair of Hutchinson's letters, minor as it was in terms of the long and bitter conflict between Great Britain and her American colonies, nonetheless does much to explain British colonial policy. Small incidents are often more revealing than great events. The Privy Councilors, who abandoned themselves so unreservedly to enjoyment of Wedderburn's envenomed rhetoric, were hardly the proper people to help direct the course of government, at least as it related to America.

Perhaps it is not too much to say that it was the British attitude toward their country cousins in America more than British policy that made the Revolution inevitable. There was soon to be evidence of the disastrous effects of such an attitude.

10

The Boston Tea Party

AFTER the excitement created by the *Gaspee* affair had died down, there was a period of calm in the colonies. For more than a year, the British government passed no new edicts relating to America. As a result no mobs roamed Boston's streets, no effigies were burned in New York, no inflammatory pamphlets came off Philadelphia's presses. But it was an eerie, unnerving calm.

What disturbed the patriot leaders was the strong sense that British policy remained substantially unchanged, and whatever relief the colonists enjoyed was due to indecision or inattention and was thus temporary. They were uncomfortably aware by now that the British government could not comprehend the reasons behind colonial opposition to the Stamp Act and the Townshend Duties. They knew it was only a matter of time before Lord North and his cabinet proposed some new law that would once again stir up trouble.

The other shoe dropped in the fall of 1773, in the form of an edict that gave the East India Company a monopoly on the sale of tea to the colonies. The monopoly had its roots in one of the most extraordinary episodes in modern history—the subjugation and exploitation of the states of India by a stock company chartered by Parliament for that purpose. Remarkable as such an arrangement would appear today, when exploitation is far less gross and uninhibited, the arrangement was a common one in the seventeenth and eighteenth centuries. Indeed, most of the American colonies had been started by chartered companies whose purpose had been profit for the investors, or "adventurers." What was novel about the activities of the East India Company was that it set about to conquer, govern, and exploit not a wilderness but a series of ancient and wealthy cultures extending over the entire subcontinent of India. It was rather as though Congress had given General Motors a charter empowering it to take over the continent of Africa by whatever means it found necessary, and to run it quite without supervision or restraint for the benefit of G.M.'s stockholders.

The nineteenth-century British historian, William Lecky, wrote a vivid description of the activities of the East India Company's agents: "They defied, displaced, or intimidated all native functionaries who attempted to resist them. They refused to permit any other traders to sell the goods in which they dealt. They even descended upon villages, and forced the inhabitants, by flogging and confinement, to purchase their goods at exorbitant prices, or to sell what they desired to purchase, at prices far below the market value. . . . Monopolizing the trade in some of the first necessaries of life, to the utter ruin of thousands of native traders, and selling those necessaries at famine prices to a half-starving population, they reduced those who came under their influence to a wretchedness they had never known before."

A committee of Parliament that investigated the East India Company estimated that in the period from 1757 to 1766 the company had drained from the treasury of the Indian state of Bengal, through forced grants and bribes alone, more than 5,900,000 pounds. To this sum must be added private fortunes illegally accumulated by functionaries of the company, as well as the vast revenues of the company itself, which kept its own army, made up largely of native troops, and distributed a yearly dividend of 10 per cent to its stockholders.

So many of the East India Company's officials spent their energy making themselves rich rather than attending to business that the company was constantly on the verge of bankruptcy. Financial collapse seemed imminent in 1773. At this juncture, the British government stepped in to preserve the East India Company by trying to help it sell one of the India commodities that the company had stockpiled—tea. Some seventeen million pounds of tea lay in its London warehouses without prospective buyers. The surplus had accumulated partly because the company was forced to charge high prices for its tea in the colonies—a duty had to be paid when the tea was landed in England for sale or transshipment, and the Townshend Acts imposed a three-penny tax on each pound of tea brought into America—but also because East India tea was boycotted by the colonists, who refused on principle to pay the tax. It occurred to Lord North that a clever solution to the problem of disposing of the East India Company's tea would be to remit the English duty on tea, and then ship the tea to the colonies for sale there with only the Townshend Acts' three-penny tax and no duty. The East India tea would, in consequence, cost less in America than in England and also be even cheaper than smuggled tea. North knew by report that Americans were great tea drinkers, and he counted on their addiction and their thrift to sweep away any minor scruples the more ardent patriots might have against paying a token tax. In effect, he sought to bribe the colonists with cheap tea in order to induce them to pay the tax.

The granting of the East India monopoly was of course a mistake— and Lord North soon made another one, perhaps more serious. He permitted most of the tea to be consigned to Tory merchants, such as the sons, relatives, and friends of Governor Hutchinson, who were anathema to the patriots. By doing this, he further alienated the great majority of patriot merchants who, in general, represented the more moderate wing of the patriot party. It quickly became evident that North and the Tories had seriously underestimated colonial opposition to the whole importation scheme.

Once again, a clever but misguided expedient had taken the place of a generous and enlightened policy. Each such action on the part of the British ministry seemed to the colonists to give further substance to their charge that the British government did not understand the nature of their protests and, most important and most wounding of all, did not really take them seriously. The colonists' suspicions were correct; the British ministers could never get it through their heads that the colonists were not simply contentious troublemakers, greedy merchants, cloddish farmers, presumptuous bumpkins, and insolent planters who prated about liberty but were interested primarily in feathering their own nests. Doubtless more disasters have overtaken mankind as a consequence of not taking seriously the claims of the "other side" than from any other single cause.

As in the case of the Stamp Act and the Townshend Duties, the reaction of the colonists to the tea monopoly was immediate and vocifer- ous. From newspapers, pulpit, and printing press came exhortations against the importation of East India Company tea. The committees of correspondence labored overtime writing one another, "ripening councils," and preparing common resistance. Physicians, recruited to the antitea cause, stated that the drink weakened "the tone of the stomach, and therefore of the whole system, inducing tremors and spasmodic affections." Drinking tea, they claimed, would make Americans "weak, effeminate and valetudinarian for life." And an essayist warned, "Do not suffer yourself to sip the accursed, dutied STUFF. For if you do, the devil will immediately enter into you, and you will instantly become a traitor to your country."

The unsavory reputation of the East India Company was also cited as an argument against accepting the tea. "It is shocking to Humanity," a New Yorker wrote, "to relate the relentless Barbarity, practised by the Servants of that Body, on the helpless Asiatics; a Barbarity scarce equalled even by the most brutal Savages, or *Cortez,* the *Mexican* Conqueror." The company had "monopolized the absolute Necessaries of Life" in India, with the consequence "that thousands perished by this black, sordid and cruel Avarice." The watchmen of Philadelphia, John Dickinson wrote, should cry out "Beware of the East-India Company" as they made their rounds.

One of the causes of colonial anxiety, particularly on the part of businessmen, was fear of the tea monopoly's implications. If the British government could consign tea to Tory dealers, could it not also consign to certain favored merchants wine, spices, and other commodities that came to the colonies via Great Britain? Even broader implications were foreseen by one editorial writer. If the tea were allowed to be sold in America, he wrote, the British ministers would, under its cover, "enter the Bulwarks of our sacred Liberties, and will never desist, until they have made a Conquest of the whole." Thus the main objection to the East India Company's tea rested on principle. The colonists refused to pay the tax, even for cheap tea.

Thomas Hutchinson wrote to Lord Dartmouth, "The people of Boston and all the neighboring towns are raised to the highest degree of enthusiasm in opposition to the duty on tea. If our advices are to be depended upon, the spirit is not much lower in several other Colonies. . . . At and near Boston the people seem regardless of all consequences. . . . To enforce the Act appears beyond all comparison more difficult than I ever before imagined."

Hutchinson, like most royal officials and colonists of Tory persuasion, had seriously miscalculated the extent and the strength of the opposition to the landing of the tea. The natural question, of course, is why. With a vast amount of experience with colonial resistance to draw upon, and with presumably reliable advisers to supplement their own observations, why were Hutchinson and so many others so far wide of the mark?

An explanation might be the hardening of "revolutionary sentiment"—or whatever we wish to call the determination to resist impositions of Parliament and the British ministers that appeared to the colonists to be tyrannical and unjust. This resistance had formed into a kind of rock of resolution; it had become internalized, part of the consciousness of all who thought of themselves as patriots. Thus it did not depend on constant and fiery exhortations, on inflammatory incidents or colorful demonstrations. It was there, firm if undemonstrative, ready to assert itself whenever the occasion clearly required.

The imposition of the tea monopoly was just such an occasion, and patriot outrage quickly manifested itself. In Boston, Will Molineux, Dr. Joseph Warren, and other leading Sons of Liberty met at the sacred Liberty Tree on November 3, 1773, and then, accompanied by a crowd of 400 or 500, marched to the agents for East India tea. At the store of Richard Clarke & Sons, Molineux and the other members of the self-styled Committee of the People found not only Clarke but also several other merchants. Warren and Molineux made it clear to them that "the people are greatly affronted" that they had not resigned their commissions as tea importers. Clarke replied with some spirit that his callers could not constitute a Committee of the People since there were "Townspeople . . . present in this room who knew nothing of any such Committee."

Molineux then read a letter asking the merchants to agree to return the tea to England when it arrived. Clarke replied heatedly, "I shall have nothing to do with you," and the other merchants present, including one of Governor Hutchinson's sons, answered in a similar vein.

With that Molineux declared the merchants to be enemies of their country and subject to the displeasure of the people. He withdrew to report the failure of his mission to the crowd that waited outside. The uneasy tea sellers, watching from the window, could see Molineux speaking to the crowd, although they could only guess at his words. But they could clearly hear the crowd shouting "Out with them," and they had no doubt who "them" meant. Surprisingly, the mob soon began to move off toward the Liberty Tree.

Apparently Molineux and the other leaders, attempting to prevent violence, had persuaded the patriots to rally at the Tree. But then a sizable part of the crowd—largely boys and young men—ran back to the store, and before the doors could be locked, forced them open and removed them from their hinges. There followed much shouting and confusion and sharp exchanges with sticks and clubs between those few in the building who tried to defend it and the larger group attempting to storm it. With the doors gone, people crowded into the store and ran up and down the stairs, crying "Out with them, Out with them." Clarke and the other merchants made their escape, however, and Molineux and his fellow committee members managed to cool the temper of the crowd and restore order.

In every colony, protests followed the Boston pattern. In New York, patriot merchants were determined that the tea should not be sold. And their word had weight. The New York Tories feared that the patriot merchants could instantly raise "a considerable Mob, including a great number of retainers, such as Boatmen, Along-Shore men, Carmen and Porters, who are all paid highly for their services and therefore interested against us." The patriot faction that prevailed, according to an embittered Loyalist, was made up of "the outcasts of society" who carried their points "by putting individuals in fear of their lives."

The patriotic citizens of Philadelphia, following New York's lead, met on October 16 to adopt resolutions declaring that since "the duty imposed by Parliament upon tea landed in America is a tax on the Americans, or levying contributions on them without their consent . . . it is the duty of every American to oppose this attempt." Americans who "in any wise aid or abet in unloading or receiving or vending the tea" were declared enemies to their country, and a committee was appointed to wait upon the consignees and request them to resign "from a regard to their own characters and the peace and good order of the city and province."

More explicitly worded handbills circulated. One, warning Delaware River pilots that any who guided a tea ship into Philadelphia's harbor would be "tarred and feathered," was signed by "The Committee for Tarring and Feathering." A special object of wrath was one Captain Ayres, skipper of the *Polly,* which was known to be headed for Philadelphia with its hold full of tea. Ayres, a pamphlet stated, "was here at the time of the Stamp Act and ought to have known our people better than to have expected we would be so mean as to suffer his rotten tea to be funnelled down our throats with the Parliament's duty mixed with it." Attached was an open letter to Captain Ayres. "What think you Captain," it read, "of a halter around your neck—ten gallons of liquid tar decanted on your pate—with the feather of a dozen wild geese laid over that to enliven your appearance?" The captain was urged to "fly to the place from whence you came . . . above all . . . let us advise you to fly without the wild geese feathers."

Such widespread opposition brought results. In Charles Town, South Carolina, the patriot faction could report that "the Gentlemen who were appointed Agents for the East India Company were prevailed upon by threats and flattery to decline the trust." Everywhere under pressure, as a Tory merchant wrote, from "the insults of many rascally Mobbs Convened in the Dark high charged with Liquor to do every act of Violence their mad Brain could invent," most tea agents gave up their offices with alacrity. And if the agents insisted on business as usual, they found difficulty in getting tea to sell. When the tea ships arrived, their skippers found the patriots determined that the cargoes should not be unloaded. Many captains reminded themselves that their responsibilities to their owners and their crews were greater than their loyalty to the East India Company. The master of the ship carrying tea consigned to New York, finding himself and his cargo unwelcome, turned about and set sail for England. In South Carolina, after lengthy and tedious negotiations, the tea was landed and locked up in a warehouse. And Captain Ayres, naturally averse to tar and feathers, turned the *Polly* around before reaching Philadelphia and headed back to England.

Boston, as usual, was to be a very special case. Although Hutchinson wrote to Lord Dartmouth that "Massachusetts Bay has raised a higher spirit than I have ever seen before," the governor was determined to do all in his power to see that the tea was landed. With Hutchinson's active support, a number of Boston merchants refused to renounce their intention to sell the tea, and they took refuge in Castle William, the island fortress in Boston Harbor, along with the customs commissioners. When the *Dartmouth*, under the command of a Captain Hall and loaded with tea, arrived in Boston Harbor, Hutchinson ordered Admiral Montagu, Commander of the British fleet, to block the exit from the harbor and prevent the *Dartmouth* from returning to England. The tea must be unloaded.

At the same time, the citizens of the city and the neighboring towns were alerted by a broadside proclaiming: "Friends! Brethren! Countrymen! That worst of plagues, the detested TEA . . . is now arrived in this harbour. The hour of destruction, or manly opposition to the machinations of tyranny, stares you in the face. Every friend to his country, to himself and posterity is now called upon to meet at Faneuil Hall at nine o'clock THIS DAY . . . to make a united and successful resistance to this last, worst, and most destructive measure of adminstration."

The crowd overflowed Faneuil Hall and, as so often before, proceeded to the Old South Meetinghouse. There it was resolved that the tea should "never be landed in this province, or one farthing of duty" be paid. The consignees were called upon to resign, and after an orgy of patriotic oratory, the meeting adjourned. As reported by a visitor from Philadelphia, the speeches "of some tended in a very different direction from that of others; for while some advised to moderation, and by all means to be abstaining from violence, a few talked in a style, that was very virulent and inflammatory."

When the Boston town meeting reconvened the next day to hear the response of the consignees, the sheriff of Suffolk County appeared with a proclamation from Hutchinson stating that the meeting was unlawful and ordering the crowd to disperse. The reading of the proclamation was greeted with hisses and howls of derision, and a vote was passed unanimously not to adjourn. John Singleton Copley, the artist whose father-in-law was one of the consignees holed up in Castle William, offered to act as a mediator, but his effort was judged "not in the least degree satisfactory." The owner of the *Dartmouth* and the vessel's captain agreed at last that the tea would be returned to England, and similar promises were extracted from the owners of two other vessels, the *Eleanor* and the *Beaver*, that were en route.

Abigail Adams, hearing of the resolutions of the town meeting, wrote to Mercy Otis Warren, sister of James Otis and sister-in-law of Dr. Joseph Warren: "The tea, that baneful weed, is arrived. Great and I hope effectual opposition has been made to the landing of it . . . the proceedings of our citizens have been united, spirited and firm. The flame is kindled and like lightening it catches from soul to soul. Great will be the devastation if not timely quenched or allayed by some more lenient measures."

Abigail Adams' fears were prophetic—the crisis was far from over. Soon the Bostonians learned that Admiral Montagu had blocked the harbor on Hutchinson's orders and would not allow the tea-bearing vessels to leave until they had been unloaded. Immediately, word went out again for a meeting at the Old South Church. Captain Francis Rotch, whose ship had been turned back when it attempted to leave the harbor, confirmed the report that the harbor entrance was sealed off. The captain was asked by the leaders of the meeting to appeal directly to Hutchinson. While the patriots waited for Captain Rotch's return, the crowd grew constantly larger until by midafternoon an estimated seven thousand people were packed elbow to elbow in the Old South and in the street outside. It was by far the largest crowd in the history of Boston. Samuel Adams and his fellow patriot-lawyers Josiah Quincy and John Rowe kept the assemblage diverted, and Rowe elicited a shout of approval when he asked: "Who knows how tea will mingle with salt water?"

It was six o'clock before Captain Rotch was back with the word that Hutchinson was obdurate. In anticipation of such a response, plans had quietly gone ahead. As soon as Rotch had delivered his message, Samuel Adams stepped into the pulpit and said to the assembly, "This meeting can do nothing more to save the country." As though on cue, a war whoop answered him from outside the church, and a band of "Mohawks" dashed past the windows and down Milk Street to Griffin's wharf. There three companies, each of fifty "Indians," swiftly rowed out to the ships riding at anchor in the harbor. George Hewes, one of those who decked himself out as an Indian that night, recalled that he equipped himself "with a small hatchet, which I and my associates denominated the tomahawk, with which, and a club, after having painted my face and hands with coal dust in the shop of a blacksmith, I repaired to Griffin's wharf, where the three ships lay that contained the tea." The raiding party, Hewes remembered, was quickly sorted into three divisions and "immediately ordered ... to board all the ships at the same time, which we promptly obeyed."

Hewes was appointed boatswain and sent to demand from the captain of the vessel the keys to the hatches and a dozen candles. "We were then ordered," Hewes later wrote, "to open the hatches and take out all the chests of tea and throw them overboard, and we immediately proceeded to execute orders, first cutting and splitting the chests with our tomahawks, so as thoroughly to expose them to the effects of the water." The Indians, having accomplished their mission in three hours' time, withdrew as quickly as they had assembled. "There appeared to be an understanding," Hewes noted, "that each individual should volunteer his services, keep his own secret, and risk the consequences for himself. No disorder took place during that transaction, and it was observed at that time that the stillest night ensued that Boston had enjoyed for many months." The only other Indian whose name Hewes knew was Leonard Pitt, "the commander of my division."

When John Adams, who had been out of town, returned and heard the news, he turned to his diary to record his feelings. "Last Night," he wrote, "3 Cargoes of Bohea Tea were emptied into the Sea. This is the most magnificent moment of all. There is a Dignity, a Majesty, a Sublimity, in this last Effort of the Patriots, that I greatly admire. The People should never rise, without doing something notable and striking. This Destruction of the Tea is so bold, so daring, so firm, intrepid and inflexible, and it must have so important Consequences, and so lasting, that I can't but consider it as an Epocha in History."

Adams, like his fellow citizens of Boston, had in the cold light of day some sobering thoughts as well. "What Measures," Adams asked himself, "Will the Ministry take, in Consequence of this?—Will they resent it? Will they dare to resent it? Will they punish Us? How? By quartering Troops upon Us?—by annulling our Charter?—by laying on more duties? By restraining our Trade? By Sacrifice of Individuals, or how?"

Others in the days ahead wondered whether the Tea Party had been necessary. For Adams' part, "it was absolutely and indispensably so. . . . There was no other Alternative but to destroy it or let it be landed. To let it be landed, would be giving up the Principle of Taxation by Parliamentary Authority, against which the Continent have struggled for 10 years, it was loosing all our labour for 10 years and subjecting ourselves and our Posterity forever to Egyptian Taskmasters—to Burthens, Indignities, to Ignominy, Reproach and Contempt, to Desolation and Oppression, to Poverty and Servitude."

Whether to have allowed the tea to be unloaded would have brought with it such a string of calamities may well be questioned. What can much less be questioned is the fact that John Adams and most of his fellow patriots sincerely believed such consequences inevitable. That they should so believe could not be imagined or comprehended by Lord North, although almost any American in England, from Franklin on, could have enlightened him. So North, because he would not listen and could not learn, gave Hutchinson, who was too vengeful and embittered to learn, an opportunity to take the step that led directly to the American Revolution. It was perhaps fitting that the honor, if it can be called that, fell to Hutchinson, that learned, long-suffering, and fatally obtuse man. It took a special combination of wrongheadedness and "partial views" in England, along with a bitter and adamantine spirit on the part of Hutchinson, to ignite the tinder of revolt.

It seems clear that Hutchinson by this time welcomed a showdown with the Boston patriots. Ever since the Stamp Act crisis, he had urged the British ministry to take a hard line with the Sons of Liberty and their ilk; he had repeatedly deplored what seemed to him the weak and indecisive actions of a succession of governments in the face of colonial resistance. He was an ambitious man who had enjoyed great popularity and had seen it entirely dissipated in the course of doing his duty. The tea crisis gave him an opportunity to demonstrate to the world and to his king that if His Majesty was poorly served by other colonial officers, there was at least one who refused to yield to popular pressure.

Hutchinson knew enough of the temper of his fellow colonists to realize that they would not stand idly by while tea was landed in Boston. What Boston patriot could hold up his head if, conscious that Philadelphia and New York had turned back the tea-carrying vessels, Boston allowed the tea to be unloaded and offered for sale? Hutchinson was aware of plans for direct action by the citizens of the city, even if he was not privy to the details of the projected raid. And he knew that if the people of Boston boarded the three ships riding in the harbor and destroyed their cargoes—cargoes in which the government had a direct and specific interest—Lord North and his ministers could not avoid taking severe punitive action against the city. The only explanation for Hutchinson's action seems to be that he wanted the patriots to call parliamentary wrath down on their heads.

Hutchinson's obtuseness prevented him from realizing how much risk his misguided firmness entailed. If he had done what the other royal governors did—stood aside and let the ships' owners, captains, and consignees thrash out the issue of landing and selling the tea with the colonists themselves—it is clear that the *Dartmouth, Eleanor,* and *Beaver* would have been, like Captain Ayres and the *Polly,* headed back across the ocean for England. Faced with such widespread resistance to importing the tea, North would have had no choice but to capitulate once more. Parliament would hardly have supported the dispatch of regiments of British soldiers to North America to try to force the colonists to drink tea. From the moment of the Stamp Act on, the only hope of avoiding an ultimate showdown on the issue of Parliamentary authority over the colonies (most particularly, of course, as it related to the power to tax) lay in the possibility that the British government would accept a de facto limitation on its authority rather than alienate its American subjects.

But the Boston Tea Party was an action that the British government could not leave unpunished, and the actions of Thomas Hutchinson in blockading the port and insisting that the tea be landed, as surely as the actions of any individual have occasioned great historical events, brought on the Tea Party and its manifold consequences.

The Boston Tea Party was what we today would call guerrilla theater, a striking and dramatic enactment of an ideological position, an episode, as John Adams at once discerned, that would capture the popular imagination as few acts in history have. Measured against the dangerous and sporadic violence occasioned by the Stamp Act, or against the uncontrolled violence of the rioters on the night of the Boston Massacre, the Tea Party showed more clearly than volumes of exposition how far the patriot cause had come from its tumultuous beginnings some eight years before. By now the patriot leaders had established firm control. There were no rioters among the carefully drilled Mohawks who dumped the tea in Boston Harbor; they were rather a corps of irregulars who might, on the next occasion, carry loaded muskets. But if they did so it would be in response to orders, not to the volatile passions of a mob.

The Boston Port Bill

THE Boston Tea Party marked a new level of radical (or patriot) political organization, and the most direct and specific defiance of British authority in the ten-year-long fight over colonial rights. All Americans waited to see how the mother country would react.

They did not have to anticipate British reaction for long. When word of the Tea Party arrived in England, it was greeted with an outburst of indignation by the adherents of the government. Nobody is more apt to be mortally offended than someone who has done something venal and stupid and in consequence suffers rebuff and humiliation. In the resulting clamor for disciplining the colonies, only a few voices could be heard advising forbearance and a reformed policy in colonial affairs.

The principal advocates of the colonial cause were, as before, William Pitt and Edmund Burke. Pitt emerged from his retirement to warn England of the consequences of losing the American colonies, and Burke spoke eloquently in the House of Commons about colonial liberties. Pitt did his best to revive the argument that Parliament had no right to tax the colonies without their consent. "I fear," he wrote in 1774, "the bond between us and America will be cut off for ever. Devoted England will then have seen her best days, which nothing can restore again." At the same time, Pitt made clear, as he had before, that he had no patience with any notion of colonial Independence. "Although I love the Americans as men prizing and setting a just value upon that inestimable blessing, liberty, yet if I could once persuade myself that they entertain the most distant intention of throwing off the legislative supremacy and great constitutional superintending power and control of the British Legislature, I should myself be the very first person . . . to enforce that power by every exertion this country is capable of making."

Burke, the greatest theorist of enlightened, flexible, conservative politics, took a more radical position than his patron. The only policy with any chance of success, he argued, was one of conciliation, returning to the state of affairs that had existed before the Stamp Act and repealing all the statutes since passed that had been so obnoxious to the colonists. Burke took seriously Franklin's assurance that "a sincere disposition prevails in the people there to be on good terms with the mother-country. . . . They aim at no revolution."

"Revert to your old principles," Burke urged his fellow members of the House of Commons, and "leave America, if she has taxable matter in her, to tax herself. I am not here going into a distinction of rights, nor attempting to mark their boundaries. I do not enter into these metaphysical distinctions. I hate the very sound of them. Leave the Americans as they anciently stood, and these distinctions, born of our unhappy contest, will die along with it. . . . Let the memory of all actions in contradiction to that good old mode, on both sides be extinguished for ever. Be content to bind America by laws of trade; you have always done it. . . . Do not burthen them with taxes; you were not used to do so from the beginning."

The famous speech was an example of those doctrines of pragmatic politics of which Burke remains the most brilliant expositor. A rebuke to every ideologue and dogmatist, Burke's speech spelled out a sure basis for preserving the allegiance of the American colonies. In virtually every historical crisis, there are men who see quite clearly, as Burke did, what needs to be done, and, what is more difficult, how to do it. The problem is that, with tragic frequency, the people and their rulers will not listen. It proved impossible even for Burke to penetrate the mass of prejudices, misconceptions, and bitter animosities held by the generality of the British people and their leaders. However wisely and eloquently Pitt and Burke spoke, they did not speak for any substantial portion of the English ruling class, and certainly not for the North ministry.

It was the angry snarl of one Van that much better expressed the feelings of most of the members. Van "was of the opinion that the town of Boston ought to be knocked about their ears and destroyed. *Delenda est Carthago.*" Said he, "I am of the opinion you will never meet with that proper obedience to the laws of this country until you have destroyed that nest of locusts."

There was, except for the fruitless objections of Pitt and Burke, no question that action would be taken to punish Boston; the only point at issue was what that action should be. If the Americans could defy Parliament with impunity, there was little doubt, a member of the House Of Commons declared, that "they will without ceremony reject the whole statute books, and so save Parliament any further trouble." In due course, "if this kingdom is tame enough," the speaker concluded, "they may proceed to control and tax it, instead of Parliament regulating and taxing them." The real issue, according to Lord North, was whether the king's ministers had any power over "the haughty American Republicans." And the king himself echoed his minister's sentiments: "We must master them or totally leave them to themselves and treat them as Aliens." The means of "mastering" the colonies was the Boston Port Bill, which was intended to starve the city into submission. Until the province paid for the tea that had been destroyed and made restitution to the revenue officers for their property that had been damaged by the mob, the Boston Harbor was to be closed to all shipping. Troops were to be stationed once more in Boston while naval vessels sealed off the harbor. "Whereas," the Port bill began, "dangerous commotions and insurrections have been fomented and raised by the town of Boston . . . by divers ill-affected persons, to the subversion of his Majesty's government and to the utter destruction of the public peace and good order of the said town; in which commotions and insurrections certain valuable cargoes of teas . . . were seized and destroyed and whereas, in the present condition of the said town and harbour the commerce of his Majesty's subjects cannot be safely carried on there, nor the customs payable to his Majesty duly collected . . . be it enacted [that no further commerce be carried on in the port of Boston] ."

Under such pressure it was thought that Boston must surely capitulate. Faced at last by an angry and resolute England, "the Boston voters will scamper behind their counters . . . assume an affecting hypocritical air, clap their hands, cast up their eyes to heaven, wonder if the King knows their oppressive situation" and express dismay that the British ministry should have "so grievously vexed the hearts of the Lord's people." And the treasonous and the rebellious in other colonies, taking note of the cost of such fractiousness, would mend their ways as well.

An American who had been in Parliament when the Boston Port Bill was read wrote to a friend: "From my Soul do I feel for Boston & for all America. I was in the Parliament House and heard the Bill Brought in and Read. . . . my Dear Worthy Sir, I beg you to Encourage your people to be Strong in Opposing this Diabolical proceeding of the ministry. . . dont Expect any mercy from them for the Love of your Country, the Love of Justice, and for God's sake take all possible care that your Town dont submit tell them to hold out only six months and all will be well." By then England would be convinced of "their fatel Error." There was great popular support, he wrote, among the common people of England for their American cousins, so much so that the wicked plans of the ministers had been kept secret "through fear that had it been known, the Parliament House would have been Destroyed."

Outside the halls of Parliament the Tory press denounced the Bostonians vehemently. Sam Adams, in command of "a banditti of hypocrites," had challenged the dignity and honor of Great Britain by "a Blow in full Face of the world." It was "the most wanton and unprovoked insult offered to the civil power that is recorded in history." England could not, indeed, hold up her head as a great nation if she were to allow "a petty little province, the creature of our own hands, the bubble of our own breath," to defy her. The Bostonians had been "the first movers, and the main spring of all this contention," "a nest of rebels and hypocrites."

Not all the British reacted to the Boston Tea Party in the spirit of the ministry. Especially among the enemies of Lord North's government, there was substantial support for the action of the Bostonians in destroying the tea. The *London Packet* expressed the view that the resistance of the colonies to the importation of the tea reflected "equal honor on the spirit and understanding of the Colonists," and another correspondent in the same paper declared that the Tea Party showed that "the ministers, or rather that miserable Cabinet Junto in whom *only* the King thinks proper to confide, are as cordially despised in America as they are detested in England. . . . The passion for power on one side and the resolution to preserve liberty on the other, give a very serious . . . a very dreadful complexion to this dispute."

In the ranks of ordinary Englishmen, there were strong indications of sympathy and support for the Americans. Much emphasis, of course, was placed on the value of the colonies to the mother country: "America is a Hen that lays her Golden Eggs for Britain; and . . . she must be cherished and supported as part of the great family of Britain." British merchants were owed some four million pounds by their American customers, and any action by the ministry that put this debt in hazard was a disservice to the nation. However, a Londoner in *The Gazetteer and New Daily Advertiser* probably spoke for the majority of his countrymen when he wrote: "I would rather all the Hamilcars, and all the Hannibals that Boston ever bred; all the Hancocks, and all the Sad-Cocks, and sad dogs of Massachusetts Bay; all the heroes of tar and feathers, and the champions, maimers of unpatriotic horses, mares, and mules, were led up to the Altar, or the Liberty Tree, there to be exalted and rewarded according to their merit or demerit, than that Britain should disgrace herself by receding from her Just authority."

The principle objection to the Boston Port Bill in those circles favorable to America was that it would punish the innocent with the guilty, or, worse, punish the innocent while the guilty went free. Diametrically opposed to the English concern for justice and instinct for fair play, it was a clear case of the punishment not fitting the crime. To close the port of Boston was much too severe. "Pacificus," a liberal journalist, declared that the "general opinion of the People of England" was that the punishment of Massachusetts Bay was "unjust and oppressive, as well as senseless and impolitic."

Perhaps the most notable effect of the debate carried on in British newspapers was that it served to encourage and mislead American opinion. British newspapers were read avidly by the patriot leaders, many of whom gained thereby a false notion of the degree of support that could be mustered in England for the colonial cause. The patriot leaders, clutching at straws, often read and took heart from pseudonymous letters in English journals that had actually been written by Americans resident in England for the purpose of helping to create a favorable opinion in England. Much of the faith of the colonial leaders that economic pressure exerted in America would force Parliament to withdraw the Boston Port Bill was based on a hopeful reading of English journals.

Despite evidence of substantial support in England for the Americans, and despite opposition to a measure as severe as the Boston Port Act, that bill passed Parliament on its second reading without debate.

When word of the bill reached Boston on May 11, 1774, even those who had little or no sympathy with the destroyers of the tea were shocked at the severity of the British reaction. Boston was to be "inhumanly murder'd in cold blood . . . and by such an act of despotism as an eastern divan would blush at." Governor Hutchinson himself was startled by the provisions of the bill.

The Boston Committee of Correspondence promptly sent off word to the committees in nearby towns summoning them to a meeting at Faneuil Hall, at the same time dispatching Paul Revere to New York and Philadelphia with requests for support. The Boston town meeting was hastily convened, and a circular letter was drafted to be sent to the other colonies. "We have just received the copy," it began, "of an Act of the British Parliament . . . whereby the town of Boston is treated in a manner the most ignominious, cruel, and unjust." The province had been condemned without a hearing. Parliament had "ordered our port to be entirely shut up, leaving us barely so much of the means of subsistence as to keep us from perishing with cold and hunger. . . . This attack, though made immediately upon us, is doubtless designed for every other colony who will not surrender their sacred rights and liberties into the hands of an infamous ministry. Now therefore is the time when all should be united in opposition to this violation of the liberties of all." The clear intention of the government was to separate Massachusetts Bay from her sister colonies. If Boston were humbled, the other colonies would in turn be forced to surrender their rights. "The single question then is," the letter continued, "whether you consider Boston as now suffering the common cause, and sensibly feel and resent the injury and affront offered to her?"

The gesture of solidarity that Boston sought was a "Solemn League and Covenant" that other colonies would voluntarily suspend all trade with Great Britain. Such action would "effectually defeat the design of this act of revenge."

The fact that the Bostonians could have believed at this point in the controversy with the mother country that a revival of colonial nonimportation would force Great Britain to repeal the Port Bill is an indication of how far the colonists themselves were from perceiving the true situation; also of how far they were from some bold plan of independence. It is not likely that men of the shrewdness of Sam Adams or Will Molineux had such delusions. The point was that the other colonies must be persuaded to give some substantial evidence of support for the beleaguered Bostonians. Nonimportation had at least been tried and had been, within limits, a success. It would be something positive and something familiar that might in time lead to more hazardous and less familiar forms of common action. The Boston Port Bill was thus for Massachusetts certainly, and doubtless for the patriot cause as a whole, the moment of truth. Was there a solid foundation of sentiment in every colony that would be evoked by such an appeal? The answer was a ringing affirmative. The Bostonians, often looked at askance by other colonies for their radical and combative ways, became overnight "an innocent, a virtuous, a religious and loyal people, ever remarkable for their love of order, peace and good government." Newport, Rhode Island, assured its "virtuous brethren in the capital, who have so nobly stood as a barrier against slavery" of its support. The *Essex Gazette* of Salem, Massachusetts, declared, "The blow struck at that truly magnanimous Community, the respectable Town of Boston, is a Blow at all the colonies." As the editor of the *Massachusetts Spy* was quick to point out, the Port Act, instead of humbling Boston, appeared to be "the very means to perfect that union in America, which it was intended to destroy, and finally restore the excellent constitution even of the mother country itself."

In Farmington, Connecticut, the citizens of the town turned out in the number of "near one thousand" to honor "the immortal goddess of Liberty" by erecting in her honor a pole "just forty-five feet high" and to burn the Port Bill. A set of resolves, which were passed without objection, denounced "the present ministry" as "being instigated by the devil and led on by wicked and corrupt hearts" to enslave the colonies, and indicted "those pimps and parasites who dared advise their master to such detestable measures. . . ."

The town of Brooklyn, Connecticut, gave assurance of its support. It was a small and unimportant town whose "abilities and opportunities do not admit of our being of that weight in the American scale as we would to God we were." Nevertheless they were "ready to march in the van and to sprinkle the American altars with our hearts blood, if the occasion should be. . . . You are held up as a spectacle to the whole world. All Christendom are longing to see the event of the American contest. And do, most noble citizens, play your part manfully. . . ."

The letter was doubtless drafted by Israel Putnam, a seasoned veteran of the French and Indian War. It expressed, in the most touching way, sentiments similar to those that poured in from every town and parish in New England, accompanied, in most instances, by food and money. From Durham, New Hampshire: "We take pleasure in transmitting to you . . . a few cattle, with a small sum of money, which a number of persons in this place, tenderly sympathizing with our suffer-

ing brethren in Boston, have contributed towards their support."
Together these letters make a very remarkable literature, quite unique
in history. These meetings, with their declarations so expressive of the
spirit and temper of a people, took place, for the most part, off the
center stage of history, in remote and obscure towns and villages,
starting in New England and spreading throughout every province of
colonial America.

In Philadelphia and New York, there were widespread expressions
of indignation and of support for Boston. When word reached the
Quaker city, the standing committee of patriot leaders met to consider
the proper response to Boston's plea for help. Clearly the problem was
that whatever action was to be taken should be taken in concert with the
other colonies. Philadelphia thus delayed action until communication
could be established with Maryland, Virginia, and the Carolinas.

In Virginia, George Washington saw the issue as whether Americans should "supinely sit and see one province after another fall a prey
to despotism?" Washington wrote to his friend George Fairfax urging
that the colonies stand together with Boston and "not suffer ourselves to
be sacrificed by piece meals though god only knows what is to become of
us, threatned as we are with so many hoverg. evils as hang over us at
present. . . ."

Some of Washington's fellow Virginians expressed their support
for Boston by fasting (although unfriendly Tories reported they did so
by shifting the main meal of the day from luncheon to supper so
"nothing was gained by the Fast but full bellies at night instead of the
day"). When the Virginia House of Burgesses made clear that it
intended to take action in behalf of the Bostonians, the royal governor
dissolved the assembly. The burgesses then moved to the Raleigh Tavern, where they passed resolutions condemning the Port Bill as an attack
on all the colonies and joined in the call for a congress. They went
further. At a continental congress they would throw their support, they
declared, behind the Solemn League and Covenant. The Boston Port
Bill was "a most dangerous attempt to destroy the constitutional liberty
and rights of all North America. . . . We are further clearly of opinion,"
the "Association" stated, "that an attack, made on one of our sister
colonies, to compel submission to arbitrary taxes, is an attack made on
all British America, and threatens ruin to the rights of all, unless the
United wisdom of the whole be applied."

Everywhere the reports were much the same. In Maryland, "a few
of the first class of people adhered firmly to Government"[that is to say,

to Great Britain], while "the people in general" were "wrought up to a high pitch of extravagance." In North Carolina the people were forming companies and drilling under the direction of the veterans of the French and Indian War. A representative assembly, meeting in Beaufort, had advised the citizens of the colony to pay no taxes to any royal official. South Carolina was no less zealous in the cause. "Where is the mighty difference," a South Carolinian asked, "between destroying the tea, and resolving to do it, with such a firmness as intimidated the Captains to a return? Besides did not every province applaud the Bostonians?" If Boston capitulated, South Carolina would soon see "our courts of Justice removed—our harbor blockaded—navigation stopt—our streets crowded with soldiers . . . and, after a little time, the now flourishing Charles-Town reduced to a neglected plain."

Despite widespread support for Boston, there was evident reluctance to join the Solemn League and Covenant and pledge nonimportation and nonexportation. That the Solemn League was resisted in other colonies is not surprising. It was bad enough that Boston should suffer from externally imposed nonimportation and nonexportation. It seemed to many good patriots the height of folly to impoverish the rest of the colonies by in effect doing voluntarily what Boston had been forced to accede to by the presence of the British navy. In addition, such measures would fall most heavily on one class of men, the colonial merchant, a class that, it might be assumed, was least likely to have viewed sympathetically the dumping of the tea in Boston Harbor.

Meanwhile some expression of support was vital for the morale of the Bostonians, even if no practical effect was to be served. In Philadelphia on May 30, "a number of inhabitants composed of most of the different societies in [the] city mett and agreed that it would be proper to express their sympathy for their brethren at Boston by suspending all of the business of that day," the first of June, when the Port Act was to go into effect. Flags were hung at half-mast, church services were held in which divine intervention was implored and the blessings of God-given liberty extolled. The bells of Christ Church tolled a dirge at intervals throughout the day. In the words of Christopher Marshall, a Philadelphia merchant, "Sorrow mixed with indignation seemed pictured in the countenance of the inhabitants and indeed the whole city wore an aspect of deep distress, being a melancholy occasion."

Other colonies took similar action. Connecticut patriots in New Haven publicly burned the Port Act "In honour to the immortal goddess of liberty." In New York, effigies of "that blood-thirsty wretch"

Lord North, of Governor Hutchinson, and, interestingly enough, of Solicitor General Wedderburn (presumably because of his humiliation of Franklin), accompanied by an effigy of the devil, were dragged through the streets and then ceremonially set afire. There was in New York, however, the familiar split between radical and conservative factions. A town meeting was called to discuss what practical action might be taken in support of the Bostonians. Before the town meeting there was a meeting of the "Mechanicks etc." under the leadership of Alexander MacDougall and Isaac Sears, who selected a slate of twenty-five reliable patriots to form a committee to recommend action. In the regular town meeting that followed, however, the twenty-five names proposed by the earlier meeting were swamped by twenty-five more, the great majority both conservative in their views and representatives of the merchants and propertied class of the city. "You may now be assured," Benjamin Booth, a merchant and leader of the conservative faction, wrote his allies in Philadelphia, "that such a committee will enter into no intemperate hasty Resolutions. . . . It is expected that the first Business this Committee will go upon . . . will be to propose a Convention to all the neighbouring Colonies save Boston, to advise the Bostonians what they ought to do in their present critical situation." There was at least the intimation that with Boston absent, Booth and his allies might hope to advise the Bostonians to pay for the tea and humbly seek pardon of His Majesty. The substantial citizens of the city were determined "to guard *against* a species of Tyranny exercised under their noses, which they conceive to be more dangerous to their liberties than anything hitherto attempted by the British Parliament." It was painfully evident to them that "a spirit of libertinism once raised among the common people, is not so easily suppressed as we now find to our sorrow."

The New Yorkers thus issued a call for another congress like that which had met at the time of the Stamp Act. In such a body, somewhat removed from popular pressures, the various courses of action might be reviewed and discussed (to a degree) dispassionately, and a line of action settled upon that would rally patriots of all persuasions. A very substantial subsidiary benefit would be to cool those extremists who were most inclined to rash and hasty deeds. There was, in fact, everything to recommend the calling of a congress. The patriot leaders from each colony much needed to ripen their counsels. The conservatives hoped to use the occasion to impose firm restraints on the more radical faction;

THE BOSTON PORT BILL / 395

the more militant patriots welcomed an opportunity to try to sway the congress toward bolder measures.

The New York merchants put forth a set of resolutions that, among other things, stated, "We are not ashamed to declare our difference in opinion with many persons on the Boston Port-Bill: for however unwilling we may be to insult our fellow-subjects in distress, we have always thought that restitution for the damage done to the property of the East India Company, is no more than a common act of justice; and that this ought to be complied with, previous to our joining the Bostonians in any measure that should be proposed; lest it should admit of a strong presumption, that we justify and applaud the destruction of the East India Company's tea, a bare approbation of which no circumstances whatever shall be able to draw from us."

Benjamin Booth was so encouraged by the success of the conservative party in New York that he wrote to his friends in Philadelphia that the "conduct of the Republicans here is one continued chain of absurdities, and while they are crying out for union they are doing everything in their power to prevent it; at the same time they cannot or will not see that they are become the laughing stock of two thirds of the inhabitants. . . . That the *ultimatum* of their plan is to establish a Commonwealth Independent of Great Britain, I have no longer a Doubt; but Providence seems to have ordered it so, that they should defeat their own schemes."

It must be remembered that fear, confusion, and uncertainty were the dominant emotions of the colonists. Only a few of the most doctrinaire at either end of the political spectrum were entirely clear in their own minds as to the proper course of action. The vast majority, Tory and patriot alike, were beset in their waking hours and in their dreams by the most agonizing doubts and misgivings. They had talked boldly of their liberties, but they had persistently deluded themselves into believing that the ministers, Parliament, or, as a last resort, a benevolent king would rescue them from injustice and oppression.

Patriot leaders in other colonies were pulled a dozen ways at once: admiration for Boston, distrust of Boston, a constantly revived hope of reconciliation with the mother country, a genuine fear of British power—the mightiest power in the world—and, mixed in, a strange brew of personal fears and ambitions.

It is difficult for people living in a relatively stable society to imagine the anxieties that must be aroused when that order is imperiled. What is to happen to one's children? Will the sons march off to war to be maimed or killed? Will daughters be raped by licentious soldiers? How will one's family be fed and clothed? And all one's cherished personal possessions—how will they fare in civil disorder and war? Would patriot leaders be taken to England and tried and hanged as traitors, their families and their fortunes proscribed?

In this atmosphere, the call for a congress came as a great relief to most colonists, but there were some for whom even a congress was too bold and dangerous a step. One of these was John Dickinson, the "Pennsylvania Farmer" whose pamphlet had touched the deepest levels of colonial consciousness and, in fact, had embodied and perpetuated a fallacy dear to the great majority of colonists—that Parliament and the ministers of the Crown would in time be moved by humble, discreet, and closely argued petitions to restore to the colonists all their lost liberties. Dickinson's prestige was so great in Pennsylvania, where he was allied by marriage to one of the leading Quaker families, that there was little hope of getting the citizens of that city to concur in the call for a congress without Dickinson's endorsement. Preliminary soundings showed him reluctant if not openly opposed.

Charles Thomson, "the Sam Adams of Philadelphia," Thomas Mifflin, and Joseph Reed, all active Sons of Liberty, called a meeting at Philadelphia's recently completed City Tavern for the evening of May 20, 1774, to consider what action might be taken in support of Boston. The three men rode out to John Dickinson's estate at Fairhill a few hours before the meeting to try to persuade the Farmer to attend. They fortified Dickinson's "weak nerves" by "circulating the glass briskly"; when Dickinson finally consented to come, it was so late that Reed and Mifflin rushed back to the city to announce that the Farmer was coming while Thomson stayed behind to prevent Dickinson's wife and mother-in-law from undermining his shaky resolve. Dickinson and Thomson appeared just as the crowd was about to disperse. Thomson, overcome by the heat and excitement, fainted dead away, while Reed rose and "urged the most spirited measures." This was done to set the stage for Dickinson's more moderate proposals. It was his view that the meeting should request that the governor call the assembly into session to deal with the matter of the Boston Port Bill.

The City Tavern meeting also issued a call for a general meeting of citizens on June 18. Here the Boston Port Act was declared unconstitutional, and a Committee of Correspondence was appointed, with John Dickinson as chairman, to sound out "the sense of the people." The intention was to bring pressure to bear on the governor and the assembly to provide for the election of delegates to a continental congress. When a "Provincial Convention" gathered in Carpenters' Hall in the middle of July, it began by affirming its allegiance to His Majesty, King George the Third, and disavowing as "utterly abhorrent" the idea of an "unconstitutional independence." The delegates then resolved unanimously that "there is an absolute necessity that a Congress of Deputies from the several colonies be immediately assembled . . . for the purpose of procuring relief for our suffering brethren, obtaining redress of our grievances, preventing future dissentions, firmly establishing our rights, and restoring harmony between *Great Britain* and her Colonies on a Constitutional foundation."

That was as far as Pennsylvanians were willing to go. They would not swallow the Solemn League and Covenant, and Thomas Mifflin wrote to Sam Adams that "a Non Importation to be urged immediately, without some previous Step taken to obtain Redress may disunite us and ruin the Cause of America." Lord Dartmouth in England wrote to Philadelphia's Joseph Reed: "I will still hope that . . . a little time will convince you, & all that can think with coolness & temper, that the liberties of America are not so much in danger from any thing that Parliament has done or is likely to do here, as from the violence & misconduct of America itself. I am persuaded I need not take pains to convince you of the absurdity of the idea . . . that the intention of government is to enslave the people of America." If the colonists were "wise enough to submit" and to promise to cause no more trouble, "they will turn [Britain's] indignation into sympathy & good will . . . they will perhaps obtain all they wish, & receive that indulgence & compliance with their desires, which they never can extort by sullen opposition or undutiful resistance."

John Dickinson's contribution was another essay on colonial rights. The tone was that of the famous Farmer's *Letters*, and many of the arguments were the same. "So alarming are the measures already taken for laying the foundations of a despotic authority of *Great-Britain* over us," Dickinson wrote, "and with such artful and incessant vigilance is the plan prosecuted, that unless the present generation can interrupt the work, *while it is going forward,* can it be imagined that our children, debilitated by our imprudence and supineness, will be able to overthrow it, *when completed?*"

The words seem to be those of a fearless and unflinching patriot. The most radical patriot could hardly have done better. But Dickinson was no radical. It turns out, he said, that "this is not a time, either for timidity or rashness. We perfectly know, that the great cause now agitated, is to be conducted to a happy conclusion, only by that well tempered composition of counsels, which firmness, prudence, loyalty to our sovereign, respect to our parent state, and affection to our native country, united must form."

What is one to make of such fiery language and such mild actions? It must have seemed to some of the more impatient patriots, as well as to the British ministers, that Americans were braggarts and loudmouths, ready to mob a frightened and defenseless customs official but reluctant to risk their own necks in defense of their precious liberties. Several things might be said in justification of the extreme caution with which the great majority of the patriots proceeded. Their leaders were haunted by what they believed they had learned from history, and especially from the historians of ancient Greece and Rome, about the dangers of overturning an existing political power. History, that tireless if ambiguous pedagogue, instructed them that when the delicate fabric of a society was torn apart, men became wolves, and bloodshed, anarchy, and mindless violence became the order of the day.

Today revolutions are old hat. In many countries revolutions are an almost yearly occurrence; we use the world "revolution" as casually as we pick up a spoon. We have revolutions in dress, in morals, in reading habits; we have "revolutionary" new shaving creams, razor blades, and underarm deodorants. But in the eighteenth century, the word as we most commonly use it today had hardly been discovered. Its ordinary meaning was the turn of a circle, of a wheel on its axis, the "revolutions" of the celestial bodies in their fixed orbits. Today there are only a few "colonies" left. Nearly every colony has thrown off, by one means or another, at least the direct control of the nation that held it as a colony. In the eighteenth century no such thing had happened, nor was it imagined by most people that it could happen.

So while the colonists, both individually and collectively, yearned for "independence," it was a social and, if you will, a psychological, not a political, independence that they yearned for. They wished most sincerely and devoutly to sit "every man under his own fig tree and under his vine," but they wished to sit there as Englishmen shaded by the might and majesty of the British Empire, sustained by a benevolent Father-King who wished only good for them. George III was not, to be sure, the ideal father. But there are no ideal fathers on earth, only in heaven, and George had to do. Thus, in all the stream of agitational literature that flowed from the colonist presses there is to be found hardly a word of criticism of or animosity to the king. And yet virtually everything that was done in the American colonies of Great Britain was done in the name of His Majesty, the king of England and all his dominions beyond the sea.

Since England was a constitutional monarchy, it was, of course, perfectly well understood in the colonies that the powers of the king were quite narrowly circumscribed—that, indeed, was what the English Civil War of 1640 had been about, as well as the Glorious Revolution of 1688—and that it was an elaborate fiction that the flood of instructions as well as of restrictive measures that arrived in the colonies actually proceeded from the pen or the mind of the monarch himself. But it took very little acumen and no very sophisticated knowledge of the strange and often intricate workings of the British government to discern that the king had substantial if limited power, and that policies of his ministers, particularly in regard to colonial matters, usually had his support if they did not, in fact, reflect on more than one occasion some royal initiative. Yet such was the power of the idea of kingship in the middle of the eighteenth century that the king remained virtually immune to criticism. He was invariably referred to by his subjects— many of whom certainly knew better—as "the best and wisest of monarchs," "that most generous and noble of men," and similar inaccurate and far-fetched phrases.

It is only in the light of this "magic quality of kingship" that much of the otherwise inexplicable behavior of the colonists can be understood. All those Americans, patriot or Tory, who feared actual political independence of the mother country like the plague (as opposed to a proper independence under her capacious wing) fixed their hopes upon the universally agreed benevolence of the king. He was the refuge of their subconscious minds, which allowed them to speak in the bitterest and most hostile ways of Parliament and the ministers while affirming their unwavering loyalty as the subjects of His gracious Majesty, George III. Loyalty to the monarch allowed them to believe that their actions were not the actions of rebels and traitors but of true Englishmen; for did they not preface every inflammatory document with the most sincere and humble affirmations of their loyalty to him?

Since the king existed, in a sense, as a fictitious personality who was not permitted to express his views publicly in matters of state, it was impossible for the colonists to be disillusioned. Had it been possible for George III to write a letter to the colonies saying, if effect: "As the King of England and the nominal head of the country and the empire, I have in every instance strongly supported the actions of my ministers designed to reduce you to a proper state of subordination to the Parliament of Great Britain and my fictious self; I have absolutely no sympathy with your claims of immunity from Parliamentary taxation and my only regret is that Parliament did not, at the time of your mutinous resistance to the Stamp Act, take bold measures to bring you to your collective senses"; had George III, in other words, been able to speak publicly what he felt privately, the colonists would have had to face much sooner and more starkly the fact that their resistance to the acts of Parliament constituted rebellion.

The notion of revolution against the mother country—had the colonists been forced to confront the true nature of their acts and the consequences that must inevitably follow—might well have been too formidable for the great majority of patriots; their devotion to their liberties would perhaps have melted away in the merciless light of the true situation. It was much better, certainly much easier, to go step by step, eyes fixed on the path ahead, placing one's faith in the ultimate benevolence of the King-Father. The strange nature of the English kingship in the middle years of the eighteenth century allowed them to continue to live a kind of double life—loyal revolutionaries of His Majesty, George III.

12

The Massachusetts Government Act and the Quebec Act

THE severe, punishing terms of the Boston Port Bill were, for many colonists, adequate proof of the tyrannical nature of the North Ministry. It seemed the last straw; what more could the British government do to interfere with colonial liberty? Parliament, it soon developed, could in fact do a good deal more. While the colonists were still experiencing the initial shock of the Port Bill, news came that the government in London had passed two more laws, the Massachusetts Government Act and the Quebec Act. Both, in the view of patriots, were aimed directly at the heart of colonial liberty.

The Massachusetts Government Act revoked the portion of the Massachusetts Bay charter that provided for the popular election of councilors, subject to the veto of the governor, and instead made that body one appointed by His Majesty the king and holding office during his pleasure. These were reforms long pressed for by Thomas Hutchinson. The act also put the machinery of law in the governor's hands, empowering him, without the consent of his council, to appoint and remove "all judges of the inferior courts of common pleas, commissioners of oyer and terminer, the attorney general, provosts, marshalls, justices of the peace . . . to appoint the sheriffs without consent of the Council. . . ."

The Massachusetts Government Act was followed by the Quebec Act, which extended the province of Quebec from Canada down the eastern bank of the Connecticut River to 45 degrees of latitude, through Lake Champlain to the St. Lawrence and Lake Ontario, thence to Lake Erie and the western boundaries of Pennsylvania to the Mississippi and then northward to Hudson Bay. The act had the effect of sealing off most of the western lands from colonial land speculators and emigrants. It further, in a humane and enlightened spirit, guaranteed the rights of all former Frenchmen "professing the religion of the Church of Rome." Nothing could have alarmed the New England Puritans more than having a sanctioned group of papists on their northern doorstep.

The debate in Parliament over the Massachusetts Government Act made clear enough the intentions of its proponents. Lord George Germain was all in favor of putting an end to Boston's troublesome town meetings. "I would not," he declared in a classic bit of snobbery, "have men of a mercantile cast every day collecting together and debating about political matters; I would have them follow their occupations as merchants, and not consider themselves as ministers of that country. . . . I should . . . expect to see some subordination, some authority and order." At present, Germain went on, Massachusetts was ruled by "a tumultuous and riotous rabble, who ought, if they had the least prudence, to follow their mercantile employment and not trouble themselves with politics and government, which they do not understand."

The Americans, of course, were not without their advocates. Stephen Fox, the huge and cumbersome brother of Charles James Fox, a leader of the Whigs, stoutly opposed the measure. "I rise, sir," he said, "with an utter detestation and abhorrence of the present measures. We are either to treat the Americans as subjects or as rebels. If we treat them as subjects, the bill goes too far; if as rebels, it does not go far enough. We have refused to hear the parties in their defence and we are going to destroy their charter without knowing the constitution of their Government."

Jonathan Shipley, the pro-American Bishop of Asaph, supported Fox: "My Lords, I look upon North America as the only great nursery of freemen now left upon the face of the earth." As for the colonies "whom we are now so eager to butcher," the bishop believed that all Englishmen should "cherish them as the immortal monuments of our public justice and wisdom; as the heir of our better days, of our old arts and manners, and of our expiring national virtues. What work of art, or power, or public utility, has ever equalled the glory of having peopled a continent without guilt or bloodshed, with a multitude of free and happy commonwealths: to have given them the best arts of life and government, and to have suffered them under the shelter of our authority, to acquire in peace the skill to use them." But, the bishop continued, "by enslaving the Colonies you not only ruin the peace, the commerce and the fortunes of both countries, but you extinguish the fairest hopes, shut up the last asylum of mankind. I think, my Lords . . . that a good man may hope that heaven will take part against the execution of a plan that seems big not only with mischief but impiety."

As eloquent as Bishop Shipley was—or as Fox, Burke, and Pitt had been—the spirit of Germain and North prevailed. Since the calling of meetings in townships throughout Massachusetts as well as in Boston had resulted in the inhabitants taking up matters that were none of their business and passing "most dangerous and unwarrantable resolves," the Massachusetts Government Act forbade all such get-togethers: "Be it enacted, That no meeting shall be called . . . without the leave of the Governor, or in his absence, the Lieutenant-Governor." Further, it was made the responsibility of those sheriffs appointed by the governor in effect to choose those persons suited for jury duty, since "the method at present used in the Province . . . of electing persons to serve on grand juries, and other juries, by the freeholders and inhabitants of the several towns, affords occasion for many evil practices, and tends to pervert the free and impartial administration of justice. . . ."

The Boston Committee of Correspondence was quick to denounce the Government Act as unconstitutional, and added, "No power on earth hath a Right without the consent of this Province to alter the minutest title of its Charter or abrogate any Act whatever made in pursuance of it, and confirmed by the Royal assent. . . . We are entitled to life, liberty and the means of Sustenance by the grace of Heaven and without the King's leave."

The result of the Port Bill and the Massachusetts Government Act was that instead of Boston feeling the full weight of British displeasure alone, the whole Massachusetts countryside became a hostile territory swarming with angry patriots, and British power was soon limited to the geographical confines of the city, or in other words, only as far as British soldiers could march. The so-called mandamus councilors, those who were appointed by the governor under the terms of the Massachusetts Government Act rather than elected, suffered systematic harassment.

Tory Daniel Leonard of Taunton had bullets whiz by his head—the marksmen probably intended to miss—and several of the mandamus councilors were forced to flee to Boston.

A similar fate was visited on judges across the state. Farmers stopped the proceedings of the court in Great Barrington and other towns. Judges were forced to resign their offices or were prevented from sitting by threats and the physical intervention of groups of patriots. One prominent Tory judge had broken glass placed under his saddle, causing his horse to buck and throw him; he "lighted on his head, and remained senseless for some time, to the infinite joy and amusement of the rebels," a friend reported.

In Worcester some two thousand people, many of them militia from nearby towns, assembled on the common and sent a delegation to Timothy Paine, who was a judge of the superior court, respectfully requesting him to resign his office. After some haggling, Paine put his signature to a resignation, adding, "I am very sorry I accepted and thereby have given any uneasiness to the People of the County from whom I have received many Favours, and I take this Opportunity to thank them. . . ." He was then required to read this document to the assembled crowd. The people were quiet and attentive. Paine wrote General Gage that he suffered no insult except that he was required to remove his hat as he left the common. "Thus," Paine wrote in his account of the incident, "you see an open opposition has taken place to the Acts of the British Parliament. I dread the consequences of enforcing them by a Military Power, People's spirits are so raised they seem determined to risque their lives and every thing dear to them in the opposition; and to prevent any person from executing any commission he may receive under the present Administration."

Gage's determination to send troops to insure the sitting of the court at Worcester early in September was dampened by the news that twenty thousand armed militiamen, many of them from Connecticut and New Hampshire, were ready to march to that town and prevent the court from conducting its business. A Worcester Tory wrote, "The People are universally determined almost to a man, to reassume the Old Charter, elect a Governor, etc. . . . I really fear, should the General send his troops out of Boston, he will loose them. . . . How to resist such an inraged multitude is not for me to say, or even pretend to guess."

When the day arrived for the opening of the fall session of the Court of Common Pleas at Worcester, some five thousand men assembled in the town, many of them armed, and lined the streets six deep for a quarter of a mile leading to the courthouse. Each company, representing a town, chose a committee to consult with committees from the other companies as to the proper course of action. The judges were barred from the court and forced to swear that they would not attempt to carry on any judicial business. Having accomplished this much, the committees of correspondence of the various towns of the county met in the usurped courthouse and, according to a Tory account, assumed "to themselves more Power and Authority than any Body of Men ever did." Declaring government to be at an end, they set about "making Rules and Orders for the Regulation of the People of the County. In truth the People here have taken the Government into their own hands." Whoever did not comply with their orders placed his life and property in jeopardy.

In all such local Massachusetts uprisings the degree of discipline was striking. The brutal assault on Thomas Hutchinson's house some nine years earlier stands in sharp contrast to the restraint exercised by people described as being "wild with resentment and rage." One might argue that the difference was the difference between the unruly mob of Boston and sober country folk. There was something in this, to be sure, but perhaps more important was the fact that the judges and other officials who were now forcibly prevented from enforcing the Massachusetts Government Act were men who had held important and responsible positions in their communities and had been, in most instances, respected and liked. There was thus a disposition to deal with them as charitably as the political situation allowed. Much more important, the patriot leaders in Boston as well as Worcester had established firm control over the form that resistance was to take and over what some today would call the patriot "infrastructure," an invisible and illegal "revolutionary" government. The committees of correspondence and of public safety were strictly disciplined and led by the intellectuals of the community.

The extension of the Quebec Act, which although not technically one of the Coercive or Intolerable Acts—as they were soon called in the colonies—was associated with them largely by virtue of the fact that it was passed in Parliament on the same day as the Massachusetts Government Act. Its provisions, enlightened as they were, aroused all the historic anxieties of Englishmen on both sides of the ocean about the threat of Papacy to the Protestant religion. The colonies were especially alarmed. "We may live to see our churches converted into mass houses, and land plundered of tythes for the support of Popish clergy . . . ," one writer declared. Alexander Hamilton predicted that the act would leave the colonists surrounded by "a Nation of Papists and Slaves," and an indignant Bostonian wrote: "a superstitious, bigotted Canadian Papist, though ever so profligate, is now esteemed a better subject to our Gracious Sovereign George the Third, than a liberal, enlightened New England Dissenter, though ever so virtuous."

The colonists' conviction that the extended Quebec Act was intended as a warning and rebuke to them was not entirely groundless. One member of Parliament had pointed out in the debate over the act that if the French-Canadians were promptly reconciled to British rule by a generous gesture, they might serve as a check to "those fierce fanatic spirits in the Protestant colonies." The Canadians, some Englishmen felt, might be used at the appropriate time "to butcher these 'Puritan Dogs.'" In the words of one colonist, had Lord North "stopped short of the Quebec Bill there might have been some distant prospect of less general confederacy; but that open, and avowed design of subjugating America, has alarmed the most inattentive and given us but one mind."

If there was substantial division in England about the Boston Tea Party and the heavyhanded measures of Parliament that it provoked, the English reaction to the Quebec Act was almost unanimously condemnatory. Prevailing British sentiment was expressed by a speaker addressing an audience of five hundred Freeholders of Middlesex, who declared that he recognized in the Quebec Act that "old prostitute, the whore of Babylon." And a member of the House of Lords promised that he would do his best to obtain a repeal of an act by which "Popery, arbitrary power and French laws" had been foisted on a part of the empire. A writer in the *London Chronicle* stated, "A Stroke of this kind, aimed at the Religion and Liberties of our Country must awaken the most drowsy Slumberer among us." When the king appeared in public, he was greeted with shouts of "No popery, no French Government," and bets were taken at five to four that the Coercive Acts would "turn out the ministry before Michaelmas Day next."

There was thus, by the late summer of 1774, a rising tide of sympathy for the beleaguered Americans. England's Bill of Rights Society sent five hundred pounds to the Boston patriots, and the Common Council of the City of London held a meeting in which much indignation was expressed at the Coercive Acts. The council presented a petition to the House of Lords requesting that body to reverse the actions of the House of Commons and the ministry. A rather seditious handbill was printed for distribution in the British army, urging soldiers to refuse to serve in America.

"There never was a time," the St. James Chronicle declared, "when the citizens of London so universally inclined to the patriot side. The late unpopular American acts have totally sunk the ministry in the esteem of all ranks of the people that wish well to their country."

In the Intolerable, or Coercive, Acts which followed each other in the space of little more than three months, the British ministry, with the same fatal obtuseness that had characterized its policy toward the American colonists from the beginning of the Revolutionary crisis, took precisely those steps best calculated to arouse the determined resistance of all the colonies. The Boston Port Bill demonstrated the government's willingness and capacity to destroy the economic foundations of a colony that sufficiently offended it. The Massachusetts Government Act was an arbitrary alteration of the constitutional arrangements existing between the mother country and a particular colony. The Quebec Act seemed to threaten what was dearest to many colonists from New Hampshire to Georgia—their sacred Protestant faith. Thus the colonies' economy, government, and religion were, it appeared, all imperiled, all subject to the whims of a remote and unfriendly set of officials and a thoroughly unsympathetic Parliament. It is hard to see how Great Britain could have done more to dramatize the essential powerlessness and dependence of the colonies—indeed, the complete subordination of the colonists to the mother country; and that, of course, was precisely what Lord North and his supporters in Parliament intended to demonstrate. The demonstration cost England the principal jewel in its imperial crown.

Colonists everywhere were warned that once Parliament had broken the spirit of resistance in America, its members would not hesitate to load the colonies with all kinds of onerous taxes. If the colonists refused to pay, British tax collectors would "take your land for the rates, and make you and your children slaves." The tax collectors would be accompanied by "a voluptuous crew of harpies . . . with a parcel of scoundrels, the off-scouring of the earth" who would grab "your pleasant habitations, your orchards and gardens, your wives and daughters." "If a few ill-minded Persons take upon them to make water against the Door of a Custom-house Officer, or of the Cellar where the Tea is lodged," wrote a correspondent of the South Carolina Gazette, "upon the same Principle all in Charles-Town ought to be laid in Ashes."

One of the most offensive sections of the Boston Port Bill called for troops to be stationed in Boston to enforce the bill's provisions. General Gage was thus ordered from New York with a regiment of infantry, to be augmented as speedily as possible by other units from Canada and England. The reoccupation of Boston was of course bitter medicine for the Massachusetts colony.

There was, to be sure, a modicum of comfort in the fact that General Gage was in command of the British forces. Gage, who was married to a New Jersey lady, was popular in the colonies, and if a military officer was to be placed in command of the city, the Bostonians were glad that it was he. In addition, the patriot leaders were determined to make every effort to prevent another Boston Massacre or any incident that might place Boston in a bad light, thereby lessening its support in other colonies and imperiling colonial unity. However bitterly they might resent the occupation of their city by large numbers of redcoats, they made a special effort to be mannerly in their reception of Gage and, in acting such a part, to emphasize to the more volatile elements in the populace that restraint was essential.

Thus Will Molineux, Paul Revere, Joseph Warren, and other patriot leaders were on hand to greet Gage when he arrived in the city from New York. Bells pealed and flags and banners flew in defiance of a menacing sky that soon produced a deluge of rain. The Boston Cadets, a smartly turned out drill unit commanded by Colonel Henry Knox, and a regiment of Boston militia under the command of Colonel William Coffin made a guard of honor. There was an elegant entertainment provided for Gage at Faneuil Hall, marred only when the general proposed a toast to Governor Hutchinson, "which was received by a general hiss." Gage had been particularly enjoined to moderation by Lord Dartmouth—"the amiable Gentle, the punctilious, the meticulous Dartmouth"—who urged him to make concessions wherever possible and to be mild and conciliatroy in his dealings with the Bostonians.

Despite his correct greeting, Gage found that he could expect no assistance from the town. No quarters were provided, and the troops were forced to camp on the Common. Merchants refused to sell supplies, and artisans declined to work. People in the surrounding country declined to sell timber and straw for the barracks; then the workmen and carpenters who were building the barracks stopped work in order to preserve "the union now subsisting between town and country."

Dismayed by this indication that patriotism could triumph over self-interest, Gage summoned the selectmen of Boston. Their own preference, the selectmen said, would be to have the troops in barracks, on the grounds that they could be better kept in order in barracks than "*scattered* over the town in private dwellings," but they declared themselves powerless in the matter. Gage was clearly upset: "Good God! for God's sake, Gentlemen!" he burst out, "Do, consider, Gentlemen!" But there was nothing Gage could do.

The Committee of Correspondence began to keep an inventory (doubtless somewhat inflated) of the indignities suffered by citizens of the city at the hands of the soldiers. The newspapers were filled with stories of rape and robbery. The patriots predicted that "neither our Wives, Daughters, nor even Grand mothers would be safe." There was no telling when a father might see "a ruffian's blade reaking from a daughter's heart, for nobly preserving her virtue." The soldiers tempted the less resolute Bostonians to "frolick and revel, frequent bawdy houses, race horses, fight cocks on Sunday, drink profane and obscene toasts, damn the sons of liberty." It was reported that a coach from Providence had been attacked, its windows broken, and the passengers bullied and abused by soldiers. Another account told of a number of British officers who, "heated with liquor . . . with drawn swords, ran through the streets like what they really were, madmen, cutting everyone they met."

Gage's efforts to be fair and moderate irritated those Tories who wished for revenge against their tormentors. Some thought him too plain and direct a man to win over the patriots. In the opinion of one British officer, it would have been much better to have "sent out as Governor a Man of Fashion and Politeness, who would have complimented, entertained, flattered and danced us all into a good Humour." Even among his own officers, Gage was "at a Loss . . . for common Chit-Chat."

Sir Hugh Percy was Gage's second-in-command, and the soldiers encamped on the Common were under his direction. Percy found the people of Boston "by all accounts . . . extremely violent and wrongheaded; so much so that I fear we shall be obliged to come to extremities." It was Percy's opinion that until Great Britain made the colonists' "committees of correspondence and congresses with the other colonies high treason, and try them for it in England, you must never expect perfect obedience . . . to the mother country."

Gage wrote to Lord Dartmouth at the end of August, 1774, giving an account of the growing resistance outside of Boston and the activities of the patriots in "casting ball and providing powder." He reported the action of the Worcester patriots in preventing the superior court session from sitting in their town, and declared his intention to "march a body of Troops into that Township and perhaps into others, as occasion happens to preserve the peace" and assure the proper functioning of the courts.

Gage found Boston itself a tough nut. Things had gone so far, he wrote glumly to Dartmouth at the end of September, 1774, that only extraordinary measures could put them aright. "The enfeebled state in which I found every Branch of Govt astonished me," he noted. He had just set about to try to repair the damage caused by the Port Bill when the Massachusetts Government Act and the Quebec Act "overset the whole & the flame blazed out in all parts at once beyond the conception of everybody." In Gage's opinion the colonists thought themselves much more important to Great Britain than in fact they were. "Were they cast off & declared alien," he wrote "they must become a poor & needy people."

To imagine the frame of mind of most Bostonians, it is necessary to recall that Boston was almost an island in the eighteenth century, virtually surrounded by water and connected to the mainland only by a narrow spit of land known as Boston Neck. Thus wherever Bostonians looked, they could see British warships, a silent and perpetual menace. It was demoralizing and worse to see the ships of Boston port, the city's lifeline to the outside world, swinging at their anchors or moored at abandoned docks. The town, if fitfully supplied by its sister colonies with food, suffered severely from the constriction of its trade. Some merchants went so far as to have West Indian molasses landed at Marblehead, carried by wagon to Boston, refined into rum, and then trundled back to Marblehead once more for shipment to the Indies. With Boston's merchant fleet constrained if not idle, large numbers of sailors were at loose ends. Their ranks were swelled by unemployed mechanics and apprentices.

Gage and his lieutenants seemed determined to interpret the Port Bill in the strictest way. The bill allowed fuel and food to be brought to the city by water, but coastal vessels carrying such supplies into the city were subject to constant harassment. Those coming from the north loaded with wood for the city were required to stop at Salem, unload their cargoes, and reload. A shipload of wheat sent by patriots at Marblehead for the relief of the Boston poor was not allowed to cross the Charles River by ferry, but had to be carried around in carts by way of Roxbury. Not only did Boston have a noose of British warships about its neck, but twelve or thirteen smaller ports along the fringe of the harbor, such as Hingham and Weymouth, were placed under the same interdict.

Thirty or forty wagons a day moved from Salem to Boston transporting essential supplies to the city. It would not have been consistent with the Puritan ethic of thrift and hard work to simply hand out food to those who needed it. The distribution of food to the poor was carried out under the direction of a committee appointed for the purpose, and the committee required the poor to work for their rations. Various public works were undertaken, such as the paving of streets and the building of ships to be sold by the city for the purchase of more supplies.

As the full effect of the Port Bill began to be felt, there were conflicting reports about conditions in Boston. By one account, "nine tenths of the inhabitants are render'd wretchedly miserable." But this seems doubtful. Supplies soon poured into the city. New York had promised a ten years' supply of food, and the patriots of Brooklyn sent 125 sheep with the words that they themselves were "ready to march in the van, and sprinkle the American altars with our heart's blood." An indignant Tory reported that the patriots were "bullying and insulting us with the Plenty they enjoyed, boasting that their Sheep and their Flour, with Fish and . . . Rice came faster than they could use them." The Boston traitors were, the Tories complained, "as sleek and as round as robins."

If the political leaders of England had by chance been responsive to the ideas of an Irish peddler recently arrived in America, they might have learned enough to avoid the loss of an empire. "There is the greatest Unanimity here, among all Ranks of People," he wrote to a friend in Ireland, "and except a *very few,* all the Americans of every Denomination are warm in the cause and determined to defend their Natural and Constitutional Rights to the last drop of their Blood . . . it is really Amazing to see the Spirit of these People, from the highest to the lowest. I have had a pretty good Oppty of being acquainted with the Sentiments of the People in general as I have Rode above Four Thousand Miles thro' this Province [Pennsylvania], Maryland, and East and West Jersey, and there is hardly a Farmer or tradesman in any part of the Country that wont talk of the Rights of the Americans, the Encroachments of the British Parliament and tell you they have no Right to tax us without our Consent, and each of these, both Men & Women with pleasure would Sacrifice something for the good of their Country. . . . I profess myself a Friend to this Country and would, if there were a necessity for it take up Arms against either Eng. or Ireland in defence of American Rights."

In each town, as surely as in Boston or Philadelphia where the attention of the world was focused, people, most of them simple folk, faced the terror of a plunge into the unknown abyss of civil war and revolution, of hunger, anarchy, and possible death. In each such town, they inscribed the magic words that would affirm their determination to be free men and women and to be independent of the authority of Parliament; words that expressed the transformation that had taken place in their own consciousness of themselves as sentient beings determined to assert some modest measure of control over their own lives; to no longer be blind masses thrust about at the whim of their "betters," counters in some intricate dynastic struggle, or the victims of policies of brutal aggrandizement by a class or "interest." This is what no one knew, neither Samuel Adams and Joseph Warren in Boston, pursuing their plans and stratagems in a self-centered preoccupation with Boston and its immediate environs, nor North and his ministers, concocting new chastisements for the king's unruly subjects in Massachusetts Bay. And this is what everything hinged on. The plans of the ministry, the fate of Boston and of the colonies, the fate of America, and possibly the fate of the world rested on one simple question: Were the ordinary people of America, 90 per cent of them farmers in modest circumstances, distributed over a vast extent of land—of forest and mountain and field and farm—were they free born "Americans"? Did they care about the principles of abstract justice? Was freedom a word that evoked for them a powerful reality, or was it a cant word of philosophers and political theorists?

Historians have offered many tendentious explanations of how or why the American Revolution came about. They have talked in terms of the patriot leadership, the role of the merchants in protecting their trade, the schemes of land speculators, the diffusion of "ideas," and a dozen more "factors" or "causes," but they have given comparatively little attention to the most important phenomenon of all: the formation of a national consciousness between 1765 and 1774. This new breed of man—the American—responded with determination and courage to all threats to what he understood to be his freedom.

In a sense the summer of 1774 was the purest moment of the Revolution as well as the most crucial. Later there would be factions and divisions, inevitable falls from noble ideals to the difficult and often seriously compromised achievement of them, bitter disappointments and failures. But for the present the determination of Americans to resist Parliamentary taxation, by force of arms if necessary, was a fact as substantial as any politician could wish for. This spirit, far from being confined to a few traitors and malcontents, was most emphatically the will of a people rushing to join the grand march of history. Charles Lee—formerly an English officer, now living in America—hearing of Gage's prediction that the colonists could be readily subdued, wrote from Pennsylvania to a whig friend in England: "What devil of a nonsense can instigate any man of General Gage's understanding to concur in bringing about this delusion? I have lately, my Lord, run through almost the whole colonies from the North to the South. I should not be guilty of an exaggeration in asserting that there are 200,000 strong-bodied active yeomanry, ready to encounter all hazards. They are not like the yeomanry of other countries, unarmed and unused to arms. They want nothing but some arrangement, and this they are now bent on establishing. Even this Quaker province is following the example. I was present at a review at Providence in Rhode Island, and really never saw anything more perfect. Unless the banditti at Westminster speedily undo everything they have done, their royal paymaster will hear of reviews and manoeuvers not quite so entertaining as those he is presented with in Hyde Park and Wimbledon Common."

Another correspondent in Pennsylvania wrote to a member of Parliament that the opposition to that body was so widespread in the colonies that there were "several hundred thousand Americans who would face any danger with these illustrious heroes to lead them. It is to no purpose to attempt to destroy the opposition to the omnipotence of Parliament by taking off your Hancocks, Adamses and Dickinsons. Ten thousand patriots of the same stamp stand ready to fill their places."

PART IV

1

The Continental Congress: Nursery of American Statesmen

NEW York conservatives had proposed an intercolonial congress modeled on the one occasioned by the Stamp Act. As the other colonies joined in the call for a congress and selected their delegates, patriots of different persuasions began to make plans to push the congress in this direction or that. The more conservative hoped that Boston would be encouraged to make its peace with the government by paying for the tea. A plan for constitutional union should also be framed that would include an American Bill of Rights guaranteeing American liberties. The congress should then frame "a Message of Peace unmixt with Threats or threatening Behavior."

But the moderates got little help from Lord North. Every packet from England brought fresh news of a hardening attitude toward the Americans. The Administration of Justice Act had been revived. It protected all British officials and soldiers who took part in suppressing riots from trial by colonial juries by stipulating that when, in the opinion of the governor, a fair trial could not be had in the colony, it could be transferred to England or to another colony.

On May 25, 1774, the Massachusetts General Court elected the members of the Governor's Council. Governor Hutchinson immediately vetoed twelve of the chosen men, among them John Adams, and sailed

417

for London to report to North, leaving the direction of the colony in the hands of General Gage. Gage promptly adjourned the assembly to Salem. Despite Gage's peremptory order, the council met, and on the tenth of June the members went ahead to vote for a congress of the colonies. "In Consideration of the unhappy Differences" between the colony and the mother country, the council resolved that "It is highly expedient and necessary that a Meeting of Committees from the several Colonies on this Continent be had on a certain Day to consult upon the present State of the Colonies and the Miseries to which they are reduced by the Operation of Certain Acts of Parliament. . . ." The delegates from Massachusetts were to be Thomas Cushing, James Bowdoin, Robert Treat Paine, and Samuel and John Adams.

Brooding about the forthcoming meeting of the congress and his own responsibilities, John Adams wrote in his diary: "We have not Men, fit for the Times. We are deficient in Genius, in Education, in Travel, in Fortune—in every Thing. I feel unutterable Anxiety—God grant us Wisdom and Fortitude!" Should the patriots be suppressed, Adams continued, "should this Country submit, what Infamy and Ruin: God forbid. Death in any Form is less Terrible." John Adams had one sobering reflection: "Brutus and Cassius were conquered and slain," he wrote James Warren. "Hampden died in the Field, Sidney on the Scaffold, Harrington in Jail, etc. This is cold comfort. Politics are a path among hot-ploughshares. Who, then would be a Politician for the Pleasure of running about Barefoot among them? Yet somebody must. And I think those whose Characters, Circumstances, Educations, etc. call them, ought to follow."

Gage, now governor, dissolved the Great and General Court as soon as he heard that it had voted to send "a committee" to the continental congress, and he warned them that he intended to go himself. He wrote to Lord Dartmouth informing him of the plan for a "General Congress" and added, "It is not possible to guess what a Body composed of such heterogeneous matter, will determine; but the Members from hence, I am assured, will promote the most haughty and insolent Resolves; for their plan has ever been by high-sounding sedition, to terrify and intimidate." Gage spoke of the patriots in the other colonies as "strangely violent in support of Boston. . . . Popular fury was never greater in this Province than at present." The leaders (or as Gage called them, "the Demogogues"), confident that they would not be arrested, "chicane, elude, openly violate or passively resist the Laws. . . ." The infection of Boston and Massachusetts had spread to Connecticut, and Gage warned that military force might well have to be used against those two colonies—though he did not "apprehend any assistance would be given by the other Colonys."

The congress of committees or delegates from the various colonies was to meet in Philadelphia on the fifth of September, 1774. The members from the more distant colonies had therefore to start early in August to cover distances of as much as, in some instances, 500 miles. From fifteen to forty miles, depending on the state of the roads and the weather—as well as the frequency of ferries at rivers—was a good day's journey.

John Adams and his fellow delegates, with the exception of James Bowdoin, set out on August 10 from Boston. I think it worthwhile to accompany them on their journey to Philadelphia. We can do so readily because John Adams kept a detailed account of the trip in his ever-present diary. From Adams, we get an extraordinary sense of the drama of different people from thirteen different colonies coming together, having little in common except a devotion to what they understood—often in somewhat different ways and with widely varying degrees of intensity—to be their rights as Englishmen and as human beings.

The little contingent of Boston radicals set off in a comfortable coach-and-four attended by four servants. The patriot faction gave a party to speed them on their way—"a most kindly and affectionate meeting . . . and fervent prayers of every man in the company for our health and success." Adams added that "this scene was . . . beyond all description affecting." The members of the committee were off on a most momentous mission; the future of America, as well as of Massachusetts, hung in the balance.

As the Massachusetts committee rode out of Boston past the Common, Lord Percy, commanding officer of His Majesty's troops, noting their departure, predicted that "instead of agreeing to any thing, they will all go by the ears together at this Congress." If they do not, he added, "there will be more work cut out for the administration in America than perhaps they are aware of." "In short," he wrote, "I am certain it will require a great length of time, much steadiness and many troops, to re-establish good order and government."

Adams and his traveling companions discussed what could be done at the congress. Would it be possible to arrange for "an Annual Congress of Committees" to draw up petitions? Was not the time for petitions, in fact, past? "The ideas of the People," Adams noted, "are as various, as their Faces. One thinks, no more petitions," since those that have been drawn up before have been ignored or ridiculed. Some were for resolves, "Spirited resolves—some are for bolder Councils." So the Massachusetts men must feel their way cautiously, not offending or alarming more conservative delegates, sounding out their counterparts from other colonies, drawing together the bolder spirits, devising strategies, cultivating and encouraging the waverers, avoiding at all costs quarrels and factions that would split delegates and set back the cause.

Connecticut was the first "official" stop. At Hartford, the Massachusetts delegates met one of the leading patriots of that colony, Silas Deane, "a gentleman of a liberal education, about forty years of age, first kept a school, then studied law, then married the rich widow of Mr. Webb, since which he has been in trade." In the party were Deane's two stepsons, both prosperous merchants but good patriots, "willing to renounce all their trade." Deane assured the Bostonians that Connecticut patriots were prepared to regard the resolutions of the forthcoming congress as "the laws of the Medes and the Persians; that the Congress is the grandest and most important assembly ever held in America, and that the all of America is intrusted to it and depends upon it." Silas Deane then gave his fellow New Englanders a detailed briefing on the character and political dispositions of the New York delegates to the congress.

The Massachusetts delegates sat down to a handsome dinner at the Hartford Tavern, "with upwards of thirty Gentlemen of the first character in the Place," and when they set off at four in the afternoon they had an escort of gentlemen in carriages and on horseback who accompanied them to Weathersfield, where they "were most cordially and genteely entertained with Punch, Wine, and Coffee."

As they approached New Haven the next day, a great crowd came to meet them, "the Sheriff of the County and Constable of the Town and the Justices of the Peace" among them. "As we came into the Town," Adams noted, "all the Bells were set to ringing, and the People Men, Women and Children, were crouding at the Doors and Windows as if it was to see a Coronation. . . . No Governor of a Province, nor General of an Army was ever treated with so much Ceremony and Assiduity, as We have been, throughout the whole Colony of Connecticut. . . ."

As soon as they passed the boundaries between Connecticut and New York, the New Englanders could sense a difference. In the highlands of Rye, the first town in the province of New York, they were told by the barber who shaved them "that Religion dont flourish in this

Town." The church had no minister and there was no grammar school, in striking contrast to a New England town of similar size.

The Massachusetts delegates approached New York City with some uneasiness. The power of the De Lancey family made it a stronghold of Toryism, and while their influence was more than counterbalanced by the patriot Livingstons, the Livingstons were aristocratic highbinders who looked very much askance at the "levelling" tendencies of the New Englanders.

Significantly perhaps, their first visitor after their arrival in New York City was Alexander MacDougall, "the Sam Adams" or, alternatively, "the John Wilkes" of New York, who had been jailed for his defiance of the New York Assembly. MacDougall impressed Adams as "a very sensible Man, and an open one." After lunch MacDougall and a friend gave the Massachusetts visitors a guided tour of the city. They visited the fort and from there looked out over the Hudson River, the East River, Long Island Sound, and the harbor. They also visited Broadway, "a fine street, very wide, and in a right Line from one end to the other of the City," and admired a handsome statue of George III in gilded lead standing on a high marble pedestal. They then saw the prison (a "large and handsome stone building"), the barracks, King's College (later Columbia), a new hospital, and then the market and business district, where the Coffee House Tavern was full of businessmen drinking coffee and reading the newspapers. It was there that they met another of the leading radicals of New York, John Morin Scott. Scott seemed a "sensible Man, but not very polite," since he promptly upbraided MacDougall for not insisting that the delegates to Congress be chosen by ballot. The result was a delegation too conservative for Scott's taste and, perhaps more important, one that did not include Scott or MacDougall. On Sunday after church, they met Peter Livingston, "an old Man, extreamly Stanch in the Cause, and very sensible."

The New Englanders were plainly impressed by the richness and elegance of New York. Among the city's most striking features were its streets, laid out in a grillwork of parallel and intersecting avenues, in contrast to the narrow rambling streets of Boston that followed, for the most part, old cow paths. The houses were "more grand" as well as neater than those of Boston.

New York turned out to be a round of elegant dinners, of meetings and discussions with patriots of all ranks and persuasions. "The Way we have been in," Adams observed ruefully, "of breakfasting, dining, drinking Coffee, etc. about the City is very disagreable on some Accounts . . . it hinders us from seeing the Colledge, the Churches, the Printers Offices and Booksellers Shops, and many other Things which we should chose to see."

Beyond that there was a kind of cheerful hedonism among New Yorkers that grated on the Massachusetts delegates' nerves. "With the Opulence and Splendor of this City, there is very little good Breeding to be found," Adams noted. "At their Entertainments there is no Conversation that is agreable. There is no Modesty—No attention to one another. They talk very loud, very fast, and alltogether. If they ask you a Question, before you can utter 3 words of your Answer, they will break out upon you, again—and talk away."

Yet the company was congenial. Scott, William Smith (the historian of New York, "a plain composed Man"), and William Livingston were all Presbyterians and all graduates of Yale, and they waged war against the overweening influence of the Church of England in the colony. At John Morin Scott's home the New England delegates met John Jay, "a young Gentleman of the Law of about 26 . . . a hard Student and a good Speaker." MacDougall warned the Massachusetts delegates to tread lightly in New York. There was, he told them, a "powerful Party here, who are intimidated by Fears of a Civil War." These had been persuaded to go along with the call for a congress only by assurances "that a peaceful Cessation of Commerce" would once again force Parliament to back down. "Another Party . . . are intimidated lest the levelling Spirit of the New England Colonies should propogate itself in N. York."

Three days after the arrival of the Massachusetts committee of delegates in the city, their New York counterparts came to pay their respects: James Duane, who had "a sly, surveying Eye, a little squint Eyed . . . very sensible and very artful"; John Alsop, "a soft sweet Man"; William Livingston, "a down right strait forward Man." They later met several more Livingstons, among them Phillip, "a great, rough, rappid Mortal," who spoke "at" rather than "with" the New Englanders, blustering away and announcing that "If England should turn us adrift we should instantly go to civil wars among ourselves to determine which Colony should govern all the rest." He seemed, John Adams noted, "to dread N. England—the Levelling Spirit, etc. Hints were thrown out of the Goths and the Vandalls—mention was made of our hanging the Quakers, etc."

But if New York was more than a little daunting to the New Englanders, there was hopeful news from the South. At the Coffee House, the committee read in the *Virginia Gazette* the bold resolutions of the House of Burgesses. "The Spirit of the People is prodigious," Adams wrote. "Their Resolutions are really grand."

The committee, before it left the city for Philadelphia, made a courtesy call on one of the great men of the province, William Smith, a lawyer and, though a member of the governor's appointed council, a man who had nonetheless maintained his standing as a staunch patriot. Smith had played the role of a conciliator at the time of the Stamp Act, and he had been a good friend of General Gage when Gage commanded the American garrisons of the British army from his headquarters in New York. Gage, he told his attentive auditors, "was a good natured, peacable and sociable Man. . . . But . . . he was altogether unfit for a Governor of the Massachusetts. . . . He would loose all the Character he had acquired as a Man, a Gentleman and a General and dwindle down into a mere Scribbling Governor, a mere Bernard, or Hutchinson."

After six days in New York, Paine, Cushing, and the two Adamses pushed on through the lush, flat fields and meadows of New Jersey. Their goal in that province was the town of Princeton, where they put up at the Sign of Hudlbras, near Nassau Hall. The son of a friend from Watertown, Massachusetts, who was attending Princeton, took them through the college. They met William Churchill Houston, professor of mathematics and natural philosophy, who showed them the library and then the pride of the college, an orrery or planetarium, built by David Rittenhouse of Philadelphia, a strong patriot. The New Englanders were charmed. "It exhibits allmost every motion of the astronomical World," Adams wrote, "The motions of the Sun and all the Planetts with all their Satellites. The Eclipses of the Sun and the Moon etc."

When the bell rang for prayers, they all filed into the chapel where, Adams remarked, "The Schollars sing as badly as the Presbyterians at New York." From chapel they went to President John Witherspoon's house for a glass of wine. Witherspoon, a Scottish Presbyterian minister imported to head the College of New Jersey, was also a member of the colony's Committee of Correspondence and Provincial Congress and was "as high a Son of Liberty, as any Man in America." He was convinced that Congress should "raise Money and employ a Number of Writers in the Newspapers in England, to explain to the Public the American Plea, and remove the Prejudices of Britons." "The Government of this College is very Strict." Adams noted, "and the Schollars study very hard. The President says they are all Sons of Liberty."

From Princeton the committee pushed on to Philadelphia, stopping at Frankford, some five miles from the city, where they were met by a large company of Sons of Liberty. Prominent among them were Thomas McKean, a delegate to the Congress, and Thomas Mifflin. Also in the group was John Rutledge, a delegate from South Carolina, and the two New Hampshire delegates. At last, after interminable introductions, the New Englanders pushed on to Philadelphia.

Arriving in the city "dirty, dusty, and fatigued," they could not resist an invitation to go to the famous City Tavern, "the most genteel one in America," to meet a large assemblage of patriots. There they were officially welcomed to the City of Brotherly Love, and after lively conversation, as Adams noted, "a curtain was drawn, and in the other Half of the Chamber a Supper appeared as elegant as ever was laid upon a Table." Until eleven o'clock the guests ate the sumptuous fare, drank innumerable toasts, beginning with one to "his Majesty, the King of England," and plotted resistance to Parliament.

So, some twenty days after they had set out from Boston, the members of the committee arrived in the city where the fate of their province and of America would be decided. There would be, it appeared, about fifty-six delegates, of whom twenty-two were lawyers. The proposal had been made to meet at Carpenters' Hall rather than the State House—in order, the Tories said, to curry favor with the working men of the city, since the hall had recently been built by the subscriptions of Philadelphia's carpenters who were understandably proud of the handsome structure.

Most of the delegates stayed in taverns, and when these were filled, they lodged in private homes or with friends. Christopher Gadsden, Thomas Lynch, and Arthur Middleton were there from South Carolina. The delegates from Virginia, North Carolina, Maryland, and New York were yet to arrive. Arthur Middleton of South Carolina was "silent and reserved," John Adams noted, but young John Rutledge "was high enough." When someone mentioned that the king had made a promise, Rutledge was rash enough to say, "I should have no Regard to his Word. His Promises are not worth any Thing. . . ." He impressed the Adamses as "a young, smart, spirited body." Later John Adams added: "He has the most indistinct, inarticulate Way of Speaking. Speaks through his nose—a wretched Speaker in Conversation. . . . He seems good natured, tho conceited." Adams found Joseph Reed, one of the leading patriots of Philadelphia, "a very sensible and accomplished Lawyer of an amiable Disposition—soft, tender, friendly, etc. . . . a friend to his Country and to Liberty."

Some of the delegates had met years earlier at the Stamp Act Congress, and for these it was a matter of renewing old, if brief, friendships. Others had corresponded but had never met each other, and some from neighboring colonies were old friends, or sometimes kin.

Philadelphia, the most progressive and cosmopolitan city of the New World, offered many interesting sights. Like the streets of New York, those of Philadelphia were all "exactly straight and parallel to the [Schuylkill] River." Under the leadership of doctors Phillip Physick and William Shippen, medicine flourished here as in no other colony. Shippen took the New England delegates to the hospital, where all the newest medical practices were followed. There, "in the lower Rooms under the Ground," they saw "the Cells of Lunaticks, a number of them, some furious, some merry, some Melancholly," among them John Ingham, whom Adams had once saved at Taunton court from being whipped and sold into bondage for horse stealing.

They were then conducted to the wards, or "Sick Rooms," a recent innovation—"very long walks with rows of Beds on each side, and the lame and sick upon them—a dreadfull Scene of Human Wretchedness. The Weakness and Languor, the Distress and Misery, of these Dejects," Adams noted in his diary, "is truely a Woefull Sight."

Two days after their arrival, the New England delegates met the famous Pennsylvania "Farmer," John Dickinson, who was hardly the picture of the simple husbandman as he arrived "in his Coach and four beautiful Horse." Dickinson was the antithesis of a bold patriot. "Slender as a Reed—pale as ashes," he looked at first sight as though he could not live a month, and, indeed, he gave a rather tedious recital of "his late ill Health and present Gout." As one hypochondriac viewing another, however, Adams was impressed with a certain tough resiliency, "as if the Springs of Life were strong enough to last many Years."

Thomas Lynch of South Carolina was an ardent patriot. Talking with him, the Bostonians were greatly reassured. He was "a solid, firm, Judicious Man," who told John Adams and his colleagues that Colonel George Washington had made the most eloquent speech in the Virginia convention, declaring, "I will raise 1000 Men, subsist them at my own Expence, and march my self at their Head for the Relief of Boston." Such bold talk was most heartening.

On Thursday, September 1, the delegates from the various colonies who had already arrived in Philadelphia met at the New City Tavern. There the Bostonians had an opportunity to meet one of the New Jersey delegates, William Livingston, "lately of New York," "a plain Man, tall, black, wears his Hair [that is, went without a wing]—nothing elegant or genteel about him . . . but very sensible, and learned, and a ready writer," if an indifferent speaker.

Pennsylvania, like every other colony, had its quota (and indeed more than its quota, if one counted the Quakers, as one surely must) of "trimmers" of those who professed "to be against the Parliament-army claims of Right to tax Americans, to be Friends to our Constitutions, our Charter, etc." These men only bided their time to try to frustrate the plans of the patriots for resistance. Most of them had been smoked out, however, when the Boston Port Bill was passed. "Then, thinking the People must submit immediately and that Lord North would carry his whole System triumphantly, they threw off the Mask." Joseph Galloway, one of Pennsylvania's delegates to the congress was, in John Adams' view, just such a man. So, he had been warned, were Dr. William Smith, provost of the College of Philadelphia, and certain members of the powerful Shippen family.

While the soundings-out, the exploratory conversations, and the forming of tentative alliances continued, the steadiest patriots, those who saw most clearly where the road ahead lay, drew together. At lunch on Friday, September 2, the Massachusetts delegates were part of a most congenial company at the Mifflin's handsome home. There, with the South Carolinians and their wives and the governors of Rhode Island and Connecticut, they felt in the company of friends.

The Virginia delegates arrived the same day, Friday, September 2, and Cushing, Paine, and the two Adamses hurried off to the New City Tavern to meet them. The encounter of the two delegations was undoubtedly the most significant event of the congress. If Massachusetts was the northern axis of the resistance to the authority of Parliament, Virginia was the southern. The two oldest colonies epitomized the most striking features of their respective sections.

Massachusetts was the birthplace of New England Puritanism, that tough ethic of thrift and self-denial—at its worst meager and pinched, at its best a noble vision of Christian harmony—that came to be such a basic ingredient of the American character. Massachusetts was the exemplar of that spirit of the modern age that we denominate as capitalism, the home of the spirit to whom the future was destined to belong, the "inner-directed," "aggressive," "ambitious," "upwardly mobile" individual, striving to achieve sanctification by mercantile enterprise.

Virginia, on the other hand, was agricultural and semifeudal; a clear, if not rigid, class society, in which the great plantation owners presided, on the whole in a quite benevolent and enlightened spirit, over those independent yeoman farmers so adored by Jefferson, and over the masses of blacks whose servitude was deplored by all enlightened slave owners. Virginia was the dominion of the planter, the American version of the English country gentleman. Its tradition was one of openhandedness, of gracious hospitality, and of liberal politics.

It would have been difficult to have found, at least within the Western World, two ways of life in sharper contrast, two styles or tempers more divergent than those of Puritan Massachusetts and Cavalier Virginia. They had, it might be argued, only one thing in common—their devotion to their American freedoms. And this turned out to be enough to overcome their innumerable incompatibilities. They met, then, on Friday, September 2, 1774, in Philadelphia. The date is as important in its own way as July 4, 1776. Certainly, if at that initial meeting they had discovered their differences to be irreconcilable, there would have been no July 4 to commemorate.

There was Peyton Randolph, Speaker of the Virginia House of Burgesses, an astute scholar with the manners of a grand lord and the political skills of a ward boss; Colonel Benjamin Harrison, vast and rather gross, stuffed with the consequences of a lifetime of gastronomical self-indulgence: Richard Henry Lee, "a tall, spare Man," as thin as Harrison was fat, one of the Virginia firebrands, a member of the apparently limitless tribe of Lees—all "sensible and deep thinkers." Colonel Richard Bland, the pamphleteer, was "a learned, bookish Man," John Adams noted. These were just a sampling. Virginia, as distinguished from most colonies, had patriots to spare. Among those missing were Patrick Henry, Thomas Jefferson, George Washington, George Mason, and several more Lees. With so much talent, the second team served quite as well as the first.

Richard Henry Lee declared that he was for "making the Repeal of every Revenue Law, the Boston Port Bill, the Bill for altering the Massachusetts Constitution, and the Quebec Bill, and the Removal of all the Troops" the purpose of the congress. "He is absolutely certain," Adams noted, "that the same Ship which carries home the Resolution will bring back the Redress. . . . He thinks We should inform his Majesty that We can never be happy, while the Lords Bute, Mansfield and North are his Confidants and Councillors." Lee then took up a pen and calculated that the forthcoming congress could be said to represent

2,200,000 people. The king and Parliament simply could not afford to ignore the collective will of so many loyal subjects.

In order for a great conflagration to be ignited in human society, it is usually necessary that each party to the dispute make miscalculations concerning the intent and the courage of its adversary sufficiently profound to allow it to proceed on a course that will inevitably bring disaster. The misconceptions of the North cabinet, and of Parliament generally, in regard to the intentions and the determination of the colonies were profound. Richard Henry Lee's confident speculations make clear that many colonists had as naive and inaccurate a notion of the British temper as the British did of the colonists'.

So it went, with Adams carefully noting each event in his diary: "This Forenoon, Mr. Caesar Rodney, of the lower Counties on Delaware River and two Mr. Tilghmans from Maryland, were introduced to us. We went with Mr. Wm. Barrell to his Store and drank Punch and eat dryed smoaked Sprats with him, read the Papers, and our Letters from Boston. . . . Dined with Mr. Joseph Reed the Lawyer, with Mrs. Deberdt and Mrs. Reed, Mr. Willing, Mr. Thom. Smith . . . etc. . . . Spent the Evening at Mr. Mifflins with Lee and Harrison from Virginia, the two Rutledges, Dr. Witherspoon, Dr. Shippen, Dr. Steptoe, and other Gentlemen." The supper was elegant, and the company drank toasts until eleven o'clock; Richard Henry Lee and Benjamin Harrison got "very high." Harrison proposed as a toast "a constitutional Death to the Lords Bute, Mansfield and North." Robert Treat Paine offered, "May the collision of British Flint and American Steel, produce the Spark of Liberty which shall illumine the latest Posterity." Others followed in almost endless succession: "wisdom to Britain, and Firmness to the Colonies. May Britain be wise and America free"; Union to the Colonies. Unaminity to the Congress"; "The Friends of America throughout the World"; "The union of Britain and the Colonies, on a Constitutional Foundation." But none to "Independence."

The Boston delegates gravitated to the Virginians. When Patrick Henry arrived, the New Englanders found him somewhat flamboyant, but a solid patriot with a shrewd sense of the realities of the colonial situation. He had had no public education, he told them; at fifteen he had read Virgil and Livy, and he had not looked into a Latin book since. His father had abandoned the family when Henry was fifteen, and he had been "struggling thro Life ever since." John Adams noted that Henry had "a horrid Opinion of Galloway, Jay, and the Rutledges. Their system . . . would ruin the Cause of America. He is Impatient to see such Fellows, and not be at Liberty to describe them in their true Colours." "I expect no redress, but, on the contrary, increased resentment and double vengeance," Adams said to Henry. "We must fight." "By God," replied Henry. "I am of your opinion."

John Adams wrote James Warren on the eve of the first official meeting of the Continental Congress: "It is to be a school of Political Prophets, I suppose, a Nursery of American Statesmen. May it thrive and flourish, and from this Fountain may there issue Streams which shall gladden all the Cities and Towns in North America forever! I am for making it Annual, and for sending an entire new Set every Year, that all the principal Geniuses may go to the University in Rotation, that we may have Politicians in Plenty. Our great Complaint is the Scarcity of Men fit to govern such mighty interests as are clashing in our present Contest. . . . Our Policy must be to improve every Means and Opportunity for forming our People and preparing Leaders for them in the grand March of Politics."

A delegate, presumably Galloway, on September 3, 1774, reported to Governor William Franklin, Benjamin's son, on the "temper of the Delegates." The Boston delegates, he reported, were "in their Behaviour and Conversation very modest, & yet they are not so much so as not to throw out hints, which like straws and feathers, tell us from which Point of the Compass the Wind comes." The way the wind came was that the Bostonians wished for a nonimportation agreement and that the other colonies should support them in their refusal to pay for the tea. Any such move would be stoutly resisted by the more conservative delegates from every colony, Franklin's correspondent assured him.

2

Down to Business

O<small>N</small> Monday, September 5, the delegates all met at the City Tavern and walked to Carpenters' Hall to inspect their accommodation. The general sentiment judged it a thoroughly satisfactory room, and the question being put whether the Congress should meet there, it was carried by a large majority. Thereupon, the meeting of the first session of the first "Continental" Congress in North America convened. Thomas Lynch of South Carolina rose to propose Peyton Randolph for chairman. The question was put, and Randolph was unanimously chosen. The Virginian took the chair, and the commissions of the delegates were produced and read. Lynch then proposed Charles Thomson, "the Sam Adams of Philadelphia," as secretary, and after a brief and unsuccessful skirmish led by John Jay and James Duane of the New York delegation to add other names, Thomson was chosen unanimously. As a conservative delegate noted, Charles Thomson, "one of the most violent Sons of Liberty (so-called) in America," was chosen secretary "to my surprise." The election of Thomson and the decision to meet in Carpenters' Hall were "It seemed . . . privately settled, by an interest made out of doors"—that is, before the delegates were convened. "I cannot say but from this day's Appearance & proceedings, I have altered very much my last sentiments. The Virginians and the Carolinians, Rutledge excepted, seem much among the Bostonians."

The aggressive patriots had thus won the first three preliminary engagements. They had had their way with the place of meeting, they had placed Randolph in the chair, and they had secured the election of one of the most ardent patriots of Philadelphia as secretary.

The first issue to perplex the delegates was whether they should vote as individuals or by colony. Patrick Henry rose to point out that this was the first general Congress that had been called, and that since there would undoubtedly be others, it was important to decide on the question of how the colonies should vote. He left no question of his own feelings by adding that "it would be a great injustice, if a little Colony should have the same Weight in the Councils of America, as a great one. . . ." To which Major John Sullivan, a delegate from New Hampshire, replied that "a little Colony had its All at Stake as well as a great one." And so the lines were drawn on one of the most crucial and complex issue that the politicians of America would have to decide over the course of the next fifteen years.

John Adams listed some of the problems involved in his diary. "If We vote by Colonies, this Method will be liable to great inequality and injustice, for 5 small Colonies with 100,000 People each may out-vote 4 large ones, each of which has 500,000 inhabitants. If We vote by the Poll [that is simply as individuals], some Colonies have more than their Proportion of [Delegates], and others have less. If we vote by interests, it will be attended by insuperable Difficulties, to ascertain the true importance of each Colony—is the Weight of a Colony to be ascertained by the number of inhabitants merely—or by the Amount of their Trade, the Quantity of their Exports and Imports, or by any compound Ratio of both. This will lead us into such a Field of Controversy as will greatly perplex us." It was not even possible to obtain a true count of the population of each individual colony.

The delegates were treated almost immediately to an example of the famous oratory of Patrick Henry. He began boldly enough, chilling the heart of the conservative Galloway. "The distinctions between Virginians, Pennsylvanians, New Yorkers and New Englanders," Henry said, "are no more. I am not a Virginian, but an American."

The Virginia orator justified his reputation. He had at once evoked the spirit of a new nation with his bold rhetoric: "I am not a Virginian, but an American." Saying the words did not make it so, but they made it possible. They began the slow, strange process that would in time make America out of this odd jumble of colonies. The immediate issue was a mundane one, but Henry, with the true visionary's gift for drawing the particular into the universal, had seized the opportunity at the beginning of the convention to take a potentially divisive issue and use it to give the delegates a sense of a common purpose nobler than all their petty insularities.

Since Virginia was the largest colony, it wished to have the vote determined by size; since South Carolina, though comparatively thinly settled, was the wealthiest colony, it wished to take into consideration property as well as population. Governor Samuel Ward from Rhode Island, the smallest of the colonies, wished to see representation by colonies—one colony, one vote. Colonel Bland pointed out that the delegates were presently without very satisfactory evidence about either population or property. They must not, in a discussion about voting, lose sight of the fact that they were there mainly to decide "whether the Rights and Liberties of America shall be contended for, or given up to arbitrary Power."

Henry repeated his view that "the Government is at an End. All Distinctions are thrown down. All America is thrown into one Mass." John Jay was uneasy at such talk. One might suppose that the delegates had been assembled for the purpose of framing an American constitution instead of endeavoring to correct the faults in an old one. The Measure of arbitrary Power is not full, and I think it must run over, before we can undertake to frame a new Constitution."

Richard Henry Lee declared that the rights of the colonies were built "on a fourfold foundation—on Nature, on the British constitution, on Charters, and on Immemorial Usage." The Americans should "lay our Rights upon the broadest Bottom, the Ground of Nature." "It is contended that the Crown had no Right to grant such Charters as it has to the Colonies—and therefore We shall rest our Rights on a feeble foundation, if we rest em only on Charters. . . ."

Rutledge, however, was convinced that "our claims are well founded on the British Constitution, and not on the Law of Nature." The law of nature was too vague; it smacked of deism and foreign philosophies. Yet there were obvious problems from a legal and constitutional point of view with putting all the eggs of colonial argument in the basket of the British Constitution. William Livingston pointed out that a corporation could not create a corporation, and therefore it would not do for America "to rest wholly on the Laws of England."

James Duane wanted to place the principal emphasis on the colonial charters. They were, in effect, "Compacts between the Crown and the People and I think on this foundation the Charter Governments stand firm. . . . The Priviledges of Englishmen were inherent, their

Birthright and inheritance, and [the colonists] cannot be deprived of them without their Consent." To this it might be argued that a strict interpretation of such a principle would make the colonies independent, but it was Duane's hope that a line could be drawn short of independence that would allow proper authority to the Crown and sufficient liberty to the colonies. Lee reminded the delegates that "Life and Liberty, which is necessary for the Security of Life, cannot be given up when we enter into Society."

On the third day of the discussions, Joseph Galloway, the most formidable of the conservative faction, rose to speak. His address was a long and able one. He was skeptical of the argument based on natural rights or on the laws of nature; they were too abstract and theoretical to be of much use in the present crisis. The issue was, in essence, one of the distribution of power. Power resulted from the landed property of a society. A review of British history illustrated how the owners of landed property had fought for and won protections for their estates against rapacious monarchs. It was thus the essence of the British constitution "that no Law shall be binding, but such as are made by the Consent of the Proprietors in England." Following this line, it could be properly argued that the colonies were not bound by any laws made in England since the time of the first great emigrations. "I am well aware," Galloway concluded, "that my Arguments tend to an Independency of the Colonies, and militate against the Maxim that there must be some absolute Power to draw together all the Wills and strengths of the Empire."

What were the radicals to make of that? Galloway had adumbrated the most radical position yet taken by any of the delegates with the exception of Patrick Henry. Was it a ruse to smoke out the real sentiments of the patriotic leaders? Or was Galloway a man too timid to follow where his logic led him and too fastidious to countenance the means by which revolutions are effected?

By the end of the week the more aggressive patriots were ready to take stock. The tide of feelings seemed to be moving their way within Carpenters' Hall and without. Joseph Reed and the two Adamses held a council of war, albeit "a very sociable, agreeable and communicative" one. Reed stated, "The Sentiments of the People are growing more and more favourable every day."

Galloway lobbied for his notion of sending commissioners to the British court, "a mode pursued by the Romans, Grecian, and Macedonian Colonies on every occasion of the like nature." Through such commissioners, the colonies would get accurate information and not have to rely on newspapers and private letters. All the tactics of the conservatives were directed to one end—to buy time, time for England to awaken to a true understanding of the colonial position, time for the haste and impatience of the colonists to be moderated. Governor Franklin, writing to Lord Dartmouth to inform him of the proceedings of Congress, noted that his information came from "a very prudent and moderate man, extremely averse to the violent and rash measures proposed by the Virginians and Bostonians." This man, certainly Galloway, "was in hopes to have formed a Party among the Delegates sufficient to have prevented a Non Importation Agreement, for the present, but he seems now [September 6] to despair of Success." The conservative delegates—primarily from Pennsylvania, New Jersey, and New York—counting noses, found themselves in a clear minority. Under such circumstances, it seemed inexpedient to resist the majority. So clear was the majority sentiment that Galloway, who had already had his proposal for sending commissioners to Great Britain to petition for a representative intercolonial parliament printed, decided not to publish it.

Galloway's gloomy apprehensions were confirmed by Benjamin Booth's Pennsylvania correspondent, Henry Drinker. A majority of the colonies and the delegates appeared to favor nonimportation. "The Virginia Delegates," Drinker wrote, "eclipse all others as well in Oratorical Abilities as in a more deep & thorough knowledge of the subjects which come before them—manifesting their acquaintance with the History and Constitution of Antient & modern States & shewing much capacity in their inferences from & references thereto." On the other hand, the delegates from New England, or more particularly from Massachusetts, "show that they have but a superficial knowledge of what they came about and are at the same time but indifferent Orators."

In the midst of the deliberations of the Continental Congress, there arrived from Massachusetts a set of resolves that had been drawn up by the Suffolk County convention, a body of more than doubtful legality that had pre-empted the role of the Massachusetts assembly after that body had been dismissed by Governor General Gage.

The Suffolk Resolves, drafted by Joseph Warren, began: "*Whereas* the power of but not the justice, the vengeance but not the wisdom of Great Britain, which of old persecuted, scourged, and exiled our fugitive parents from their native shores, now pursues us, their guiltless children, with unrelenting severity: And whereas this, then savage and uncultivated desert, was purchased by the toil and treasure, or acquired by the blood and valor of these our venerable progenitors; to us that bequeathed the dear bought inheritance, to our care and protection they consigned it, and the most sacred obligation are upon us to transmit this glorius purchase, unfettered by power, unclogged with shackles, to our innocent and beloved offspring." The Americans must resist "that unparalleled usurpation of unconstitutional power," with all its attendant miseries. Only thus will they "enjoy the rewards and blessings of the faithful, the torrent of panegyrists [that] will roll our reputations to that latest period, when the streams of time shall be absorbed in the abyss of eternity."

Then followed a series of resolves. No obedience was due to any of the Coercive Acts, "the attempts of a wicked administration to enslave Americans. . . ." All public monies should be kept in the hands of "collectors of taxes, constables and all other officers . . . until the civil government of this province is placed upon a constitutional foundation, or until it shall otherwise be ordered by the proposed provincial Congress. . . ." The Quebec Act was "dangerous in an extreme degree to the Protestant religion and to the civil rights and liberties of all America," and the colonists were thus obliged to "take all proper measures for our security"—whatever that might mean. The eleventh resolve was that all royal commissions be taken away from the militia officers and that men be elected officers in their place who had shown themselves "the inflexible friends to the rights of the people." Moreover, the inhabitants of every town should "use their utmost diligence to acquaint themselves with the art of war as soon as possible, and do, for that purpose, appear under arms at least once every week."

Finally, until the rights of the citizens of Massachusetts were fully restored to them, the resolves urged a strict policy of nonimportation and nonexportation with "Great-Britain, Ireland, and the West Indies, especially of East-India teas and piece goods. . . ." If a patriot leader was arrested by the British, the people of Massachusetts would be justified in seizing "every servant of the present tyrannical and unconstitutional government."

On Sunday, September 18, Congress replied to the Suffolk Resolves, commending the resolvers for the "wisdom and fortitude" with which they had resisted "these wicked ministerial measures"; and after several weeks of debate, the delegates formally approved the resolves, while cautioning against any hostile act directed against Gage and the soldiers "as far as possibly can be consistent with their immediate safety, and the security of the town." John Adams wrote in his diary:

"This was one of the happiest Days of my Life. In Congress we had generous, noble Sentiments, and manly Eloquence. This Day convinced me that America will support the Massachusetts[sic] or perish with her."

Outside of Carpenters' Hall, the delegates enjoyed the social life of Philadelphia, while a subcommittee prepared a report stating the rights of the colonies. The Massachusetts delegates dined with Mifflin and Thomson at John Dickinson's handsome estate, which offered a fine view of the city, the Schuylkill River, and the countryside—"a convenient, decent, elegant Philosophical Rural Retreat," Robert Treat Paine called it. And John Adams, encouraged by the resolute line that the Congress was taking and consequently inclined to be pleased with the world and everything in it, found the master of Fairhill "a very modest Man, and very ingenuous, as well as agreeable. He has an excellent Heart and the Cause of his Country lies near it."

Despite all the glittering allurements of Philadelphia, the Massachusetts delegates—or John Adams at least—were not seduced. Adams remained infatuated with Boston. "Philadelphia," he noted in his diary, "with all its Trade, and Wealth, and Regularity is not Boston. The Morals of our People are much better, their Manners are more polite and agreable—they are purer English. Our Language is better, our Persons are handsomer, our Spirit is greater, our Laws are wiser, our Religion is superiour, our Education is better. We exceed them in every Thing, but in a Markett, and in charitable public foundations."

The New England delegates dined with Miers Fisher, a young Quaker lawyer, and John Adams had a little difficulty reconciling the luxuriousness of their style of life with the reputed simplicity of their faith. "This plain Friend, and his plain, tho pretty wife with her Thee's and Thou's," Adams noted, "provided us the most Costly Entertainment—Ducks, Hams, Chickens, Beef, Pigg, Tarts, creams, custards, Gellies, fools, Trifles, floating Islands, Beer, Porter, Punch, wine. . . . etc." The delegates were lavishly entertained at the splendid home of Richard Penn, grandson of the founder of the colony—"a magnificent House, and a most splendid Feast, and a very large Company." But grandest of all was the visit to the townhouse of Benjamin Chew, the chief justice of Pennsylvania. "We were shown," Adams wrote, "into a grand Entry and Stair Case, and into an elegant and most magnificent Chamber, until Dinner. About four o'clock We were called down to Dinner. The Furniture was all rich,—Turttle, and every other Thing— Flummery, Jellies, Sweetmeats of 20 sorts, Trifles, Whip'd Syllabubbs, floating Islands, fools, etc., and then a Desert of Fruits, Raisins, Almonds, Pears, Peaches—wines most excellent and admirable. I drank Madeira at a great Rate and found no Inconvenience in it."

All this wining and dining, which seemed excessive to the rather frugal New England delegates, had a useful political as well as social purpose. Such convivial occasions bound the delegates together and fortified their sense of being engaged in a common cause. The amount of food and wine they consumed on such occasions was prodigious. Dinner in midafternoon was ordinarily the principal meal and commonly lasted several hours, but it was by no means unusual to follow such a lavish repast with a supper that might begin at eight o'clock and last until eleven, when the diners would rise stuffed almost to insensibility with good food, and often more than slightly tipsy with wine.

When we add to these meals the very ample breakfasts, it is clear that the revolutionary statesmen spent a considerable part of each day eating and drinking. The results are evident in their portraits. Most were inclined to be pleasantly globular. Thin men, like Dickinson, Lee, and Caesar Rodney were rather the exception. I suppose a society might be judged as much by its attitude toward food as toward sex or money. The colonial upper classes considered the securing, preparing, and eating of food a central aspect of their lives. More than that, they treasured the company and the conversation occasioned by such repasts, the flow of good humor, the witty sallies, the skillfully presented arguments, the learned allusions, the precise steps in a logical analysis, the neat turns of phrase that might support a delicately balanced proposition. In short, they relished that noble and proper accompaniment of good food, good talk. And that good food and wine and talk wove a subtle but powerful web among their affections, binding them into a unity of spirit and a bond of concord, in which agreeable harmony lay the seeds of a nation.

The political and the social lie very much closer than we suspect. Democratic politics rest, in considerable part, on trust, and trust quite clearly rests on the mutual confidence that comes most commonly out of knowing the people that one trusts. To put the matter simply, if South Carolina was to support Massachusetts, or Virginia join with Rhode Island, it was necessary that Christopher Gadsden and Richard Henry Lee like or at least trust Thomas Cushing and Stephen Hopkins.

By the end of September, the delegates, having heard from the several subcommittees, were ready for a boycott of British goods; Richard Henry Lee made the proposal. The debate centered primarily on when the agreement should go into effect. Samuel Chase of Maryland expressed his conviction that a "total Non Import and Non Export to G. Britain and W. Indies must produce a national Bankruptcy [of Great Britain] in a very short Space of Time." Lynch reinforced Chase; the sooner nonimportation went into effect the better, "I believe," he declared, "the Parliament would grant us immediate relief. Bankruptcy would be the Consequence if they did not."

Christopher Gadsden followed his fellow Carolinian. "By saving our own Liberties," he said, "we shall save those of the West Indies. I am for being ready, but I am not for the sword. The only Way to prevent the sword from being used is to have it ready. . . . Boston and New England can't hold out—the Country will be deluged in Blood, if we don't act with Spirit. Dont let America look at this Mountain, and let it bring forth a Mouse."

Edward Rutledge stated that as naval stores were vital to the economy of North Carolina, so was rice to her sister to the south. Every colony must suffer some hardship if Parliament was to be forced to restore colonial liberties. Rutledge was thus for immediate nonimportation and nonexportation. He was supported by John Jay, who stated that only three choices faced the Congress, "negotiation, suspension of Commerce, and War." The delegates were generally agreed that for the present war was to be avoided. To Eliphalet Dyer, the rather dour and tough-minded delegate from Connecticut, it was all very well to talk of economic pressures, but the fact was that the British "have now drawn the Sword, in order to execute their Plan, of subduing America, And I imagine they will not sheath it, but that next Summer will decide the Fate of America." Nonetheless he had been persuaded by the array of statistics quoted by the delegates that Great Britain "is much more in our Power than I expect." It seemed clear that "to withdraw all Commerce with Great Britain at once, would come upon them like a Thunder Clap." And so the delegates continued to delude themselves that they could, by economic measures, soon force the British to rescind the objectionable statutes.

September 28 was an important day for the Massachusetts delegates. That day they met the recently arrived Colonel Washington, who made a typically laconic entry in *his* diary: "Dined at Mr. Edward Shippen's. Spent the afternn. with the Boston Gent." Washington, as reserved and taciturn as any New Englander, hit it off well with the

"Boston Gent." His lack of airs, his candor and directness, his manner of weighing each sentence before he uttered it—he was cautious and reflective but never ponderous—his soberness and discretion, all these qualities in the Virginia militia colonel impressed the New Englanders. For his part, Washington, who had half-expected to encounter a group of radical agitators, was most reassured to meet the men from the Bay Colony. Even their appearance was reassuring. Samuel Adams looked a bit like a clerk in a mercantile house. Except for his dark, slightly protuberant eyes, which read faces as avidly as his cousin John read books, there was little about him to suggest the fiery revolutionist. John Adams looked very much like what he was—a short, stout provincial lawyer—and, carefully minding his tongue so as not to alarm Washington, he sounded both learned and eminently sensible. Cushing was a florid, handsome man, more cosmopolitan in his manners than his companions but equally reassuring in his temper. Washington and the Bostonians came away mutually impressed, and another very crucial link was forged between Massachusetts and Virginia—perhaps, in retrospect, the most crucial link of all.

In the debates at Carpenters' Hall the same day, Joseph Galloway got up to offer his plan of union, and to subject the plans of the delegates for nonimportation and nonexportation to a brilliant and searching scrutiny. The nonimportation agreement that the delegates had already adopted would be "too gradual in its Operation for the Relief of Boston." The notion of nonexportation was poorly thought out; it would be impossible for America to exist under a total nonexportation. "We in this Province," he declared, "should have tens of Thousands of People thrown upon the cold Hand of Charity—Our Ships would lie by the walls, our Seamen would be thrown out of Bread, our Shipwrights etc. out of Employ and it would affect the landed interest. It would weaken us in another Struggle which I fear is too near." All the great authorities on the nature of government—Burlamaqui, Grotius, Pufendorf, Hooker—agreed that a government must contain "an Union of Wills and Strength." That was what distinguished a settled social order from an unruly multitude. The center, the focus of such will and strength must be Great Britain, and the Americans must come to terms with the mother country. The answer was "a British American Legislature" that would act on all occasions in which more than one colony was concerned, such as raising money for war or levying other proper taxes. No taxes could be imposed or laws passed by Parliament affecting the colonies without the concurrence of the American legislature. The legislature, or Grand Council, would be chosen "by the representatives of the people of the several colonies in their respective Assemblies, once in every three years." All matters, civil, criminal, and commercial, that affected "the colonies in general, or more than one colony" should come under the jurisdiction of the President-General and the Grand Council.

The problem with the Galloway Plan of Union was that it was, in essence, a diversionary tactic, and it was understood as such by most of the delegates. At the same time, it had a very strong appeal. Men faced with taking difficult and costly actions are prone to grasp at straws. Most men prefer to avoid or delay hard decisions. This, in the view of the more resolute patriots, was the iniquitousness of the Galloway proposal. The appeal of the plan was heightened by the fact that many of the delegates had in their hearts little taste for nonimportation and nonexportation. They shrank from the dismal and demoralizing task of bullying their neighbors into conformity, and the more realistic of them knew, if they dared not say so, that it was a futile palliative, a mild poultice on a gaping wound. The British army was occupying Boston, the navy blockading its port; the government of the colony was altered by fiat; the province of Quebec was wrapped around the northern provinces like a noose around the neck of a condemned man. Elaborate schemes for some intercolonial government would take years of discussion and negotiation and even then had little chance of coming to anything, given the temper of the British government. Meantime what would happen to Boston and to colonial liberties in general?

The seductiveness of the Galloway plan lay almost wholly in the inadequacy of the alternative. James Duane announced his intention of seconding the proposal, and John Jay, following his New York colleague, declared his support. "Does this Plan give up any one Liberty?— or interfer with any one Right," he asked. (To which the Bostonians might have replied that it simply gave up Boston.)

The radicals, led by Patrick Henry, took up the cudgels against the Galloway plan. "We shall liberate our Constituents from a corrupt House of Commons, but throw them into the Arms of an American Legislature that may be bribed by that Nation which avows in the Face of the World, that Bribery is a Part of her System of Government," Henry said. When Henry had finished, Edward Rutledge of South Carolina rose to endorse the plan of union: "I think the Plan may be freed from almost every objection. I think it is an almost perfect Plan." And Galloway had the last word of the session, ending with the admonition:

"There is a Necessity that an American Legislature would be set up, or else that We should give the Power to Parliament or King." Power there must be.

After several days of heated debate, however, Galloway's plan died for want of sufficient support (and doubtless from judicious politicking out-of-doors). Indeed, the more determined patriots went further and had all references to the Galloway plan expunged from the official records of the Congress. As a force in American politics, Galloway was finished. A Pennsylvania Quaker wrote to an English friend, "The Warmth of the Virginians added to the craft of the New England Men with some other fiery Spirits defeated this rational proposal."

It was odd also that no one picked up Galloway's warning, i.e., that if war was to come, nonimportation and nonexportation, far from being the means by which the British government was to be brought to terms, might be the means of fatally weakening the colonies and leaving them an easy prey to the armed might of the mother country. Perhaps the patriot party felt that since it would be disastrous for Congress either to espouse the Galloway plan or to return home empty-handed, weak and ineffective action was the best that could be gotten and better than none at all.

The clearest division among the delegates was over the issue of whether or not Parliament had the right to regulate trade. All those who were delegates were in Philadelphia presumably because they were agreed that Parliament had no right to tax the colonies without their consent. But, just as at the time of the Townshend duties, there was a substantial and articulate group who insisted that it was necessary to acknowledge and accept the power to regulate trade, as opposed to the power to tax. Similarly, there was a strong faction that opposed all power of Parliament over the colonies and that wished to go back and rake over old coals, listing the impositions of Parliament on the American colonies from the beginning and rejecting them in all cases, past, present, and to come. It might be assumed that these patriots were, as a logical consequence of their position, in favor of immediate independence for the American colonies. But to presume that would be to assume that men are ruled by logic, and history gives no support to that assumption. The fact was that many of those who rejected the authority of Parliament over the colonies *in all cases whatsoever* rejected the idea of independence, wished to remain within the British Empire, and somehow believed that they could.

Thomas Lynch of South Carolina was a spokesman for those who wished at least to reject the authority of Parliament over all trade. He hammered away during the debates at the fact that he "came here to get Redress of Grievances, and to adopt every Means for that End" that could be adopted with a Good conscience. "In my idea," he reiterated, "Parliament has no Power to regulate Trade. . . . These Duties are all for Revenue not for Regulation of Trade."

Isaac Low of New York was dismayed by such reckless talk. "We ought not," he declared, "to deny the just Rights of our Mother Country. We have too much Reason in this Congress, to suspect that independency is aimed at." He was in favor of adjourning Congress for six months to allow tempers to cool and to see how the course of events might run. Could or would the people of the colonies "live without Rum, Sugar, and Molasses?"

Congress did not adjourn, however, and the delegates labored on. Their principal task was to draft another petition to the king. Richard Henry Lee, as a member of a subcommittee appointed for that purpose, wrote one after consulting with the Adamses, Cushing, and Paine, but it was too strong for many of the members of the Congress—"written in language of asperity very little according with the conciliatory disposition of Congress"—and John Dickinson, the master of conciliatory language, was induced to try his hand.

Meanwhile a vote in Congress on the question of conceding the power of parliament to regulate trade failed, with five colonies for allowing it, five opposed, and two, Massachusetts and Rhode Island, divided among themselves.

Finally, on October 14, the delegates passed the Declaration and Resolves that began, "whereas, since the close of the last war, the British Parliament, claiming a power, of right, to bind the people of America by statutes in all cases whatsoever, hath, in some acts, expressly imposed taxes upon them . . . established a board of customs commissioners with unconstitutional powers, and extended the jurisdiction of the courts of admiralty. . . ."

Subsequent "whereases" listed further grievances: making judges dependent on the Crown alone for their salaries, quartering standing armies on a civilian population in time of peace, passing the Coercive Acts—"impolitic, unjust, and cruel, as well as unconstitutional, and most dangerous and destructive of American rights"—dissolving colonial assemblies "when they attempted to deliberate on grievances," and, finally, treating "their dutiful, humble, loyal, and reasonable petitions with contempt." (It is certainly not clear why the delegates thought this petition would be treated any differently.)

As a consequence of these oppressive and unconstitutional acts, "the good people of the several colonies" had appointed deputies "to sit in a general Congress, in the City of Philadelphia" to take the necessary measures to protect "their religion, laws, and liberties."

To this end, the delegates had deliberated and did now *declare* That the inhabitants of the English colonies in North America, by the immutable laws of nature, the principles of the English Constitution, and the several charters of compacts, have the following rights:

"That they are entitled to life, liberty and property, and they have never ceded to any sovereign power whatever, a right to dispose of either without their consent." (This was almost pure Locke.) Their ancestors, who had first settled the colonies, had brought with them "all the rights, liberties, and immunities of free and natural-born subjects." It was, moreover, a basic right of all Englishmen and indeed "of all free government . . . to participate in their legislative council." Since this was impossible, the colonists rejected as unconstitutional "every idea of taxation, internal or external, for raising a revenue on the subjects in America without their consent."

The petition closed with a list of those acts of Parliament that were "infringements and violations of the rights of the colonists . . . the repeal of them is essentially necessary, in order to restore harmony between Great Britain and the American colonies." Then followed a formidable list of eleven Parliamentary statutes that, in the view of the colonists, must be repealed. To emphasize the strength of their convictions, the colonists were resolved "to enter into a nonimportation, non-consumption, and non-exportation agreement or association: (2) to prepare an Address to the people of Great Britain, and a Memorial to the inhabitants of British America; and (3) to prepare a loyal address to His Majesty, agreeable to the resolutions already entered into."

Six days later came the Association of the Colonies that spelled out the details of nonimportation, nonconsumption, and nonexportation. The nonimportation agreement was to go into effect on the first of December, 1774. Among those items not to be imported were slaves— "we will wholly discontinue the slave trade." And then the sweetening that would make the bitter medicine of nonimportation go down more easily: nonexportation would be deferred until the following September of 1775, a year away, "in order," the resolutions stated with more than a touch of hypocrisy, "not to injure our fellow-subjects in Great Britain, Ireland, or the West Indies."

In order to ameliorate the effects of a boycott, the delegates pledged themselves to "encourage frugality, economy, and industry, and promote agriculture, arts and the manufactures of this country, especially that of wool"; to "discountenance and discourage every species of extravagance and dissipation, especially all horseracing, and all kinds of gaming, cock-fighting, exhibtions or shews, plays, and other expensive diversions and entertainments." Further, none of them would wear mourning clothes at funerals other than "a black crape or ribbon on the arm or hat, for gentlemen, and a black ribbon and necklace for ladies. . . ."

It was recommended that each county, city, and town appoint committees to ride hard on possible violators of the Association, and that respective committees of correspondence check customhouse entries periodically to be sure that the agreements were being observed. Domestic manufacturers were warned not to be tempted by the scarcity of British imports to try to profiteer by charging high prices for their current inventories.

So the First Continental Congress (we except the Stamp Act Congress because of its inadequate representation) drew to a close. Its main business out of the way, it went on "nibbling and quibbling—as usual." "There is no greater Mortification," John Adams noted, "than to sit with half a dozen witts, deliberating upon a Petition, Address or Memorial. These great witts, these subtle Criticks, these refined Genius's, these learned Lawyers, these wise Statesmen, are so fond of shewing their Parts and Powers as to make their Consultations very tedius." Worst of all was young Ned Rutledge, "a perfect Bob O'Lincoln—a Swallow—a Sparrow—a Peacock—excessively vain, excessively weak, and excessively variable and unsteady—jejune, inane, and puerile."

Adams' nerves, like those of his fellow Massachusetts delegates, were wearing raw at the endless "nibbling and quibbling." But finally the work was done. The Congress voted a resolution of thanks to the Pennsylvania assembly "for their politeness" and "then dissolved itself," almost two months after it had convened. The Pennsylvania assembly gave a dinner for the delegates at the City Tavern. The toast was, "May the sword of the Parent never be Stain'd with the Blood of her Children." Adams noted that a Quaker, sitting nearby, said to his companion, "This is not a Toast but a Prayer, come let us join in it."

After making their farewells, the delegates who had come as provincial politicans rode off with some claim to having become continental statesmen. Their sense of accomplishment as they rode away from "the happy, the peaceful, the elegant, the hospitable, and polite City of Philadelphia" was hardly dampened by a torrential downpour. A recently arrived Irishman, who was working as a traveling salesman for "one of the most Capital Dry Goods Merchts in America," was much impressed with their proceedings. "It is said," he wrote a friend in the homeland, "that such an August Body as form'd our late Congress, never before was conven'd together, nor was there ever before a subject of such importance in its consequences to be consider'd by any part of the World, come under the notice of any part of the World—The Spirit of Resistance is Universal, and those Men that compos'd the Congress were the real Representatives of the People, therefore their Resolves and Opinions are those of all America."

In practical fact their achievements, measured in any realistic terms, were very modest. They had spent an inordinate amount of time talking about how to provide some relief for the embattled Bostonians and turn back the progressive erosion of colonial liberties. Their remedy—nonimportation and nonconsumption with a threat of nonexportation—was woefully inadequate to the disease. There was not the slightest prospect that it would succeed. Perhaps the only substantial achievement of the Congress was to have come together, to have established a basis, at least among the bolder delegates, of mutual understanding and trust. The British would be much more impressed (though still insufficiently) by the demonstration of colonial unity offered by the fact that the Congress had convened, and that it had drawn together many of the ablest men in the various colonies, than by anything that happened.

The Congress was more notable for the pitfalls that it had avoided than for the positive actions it had taken. The principal pitfall was Galloway's plan, which, whatever its theoretical virtues may have been, would have left Boston to stew in its own juices—which presumably would not have distressed Joseph Galloway. The conservatives had been routed. They had made their bid to control the nature and, above all, the degree of colonial resistance, and they had failed signally. They would never again be a serious threat.

As ineffectual as the Congress was in terms of bringing Great Britain to terms, it was highly successful in drawing the colonists together. It was essential that the colonies have at least the illusion that they were accomplishing something. The fact that they were called on to

make common sacrifices had a salutary effect on patriot morale. It is to
be feared that spying on their neighbors—mostly neighbors of Tory
sentiments whom they feared and distrusted—was an additional pleasure. They developed the means and the temper of cooperation and
mutual confidence, the rudimentary organs of self-government. So,
although the various pronouncements of Congress weighed as a feather
in England, they performed a very useful function in America; they
kept the patriots occupied, gave them the illusion of accomplishment,
and developed further those "shadow governments" that would in time
become legitimate.

As with all deliberative bodies, the discussions of the delegates to
the First Continental Congress were extensive and at times tedious. The
delegates were, as time would prove, a remarkably able group of men; it
has been common to call them the ablest in history who have gathered
together to contemplate some form of political action. They were, on
the whole, remarkably learned. They had read most of the great classical authors—Vergil and Cicero especially, but the historians Herodotus,
Thucydides, Polybius, Tacitus, and Livy as well. They knew modern
writers on law and government—Locke, of course, and Harrington, and
the authorities on jurisprudence that Galloway had referred to in
introducing his plan of union. Perhaps most important, they were all
practical politicians with many years of experience in the arduous school
of provincial politics. Nonetheless, they rehearsed the same arguments,
worried at niggling points like a dog at a bone, lost their tempers on
occasion, and in general behaved like human beings faced with a
particularly difficult and frustrating problem. John Adams, after some
six weeks of debate, expressed his irritation in his diary. "The Deliberations of the Congress," he wrote, "are spun out to an immeasurable
Length. There is so much Wit, Sense, Learning, Acuteness, Subtlety,
Eloquence, etc. among fifty Gentlemen, each of whom has been habituated to lead and guide in his own Province, that an immensity of Time
is spent unnecessarily."

After the results of the deliberations of the Continental Congress
became known, a chastened and gloomy Benjamin Booth wrote to his
friends in Philadelphia, "I now think the Non-importation Association
will be faithfully observed here. . . . This Town will shortly be put under
the direction of a new Committee, consisting mostly of forward, busy
spirits, who I make no doubt will rule us as with a rod of iron."

It was Governor William Franklin's view that the resolves of Congress left England "no other alternative than either to consent to what must appear humiliating in the eyes of all Europe, or to compel obedience to her laws by a military force." When General Gage read the resolutions and memorials of Congress, he wrote to Lord Dartmouth that "the proceedings of the Continental Congress astonish and terrify all considerate men."

The Tories, who were by no means intimidated, were furious at the outcome of the Continental Congress, the more so since many of them had supported the calling of the Congress in the hopes that it would be dominated by the moderate faction and take the leadership away from the extremists. They charged the Congress with producing at home the tyranny it denounced in England. In place of the king, loyal Americans had to contend with "their *High Mightinesses* the MOB."

To the Tories, the action of Congress meant "the utter subversion of all Law, and the total destruction of all LIBERTY." The meddling Associators would soon proceed, one Loyalist warned, from inspecting warehouses to examining "your tea-cannisters and molasses-jugs and your wives and daughters petty-coats." The patriots were in virtually that "state of nature" they were always prating about; they "swear and drink, and lie and whore and cheat, and rob, and pull down houses, and tar and feather, and play the devil in every shape, just as the devil and their own inclination lead them," wrote Jonathan Sewall, John Adams' once-close friend, "and yet they cry out for liberty." Instead of taking a peaceful and conciliatory line, they had spoken of Parliament as little better than "a Pack of Banditti" and made the "breach with the parent state a thousand times more irreparable than it was before." The delegates had fallen into the snare of the "sly favourers of an America Republic" and produced "a venemous brood of scorpions, to sting us to death."

In the aftermath of the Congress, the pamphlet warfare between Tories and patriots flared up with fresh vigor. Samuel Seabury, the New York Tory, attacked Congress for having "*erected itself into the supreme legislature of North America,*" overriding in the process the rights of both colonial assemblies and the British government. "Virginia and Massachusetts madmen," he wrote, "met at Philadelphia, have made laws for the Province of *New York* and have rendered our Assembly *useless.*" Harrison Gray of Boston, who styled himself "A Friend to Peace and good Order," produced a pamphlet entitled "The Two Congresses Cut Up: Or a Few Remarks upon Some of the Votes and Resolutions of the Continental Congress, Held in Philadelphia, in September, and the

Provincial Congress, Held in Cambridge, in November, 1774." Gray did not, he wrote, pretend to be competent to judge the constitutional question of the right of Parliament to tax the colonies. He could only say "that the *opposition* that hath been generally made to it, is inconsistent with our profession of *christianity,* with the *loyalty* we owe to our Sovereign, and the reverence and respect that is due to the British Parliament. . . ." The destruction of the tea, Gray declared, was "an action of such a gross immoral nature as cannot be justified upon the principles of equity or policy."

Another Tory pamphlet, written by the Reverend J. B. Chandler, expressed the opinion that "even a final victory would effectually ruin us: as it would necessarily introduce civil wars among ourselves, and leave us open and exposed to the avarice and ambition of every maritime power in Europe or America. Until one part of the country shall have subdued the other, and conquered a considerable part of the world beside, this peaceful region must become, and continue to be, a theatre of inconceivable misery and horrour." The Americans were "without fortresses, without discipline, without military stores, without money. These are deficiencies which it must be the work of an age to remove; and while they continue, it will be impossible to keep an army in the field. . . . It is not in the power of all the friends of Congress, to introduce what deserves the name of discipline into any of the colonies to the southward of New-England and the New Englanders could only be half-disciplined and kept in the field until the appearance of the British or the rumor of a small-pox epidemic caused them to flee for their lives."

On the patriot side, John Adams and Thomas Jefferson both took up their pens. Under the pseudonym Novangius, Adams replied to a pamphlet by Daniel Leonard, a Tory spokesman. Leonard had attacked the committees of correspondence as "the foulest, subtlest, and most venemous serpent that ever issued from the eggs of sedition." Adams defended them warmly. "Almost all mankind," he wrote, "have lost their liberties through ignorance, inattention, and disunion. These committees are admirably calculated to diffuse knowledge, to communicate intelligence, and promote unanimity. . . . The patriots of this Province desire nothing new: they wish only to keep their old privileges. For one hundred and fifty years they had been allowed to tax themselves and govern their internal concerns as they thought best. Parliament governed their trade as they thought fit. This plan they wish may continue forever."

Adams indignantly rejected the charge that certain colonists wished for independence. If Leonard meant by independence "a independent republic in America or a confederation of independent republics," no accusation could be "a more wicked or a great slander on the Whigs." Adams knew in his own heart that " there is no man in the province among the Whigs, nor ever was, who harbors a wish of that sort. . . . The Whigs acknowledge a subordination to the King in as strict and strong a sense as the Tories. The Whigs acknowledge a voluntary subordination to Parliament, as far as the regulation of trade."

Leonard had in fact seized on a serious weakness in the arguments of those who declared that the colonists owed allegiance simply to "the Crown" of England. "The Crown," properly understood, Leonard said, meant Parliament as well as the royal ministers. To this Adams replied that colonists owed their loyalty and subordination to the "person of the King, not to his crown . . . to his natural, not his politic capacity." The truth was that "the people of England were depraved, the Parliament venal, and the ministry corrupt." The colonies were neither part "of the English realm, dominions, state, empire, call it what you will," or corporations, or conquered territory, or annexed lands. "Thus Parliament could assert no lawful claim on their subordination."

Then Adams came to the heart of the matter. The "noblemen and ignoblemen [of England]," he declared, "ought to have considered that Americans understand the laws and politics as well as themselves, and that there are six hundred thousand men in it, between sixteen and sixty years of age; and therefore it will be very difficult to chicane them out of their liberties by 'fictions of law' . . . no matter upon what foundation." The theoreticians of the mother country might, before some impartial tribunal, carry all the arguments in law and constitutional precedents (although the Americans were clearly not willing to make any concessions on the constitutional issue). But the fact was that when all was said and done, the colonists were determined to have a large measure of control over their own destiny. It was really that simple.

3

England

EVEN before the end of its deliberations, word of the meeting of the Continental Congress had brought strong reactions in England. On December 13, 1774, when the text of the Suffolk Resolves reached England, the attorney general declared it to be treason. Indignation and surprise turned to astonishment when it was learned a few weeks later that the Congress at Philadelphia had endorsed the seditious resolutions. Lord Dartmouth professed to be "thunderstruck," and he wrote to General Gage agreeing that the situation in Massachusetts constituted "actual Revolt, and show a determination in the People to commit themselves at all Events to open Rebellion." Four more regiments of infantry and seven hundred marines were on their way. Gage was instructed to arrest the leaders of the Massachusetts Provincial Congress, who were to be tried as traitors. This should be done, if possible, without bloodshed, "but however that may be, if resistance occurs, it cannot be too formidable," he added. If there was to be a conflict it was better that it "should be brought on, upon such ground, than in a riper state of Rebellion." Having been so bold, Dartmouth then backed off and left any action to Gage's discretion.

When word reached London of the action of the Continental Congress in regard to nonimportation, one Englishman wrote an American friend, "From curiosity I strolled upon the 'Change, and for the first time saw concern and deep distress in the face of every merchant engaged in the American trade. This convinced me of the truth of what I may have said before, that the merchants will never stir until they feel. . . ."

At first the British affected to scorn reports of nonimportation agreements. *The Political Annotator,* reflecting on the news that the merchants of New York had rejected the nonimportation agreement, noted "To suppose that any people will keep an agreement which interest prompts or necessity urges them to break, is an absurdity truly patriotic."

But even before the effects of nonimportation had a chance to be felt, a number of British merchants engaged in colonial trade began to draw up petitions to Parliament requesting repeal of the Coercive Acts. They were immediately denounced as "a cat's paw for the American rebels," who "humbly submitted to be handled in the same contemptible manner by the Bostonian monkeys twice since." They were accused of yielding to pressure from their American counterparts and of putting their own profits ahead of the good of the empire. The merchants of Birmingham sharply rebuked those who wished to capitulate, and urged that the measures taken against the Massachusetts colonists be persisted in until those rebel subjects capitulated.

"The Birmingham Knaves" were promptly attacked as wishing to bring about a war so that they could sell arms to the British army as well as to the Americans. Indeed, they were accused of doing so already through Dutch merchants. As a versifier in the *London Packet* wrote:

> Since you pray'd our good Monarch to cut all their throats.
> And plunge them at once in a sea of despair;
> I suppose as he kindly attended your votes;
> The arms that you sent them were Birmingham ware.

When the hangman and two sheriffs appeared in the Royal Exchange to burn publicly copies of a journal called *Crisis,* which espoused, among other things, the cause of the colonists, the fire was immediately extinguished by the crowd, and the officers were pelted with dead dogs and cats. It was reported that more than three hundred ships were lined up at wharves between London Bridge and the Lime-House with brooms tied to their masts, thereby advertising them for sale by merchants whose business had been destroyed by the nonimportation agreements.

Another significant indication of British feeling might be found in the fact that most politicians running for office in 1774–75 endorsed a policy of conciliation with America.

While a preponderance of those classes in England who had a public voice—the country gentry, the greater part of the merchants, and most of the great lords—supported the measures taken against the Americans, among the voiceless masses of England, Ireland, and Scotland there was a very different feeling. They did not write pamphlets or letters to the newspapers, they did not speak in Parliament or give expression to their feelings in script or print, for they were largely illiterate. They voted the only way they knew how: substantial numbers refused to enlist in the army or navy to serve against the Americans, who, they felt instinctively, were fighting their battle.

When Parliament convened in January, 1775, the first subject for debate was American affairs. Pitt appeared dramatically in defense of the colonies. He spoke boldly in praise of the "papers transmitted to us from America," their "decency, firmness and wisdom. . . . For myself," he declared, "I must avow that in all my reading and observation—and it has been my favourite study—I have read Thuycidides, and have studied and admired the master-states of the world—that for solidity of reasoning, force of sagacity, and wisdom of conclusion, under such a complication of difficult circumstances, no nation or body of men can stand in preference to the general Congress at Philadelphia. . . . This glorious spirit [of resistance to taxation] animates three millions in America; who prefer poverty with liberty to gilded chains and sordid affluence; and who will die in defence of their rights as men, as freemen." The cause of the colonies, Pitt declared, was "an alliance of God and nature" on principles that were "immutable, eternal—fixed as the firmament of heaven." The thought that the ministers could suppress such a spirit was ridiculous. Nor can "such a national and principled union be resisted by the tricks of office, or ministerial manoeuvre. . . ." The hour of danger must inevitably come "unless these fatal acts are done away; it must arrive in all its horrors, and then these boastful ministers, spite of all their confidence, and all their manoeuvers, shall be forced to hide their heads." Even at the moment, "they cannot . . . stir a step; they have not a move left; they are check-mated."

The proper course for the government to follow, Pitt went on, was to take the initiative in a policy of conciliation: "With a dignity becoming your exalted situation, make the first advances to concord, to peace and happiness; for that is your true dignity, to act with prudence and justice.

That you should first concede is obvious, from sound and rational policy. Concession comes with better grace and more salutary effect from superior power; it reconciles superiority of power with the feelings of men, and establishes solid confidence on the foundations of affection and gratitude."

Edmund Burke joined his own voice in the plea for conciliation. "The use of Force alone," he reminded the members, "is but temporary. It may subdue for a moment; but it does not remove the necessity of subduing again; and a nation is not governed, which is perpetually to be conquered. . . ." After dwelling on the devotion of the colonists to liberty, Burke summarized the reasons why a close control of the colonies by the mother country was impractical: "Then, Sir, from these six capital sources: of descent; of form of government; of religion in the northern provinces; of manners in the southern; of education; of the remoteness of situation from the first mover of government; from all these causes a fierce spirit of liberty has grown up. It has grown with the strength of the people in your colonies, and increased with the increase of their wealth; a spirit that unhappily meeting with an exercise of power in England, which, however lawful, is not reconcilable to any ideas of liberty, much less with theirs, has kindled the flame that is ready to consume us. . . ."

Burke then went on to deliver one of those marvelous lectures on the nature of politics that represent a kind of distillation of all that the English knew about that complex and fascinating art—but, like the rest of mankind, too seldom practiced. As long as England remained true to its historic devotion to liberty, it would be a wise and benign ruler of her people ("they will turn their faces toward you"). That spirit was the true essence of the constitution, the true source of legitimacy. Turning to the ministers of the government, Burke admonished them not "to entertain so weak an imagination as that your registers and your bonds, your affidavits and your sufferances, your crockets and your clearances, are what form the great securities of your commerce. Do not dream that your letters of office, and your instructions, and your suspending clauses, are the things that hold together the great contexture of the mysterious whole. These things do not make your government. Dead instruments, passive tools as they are, it is the spirit of the English communion that gives all their life and efficacy to them. It is the spirit of the English constitution which, infused through the mighty mass, pervades, feeds, unites, invigorates, vivifies every part of the empire, even down to the minutest member. . . ."

Burke was aware that he was talking to practical politicians. "All this I know well enough," he declared, "will sound wild and chimerical to the profane herd of those vulgar and mechanical politicians who have no place among us; a sort of people who believe that nothing exists but what is gross and material; and who therefore, far from being qualified to be directors of the great movement of empire, are not fit to turn a wheel in the machine." Such individuals had no real concept of the true nature of government. "Magnanimity in politics is not seldom the truest wisdom; and a great empire and little minds go ill together," Burke concluded, appealing to his fellow delegates in the Commons to reverse the disastrous policy of the government.

Truth and justice were with Chatham and Burke, but the votes were with North. Parliament gave solid support to that minister's determination to bring the rebellious colonies to heel. Yet there persisted two repetitious themes in all the speeches and addresses, in Parliament and out, in opposition to the policies of the administration: first, they were tyrannical and unjust; second, they would not succeed in their object of subduing the colonies, and they might very well ruin England in the process.

North, anxious to muster at least an appearance of public support, busied himself rounding up petitions in favor of the government's policy toward the colonies. Oxford dutifully produced an "Address of the Chancellor, Masters and Scholars of the University of Oxford," which condemned in ritual language the "profligate licentiousness" of the Americans and deplored the actions of "our deluded fellow-subjects . . . which have been by . . . seducing arts, betrayed, plunged . . . in all the horrors of a civil war, unnaturally commenced against the State which gave them birth and protection." Cambridge, ancient seat of libertarian principles, followed suit, more briefly and reluctantly.

4

The Lull Before the Storm

IN Boston, events moved inexorably toward armed conflict. In response to Gage's requests, the Boston garrison was constantly being reinforced, until by the end of 1774 there were eleven battalions in the city. Gage then had under his command some 4,000 soldiers. In addition to the Fourteenth and the Twenty-ninth, quartered at Castle William ever since the massacres, he commanded the Fourth, Fifth, Thirty-eighth, Forty-third, and Fifty-ninth regiments, and portions of the Sixty-fourth and Sixty-fifth. Plainly, 4,000 rough and belligerent soldiers in a city of some 16,000 people had a very decided impact.

Further, like Parliament and British political life generally, the army was riddled with graft and corruption. Everyone seemed to have his hand in the military till. The paymaster general was allowed to lend government funds on interest and pocket the interest for himself, hardly the best way to assure the prompt payment of expenses. Nonexistent soldiers were carried on the rolls and their pay, small as it was, kept by their officers. Of the soldiers' penny-a-day, a contemporary gave the following accounting: "When the deductions are made for cloathing, for necessaries, for washing, for the paymaster, for the surgeon, for the multiplied articles of useless and unmilitary fopperies (introduced by many colonels to the oppression of the soldier for what they call the

455

credit and appearance of the Regiment) there is not sufficient overplus for healthful subsistence; and as to the little enjoyments and recreations, which even the meanest ranks of men can call their own in any country, [these] the brave, the honorable, the veteran soldier must not aspire to."

Other corruptions also weakened the army line officers; these professional soldiers, who had often served with bravery and enterprise in arduous campaigns, were apt to be superseded at any moment. As one critic of the army put it: "When the road seems smooth towards [command of] a regiment, an inundation of captains of the guards . . . by dint of court rank, and etiquette of precedence, step in between, defeat all the prospects of the actual soldier, and trample upon a life of dangers." In other words, friends and influence, far more than experience and ability, determined advancement in the British army.

If the army paid meagerly, it did, at least for some soldiers, partly make up for this deficiency by allowing them to have their wives or mistresses accompany them on campaigns. Women in considerable numbers were carried on the British payroll in Boston at half-rations, and their children at one-quarter. Long stays in garrison not unnaturally encouraged the accumulation of such "wives" and children, and when the British finally evacuated Boston in 1776, they carried on their rolls 567 women and 553 children. The women were not a total liability; they washed, mended, and often cooked for their soldier-husbands. One observer believed that the ragged appearance of the Americans in the field was due to the fact that "they in general not being used to doing things of this sort, and thinking it rather a disparagement to them, choose rather to let their linen, etc., rot on their backs than to be at the trouble of cleaning 'em themselves."

An officer complained that there was "nothing remarkable" in Boston, "but the drunkenness among the soldiers, which is now at a very great pitch; owing to the cheapness of the liquor, a man may get drunk for a copper or two." The officers spent most of their time gambling, and Gage, disturbed at the infatuation, tried to form an Anti-Gambling Club with limited stakes.

The colonists of course encouraged desertions; one handbill distributed to the soldiers read, "Friends and Brothers . . . you may have Liberty and by a Little Industry may obtain Property. . . . March up either Singly or in Companys. . . . The Country People are Determined to Protect you and Screen you. . . ." Colonel Alexander Leslie of the Sixty-forth Regiment was convinced that the social equality in Massachusetts was the main attraction to British deserters. The problem of desertions became so serious for the British that one deserter who was recaptured was sentenced to 1,000 lashes in lieu of execution, 250 to be delivered each week for four weeks.

The soldiers encamped on the Common held target practice by firing at a target in the bay. According to a story that went the rounds, a farmer who was watching them began to laugh "very heartily at a whole regiment's firing, and not one being able to hit it."

A British officer asked the man why he was laughing. "Why then," the farmer was reported to have replied, "I laugh to see how awkward they fire. Why, I'll be bound I hit it ten times running."

"Ah! will you? Come try. Soldiers, go and bring five of the best guns and load 'em for this honest man."

"Why, you need not bring so many! let me have any one that comes to hand, but I chuse to load myself."

After he had loaded the gun, the farmer turned to the officer and asked which part of the target he should aim at. "The right." The farmer fired and hit the exact spot.

The farmer loaded his musket again and asked where he should fire.

"To the left." Again he hit the target in the designated spot.

"Come! Once more."

"Where shall I fire naow?"

"In the center."

Again he hit the mark as the soldiers and officers stared at him open-mouthed. Then, adding a final touch of bravado, the countryman declared, "Why, I'll tell you naow. I have got a boy at home that will toss up an apple and shoot out all the seeds as it's coming down."

Such a tale, to be repeated in a thousand forms, with heroes ranging from Mike Fink and Davy Crockett to Paul Bunyan and Wild Bill Hickok, was already a classic American story. If it was apocryphal, it nonetheless contained, as most tall tales do, a substantial element of truth. Many American farmers were far better shots than the trained soldiers of His Majesty's regiments.

Increasingly the British troops in Boston—"too numerous . . . for Ambassadors, and too few for soldiers"—instead of overawing the countryside found themselves in a state of virtual siege. No soldier dared venture outside the city, and within they were safer in groups. It was evident that the colonists were arming and drilling in preparation for open warfare. Every time a platoon of soldiers was dispatched on a military mission beyond the immediate environs of Boston, they ran the risk of being fired upon, and on several occasions skirmishes were narrowly avoided.

When Gage undertook to fortify Boston Neck, he was besieged by the selectmen of Boston, who pressed him for a statement of his purpose in erecting the fortification. The site was picketed, the workmen were persuaded to lay down their tools, and materials collected for the fortification were systematically pilfered.

Gage's fortification of the Neck, which in light of his intelligence that militia units were drilling in every town throughout the colony seemed common prudence, nevertheless gave rise to the rumor that the British commander intended to starve the city of Boston into submission. Such gossip greatly increased the general uneasiness of the people. Hannah Winthrop wrote to Mercy Warren that she shed tears of anxiety over the news from Boston. "The dissolution of all Government gives a dreadful Prospect, the fortifying Boston Neck, the Huge Cannon now mounted there, the busy preparation, the agility of the Troops, give a Horrid prospect of an intended Battle. Kind Heaven avert the Storm!" And her husband wrote John Adams that he must soon "beat my plow shares into Swords, and pruning Hooks into Spears." The Massachusetts Provincial Congress, an extralegal body acting in place of the prorogued assembly, undertook to call up twelve thousand men and invited New Hampshire, Rhode Island, and Connecticut to add levies of their own.

In Rhode Island, the inhabitants of Newport had commandeered the forty cannon that defended the harbor, while in New Hampshire, a fort at Piscataqua Harbor was seized with its supplies.

At Portsmouth, New Hampshire, the news, brought by Paul Revere, that Gage had seized powder and bullets belonging to the Massachusetts colony on Castle Island brought a quick reaction. On Wednesday, December 14, Governor Wentworth heard a drum beating through the town, assembling the citizens for the purpose of taking away the powder from, and then dismantling, the fort that commanded Portsmouth's harbor. The governor sent the chief justice of the province to explain to the crowd of several hundred people "the nature of the offense they proposed to commit [treason], told them it was not short of Rebellion, and intreated them to desist from it and disperse." But it was all to no avail. The crowd, swelled by inhabitants of nearby Newcastle and Rye to the number of some four hundred, descended on the fort, which was defended only by a Captain Cochran and five soldiers. Despite Cochran's stout defense (he fired the cannon at the

men besieging the fort), the patriots swarmed over the walls and overcame him, one of them jumping from the wall onto his shoulders, Wild
West style, as he was fighting off several others.

"After they entered the Fort," Governor Wentworth wrote Lord
Dartmouth, "they seized upon the Captain, triumphantly gave three
huzzas, and hauled down the King's Colours . . . broke open the Gun
powder Magazine and carried off about 100 barrels of Gunpowder."

The distressing fact to Wentworth was that none of those who had
participated in the raid could be brought to justice, although the names
of many of them were well known to the governor. "The Country,"
Wentworth wrote Dartmouth, "is so much inflamed especially since the
return of the Delegates from the Congress, that many Magistrates and
Militia Officers who ought to have given their aid and assistance in
restraining and suppressing this uproar, were active to promote and
encourage it." Wentworth was powerless to punish any of those who
openly flaunted the authority of the Crown; he would need at least two
regiments of soldiers, he advised Dartmouth, if he were to maintain
order in the town.

The Suffolk Resolves had recommended "purging" the militia of
officers anything less than 100 per cent patriotic, and simultaneously
stepping up militia drills. The seeds of the famous Minutemen lay in the
resolves.

The Worcester County convention, made up of resolute patriots,
led the way in purging the militia officers in that county. It stipulated
that all officers, from company-grade officers up to colonels, must
resign their commissions. The convention, acting on the recommendation in the Suffolk Resolves, decided that the towns should elect their
officers, and that these in turn should elect the field-grade officers. The
militia should be organized in companies of "fifty privates, at the least,
who shall equip and hold themselves in readiness, on the shortest notice,
to march to the place of rendezvous." At indeed a minute's notice;
hence, "minute men."

Since these arrangements were all to be kept secret—even to the
names of the officers—in order to prevent retribution by the British,
very little is known about the so-called Minutemen. What, in effect, took
place was a reconstitution of the old militia, purged of all those who had
Tory sympathies or who were lukewarm in the cause of liberty. It was a
silent struggle, doubtless attended by considerable bitterness and soul-
searching, by means of which the stoutest patriots took control of
the apparatus of the militia.

Ephraim Doolittle, writing to John Hancock, who had been elected a colonel of the Minutemen, deplored "the difficulties that arise among us by ambitious men who are endeavoring to break our companies to pieces, in order to get promotion. . . . A number of companies in my Regiment are now in such circumstances; and I fear if we are not called to action, we shall be like a rope of sand, and have no more strength."

At the same time that the Minutemen were being organized, a number of towns created "Alarm Companies" made up primarily of boys and old men, "our aged sires," as one militia officer called them—home defense units that were to be ready to turn out and defend their towns in the event that the militia marched off to campaign elsewhere.

Connecticut was, of all the New England colonies, the one best provided with men and arms. It boasted of twenty thousand men enlisted in eighteen regiments, "with a Troop of Horses to each, and to some, Two Troops." In the fall of 1774, the Connecticut assembly took steps to make their force, at that point more formidable on paper than in fact, ready for whatever action might be necessary. The regiments were immediately to undertake extensive drill and training. The towns "as soon as may be" were to "double the quantity of Powder, Balls and Flints, that they were before by law obliged to provide." It was rumored that "In most Towns, they have a deserter from his Majesty's Forces, by way of a drill-sergeant."

To the British and the Tories, the fact that patriots were quite evidently busy preparing for war—while at the same time still declaring their undying allegiance to George III—was prima facie evidence of a quality that had been attributed to the New Englanders since the Puritans first landed in the Bay: hypocrisy. "The inhabitants of this colony," a British officer wrote, "with the most austere show of devotion are void of every principle of religion or common honesty, and reckoned the most arrant cheats and hypocrites in America."

When Boston set aside a day of prayer and fasting for its lost liberties, Gage, in a calculated insult, issued a "Proclamation against Hypocrisy," and on the appointed day soldiers of the King's Own Regiment pitched two "marquee tents" under the windows of one of the churches and sounded their fifes and drums throughout the service. A few days later, a party of officers broke the windows of Hancock's house and slashed at the railing in front of it with their swords. A farmer who had bought a gun from a soldier was tarred and feathered by soldiers and carried about the streets in a cart by a group of redcoats that

included their commanding officer and a band playing "Yankee Doodle."

Thus incident followed incident, and preparation for armed conflict went ahead. The Sons of Liberty in Massachusetts were convinced
that with the first hostile, offensive act by the British soldiers, the
colonists would rise as a man and drive the intruders into the sea. They
assured themselves that the redcoats were more notable for lechery than
bravery; their officers were effeminate fops, interested in balls and
parties rather than in fighting. It was well known that the British army
was recruited from the lowest levels of English and Irish society.
According to one colonist, they were "the most debauched Weavers
'prentices,' the scum of Irish Roman Catholics, who desert upon every
occasion, and a few, a very few Scotch who are not strong enough to
carry packs." All together they were "more like the frog eaters of
France, than the hale, lusty Englishmen nurtured by beef and Sir John
Barleycorn." Those colonials who had fought beside British soldiers in
the French and Indian War came forward with reassuring tales of
ineptness, cowardice, and stupidity, all adding up to the fact that the
English "knew not how to fight." Instead of toughening themselves for
long campaigns and "seeking glory on the blood stained field," the
British officers made their boldest conquests in boudoirs, seeking "to
captivate the softer sex, and triumph over virtue." Such "imprudent
ravishers" would be no match for hardy farmers skilled in the use of
musket and rifle. One colonial military expert announced, "We can bush
fight them and cut off their officers very easily and in this way we can
subdue them with very little loss." Benjamin Franklin offered a more
reasoned, more conclusive argument; Americans, he pointed out, were
breeding faster than the British could kill them off.

The Tories read such braggadocio with contemptuous amusement.
Tell Americans that British veterans would fly before "an undisciplined
multitude of New England squirrel hunters," a Tory wrote, "and they
will swallow it without a hiccough." Of course, the British were, if
anything, even more contemptuous of the colonials than the colonials
were of them. Their experience in the French and Indian War was that
the colonials were poorly trained and unreliable. It was common knowledge, they declared, that the New Englanders would not fight without
large quantities of rum. "Without rum they could neither fight nor say
their prayers"; there were "no meaner whimpering wretches in this
universe" than New Englanders sober. United "by an enthusiastic fit of

false patriotism—a fit which necessarily cools in time," they were never-theless too cowardly to fight. At the first volley from trained British soldiers, the New Englanders and the Virginians, who were little better, would run for cover to those "extensive woods which they are too lazy or feeble to cut down."

The British attitude was colored by class prejudices that held, in effect, that courage was a consequence of good breeding. The common people of every nation were, for the most part, cloddish and cowardly. With firm discipline and thorough training, and led by their betters, they could be counted on to give a good account of themselves. But the lower classes (that is to say, in this instance, the colonists), untrained and led by officers very little better than themselves, were hardly to be taken seriously. "I am satisfied," wrote Major John Pitcairn, an officer in the Royal Marines, "that one active campaign, a smart action, and burning two or three of their towns, will set everything to rights." One British officer wrote to a friend in England: "As to what you hear of their taking arms, it is mere bullying, and will go no further than words. Whenever it comes to blows, he that can run fastest will think himself best off. And any two regiments here ought to be decimated if they did not beat in the field the whole force of the Massachusetts province: for though they are numerous, they are but a mere mob without order or discipline, and very awkward in handling their arms."

Another British officer, observing the Boston militia at drill, wrote: "It is a curious Masquerade Scene to see grave sober Citizens, Barbers and Tailors, who never looked fierce before in their Lives, but at their wives, Children, or Apprentices, strutting about in their Sunday wigs in stiff Buckles with their Muskets on their Shoulders, struggling to put on a Martial Countenance. If ever you saw a Goose assume an Air of Consequence, you may catch some faint idea of the foolish, awkward, puffed-up Stare of our Tradesmen; the wig, indeed, is the most fright-ful Thing about them, for its very Hairs seem to bristle in Defiance of the Soldiers."

An English lady travelling in North Carolina had similar observa-tions. The "American clowns" that she observed were "tall and lean, with short waists and long limbs, sallow complexions and languid eyes, when not enflamed by spirits. Their feet are flat, their joints loose and their walk uneven." She observed some two thousand such militiamen maneuvering on a field of scrub oak. The exercise, she was told, was "that of bush-fighting." She could not tell whether it was done well or ill, but she did know "that they were heated with rum till capable of committing the most shocking outrages." "I must really laugh," she continued, "while I recollect their figures: 2000 men in their shirts and trousers, preceded by a very ill-beat drum and fiddler . . . who played with all his might. They made indeed a most unmartial appearance. But," she added shrewdly, "the worst figure there can shoot from behind a bush and kill even a General Wolfe."

Gage himself believed that the Massachusetts men "will be Lyons, whilst we are Lambs but if we take the resolute part they will undoubtedly prove very meek." At the same time he was convinced that a strong show of force was necessary. "If you think ten Thousand Men sufficient," he wrote to the Secretary of State, "send Twenty, if one Million is thought enough, give two; you will save both Blood and Treasure in the End." He had warned the patriot leaders that "by the living God . . . if there was a single man of the King's troops killed in any of their towns he would burn it to the ground." In the Seven Years' War, Great Britain had put 300,000 men into the field, and, he continued, she "will do the same now rather than suffer the ungrateful people of this country to continue their rebellion."

Lord Barrington, who perhaps understood as much about the American colonies as any Englishman, expressed his doubts to Lord Dartmouth "whether all the [British] troops in North America, though probably enow for a pitched battle with the strength of the Province, are enow to subdue it; being of great extent, and full of men accustomed to fire-arms. It is true they have not been thought brave, but enthusiasm gives vigour of mind and body unknown before."

The Massachusetts assembly (which met illegally at Concord and kept their deliberations secret), judging that the time had come to lay in military supplies, voted in the fall of 1774 to purchase twenty fieldpieces and four mortars, twenty tons of grapeshot and round shot, and five thousand muskets and bayonets, although it was not clear how they were to pay for them or where they might secure them. A Committee of Public Safety was appointed under the direction of John Hancock with authority to summon the militia, every fourth man of which was charged with being ready to march at a moment's notice. When they met again in November, the Committee of Public Safety had acquired a substantial amount of ordnance and 350 spades and pickaxes. In organizing the province on a wartime footing, they instructed "the Militia in general, as well as the detached part of it in Minute-men, in obedience to the great law of self-preservation," to be diligent in their drills and exercises.

In spite of the menacing presence of British troops, Boston was the headquarters for the patriots. Beacon Hill was reactivated, so to speak, and a system of telegraphy devised in which signal flares would be used to alert the countryside in the event of an outbreak of armed hostilities. The Green Dragon Tavern became the central meeting place for the patriots. This tavern was doubtless chosen because patriot organizer Joseph Warren was also Grand Master of the Boston Masonic Lodge, and the Masons had their headquarters there. In addition, the tavern served as a kind of intelligence center for Paul Revere and some thirty "mechanics," who circulated about the city keeping watch on British troop movements and dispositions and listening for any word of British forays into the countryside.

Broadsides or printed handbills were published in considerable numbers attacking Gage and the troops under his command, and it was reported that one mother who dared to name her infant Thomas Gage was threatened with tar and feathers for both herself and the child. As preparations for armed resistance went ahead, even the farmers' almanacs carried instructions for making gunpowder. John Adams, who was delegated the task of incorporating friendly Indians into the companies of Minutemen, signed up the Stockbridge Indians.

Abrasive incidents continued day after day. Early in 1775, there was a brawl between the butchers at the public market and a group of soldiers; it began when one of the butchers tripped while carrying a piece of beef and went crashing into the muck and mire of the street, while the soldiers roared with laughter. The butchers immediately abandoned their stalls and began to close in on the soldiers. Trouble was averted only by an officer of the guard who ordered the soldiers to their barracks, seized the most belligerent butcher by the collar, and tried to force him toward the guardhouse. Young Ned Gray, who had been present at the Boston Massacre, intervened and persuaded the officer to take the butcher to Miss Foster's store and there call the sheriff if he wished to make charges against him.

The first week of March, 1775, saw the annual commemoration of the Boston Massacre. Joseph Warren was once more chosen to give the oration in the Old South Meeting House. The circumstances of the city gave an increased meaning, a heightened impact to Warren's words. Some British officers stood on the top of the pulpit stairs near Warren and "frequently interrupted [him] by laughing at the most ludicrous parts, and coughing and hemming at the most seditious, to the great discomfort of the devoted citizens," in the words of a Tory observer.

When the address was over, Sam Adams moved that an orator should be chosen for the following year. "At this the officers could no longer contain themselves, but called 'Fie! Shame!' and 'Fie, Shame!' was echoed by all the Navy and Military in the place. This caused a violent confusion and in an instant the windows were thrown open and the affrighted Yankees jumped out by fifties," according to a Tory account.

James Warren, brother of Joseph, wrote his wife, Mercy, from Concord: "We are no longer at a loss what is intended to us by our dear Mother. We have ask'd for Bread and she gives us a Stone and a serpent for a Fish. However my Spirits are by no means depressed, you well know my Sentiments of the Force of both Countrys, you know my opinion of the Justness of our Cause, you know my Confidence in a Righteous Providence. I seem to want nothing to keep up my Spirits . . . but seeing you in Spirits, and knowing they flow from the heart. . . . All things wear a warlike appearance here. This Town is full of Cannon, ammunition, stores, etc., and the Army long for them and they want nothing but strength to Induce an attempt on them. The people are ready and determined to defend this Country Inch by Inch. . . . I long to sit with you under our Vines etc. and have none to make us afraid."

In this atmosphere, a dangerous incident took place on the night of January 20. As Lieutenant Myers, an officers of the Thirty-eighth Regiment, was walking to his quarters, a group of men intercepted him and began to abuse him as a "bloody-backed Irish dog," and then proceeded to beat and kick him. The shouts and cries attracted the Boston night watch and also brought out some British officers who had been drinking a nightcap at Ingersol's Tavern nearby. When the watch seemed inclined to arrest Myers rather than his attackers, the indignant officers intervened. A sharp scuffle ensued, during which one member of the watch cut an officer's head with a billhook, while another made an apparent attempt to run an officer through. A crowd gathered, soldiers arrived from the main guard, and only the resolution of the officer in command, Captain Gore, prevented further violence. Despite cries from the crowd of "fire! fire!" Gore, doubtless with the Boston Massacre in mind, gave "positive and repeated order not to fire on any account." And so a crisis was narrowly averted.

A month or so later, Colonel Leslie sailed with several squads of soldiers and a military band—a full-dress expedition—to Salem to seize some fieldpieces that Gage's spies told him were hidden there. The soldiers landed near Salem on a Sunday morning, at a point where a creek flowed into Massachusetts Bay.

Colonel David Mason, commander of the militia, who had received word that the British were coming, ran to a church that lay in the British line of march. A service was going on when the colonel called out, "The reg'lars are coming after the guns and are now near Kelloon's Mills!" David Boyce, a Quaker who lived near the church, turned out with his team to help move the guns out of range of the British. Little Billy Gavett was surprised that his father came home from church sooner than usual. He followed him into the kitchen and heard him say to his wife, "The reg'lars are come and are marching as fast as they can towards the Northfields bridge." And then very solemnly, "I don't know what will be the consequence but something very serious, and I wish you to keep the children home." While they talked, they heard the tramp of feet and saw the British marching by at the end of the yard.

Colonel Leslie, finding the Northfield drawbridge raised, threatened to fire on the townspeople clustered along the opposite bank if the leaf was not immediately lowered. Captain Felt, a militia officer who had approached Leslie, answered boldly that if any British soldier dared to fire they would all be dead men. He meant, he said later, to seize Colonel Leslie and jump into the river with him—"I would willingly be drowned myself to be the death of one Englishman. . . ."

While Colonel Leslie and Captain Felt argued about lowering the drawbridge, some townspeople who were on the western side of the river ran down the bank to scuttle two small barges that might have been used to ferry the soldiers across. A group of soldiers moved to intercept them, and Joseph Whicher, a foreman in Colonel Sprague's distillery, who was busy hacking at one of the boats with a hatchet, was ordered by the soldiers to desist before he was run through. At this Whicher bared his chest and dared the soldiers to strike. One did, a short jab which drew blood. At the sight of the blood, the people began to shout at the soldiers, some of them climbing on the drawbridge. One man yelled, "Soldiers, red-jackets, lobster-coats, cowards, damnation to your government!" Others in the crowd rebuked him. It was better to do nothing to inflame the troops, else innocent people might be hurt.

Colonel Leslie, seeing the Reverend Mr. Barnard in his clerical attire, said to him, "I will get over this bridge before I return to Boston, if I stay here till next autumn." "I pray, Sir," said Barnard, that "there will be no collision between the people and the troops." "Well, I will break into those buildings," Leslie replied, indicating two nearby stores on the west side of the river, "and make barracks of them until I can get over the river." Then, turning furiously on Captain Felt, he declared, "By God! I will not be defeated."

"You must acknowledge you have already been baffled," Felt replied, looking insolently at the furious colonel.

Leslie decided to take another tack. "It is the King's Highway that passes over that bridge and I will not be prevented from crossing it."

At this old James Barr broke in: "It is not the King's Highway; it is a road built by the owners of the lots on the other side, and no king, country, or town has anything to do with it."

"There may be two words to that," Leslie answered lamely.

"Egad," Barr said, "I think it will be the best way for you to conclude that the King has nothing to do with it."

There the matter seemed to stand, an impasse. Leslie had so far committed himself that he could not keep face with his own soldiers if he allowed himself to be held in defiance by a handful of countrymen. The colonials were equally determined that the British should not pass. Finally Leslie, whose only choices seemed to be to retreat or to open fire on the people—thus, in effect starting a war, with no guarantee that the latter course would get him and his men over the bridge—persuaded Captain Felt to use his influence to arrange a compromise. If the leaf of the bridge were lowered and the British soldiers allowed to pass over it, the colonel gave his word they would advance no more than a few hundred feet and then return at once, "without troubling or disturbing anything."

After a lengthy debate, Felt consented to try to persuade the guardians of the drawbridge to lower it. The minister joined with the militia captain in urging that it be dropped to allow the passage of the British under such terms. The bridge was lowered into place, the British marched across, "then wheeled and marched back again" and off toward Marblehead. As they turned about, Nurse Sarah Tarrant threw up the window of her house and called out to them: "Go home and tell your master he has sent you on a fool's errand and broken the peace of our Sabbath. What do you think? We were born in the woods to be frightened by owls?" When one of the soldiers pointed his musket at her, she stood her ground. "Fire if you have the courage," she cried. "But I doubt it."

The incident may have been a trivial one, but only because it did not result in the first open engagement between Americans and British troops. The moral was clear enough. British soldiers, marching out on a mission, had been frustrated in their purpose by a group of determined inhabitants in the little town of Northfield. They had, in effect, been forced to retreat under the cover of a patently face-saving formula. They had marched up with their band playing "Yankee Doodle"; they withdrew playing "The World Turned Upside Down."

In the same month a British captain and a young army ensign were given the mission of mapping the roads and preparing a rough map of the salient terrain features in Suffolk and Worcester counties. Attired as farmers in "brown clothes, and reddish handkerchiefs," the officers were too plainly English gentlemen to fool anyone—except General Gage and his staff upon their return. Stopping at a tavern for dinner at the beginning of their expedition, they were waited on by a black woman. "At first she was very civil, but afterwards began to eye us very attentively," one of them recalled. "We observed to her that it was a very fine country, upon which she answered, 'So it is, and we have brave fellows to defend it.'"

That evening the party, which included a batman, or soldier-servant—without which a British officer, even in the disguise of a farmer, was hardly able to proceed—stopped at the sign of the Golden Ball, a roadside inn. "But," the Captain wrote, "The landlord pleased us so much, as he was not inquisitive, that we resolved to lie there that night; so we ordered some fire to be made, and to get us some coffee. He told us we might have what we pleased, either Tea or Coffee." A Tory in sentiment, the landlord by offering the two men tea indicated that he had penetrated their disguise as readily as the black woman. In Worcester another innkeeper again indicated his loyalist sympathies by offering them tea. "At Shrewsbury we were overtaken by a horseman who examined us very attentively, and especially me, whom he looked at from head to foot as if he wanted to know me again, and then rode off pretty hard."

At a tavern where they got their supper that night, the two officers watched from the windows while a militia company drilled on the common. "The commander made a very eloquent speech, recommending patience, coolness, and bravery (which indeed they very much wanted), quoted Caesar, Pompey, and Brigadiers Putname and Ward; recommended them to wait for the English fire, and told them they would always conquer if they did not break! . . . and observed that the [British] Regulars in the last war must have been ruined but for them. After a learned and spirited harangue he dismissed the parade, and the whole company drink until nine o'clock, and then returned to their homes full of pot-valour."

Riding on, the two British officers were overtaken by a group of men whose leader asked them pointblank if they were British soldiers. They denied it, and the men rode off. When they arrived at the town of Marlborough in the midst of a storm, they found the town buzzing like a beehive. A baker, whom they later learned was harboring a British deserter from their own regiment, accosted them and bombarded them with questions, and when they put up for the night at the home of a prominent Tory, the town doctor invited himself in and set to quizzing the children of the house about the newly arrived guests. Their host, now thoroughly alarmed, persuaded them to depart as soon as it was dark. They had scarcely cleared the premises when the local Committee of Correspondence stormed into the house, searched it from top to bottom and assured the owner that if they had caught the officers they would have torn his house down. Indeed, when hostilities did break out, the officers' host was proscribed and banished; he ended his life in London.

Meanwhile the officers, hungry and exhausted, had to travel some thirty miles through bitter weather to reach a place where it was safe for them to tarry. The next day, their horses exhausted, they found their way on foot back to Boston, where they appeared so travel-stained and weary that Gage and his staff did not recognize them. But they were, it seems, the only ones fooled by the disguise—a very modest triumph for the two spies.

5

Lexington

WHILE the Bostonians and their British jailers sat on a powder keg waiting apprehensively for the explosion, the patriot cause began to languish elsewhere. In many colonies, it was clear that a reaction had set in as the full implications of the course plotted by the Continental Congress became more apparent. By February, 1775, the moderates, who were more and more inclined to line up with the hard-core Tories, were congratulating themselves on a significant change in the tide of popular feeling. Pennsylvania's Joseph Galloway wrote to New Jersey's Governor Franklin that "the People of this Province are altering their sentiments and conduct with amazing rapidity. We have been successful in baffling all the attempts of the violent Party to prevail on the People to prepare for war against the Mother Country." New York also reported a strong reaction among the citizens of that colony against the proceedings of Congress. "The Tories (as they are called)," Galloway wrote, "make it a point to visit the Coffee House dayly and maintain their ground, while the violent independents are less bold & insolent as their Adherents are greatly diminished."

The atmosphere had so far changed that Galloway dared to speak out boldly in the Pennsylvania assembly, censuring "the measures of the Congress in every thing" and declaring that the actions of the delegates "all tended to incite America to sedition, and terminate in Independence." He went on to "prove" the "necessity for Parliamentary jurisdiction over the Colonies in all cases whatsoever." Galloway got angry rebuttals from the leading patriots in the assembly, chief among them John Dickinson; but on a vote, fourteen members out of the thirty-eight in the assembly supported Galloway's effort to condemn the proceedings of the Continental Congress.

The same word came from Governor Josiah Martin of North Carolina in a letter to General Gage. "The people in some parts," he wrote, "begin to open their eyes and see through the artifice and delusions by which they have been mislead and they discover good dispositions to renounce the powers and authority of the Committees that have been appointed by the recommendation of Congress. . . . Many of the Inhabitants in several Counties of the Province, have already by their addresses to me disclaimed all obedience to these illegal Tribunals."

The committees of correspondence and those numerous committees appointed to enforce nonimportation did not always find easy sailing. Their authority, after all, rested on very precarious grounds. Government, to be accepted, must be legitimated, otherwise it is simply a matter of your neighbor trying to tell you what to do—in which case all kinds of awkward personal matters enter the picture. Moreover, the members of such committees were, for the most part, little trained in the art of politics; they were, by and large, the "warmest"—which is to say the most zealous and, one fears, often the most intolerant—patriots, who were not inclined to exercise their uncertain authority with tact and discretion. Indeed, it might be said as a rule of political life that the less legitimate the authority, the more brutal the exercise of it is apt to be. If you are without the support of courts and magistrates, sheriffs and jailers, you are very apt to resort to direct force and intimidation to achieve your ends.

Many unpleasant incidents took place in all the colonies, actions that were no credit to the cause of liberty. The committees of correspondence and the committees of safety and the committees of inspection and a dozen other committees that sprang up in every town and county throughout colonial America were plainly illegal, although they derived a very uncertain kind of legitimacy from the fact that their members had been elected by other patriots. A very substantial number of colonists remained aloof from the whole business, and those of Tory persuasion were, of course, actively opposed to it and did all they dared to undermine the ubiquitous committees that had usurped the prerogatives of the Crown.

It was only natural that a peaceful, law-abiding German-American from, say, Lancaster, Pennsylvania, should resent being told what to do by a man named Jonathan McDougall whom he had never liked, who drank too much, and who now appeared clothed with the dubious authority of an illegal body, the Continental Congress. It is thus not surprising that a reaction to amateur and illegal government by committees set in throughout colonial America.

The more time that passed without an outbreak of open warfare, the more inclined the faint-hearted, the irresolute, and the uncertain were to recant the heresies that their hotheaded neighbors had hurried them into. The Tories, observing this wavering, plucked up their spirits and grew bolder in denouncing that combination of treason and tyranny that, as it seemed to them, the patriots were trying to foist upon all Americans. If only armed hostilities could be prevented or delayed, the patriot faction must, sooner or later, molder away, its self-assumed authority eroded, its ranks split by quarrels and jealousies.

On the other hand, there were those Tories, particularly in Boston, who were impatient for Gage to take a firm line, indeed to seek an occasion to suppress once and for all those vociferous and cowardly colonials who would never be properly obedient until they had been soundly thrashed.

An example of British power was needed. While Gage was seeking an occasion for a display of British authority, his spies informed him that ammunition was being collected by the colonists at Worcester and Concord. Worcester was some fifty miles from Boston, and it was estimated that it would take virtually all of the four thousand soldiers in Boston to make such an extended foray. Concord was much closer. A military force, by starting early in the morning, could march to the town, seize or destroy the munitions stored there, and return to Boston by nightfall, thus avoiding the problem of making an overnight encampment in what was plainly hostile territory. Moreover, the Provincial Congress of the colony had been meeting at Concord, and a quick raid might succeed in seizing some of these gentlemen as well as military supplies.

Gage and his staff, preserving the strictest secrecy, proceeded to make careful plans for a raid on Concord. A reinforced company under the command of young Hugh Percy was to be used for the raid. There were two routes that could be followed in striking at Concord. One led over Boston Neck through Roxbury and Brookline and across the Charles River to Cambridge, and thence to the Concord Road. But this course was too roundabout and slow. The alternate route, by boat from the foot of the Commons directly to East Cambridge, was clearly the better one, and warships in the harbor were alerted to have longboats and marines ready to transport soldiers.

The patriots were, of course, as well aware as the British of the egresses from the city, either across Boston Neck or by boat. Patriot spies kept close watch on both avenues—the narrow corridor over the Neck and the much broader area of the harbor and river. Somehow, perhaps by observing longboats being run out and refurbished, the patriots were alerted to the possibility of substantial troop movement by water, and word went out from the headquarters of the Provincial Congress at Concord to the adjacent towns to be on the lookout for British troops either by water or land.

Word arrived from Dartmouth on the eleventh of April that heavy reinforcements were on their way for Gage's army. Dartmouth urged Gage to try to seize the leaders of the extralegal Provincial Congress, who were known to be meeting in defiance of the Massachusetts Government Act. The Provincial Congress was scheduled to adjourn on the fifteenth, to allow those of its members who were to be delegates to a Second Continental Congress, scheduled for May, time to make their way to Philadelphia. If Gage were to capture any of the delegates, he would have to strike quickly. The grenadier and light infantry companies of each regiment were relieved of garrison duty in order to carry out certain exercises and "new evolutions" and were ordered to hold themselves in a state of readiness. Again the disturbance of camp routine was immediately noted by observant patriots in Boston. Since the grenadier and light infantry units were the most mobile, it was logical to assume that a raid was in prospect. From this inference and from the activity that had been observed on naval vessels in the harbor, the logical deduction was that there was to be an expedition carried by longboats. Such suspicions were confirmed when a number of longboats were observed secured to the sterns of warships on the morning of April 16. Meanwhile the Provincial Congress disbanded, and Samuel Adams and John Hancock started off on a leisurely journey to visit Hancock's Aunt Lydia and his fiancée, Dorothy Quincy, in Lexington, and then to pick up John Adams and Robert Treat Paine on Wednesday, April 19, to head for Philadelphia.

The sixteenth of April was Easter Sunday. Boston Selectman

Joseph Greenleaf sent word to Robert Treat Paine that two regiments plus the grenadiers and light infantry were scheduled to slip out of the city that night. The Concord Committee of Correspondence was instructed to take special pains in hiding the munitions.

However, for reasons best known to himself, Gage gave no orders on the sixteenth or the seventeenth. It was Tuesday, the eighteenth, before he gave the order that started redcoats on the way to Concord. Lieutenant Colonel Francis Smith was to command the troops that would embark at the foot of the Common to be carried by longboat to the shore near Cambridge. Lord Percy was directed to lead a support force over the Neck, through Roxbury to Cambridge. Percy, who was receiving his orders from Gage when Smith's grenadiers and light infantry were already embarking, was walking home to his quarters when he encountered eight or ten men on the Common who were talking about the British raid. He heard one of them say, "The troops have marched, but will miss their aim."

"What aim?" Percy asked, stepping up to the men in the darkness.

"Why, the cannon at Concord," the speaker replied. Percy hastened back to Gage's headquarters to tell him that the news of the departure of the detachment under Lieutenant Colonel Smith was already common knowledge in the town and doubtless in the countryside as well. The fact was that one of the first indications that the British soldiers would be on the move on the night of April 18 came from a Mrs. Stedman, who, with servants hard to come by, had employed the wife of a British grenadier named Gibson. On the evening of the eighteenth, a grenadier in full uniform knocked at Mrs. Stedman's door and asked for Gibson. The soldier was absent but expected soon, and the grenadier left word for him to report at eight o'clock at the bottom of the Common in full field dress, ready to march. Mrs. Stedman told her husband, who passed the word to Dr. Benjamin Church, one of the network of patriot spies.

When Gibson returned and received the message from his wife, Mrs. Stedman, who had grown fond of the young soldier, asked, "Oh, Gibson! What are you going to do?"

"Ah, madam," he replied. "I know as little as you do. I only know that I must go." And go he did, to die in the retreat from Concord.

Aware that Boston was by now thoroughly alerted to some move, Gage sent off several patrols to try to intercept any messengers that might be dispatched to warn the countryside. Joseph Warren, acting as chief of staff in Boston, had received persistent reports that the British troops would march under cover of darkness. Warren therefore directed a courier, William Dawes, to leave Boston at nightfall by way of the Neck and warn the inhabitants along that route and at Concord that the redcoats might be expected. At ten o'clock Warren summoned Paul Revere and directed him to row to Charlestown and give the word that the British were embarking at the foot of the Common—"and it was supposed they were going to Lexington, by way of Watertown to take them, Mess. Adams and Hancock on to Concord."

Two of Revere's fellow spies hung a lantern in the tower of Christ Church to warn patriots in Charlestown who were watching for this agreed-upon signal that the British were leaving Boston by water. Meanwhile, Revere and a friend hurried through the North End, picked up a boat that Revere had hidden a year ago for just such an emergency, and rowed past the British man-of-war *Somerset*. It was a moment of real peril. In Revere's words: "It was then young flood, the Ship was winding, and the moon was Rising." Somehow the watch on the *Somerset* missed seeing Revere's boat, and the two men made it safely to the Charlestown shore. Landing at the battery, Revere made his way to the town and borrowed Deacon Larkin's horse, discovering in the process that nine British officers "well mounted and Armed," had already been observed heading for Concord.

An almost full moon cast a pale light over Charlestown as Revere mounted and started off. He had hardly traversed the Charlestown Common when he saw the dim figures of two mounted officers under the dark shadow of a tree; before he could turn or rein his horse, he was close enough to see their holsters and the cockades in their hats. As both officers started toward Revere as though to head him off, he whirled his horse around and rode at full gallop toward the Mystic Road with the British in pursuit. Revere soon outdistanced them and rode on to Lexington.

The house of the Reverend Jonas Clarke, where Hancock and Adams were staying, was guarded by militiaman William Munroe, who intercepted Revere as he rode up. "Please," Munroe said, "not so loud. The family has just retired and ... requested that they might not be disturbed by any noise about the house." "Noise!" Revere replied, "You'll have noise enough before long. The regulars are coming." Adams and Hancock were at once awakened; they dressed, their horses were saddled, and they prepared to decamp. While Revere was still at Lexington, Dawes, having taken the longer route, arrived. Dawes and Revere, accompanied by a young man named Prescott, then set off together to warn the inhabitants of Concord.

Dawes and Prescott stopped to rouse a family along the way, and Revere rode on several hundred yards. Again he saw two British officers under a tree beside the road. He called for Prescott and Dawes; the three of them would be a match for the officers. Then he saw two more British soldiers, all with their pistols in their hands. "God damn you, stop! If you go an inch farther you are a dead man," one of the British officers cried. At that point young Prescott rode up, and the officers, still threatening, tried to surround them. For a moment or two Revere and his companion tried to find a way through, but, as Revere wrote, "they kept before us and swore that if we did not turn in to that pasture, they would blow our brains out." As they turned into the pasture, Prescott whispered. "Put on" and started to the left, while Revere turned to the right, intending to rush the fence at the bottom of the pasture, jump, and make his escape. As he approached it, six other mounted soldiers rode out of the shadows with their pistols at the ready, "put them to my Breast, siezed my bridle and ordered me to dismount." Prescott, knowing the lay of the land, escaped into the darkness. Dawes, warned by the commotion, rode on to Concord by a side road.

The officer in command rode up and quizzed Revere. Where had he come from? Boston, Revere replied.

"When did you leave?"

"About ten o'clock."

"Sir, may I crave your name?" the officer asked courteously.

"Revere."

"What, Paul Revere?"

"Yes."

Revere's name was well known to the British as a patriot courier and spy, and the other men in the patrol began to curse and denounce him.

"Don't be afraid," the officer assured him. "They will not hurt you."

"You've missed your purpose," Revere replied boldly.

"Oh, no. We're after some deserters who've been reported on this road." the officer said.

"I know better," Revere answered. "I know what you're after. You're too late. I've alarmed the country all the way up. . . . I should have five hundred men at Lexington soon."

At this alarming news, the officer rode off to confer with the two soldiers who had initially stopped Revere. The three returned at full gallop, and Major Mitchell, the senior officer in the little detachment, placed his pistol at Revere's head and told him that if he did not answer his questions truthfully he would blow his brains out.

"I call myself a man of truth. You stopped me on the highway and made me a prisoner. I know not by what right," Revere replied with all the dignity a man might be expected to muster under such circumstances. "I will tell the truth, for I am not afraid."

The original questions were put once more with additional queries, and Revere gave the same answers. The officers were by now thoroughly alarmed. The success of the British mission had depended largely on secrecy. If the whole countryside was notified, with the Minutemen even then looking to their arms and powder, the soldiers on the march might find themselves in a dangerous trap.

The three officers conferred once more in hushed voices. Then Revere was searched for arms and told to mount his horse. As he took his reins, the major rode up and took them from his hand: "By God, Sir, you are not to ride with reins," he declared, handing them to an officer on Revere's right.

"Please let me have my reins," Revere said. "I will not run from you."

"That may be, but I do not trust you."

At that, the soldiers brought out of the bushes four farmers who had been intercepted earlier and ordered them to mount their horses.

The major came up to Revere and said, "We are now going towards your friends and if you attempt to run, or we are insulted, we will blow your brains out."

Back on the road, the British formed a circle with the colonials in the center—except for Revere, who was placed at the head of the little company. "We rode down to ward Lexington prittie smart," Revere recalled. "I was often insulted by the officers calling me a damned Rebel, etc., etc."

The officer who held the reins of Revere's horse reminded him that he was "in a damned critical situation."

"I am sensible of it," Revere replied.

After the party had gone about a mile, the officer turned Revere over to a sergeant with instructions to shoot him if he tried to escape. A few minutes later, a shot rang out from the direction of the Lexington meeting house. The party halted, and the major asked Revere what the shot was for. "To alarm the country," Revere replied. The major then ordered the four farmers to dismount, cut the bridles and saddles off their horses, and told them "they might go about their business." Revere asked to be released also but the major refused, and the party pushed on.

As they approached the meeting house, a volley of shots rang out, apparently fired from the tavern as an alarm. The group halted once more while the major questioned Revere about the distance to Cambridge, the best route, and so on. Then he turned to the sergeant and asked if his horse was tired.

"Yes," the Sergeant replied. The major then ordered the sergeant to mount Revere's horse, and Revere, his usefulness over and now an impediment, was set free. While the British patrol headed back to Cambridge, Revere made his way to the Clarke house in Lexington, where Samuel Adams and John Hancock, who had not yet left, were discussing the best course of action. Revere joined with Hancock's aunt, fiancée, and friends in urging the two men to lose no time in getting out of the area. They were finally persuaded, and Revere accompanied them and their servants to a crossroad some two miles away, where the way seemed clear. Then, after a brief rest, he set off for the Lexington tavern to get the latest word on the progress of the redcoats.

In the hours during which Revere and Dawes were spreading the alarm, the British expeditionary force slowly got underway. The grenadiers and light infantry under Smith's command were ferried across to Cambridge, where they landed in a marsh and then, wet to the knees, stood shivering in the night air for an hour or more, waiting, as soldiers do, for orders and, as it turned out, for the distribution of food. Some soldiers had been given rations before they left their units, and most of these munched on some of the food and threw the rest away, littering the dirt road where they stood, chilled to the bone. When the order came to move off, they had to cross a ford, this time up to their waists in frigid water. At last they were on their way to Lexington.

At Lexington, the militiamen had been mustered on the common in the early morning hours to the number of perhaps a hundred or so, including the alarm men (the aged and those excused from service except in extreme emergency). It was damp and chilly, and since no further word came of the movement of British troops, the men were cautioned to be ready for a later summons and dismissed. A beating of drums would summon them when they were needed.

As Revere rode back to the tavern at Lexington, a farmer arrived with the news that Smith's soldiers were within two miles of the town. Revere entered the tavern to collect a small trunk of papers belonging to

Hancock, and before he had time to leave he saw through a window in the misty light of early morning the bright figures of the approaching soldiers far down the road. Hurrying out a rear door of the tavern, he passed through some fifty or sixty Minutemen forming on the green immediately behind the inn. As he passed, Revere heard the captain in command saying to his men. "Let the troops pass by and don't molest them with out they begin first."

The militia, formed in a nervous clot on the common, chilled by the sharp morning air of early spring, looked to the priming of their muskets and waited. As the British approached Lexington they could hear alarm guns firing, and scouts and British spies brought reports that armed men to the number of several hundred had been mustered on the common. At the sight of the Minutemen, barely visible in the growing light, the British advance guard stopped, uncertain of its next move. When Major Pitcairn, whose contempt for the colonials was notorious, rode up to the head of the advance guard, the soldiers told him that a militiaman had marched out from the company assembled on the common, aimed his musket, and attempted to fire on them, but there had only been a flash in the pan; the weapon had misfired. Pitcairn then ordered the troops to advance, but on no account to fire without orders. As the advance guard of British soldiers approached within one hundred yards of the common, the Minutemen began to file off to the cover of a stone wall that ran along the right margin of the green. Pitcairn rode toward them, shouting, "Ye villains, ye rebels disperse! Lay down your arms! Why don't ye lay down your arms?" At the same time a detachment of light infantry began to run forward as though to intercept the militia. Pitcairn called to the soldiers not to fire but to surround the men and disarm them. The militia made it to the wall well in advance of the redcoats and then turned. Five or six shots were fired by the Minutemen, wounding a soldier and Major Pitcairn's horse in two places. At this point the light infantry fired a deadly volley that killed ten of the militiamen, four of them members of two families, and wounded nine others, among them Prince, a black man.

When those first shots rang out, all the pent-up bitterness and hostility of the British soldiers toward the hated colonials who had abused and tormented them—staying always, like dogs baiting a bear, just out of range of their victim—burst forth. Now the bear was loose, and for a few moments the British officers lost all control. As one officer put it, "the men were so wild they could hear no orders." In the words of another, "Our men without any orders, rushed in upon them, fired and put 'em to flight." Given the dim light of morning and the very imperfect aim of the average British soldier, in order to have produced so many colonial casualties virtually the entire advance guard of between fifty and one hundred men must have fired in the first ragged volley. And having routed the rebels, it was almost impossible for their officers to re-form them. Milling around on the common, intoxicated by their "victory," they fired their guns and gave three cheers "by way of triumph and as expressive of the joy of victory and the glory of conquest."

The British soldiers had opened a heavy fire without orders. As for the Minutemen, it is clear that there was no order for them to fire and no general firing on their part. For them to have fired on the British advance guard in the open and without provocation would have been suicidal. So, regardless of the question of whether a stray bullet or two may have come initially from the colonial side, the evidence is that the British soldiers gave vent to their own pent-up rage by blasting the Minutemen with a withering volley. By their undisciplined actions, the soldiers provoked that nightmare of death and suffering that they and their companions were to live through that day. Because the advance guard broke ranks, acted without orders, and allowed their fury free rein, the entire British force, including Smith's main body and Percy's support brigade, had to suffer the bloody consequences.

It was perhaps fitting that the episode that triggered the military phase of the American Revolution should have come about as the consequence of an ill-planned and ineptly executed foray, marked, at least in its initial phase, by poor discipline and heavy-handed brutality. On the political level, British policy toward the colonies had been characterized by many of the same qualities.

Although Smith's advance guard under Pitcairn had easily routed the forlorn detachment of Minutemen on the Lexington green, his whole force was in a much more precarious situation than that officer could have guessed. His supporting troops under Percy, instead of being a few miles in his rear, were hours behind. As Smith's men had embarked at the foot of the Boston Common, Percy, already somewhat late, was forming his infantry regiments for the march to Lexington by land. Under his command were the Fourth, Twenty-third, and Seventeenth regiments. These were to be joined by a detachment of Royal Marines under Major Pitcairn. A message had gone from Percy to Pitcairn, directing him to bring his marines to the assembly point on Tremont Street. But Pitcairn already had gone off with Smith as commander of the advance guard. The messenger, not knowing this, simply left the message to be delivered to Pitcairn and returned to Percy's headquarters. As a consequence the order to the marines remained undelivered for several hours, while the regiments assigned to Percy's command waited impatiently in Tremont Street, cold and restless at the delay, the end of the column a few yards from the schoolhouse on School Street run by Mr. Lovell. When the marines were finally routed out and joined Percy's detachment, it was after eight o'clock in the morning, and the first young scholars on their way to school saw the British soldiers, looking considerably larger than life in their bright uniforms and tall hats, their webbing freshly whitened with pipe clay, their muskets and bayonets flashing in the morning sun. The students arrived to find school dismissed for the day. Mr. Lovell had put the matter simply (and prophetically) enough: "War's begun, and school's done." As Percy's column, with the band playing "Yankee Doodle," wound its way through Roxbury, a local schoolmaster also dismissed his students, locked the schoolhouse, and went off to join his militia company and serve for the next seven years in the army.

It was after twelve when Percy's force came to the bridge across the Charles River between Brighton and Cambridge. By the orders of William Heath, general of the Massachusetts militia, the planks of the bridge had been removed, but the thrifty members of the Committee of Public Safety could not bring themselves to throw the boards away, and they were neatly piled on the Cambridge side of the river. Soldiers went across on the stringers of the bridge and quickly relaid the planking, and the British marched on, with the soldiers of the baggage train left to complete the rebuilding of the bridge. At Cambridge Common, where roads diverged in half a dozen different directions and there were no road signs, Percy was puzzled. The town of Cambridge was virtually abandoned, so there was no one in sight to ask directions. Finally Isaac Smith, a tutor at Harvard College, was routed out and gave Percy directions to Concord. Percy, informed of the incident at Lexington, pressed on as fast as the heat of the day would permit.

Meanwhile at Lexington, after one of those seemingly interminable delays so familiar to the soldiers of every army in the world, the whole force under Smith's command set off for Concord, leaving the citizens of Lexington to gather up their dead and care for the wounded. For many British officers as well as men, this was the first knowledge they had of their primary mission—to seize the reported arsenal at Concord.

6

Concord

Even before the first shots rang out on the Lexington Common, Minutemen were stirring in neighboring towns. All through the early morning hours of April 19 and increasingly after the sun rose, Minutemen tested the appropriateness of their appellation. They took down their muskets, loaded them, gathered precious powder and ball, formed up in companies in their town commons, and headed for Lexington and Concord. By the time the British had taken up the march to Concord, the militia of that town had been augmented by contingents from a half-dozen communities, to the number of two battalions, which stationed themselves on a small hill just east of the town.

The men had scarcely taken their positions when they saw, in the words of the Reverend William Emerson, grandfather of Ralph Waldo Emerson, "the British troops at the distance of a quarter of a mile, glittering in arms, advancing towards us with the greatest celerity. Some were for making a stand, notwithstanding the superiority of their number; but others more prudent thought best to retreat till our strength should be equal to the enemy's by recruits from neighboring towns that were continually coming to our assistance." The same scene of strategic retreat was repeated several times, each time with the militia withdrawing as the British sent out skirmishers. Finally the militia stationed itself on a ridge overlooking the North Bridge, which crossed a stream northwest of Concord.

When the British reached Concord a light infantry company was dispatched to search for cannon in the town and another guarded a line of retreat over the South Bridge, while six companies followed the Americans across the North Bridge. Three of these companies proceeded to march beyond the town to the fort of militia Colonel James Barrett, where, rumor had it, rebel military stores were cached. Instead of an arsenal the British searchers found only two small cannon. They knocked the trunnions off these, confiscated some powder and ammunition, burned a supply of wooden spoons and trenchers, and chopped down the town's Liberty Pole.

While Colonel Francis Smith, in command of the detachment of redcoats at Concord, lingered on hoping to turn up a larger cache of munitions, time slipped away and the colonial militia collected in rapidly growing numbers on the high ground above Concord. The town of Woburn "turned out extraordinary," 256 men strong. Dedham sent a company made up of a number of seasoned soldiers who had fought in the French and Indian War, plus raw recruits. Their departure left "the town almost literally without a male inhabitant before the age of seventy, and above that of sixteen."

The three British companies stationed by the North Bridge faced the militia on the gently sloping hill above them. For nearly an hour, the two forces confronted each other. Finally the British officer commanding the detachment at the bridge, alarmed by the steadily growing numbers of Americans, whom he estimated at more than a thousand, sent off a messenger to Colonel Smith requesting reinforcements. Smith, unfortunately for the detachment waiting at the bridge, placed himself at the head of the relief force of grenadiers, thus slowing its progress. As a British officer later wrote, Smith, "being a very fat heavy man he would not have reached the bridge in half an hour, tho' it was not half a mile to it."

Before the requested reinforcements could arrive, the Americans began to advance. As they approached, the British commander ordered his men back over the bridge, a step he should have taken sooner, for now, in withdrawing across the bridge, the fire of the first two companies to cross was blocked by the third. The Americans took advantage of the situation to open fire on the rear company, which, as four officers fell wounded in the first exchange, came near to panicking, pressing hard on the companies behind it. The grenadiers under Smith, coming up in support, managed to hold off the colonials long enough to allow the fleeing soldiers of the light infantry to reform and make their way in relatively good order back to the center of Concord, but the British had lost a total of four officers and three soldiers killed and five wounded at the bridge.

Colonel Smith was by now well aware of his danger. Nothing could be gained by lingering. He prepared to march back to Boston, but first provision had to be made for the British wounded. Carriages were commandeered, the injured soldiers were placed on them, and the withdrawal finally started about noon.

Smith's troubles were far from over. The Minutemen from the North Bridge took a short cut across country north of Concord and caught up with the retreating British column at Meriam's Corner, a mile east of town. Joined there by reinforcements, the rebels took positions behind stone walls, hedges, trees, and in houses and kept up a galling fire on the British. A British Lieutenant, John Barker, reported that his men were fired upon "from all sides but mostly from the rear, where people had hid themselves in houses till we had passed, and then fired. The country was an amazing strong one," he added, "full of hills, woods, stone walls, etc., which the Rebels did not fail to take advantage of, for they were all lined with people who kept an incessant fire, upon us, as we did too upon them, but not with the same advantage, for they were so concealed there was hardly any seeing them."

The men of Smith's brigade arrived at Lexington with their ammunition virtually exhausted and, in the words of one officer, "so fatigued that we could not keep flankering parties out, so that we must soon have laid down our arms or been picked off by the rebels at their pleasure." There they found Lord Percy with his relief force. Brigadier General Percy, informed of the events at Concord, had formed a square on the Lexington Common and put into action two artillery pieces loaded with grapeshot and canister to hold off the colonials. Smith's soldiers filed into the square and dropped to the ground, utterly worn out after some fourteen hours on the march without food or rest. They had all suffered from the debilitating effects of garrison life in Boston and were woefully ill prepared for their ordeal. Though every minute was precious, Percy could not start the retreat from Lexington to Boston until the exhausted men had recovered their strength and morale. During the interval, Percy sent out parties to seize carriages from farmhouses in the vicinity of Lexington to carry those soldiers that had been killed or wounded on the retreat from Concord.

The citizens of Boston had, of course, waited anxiously throughout the long day for some news of the fate of the British soldiers and of their countrymen. By late afternoon the thump of distant musket fire was intermittently audible to those who lined the shore; they could also see the flashes of fire from firing pans and the muzzles of muskets: first the flash of the pan, then the muzzle flash, and then seconds later the deep cough of the musket.

The patriots had better intelligence than Gage's headquarters. Dr. Joseph Warren, who had been in charge of the patriot intelligence system in the city, had heard of the clash at Lexington by eight o'clock in the morning. He left his patients and crossed on the ferry to Charlestown. As he left the boat, he turned to a friend and said, "Keep up a brave heart! They have begun it—that either party can do; and we'll end it—that only one can do." Another physician, Dr. Thomas Welch, joined Warren, who kept a horse in Charlestown. "Well, they are gone out," Welch recalled saying, and Warren answered, "Yes, and we will be up with them before night." For him, for Samuel Adams and John Hancock, as well as for scores of patriots, the fateful hour had finally come. We can only guess at their sensations: relief of a kind that the issue was at last joined; and various fears—for themselves, their families, and friends, for the cause, for the fortitude of those upon whom they must depend for help if they were not to be isolated and beaten into submission by the whole weight of British power; and hope, hope for colonial liberties, and faith that their cause was just and that the all-powerful Ruler of the Universe would carry them safely through the stormy waters ahead.

At Cambridge, the two doctors came on Percy's baggage train. When they tried to pass it their way was blocked by bayonets. Two British officers rode up to Warren to inquire if he knew where the main body of Percy's force was. Warren did not. The British officers were obviously too worried and alarmed to pay any further attention to the two civilians, and Warren and Welch rode off to join the militias who were accumulating in large numbers around Lexington.

As soon as the troops of Smith's brigade had had a brief respite, Percy took full command, formed up the troops, and began the withdrawal from Lexington to Cambridge. Advance and rear guards, along with flanking parties, afforded some protection to the main body of troops and bore the brunt of colonial fire. The British, as one officer reported, received "heavy fire from all sides, from Walls, Fences, Houses, Trees, Barns, etc." The retreat, orderly at first, soon approached a rout. While the main body lurched along, choking in the dust stirred up by their heavy boots, their faces streaked with grime, their thick woolen uniforms soaked with sweat, detachments or, more often, a half-dozen or so soldiers, acting without direction or orders, would break off to pursue their tormenters.

Strangely, the soldiers began to loot. Fleeing for their lives, walled on every side by rebel fire, frightened and near the limits of their strength, they nonetheless filled their arms and pockets with everything they could carry away. "Many houses," Lieutenant Mackenzie reported, "were plundered by the soldiers, notwithstanding the efforts of the officers to prevent it." He added, "By all accounts some soldiers who staid too long in the houses were killed in the very act of plundering by those who lay concealed in them."

One soldier noted that "even women had firelocks. One was seen to fire a blunder bus between her father and her husband from their windows; there the three with an infant child soon suffered the fury of the day." The whole long column was delayed time and again while the advance guard cleared out the colonials, house by house. "They suffered for their temerity," Lieutenant Barker noted grimly, "for all that were found in the houses were put to death."

Under such circumstances it was not surprising that the frantic soldiers failed to make careful discriminations. Some Americans were butchered in their homes because of a suspicion that firing had come from thence or because it might come. Retreating toward Cambridge, soldiers, convinced that they had been fired upon from the tavern of Benjamin Cooper, smashed down the door and bayoneted and smashed the skulls of two unarmed men who had taken refuge there.

John Raymond, a cripple left in charge of William Munroe's tavern while Munroe went off to fight, found himself beset by British soldiers who entered his shop and demanded punch. Raymond served them and then tried to slip off through the garden. Two of the soldiers fired, and he dropped dead. Frustrated in their search for arms, British soldiers entered the house of Deacon Joseph Adams, known as a leading patriot, and forced his wife Hannah, who had recently given birth to an infant, to flee with the child while they set the house on fire. Simple-minded William Marcy, the village idiot of Cambridge, was sitting on a fence watching the soldiers and making such cheerful observations as occurred to him when a redcoat fired at him and killed him instantly. As the troops made their weary way on to Charlestown, one of William Barber's children, a boy of fourteen, who was sitting in a window looking down at the soldiers, was killed by a casual musket shot from one of the passing men. These are the incidents of war, but they horrified the patriots and, widely repeated, confirmed the image of the British soldiers as cruel and ruthless instruments of a distant tyranny.

Probably the most effective work was done by those militia who depended on stone walls and tree trunks for cover. They fought like the Indians, firing and then withdrawing to load their cumbersome pieces with nervous, fumbling fingers, find a new position, and fire again. What was most disheartening of all to the British was the accuracy with which these farmers fired their muskets. As the effective British force dwindled away through casualties and exhaustion, the number of colonists, fresh and eager to have a shot at last at the hated redcoats, swelled by the hundreds. There were many near-misses as well as hits. Joseph Warren, fighting as a volunteer with a militia unit had a bullet pass so close that it knocked a hairpin out of his wig. On the British side Lord Percy had a button shot off his waistcoat. And Colonel Smith, the British commander at Concord, was badly wounded in the leg.

Credit for extricating the demoralized troops was plainly Percy's. He kept his head and kept the weary men under his command moving when they could easily have bogged down and been forced to surrender or be destroyed. The boats that had brought Smith's force to Cambridge were still lying at Phip's Point, but there were not enough of them to carry off all the troops, and it would have been most hazardous to try to evacuate the soldiers by water when they were being pressed so hard by the colonial militia. It was Percy's good judgment to avoid trying to move through Cambridge and across the bridge that he had passed over in the morning, for the bridge had now been thoroughly destroyed, and he and his men would certainly have been trapped if they had tried that line of retreat. He turned rather toward Charlestown. The crucial point in the British retreat came when the battered force reached the causeway that connected Charlestown peninsula to the mainland. Once over the causeway, the soldiers would be protected by the guns of the British fleet. Percy barely got his force across ahead of a large body of militiamen sent to intercept them.

It was George Washington's opinion, when he retraced the events of April 19 some six weeks later, that "the fact, stripped of all colouring . . . [is] plainly this: that if the retreat had not been as precipitate as it was, (and God knows it could not well have been more so,) the ministerial troops must have surrendered, or been totally cut off. For they had not arrived in Charlestown, under cover of their ships, half an hour before a powerful body of men from Marblehead and Salem was at their heels, and must, if they had happened to be one hour sooner, inevitably have intercepted their retreat to Charlestown."

The question must occur to the reader: what would have been the reaction of the British government if, in the first engagement of the war, half of Gage's entire command had been captured or destroyed? There were, at this moment, scarcely twenty thousand soldiers in the entire British army, at home and in all the widespread empire. Would the Lord North ministry, in the face of such an unimaginable disaster as losing, in one day, nearly a tenth of this force, have discovered a spirit of conciliation? Such a defeat would have been a staggering setback to the British, with results that are hard to estimate.

By the same token the very style of fighting adopted by the Americans doubtless made it impossible for them to take advantage of the demoralization of the British troops. They did not constitute an army, but rather a horde or a swarm of individuals who stung and flew on to sting again. At Bunker Hill they would fight much in the same fashion. Indeed it would be Washington's principal task to make these individuals cohere into an army capable of carrying on sustained campaigns, pursuing an advantage, or extricating itself from a defeat.

As Percy's force made its way over the Charlestown Neck, it encountered streams of refugees pouring out of Charlestown, afraid that the British would burn the town. The soldiers entertained themselves by cursing the people and firing off their muskets to frighten them. The Charlestown selectmen sent word that if Percy would refrain from attacking Charlestown, they would promise that no hostile action would be taken against his soldiers and would do all in their power to help get his men across the ferry to Boston.

Passing peacefully through the town, Percy led his men up the gently sloping ground to Bunker Hill, where they made a rough camp and tended the wounded, some of whom had died in the long jolting ride from Lexington. Exhausted and hungry, the redcoats fell asleep where they dropped. One soldier expressed a common experience: "I never broke my fast for forty-eight hours, for we carried no provisions. I had my hat shot off my head three times. Two balls went through my coat, and carried away my bayonet from my side." The *Somerset*, beneath whose bows Paul Revere and his companion had rowed silently not many hours before, sent her boats first to carry over the wounded and then to evacuate the rest of Percy's force.

Some 1,800 men and officers had set out for Concord on the morning of April 19, more than half the Boston garrison of 3,500 soldiers, and those the best trained and most experienced. By the end of that long, long day—more than twenty-four hours for the troops of Smith's command—they had suffered 73 killed and nearly 200 wounded. The Americans had lost 49 killed and 41 wounded. Small as were the numbers involved, it is doubtful that the British had ever suffered a more humiliating setback. A miscellaneous collection of armed peasants had routed His Majesty's finest troops.

Aside from ten men who died on the Lexington Common or soon afterwards, the roll of colonial casualties tells eloquently how quickly the militiamen of adjacent towns turned out. Cambridge listed five dead or wounded, Charlestown one, Sudbury three, Bedford two, Woburn five, Medford two, Billerica two, Chelmsford two, Concord five and on through Framingham, Dedham, Needham, Roxbury, Salem, Danvers, Beverly, and Lynn. Twenty-six towns in all made up the company of those who had been killed or wounded in the first engagement of the Revolution.

In the aftermath of the events at Lexington and Concord, there was a widespread feeling of pride in the courageous performance of the New England militia, who had forced the finest soldiers in the world to retreat. The day after Lexington and Concord Lord Percy wrote: "Whoever looks upon them as an irregular mob, will find himself much mistaken. They have men amongst them who know very well what they are about, having been employed as Rangers agst the Indians & Canadians, & this country being much cov'd w. wood, and hilly, is very advantageous for their method of fighting." Nor were the Americans without courage. During the retreat some Americans had rushed toward Percy and other officers to fire at them, knowing that they could not avoid being riddled with British musket balls. It seemed clear enough to Percy that "the Rebels have now had time to prepare" and were "determined to go thro' with it." "Nor," he added, "will the insurrection here turn out so despicable as it is perhaps imagined at home. For my part, I never believed, I confess, that they wd have attacked the King's troops, or have had the perseverance I found in them yesterday."

Colonial pride in New England's soldiers was coupled with dismay at the realization that the colonists were at last engaged in open warfare with the mother country. Many citizens of Massachusetts would have echoed John Adams' somber words to James Warren: "When I reflect and consider that the fight was between those whose parents but a few generations ago were brothers, I shudder at the thought, and there's no knowing where our calamities will end."

The events of April 19 led to considerable foreboding on the British side. Captain John Crozier, the master of the *Empress of Russia*, a British naval vessel that assisted in carrying the battered soldiers back to

Boston, wrote a friend, "The enthusiastic zeal with which those people have behaved must convince every reasonable man what a difficult and unpleasant task General Gage has before him." On the other hand, Captain A. Glanville Evelyn of the King's Own Regiment, preserving the famous British aplomb, wrote to his father about "the little fracas that happened here a few days ago, between us and the Yankey scoundrels . . . although they are the most absolute cowards on the face of the earth, yet they are just now worked up to such a degree of enthusiasm and madness that they are easily persuaded the Lord is to assist them in whatever they undertake, and that they must be invincible. . . ."

General Gage had his share of British sangfroid. On the twenty-second of April he mentioned with incredible casualness in a dispatch to Barrington, "I have now nothing to trouble your Lordship with, but of an affair that happened here on the 19th Instant." Then followed a brief account of the engagement at Concord and the retreat of the British troops, with warm praise for the skill and bravery of Lord Percy.

How does one explain the general's offhandedness? In part, perhaps, because to a soldier, warfare is normal, peace abnormal. A professional soldier is trained to fight and lives to fight. Gage quite correctly considered that a state of war had in fact existed for some time between the colonists and the mother country. He had been instructed to take stern measures and had assumed they were necessary. The fact that one particular expedition brought on the grim reality of men dead and dying was in no way remarkable to Gage.

It is instructive to place the American reaction beside that of the British general. For the colonists, Lexington and Concord were and would continue to be facts of transcendent importance. Crude and rough as American society was in many ways, its experience of war had been as a fairly remote reality. A portion of its young men had gone off to fight with the British in Canada, or on the frontier against the Indians and the French, but it had been generations since the seacoast towns had known anything but peace. What to the British was simply an unfortunate skirmish involving the death of a few soldiers, was to the colonists the most piercing and agonizing assault upon their homes, families, and friends. To hear that Hannah Adams had been driven from her bed with her infant child by brutal British soldiers intent on burning down her house—for what offense?—was more shocking to an American than the record of one hundred men lost in battle could be to an English officer or a minister of His Majesty's government. To the latter it meant a setback, an inconvenience, more trouble and expense, explanations, and the usually embarrassing problem of fixing blame. To the colonist it seemed as though the whole order of the universe had been disturbed; he felt imperiled in the most sacred recesses of his personal life—the safety of his wife and children, of a son or a brother. He found himself arrayed against the most awesome power in the world, and that power, more cruel and bloody-minded than he had dared imagine, had murdered innocent old men by their firesides, plundering and pillaging in the name of the king.

Once the engagements of Lexington and Concord were over, it remained for the Massachusetts Committee of Safety to spread the word to every part of British America. Israel Bissel, Paul Revere's principal rival as a courier, was on his way with the news of Lexington before the British had begun their retreat from Concord. He reached Worcester, where his horse fell dead of exhaustion, at noon on the nineteenth. The next day he was in New London, Connecticut, a distance of more than a hundred miles from Boston, spreading the word through every little town on his route, and by April 23, four days after the battle, Bissel had reached New York. Picking up more fresh horses along the way, he arrived in Philadelphia on the twenty-fourth.

Benedict Arnold, hearing the news in New Haven, abandoned his shop and led his militia company northward by forced marches, arriving at Cambridge on the twenty-ninth. General Israel Putnam was quite literally called, like the ancient Roman hero Cincinnatus, from labors on his farm, which was at Pomfret, Connecticut. He gave word for the Connecticut militia to turn out, and then he set off for Cambridge, riding a hundred miles in eighteen hours on the same horse. Word of the events at Lexington and Concord reached New Hampshire by noon of the twentieth, and the boats that had crossed the Merrimack River with the news were jammed with Colonel John Stark's Minutemen on their return trip. By dusk several companies of Stark's militia had reached Haverhill ferry, twenty-seven miles from the south bank of the Merrimack; they had covered the distance in some five hours at what was more of a trot than a march. (In World War II, the famous Truscott Trot, a speed march for conditioning troops, required five miles in one hour, ten in two, and twenty-five in seven). Stark's men stopped at Andover, Massachusetts, only long enough to eat, and then pressed on, reaching the Cambridge Common by sunrise on the twenty-first, having come fifty-five miles in less than twenty hours.

Other militia contingents were not so prompt as Colonel Stark's, but the army around Boston grew every day. James Warren wrote to his wife: "It is Impossible to describe the Confusion in this place, Women and Children flying into the Country, armed Men, going to the field, and wounded Men returning from there fill the streets."

Everywhere that the news of the fighting spread, it had a profound effect on those who heard it. Ezra Stiles, a Connecticut friend and collaborator of Benjamin Franklin, wrote another friend that when word of Lexington and Concord arrived in New Haven it produced "universal anxiety and solicitude in town. All business is laid aside." A Philadelphia lady wrote to a British officer in Boston whom she knew, informing him of the spirit of the people of that city. "I have retrenched every superfluous expense in my table and family," she wrote; "tea I have not drunk since last Christmas, nor bought a new cap or gown since your defeat at Lexington, and what I never did before, have learnt to knit, and am now making stockings of American wool for my servants, and this way do I throw in my mite to the public good. I know this, that as free I can die but once, but as a slave I shall not be worthy of life. . . . It is not a quibble in politics, a science which few understand, which we are contending for; it is this plain truth, which the most ignorant peasant knows . . . that no man has a right to take their money without their consent. . . . All ranks of men amongst us are in arms. Nothing is heard now in our streets but the trumpet and drum; and the universal cry is 'Americans, to arms!'"

Philadelphia produced five regiments from the city and surrounding country, complete with arms and uniforms "and very expert at the military manoeuvres." There were companies of "light-horse, light infantry, grenadiers, riflemen and Indians, several companies of artillery, and some excellent brass cannon and field pieces." In addition it was estimated that two thousand more militia would be mustered in the rest of Pennsylvania. As Joseph Barroll put it, writing to a friend on May 24, 1775: "We are ready to die free, but determined not to live slaves. We ardently wish the people of England, (who we still love as a people, for take them from their venal Parliaments, & they are just) would arouse before it is too late. . . . 'Tis not Boston, 'tis not the prov. of the Masst Bay, 'tis not the four N.E. Provinces only, but 'tis the continent of America joined in the Opposition. . . . We have many & Daily Reports from every part of this Extended Continent. They all seem determined and more awake than ever. *Oppression will make a wise man mad;* you will soon be made acquainted with the Spirit of the times."

The patriots were quick to put their case before the court of world opinion. The prose with which the colonists described the actions of the

British soldiers on the retreat from Concord seems lurid and overblown to us today; as with the Boston Massacre, we profess to admire their skill as propagandists, their instinct for playing upon susceptible emotions. It seems seldom to occur to us how genuinely distressing and bewildering the colonists found their situation to be; how little it might appear to them that the boldest language was adequate to describe the reality in its full horror. On the American side, there was deep dismay and equally deep determination, a full realization that the fateful moment had arrived, that it was impossible to turn back and foolish to hope for a speedy reconciliation—although, since men are frequently hopeful and foolish in equal measure, many colonists continued to do so.

In addition to boldness and resolution in the ranks of the patriots, there was also fear and anxiety that sometimes approached panic. This was especially true of the little port and seacoast towns that dotted the New England shoreline from Westport and Saybrook in Connecticut to Kittery in Maine. Each town was convinced, rather egotistically, that the British fleet was planning to descend upon it and destroy all its people in their beds. The towns kept their militia constantly on the alert against a seaborne invasion and frantically petitioned their respective provincial congresses for more men and arms. If, in the first rush of enthusiasm, they had dispatched their militia to Cambridge, they now tried to recall them. A Durham, New Hampshire, militia officer wrote that six or seven urgent messages had arrived in Durham, "some desiring us to march to Kittery, some to Hampton, some to Ipswich etc. which places they said sundry men-of-war were ravaging. The whole country was in a continual alarm. . . . Master Smith being under the same apprehension, did actually lay in ambush behind a warehouse, and came very near sinking a fishing boat anchored off in the river, which he supposed heaped full of marines."

Some seaport towns, however, responded nobly, like Newburyport, which, although quite vulnerable to enemy assault and a not unlikely object for attack, declared itself willing to send its small but precious supply of powder to Cambridge if "the publick cause renders it absolutely necessary, in which case we shall readily give up the last ounce, the destruction of this Town being a trivial matter in our estimation, compared with a final defeat of the Army."

When the colonists' version of the events at Lexington and Concord reached England—some twelve days prior to Gage's official account—it caused a variety of reactions. When word was sent to the king, he refused to be dismayed. "I am not apt to be over-sanguine, but I cannot help being of opinion that with firmness and perseverence America will be brought to submission. If not, old England . . . yet will be able to make her rebellious children rue the hour that they cast off obedience. America must be a colony of England or treated as enemy." The foes of the North ministry, on the other hand, did not try to conceal their pleasure at the news. "It is strange," Lord George Germain wrote, "to see the many joyful faces upon this event, thinking, I conclude, that rebellion will be the means of changing the Ministry." He noted several days later, "Great betts are laid that the Ministry will be changed in two months." When Colonel Dalrymple of the earlier army of occupation in Boston encountered Adjutant General Edward Harvey, Dalrymple, got the rough edge of Harvey's tongue. "How often," Harvey asked Dalrymple, "have I heard you American Colonels boast that with four battalions you would march through America; and now you think Gage with 3000 men and 40 pieces of cannon, mayn't venture out of Boston!"

One Whig newspaper correspondent wrote gleefully that "Lord North when he received the unhappy news to government, that the Provincials had defeated General Gage's troops, turned pale, and did not utter a syllable for some minutes." John Horne Tooke, the English radical, appealed for contributions "for the relief of the widows, orphans, and aged parents of our beloved American fellow-subjects who, faithful to the character of Englishmen, preferring death to slavery, were, for that reason only inhumanly murdered by the King's Troops at or near Lexington and Concord." The appeal produced a hundred pounds; Tooke, for his rashness, was sentenced to a year in prison.

When Gage's official dispatches arrived, North did indeed offer to resign. The king, however, persuaded North that the moment had arrived for resolution, not retreat. There were unpleasant facts that had to be faced: It appeared that Great Britain, based on the experience of Lexington and Concord, simply did not have enough soldiers available to subdue its American colonies. At this juncture the attitude of the king himself was decisive. North was thoroughly demoralized by the news of Lexington and Concord. Matters were at the precise point where the king could clearly affect the course of events. Had the King himself been weak or indecisive, or if he had been wise and prescient, seeing the cost and anticipating the outcome, he undoubtedly could have taken the initiative through his ministers to attempt the reconciliation that the colonists wished for so devoutly and that they persisted in believing the king favored. The fact was that the king was a courageous and resolute man who, while by no means unintelligent, suffered from a certain kind of moral obtuseness, and who was, in addition, stubborn and vain. His inclination, like a good leader, was to buck up his subordinates in adverse times. "I am certain," he wrote after news of Lexington and Concord, that "any conduct but compelling obedience would be ruinous and culpable, therefore no consideration could bring me to swerve from the present path which I think Myself in Duty bound to follow." He was convinced that "once these rebels have felt a smart blow, they will submit."

Thomas Hutchinson, the one-time governor of Massachusetts now in exile in England, who knew so much and yet so little about his fellow New Englanders, wrote to the great historian Edward Gibbon that the colonists would not long maintain their siege of Boston. For, Hutchinson predicted, "unless fanaticism got the better of self preservation, they [the people] must soon disperse, as it was the season for sowing their Indian corn, the chief subsistence of New England."

7

Boston Besieged

In the weeks immediately following the incidents at Lexington and Concord, New England militia poured into Cambridge and the adjacent towns. The Massachusetts Provincial Congress, to relieve itself of the imputation that it was forming a revolutionary army to make war on Great Britain, referred to those militia that it was so busy organizing, or reorganizing, as an "Army of Observation," suggesting that its soldiers were armed with spyglasses instead of muskets. The Connecticut militia were enlisted in "the new service" as "in His Majesty's Service . . . for the preservation of the Liberties of America."

Typical of those who poured into Cambridge was a little group of twenty-nine men from Southwick, Rhode Island, who left the town four days after Lexington and Concord and arrived at their destination nine days later on the first of May, having "Borded and Bedded and Vittled our Selves during the Whole of the March which is one Hundred and Ten miles upon our own Count." Arriving at Cambridge and finding no fighting to do immediately, eleven of their number were persuaded to enlist in the new eight-months' service, and the remainder were "Dismisst . . . and Returned Home."

Rhode Island men led by newly appointed Brigadier General Nathaniel Greene began arriving on the twenty-third of May. As an officer noted, "the Troops from Rhode Island Govmt are Comeing in Every Day in Small Parteys." The scene at Cambridge was one of general confusion. James Warren wrote that the members of the Provincial Congress were as "busy as piss-mires on a molehill," and Benjamin Thompson, writing about the efforts to form the militiamen who filtered in every day into an "Army," added, "if that mass of confusion may be called an Army."

When the militia forces were finally assembled, Connecticut had provided some 2,300 men and New Hampshire and Rhode Island, much smaller colonies, approximately the same number between them. The Minutemen predominated, especially among the Massachusetts militia. They considered themselves an elite corps and were inclined to hold themselves aloof from the common run of militia, thus causing a number of problems and moving James Warren, writing to John Adams, to regret that they had ever been recruited.

As the ranks of the army filled up, the highest-ranking officer, General Artemas Ward, divided them into three divisions. General John Thomas commanded some four thousand men in the Roxbury sector, including troops from Connecticut and Rhode Island and some ancient artillery pieces. The main body of Rhode Islanders under General Greene occupied a rough line from Roxbury to Brookline. Ward, as commander in chief, held fifteen regiments at his headquarters in Cambridge. War had served as colonel of militia in the French and Indian War, and he had risen from a sickbed to ride to Cambridge on hearing the news of Lexington and Concord. In east Cambridge, toward Charlestown, Israel Putnam commanded a regiment of Connecticut militiamen.

Nathanael Greene was purely a textbook soldier. Raised by his preacher father to read the Bible as the source of sufficient wisdom, Greene had educated himself in military history, in mathematics, and in political theory. He was a Quaker, but his belief that tyranny should be resisted by force if necessary had led to his being read out of the pacifist Society of Friends. In the Rhode Island militia he had held no higher rank than that of private, and he had the further disadvantage of a gimpy knee. When he went to Boston in 1773 to buy himself a gun, he also purchased a work on the life of the great French general Henri Turenne, and he brought back with him a British deserter to instruct his company in drill. Unlike Joseph Warren, he had not been an outstanding political figure or a man who had enjoyed public patronage. Apparently his being chosen as general of the Rhode Island militia was the consequence of his intelligence, his quiet authority, and his confidence in himself and in his ability to lead others. It was a confidence by no means misplaced. Greene was to become Washington's most brilliant general.

Returning to camp in late May after a visit to Rhode Island, Greene found his men thoroughly demoralized by camp life. "A few days longer in the state of excitement in which I found our Troops," he wrote a friend in Rhode Island, "would have proved fatal to our campaign. The want of government, and of a certainty of supplies, have thrown everything into disorder. Several Companies had clubbed their muskets [reversed them] in order to march home. I made several regulations for introducing order and composing their murmurs; but it is very difficult to limit people who have had so much latitude, without throwing them into disorder . . . I believe," he added, "there never was a person more welcome, who was so little deserving, as myself." The men needed and wanted leadership and responded strongly to it when it was exercised by officers as firm and wise as Greene.

Another of Artemas Ward's generals was fifty-seven-year-old Israel Putnam. Putnam had a slight stutter and grew faint, it was said, at the sight of blood. He had served with Gage during the French and Indian War and maintained a close friendship with the British general. Gage, indeed, had offered Putnam the rank of major general in the British army when he arrived in Boston, and Putnam, when meat became scarce during the siege of the city, sent a side of beef to Mrs. Gage to help feed her large household.

Putnam had a wry sense of humor. When a British friend jollied him about the report that a member of Parliament had said four regiments of British regulars could march from one end of the colonies to the other without meeting opposition, Putnam replied, "Oh, probably true enough. They would meet no opposition if they let the women folk alone. But if they annoyed the women, a few brigades of females with broomsticks would chase them right into the ocean." It was Putnam who wisely insisted in keeping the militia busy with fortifications. "It is better to dig a ditch every morning and fill it up at evening," he told Joseph Warren, "than to have the men idle."

The Stockbridge Indians had been recruited as Minutemen, and several groups joined the colonists around Boston, along with a troop of Mohawk warriors. They were placed under white officers, which was not entirely satisfactory to them. As the Stockbridge Indians wrote to the Massachusetts Provincial Congress: "Brothers, one thing I ask of you, that you will let me fight in my own Indian way. I am not used to fight English fashion, therefore you must not expect I can train like your men. Only point out to me where your enemies keep, and that is all I shall want to know."

The Stockbridge Indians were "domiciled" Indians, that is, Christianized agricultural Indians who had settled as farmers in proximity to the whites. They were thought to be much less fearsome warriors than "the savages" who maintained their nomadic, tribal life. The Indians' principal contribution was to frighten British sentries. They killed a few and apparently enjoyed coming dangerously close to the British lines, where they would "flourish their scalping knives, and yell by Way of Insult." But the Indians were even less suited to camp life than the Yankees. As one militia officer put it, "They were too fond of Liquor; they grew troublesome . . . there was no Bush fighting to employ them in; and they were dismissed."

Supplying the troops was a constant problem. The weekly ration of the American soldier was supposed to be: "One pound of Bread; half a pound of Beef, and half a pound of Pork, and if Pork cannot be had, one pound and a quarter of Beef, and one day in seven they shall have one pound and a quarter of salt Fish, instead of one day's allowance of Meat: one Pint of Milk, or if Milk cannot be had, one gill of Rice; one quart of good spruce or malt Beer; one gill of Beans or Peas, or other sauce equivalent." In addition, the soldiers were to get "six ounces of good Butter per week; one pound of good common Soap for six men per week; half a pint of Vinegar per week per man, if it can be had." The operative phrase was: "if it can be had."

Sailcloth for making tents was in short supply and much needed, because the available houses were full, and the crowding of men into improvised barracks had already caused much sickness. Personal cleanliness was a major problem. Soldiers refused to take proper sanitary precautions and seemed content to live in filth. John Adams was obsessed with the physical fitness of the troops, and he wrote to James Warren: "It is of vast importance that the officers of our Army should be impressed with the absolute Necessity of Cleanliness, to preserve the Health of their Men. Cleanliness is one of the three Cardinal Virtues of a Soldier, as Activity and Sobriety are the other two. They should be encouraged to go into Water frequently, to keep their Linen washed, and their Beds clean. . . ." Either Warren did not pass on the advice or the officers did not heed it. Dirt, infection, and disease began to haunt the American encampments.

In addition, there was rather too much drunkenness among the militiamen, who were restless with too little to do—there was a limit, Putnam's dictum aside, to the building of fortifications. The men were at loose ends away from home. It was therefore ordered "That no person presume to sell any spirituous liquor in your camp, but such as have been heretofore licensed for that purpose. That all persons immediately break off this iniquitious practice, which has a tendency to destroy the peace and good order of the camp. . . ."

More awkward was the fact that the soldiers who were encamped around Boston had no official commander in chief. Artemas Ward was senior Massachusetts officer, but his authority was limited to the soldiers of this own colony. The ragtag army, Warren reported to a friend, was "in such a shifting, fluctuating state as not to be capable of perfect regulation. They are continually going and coming. . . . They seem to me to want a more experienced direction . . . it is difficult to say what Numbers our Army consists of. If a return could be had one day, it would by no means answer for the next. . . . I believe there are about 6,000 in Camp at present. They are employed at Cambridge in heaving up Intrenchments."

The sight of "the New England army," as John Adams called it, would have made a professional soldier weep or laugh, depending on his sympathies. The troops were without proper uniforms, in every kind of raggle-taggle attire, without sufficient powder or flints or even guns, and without proper shelter. To supply their wants, they fashioned improvised lean-tos on Cambridge Common, and made off under cover of night with pigs and chickens purloined from indignant housewives. They bobbled across the common hour after hour in thoroughly unmilitary drill, some tall, some short, some thin as fence rails and others fat and puffing, almost all awkward, hardly knowing their left feet from their right. The story was that one ingenious officer, cursed with a particularly dense collection of hayseeds who could not untangle their feet, ordered his men to tie hay to the right foot and straw to the left and then gave his marching order smartly enough. Instead of "right, left"— "hay foot, straw foot."

Gunpowder was in especially short supply, and the colonies were ransacked for every available pound. Six hundred and fifty pounds were discovered in New Jersey and sent to Connecticut. General Ward issued orders that no volunteer returning home from Cambridge be allowed to take any ammunition with him. The Provincial Congress authorized the Committee of Safety to buy powder "not only at Connecticut and Rhode Island, but at New York, or any other Colony on the Continent." Massachusetts sent off urgent requests to the Continental Congress, which had met again in Philadelphia, and to the New York assembly appealing for powder, "not because we suppose you have a surplusage, but because we are in very distressing want." But New York replied that there were not one hundred pounds of powder to be purchased or requisitioned in the city.

Much of the time and attention of the Committee of Safety and, subsequently, of the Provincial Congress was taken up with the matter of procuring enlistments. Commissions as colonels were offered to those men who could enlist a regiment. Anyone who could bring into camp at least fifty-six men, including noncommissioned officers, would be made a captain and immediately entered with his men on the payrolls. In the army organized by the Committee of Safety, a company was to be made up of "a captain, one lieutenant, one ensign, four sergeants, one fifer, one drummer, and seventy rank and file." The seventy was soon lowered to fifty. Nine such companies were to make up a regiment, commanded by a colonel, a lieutenant colonel, and a major.

Compared with the state of affairs in the ragged and poorly disciplined militia surrounding them, the British troops in Boston lived most agreeably. Most of the British soldiers were quartered on the Common. George Harris, captain of Fifth Grenadier Company, wrote a friend in England: "I have now before me one of the finest prospects your warm imagination can picture. My tent-door, about twenty yards from a piece of water, nearly a mile broad, with the country beyond most beautifully tumbled about in hills and valleys, rocks and woods, interspersed with straggling villages, with here and there a spire peeping over the trees, and the country of the most charming green that delighted eye ever gazed on. Pity these infatuated people cannot be content to enjoy such a country in peace. But, alas! this moment their advanced sentinels are in sight."

The British soldiers and officers supplemented their scant supplies of fresh food by growing vegetables in little gardens that they planted. Captain Harris was rhapsodic about the one that his servant had planted for him: "Such salads! such excellent greens the young turnip tops make! Then the spinach and radishes, with the cucumbers, beans, and peas so promising."

Meanwhile the British staff was augmented and reorganized on the twenty-fifth of May. Gage was joined by three generals, Sir William Howe, Sir Henry Clinton, and John "Gentleman Johnny" Burgoyne.

Gage remained as governor of the province, while General Howe took command of the British forces, with Clinton and Burgoyne serving under him.

Howe was a tall, dark-complexioned, stout man with a prominent nose and black eyes. The British ministry could hardly have sent a general more congenial to the tastes of the colonists had his mission not been to subdue them. The Americans knew him as one of three brothers, all of whom had served with distinction in the French and Indian War, and who had shown a very unusual delicacy of feeling in all their dealings with the colonists. Further, William Howe had been instrumental in the British victory at Quebec. The victory of General James Wolfe on the Plains of Abraham, followed by his death on the field of battle, exercised a very powerful hold on the imaginations of Americans. On that almost mythical occasion fifteen years before, Howe had led 25 volunteers up the sheer face of the Quebec bluffs and surprised the French guarding that supposedly impassable route. The heights secured, Wolfe had followed with the rest of his army. While Wolfe with 3,000 men repulsed the French frontal assault, Howe, now commanding a detachment of 400 men, had skillfully held off 2,000 French reinforcements. As a member of Parliament after the French and Indian War, Howe had placed himself squarely among the friends of American liberty.

In addition to the admiration of the colonists for his own achievements, Howe enjoyed the reflected glory of his two older brothers. "Black Dick" Howe, with the dark visage characteristic of the family, was one of the most successful and popular admirals in the British navy. It was he who at Nova Scotia had fired the opening shot in the "Great War for Empire." But it was George Augustus Howe who, most of all, had won the affection of the colonials who fought with him during the French and Indian War. Wolfe called him "the noblest Englishman that has appeared in my time and the best soldier in the army." George Howe discarded the ornate uniform of a British general for the leather breeches and buckskin shirt of a frontiersman. He learned from the colonials the Indian tactics of woods fighting and guerrilla warfare. He accompanied Robert Rogers and his Rangers on patrols "to learn," in Rogers' words, "our methods of marching, ambushing, retreating, etc. . . ." A colonial carpenter wrote of him: "It was not extravagant to suppose that every soldier in the army had a personal attachment to him, he frequently cam among the Carpenters and his manner was so easy and fermilier, that you loost all the constraint or diffidence we feale when addressed by our Superiors whose manners are forbidding."

At Ticonderoga in 1758, as one of his colonial officers, Major Israel Putnam, tried to prevail on him not to expose himself so recklessly. George Howe was struck in the heart and died almost instantly in Putnam's arms. Now Putnam, having learned his trade from George Howe, waited in Cambridge for the moment he would meet Howe's younger brother in battle.

This younger Howe must certainly have had very mixed feelings when he accepted the command of the British troops in America. Standing for re-election to Parliament a year earlier, he had assured his constituents in Nottingham that he would never fight against "our American brethern." When it was known in England that he had failed to honor his election pledge, some of the voters who had supported him let him know that they considered he had welshed on his promise. And some went further and in their bitter resentment hoped he would leave his bones on American soil. "If you should resolve, at all events to go," one of his Nottingham constituents wrote, "I don't wish you may fall as many do; but I cannot wish success to the undertaking." "My going thither [to America] was not of my seeking." Howe wrote in reply. "I was ordered, and could not refuse without incurring the odious name of backwardness to serve my country in distress. So contrary are men's opinion here, to some with you that instead of the grossest abuse, I have been most highly complimented upon the occasion by those who are even averse to the measures of Administration! Every man's private feelings ought to give way to the service of the public at all times, but particularly when of that delicate nature in which our affairs stand at present." So much for Howe's rationalizations.

Howe considered himself an honorable man, and the barbs directed at him by the voters of Nottingham (and other friends of America as well) must have left festering wounds. The reasoning by which he squared his mission with his conscience was that, if the colonists must be subdued, it was better done by a friend than an enemy, a view with which the colonists could hardly have been expected to sympathize. Howe apparently saw his task as that of bringing the colonists to their senses by administering a sharp defeat and then stepping forward as peacemaker and conciliator, prevailing upon the ministry to grant generous terms, and persuading the Americans to return to the fold. This, in fact, is the course he attempted to follow, but it is measure of his simplicity and innocence that he would have imagined such a policy could succeed. It must be said in his defense, however, that he was no more mistaken in his reading of the colonial temper than that succession of British ministers who had been responsible for directing American affairs since the Treaty of Paris in 1763.

Sir Henry Clinton, a smallish, fleshy, fair-haired man with a florid complexion, was an experienced soldier. The son of Admiral George Clinton, who had been governor of the province of New York during his youth, Henry Clinton was almost as much an American as an Englishman. His first military duty had been as a captain-lieutenant in the fashionable militia company of New York City, and he had many childhood friends from that province. Clinton, like Howe, had been a member of Parliament, albeit an undistinguished one who dutifully voted on most issues as his cousin and patron, the Duke of Newcastle, wished him to. Reserved and rather colorless, he had a keen military instinct and was a skillful tactitian with a meticulous eye for detail. Under his reserved exterior, Clinton was sensitive and introspective. The death of his wife, to whom he was devoted, brought on a breakdown that seems to have carried him to the edge of insanity. Like many introspective men, he seems to have suffered from a deep sense of insecurity, which produced an alternation of rashness and extreme caution—in response, apparently, to the tides of his own emotional life rather than to the military situation. On the warship that carried him, along with Howe and Burgoyne, to Boston, he wrote a friend, "At first (for you know I am a shy bitch) I kept my distance [and] seldom spoke out until my two colleagues forced me out."

The third general, John Burgoyne, had begun his career as that familiar English specimen, a young man of good family and good abilities without money. He had scraped together enough to buy a lieutenant's commission in 1741, when he was nineteen years old. When his regiment was stationed at Preston, England, Burgoyne often visited the great mansion of the Earl of Derby, whose son had been a schoolmate. There he fell in love with his friend's sister, the charming Lady Charlotte, and eloped with her. The indignant earl gave his daughter a small settlement (which Burgoyne used to buy himself a captain's commission) and then cut her off without further income. After three years of struggle to keep up appearances on a captain's pay (aristocratic Englishmen had a profound prejudice against doing any kind of "work" for a living), Burgoyne was forced to sell his commission to pay his debts, and he and his wife moved to France, where the living was cheaper.

France suited Burgoyne. He learned the language and plunged into French life and culture with gusto. Finally, his father-in-law relented and used his influence to get Burgoyne a commission, once more as a captain, in the Eleventh Dragoons, which Burgoyne a year later exchanged for a lieutenancy-colonel in the Coldstream Guards. In the Seven Years' War he rose rapidly in rank. He was a charming man, intelligent and witty, and he made a. modest name for himself by introducing the first light horse units in the British army, giving it thereby a new mobility and the capacity for quick reconnaissance in force. His most notable accomplishment in the war was a daring raid with his light horse on the Spanish garrison at Valencia de Alcántara, for which the king of Portugal gave him the captured flags and a large diamond ring.

Back in London after the war, he won a seat in Parliament and cut a wide swath through London society as a member of fashionable clubs, a reckless gambler, a playwright, and an actor of some talent. His principal dramatic effort, *Maid of the Oaks*, a rather foolish romantic play, had been produced by David Garrick at the Drury Lane Theatre not long before Burgoyne set sail for America. The "Gentlemen" in Johnny Burgoyne's nickname, however, did not refer to the figure he cut in London high life, but to the care and attention he paid to the soldiers under his commmand. Strongly opposed to brutality and corporal punishment as a means of disciplining soldiers, he wrote a treatise attacking the treatment of enlisted men in the British army that, in its humane spirit, was far ahead of its time. Of the three officers who joined Gage in Boston, Burgoyne was certainly the most colorful and appealing. Everything he did was done with a flair, whether on parade, in battle, or in the officers' mess. He was the kind of leader soldiers adore—flamboyant and dashing, but always attentive to their needs and comfort.

It tells a good deal about the relations between England and the colonies that Gage, who had spent seventeen years in America, had married an American, the delightful Margaret Kemble of New Jersey, had ten children born in America, and owned nineteen thousand acres of land in the province of New York; that Henry Clinton had been born and raised in New York; that William Howe, through his brothers and in his own right, had the closest of ties with the colonies. The fact was that among the general officers charged with suppressing the American rebellion, only Burgoyne lacked strong connections with the American colonists. All, despite their individual shortcomings and eccentricities, were experienced professional soldiers.

In the weeks following Lexington and Concord, a strange two-way traffic passed in and out of the city. Patriots applied for permission to leave Boston, and Tories from Boston's outlying towns, no longer safe in their own communities, poured into the city. Gage would allow Bostonians to leave the city only if they first surrendered all firearms to the selectmen. He would then do what he could to help the evacuation with boats and wagons. Under these terms residents of the city turned in 1,778 muskets, 634 pistols, 973 bayonets, and 38 blunderbusses, a very substantial armory for a city of some 16,000, many of whom were women and children. If we take into account those weapons that had already been taken out of the city by patriots, it is probably not far off the mark to say that every other male Bostonian over the age of eighteen possessed some sort of firearm.

The Loyalists, some of whom formed themselves into infantry companies, protested Gage's policy of allowing Bostonians to leave. Once the patriot families had departed, they argued, the colonials would not hesitate to attack the city. Patriot families should be forced to remain as hostages and as a means of keeping the city supplied with food. Gage's only concession was to require that all those departing from the city leave their belongings behind. The exodus was so great that by the middle of the summer there were only 6,753 civilians left from the normal population of some 16,000. "You'll see parents that are lucky enough to procure papers," a patriot wrote, "with bundles in one hand and a string of children in the other, wandering out of the town (with *only suffrance of one day's* permission) not knowing wither they'll go. . . ."

The besieging colonials around Boston and the besieged British waited uneasily day after day for the other side to take the initiative. Having underestimated the determination of the colonists and the degree of their solidarity, Gage now overestimated their numbers and their ability to mount an attack. For their part, the colonists daily anticipated a massive assault by the British, supported by the guns of the naval vessels in the harbor.

Yet while Gage anticipated a massed attack by thousands of colonials, he still clung to the notion that all the trouble was the work of a few wicked men who had deluded the ignorant multitude. In line with this theory, he issued a pardon to all those in a state of rebellion against His Majesty on June 12 that began: "Whereas, the infatuated multitude, who have long suffered themselves to be conducted by certain well known incendaries and traitors, in a fatal progression of crimes against the constitutional authority of the state...." This "infatuated multitude" was now making, Gage declared, "a preposterous parade of military arrangement" by which they pretended to hold the British troops besieged. In spite of such outrageous behavior, Gage was willing to promise the king's "most gracious pardon to all persons who shall forthwith lay down their arms and return to their duties ... excepting only ... *Samuel Adams* and *John Hancock*...." The proclamation was highly flattering to Adams and Hancock—and doubtless irritating to Joseph Warren, John Adams, and a host of other patriots who were by it relegated to the position of being tools of Hancock and Samuel Adams.

If the proclamation was nothing else, it was a measure of how far General Gage was divorced from reality. Perhaps the poor General felt that it was better than doing nothing. But something foolish is often infinitely worse than nothing. Boston greeted the proclamation with cheerful derision and an ingenious variety of obscenities chalked on walls and fences.

The tedium of waiting was relieved by a bravura display put on by Israel Putnam. On May 13 he paraded all the colonial troops, excepting those actually manning the fortifications, from Cambridge to Charlestown, over Bunker Hill, and back to their camps—in full view of the soldiers and remaining inhabitants of Boston and in range of the British warships anchored in the harbor. The militiamen at several points passed so close to British vessels that they could see sailors standing by loaded cannon, with lighted matches held near the touchholes. It was a bold gesture that strengthened the morale of the colonials; they were, their orderly march proclaimed, not afraid of the British with all their cannons and guns.

On May 27 the engagement of Noodle Island took place. British soldiers in Boston, hard-pressed for food and fodder for their horses, had taken to raiding the islands in Boston Harbor and carrying off everything that squealed or mooed or was movable. On the twenty-seventh, at low tide, a group of militiamen waded to Hog Island and began driving off the pigs that gave the island its name, and the other livestock as well. Admiral Samuel Graves, who had taken command of the British fleet in American waters in 1774, observing the militiamen and concerned for a cache of military supplies on nearby Noodle Island, sent forty marines on a small schooner, the *Diana,* under the command of his son, Lieutenant Thomas Graves, to defend Noodle Island against possible attack. When the marines on the schooner fired on the Americans on Hog Island, the colonials took cover. One of the party, Amos Farnsworth, a pious farmer, noted in his diary that when he and his fellows saw the *Diana* approaching, "about fifteen of us Squated Down in a Ditch on the mash and stood our ground. And thare Came A Company of Regulars on the mash on the other side of the river. . . . And we had a hot fiar untill the Regulars retreeted. But notwithstanding the Bulets flue very thitch thare wasnot A Man of us Kild. Suerly God has a favor towards us . . . thanks be unto God that so little hurt was Done us when the Bauls Sung like Bees Round our heds." Farnsworth, like many Puritan soldiers, often seemed more concerned about his state of grace than about the British. His journal abounds with his "Anchous Desires after Holiness," and his inability "to Performe Some Privit [Religious] Duties But was Cold and Ded in Duty . . . Alas my Backsliding Hart; Oh how have I Revolted from the Liven God Alas Alas."

Gage, observing the engagment from the Boston shore, ordered eighty more marines with two 12-pound cannon to support young Graves and his force. Before they reached Noodle Island, the British schooner began to be carried by the tide toward the shore, where American militia lay in wait for it. Putnam, getting word in Cambridge of the rapidly expanding action, came up in an hour with a thousand men and two cannon. When the *Diana* was within a hundred yards of the shore, Putnam called on the crew to surrender. For response, they fired their swivel gun and cannon at the colonials, and Gage's relief force joined in the cannonading from Noodle Island. Putnam's two cannons meanwhile were leveled at the schooner. In all the hail of fire from both sides, there were few casualities—the range was too great.

At dusk the *Diana* finally ran aground and her crew abandoned her, leaving her to be stripped down to the bare boards and burned to the water line by the Americans. It did nothing for the temper of the British to stand by, helpless observers, while one of His Majesty's ships was pillaged by the rebels. When the sloop *Britannia* ventured back to try to drive off the militia, it was put out of action almost immediately by the colonial cannoneers and (most humiliatingly) had to be towed out of range by sailors in longboats.

The so-called Battle of Noodle Island lasted all day and far into the night and saw the exchange of thousands of rounds of musket ammunition and hundreds of cannon balls; yet as darkness fell not a single American had been killed, while the British had suffered no more than a dozen casualties. The fray had a splendid effect on colonial morale. Whatever modest laurels were to be gathered, they clearly belonged to Putnam's troops, not to the British who had been surprisingly inept in their maneuvers.

8

Bunker Hill

GENERAL Howe, who had arrived in Boston only three days before the "Battle" of Noodle Island, very promptly produced a bold strategy for routing the poorly disciplined and tatterdemalion militiamen clustered around Boston. The center of the British assault would be on the colonial command headquarters and supply depot at Cambridge. With the guns of the fleet covering his advance, Howe intended to personally lead an amphibious landing at Dorchester Point. He would seize Dorchester Heights with his brigade and then follow the course that Percy had taken through Roxbury and Brookline to Cambridge, rolling up the thinly held lines as he went. Sir Henry Clinton was to lead another force, landing at Willis Creek on the left flank of the main positions at Cambridge. Clinton would secure the high ground on the Charlestown peninsula and then be prepared to join with Howe in a combined attack on the flanks of the crude fortifications around Cambridge.

Of course, word of the intended attack leaked out. As it came to the Committee of Safety, its aim was understood to be the seizure of Dorchester Heights. The colonials displayed an encouraging capacity to make a difficult decision quickly. It was decided to anticipate the British attack on Dorchester by securing Bunker Hill above Charlestown,

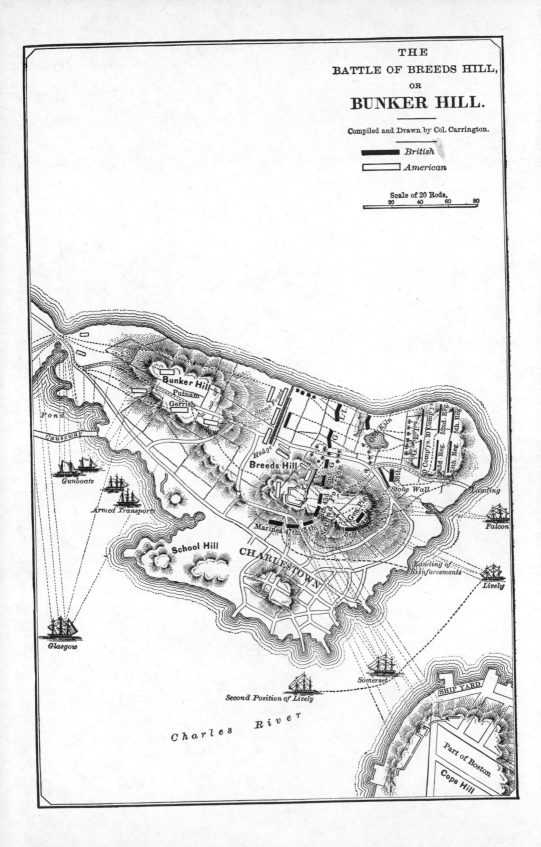

THE
BATTLE OF BREEDS HILL,
OR
BUNKER HILL.

Compiled and Drawn by Col. Carrington.

British
American

Scale of 20 Rods.
20   40   60   80

Bunker Hill
Putnam
Gerrish

Stone Fence

L.I.

Kiln

10 Comp'ys. 10 Comp'y
52nd. Reg
5th. Reg
43rd. Reg
48th. Reg
Landing

Hedge

Breeds Hill

Stone Wall

48th

Gen'l Pig

Marines 47th

Pond
Causeway

Gunboats

Armed Transport

School Hill

CHARLESTOWN

Falcon

Landing of
Reinforcements

Lively

Glasgow

Somerset

Second Position of Lively

Charles River

SHIP YARD

Part of Boston

Cops Hill

thereby bringing Boston within range of American cannon. Once the decision had been made, the colonial units designated for the mission, unencumbered by elaborate staff work or heavy equipment, were soon ready to march. Colonel William Prescott, a farmer from Pepperell, Massachusetts, a lean, taciturn man with cool blue eyes, was in command of the operation. Prescott had fought as a lieutenant in one of the colonial regiments that had participated in the siege of Louisburg during the French and Indian War. He had, indeed, fought so well that he had been offered a commission in the British army, but he had preferred the life of a farmer.

Prescott's second-in-command was the older and more experienced Israel Putnam. Putnam, it will be recalled, was major general of the Connecticut militia, but on Massachusetts soil and with the great majority of the men involved being Massachusetts militia, Prescott had been given first command. Perhaps the most gifted of the senior officers assigned to occupy and fortify the high ground above Charlestown was Colonel Richard Gridley, a brilliant engineer who, in the French and Indian War, had performed the heroic task of getting two cannon up the sheer cliffs that rose to the plains of Abraham—cannon that, directed by Gridley, gave crucial support to Wolfe's Infantry in the battle for Quebec that followed. In recognition of his services at Quebec, Gridley had been given the rank of colonel at half-pay in the British army, plus the Magdalen Islands in the Gulf of St. Lawrence and three thousand acres of land in New Hampshire. A few months before, Gridley had gotten a letter from the war ministry asking if he would take up his commission in the event of war between the mother country and her colonies. Gridley's answer was: "I have never drawn my sword except on the side of justice and justice lies I believe with my countrymen." In a day when fifty was considered old, Gridley at sixty-five was the oldest officer in the American forces. It was his job to direct the fortifications on the top of Bunker Hill once that promontory had been occupied by the Americans.

Prescott, with a force numbering fewer than twelve hundred men, left Cambridge at nine o'clock on the evening of June 16. Putnam met the column at Charlestown with several wagonloads of picks and shovels, along with barrels that were to be filled with earth and used to reinforce the works, and fascines—bundles of stiff twigs woven together and placed to absorb the impact of cannon balls. Charlestown was virtually deserted: most of its inhabitants, acutely aware after Lexington and Concord of their vulnerability both to attack by British soldiers and bombarding from ships in the harbor, had taken refuge with friends and relatives on the mainland.

The advance guard of Prescott's force moved through the town without incident and waited in the open fields beyond while the main body came up and their leaders tried to decide which of the three modest hills above the town they were supposed to fortify. Morton's Hill, the lowest of the three, was quickly identified and ruled out. But Prescott, Putnam, and Gridley could not agree which of the two remaining promontories was in fact Bunker Hill—a confusion that, as it turned out, was to persist in all accounts of the events that followed. Prescott was convinced that the hill that Gridley and Putnam wished to fortify was not Bunker Hill but another. Bunker Hill, he insisted, lay above and beyond, and his orders were to fortify Bunker Hill. Putnam and Gridley grew increasingly impatient as they tried to persuade Prescott that whatever its name, the hill they had reconnoitered and now stood upon was the most advantageous site for their fortifications. If calling it Bunker Hill would expedite matters, they were perfectly willing to do that. It rose, in any event, only sixty-seven feet above the water of the harbor, but in their opinion it lent itself much more readily to defense than the hill running down the center of the peninsula like a spine—which Prescott insisted was Bunker Hill.

Finally, after more than an hour of debate, Putnam and Gridley overcame Prescott's objections, and the decision was made to fortify the lower hill—Breed's Hill, as it was called. The soldiers were brought up, tools were distributed, and the digging began under the direction of Gridley, cautiously at first lest the sound of pick striking rock alert the British, but soon more rapidly as the night wore on and it became evident that it was more important to make substantial progress on the fortifications than to preserve an increasingly doubtful secrecy. (The fact was that Howe had heard a report of the occupation of the peninsula by the Americans before he retired to bed, but he had dismissed it as a rumor.)

Troops from Prescott's force were dispatched to patrol the little village of Charlestown, especially the waterfront, and instructed to sound the alarm at any unusual activity on the part of the British. The American militia had yet to demonstrate whether they would stand fast in the face of an attack by British soldiers, but of their ability to dig there was no question. In a few hours they accomplished more than their British counterparts could have done in twice the time. As the war progressed, it came to be a truism that the colonial farmer-soldier was not only a fast digger, but also that he would fight stoutly if his legs were protected. A farmer with one leg or a mangled foot was of little use, and the great majority of the American soldiers were farmers first and soldiers second.

Gridley had sketched out plans for a reinforced earthwork some 160 feet long and 80 feet wide, with walls six feet high and at least a foot thick. A simpler breastwork of earth thrown up to the height of three or four feet was to run from the fort itself down along a rail fence to a marsh at the foot of the hill. Gridley, alarmed at the slowness—despite the colonial diggers' sweat—with which the fortification was rising, urged Prescott to assign all his men to digging, but Prescott, following standard if hardly applicable military procedure, insisted on having half his command stand guard in half-hour shifts while the other half dug. However, Prescott exhorted his officers to dig, and Prescott himself took his own turn with a shovel to encourage his men. "Dig men, dig," he urged. "Dig for your lives."

The fortification slowly took shape in the waning darkness. On the southern side, facing Charlestown and Boston across the channel, Gridley placed a redan, an angled projection designed to hold cannon. Although the militiamen had no cannon with them, the intention was to secure cannon that could command the ships in the harbor and the British garrison in Boston. Gridley also intended a sally port at each end of the fortification. The one on the northeast was to provide an exit from the fort for a counterattack. The sally port on the south side was for the purpose of allowing the defenders to man the breastworks that extended down the hill. But while Gridley fussed over the failure to start work on the sally ports and breastworks, Prescott stubbornly kept the men working on the main defenses.

From time to time the anxious Prescott, knowing how important it was that the fortification be substantially finished before the light of day revealed what the Americans were up to, walked to the shore to listen for sounds that might indicate the British had taken alarm. But all he heard was the periodic cry, "All's well," of the sailors on watch.

As dawn broke and the figures of the militiamen—looking in their dark clothes like industrious ants as they dug on—became visible, the ship *Lively* fired a shot that alerted the British on ship and on shore. The light that revealed the activities of the Americans also made clear the vulnerability of their position. It was easily accessible to attacks from both flanks, with poor fields of fire and inadequate breastworks. To try to forestall an attack on his flanks, Prescott set his men to digging a trench running from the east side of the fort in a northerly direction some twenty rods, "under a very warm fire from the enemy's artillery." Both the ships in the harbor and the British battery across the channel on Copp's Hill kept up a continuous fire. But the ships were hampered by the fact that they could not elevate their cannon high enough to reach the fort without withdrawing to a distance that, while it allowed the trajectory of their balls to reach the hill, sacrificed a good deal of accuracy. The cannon fire was thus largely ineffective.

But the colonials were beginning to feel the effects of their night's labor on empty stomachs. Food was supposed to have been sent up along with more ammunition, cannon, and replacements for the weary men. With the shelter of darkness gone, they felt extremely vulnerable on their bare promontory in the harbor, as though the whole world were looking down upon them. They were conscious that their retreat could readily be cut off if the British landed a substantial force on Charlestown Neck. And while the constant bombardment did little damage, it was demoralizing to men who had no experience under such fire. The men in Prescott's command could see that some of the officers and men of other Massachusetts regiments were slipping off, feeling that they had done their duty by their stint of digging. They were hungry and tired; it was time for others to do their part. As one soldier later wrote, "The Danger we were in made us think there was Treachery, and that we were brot there to be all slain, and I must and will venture to say there was Treachery Oversight or Presumption in the Conduct of our Officers. . . . [The cannonading] caused some of our Young Country p[eo]ple to desert, apprehending the Danger in a clearer manner than the rest, who were more diligent in digging and fortifying ourselves. . . ."

It was not an encouraging beginning. Under the stress of field conditions, in battle or faced with the threat of battle, small things make a large difference to soldiers: a ration of food, however tasteless and meager, is a comfort and a reassurance, representing, as it does, the fact that someone knows you are there and has taken pains to meet your needs. For the soldier in combat, one of the most distressing experiences is the sense of being isolated. A battlefield is a lonely place where terror lurks even for the most resolute. Prescott himself was weary to the bone. His mission had been to supervise the construction of the fortifications; he, like his men, was supposed to be relieved, and his junior officers, observing his exhaustion, urged him to request to be relieved so he could get some much-needed rest. But he refused. Prescott was conscious that his departure would be the last blow to the morale of the men under his command; it would simply increase their sense that they had been abandoned.

Gridley had been gone for hours, perhaps to expedite the movement of additional supplies and cannon, or perhaps, feeling that his task was done, to catch a few hours of sleep. He was too old for all-night vigils. Putnam had spent the night riding between Cambridge and Charlestown, trying to round up reinforcements. Near noon the cannon were finally brought up, six fieldpieces under the command of three captains. The sight was vastly cheering to the soldiers. When one gun was wheeled into position on the embrasure, "The Captain fired but a few times, and then swang his Hat round three Times to the Enemy, and then ceased to fire."

When the British staff, headed by Gage, Howe, and Clinton, gathered early on the morning of June 17 for a council of war, there was unanimous agreement that the Americans must be driven off the high ground in Charlestown; otherwise their guns would command most of the city. The only point at question was how this might best be accomplished. The practical Clinton had proposed that while Howe attack from the Charlestown side, "he might be landed with 500 men and taking possession of the Jews burying ground near Charlestown Neck where he would have been in perfect security and within half a gun shot of the narrow neck of communication of the Rebels." The British navy under the direction of Admiral Graves had the means to close off the Neck—which at its narrowest was only some thirty yards wide—with enfilade fire.

Clinton's suggestion was brushed aside. In the discarding of it, there was the implication that it was too devious, a slightly unmanly approach to the problem. "The hill was open and of easy ascent and . . . it would be easily carried." Subconscious assumptions often influence conscious decisions. It was simply inconceivable to the British generals that the untrained rebels would stand in the face of a vastly superior force of British soldiers supported by artillery and by the guns of the entire fleet. Howe may have welcomed the opportunity to teach the colonials the crushing lesson that he had planned for a few days later. To outmaneuver and catch them in a noose would hardly be as instructive as to drive them in full flight from the silly little redoubt that they had erected so insolently right under British noses.

Beyond this consideration, there was the fact that an attack on the rebel redoubt offered an opportunity for that marvelous pageantry so

dear to the hearts of eighteenth-century generals. They loved a parade
almost as much as they loved the glory of war. Gage and his generals
were proud of their troops. They liked to play "soldiers," almost as
though the brightly colored figures, each one a kind of art object in
itself, were toy counters in a splendid game. We cannot of course know
what went through the minds of the British generals (except for Clinton's sensible proposal), but their actions spoke for them.

Complicating Howe's plan was the delay between the time, well
before six in the morning, when the activities of the colonials were first
revealed, and the actual assault. One of the basic principles of military
action is speed. But the British generals thought otherwise. Things had
to be done with "decency and order"—virtues that ranked high in the
eighteenth century, certainly higher than speed.

In fairness to Gage and Howe, it must be said that soldiers cannot
be turned out in an instant. To put a large garrison force in the field
takes time. The British soldiers were scattered throughout the city.
They had to be routed from hundreds of houses, many from the arms
of sleepy wives or, possibly more frequently, from the beds of indignant
doxies. They had to be assembled, their equipment inspected, rations
and ammunition distributed, their heavy field packs packed. Howe had
ordered that the soldiers should take with them not only their blankets,
but also "the provisions Ordered to be Cooked this morning." Always
attentive to the comfort of his men, he wanted them to be warm and
well-fed when they occupied the colonial fortifications. The soldiers,
including the so-called light infantry, were "incumbered with three days
provision, their knapsacks on their backs, which, together with car-
touche-box, ammunition and firelock, may be estimated at one hundred
and twenty-five pounds weight." The barges that were to carry them
had to be requisitioned and then run out and made shipshape; sailors
had to be assigned to man them, and they had to be rowed to Boston to
await the loading of the troops. All these steps took time, and while
Howe could certainly have moved several hours sooner against the
Americans, it is doubtful, given his tactics, that an earlier attack would
have materially affected the outcome of the battle.

The ten senior companies of grenadiers and the ten senior companies of light infantry had the honor of carrying out the assault; they,
with the Fifth and Thirty-eighth regiments, were to march to the Long
Wharf and embark from there. The remaining grenadiers and light
infantry, with the Forty-third and Fifty-second regiments, were to proceed to the North Battery. When these troops were embarked, the

Forty-seventh Regiment and the first battalion of marines were to stand by at the North Battery for further orders. The engineers were to wait at the South Battery, prepared to act under the orders of the chief of artillery.

The grenadiers got their name from the fact they had originally been formed to throw the heavy "hand bombs" that were first used in the early seventeenth century. They had long since ceased to be armed with grenades, but they were still the largest and most powerful soldiers, who, with the light infantry, were sent on special missions. The light infantry was also made up of men chosen for stamina and agility. Howe himself had recently developed special maneuvers for the light infantry that made use of their greater mobility and higher esprit.

The crossing of the troops from Boston in rows of barges made a brilliant spectacle. The scene was given a heightened drama by the leaping flames from buildings in Charlestown that had been set on fire by British cannonading. Burgoyne wrote a friend after the battle: "And now ensued one of the greatest scenes of war that can be conceived." He described the movements of soldiers, the cannonading of the British ships, and "straight before us a large and noble town in one great blaze—the church steeples, being timber, were great pyramids of fire above the rest; behind us, the church-steeples and heights of [Boston] covered with spectators . . . the hills round the country covered with spectators." There was the sound of all this, the crescendo of battle noises, "the crash of churches . . . and the whole streets falling together to fill the ear; the storm of the redoubts . . . to fill the eye; and the reflection that, perhaps, a defeat was a final loss to the British Empire in America, to fill the mind—made the whole picture, and a complication of horrour and importance, beyond anything that ever came to my lot to be witness to."

The available boats had room for only eleven hundred men, so they had to make two crossings. Howe and his second-in-command, General Robert Pigot, went on board Admiral Graves's flagship, the *Somerset,* to direct supporting fire. Finding that the ship had too deep a draft to get within effective range of the hill, they went ashore at Charlestown peninsula in the second crossing. Having landed his main force, Howe then sent for his reserves and waited.

Meanwhile the Americans were heartened to see Colonel Stark's New Hampshire regiment crossing Charlestown Neck. That these soldiers had arrived at all was something of wonder, since their march had been marked by a succession of misunderstandings, miscarried orders, poor discipline, and general confusion. Prescott and Putman, as they had observed the British preparations, had sent a series of dispatches to Artemas Ward in Cambridge urging that he send substantial reinforcements immediately. Ward, in response, had issued orders to various regiments who were, in consequence, marching about, "some under the vaguest notion of what they were expected to do." Stark's regiment was one of the few that seemed to have any notion of what its mission was and how to accomplish it.

As the colonel and his men in measured pace marched across the Neck under the intermittent fire of British warships, Henry Dearborn, who commanded the company at the head of the column, asked Stark why he did not hurry the men along that they "might be sooner relieved of the galling crossfire of the enemy." Stark replied cooly, "Dearborn, one fresh man in action is worth ten fatigued ones."

Once Stark had arrived on Bunker Hill and looked down from that slightly higher elevation on the fortifications below and on the British dispositions, he understood immediately where his small force was most needed and moved off to station the New Hampshire men with Captain Thomas Knowlton and the Connecticut militia at the rail fence. Cut hay lying in the field nearby was collected and piled over the fence, giving the appearance of breastworks where none in fact existed. Stark also noted that where the fence terminated, a bank eight or nine feet high dropped to the beach below where, with the tide out, there was a passage sufficiently wide for British soldiers to pass unobserved and take the American position in the rear. Some soldiers were detailed to block the narrow strip of beach with boulders and to defend the spot.

Instead of the thirty rounds of ammunition commonly issued prior to an engagement, Stark's men, according to Dearborn, were "destitute of ammunition" when they came up and were given, instead of cartridges, "a gill cup full of powder, fifteen balls, and one flint," a tragically inadequate supply, as events were to prove.

Prescott was the crucial figure in the unfolding drama. It had frequently been observed during the French and Indian War that Americans would fight well if they were well led. They would be well led on this day. Prescott was constantly among his men, a conspicuous figure in his blue uniform (indeed one of the few American officers in a uniform), encouraging them and directing their digging. When the bombardment began, he exposed himself conspicuously on the parapets to reassure the soldiers. Gage, studying Prescott from Boston through his spyglass, handed it to Abijah Willard, Prescott's Tory brother-in-law, and asked him if he knew the man in the blue uniform. When Willard identified him, Gage asked, "Will he fight?" "I cannot answer for his men," Willard answered, "but Prescott will fight you to the gates of hell."

As Prescott and his men watched anxiously, the British landed near Morton's Hill. Captain Knowlton and two hundred men were sent with cannon to try to forestall a British movement to Prescott's flank. The initial disposition of the British was alarming to Prescott. Instead of landing on the Charlestown side of the peninsula nearest Boston, they had disembarked and formed up at Morton's Point, and then advanced up the hill in three long lines. From Morton's Point they were only a few hundred feet from the rail fence where the colonials with two fieldpieces and Knowlton's two hundred Connecticut militia formed a thin barrier. But having formed, the British did not at once move forward.

Between the fort itself and the rail fence, someone had had the presence of mind to construct three flèches—tiny, separate, hastily erected embrasures, built of earth and fence posts, where a few dozen men could kneel or stand and fire enfilade or flanking fire down on any line of British soldiers that might advance to the rail fence. The flèches were a minor stroke of genius. They could only have been the inspiration of an experienced engineer, and it was thus probably Gridley, who had returned to the field at dawn, who proposed their construction. In any event, they played a crucial role in the action that followed.

While more small groups of soldiers filed up during the morning and took up posts where they could find them to reinforce Prescott, others were daunted by the heavy fire of British ships across the Neck and lingered on the mainland, afraid to cross. If Artemas Ward had shown skill and enterprise in supporting Prescott with major reinforcements, and all available cannon and ammunition had been rushed to Charlestown, ideally under Ward's own direction, the America positions might have been made vitually impregnable.

The colonial lines were in a state of confusion—the same disorder that characterized all of the events of that day on the American side. No one was sure who was in overall command, whether Putnam, who hurried about the field performing the functions of an entire staff—giving orders, chivvying laggards, placing late comers in position, dashing to Charlestown to speed up the movement of reinforcement—or Prescott, who concentrated all his attention on completing and extending the fortifications on the hill. More serious, since there was no chain of command, there was no way of assuring that orders were carried out except by personally supervising them or doing them oneself. As one eyewitness wrote to Samuel Adams a few days later, "To be plain it appears to me there never was more confusion and less command." There was a strange mixture of skill, enterprise, and military acumen combined with the most amateurish, muddled ineptitude. The ineptitude, surprisingly, turned out not to matter very much. The British persisted in such rigid and suicidal tactics that almost every American error and deficiency was redeemed.

In addition to the regiments and companies that were rounded up and dispatched to Charlestown to fill up Prescott's lines, a number of individuals simply took up their muskets and strode off to join in the defense of the American positions. Seth Pomeroy, a veteran of the French and Indian Wars, nearly seventy years old, recently elected a general of the Massachusetts line but not yet formally commissioned, had received word at his home in Northampton of a British plan to attack the colonial lines around Boston and had set out on horseback for Cambridge. He had ridden almost twenty-four hours when he appeared at the American lines. Putnam offered him the command, but Pomeroy, armed "with a gun of his own manufacture," which he had carried thirty years before at the siege of Louisberg, refused and took his place with Stark's New Hampshire men at the rail fence. Joseph Warren was another volunteer. President of the Massachusetts Provincial Congress, he had been acting as the chief executive officer of the colony; like Pomeroy, Warren had been elected major general but was not yet commissioned. He woke up on the morning of the seventeenth with a bad headache, but when he heard of the impending British attack, he rode to Charlestown and reported to Prescott at the redoubt. Prescott offered him command of the position, but Warren declined, as Pomeroy had done, and stationed himself with the other soldiers at the rim of the redoubt.

Other prominent Bostonians joined Warren in the breastworks. Joseph Otis, brother of Mercy and James, borrowed a gun and powder and took his place with the riflemen. James Winthrop, the librarian of Harvard College, also joined the defenders and was later wounded in the hand by a musket ball.

As the long, formidable lines of grenadiers and light infantry, the finest soldiers in the British army, began their orderly, disciplined advance across the open fields in the front of the colonial defenses, drums beating and regimental flags fluttering in the light breeze, the American officers passed among their men ordering them not to fire until the British were well within range. They were also to aim low—at the crossings of the soldiers' belts. They should pay particular attention to the officers. Marksmen had been designated to fire at the officers and guns given them with a soldier to load so that they could maintain their fire. In each unit, one line of men was ticked off to fire first, then to retire and load while the line behind them stepped up to blaze away.

With his reinforcements, Howe had some twenty-two hundred men ready to advance on the hill. As the attack began, he sent word to the commanders of the British ships whose fire had been sweeping the Neck to raise anchor and move to take the soldiers along the rail fence under enfilade fire. Fortunately for the colonials, the tide had turned, and the vessels found it impossible to carry out this mission.

Howe commanded the right wing of the advance, General Pigot the left. It was apparently Howe's intention, by taking command of the right wing, to force the left of the American position along the rail fence and thereby envelop the redoubt. But Howe made a key mistake in failing to cover the advance of his infantry on the rail fence by artillery. This oversight can perhaps be attributed to his having been deceived by the hay piled along the fence into believing that substantial earthworks had been thrown up that would be proof against cannon fire. Careful observation would have told him otherwise. Or, perhaps as likely, Howe believed that the colonials would not, in any case, stand fast against his infantry. If the hay were perceived to be hay and not earthworks, the men stationed behind it were almost as vulnerable to the massed fire of muskets as to artillery shrapnel. Further, to have preceded the attack on the fence with an artillery barrage would presumably have delayed the attack on the redoubt or sacrificed the coordinated attack of the two wings.

Howe sent eleven companies in column along the narrow beach. On the field above the bank, ten companies advanced in line, dressed right at intervals to preserve their order. To march so, in steady ranks across uneven ground with almost parade-ground regularity, was the supreme mark of disciplined, well-trained soldiers.

The tactic of sending the companies in column along the beach was a dubious one. The men were, to be sure, in defilade, that is, below the line of fire of the Americans manning the fence, and thus protected from fire to their left, with the harbor to their right. But the beach was blocked by boulders far more formidable than the rails and hay that provided such a flimsy shield for Stark's and Knowlton's men crouched along the fence. Only the first company, the famous Welsh Fusiliers, could return fire from the militiamen guarding the stone barricade. The company behind them had to take fire without being able to return it for fear of striking their own soldiers to their front. Howe would have done far better to have held ten of the eleven companies that he dispatched along the beach in reserve.

Howe's light six-pound artillery pieces bogged down in a marshy area as they were brought forward to fire on the fence, and it was impossible to fire them. The advance was almost painfully slow. The line was halted frequently to allow the heavier cannon in the rear to fire. Nevertheless, on came the redcoats, soon soaked with sweat (the garments from which they took their nicknames were thick woolen jackets), weighed down with their heavy packs and accouterments, which common sense would have left behind at their point of debarkation, while the Americans, sweating with the cold sweat of apprehension, waited for them.

Over the whole scene there hung what could not be called silence, for the cannon still thumped and thudded and the bands played, but a strange and heavy air of expectancy. A formidable and essential silence pervaded the ranks of the men who faced each other across the open field.

The first point of contact was on the beach, where, it must be presumed, Howe expected the Americans to give way promptly, thus rolling up the whole left flank along the fence. When the Fusiliers, with bayonets at the ready, were almost close enough to begin their final charge, a sustained fire poured out from the line of rocks in front of them with devastating accuracy. The timing was crucial; had the raw and inexperienced Americans fired too soon, their fire would have been far less effective and they undoubtedly would have provoked a bayonet charge—which would have swept them from their positions. To stop the British in their tracks, it was necessary only that the Americans should wait long enough, and wait they did. This was, as it turned out, the only bit of discipline they needed. It was also the most difficult discipline of all. Beside it the fact that they were in the highest degree unmilitary, that they often received orders resentfully and carried them out indifferently, faded into insignificance. They understood very well the point of waiting "until they could see the whites of their eyes," or whatever else served to properly calibrate the most precise and deadly distance at which they must fire, and they waited. And then they fired. And as inevitably as the climax of a Greek tragedy, the British soldiers fell down, some killed instantly, others mortally wounded, others wounded seriously enough to bear the scars the rest of their lives. Most demoralizing of all, officers and noncommissioned officers fell first, a devastating loss for an army trained to obey commands like robots. What was left of the front ranks fell back on the rear, as any amateur strategist could have predicted.

As the Welsh Fusilier officers tried to rally their men, they fell in the very act of urging them forward. The narrow beach was within seconds piled with bodies, and the proud companies of light infantry broke and ran headlong down the beach they had just marched up so splendidly, discarding their arms and equipment as they went until, well out of range, their frantic officers, with "the most passionate gestures and even to push forward ye men with their swords," at last rallied them.

The grenadiers marching above, although they could hear the constant thumping of musket fire, could not see the debacle below them on the beach. They continued their deliberate march towards the rail fence, obeying the shouted orders of officers and noncommissioned officers to close ranks and hold formation. They had to cross several fences, and after each crossing the lines had to be re-formed and dressed up smartly before the advance could be resumed. At last, after what seemed to all who observed the strange scene an infinity of time, they came to that spot where they faced the pointblank fire of the Americans along the fence. The colonials who watched them come on so boldly—among them Pomeroy and Stark and a number of veterans of the French and Indian War—must have watched with awe and incredulity, hardly believing their eyes, exulting at the sight of their enemy delivered into their hands—yet with a nagging fear that those splendid figures might somehow be invulnerable to musket fire and, like the figures in a nightmare, march on untouched, over and through the defenders, skewering them with their bayonets as they passed.

At last, when the redcoats were less than twenty yards away, the command was given and the colonials fired. Their bullets, they were relieved to observe, did penetrate. The fearsome British soldiers were, after all, flesh and blood. Like the light infantry on the beach, they fell down—tall, fine, brave men, trained to commit whatever folly they were ordered to commit; and now, having committed one of the greatest of those follies, they fell like slaughtered animals, a dreadful sight even to those who slaughtered them. The grenadiers, unlike the Welsh Fusiliers on the beach and the other light infantry companies behind them, fired, though with little or no effect, and then came on with their bayonets fixed. But they could have much more easily surmounted earthworks than the rail fence behind which the Americans crouched. Under relentlessly accurate short-range fire the grenadiers broke, some preserving a semblance of military order, the others in full retreat. The colonials, seeing the grenadiers in retreat, made as though to pursue them, but by "the prudence of the officers they were prevented leaving so advantageous a post."

Howe meanwhile watched the scene with horror. He saw the careful order, on which the success of any such operation rested, broken as the first and second lines of the light infantry "fell into disorder" and became hopelessly entangled and confused. "The Light Infantry," a veteran soldier later wrote, "at the same time being repulsed, there was a Moment that I never felt before."

That moment must rank in military history with the battle of Agincourt in 1415, where heavily armored French knights were cut down by English bowmen. The misnamed Battle of Bunker Hill was the symbolic military enactment of a profound change in Western history.

Such reflections could hardly have preoccupied Howe's mind at that moment. His only concern was how to retrieve an unthinkable disaster, the repulse and flight of British soldiers. The left of the British force, under the command of Pigot, had been too preoccupied with snipers' fire from Charlestown to make much progress. In addition, Howe's strategy called for turning the colonials' flank at the fence, rather than for a direct assault on the redoubt itself. That was to come after the left had been turned.

Howe now re-formed his forces for a second attack. Pigot's regiments were virtually intact. The light infantry had lost heavily in a few advance companies, but a number of companies from the beach were intact. So once more the British moved forward in two long red lines. This time fear must have lain in the hearts of the redcoats; their steps must have been a bit more weary, now faltering and uncertain, but locked still into that terrible precision by their training, their pride, and, at the lowest level, their basic reflexes. One Englishman wrote of the advance, "As we approached, an incessant stream of fire poured from the rebel lines. It seemed a continued sheet of fire for near thirty minutes. Our Light-Infantry were served up in Companies against the grass fence, without being able to penetrate—indeed how could we penetrate? Most of our Grenadiers and Light-Infantry, the moment of presenting themselves [within range] lost three-fourths, and many nine-tenths, of their men. Some had only eight and nine a company left;

some only three, four and five. On the left Pigot was staggered and actually retreated." This time the shattered remnants of the British companies held their ground, those who were left, until ordered by their officers to retire.

As Prescott later told the story of the action at the redoubt during the second British attack, he was left with "perhaps one hundred and fifty men in the fort. The enemy advanced and fired very hotly on the fort, and meeting with a warm reception, there was a very smart firing on both sides. After a considerable time, finding our ammunition was almost spent, I commanded a cessation till the enemy advanced within thirty yards, when we gave them such a hot fire that they were obliged to retire nearly one hundred and fifty yards before they could rally."

On Pigot's left were two buildings close together. One was a barn in which some of the militia who had been harassing Pigot's force from Charlestown had taken up positions after they were driven from the town by the fire. These improvised strongpoints not only prevented Pigot from outflanking Prescott's redoubt, they inflicted numerous casualties on the flank units during Pigot's advance to the redoubt. A British engineer and draftsman who drew a map of the peninsula after the battle circled an area near the buildings and wrote by it, "the Rebels behind all the Stone walls, Trees, and brushwood, etc. their numbers uncertain. . . ." The point is an important one. It shows that, as at the retreat from Lexington, the militia were able during the course of an engagement to take an initiative without formal orders from above when they saw an opportunity to play an effective part in the unfolding of the action. This is the most desirable quality in a soldier—the ability to see where some pressure, however slight, if skillfully applied can change the whole course of battle. Such action, because it must be improvised on the spot, is seldom the result of a command decision. The lack of formal organization on the American side, and the lack of control by the officers in command owing to primitive and amateurish staffwork, while often a grave handicap in conventional actions, was an asset in engagements where strategies had miscarried or where the changing pattern of combat had made such strategies obsolete.

Howe had twice tried and twice failed, terribly. A stream of wounded made their way to the boats to be evacuated to Boston. The field was littered with dead and dying. Howe's officers were said to have pleaded with him not to renew the attack, but with a stubbornness little characteristic of him, Howe persisted. Something must still be salvaged from what would otherwise appear to be one of the most devastating defeats in British military history. Indeed, to have suffered such losses and still have failed of the objective might have been enough to have finished Howe's career.

But it would be unfair to assume that Howe's thoughts at that moment were of his own reputation. He was probably in what might be described as a state bordering on shock. It must have seemed to him that the power and might of Great Britain, the pride and honor of Englishmen, the ability of every officer in the army to hold his head up, rested on renewing the attack until at last either the hill was captured or there was hardly a soldier left alive. And so, incredibly to the shaken soldiers and their officers and to the militiamen who watched from the fence line and the redoubt—and incredibly to us who read of it two hundred years later—the British lines were re-formed once more. The soldiers at last took off their packs. The artillery struggled to get its guns in position to rake the colonial defenses. The light infantry were to make a feint toward the fearsome rail fence; the main attack, led by Howe and finally supported with effective artillery, was to be against the redoubt itself.

Henry Clinton, who with Burgoyne had witnessed the whole extraordinary scene from the British batteries on Copp's Hill, could stand the role of spectator no longer. Leaving Burgoyne to make his excuses to Gage, Clinton secured a skiff and, rounding up a dozen or more soldiers, made for the shore near Charlestown—where his boat came under fire and two of his men were wounded before they could disembark. Once landed, Clinton added to his little detachment those of the wounded who were not too badly injured to walk and set off, with desperate and quixotic courage, to join in Howe's final assault. Clinton's action tells more eloquently than words the anguish that he and his fellow officers felt at the terrible spectacle they had witnessed. His pathetic little troop could not possibly affect the course of battle. Clinton wished to stand on Breed's Hill with Howe or die with him in the attack.

In the American positions, the principal problems were the overconfidence of the men and the low supplies of ammunition. The defenders had suffered few casualties and had shattered the enemy. There was every reason for them to feel euphoric. For many of them, it must have seemed that the British would now surely redress colonial grievances and grant the Americans that degree of independence within the British Empire that was consistent with sound constitutional principles.

Prescott, rummaging for powder, broke open several cartridges for the cannon and distributed them to the men in the redoubt. Some militia still hung back from crossing Charlestown Neck, and others, across, hovered on Bunker Hill, afraid to join their fellows on Breed's Hill or inhibited by what they conceived to have been their orders. Some of these began halfheartedly to fortify Bunker Hill, and a few of the bolder officers led small detachments down to reinforce the redoubt. But of ammunition and other supplies there was no sign. If the laggards who remained out of the battle had done no more than send their powder and bullets forward to the men under Putnam and Prescott, they would have done a service probably greater than their presence.

Putnam, riding his apparently endless circuit in search of men and supplies, overtook an officer and men rushing back down Bunker Hill toward the Neck with their cannon. Putnam ordered the officer to stop. Why was he fleeing from the field of battle? He had no ammunition for his pieces. Putnam dismounted and opened the boxes on the caisson. There were a number of cartridges in their compartments. Putnam ordered the officer back up the hill, and when this hero refused, Putnam threatened to shoot him if he did not obey. Reluctantly, the officer and his men returned to the crest of the hill, placed their cannon in position, and then, at the first opportunity, slipped off again. Another cannoneer behaved in much the same fashion. Putnam was convinced that the eventual defeat of the colonials was due to the refusal of the artillery officers to obey his orders. One immediate consequence was that militiamen, ordered to move up as reinforcements, cited the absence of artillery as their principal reason for refusing. Putnam was so incensed by their behavior that he believed the culprits should be punished by death and threatened to resign his commission "unless some exemplary punishment was inflicted" on them.

We have one shrewd eyewitness account of the confusion behind the American lines on Breed's Hill. John Chester was captain of the Wethersfield, Connecticut, company of militia, the only unit in the battle to be outfitted with uniforms. Chester had barely finished lunch in his lodgings at Cambridge when drums began beating to arms and bells ringing. The startled Chester saw Captain Putnam, the son of the general, galloping up and called out to ask what was going on. "Have you not heard." Putnam asked, reining up. "No." "Why the regulars are landing at Charlestown . . . and father says you must all meet, and march immediately to Bunker Hill to oppose the enemy."

Chester grabbed his own arms and ammunition and then ran to the church where his company was quartered. There the men had already been alerted and were almost ready to march. Feeling too conspicuous in their smart blue and red uniforms, they had put their frocks and trousers on over the uniforms. The road to Charlestown was jammed with men, but whether to witness the fighting or to engage in it, it was hard to tell. In the rush, companies got mixed together, men separated from their officers, and civilians mixed in with militia. When Chester and his men arrived at Bunker Hill, there was hardly a unit in the crowd that had preserved its identity. "Here they were scattered," Chester wrote, "some behind rocks and hay-cocks, and thirty men, perhaps, behind an apple tree, it was a common sight to see fifteen or twenty men assisting a wounded man from the battle field, where two or three could have done the job, and by their crowding and jostling and curiosity putting the poor wretch's life more in danger from suffocation than from his wounds." What had it been like? Were the British running? How had he been hit? A trickle of men passed Chester's company who had no better excuses for abandoning the field than that they "had been all night and day on fatigue, without sleep, victuals, or drink; and some said they had no officers to head them."

Finally Chester encountered the better part of a company, with its captain in the lead, headed for the rear. When Chester called out to ask him why he was leaving, the officer did not answer. The Connecticut captain stopped his own men and pointing his pistol at the captain ordered the officer to halt on peril of his life. When the officer and his men continued on, Chester's soldiers cocked their muskets, and one called out that they were ready to fire on command. At this the company finally halted and the officer began to make excuses, but Chester shut him up impatiently and ordered him back up the hill. "He complied," the captain wrote laconically.

For all his determination, Chester arrived only at the very tail end of the battle. For as he was approaching Bunker Hill, Howe launched his third and final assault.

The Americans in the redoubt and along the rail fence appeared more demoralized by their success than the British by their losses. While some soldiers had simply withdrawn, perhaps confident that the British could not renew the assault, and some had left the field because they were out of ammunition and could get no more, others came up to the line, anxious to be involved at least in the closing stages of the battle. Many who wandered about behind the American lines and even onto the fringes of the battlefield itself were no better than sightseers and sensation-seekers. In defense of the Americans, it should be said that while simple cowardice was undoubtedly the motive of a good many individuals or even small units that failed to reinforce Prescott and Putnam despite orders, the greater fault lay in the hopelessly inadequate staffwork. There were not enough officers to keep any account of the movement of various units or to supervise orders once they had been delivered. Many orders were simply carried by word of mouth and were badly garbled in transmission.

In the final British assault, Captain George Harris, commanding a company of the Fifth Grenadiers, prodded his unit as far as the redoubt. The British artillery had driven most of the American defenders from the breastworks running to the left of the redoubt. Harris found a breach in the works and tried to lead his men through. Twice they hung back as he advanced alone; finally a bullet grazed his head and knocked him unconscious. Assigning four soldiers to evacuate him, three of whom were themselves wounded in the process, young Lord Francis Rawdon, his lieutenant, took command of the company. The soldiers huddled under the breastwork, out of sight of the defenders, until some men began to cry impatiently, "Push on, push on." As soon as the grenadiers exposed themselves, the Americans in the redoubt "rose up and poured in so heavy a fire upon us that the oldest officers say they never saw a sharper action. They kept up this fire until we were within ten yards of them," Rawdon wrote. "Nay they even knocked down my captain, close beside me, after we had got into the ditch of the entrenchment. . . . There are few instances," Rawdon added, "of regular troop defending a redoubt until the enemy were in the very ditch of it, and [yet] I can assure you that I myself saw several pop their heads up and fire even after some of our men were upon the brim." In one British company there were only five privates left; the oldest assumed command of the others, and together they pressed on.

While the grenadiers had at last gained a foothold in the redoubt, the marines on Pigot's left were in serious straits. In the words of their adjutant, "When we came immediately under the work, we were checked by the severe fire of the enemy, but did not retreat an inch. We were now in confusion, after being broke several times in getting over the rails, etc. I did all I could to form the two companies on our right, which at last I effected, losing many of them while it was performing." The adjutant of the marines, believing it was safer to advance than to stand still, persuaded the officer commanding the unit on his right to order a bayonet charge on the redoubt, "and when we had got a tolerable order, we rushed on, leaped the ditch, and climbed the parapet, under a most sore and heavy fire."

The Americans had very few bayonets and none of the spears that were used in conventional eighteenth-century warfare to repel such a final charge. They were now without ammunition and without adequate reinforcements, and they had stood their ground longer than most trained troops would have done under similar circumstances. With a final volley aimed at the grenadiers as they rose above the parapet, the American fire "went out," in that famous and vivid phrase, spoken by a veteran of the battle years later, "like an old candle."

In this last charge Major Pitcairn, who had commanded the advance guard at Lexington, was shot and died in the arms of his son, an ensign in the marines, who carried his body to a boat, along "with a captain and a subaltern; also a sergeant, and many of the privates; and had we stopped there much longer, the enemy would have picked us all off."

Even before Prescott could give the order to retreat, many of the militiamen were running for their lives. Peter Brown (who fled with the rest) was sure that the Lord had spared his life, "altho I was in the fort when the Enemy came in, and jumped over the walls, and ran half a mile where Balls flew like Hailstones, and Canons roared like thunder." Amos Farnsworth, a veteran of Noodle Island, where the bullets had buzzed about his head like bees, was less fortunate this time. Fleeing the redoubt, he had only gone some fifteen rods when he was hit; but he was still able to make his escape, and he was no less diligent than before in praising the Lord "in preserving my life Althoe they fell on my right hand and on my left." A few refused to run or to retreat, but fought with clubbed muskets and stones and anything they could lay their hands on until they were bayoneted to death. Some thirty fell in the redoubt, among them Joseph Warren, very much "up to his knees in British blood." Their sacrifices were not in vain, for they undoubtedly gained time for the rest of the defenders to make their escape. Prescott refused to run, though he "stepped along with his sword up," parrying bayonet thrusts that missed him but pierced his clothes. As Burgoyne wrote: "The retreat was no flight: it was even covered with bravery and military skill."

As the redoubt was broken, the soldiers along the breastworks and, beyond it, the rail fence fell back in good order, taking their own wounded with them and helping to cover the retreat of the defenders of the redoubt. The British took only thirty-one prisoners, most of whom were men so severely wounded that they later died. Captain Chester and his Wethersfield militia, who had persevered so stoutly in their advance, arrived in time to help cover the American retreat. His lieutenant recorded his own emotions: "Good God, how the balls flew—I freely acknowledge that I never had such a tremor. . . . I confess, when I was descending into the Valley from off Bunker's Hillside by side of Captain Chester at the head of our Company, I had no more thot of ever rising the Hill again than I had of ascending to Heaven as Elijah did, Soul and Body together."

Captain Chester found a rather meager shelter behind a crumbling stone wall, and there he stationed his company "every man loading and firing as fast as he could . . . We covered their retreat till they came up with us . . . by a brisk fire from our small arms." The five or six minutes that the frightened company fought seemed like half an hour, but they had done well in their baptism of fire.

With the British at last in possession of the crude and simple fort and the Americans in retreat, it was time for an accounting. Howe had lost all his aides and most of his officers. Frequently exposed to colonial fire, he himself was unscathed, but some noticed that the general's leggings were streaked with red where he had walked through grass stained with the blood of his soldiers. Clinton came up just as Howe entered the captured redoubt and got permission from his exhausted superior to press on in pursuit of the retreating Americans. Clinton found this no easy task, but he pushed forward until he had driven the last colonial soldier from the Charlestown peninsula. Under Putnam's tireless direction, Winter Hill, which commanded the egress from the Neck, was fortified before the exhausted Americans fell asleep under a serene and peaceful June sky.

Clinton, reflecting on the hazards of that day, wrote a trenchant summary of the battle: "A dear bought victory, another such would have ruined us."

The Tories in Boston, when the wounded began to arrive in the city, "sent out every sort of carriage they had, as coaches, chariots, single-horse chaises, and even hand-barrows, to the water-side to assist in bringing to Boston, the wounded and killed officers and soldiers to their respective homes; likewise all the Physicians, Surgeons, and Apothecaries of Boston, instantly attended the wounded Officers, and gave them every assistance in their power." Then followed, according to a British officer, John Clarke, "a melancholy scene of several carriages, with the dead and dying officers; in the first of which was Major Williams bleeding and dying, and three dead Captains of the 52nd regiment. . . ." It was two days before all the wounded soldiers could be ferried over to Boston. The city was filled with the agony of war. It became a vast hospital and mortuary for the injured and the dead. Peter Oliver, a Boston Tory, wrote, "It was truly a Shocking Sight and Sound to see the carts loaded with those unfortunate Men and to hear the piercing Groans of the dying and those whose painful Wounds extorted the Sigh from the firmest minds." Oliver saw a soldier walking toward him with his white waistcoat, breeches, and stockings soaked with blood.

"My friend, are you wounded?" Oliver asked.

"Yes, Sir, I have three bullets through me," he replied, indicating to Oliver where he had been hit. And then, in Oliver's words, "he . . . with a philosophical Calmness began to relate the History of the Battle; and in all probability would have talked 'till he died, had I not begged him to walk off to the Hospital; which he did, in as sedate a Manner as if he had been walking for his Pleasure."

A Tory lady wrote bitterly that there were many in the British army who fell that day who were "of noble family, many very respectable, virtuous and amiable characters, and it grieves me that gentlemen, brave British soldiers, should fall by the hands of such despicable wretches as compose the banditti of the country, amongst whom there is not one that has the least pretension to be called a gentleman. They are the most rude, depraved, degenerate race, and it is a mortification to us that they speak English and can trace themselves from that stock."

The British casualties were staggering. They amounted to a total of 1,054, of whom 226 were killed and 828 wounded, or between 46 and 48 per cent of the British troops engaged. The officer corps suffered disproportionately; 19 had been killed and 70 wounded, among them all of Howe's own aides, who were struck down beside him. Regiments were far more than decimated. All except four of the grenadiers of the King's Own Regiment were killed or wounded. Only three of the Welsh Fusiliers who had led the attack along the beach survived unscathed. In companies with a normal strength of thirty-nine there were often only five or ten men left. The percentage of losses was so great that the British officers could suggest the carnage only by comparing Bunker Hill to the terrible battle of Minden in Westphalia in the Seven Years' War, which had become a byword as a result of its disastrous casualty rate. In no other engagement in history had the British lost so high a percentage of the troops engaged.

A British officer put the matter most acutely: "From an absurd and destructive confidence, carelessness, or ignorance, we have lost a thousand of our best men and officers and have given the rebels great matter of triumph by showing them what mischief they can do us." Another wrote: "We are all wrong in the head. My mind cannot help dwelling upon our accursed mistakes. Such ill conduct at the first set-out argues a gross ignorance of the most common rules of our profession, and gives us, for the future, anxious forebodings. . . . This wanton madness of ignorance nothing can excuse. The brave men's lives were wantonly thrown away." At a crucial juncture when artillery might have been of very material help, it was discovered that twelve-pound shot had been provided for the six-pounders, because, as one British officer wrote bitterly, of the "dotage of an officer of rank . . . who spends his whole time in dallying with the schoolmaster's daughters. God knows he is old enough—he is no Sampson—yet he must have his Delilah."

It fell to Gage, of course, as the commanding general, to write the official dispatches to Lord Barrington, Secretary of State for War. "These people," the chastened general wrote, "shew a spirit and conduct against us they never shewed against the French, and every body has judged of them from their former appearance and behaviour when joyned with the Kings forces in the last war, which has led many into great mistakes. They were now spirited up by a rage and enthusiasm as great as ever people were possessed of, and you must proceed in earnest or give the business up. . . . The loss we have sustained is greater than we can bear. . . . I have before wrote your Lordship my opinion that a large army must at length be employed to reduce these people, and mentioned the hiring of foreign troops. I fear it must come to that. . . ."

The official British reports quite understandably emphasized the heroism of the army and vastly exaggerated the number of colonials opposing them. Howe wrote to a friend in England, "I freely confess to you, when I look to the consequences of it, in the loss of so many brave officers, I do it with horror. The success is too dearly bought. . . . *Entre nous*, I have heard a bird sing that we can do no more this campaign than endeavour to preserve the town of Boston. . . . The intentions of the wretches are to fortify every post in our way; wait to be attacked at every one, having their rear secure, destroying as many of us as they can before they set out to their next strong situation, and, in the defense mode (the whole country coming into them upon every action), they must in the end get the better of our small numbers."

Howe, reflecting on the lessons taught by the Battle of Bunker Hill, advised Lord George Germain, Secretary of State for the Colonies, against trying to use Boston as a base for suppressing the rebellion. It would make far better sense, he wrote, to send some 12,000 soldiers to

New York to drive up the Hudson assisted by Canadians and Indians, with another 3,500 "to act upon the Connecticut River, and an equal Number to Garrison this Town and Environs. With this force of 19,000 Rank and File, an End to this, now formidable, Rebellion might take place in one Campaign. . . . With a Less Force than I have mentioned, I apprehend this war may be spun out untill England shall be heartily sick of it." Prophetic words.

On the American side, the principal achievements of the defenders of Bunker Hill (or, more accurately, Breed's Hill) flowed from the inability of the colonists to fight as the rules of eighteenth-century warfare indicated they should, holding their formations at all costs, loading and firing "by the numbers" and on command. Captain John Chester's words are most revealing in this respect. Coming up with his company at the end of the battle, he noted, "Here we lost our regularity, as every company had done before us, and fought as they did, every man loading and firing as fast as he could." This was not what they had been taught to do. They had been instructed to stand shoulder to shoulder, to load and fire together on orders from their captain. If they had been properly trained and disciplined like their counterparts, the British redcoats, they would have stood in formation, in two lines, one firing while the other loaded. And doubtless most of them would have been shot down in their tracks by the more numerous British, "since the small as well as the cannon shot were incessantly whistling by us." Improvisation was the strength of the Americans: the ability to respond to novel situations with novel solutions, on the spur of moment, without orders or directions; to take cover, to see the opportunity for a flanking maneuver, even to "aim" their muskets at a particular enemy soldier. On the battlefield that was, in some ways, the severest test of the new consciousness—of the independent, self-reliant individual—two modes of life met in one of the most dramatic confrontations in history. What had been hinted at by Lexington and Concord was proved in one of the most decisive engagements of modern times. The formal order encountered the instinctive, and spontaneous; expedients proved stronger than all the complex, intricate, and awesome formalisms that lay behind the British soldiers who marched like automatons toward the American lines and died like brave men condemned to death; "murdered," as a bitter British officer put it, by the stupidity and arrogance of their leaders—and murdered, in the words of the Tory lady, by men not one of whom had "the least pretension to be called a gentleman."

If all the events that occurred between 1765 and 1775 were contained in the initial episodes of resistance to the Stamp Act, the eventual outcome of the American Revolution was equally contained in the battle for Breed's Hill, a relatively worthless piece of real estate, militarily speaking, which was paid for by the lives of more than two hundred men and the grievous wounds of many more. Bunker Hill proved that, ultimately, the Americans must triumph, however long it might take and whatever the cost.

So far as it is possible to estimate, the colonials on Breed's Hill never numbered more than between 1,500 and 1,700 men, of whom some 450 were either killed or wounded. Most of these casualties were incurred in the redoubt and at the breastworks during the last charge, and in the flight that followed. Although lower than the British, the casualty rate of the Americans was very high.

Initially, the triumph of the Americans was tempered by the fact that they had been driven from their fortifications by the British and had suffered heavy casualties, the most grievous being the death of Joseph Warren. The brillant, charming, and courageous Warren had died, in his cousin's words, "with as much Glory as Wolfe on the Plains of Abraham," and that, simply, was as much glory as could fall to human lot. A British officer wrote that "he died in his best clothing; everybody remembers his fine, silk-fringed waistcoat." He was buried on the field of battle. The British officer detailed to bury the dead reported, "Doctr. Warren . . . I found among the slain, and stuffed the scoundrell with another Rebel into one hole and there he and his seditious principles may remain."

Warren was certainly one of the most attractive figures in the gallery of patriot leaders. A handsome, gifted man, an excellent physician, a brilliant speaker, and a scion of one of the oldest and most respected families of the Bay Colony, he was known all over Boston for his generosity in treating the poor without pay and for his lack of any "side" or stiffness of manner. He and Paul Revere had formed a strange but close alliance—the stout, muscular craftsman and the aristocratic doctor. It was Warren who had proposed Revere for the Long Room Club, a society of Harvard men, amateur scholars, and prosperous merchants—the elite of the city. After the Tea Party a popular ballad most appropriately linked their names:

Our Warren's there and bold Revere
With hands to do and words to cheer
For Liberty and laws.

Even Gage could not resist Warren; and Warren wrote generously of the general: "I have frequently been sent to him on committees, and have several times had private conversations with him. I have thought him a man of honest upright principles, and one desirous of accommodating the difference between Great Britain and her colonies in a just and honorable way." However, Gage was, Warren also thought, too much influenced by "that malicious group of harpies whose disappointments make them desirous to urge the Governor to drive every thing to extremes"—the Tories of Boston.

Warren had been the first doctor in the colony to set up a course of instruction for young men who apprenticed themselves to him. Moreover, he carried on his political activities without stinting his practice. His medical records show that he seldom made fewer than ten or twelve house calls a day, and sometimes as many as twenty. Samuel Adams' son was one of his apprentices. John Quincy Adams, John Adams' eldest son, was devoted to him; he had saved young John Quincy's right hand when a serious fracture had become infected and other doctors had advised amputation. To John Adams he was "our dear Warren," as beloved as a member of the family. Warren bitterly resented imputations by the British that the Americans were cowards who would refuse to fight. His pupil William Eustis recalled him exclaiming, "They say we will not fight. By God I hope I die up to my knees in British blood."

Under such circumstances there was little inclination on either side to exult. The battle had demonstrated many shortcomings among the colonials. How was it to be explained that with 15,000 American militia camped around Boston, only some 1,500 or 1,700 could be marched to Breed's Hill to assist in its defense? Staffwork was nonexistent. Putnam was his own entire staff; Prescott did without. Artemas Ward, the commanding general, showed little energy or enterprise. A number of units, ordered to battle, found excuses for not crossing Charlestown Neck, and others lingered on Bunker Hill, quite literally above the strife. Still others abandoned the field of battle. The triumph was thus due far less to the skill and initiative of the colonials than to the colossal blunders of the British. At the same time, much credit must be given to Prescott for his leadership and courage, to Gridley for laying out defenses that proved to be remarkably effective, and to Putnam for his inexhaustible efforts at rallying support for Prescott; but most of all to the militia and their officers who manned the American defenses, especially Stark and his New Hampshire men at the rail fence, which turned out to be the most crucial area on the battlefield.

For the British, it must be said that they made almost every error it was possible to make. If we assume the original strategic error of failing to cut off Charlestown Neck as Clinton had suggested and thus putting the colonials "in a bag," as a British officer put it after the conflict, we must add a number of tactical errors on the part of Howe. The most serious of these was failing to place gunboats in position to deliver enfilade fire along the line of the rail fence, which would have driven the defenders to retreat or to take cover, or would at least have greatly diminished their effectiveness. The second major error, and perhaps the most decisive one of the day, was sending the light infantry along the beach in a column of companies while the grenadiers above attacked in line. The eleven companies of light infantry, had they been added to Pigot's force and directed against the redoubt, would probably have broken that position in the first assault.

In defense of Howe, it must be said that there was every reason to believe that the redoubt was the most formidable point in the colonial defenses. It was sound tactics, therefore, to avoid a frontal attack on it, and to attempt to turn the flank.

In every battle there is a key to the enemy's defensive system. Usually that key is unperceived by the defender as well as by the enemy; both are distracted by the formal aspects of the engagement. The defenders fortify what they have been taught to fortify—the dominant or commanding feature of the terrain. The attackers almost invariably accept the decision of the defenders by attacking the major fortified zone or trying to outflank it. The key to the defensive position in the case of a successful attack is discerned by a certain genius, the essential element of which is careful reconnaissance or, more frequently, luck. The redoubt, which looked the most formidable part of the American defenses, was actually the most vulnerable. The rail fence, which attracted Howe's attention as being the most easily broken part of the colonial defenses, was virtually impregnable. It is safe to say that Howe could have attacked it frontally all day without success. The first sustained attack against the redoubt succeeded. And this success was by no means entirely due to the Americans' lack of ammunition. It would be unfair, however, to blame Howe for believing the rail fence to be the weakest part of the Americans' defense. Most commanders of the time, however experienced, would have made the same error. A proper reconnaissance would have cleared up the impression that the hay piled against the fence was earth. It would also have disclosed the fences and some of the other terrain features that impeded the progress of the British soldiers and delayed the attack. With that information Howe might have decided to direct his artillery at the fence, which was extremely vulnerable to artillery fire, rather than at the redoubt, which was well protected against cannon and shrapnel. Canister directed against the fence would have had a devastating effect on the relatively unprotected defenders.

Perhaps Howe did not bother to reconnoiter the terrain in front of the American lines because of the illusion that it was all entirely visible, laid out like a relief map open to inspection from a hundred vantage points. But there is no substitute—map or photograph—for a reconnaissance of the terrain. Perhaps Howe did not bother with a reconnaissance because basically he held the colonials in such contempt that he did not think it necessary to obey the most basic rules of warfare. These rules were, after all, devised to cope with real soldiers, not disorderly civilians. However, having made the initial error of sending the light infantry in column along the beach, Howe compounded that by sending the grenadiers off in line. They should certainly have gone forward in column, covered by fire from skirmishers between the columns and formed into line only as they approached within musket range of the fence—where again, by the accepted tactics of the day, they might have received covering fire from small detachments as the main body advanced.

But every tactical error flowed from the original error of holding the colonials in contempt, and this was an error that lay in the bones rather than the conscious minds of the British.

After the battle, life in Boston returned, it could not be said to normal, but to that of a besieged city. Peter Oliver expressed the situation rather sardonically: "in the mean Time, both Armies kept squibbling at each other, but to little Purpose; at one Time a Horse would be knocked in the head, and at another Time a Man would be killed, or lose a Leg or an Arm; it seemed to be rather in Jest than in Earnest; at Times a shell would play in the Air like a Sky Rocket, rather in Diversion and there burst without Damage; and now and then, another would fall in the Town, and there burst, to the Terror [of the populace] or breaking of a few Panes of Glass; and during the whole Blockade, little else was done but keeping both Armies out of the way of the Idleness, or rather the whole Scene was a idle Business."

The burning of Charlestown became a particular grievance to the colonists. A popular song expressed the common sentiment.

> To see a town so elegantly form'd.
> Such buildings graced with every curious art,
> Spoil'd in a moment, on a sudden storm'd,
> Must fill with indignation every heart. . . .

And such chastisement coming from a state
Who calls herself our parent, nurse and friend—
Must rouse each soul that's noble, frank, and great,
And urge us on our lives and all to spend!
But God "whose laws are still the same" will come
To the aid of his tormented children.

Thy crimes, oh North, shall then like spectres stand,
Nor Charlestown hindmost in the ghastly roll,
And faithless Gage, who gave the dread command,
Shall find dire torments gnaw upon his soul.

The Battle of Bunker Hill provided the strongest possible incentive for the colonials to fortify every promontory that looked down on Boston, and they were not slow to respond. Under the direction of bookseller Henry Knox, they dug like industrious moles until Gage wrote gloomily, "they have fortifyed all the Passes and Heights round this Town from Dorchester to Medford or Mystick." They needed only sufficient heavy cannon to make Boston untenable for its British garrison. Knox, indeed, had sold Nathanael Greene the volumes in which he studied "the military art." Knox was a tall man with an impressive bearing and ruddy complexion, who had courted Lucy Flucker, the daughter of the Loyalist secretary of Massachusetts. They married over the strenuous objections of Lucy's parents, and a few weeks after Lexington escaped from Boston with Knox's sword sewn into the lining of his wife's cape.

The busy and ingenious Burgoyne chaffed under the increasingly morose and withdrawn Gage. He proposed to North that he be dispatched "as an individual member of Parliament, a friend to human nature" to confer with Congress in "the great work of conciliation." He also did his best to weaken Gage's increasingly shaky standing with his superiors in England by criticizing his administration in considerable detail and implying that he, Burgoyne, would have done infinitely better. Burgoyne was distressed at the lack of funds to do those things that needed to be done. There was not even enough money to pay spies: "Very few or no spies," he wrote. "We are therefore intirely ignorant of what they are about in the neighborhood. . . . And what renders the reflection truly provoking," Burgoyne added, "is that there was hardly a leading man among the rebels, in council, or in the field, but at proper time, and by proper management, might have been bought." Burgoyne's behavior reminds us that there is nothing more mischievous than a clever and energetic man with too much time on his hands.

PART V

The Second Continental Congress

THE Second Continental Congress was faced with the fact of a country at war. It had to take on all the responsibilities of a national government in a time of severe crisis, and it had to do so with powers entirely inadequate to the task.

While the colonial forces around Boston began the tedious and demanding task of trying to convert themselves from civilian levies into a reasonably disciplined army and their leaders struggled to find ways of feeding and equipping them, the Second Continental Congress began to assemble. The progress of the Massachusetts delegates to the meeting of the Congress was another triumphal procession. John Hancock had replaced James Bowdoin, but the two Adamses, Thomas Cushing, and Robert Treat Paine were once more delegates. "We are treated with great Tenderness, Sympathy, Friendship, and Respect. I have no Doubts now of the Union," John Adams wrote to his wife. The news of Lexington and Concord had made the delegates heroes.

Silas Deane and the delegates from Connecticut were greeted on the outskirts of New York, Deane wrote, by "a battalion of about eight hundred men in uniform and bayonets fixed, with a band of music. . . . You can easier fancy than I describe the amazing concourse of people: I believe well nigh every carriage in the city, and thousands on foot

543

trudging and sweating through the dirt. . . ." In the city itself, "the doors, the windows, the stoops, the roofs of the plazzas, were loaded with all ranks, ages, and sexes: in short I feared every moment lest someone would be crushed to death; but no accident . . . the populace insist[ed] on taking out our horses and drawing the carriages by hand."

In Philadelphia, John Adams was delighted with the activity he observed in the City of Brotherly Love. "The Martial Spirit throughout this Province," he wrote James Warren, "is astonishing. It rose all of a Sudden, Since the News of the Battle of Lexington. Quakers and all are carried away with it. Every day in the Week Sundays not excepted they exercise, in great numbers. The Farmer [John Dickinson] is a Coll. [Colonel] and Jo. Reed another. . . . Uniforms and Regimentals are as thick as Bees, America will soon be in a Condition to defend itself by Land against all Mankind."

When Congress assembled on May 10, there were "a number of new and very ingenuous faces" among them. The most famous addition was Benjamin Franklin, who had resigned his duties as colonial agent in London and had arrived in Philadelphia only five days before Congress convened. Franklin, "a great and good man . . . composed and grave . . . very reserved," was not, however, the equal "in fortitude, rectitude and abilities," in Adams' opinion, to young James Wilson, a Scottish immigrant, who had studied law with John Dickinson. George Washington's tall and commanding figure, attired in the blue and buff uniform of a Virginia militia officer, was much in evidence. Washington, John Adams wrote, "by his great experience and abilities in military matters is of much service to us." However, in the Second Congress, as in the first, the Massachusetts delegates found "a great many Bundles of weak Nerves. We are obliged to be as delicate and soft and modest as possible."

The first matter before Congress turned out to be a prickly one. The Massachusetts Provincial Congress had turned its attention to the problem of framing a constitution, and Massachusetts wished to have the sanction of Congress to proceed with this task. Urging Congress to respond to the request for support, John Adams noted that the enterprise would be a demanding one; the opportunity facing the Colonies was unique. The people of America, people of "more intelligence, curiosity, and enterprise" than history could show, must all be consulted. The framers of the new constitutions must be attentive to the "wisest writers and invite the people to erect the whole building with their own hands, upon the broadest foundations." This could be done "only by conventions of representatives chosen by the people of the several colonies," and Congress should recommend "to the people of every colony to call such conventions . . . and set up governments of their own, under their own authority, for the people were the source of all authority and of all power."

Adams' speech was one of the milestones of the Revolutionary era. Although a majority of the delegates nervously rejected the New Englander's request that Congress officially endorse the establishment of Revolutionary governments, their attention was directed (however reluctantly) to the issue of acting independently. The delegates' consideration of the making of constitutions brought to the fore the colonies' relationship with the mother country. The method that Adams proposed—the calling of constitutional conventions—came to be the course that was followed, in fact, by most colonies when they finally took up the task. Adams' insistence that the people were the legitimate source of all governmental power and must be involved as directly as possible in the framing of constitutions was an idea that had long been voiced by liberal thinkers. Now the idea of government by the people was to have a trial. In other words, "the people" had never, at least in modern times, been involved in the drafting and approval of a constitution. In fact, no such thing as a written constitution governing a nation existed in the world, if we except the rather unique case of the Swiss Confederation.

The special and unique American contribution to those arrangements under which people live together in relative harmony was to be in the framing of constitutions. For the next fourteen years, their principal intellectual energies were to flow in this direction. If the British brought parliamentary government to its highest and most expressive form, the Americans ushered in the age of constitution-making, an enterprise new in the history of the world and carried out on an unprecedented scale by several score of provincial politicians. Framing constitutions was, in a manner of speaking, the way Americans "framed" themselves, the way they formed and directed their own consciousness. In colonial America a notable and novel consciousness had come into existence that made the resistance to Great Britain possible. That consciousness had to find a practical political form; the form it found was constitutional. This making of constitutions, which culminated in the Federal Constitution, was the most striking intellectual venture in American history.

Adams' speech to the largely unsympathetic delegates at the second meeting of the Continental Congress was like a trumpet blast announcing the beginning of "a new series of ages." While most of his colleagues preferred to put their fingers in their ears (the resolution was allowed to "lie on the table"), the sound of the trumpet would go on echoing and reverberating until no American could shut it out.

If the topic was tabled in the Congress's meeting hall, it was actively canvassed "out of doors." What form should the constitutions of the respective colonies take? When John Rutledge of South Carolina asked Adams what form he thought proper for the government of a state, Adams answered that "any form that our people would consent to institute would be better than none, even if they placed all power in a house of representatives, and they should appoint governors and judges." But Adams "hoped they would be wiser, and preserve the English Constitution in its spirit and substance, as far as the circumstances of this country required or would admit."

The most pressing issue before Congress was the appointment of a commander in chief for the army at Boston. Artemas Ward was too fat, Israel Putnam too old, William Heath too inexperienced. Charles Lee, an Englishman (indeed the only prominent Lee in the American Revolution who was not a member of the redoubtable Virginia clan of Lees), was, besides Washington, the leading condidate for the command of the Continental Army. "General" Lee had, in fact, considerable military experience. As a young lieutenant in the Forty-fourth Foot, he had been with Washington on General Edward Braddock's disastrous campaign, had been adopted by the Mohawk Indians, and had married the daughter of a Seneca chief. Badly wounded at Ticonderoga in 1758 during the French and Indian War, he recovered in time to participate in the capture of Montreal, retiring after the war with the rank of major. He subsequently joined the Polish army as a soldier of fortune and there, in campaigns against the Turks, was promoted to major general. His current sympathies were entirely with the colonies in their contest with the mother country, and he believed the Americans quite capable of holding their own against British soldiers. He had written to a friend in 1774: "By all that is sacred, these are a fine people, liberal, enlightened, sensible and firm. Your Mansfields and Norths may play their wretched tricks, have recourse to their paltry finesses, may bluster and bellow, but they will never be able to frighten these men out of their liberties." After Lexington and Concord he wrote to Lord Percy that the cause of America was "the cause of Great Britain as well as of America; it is the cause of mankind." "When I see a minister violent and tyrannical like North, mowing down whole communities, merely to indulge his hereditary hatred of liberty . . . I think it is the duty of every honest man and friend to humanity to do his utmost to defeat the diabolical purpose." Such sentiments, of course, commended Lee to sincere patriots. In spite of his thoroughly eccentric appearance and foppish manners, many patriot leaders were impressed by Lee's credentials and flattered that an English officer with a distinguished military record (he had been promoted to lieutenant colonel on half-pay in the British army in 1772) should espouse the colonial cause.

The matter of selecting a commander in chief was complicated by the fact that the troops around Boston were all, at this point, New Englanders with their own traditions and their own crotchets. In addition to the differences in manners and outlook, to place them under the command of a general from another section—the Middle Colonies or the South—would seem to imply that New England could produce politicians and soldiers in abundance, but no military leader sufficiently competent to take command of "the New England army," as John Adams (and others) called it.

Overriding these considerations, at least for the New England delegates, was the need to rivet the alliance of Virginia and Massachusetts, on which the success of any intercolonial union and any joint military effort must depend. In the minds of John and Samuel Adams, it seemed clear that George Washington was the only man who completely filled the bill as commander in chief. Their determination to support the tall, reserved Virginian was somewhat complicated by the fact that both men knew that their fellow delegate, John Hancock, yearned to be commander in chief himself.

Deeply disturbed by the evident inclination of New England delegates to waffle and delay, John Adams took his cousin on a stroll around State House yard one morning before the Congress convened. He was, he told Samuel, determined to force the issue. He intended "to make a direct motion that Congress should adopt the army before Boston, and appoint Colonel Washington in command of it." Sam agreed to support him.

As soon as the delegates had been called to order, Adams asked to be recognized by Hancock, who was presiding over this Second Congress. The army around Boston, Adams declared, was badly in need of unified leadership. If Congress did not take responsibility for it, the army might well disintegrate, and the colonial cause with it. There was, Adams pointed out in the classic style of nominators, a man in that very room splendidly equipped to assume command of the army at Boston. As he described the talents of his nominee, Adams noticed, as he thought, a look of beatification pass over John Hancock's sallow features. The president of Congress was quite evidently confident that his fellow delegate was describing him. Who else better fitted the description: "an independent fortune, great talents, and . . . excellent character." When Adams, having created sufficient suspense, named Washington as his choice, Hancock's face fell; "mortification and resentment were [expressed] as forcibly as his face could exhibit them." Washington, embarrassed by the New Englander's encomiums and anxious to give free reign to debate, slipped quickly out of the room.

Adams' nomination of Washington was seconded by Sam Adams. Peyton Randolph, perhaps displaying some envy of his fellow Virginian, argued that New England already had a perfectly good general in Artemas Ward. Paine likewise supported Ward, while Cushing suggested that New England soldiers might resent being commanded by a foreigner. John Adams, seeing that there was substantial opposition to Washington, urged that the matter be put over to another session. This gave the two Adamses a chance to line up votes for Washington. In John Adams' words, "Pains were taken out of doors to obtain an unanimity." Adams did his persuading so successfully that soon there was a majority for Washington. Shortly John and Sam Adams, with help from some of the Virginia delegates, were able to persuade those members who were opposed to withdraw their opposition. On June 15, the Virginian was nominated and unanimously elected commander in chief of the Continental Army at Cambridge. Congress at the same time took the army officially under its wing. John Adams wrote to his wife two days later that "the modest, the virtuous, the amiable, generous, and brave George Washington, Esquire," had been appointed commander in chief, an appointment that would have "a great effect in cementing and securing the union of these colonies," which "the liberties of America depend upon, in a great degree."

Since Washington was to become the greatest figure in American history and one of the greatest figures in world history—in the minds of many of his nineteenth-century admirers, unquestionably the greatest—we might pause to consider what that greatness consisted of.

Washington was the younger son of a middle-aged father who died when the boy was eleven. He had grown up at Mount Vernon under the tutelage of a much older brother, Lawrence. What little formal education Washington had had ended when he was thirteen. In this respect, he was no different from most of the young men of the planter class. Some Virginians went to Princeton, some to William and Mary, and some to one of the colleges at Oxford or Cambridge. But these were what we would call today the intellectuals, the Madisons or Jeffersons. "Going away to college" did not become fashionable in the South until after Washington's youth. He had a modest talent or knack for mathematics and a natural inclination for the military life. He had seen a little of the world, accompanying his brother on a trip to the West Indies. On his brother's death in 1752, Washington, then only twenty years old, fell heir to one of the handsomest estates in Virginia, and to what was for the day a comfortable fortune.

His military experience was considerable for a colonial. At the outset of the French and Indian War, Governor Robert Dinwiddie sent him on the dangerous (and fruitless) mission of warning the French to give up their posts on the frontier in the region of Ohio. When he returned he was made lieutenant colonel in the Virginia militia. At the head of two companies he made a long march to the Ohio country and there defeated the French and Indians at the battle of Great Meadows. At Fort Necessity, he was surrounded by a much larger body of the enemy and forced to surrender. As aide-de-camp to General Braddock, he was involved in the Battle of the Wilderness, and emerged with whatever laurels were to be garnered from that mismanaged and disastrous campaign. The following year, at the age of twenty-three he was made commander of the Virginia militia. For the next two years he directed some seven hundred Virginia militiamen in the defense of the province.

In 1759, at the end of the fighting part of the French and Indian War, Washington resigned his commission and married Martha Dandridge, the widow of Daniel Parke Custis, a wealthy planter. Martha's fortune plus his own made him one of the richest men in America, and at Mount Vernon he turned enthusiastically to farming and improving his plantation.

As a young man Washington had fallen deeply in love with Sally Fairfax, the wife of his patron and close friend, William Fairfax. When he became engaged to Martha Custis, Sally Fairfax, who had, doubtless wisely, stopped writing to Washington some time before, wrote to congratulate him on his coming marriage. In reply, Washington poured out, in cryptic but unmistakable language, the tragedy of his love for his friend's wife. "How joyfully," he wrote, "I catch at the happy occasion of renewing a correspondence which I feared was disrelished on your part, I leave to time, that never failing expositor of all things, and to a monitor equally faithful in my own breast to testify. In silence I now express my joy; silence which in some cases, I wish the present, speaks more intelligently than the sweetest eloquence." He loved Martha Custis, but he wished to make clear to Sally that she was the one consuming passion of his life, and he longed for some hint from her that she felt as he did. He who had felt "the force of her thousand amiable beauties in the recollections of a thousand tender passages that I could wish to obliterate," knew that he could not blot out the memories; they would be a pain to him as long as he lived, for there was "a Destiny which has control of our actions, not to be resisted by the strongest efforts of Human Nature."

"You have drawn me, dear Madam, or rather I have drawn myself, into an honest confession of a simple Fact," Washington continued, "Misconstrue not my meaning; doubt it not, nor expose it. The world has no business to know the object of my Love, declared in this manner to you, when I want to conceal it. . . . But adieu to this till happier times, if I ever shall see them . . . I dare believe you are as happy as you say, I wish I was happy also."

This story is repeated here because it seems to give an essential clue to Washington's character. It is not how we generally think of him: a passionate, lovelorn young man who cannot resist proclaiming that love. For a man of Washington's restraint, the letter is a touchingly romantic proclamation, full of anguish, baring a wound that would never entirely heal. The importance of Washington's devotion to Sally has not been sufficiently noticed by historians and biographers of Washington. Where they have mentioned it at all, they have treated it as a colorful and romantic episode in Washington's youth, something that makes him seem more "human." The fact is that Washington's love for Sally Fairfax was one of the central experiences of his life. We know that he was a man capable of the most intense emotions, however restrained. It is clear that the two principal passions of an otherwise rather commonplace young Virginia gentleman were his military career and his love for Sally Fairfax.

Indeed, it is striking how neatly he fits here into the role of the tragic hero of the medieval *chanson de geste*. In those stories a knight found his Destiny (sometimes in the form of a magic potion) by falling hopelessly in love with the wife of his king or patron, to whom he felt deep obligations of loyalty, as, for example, in the stories of Tristan and Iseult or Lancelot and Queen Guinevere. The tragic hero of the *chanson* struggles desperately to master his passion, but since the passion, hopeless of fulfillment without violating his honor, is part of his "Destiny," he can never subdue it. Difficult as it may be to think of George Washington as a tragic hero, to do so is vital to an understanding of the man in his full dimensions. Without the passion, Washington would have been what historians have so often seemed determined, albeit inadvertently, to make him—a pompous prig.

If Washington could love passionately, he could also feel deep anger and rage. Jefferson, writing much later of a cabinet meeting, noted, "Washington got into one of those rages where he cannot command himself." The people who knew him well often saw him drop that mask of reserve, and when it was dropped in anger the effects were terrifying to those against whom that occasional rage was directed, and to those who witnessed it as well.

The secret of Washington's extraordinary moral force, then, was his passionate nature. In him was a fierce ambition that, at the same time, never compromised with "honor" and "duty." To control his passionate nature, Washington adopted a stoic reserve. This stoicism was the quality John Adams, a man with some self-control of his own, most admired about the general. Above all else he possessed "the gift of silence. This I esteem as one of the precious talents," Adams wrote to Benjamin Rush after Washington's death. "He had great self-command. It cost him a great exertion sometimes, and a great constraint; but to preserve so such equanimity as he did required great capacity." Adams was not alone in his admiration. The Protestant notion of the force of will, which Washington seemed to epitomize, was reinforced by America's admiration for the virtues of republican Rome: Stoicism and "condescension," unselfish public service, "republican" simplicity, and dignity. Washington seldom lost his self-control. It was this equanimity, this composure in the face of every setback, defeat, and disappointment, for which his countrymen honored him above all else. If he did not learn it in the suffering of a love that his destiny had made inaccessible to him, he certainly tempered it in that love. A man who has given up what is for him the dearest thing in life has always thereafter a certain aloofness, a certain detachment; having survived the keenest anguish of all, he knows himself superior to most of the tribulations that the world can place before him. Having denied him what he most wished, the world had lost, to a substantial degree, the power to wound or dismay him further.

If Washington with his disciplined will was the ultimate Protestant hero, he was also the classical hero revived. It was as though an ancient Roman had appeared in modern guise, to lead the American republic.

Moreover, a people in whose imaginations the king-father had loomed so large must have longed subconsciously for a figure as powerfully consoling as the British monarch had once been. In this sense Washington was to become the residuary legatee of George III, an image of total benevolence. Because the myth-making popular mind worked its own irresistible way with the idealized Washington, it has been difficult for historians to make much headway in peeling off those layers of pious wrapping. What is plain enough is that he is no longer a functioning hero for most Americans, and especially for those of the younger generation. And this is not simply because "the true George Washington" has been obscured by the mythical George Washington, but rather because that quality of self-control that his contemporaries so much admired, is seen today as a classic form of the "repression" that has produced the "up-tight" American society.

Certainly, one of the most important aspects of Washington's power to command was his "presence." He was very tall. He was handsome, strong as a bull, and of remarkable stamina, physical and emotional. The quite evident Roman contours of his face made a strong impression on his contemporaries. In other words, he was the almost perfect embodiment of all those qualities that his age, and several subsequent ones, most admired. Abigail Adams shared her husband's admiration for the general. After dining with Washington she gave a classic description of him: "He is polite with dignity, affable without familiarity, distant without haughtiness, grave without austerity, modest, wise, and good." Washington was no prude. He loved the theatre, elegant clothes, fine horses, handsome women—and those women invariably responded to his courtly attentions.

This was the man who took over command of what was now the Continental Army from Artemas Ward on July 3, 1775; a man restlessly ambitious, strong-willed, and passionate—all concealed beneath that Stoic equanimity. He would need all that equanimity for the task ahead of him.

Washington wrote (somewhat melodramatically) to his brother, John Augustine, "I am now to bid adieu to you, and to every kind of domestick ease, for a while. I am imbarked on a wide ocean, boundless in its prospect and from whence, perhaps, no safe harbour is to be found. I have been called upon by the unanimous Voice of the colonies to take Command of the Continental Army." It was, Washington claimed, not altogether candidly, "an honour I neither sought after, nor desired. . . . It was by no means a thing of my own seeking, or proceeding from any hint of my friends."

Eliphalet Dyer, one of the Connecticut delegates, assured Connecticut's Governor Jonathan Trumbull that Washington was "clever, and if any thing too modest. He seems discreet and Virtuous, no harum Starum ranting Swearing fellow but Sober, steady and Calm." Dyer added, "I imagine he will be very Agreeable to the Genius and Climate of New England." And Governor Trumbull in turn wrote a splendid Biblical-sounding letter to Washington congratulating him on taking command: "Now, therefore, be strong and very courageous. May the God of the Armies of Israel shower down the blessings of his divine providence on you; give you wisdom and fortitude; cover your head in the day of battle and danger; add success; convince your enemies of their mistaken measures. . . ."

The election of Washington as commander in chief was the first and, for Congress, comparatively the simplest step. He must have a staff, and a number of other officers must be appointed. John Adams wrote to James Warren that "nothing has given more Torment, than the Scuffle we have had in appointing the General Officers." Here judicious logrolling was necessary. Each colony wished to be properly represented, and its delegates constituted a determined lobby for this name or that. Having gotten Washington appointed commander in chief, Sam and John Adams fought with all the weapons at their disposal for Charles Lee as third in the chain of command, after Artemas Ward. Why the eccentric Englishman should have had such an appeal to the New Englanders is hard to account for, unless the reason was his radical politics. "There were Prejudices enough among the weak and fears enough among the timid, as well as other obstacles from the Cunning," John Adams reported, "but the great Necessity for officers of skill and Experience, prevailed."

In addition to Ward and Lee, Philip Schuyler, of the great New York family, was made third major general—Eliphalet Dyer wrote that Schuyler's appointment was intended "to Sweeten and . . . keep up the Spirit in that Province"—and Israel Putnam, fourth. Horatio Gates, another English officer who defected to the American cause, was made adjutant general and given the rank of brigadier. Eight brigadier generals were appointed in all. Seth Pomeroy, who had fought as a common soldier under John Stark at Bunker Hill, was made senior brigadier. Richard Montgomery was next in line. The son of an Irish member of

Parliament, he had been educated at St. Andrews and at Trinity College, Dublin, and had served under General Jeffrey Amherst in the French and Indian War expedition against Ticonderoga and Montreal. Deciding that his future lay in America, he had sold his British Army commission in 1772 and had moved to the colony of New York, where he became an enthusiastic and successful farmer and married into the powerful Livingston family. It was the intention of Congress that Montgomery would serve as second-in-command to his fellow New Yorker, Philip Schuyler.

Another brigadier, David Wooster of Connecticut, was a graduate of Yale who became a militia lieutenant three years later and served with the British at the siege of Louisburg. He performed so ably that he was promoted to the rank of captain in a newly formed British regiment and, after having served in several campaigns as colonel of the Connecticut militia, retired as a half-pay officer in 1774. Wooster, who was sixty-four years old at the outbreak of the Revolution, held the rank of major general in the Connecticut militia and was the only colonial major general who was commissioned by Congress at a lower rank—to his intense irritation. Still another veteran officer was William Heath, who described himself as "of middling stature, light complexion, very corpulent, and bald-headed." Heath lived in Roxbury, Massachusetts, on land occupied by his family since 1636. He was a member of Boston's Ancient and Honorable Artillery Company, a member of the Massachusetts Provincial Congress, and an ardent student, like Nathanael Greene and Henry Knox, of military history.

Silas Deane of Connecticut, having tried to disarm Wooster's irritation at having been placed below Putnam in rank, was indignant to hear that Wooster had nonetheless expressed his displeasure openly. Deane was determined to defend the action of Congress, he wrote his wife, "and will on no occasion sacrifice the good of my country to the whim of any old man, or old woman rather, or their sticklers. . . ."

Another officer discontented with his rank was Joseph Spencer, one of the senior militia officers at Cambridge. When Congress appointed Putnam a major general and Spencer only a brigadier, Spencer simply left for home in a huff; but before the month was over, he was persuaded to return to Cambridge and resume his command. John Thomas, another of the Congressional crop of brigadier generals, had advanced to the rank of militia colonel in the French and Indian War. After that war he had practiced medicine for fifteen years, served as a justice of the peace, and been an active Son of Liberty. He took the initiative to raise a volunteer regiment, and he had been appointed to the rank of general by the Massachusetts Provincial Congress.

John Sullivan, the youngest of the brigadier generals at thirty-five, was the son of poor Irish immigrants who had settled in Maine. He moved to Portsmouth, where he practiced law and became a colonel in the New Hampshire militia. Sullivan was a delegate from New Hampshire to the First Continental Congress, and he had been one of the leaders of the little expedition that captured Fort William and Mary at the entrance to Portsmouth Harbor.

Congress left it to Washington to recommend the appointments of quartermaster general and chief of artillery, but they did appoint John Adams' friend (and Joseph Warren's successor as president of the Massachusetts Provincial Congress) James Warren as paymaster general. Dr. Benjamin Church, a long-time Boston Son of Liberty who was actually an undercover agent for Gage, was named director and surgeon of a military hospital to be established as soon as possible.

John Adams, disgusted with the jealousy over rank displayed by officers of the Continental Army, wrote to James Warren, "I have read of Times, either in History or Romance, when Great Generals would cheerfully serve their Country, as Captains or Lieutenants of Single Companies, if the voice of their country happened not to destine them to an higher rank; but such exalted ideas of public virtue seem to be lost out of the world." Adams had perhaps read of such times in romance, but seldom in history.

Officers in every army and in every time have been, to the civilian mind, inordinately sensitive about matters of rank. The most evident reason is not that military men are more petty than their civilian counterparts, but that rank is to the army officer corps what oil is to the wheels of a machine; it makes the whole thing work. An army is arranged and sorted out by rank. The soldier thus becomes conditioned to a close and indeed not infrequently feverish attention to who outranks whom. Congress, not being well informed on such subjects and being in a hurry, paid little attention to such matters as when a particular officer's commission was dated and, as a consequence, stirred up a hornets' nest of offended and angry generals.

Certain things might be noted about the officers commissioned by Congress. Three—Lee, Montgomery, and Gates—were British, or, perhaps more accurately, noncolonial. With the exception of Greene and Sullivan, all had served in the French and Indian War. Since that war had ended in 1763, twelve years earlier, and the major campaigns in

1761, this meant that the generals were old men by the standards of the day, with the exception of Montgomery, who had entered military service at the age of eighteen and was thirty-seven when he was commissioned by Congress. Of course military experience is important, but it is almost invariably a mistake to try to fight a new war with veterans of the old, especially if those veterans are getting on in years. For one thing, military technology changes rapidly, and tactics with it. One of the besetting sins of the military mind is rigidity. That is because human beings love routine, and where that routine has the effect of governing almost all their actions and confirming their self-esteem, most ultimately become enslaved by it. In addition, age produces its own rigidities that compound those that typically accompany military life. Perhaps even more important, age, sadly and inevitably, brings a diminution of physical strength, energy, endurance (although that goes last), and agility. Decisions made by tired and ailing men are usually bad decisions. There is a direct correlation between physical robustness and military efficiency.

And while experience is helpful, if not essential, in the organization and ordering of military life, it is far less important, as events were to prove, than energy, imagination, and initiative. Thus the experienced older officers of the French and Indian War, while they may initially have been better than nothing, turned out to be, almost without exception, a serious liability for Washington. Moreover, of those Revolutionary generals who had fought in the French and Indian War, Washington, who was forty-three when he assumed command at Cambridge, was one of the youngest.

Once the Revolutionary generals had been appointed, Congress next decided to reinforce the army besieging Boston with ten companies of Virginia, Maryland, and Pennsylvania frontiersmen, "the most accurate marksmen in the world," armed with rifles. The rifle, as contrasted with the common musket, the standard weapon of soldiers in the eighteenth century, had a grooved or rifled barrel. While the rifle was more difficult to load—since the bullet that was rammed down the muzzle of the piece had to fit snugly enough to engage the rifling when the weapons was fired—it was far more accurate than the smooth-bored musket that dispatched a heavy projectile on a rather wobbly and uncertain flight. The theory of massed firepower from muskets was that, pointed in the general direction of the enemy and fired in a volley, they would take a heavy toll. By the same token, an individual firing his musket from behind a tree or stone wall was, because of the limited accuracy and range of the weapon, less effective.

There were ways of making even the musket more accurate. The principal way was in the loading of the weapon. The more skillful the loading, the more accurate the shot. The weapons that the colonials fired at the retreating British after the encounters at Lexington and Concord were, in the great majority of cases, muskets, although a few militiamen probably owned rifles. The rifle was, for one thing, a much heavier weapon, since in order to carry the rifling and prevent the explosion of the barrel by the backing up of gases behind the projectile, rifle barrels were made of thick, heavy steel. Rifles were also apt to be six inches to a foot longer than the average musket, since their primary virtue was accuracy, and accuracy was directly related to the length of the barrel. Making a fine rifle was a slow and highly skilled process, and rifles were, in consequence, much more expensive than muskets. Since each was made laboriously by hand, they could not be turned out at anything like the rate of muskets, where the rudiments of mass production could be used.

Another complication with rifles was that they varied greatly in caliber, so that the individual rifleman had to pour his own bullets and shape them to fit his piece as precisely as possible. Muskets, specifically the famous Brown Bess, which was the arm of the Continental infantryman, were much more standardized. They had a caliber of .75, or roughly three quarters of an inch in diameter. The ball they fired weighed about an ounce. A projectile could strike with killing or wounding force at up to eighty yards; beyond that distance its velocity as well as accuracy fell off sharply. Few soldiers were ever wounded by musket fire at 150 yards. The case was very different with the rifle. It was not unusual for an experienced marksman to drop a deer at a range of several hundred yards, and Continental riflemen became notorious for picking off British officers at distances far beyond musket range.

It is worth spending this much time on the subject of muskets and rifles because confusion on the matter of the riflemen of the Revolution is common. Congress was clearly enthralled by the notion of companies of riflemen picking off English soldiers and, more particularly, officers, one by one. The fact was that riflemen never made up more than a small portion of the Continental Army, and their role as riflemen was an important if romantic one. They did not readily adapt themselves to standard infantry tactics, which placed the emphasis on speed of reloading and firing by a series of commands in volleys, rather than on accurately aimed fire from individual weapons.

Congress, having indulged its fantasy of ten companies of deadeyes slaughtering the British, took the more practical measure of voting to raise two million dollars for the support of the army. Then, having appointed a commander in chief and taken on responsibility for an army that it had not called into existence and that was doubtless an acute embarrassment to many members of Congress, the delegates, perhaps appalled at their own boldness, fell into a kind of lethargy, squabbling and quibbling, still clearly unwilling to look independence full in the face, distracting themselves with rumors of concessions from North and his ministers.

John Adams wrote to Moses Gill in June, "We have found by Experience that Petitions, Negotiations every Thing which holds out to the People Hopes of a Reconciliation without Bloodshed is greedily grasped at and relyd on—and they cannot be persuaded to think that it is so necessary to prepare for War as it really is—However, this Continent is a vast, unwieldy Machine. We cannot force Events. We must suffer People to take their own Way in many Cases, when We think it leads wrong, hoping however and believing that our Liberty and Felicity will be preserved in the End, tho not in the Speedyest and Surest Manner. . . ."

Adams found two other metaphors to describe the colonies. They were "like a large fleet sailing under convoy. The fleetest sailors must wait for the dullest and slowest. Like a coach and six, the swiftest horses must be slackened, and the slowest quickened, that all may keep an even pace. . . ."

When an old order is in the process of being sloughed off and before a new order has taken form, there is a period of extreme vulnerability, a period that can slide quickly into anarchy if some guiding or controlling principal or person (preferably both) does not emerge. This was the case with the American colonies after Lexington. Once the de facto rejection of the old order had taken place, the crucial question became, what was to replace it? The same cantankerous individualism that had enabled the colonists to oppose the mother country with such persistence—and that at the Battle of Bunker Hill was represented so dramatically by the way in which individual soldiers instinctively fought in the mode best suited to the demands of the real battlefield situation—made the matter of establishing the new order an extremely complex and arduous one.

The problem was complicated by the sectional jealousies that lay just below the surface. The suspicion of New England that had been so evident at the first Congress was not, the Massachusetts men found, entirely dissipated. The Pennsylvanians, in particular, suspected them of seeking independence, "an American republic; Presbyterian principles, and twenty other things."

Adams wrote to James Warren in July that "the Congress is not yet so alarmed as it ought to be. There are still hopes, that Ministry and Parliament, will immediately recede as soon as they hear of the Battle of Lexington, the spirit of New York and Philadelphia, the Permanency of the Union of the Colonies, etc.: they are much deceived." Adams added, "These opinions of Some Colonies which are founded I think in their Wishes and passions, their Hopes and Fears, rather than in Reason and Evidence will give a whimsical Cast to the Proceedings of this Congress. You will see a strange Oscillation between love and hatred, between War and Peace—Preparations for War and Negociation, etc. This Negociation I dread like the Death: but it must be proposed. We can't avoid it. Discord and total Disunion would be the certain Effect of a resolute Refusal to petition and negociate . . . If we Strenuously insist upon our Liberties, as I hope and am pretty sure we shall however, a Negociation, if agreed to, will terminate in Nothing, it will effect nothing. We may possibly gain Time and Powder and Arms."

Congress, in Adams' opinion, should encourage every colony to set up its own government, then "confederate together like an indissoluble Band, for mutual defence, and open our Ports to all Nations immediately. . . . But the colonies are not yet ripe for it." And so Congress dragged on from day to day, doing too late and under duress and timidly what it should have done boldly and expediously months before.

Even John Adams could hardly have imagined that it would take Congress another full year before it could muster up enough courage to declare the colonies independent of the mother country. For those delegates who saw the situation as it really was, the delay was nerve-racking. Even from this distance in time it is only to be explained by the power of that magic word "Englishman," by a strange kind of Freudian dependence on the father-king, a dependence so strong that it was agony to reject it. So the majority in Congress went on, as Adams said, snatching at straws and deluding themselves by every means they could conceive.

Progress was further impeded by receipt of the resolution of the House of Commons in which Parliament promised to forebear "to impose any further duty, tax or assessment." A letter from Lord North stated that this was the furthest limit of parliamentary and ministerial concession. North, one delegate wrote, "rocks the cradle and sings lullaby, and the innocent children go to sleep. Next spring we shall be jockied by negotiation, or have hot work in war."

Colonel John Dickinson, the "Farmer" was now one of the more timid delegates, doing his best to try to persuade the South Carolinians, already lukewarm, to avoid all measures that might irritate the British. Philadelphia's Charles Thomson confided to Adams that Dickinson was under constant pressure from his wife and his mother, both Tory sympathizers. His strong-willed old mother had told him, "Johnny, you will be hanged, your estate will be forfeited and confiscated, you will leave your excellent wife a widow and your charming children orphans, beggars and infamous."

Under the circumstances, the atmosphere in Congress naturally grew increasingly tense. The New Englanders were at war with the mother country; their fellow citizens had died in battle, and yet the Pennsylvanians and their weak-willed friends still charged them with plotting independence. The situation was somewhere between a bad joke and a nightmare. Dickinson proposed that Congress draft another humble petition to the king, begging for a redress of grievances; John Adams opposed the suggestion in the most emphatic terms. Later, in the hall outside the room where Congress met, Dickinson taxed Adams for his militancy: "What is the reason, Mr. Adams, that you New England-men oppose our measures of reconciliation? . . . Look ye! if you don't concur with us in our pacific system, I, and a number of us, will break off from you in New England, and we will carry on opposition by ourselves in our own way."

"Mr. Dickinson," Adams replied, "there are many things that I can very cheerfully sacrifice to harmony, and even unanimity; but I am not to be threatened [into an] express . . . approbation of measures which my judgment reprobates. Congress must judge, and if they pronounce against me, I must submit."

So they parted and never spoke to each other again. Adams inadvertently widened the rift by writing to James Warren that "certain great fortune [a reference to Dickinson's wife's estate] and piddling genius, whose fame has been trumpeted so loudly, has given a silly cast to our whole doings. We are between hawk and buzzard. We ought to have had in our hands a month ago the whole legislature, executive and judicial of the whole continent, and have completely modeled a constitution; to have raised a naval power, and opened all our ports wide; to have arrested every friend to government on the continent and held them as hostages for the poor victims in Boston, and then opened the door as wide as possible for peace and reconciliation . . . Is this all extravagant? Is it wild? Is it not the soundest policy?" The indiscrete letter was intercepted and published gleefully in the Tory *Rivington's Gazette.*

One interlude entertained the delegates. A certain Major Skene arrived in Philadelphia with a royal commission appointing him Governor of Ticonderoga and Crown Point. The ministry had not yet learned that those forts were in the hands of patriot forces led by Benedict Arnold and Ethan Allen. Skene, it turned out, really came as a British agent supplied with funds to bribe the colonists to accept Lord North's conciliatory plan. Eliphalet Dyer wrote Governor Trumbull that "Skene now had unlimited orders to draw on the Treasurer in England for any sums Necessary that he was to bribe and buy over such a Number of the Congress as was Necessary to Confound the whole he was to propose [Lord North's] Conciliary plan and the dunce imagined he should have easy work to settle the whole Controversy. I dare say he told the Ministry so and they fully believed him. It is amazing how they can be so reduced as to employ such a genius as this Majr. Skene, open, exposed, unguarded, and his Abilitys but moderate."

Congress, having adopted the army around Boston and appointed Washington its commander, decided that some statement was required to justify its actions. Thomas Jefferson was asked to draft a "Declaration on Taking Up Arms." But Jefferson's statement was too militant, and John Dickinson, Mr. Moderation, was given the assignment. Once more Dickinson patiently reviewed the colonists' efforts to have their grievances redressed. Added to this now familiar inventory were the events of Lexington and Concord. As a result of action taken by the British troops, the colonies were now experiencing "the complicated calamities of fire, sword and famine," and had, of necessity, to take up arms to defend themselves and their families. "Our cause is just," Dickinson wrote, "Our union is perfect. Our internal resources are great, and, if necessary, foreign assistance is undoubtedly attainable. . . . With hearts fortified with these animating reflections, we most solemnly, before God and the world, declare, that exerting the utmost energy of those powers which our beneficent Creator hath graciously bestowed upon us . . . we will, in defiance of every hazard . . . employ for the preservation of our liberties; being with one mind resolved to die freemen, rather than to live like slaves."

And then after these bold and stirring words came a cautious disclaimer: "Lest this declaration should disquiet the minds of our [British] friends and fellow-subjects . . . we assure them we mean not to dissolve that union which has so long and so happily subsisted between us. . . ."

Dickinson once more had his way when Congress approved still another petition to the king. Dickinson was delighted when it passed and rose to express his pleasure. There was only one word to which he objected since it might possibly offend His Majesty, and that was the word "Congress." Whereupon Benjamin Harrison of Virginia promptly rose and, inclining his head to John Hancock, declared, "There is but one word in the paper, Mr. President, of which I approve, and that is the word *Congress*."

Congress also sent appeals for support to the British West Indian Islands, to Ireland, to the Canadians, and, finally, to the Six Nations, the most powerful and warlike confederation of Indian tribes in the New World. It was critically important to try to insure the neutrality of the Iroquois, whose alliance with the British had been traditional and whose assistance had been a vital factor in the French and Indian War. "The Indians are known to conduct their wars so entirely without Faith and Humanity," John Adams wrote to James Warren, "that it will bring eternal infamy on the Ministry throughout all Europe if they should excite the Savages to War. The French disgraced themselves last war by employing them. To let loose these blood Hounds to scalp Men and to butcher Women and Children is horrid."

The delegates took special pains with the speech that was to be delivered with much wampum to the chiefs of the Six Nations: "You Indians know how things are proportioned in a family—between the father and the son—the child carries a little pack—England we regard as the father—this island may be compared to the son. The father . . . apoints a great number of servants. . . . Some of his servants grow proud and ill-natured—they were displeased to see the boy so alert and walk so nimbly with his pack. They tell the father, and advise him to enlarge the child's pack—they prevail. . . . Those proud and wicked servants . . . laughed to see the boy sweat and stagger under his increased load. By and by, they apply to the father to double the boy's pack, because they heard him complain. . . ." The boy implores the father with "tears and entreaties"; the father gives no answer and, staggering under the crushing load, the boy "gives one struggle and throws off the pack. . . . Upon this, those servants . . . bring a great cudgel to the father, asking him to take it in his hand and strike the child." The speech concluded: "This is a family quarrel between us and old England. You Indians are not concerned in it. We don't wish you to take up the hatchet against the King's troops. We desire you to remain at home, and not join on either side, but keep the hatchet buried deep. . . . What is it we have asked of you? Nothing but peace."

In September, Georgia finally "came into the Union, and . . . appointed delegates to the Congress." They had done more; they had joined with South Carolina in arming a vessel that had promptly captured a ship with 140 barrels of the king's powder on board. The Maryland delegates meanwhile decamped on the twenty-first and the Virginians expressed their intention of following. "Our going," Benjamin Harrison wrote Washington, "I expect will break up the Congress. Indeed I think it is high time there was an End of it. We have been too long together. . . ." They were to be together much longer. Despite Harrison's desire to return to his plantation and a general weariness among the delegates, they had too much to do to adjourn. As John Adams put it: "when 50 or 60 Men have a Constitution to form for a great Empire at the same time that they have a Country of fifteen hundred miles extent to fortify, Millions to arm and train, a Naval Power to begin, an extensive Commerce to regulate, numerous Tribes of Indians to negotiate with, a standing Army of Twenty seven Thousand Men to raise, pay, victual and officer, I really shall pity those 50 or 60 Men."

Washington Makes an Army

WHEN Washington assumed command of the troops at Cambridge, he immediately undertook the staggering labor of creating a Continental Army. This turned out to be the most crucial enterprise of the period from the Boston Tea Party to the framing of the Federal Constitution in 1787. Upon its success or failure rested, quite literally, the future of the United States—not so much in the matter of a collection of soldiers who could fight the British to a standstill, but in the existence of a "continental" entity, in this case an army, which would represent in simple, practical terms the fact that there was a reality that transcended the particular individual colonies, a reality that could be called America. Beside this essential fact, which had to be represented in some form that everyone could grasp, the existence of the Continental Congress was of relatively minor importance. The army had appeared without any act or declaration of Congress. It clearly existed, however precarious and transitory it might be, independently of Congress; and Congress, however reluctantly, had to adopt it or go out of business.

Washington left Philadelphia for Cambridge on June 19, with Charles Lee and General Philip Schuyler of New York. After the splendid sendoff that Philadelphia gave Washington and his generals—they were accompanied by the city light horse, a number of mounted militia officers, and a military band—it was slightly disconcerting to find that the Provincial Congress of New York was expecting the colony's governor, William Tryon, back from a trip to England on the same day that Washington and his entourage were to arrive. The New York legislature solved the problem of protocol by sending two sets of honor guards, one to greet the new general of the Continental Army and his officers at their landing place on Manhattan, the other to welcome the royal governor of the province.

After landing, Washington spoke briefly to the assembled patriots, uttering his memorable sentence, "when we assumed the soldier we did not lay aside the citizen." Philip Schuyler was left in New York to take charge of military affairs there, with orders to assume command of the forts at Ticonderoga and Crown Point. If Governor Tryon attempted to disrupt patriot plans and projects during the recess of the Continental Congress, Schuyler was authorized to arrest him. Without British troops to support him, Tryon was powerless to take any action.

All along Washington's route, crowds of patriots turned out to welcome the general. Some members of his small retinue soon found the ceremonies more tiring than the journey. At Watertown, Massachusetts, Washington had his first encounter with Yankee candor. The soldiers in the army he was about to assume command of were, he was told, "naturally brave and of good understanding, yet for want of experience in military life" they had "but little knowledge of divers things most essential to the preservation of health, even life. The youth of the army [were] not possessed of the absolute necessity of cleanliness in their dress and lodging, continual exercise, and strict temperance. . . ."

When Washington arrived in Cambridge his Olympian dignity and courtly manners made an immediate impression on everyone who met him. "You had prepared me to entertain a favorable opinion of him," Abigail Adams wrote her husband, "but I thought the half was not told me. Dignity with ease and complacency, the gentleman and the soldier look agreeably blended in him. Modesty marks every line and feature of his face. Those lines of Dryden instantly occured to me:

> Mark his majestic fabric; he's a temple
> Sacred by birth, and built by hands divine;
> His soul's the deity that lodges there;
> Nor is the pile unworthy of the god."

Washington anticipated an attack on the American lines by the British, and he gave his first attention to strengthening the colonial defenses. Riding out to Roxbury, he and his staff met Henry Knox, and, as Knox wrote proudly to his wife, "when they had viewed the works [which Knox had directed] they expressed the greatest pleasure and surprise at their situation and apparent utility, to say nothing of the plan which did not escape their praise." Upon inspection Washington found the army to be "a mixed multitude of people . . . under very little discipline, order or government." "Confusion and disorder reigned in every department," he wrote Schuyler, "which in a little time must have ended either in the separation of the army, or fatal contests with one another."

General Lee established himself in a headquarters that he named Hobgoblin Hall, where Jeremy Belknap, the New Hampshire patriot, encountered him, "a perfect original, a good scholar and soldier . . . but little good manners; a great sloven, wretchedly profane, and a great admirer of dogs—of which he had two at dinner with, one of them a native of Pomerania, which I would have taken for a bear had I seen him in the woods."

The New Englanders' romance with Washington was rather one-sided. He found them "an exceedingly nasty and dirty people," which was simply to say that they had little or no camp discipline. Accustomed to the openhanded style of the Virginia aristocrats, he was also offended at the Yankee tendency to drive a sharp bargain or worse. He cashiered a number of officers, one of them a colonel, for dishonesty in drawing pay for men not enrolled, for their own children, or for soldiers on leave. In his words, he made "a pretty good slam" among dishonest or inefficient officers, "as these people seem to be too inattentive to every thing but their interest."

Nathanael Greene, a Rhode Island Yankee himself, felt that Washington was too hasty in his judgment of the New Englanders. "They are naturally brave and spirited," he wrote, "as the Peasantry of any Country, but you cannot expect Veterans of a Raw Militia from only a few months service. The common People are exceedingly avircious [sic] the Genius of the People is Commercial from long intercourse of Trade. The Sentiment of honnor the true Characteristick of a Soldier has not yet got the better of Interest." Washington had expected to find the New Englanders "a Superior Race of Mortals," Greene noted shrewdly, "and finding them of the same temper and disposition, passion and Prejudices, Virtues and Vices of the common People of other Governments they sink in his Esteem." But if the New Englanders were dirty, they were also pious. They put one in mind of Cromwell's Puritans. Their camps abounded with chaplains and visiting preachers.

General John Sullivan of New Hampshire, always a complainer, deplored his misfortune "in being Called to Comand Men of such Principles as would induce them to Betray the Freedom of their Country, and Enslave themselves and Posterity rather than Dispense with a Sight of their own habitations for a Month." The course to follow was to fill in for the time being with militia companies while pushing in every possible way to fill up the newly formed regiments with soldiers willing to enlist for a stated period. Washington himself, impatient as he became at times, was well aware of the magnitude of the task. "Search the vast volumes of history through," he wrote, "and I very much question whether a case similar to ours is to be found; to wit, to maintain a post against the flower of the British troops for six months together, without powder, and at the end of them to have one army disbanded and another raised within the same distance of a reinforced enemy."

Ralph Waldo Emerson's grandfather, the Concord minister, was charmed by the evidence he found in the camps of the soldiers' lively individualism. "They are as different in their form," he wrote, "as the owners are in their dress; and every tent is a portraiture of ye temper and taste of ye persons that incamp in it. Some are made of boards, some of sailcloth, and some partly of one and partly of the other. Others are made of stone and turf, and others again of Birch and other brush. Some are thrown up in a hurry and look as if they could not help it— mere necessity—others are curiously wrought with doors and windows done with wreaths and withes in the manner of a basket. Some are proper tents and marquees, and look like ye regular camp of the enemy. These are the Rhode-Islanders [Greene's troops] who are furnished with tent equipage from among ourselves and everything in the most exact English taste. However I think that the great variety of the American camp is upon the whole, rather a beauty than a blemish to the army."

One of the first problems Washington tackled, and one of the thorniest that faced him, was the relation between officers and men. In the simple democracy of the militia company, officers and men mixed without distinction, called each other by their first names, and, on the men's part, obeyed or disobeyed orders pretty much as they chose. Under such circumstances discipline was negligible. To tackle this problem Washington's headquarters issued a stream of orders that were read to the men each morning after prayers. "The strictest government is taking place," the Reverend Mr. Emerson noted, "and great distinction is made between officers and soldiers. Everyone is made to know his place and keep in it, or be tied up and not 1,000 but thirty or forty lashes according to his crime. Thousands are at work every day from four till eleven o'clock in the morning. It is surprising how much work has been done."

Not, certainly, without a great deal of grumbling and complaining. New Englanders were not used to "spit and polish," not accustomed to taking orders, and much averse to having to start calling Seth Williams "Captain." But there was ambivalence even in the complaints. Soldiers, like most of the rest of us, want and depend upon some order. These men had been well adapted to the particular order of civil life. In camp they lapsed into a disorder that was basically very demoralizing, and at least an important part of them responded to the demand that they "shape up."

The fact was that the officers were more of a problem than the men, as Washington was well aware. And it is hard in turn to blame the officers. Their authority rested on very precarious grounds until they were firmly supported from higher up. They had not the habit of command; they were not recruited from a class trained to expect obedience, nor did their soldiers come from one accustomed to give it. Washington was especially disturbed at the tales of officers who had shown cowardice or indecision at the battle of Bunker Hill. He took the occasion of the court-martial of John Callender for deserting his cannon at Bunker Hill to issue a stern admonition to the members of the officer corps. "It is with inexpressible concern," he wrote in his general orders for July 7, "that the General, upon his first arrival in the army, should find an officer sentenced by a general court-martial to be cashiered for cowardice—a crime of all others the most infamous in a soldier, the most injurious to an army, and the last to be forgiven, inasmuch as it may, and often does, happen that the cowardice of a single officer may prove the destruction of the whole army."

From the beginning, Washington was keenly aware of the strength of local loyalties and prejudices among troops from different colonies. He repeatedly reminded the soldiers that they were members of the army of "the United Provinces of North America, and it is to be hoped that all distinction of colonies will be laid aside, so that one and the same spirit may animate the whole, and the only contest be, who shall render on this great and trying occasion the most essential service." "Connecticut wants no Massachusetts men in her corps," Washington wrote, "Massachusetts thinks there is no necessity for a Rhode-Islander to be introduced into her: and New Hampshire says, it is very hard, that her valuable and experienced officers, who are willing to serve, should be discarded. . . ."

William Gordon, an English minister and self-appointed historian of the Revolution, remarked soon after Washington's arrival on the change in the manner and appearance of the encampments and the soldiers therein: "The regulations of the camp have been greatly for the better," he wrote. "Before, there was little emulation among the officers: the soldiers were lazy, disorderly, and dirty. The freedom to which the New Englanders have always been accustomed, makes them impatient of controul; [but now] every officer and private begins to know his place and duty."

Nonetheless, the instances of unsoldierly conduct seemed endless. Sentries had been deplorably lax about checking the casual traffic that flowed back and forth from Boston through the American lines. Officers and men talked freely with enemy pickets. The ubiquitious Jabez Fitch, who for a time was in command of the American redoubt at Roxbury, under a flag of truce met with officers from the British lines on four different occasions. Fitch inquired after officers that he had known when he had served during the French and Indian War, and "was answered to every question in the most free, affable and polite manner, and indeed we held a discourse of near half an hour. . . . I proposed to them to erect a coffee house for the convenience of such occasional conferences, upon which we held a considerable banter with good humor on both sides, and we finally parted with great appearance of friendship."

Washington issued a stern order that "the General *alone* is to judge of any propriety of such intercourse with the enemy, and no one else is to presume to interfer." Since there were few uniforms, Washington ordered generals and their aides to wear insignia of rank, and finding that an inordinate number of soldiers had been allowed to depart on leaves and furloughs granted by amiable officers, he ordered these limited to two soldiers per company on furlough at any one time.

Washington also had to contend with discontent among his officers, who showed a tendency to insubordination and offered unsolicited advice, trying to interfere with the administration of the army. "I must declare my disapprobation," Washington burst out, "of this mode of associating and combining, as subversive of all subordination, discipline, and order. . . ." When such an officers' council petitioned against the appointment of a certain young officer, Washington rebuked them sharply. To yield to such pressure "would be in effect," he wrote, "to surrender the command of the army to those, whose duty it is, and whose honor it ought to be, to obey. . . . The power which has established and which pays this army, has alone the right to judge, who shall command in it, from the general to the ensign."

Desertion and absence without leave were also troublesome problems. Washington was particularly indignant at discovering instances where soldiers were given leave to work on farms owned by their officers, which doubtless seemed to the culprits mere practicality. A soldier was better off earning some pocket money at honest labor than lolling around camp, untidy and addled with rum. Some soldiers enlisted, received their bounty, and then deserted, only to enlist again. Some enlisted, went off with their muskets, and sold them to the highest bidder. Daniel Peters, a deserter who was caught and brought back to camp, was court-martialed and sentenced to forfeit nine days pay "and that he shall do Camp Color Man's Duty for six days, and the whole of which time Shall Wear on his outside Garment plain to be Seen and Easy to read, cut out of white paper the word Deserter, and on failure thereof to be whiped on his naked back ten stripes." He was let off lightly because of his plea that he had returned home "to provide for his family, and get his shirts wash't and mended." The standard punishment for desertion was thirty-nine lashes.

The problem of the American soldiers was one of discipline. The effort to maintain good order was to plague Washington and every officer in virtually every unit throughout the Revolution. The colonists were fighting for "independence"; they were in consequence little inclined to accept any authority or any substantial degree of subordination. They would give loyalty to a particular officer that they liked and admired, and he might, through the force of his character and the affection of his troops, exercise considerable authority, or at least sufficient authority for the purpose. But to authority *as authority,* to the military chain of command or to officers other than their own, to "the rank" that is to say, they typically proved a refractory lot. General Greene, who managed through moral suasion to preserve reasonably good order among his Rhode Islanders, nonetheless reported, "There are some officers in each Regiment who exert themselves to bring the camp under regulations. There are some Captains, and many subaltern officers, who neglect their duty; some through fear of offending their soldiers, some through laziness, and some through obstinacy. . . . I have warned them of their negligence many times and am determined to break every one for the future who shall lay himself open to it. My task is hard, and fatigue is great."

Part of the trouble was that few Americans were born to command, and none, certainly were born to obey. Military discipline consists in large part of doing a number of disagreeable and tedious (and often pointless) tasks simply because one is told to do them. The tedious and useless tasks are, in practical fact, mixed in with tedious and necessary tasks and with some absolutely essential ones. If the individual soldier were to question each command, demand to be persuaded of its utility or importance, and refuse to do those that he considered plainly absurd, the whole military organization would collapse at once. No camp discipline could be maintained, no campaign carried out, no battle won. Yet that is substantially what the colonial soldier wished to do. And from a civilian point of view, it was not only eminently reasonable, but also the very quality that had made the colonists so resolute in their resistance to any impairment of their "liberties."

The colonists had, as individuals, followed the issues and arguments with a remarkably sophisticated understanding and had, as individuals, made up their minds how they meant to respond. They could not see why they should not continue to do so. The mere fact that they carried a gun and marched off with their friends and relatives to fight the British surely did not mean that they were expected to surrender the right of individual judgment. But that, of course, was exactly what it did mean, and it was small wonder that the "lack of a proper subordination"—which had so offended "upper class" Tories and amused and irritated British travelers in the colonies—should have created a perpetual dilemma for those among their fellow countrymen who had the responsibility of leading them in camp and in battle.

The results of Washington's shaking up of the army were, on the whole, encouraging, although serious problems of discipline continued. Washington himself declared that he had "materials for a good army, a great number of able-bodied men, active, zealous in the cause, and of unquestionable courage." John Dickinson's "Declaration on Taking Up Arms" was read to the troops on the fifteenth of July and evoked an enthusiastic response. On Prospect Hill, near the confluence of the Mystic and Malden rivers, Putnam's soldiers sent up such a cheer that "the Philistines on Bunker's Hill heard the shout of the Israelites, and, being very fearful, paraded themselves in battle array."

Among the recruits who poured into Cambridge were the riflemen whose fame had already preceded them. At Fredericktown, Maryland, Michael Cresap's First Maryland Rifles, on their way to join Washington, gave a demonstration of their skill. As one witness recounted it: "A clapboard, with a mark the size of a dollar, was put up; they began to fire off-hand, and the bystanders were surprised, few shots being made that were not close to or in the paper. When they had shot for a time in this way, some lay on their backs, some on their breast or side, others ran twenty or thirty steps, and firing, appeared to be equally certain of the mark." One young soldier then picked up the board and held it in his hand while his brother walked off a distance and shot at the mark. Then "one of the men took the board, and placing it between his legs, stood with his back to the three while another drove the center." The witness to these astonishing feats of marksmanship wrote a friend, "What would a regular army of considerable strength in the forests of America do with one thousand of these men, who want nothing to preserve their health and courage but water from the spring, with a little parched corn, with what they can easily procure in hunting; and who, wrapped in their blankets, in the damp of night, would choose the shadow of a tree for their covering, and the earth for their bed."

The Virginian riflemen covered six hundred miles in three weeks without, it was said, losing a single man. In the space of a few weeks some twelve rifle companies from Maryland, Virginia, and Pennsylvania arrived at Cambridge. At Cambridge they tried to relieve the tedium of camp life by sniping at the British on the picket lines or in Boston. Washington was finally forced to order "All officers commanding guards, posts, and detachments to be alert in apprehending all future transgressors," and General Sullivan declared "that no Person attempt to go down to the Lines and fire at the Enemy without leave from the Colonel of his Regiment." A few weeks later Washington noted "with indignation and shame" that the poorly disciplined riflemen were still at it, doing no more than "to waste their ammunition, expose themselves to the ridicule of the enemy, and keep their own camps harassed by frequent and continual alarms."

In addition, the riflemen believed that, as elite soldiers, they should be exempt from ordinary camp chores and discipline. When a sergeant in Captain Ross's company was placed in the guardhouse "for neglect of duty and murmering," the men in his company undertook to free him. Their leader being, in turn, arrested, the riflemen freed both; and when the colonel of their regiment arrested one and sent him to the main guard in Cambridge, "in abt 20 minutes 32 of [them] with their loaded Rifles, swoare by G-d they would go to the Main Guard and release the man or loose their lives and set off as hard as they could run."

But Washington had been warned, and he turned out such a number of soldiers that the rebels were quite disconcerted. When Washington himself ordered them to ground their arms, they did so immediately. They were then surrounded and disarmed and punished for their insubordination. Benjamin Thompson was not far from the truth when he wrote, "Of all the useless sets of men that ever incumbered an army, surely the boasted riflemen are certainly the most so, when they came to the camp they had every liberty and indulgence allowed them that they could possibly wish for. They had more pay than any other soldiers; did no duty; were under no restraint from the commands of their officers, but went when and where they pleased." They were the most "mutinious and undisciplined set of villains that bred disturbance in any camp." Artemas Ward wrote: "Gen. Washington has said he wished they had never come; Gen. Lee damned them and wished them all in Boston; Gen. Gates has said, if any capital [improvement] was to be made the Riflemen must be removed from this camp." They were, in fact, the quintessence of that individualism that so plagued Washington throughout the army.

The "mutinious and undisciplined" riflemen were, to be sure, one of Washington's lesser problems. His essential task was to create an army. And this he did.

As something created to fight the British, the army was, in purely military terms, a failure. After the colonists had been formed, at enormous cost and effort, into a more or less conventional army, they never again were as successful in any engagement with the British as they had been when they extemporized their tactics at Concord and at Bunker Hill. If a general of far more imagination and originality than George Washington had taken command of the army at Cambridge, he might have said, in effect: "There is no point trying to teach all these contentious individuals to behave like conventional soldiers. It is entirely against their temperament, their mode of life, their 'native genius.' Clearly the thing to do is to encourage the development of those tactics that they have already discovered instinctively: constant harassment by militiamen who constitute no organized 'army' but slip out to harass and raid, to wear down the British by ceaseless minor forays, and then disappear into 'those endless forests, which,' as a contemptuous Britisher wrote, 'they are too lazy to cut down.'"

Such a strategy might have succeeded far better than a strategy that called for the creation of a Continental Army modeled along a conventional line. But it would not have answered the purpose of providing a foundation for the eventual United States.

The most serious impediment to forming an army was the fact that the enlistment period for the soldiers around Boston was up at the end of the year. Unless the men could be prevailed upon to re-enlist, Washington faced the prospect of being left without an army at the beginning of 1776. Governor Trumbull of Connecticut put the matter quite plainly: "The pulse of a New England man beats high for liberty. His engagement in the service he thinks purely voluntary; therefore, in his estimation when the time of inlistment is out, he thinks himself not holden without further engagement. This was the case in the last war. I greatly fear its operation amongst the soldiers of the other Colonies, as I am sensible this is the genius and spirit of our people."

There were a dozen good reasons—or reasons that seemed good to the individuals involved—why the majority of soldiers under Washington did not intend to re-enlist. Perhaps foremost was the fact that they were homesick. Most of them had been living for seven or eight months in thoroughly unfamiliar and, for the most part, unpleasant circumstances. They were place-bound people who, in many instances, had never been farther than twenty or thirty miles from their own homes. They were an industrious people for whom work was an expression of piety and of their own reality. At Cambridge they had experienced, aside from sporadic periods of activity in digging or maintaining their fortifications, that most demoralizing of conditions for Americans, idleness. Or they did "make work"—tasks that were clearly intended to keep them busy and that were to their practical minds worse than no work at all. They missed wives and children, mothers and brothers, and the warmth and intimacy of family and community life. They had come to fight the British, and instead of fighting, they had endured months of bad food, dirt, sickness, dampness and, as winter came on, often bitter cold, and silly orders given by men who affected to be their superiors. They were poorly equipped, and their clothes were falling off them. It seemed to them that they had done enough for the cause. No one had a right to expect them to sit and rot indefinitely. If the British marched out of Boston to devastate the countryside, they would gladly come back and give the redcoats the Lexington and Concord treatment.

In addition to these major grievances, they had numerous minor ones. Washington, with the support of Congress, was determined to reform the army into companies, regiments, and divisions of uniform size. No general could command an army in the field whose companies varied in numbers from thirty-two to ninety-five, and whose regiments and divisions were equally irregular. (Rhode Island and New Hampshire had 590 men per regiment, while Connecticut regiments had 1,000.) Without a roster before him, he could not be sure whether he was ordering 1000 men or 2000 men to execute some essential maneuver.

But remodeling an army of forty odd-sized regiments into twenty-eight uniform ones meant reassigning many officers and grouping men from different colonies in the same regiment. It followed from this that some popular officers must find themselves, at least temporarily, without commands, and that many soldiers must be under the direction of unfamiliar officers who were not even from the same colony. This seemed to officers and men alike a great hardship. The officers, for the most part, could understand the necessity for such a reformation. The average soldier, on the other hand, knew simply that he was no longer to be commanded by officers he knew and trusted. As a militiaman he had normally chosen his own company-grade officers, and he had found great reassurance in the midst of a new and strange situation in being officered by men who "spoke his own language" in the most direct vernacular sense, but who, beyond that, *understood him* and his ways, his crotchets and idiosyncrasies, his "native genius," his good points as well as his bad. This was particularly true of the New Englander who resented, and often simply could not understand, the curious soft intonations of Southern officers, the odd consonants of the Pennsylvanians, or the cool accents of the New Yorkers. To soldiers from those other colonies, the nasal twang of the New Englander fell unpleasantly on the ear and indeed seemed ridiculous.

The soldiers wanted a bounty for re-enlisting, and Congress refused to grant one. As militiamen they were used to being paid by their respective colonies on a lunar month; Washington and Congress were determined they should be paid on a calendar month, which meant, in effect, a month's less pay per year. Even John Adams, a staunch supporter of Washington, was alarmed at the implications of the new modeling of the army. "Can it be supposed." he wrote, "that the private man will be easy to be commanded by strangers, to the exclusion of gentlemen whom they know, being their neighbors?"

John Adams also gave an interesting analysis of the differences between Southerners and New Englanders. "Gentlemen in other colonies have large plantations of slaves, and the common people among them are very ignorant and very poor. These gentlemen are accustomed, habituated to higher notions of themselves, and the distinction between them and the common people, than we are. I dread the consequences of this dissimilitude of character, and without the utmost caution on both sides, and the most considerate forbearance with one another, and prudent condescension on both sides, they will certainly be fatal. . . . For God's sake, therefore, reconcile our people to what has been done, for you may depend upon it that nothing more can be done here."

The New England general officers were not surprised that the soldiers were reluctant to re-enlist. Their religion taught them that men were by nature (or by original sin) selfish, greedy, envious, full of vanity and presumption. But they were no less aware than Washington of the alarming consequences of having the greater part of the Continental Army leave for home, whatever the reasons might be; and as the period of enlistment ended, they exhausted all their eloquence in trying to persuade their soldiers to sign on again.

The results were meager. At the end of the first week of the re-enlistment period, only 966 men had come forward in eleven regiments. Loyalty to their cause, concern for liberty, honor, and even self-interest should prompt them to enlist, their officers argued. "Never were soldiers whose duty has been so light, never were soldiers whose pay and provision has been so abundant and ample."

Greene noted that despite all efforts to persuade men to re-enlist, "the Connecticut men are going home in shoals this day." Even his own Rhode Islanders showed little better spirit: "I was in hopes," he wrote Samuel Ward, the governor of Rhode Island, "that ours would not have deserted the cause of their Country. But they seem to be so sick of this way of life, and so home sick, that I fear the greater part and the best part of the troops from our Colony will go home. . . . I harangued the troops yesterday, I hope it had some effect; they appear of a better disposition today. . . . I sent home some Recruiting Officers, they got scarcely a man, and Report that there are none to be had there. . . . It mortifies me to Death, that our Colony and Troops should be a whit behind the Neighbouring Governments in private Virtue or Publick Spirit."

Washington informed Congress of the desperateness of his situation, and it promptly dispatched an investigating committee that spent several days in Cambridge and reported back a disheartening story.

Washington himself burst out in a letter to his young Pennsylvania aide, Joseph Reed, who was back in Philadelphia on a brief leave: "Such a dearth of public spirit, and such want of virtue, such stock-jobbing, and fertility in all the low arts to obtain advantage of one kind or another, in this great change of military arrangement, I never saw before, and pray God's mercy I may never be witness to again. What will be the end of these manoeuvres is beyond my scan. I tremble at the prospect. We have been till this time enlisting about three thousand and five hundred men. To engage these I have been obliged to allow furloughs as far as fifty men to a regiment . . . such a dirty mercenary spirit prevades the whole that I should not be surprised at any disaster that may happen. In short, after the last of this month our lines will be so weakened that the minute-men and militia must be called in for their defence, these being under no kind of government themselves, will destroy the little subordination I have been laboring to establish. . . ."

Washington's judgment was too harsh. Allowing the accuracy of his charges and with sympathy for his own anger and despondency, he was nonetheless, as the phrase goes, fighting the problem. While he could not retreat from his determination to effect "this great change of military arrangement," he could have urged Congress to provide a substantial bounty for re-enlistment, rotated the men on leave in some more generous fashion, and accepted other accommodations that would have made further service more attractive. In place of the reality the common soldier knew best and loved, his Massachusetts or New Hampshire home, Washington was demanding that they give loyalty to a new abstraction that clearly did not exist except in the most precarious form, that was embodied by that ill-defined entity, Congress, and of course most clearly by Washington himself. Samuel Ward, a shrewd observer, warned Congress that the effort to make the army continental could very well destroy it. "Southern gentlemen," he wrote, "wish removed that attachment, which the officers and men have to their respective colonies, and make them look up to the continent at large for their support or promotion. I never thought that attachment [to the soldiers' respective colonies] injurious to the common cause, but the strongest inducement to people to risk everything in defence of the whole, upon which must depend the safety of each colony."

The conventional army of the eighteenth-century was a product of the new industrial age, which depended for its efficiency on treating people like interchangeable parts. Every soldier was, ideally, like every other soldier, just as every factory worker was to be, in time, like every other factory worker. The point was not merely to destroy personal ties when they threatened to be obstacles to proper organization; it was to destroy personal ties on principle—on the principle that in the average they were less efficient than impersonal or objective relations in that they almost invariably caused problems and complications. Any efficient officer should be able to command any company of these interchangeable soldiers. In a sense, the New Englanders were fighting to preserve an older, "personal," agricultural order, where things worked reasonably well because people knew and trusted one another. There was thus a special kind of poignance in the struggle. In order to lay a proper foundation for what was to become a continental nation, Washington had to remodel his army as a conventional army rather than as congeries of friends and neighbors fighting against a common foe. However, in doing so he had to destroy a portion of that community-based individualism that had provided, in the deepest sense, the morale to oppose the awesome power of Great Britain. It was perhaps no accident that it was Southern slave-holder politicians who provided the principal impetus for this transformation. They were already accustomed, in their relations with their slaves, to treating human beings as a work force, to organizing and exploiting the physical energies of their slaves, without, in the main, any more regard for purely personal consideration than the commander who assigned his soldiers to those units where they were needed, or, in the future, the industrialist who assigned his workers with a concern only for efficiency.

The problem of setting up military hospitals was related to the problem of establishing a Continental Army. Just as soldiers fit for duty wished to serve with their friends and neighbors and under the command of officers whom they knew, soldiers who were sick or wounded wished to be with friends and tended by doctors they knew. General Sullivan listed in a letter to Josiah Bartlett, a Massachusetts delegate to Congress, the most common objections of the soldiers to general hospitals. Bringing a number of ill persons together "in one hospital will render the air so putrid that it will not only be pernicious to the Neighbouring inhabitants but must prove fatal to the patients themselves; and reason [why hospitals were so detested] is that soldiers are taken from among their Friends and Acquaintance and put among persons with whom they have no sort of acquaintance and under Physicians they never saw." Sullivan's solution was for each brigade to have its own hospital unit.

To produce some degree of subordination and some acceptance of authority at whatever cost was a vital first step in the creation of a new order to replace the old. Even if it could have been proved conclusively (as of course it could not) that irregulars fighting a widespread guerrilla war would have been more successful than an inadequately trained and equipped army of the standard eighteenth-century type, it would still have been necessary to have created the army—because out of the drawing together and the rough fashioning of the Continental Army came the discipline, order, and unity that made a nation possible. Thus the question of Washington's genius as a military commander, while an interesting question in itself, is, strictly speaking, beside the point. Having molded an army by the most herculean efforts, by indomitable patience, by tact, by moral suasion, Washington had simply to keep it in existence to ultimately triumph. That he had created it and was able, in the face of every discouragement, to preserve the army was the seed of the new order. Congress existed for no other purpose than to supply it (rather badly), to facilitate its operations, to secure allies to aid it.

Washington's instructions from Congress authorized him to take inventory of the men and supplies in the army around Boston and to recruit sufficient additional soldiers to number twice the British force, so far as the latter's size could be ascertained. He was further authorized to purchase food and supplies for the army at the expense of Congress, and to use his own best judgment in any unforeseen contingencies that might arise.

In September, 1775, Washington had a doleful tale to tell Congress. He did not, he wrote, wish to give the slightest notion that he felt neglected. "But my Situation is inexpressibly distressing to see the winter fast approaching upon a naked Army, the time of their Service within a few weeks of expiring, and no Provisions yet made for such important Events. Added to this the Military Chest is totally exhausted. The Paymaster has not a single Dollar in Hand. The Commissary General assures me he has strained his Credit to the utmost for the Subsistence of the Army. The Quarter Master General is precisely in the same situation, and the greater part of the Army in a State not far from mutiny. . . . I know not to whom to impute this Failure, but I am of opinion, if the Evil is not immediately remedied and more Punctuality observed in the future, the Army must absolutely break up."

Congress having repeatedly failed him, Washington was forced to place his hopes in a higher power. He wrote to Joseph Reed in January to inform him that his troops still seemed bent upon "retiring into a chimney-corner as soon as their time expired." "How it will end," he added, "God in his great goodness will direct. I am thankful for his protection to this time." As week after week passed with the ranks of his army still unfilled, Washington was again overcome by despair. "My situation has been such," he wrote Reed, "that I have been obliged to use art to conceal it from my own officers." If they saw the degree of their commander's anxiety and distress, the contagion might spread through the whole army. Much of the problem revolved around the unwillingness of Congress to give a bounty for re-enlistment.

The diary of Simeon Lyman, a Connecticut soldier, gives us some hint of the anguish and bewilderment that many soldiers felt: "December, Friday, 11th," he wrote, "We was ordered to parade before the general's door, the whole regiment, and General Lee and General Sullivan came out." The men who would not stay on "after their enlistments was out they was ordered to turn out, and there was about 3 quarters turned out and we was ordered to form a hollow square, and General Lee came in and the first words was, 'Men, I do not know what to call [you] you are the worst of all creatures,' and flung and curst and swore at us, and said if we would not stay he would order us to go to Bunker Hill, and if we would not go he would order the riflemen to fire at us, and they talked they would take our guns and take our names down. . . ." when one man tried to persuade a friend to go home with him, "the general see him and he catched his gun out of his hands and struck him on the head and ordered him to be put under guard."

So were men treated who had left their communities and their families for a long and tedious service, had done their best, and now simply wished to be free to go home and let others serve their turn until they were clearly needed again. For this they were cursed and abused and accused by implication, if not more plainly, of being cowards and traitors to the cause of liberty. As a result of pleading, bullying, threatening, and promising, of eloquent and pathetic appeals to their patriotism, and of blows and curses, some ten thousand men were persuaded to re-enlist (approximately two-thirds of the besieging army); that was ten thousand fewer men than Washington felt he needed to form the nucleus of a continental army.

With enlistments lagging badly, Washington tried to infuse a little spirit into his army by raising at Prospect Hill, on the first day of the new year, a new flag. On it the crosses of England and Scotland were relegated to one corner, while the rest of the flag was composed of thirteen alternate red and white stripes. The story spread through the camp that the British in Boston, viewing the flag, thought it was a signal of surrender.

At the end of February, Washington, far from having the 20,000 men he was authorized to raise, had not even the 10,500 that he believed to be the minimum needed to maintain the siege of Boston. His enlistments numbered scarcely more than 8,000, of whom only 5,582 were present and ready for duty. He expressed his doubts and fears to Reed on the fourteenth of January: "The reflection on my situation, and that of this army, produces many an uneasy hour when all around me are wrapped in sleep. Few people know the predicament we are in, on a thousand accounts. . . . I have often thought how much happier I should have been, if, instead of accepting a command under such circumstances, I had taken my musket on my shoulder and entered the ranks, or, if I could have justified the measure to posterity and my own conscience, had retired to the back country and lived in a wigwam. . . . Could I have foreseen the difficulties, which have come upon us; could I have known, that such a backwardness would have been discovered in the old soldiers to the service, all the generals upon earth should not have convinced me of the propriety of delaying an attack upon Boston until this time."

Only half of Washington's problems involved discipline, re-enlistments, and now modeling the army. The other half had to do with items almost as important as soldiers—money, provisions, and powder. William Allen, a Rhode Island merchant who helped to supply the army at Cambridge, was disturbed, like many of his fellows, at the rapid rise in prices. "I cannot strain everything to the top of the Market at this dismal time of general Calamity while so many thousands are suffering in the depths of Poverty and distress," he wrote. "I had much rather not be in the class of the 100% Traders. I know a good Conscience is far more valuable than great sums of Continental Bills, I also know that he who makes haste to be rich shall not be innocent. But while I am attempting to escape the left hand wickedness, I shall take care to avoid the right hand Weakness. I well know every honest and fair Trader ought to have a reasonable Advance"—that is, profit—"which is to be governed upon a justifiable foundation."

John Adams sent word to Boston that "every stable, Dove house, Cellar, Vault, etc. is a Mine of salt Petre . . . The Mould under stables, etc., may be boiled into salt Petre it is said. Numbers are about it here." In early August, an inventory of all the available powder revealed that the whole army had less than ten thousand pounds, or roughly nine rounds per man. General Sullivan reported that when Washington received this tally he "was so struck that he did not utter a word for half an hour." James Warren, president of the Provincial Convention, could not think of the powder problem "without gloom and fearful apprehension," and the people of Massachusetts were urged "not to fire a gun at beast, bird, or mark without real necessity therefor."

In Boston, the British lay low with the exception of Burgoyne, who let out some of his pent-up energy by keeping up an intermittent bombardment of the American lines until a raiding party was sent that burned Burgoyne's forward observation posts and routed his pickets. "The Regulars have so hardened our people with their repeated firing, that a cannonading is just as much minded there," an officer wrote his wife, "as a common thunder shower." The British force in Boston was swelled by the arrival of a second quota of troops from Ireland in late July, bringing the army to some six thousand fit for duty with another fourteen hundred in hospitals. While the colonials continued to anticipate an attack, Gage had no serious notion of venturing beyond the city; his principal concern was preparing to repel an attack by the more numerous rebels.

A brief exchange of letters took place between Washington and Gage on the matter of the British treatment of captured American officers, who were confined with their men. Burgoyne answered for Gage and delivered a smug sermon: "Sir: to the glory of civilized nations, humanity and war have been made compatible, and compassion to the subdued is become almost a general system." And then a few admonitions for the presumptuous rebel general: "Be temperate in political disquisition; give free operation to truth; and punish those who deceive and misrepresent; and not only the effects but the causes of this unhappy conflict will be removed."

Clinton, Burgoyne, and Howe concerted their efforts to persuade Gage to move his small army from Boston to New York. They were plainly shut up in the city, and everything was at a standstill. New England was difficult terrain to fight in, and the region was swarming with patriots. New York, by contrast, offered much better strategic opportunities; it was much less susceptible to siege; and it was said to be full of Tories. As Clinton wrote: "Geografically and politically the town and island are much awed; and if there are friends of Govt. in America they are in [that] province and this step may enable them to show themselves. Staten Island [is] with you and all the Episcopal part of

America." From New York, the British could move to Pennsylvania and Virginia or, probably more profitably, up the Hudson River, destroy the American forces on Lake Champlain, and establish contact with the Canadians and the Indians of the Northwest. To stay in Boston was to invite sickness, which "has already seized us. Confinement hard duty, and want of fresh meat will increase it, and we shall in the course of a long winter, moulder away to nothing." Gage waivered. On the nineteenth of August he wrote to Lord Dartmouth reminding him that he had earlier urged "that no Expence should be spared to quash the Rebellion in it's Infancy." "You have too many amongst you," he added, "of the same stamp as the American Rebels who wish to overturn the Constitution. . . . You have gone too far to retreat therefore proceed with all the Force you can collect whether National or Foreign force, and I think you will not fail to bring the Rebellious Provinces to your terms notwithstanding all their Gasconnades."

3

Ticonderoga

I N the immediate aftermath of Lexington and Concord, some of the more militant New Englanders cast about for the means of striking a blow against British military might. Fort Ticonderoga, at the lower end of Lake Champlain, was held by a small garrison of British soldiers— some forty-eight men, among whom were a number of invalids.

What made Ticonderoga an especially tempting objective was that it contained a large number of heavy cannon, an item of ordinance very scarce in the colonies and much needed in any prolonged siege of Boston. Even before Lexington and Concord, rumors had circulated of plans for an attack on the fort, and Gage had sent a message to its commanding officer, Captain William De la Place warning him to be on the alert for an American foray.

Beyond the desperate need for ordnance and ammunition, the colonists were, of course, extremely aware of British Canada, as they had been of French Canada. They had participated so actively in the campaigns that had wrested Canada from the French that they felt a sense of proprietorship, as though Canada were somehow an extension of the colonies. For someone who had fought at Crown Point or Louisburg or had been with Wolfe at Quebec, or whose father or brother had died in one of the numerous battles with the French and the Indians, such feelings were natural enough. This attitude on the part of the colonists helps to explain their reaction to the Quebec Act—a sharp feeling (among the less creditable feelings of religious prejudice) of betrayal.

The First Continental Congress had directed a special plea to the Canadians to join with them in their resistance to British tyranny. And Samuel Adams had extended the range of the Boston Committee of Correspondence to take in Englishmen in Canada known to be sympathetic to the American cause. Ticonderoga and, just beyond it, Crown Point might be important links with a Canada disposed to cast its lot with the colonies to the south, or a point of entry, a staging area, and a jumping-off point for an invasion of Canada. Even if a majority of the people of Canada were willing to make common cause with the Americans, an invasion would certainly be necessary to help the Canadians overturn Sir Guy Carleton, the able governor of Canada, and the small force of British soldiers under his command. Finally, if the Canadians should prove immune to appeals from the south, Ticonderoga and Crown Point in the hands of a strong British garrison would be like a dagger aimed at the heart of New England. So, offensively or defensively, politically or militarily, Ticonderoga and Crown Point were crucial to the Americans.

In addition to its strategic importance, the fort had a sentimental value for the colonists: A number of them had been involved in General James Abercrombie's ill-fated effort to capture the fort in the French and Indian War.

How Ticonderoga came to be captured is, at the same time, one of the most curious and engaging stories of the Revolution, a story that demonstrates the remarkable capacity for initiative and improvisation that was the particular genius of the American colonists throughout the revolutionary crisis. The leading actors, Benedict Arnold and Ethan Allen, were almost too pat as classic American types, and the whole episode teeters wildly between the heroic and the farcical.

Benedict Arnold was the model of the aggressive, ambitious young man of modest background who, armed only with a certain shrewdness and a reckless determination to make his mark in the world, emerges from obscurity to blaze across the historical scene like a comet. In New Haven, Arnold had been variously an apothecary, a bookseller, a shipowner, and a horse trader. His military instincts were deep-seated. He had gone off as little more than a boy to fight at Ticonderoga during the French and Indian War. He was an avid reader, like Nathanael Greene, of military history. His horse-trading activities had taken him several times to Canada, where Carleton described him as "a known Horse Jockey, who has been several times in this Province, and is well acquainted with every avenue to it."

Arnold had also been one of the warmest Sons of Liberty in New Haven; the very day that word came of Lexington and Concord he set off at once for Cambridge to volunteer his services. On the way he fell in with Colonel Samuel Parsons, who was headed for the same destination. Arnold discussed with Parsons the vulnerability of Ticonderoga, which was falling into decay and guarded by a few disabled veterans of the late war. It was a plum that should be plucked as soon as possible by the colonials.

Parsons was so struck by the notion that when he arrived in Hartford he rooted about, collected some men and money, and dispatched a kind of private expeditionary force to seize Ticonderoga, one of the strongpoints in British America, from the soldiers of the Crown. Audacity and initiative, indeed a startling presumptuousness, characterized the project. Parsons had no official sanction for his little band and doubtless knew it would be risky to try to secure any formal approval.

On the way through Pittsfield, Massachusetts, Parsons' "raiders" recruited some forty more men, most important among them John Brown and Colonel James Easton. John Brown was probably New England's leading expert on Canadian affairs. He had recently been sent on a mission to Canada by Sam Adams and the Boston Committee of Correspondence to sound out the state of public opinion there. In Montreal, Brown had conferred with both the French and the English. Among them Brown found a number who were thoroughly dissatisfied with one aspect or another of the British administration, but they were more prudent than bold. Most of them were engaged in the Indian trade under royal licenses and were afraid that any open espousal of the American cause would result in the prompt revocation of their trading rights. Apparently the best the Americans could hope for was a lack of support for Carleton's efforts to raise a native military force.

When Parsons' little force arrived in Pittsfield, Brown was already an enthusiastic supporter of the idea of capturing Ticonderoga. As early as March he had written from Canada, "One thing I must mention to be kept as a profound Secret, the Fort at Ticonderoga must be seized as soon as possible should hostilities be committed by the kings Troops. . . . This will effectually curb this Province [Canada] and all the troops that may be sent here."

As Parsons' group, augmented by a Pittsfield contingent, made its way north, Benedict Arnold set his own plans in motion. As soon as he arrived in Cambridge, he presented to the Committee of Safety his own scheme for taking the fort. The members of the committee were plainly entranced, but there was a sensitive jurisdictional point involved. Lake George and the area known as the New Hampshire Grants, through which any expedition must go, was claimed by the province of New York.

The Committee of Safety thought it prudent under the circumstances to send off a message to New York, urging that the colony take advantage of the opportunity to seize the fort in its present weakened condition. Then, doubting the resolution of its neighbor, the committee commissioned Arnold as provisional colonel, the provision being that he raise not more than four hundred men for the express purpose of capturing Ticonderoga. Arnold, aware that other plans were afoot, turned over the recruiting to other officers and headed for Ticonderoga.

The third interested adventurer who had designs on Ticonderoga was a great, rough, burly, blustering character named Ethan Allen, famous in the region of the Grants for his physical strength, his eloquence, and his ability to hold large amounts of rum. When John Brown wrote from Canada to the Boston Committee of Correspondence urging that Ticonderoga be seized at the opening of hostilities with the British, he added: "The people on N. Hampshire Grants have ingaged to do this Business and in my opinion they are the most proper Persons for this Jobb."

The "Persons" on the New Hampshire Grants were led by Ethan Allen. In addition to his size and strength, Allen was the prototype of the village atheist. He was a self-taught philosopher and, like Arnold, an enterprising and tireless self-promoter. There was a kind of excess in everything Ethan Allen did, a frontier flamboyance, a boastful bravado, an expansiveness of word and gesture that made him the natural leader of his "Green Mountain Boys," or, as those less impressed by Allen and his followers called them, "the Bennington rioters."

The Parsons contingent had already made contact with Ethan Allen and his "boys" and had accepted Allen's leadership of the expedition when Arnold overtook them at the little settlement of Castleton. Allen had gone on ahead, and Arnold, producing his tentative commission from the Committee of Safety, insisted that he was the new commander of the foray. The rest of the company, described as "Shockingly surprised," made it plain that they were determined to resist the interloper. The next day Arnold and the others caught up with Allen. This was Allen's own turf, but when the two adventurers faced each other—one a cool, shrewd city boy with the air and manners of a gentleman, the other a burly frontiersman with his own brand of native cunning—Arnold did not hestitate to press his argument that his commission gave him the most substantial credentials in the group, and to insist that he take charge. Allen, however, had no intention of relinquishing command. After all, Arnold might have his somewhat tainted commission, but Allen had his boys—and it was clear that they would march under no one else.

The two men were like riverboat gamblers. Allen was full of furious bluster, even to threatening Arnold's life; Arnold, by contrast, had a quiet but deadly persistence. He intended to start his military career by capturing Ticonderoga, and he was not to be done out of the glory by a noisy backwoodsman. There was something vaguely reptilian about Arnold, a coiled waitingness, a latent violence kept in check, a sinuous and unblinking watchfulness; not an attractive quality, but one that seems to have disconcerted people. Even Allen was not immune to it; indeed he may have sensed that terrible lust for power and wealth and fame beside which his own posturings seemed like a small boy's charade. Since Allen could not retreat and Arnold would not, it was decided that they would share the command, a poor solution but the best one possible under the circumstances.

Men were sent ahead to reconnoiter the shores of the lake, searching for boats that could carry the party across to the fort; and on the evening of May 9 that strangely ill-assorted little force, some three hundred strong, collected to wait for boats at Hand's Cove in Shoreham, on the east shore of the lake, some two miles from the fort. No boats arrived. Finally, when it was almost morning, Captain Douglas appeared with a leaky barge. This, with another boat they already had, would carry some eighty men. A hasty council of war determined to cross in the barge and attack. To wait another day might mean sacrificing the vital element of surprise. Landing on the opposite shore one hundred yards or so above the fort, the raiders halted while Arnold made a last effort to assume command. Allen replied by threatening to put him in irons. Amos Callender, a militia officer finally persuaded the rivals to march side by side, an awkward and slightly ridiculous arrangement as the expedition struggled through the underbrush surrounding the fort, its leaders matching stride for stride in the misty light of dawn. The gates of the fort were open and defended by one sleepy sentry who leveled his musket at the unexpected invaders and called a quavering challenge. Allen struck the musket aside with his sword, and the colonials rushed into what had once been—and remained potentially—one of the strongest forts in the Americas without firing a shot.

Arnold and Allen quickly made for the officers' quarters, where Allen, with a notable lack of military protocol, called out to the commanding officer, "Come out, you old rat!" The figure that appeared in response to this graceless summons was only half-dressed. It was Lieutenant Jocelyn Feltham, second in command of the fort. Hearing a clamor, he had wakened the commander, Captain De la Place, and then gone out to confront the "rioters" at the foot of the stairs. Allen immediately demanded the surrender of the fort. In Allen's own vivid account of the scene, the officer replied by asking in whose name such a request was made, whereupon Allen answered with the ringing phrase, "In the name of the Great Jehovah and the Continental Congress." The lieutenant's story is somewhat different. According to Feltham it was Arnold who spoke first, saying that "he came from instructions, received from the congress at Cambridge," while Allen added loudly that "his orders were from the Province of Connecticut and that he must have immediate possession of the fort and all the effects of George the third (those were his words.)"

While Allen shouted and threatened and waved his sword over the indignant British officer's head, Arnold, appalled at such crude behavior, "begged it in a genteel manner." By this time Captain De la Place had gotten into proper uniform and had taken over the rather one-sided negotiation. Perhaps it was to him that Ethan Allen delivered the ringing phrase, or perhaps the phrase came to him later as a splendid thing to have said and he put it into his account after the fact. The matter is unimportant. It was a marvelous phrase, and it was certainly Allen's. Its combination of piety and presumption was enormously pleasing to his countrymen when they read it.

The attackers captured some one hundred cannon of various sizes with much ammunition, and forty soldiers, many of whom bore crippling wounds from ancient campaigns.

Having seized Ticonderoga in nobody's name in particular or, alternately, in the name of one agency (the Boston Committee of Safety) and a number of enterprising individuals, the Americans invested Crown Point without opposition the next day. The members of the expedition had then to decide what to do next. The control of the lake itself could not very well be claimed until the Americans had captured the armed sloop that was used to supply the posts. This vessel was moored at St. John's on the Canadian border, where Lake Champlain runs into the Richelieu River.

At this juncture a schooner arrived, having sailed up Lake George from Skenesborough. In it were a number of the recruits that Arnold's commission had authorized him to raise. After the capture of Ticonderoga, Arnold's joint leadership had been flatly rejected by the Vermont soldiers and officers. Arnold claimed it was because he tried to prevent their looting, which is not improbable. But now Arnold had a small force of which he was the legitimate commander. Since no one in the entire party save Arnold could sail a boat, Arnold took command of the schooner and set sail with his recruits for St. John's. On the way they were becalmed, and he put his men in boats and had them row all night. But surprise was complete, and Arnold caught the St. John's garrison of fourteen men by surprise. He also captured the seventy-ton armed sloop and her crew. After destroying all the boats in which the British might pursue him, he started back down the lake to Ticonderoga.

Ethan Allen, in his account of the capture of Ticonderoga, dealt with the problem of Benedict Arnold by not mentioning him at all. He and his "valiant Green Mountain Boys" not only occupy center stage, they constitute the whole cast of characters. According to Allen's recollection, when his party had arrived near the fort and he had made the decision to attack, "I harangued the officers and soldiers in the manner following: 'Friends and fellow soldiers, you have, for a number of years past, been a scourge and terror to arbitrary power. Your valour has been famed abroad, and acknowledged, as appears by the advice and orders to me (from the general assembly of Connecticut) to surprise and take the garrison now before us. I now propose to advance before you, and in person conduct you through the wicket-gate; for we must this morning either quit our pretensions to valour, or possess ourselves of this fortress in a few minutes; and, as much as it is a desperate attempt (which none but the bravest of men dare undertake) I do not urge it on any contrary to his will. You that will undertake voluntarily, poise your firelocks.'" Gratifyingly, all of his men did. There is no hint of what Arnold was doing during the harangue, or indeed at any other time during the attack. Allen, who had a definite literary flare (he wrote two books), added, "The sun seemed to rise that morning with a superior lustre; and Ticonderoga and its dependencies smiled on its conquerors, who tossed about the flowing bowl, and wished success to Congress and the liberty and freedom of America."

In Allen's script, Arnold enters the scene only with the appearance of the schooner from Skenesborough. Sailing faster than Allen's men could row, Arnold took St. John's and the sloop moored there; and on the way back down the lake, he encountered Allen and his men in their bateaux. "He saluted me with a discharge of cannon, which I returned with a volley of small arms: This being repeated three times, I went on board the sloop with my party, where several loyal Congress healths were drank. [An appealing picture of two comrades-in-arms.] We were now masters of lake Champlain and the garrison depending thereon."

At Ticonderoga, Arnold's recruits arrived daily to augment the men that he could claim as his own. Allen meanwhile played into Arnold's hands by attempting an abortive expedition into Canada that was surprised and routed at St. John's. When Allen and a remnant of his men finally got back to Ticonderoga, they found Arnold firmly in charge. With his ascendancy assured, Arnold promptly demonstrated his very real gifts for military organization and his remarkable energy. Hearing word of an impending British attack, he strengthened Crown Point and sent off requests to Cambridge for more men and supplies. "You may depend, gentlemen, these places will not be given up unless we are overpowered by numbers, or deserted by Providence, which has hitherto supported us," he wrote.

When word of these astonishing exercises in "private enterprise" reached the Second Continental Congress, it threw that body into a dither, a state with which it was not unfamiliar. There were some members who still placed their hopes on reconciliation with the mother country. Lexington and Concord had, in their view, been defensive actions, efforts of countrymen to protect their homes and families against the "ministerial troops." But the seizure of Ticonderoga and Crown Point were acts of reckless aggression against His Majesty, George III. These forts belonged to the king. How could it be hoped that he would look indulgently on his colonial children in the face of such acts of provocation? A bitter debate followed, at the end of which, over the opposition of most of the New England delegates—who realized how vital Ticonderoga and Crown Point were for the safety of their region—Congress directed that they be abandoned. The desperately needed supplies might be carried off, but a careful inventory should be made so that when harmony was restored between Great Britain and her colonies, proper restitution could be made of His Majesty's property.

This was indeed an extraordinary degree of nicety, a touching instance of the delegates' hopes for reconciliation. Connecticut lawmakers also disclaimed any responsibility for the capture of the forts, and New York followed suit. But the people themselves, and the several colonial legislatures, reacted differently. When word reached the colonies that Congress intended that the forts be, in effect, returned to the British, there was an immediate shock felt throughout New York and New England. The Albany Committee of Safety requested "blankets, pitch, tar, oakum, nails, spikes, gin, ropes" in order to build a fleet that could command the lake, and pointed out that the decision of Congress had been made without knowledge that Arnold was in command of the lake. Ticonderoga, the committee reminded Congress, was "by far the strongest and most important fortress" in North America. An obvious British strategy would be to cut off New England from the rest of the colonies by a campaign from Canada down the line of the Hudson to New York. The possession of Ticonderoga would forestall such a move. Connecticut joined forces with Massachusetts in sending a strong protest to Congress and dispatched four companies of men to the fort. New Hampshire, alarmed at the rumor that Guy Johnson, the Indian agent, was planning to enlist the Iroquois for an attack on the border settlements, joined in the protest. Massachusetts was the most emphatic of all. Joseph Hawley wrote that by an attack from Canada "the chain of the Colonies will be entirely and irreparably broken; the whole Province of New York will be fully taken into the interest of Administration [the Crown]; and this very pass of Ticonderoga is the post and spot where all this mischief may be withstood and resisted; but if that is relinquished or taken from us, desolation must come in upon us like a flood." If necessary, Massachusetts would join with Connecticut in holding the forts. Faced with explicit resistance to its authority, Congress reluctantly gave way. The forts might be held.

Meanwhile, the Massachusetts Provincial Congress, hearing of the friction between Arnold and Ethan Allen, sent off a three-man investigating committee to look into the whole matter and to place Arnold under Colonel Hinman, the officer in command of the considerable forces that had arrived from Connecticut. Arnold had been foolish enough to ask to be relieved of his command, apparently in the hope that the request would bring a confirmation of his ambiguous authority. He was dismayed and indignant to be superceded by Hinman. As the

Massachusetts mission reported, "He seemed greatly disconcerted, and declared he would not be second in command to any person whomsoever; and after some time contemplating upon the matter, he resigned his post . . . and at the same time he ordered his men to be disbanded which, he said was between two and three hundred." Arnold had not been treated well; he nourished his sense of grievance.

4

The Invasion of Canada

Wₕᵢₗₑ Washington continued to keep watch on the British in Boston, Congress began to dream of an invasion of Canada. Benedict Arnold wrote letters to Philadelphia urging such a step. New York's Philip Schuyler, just promoted to major general, also pointed out the advantages of such a bold move. To Congress, the most appealing aspect of a Canadian invasion was the thought that with Canada in American hands, Great Britain might be persuaded to redress American grievances and a reconciliation might be effected. So before Schuyler left Philadelphia to take up his duties in Albany, Congress gave him permission to plan a northward thrust.

The omens for the success of this rather daring scheme were not very favorable. First of all, Schuyler was not the ideal man for the job. One of the great aristocrats of New York, he was a handsome and urbane man, famous for his open-handed hospitality, and a shrewd politician. However, he lacked actual fighting experience, and he was also lacking in physical vigor. As a consequence, he was without the capacity for decisiveness and forceful leadership. The Canadian venture was the kind of quixotic enterprise that, if it was to succeed at all, had to be pushed with great energy and resourcefulness. Second, Schuyler was hampered by Congress's faltering and uncertain support. Among the

594

most outspoken critics of the proposal to invade Canada was Philadelphia's John Dickinson. Dickinson had been one of the leading advocates
of returning Ticonderoga and Crown Point to the British, and by the
same token he opposed any talk of invading Canada. While he did not
prevail, in John Adams' view he caused sufficient doubt and uneasiness
among the delegates to substantially weaken their support for the
venture.

The main hope of success lay in Schuyler's second-in-command, the
forceful Irish officer Richard Montgomery. Montgomery, at forty, was
one of the youngest general officers in the American army, and he was a
dashing and romantic figure. A tall, handsome, agile man in the prime
of life, he had great physical stamina and the kind of bravura that
soldiers most admire in their leaders. Together Schuyler and Montgomery, aided by the New York Provincial Congress and the Committee of
Safety, set to work to improve the defenses of the colony and to make
preparations for an invasion of Canada should the auguries prove
favorable.

Benedict Arnold, while still in command of Ticonderoga, had
prepared a plan of his own for a campaign directed against Montreal.
He had reliable information, he told Congress, that the Canadian
Indians were determined to remain neutral. "They have made a law,"
he noted, "that if any of their tribe shall take up arms for that purpose,
he shall immediately be put to death; this confirmed by five of their
chief men, who are now here with their wives and children, and press
very hard for our Army to march into Canada, being much disgusted"
with the British. Arnold calculated that Canada's governor general, Sir
Guy Carleton, had no more than 500 or 600 soldiers capable of action
duty; an American force of 2,000 men could, Arnold insisted, take the
whole vast region. Such an expedition could go by boat up Lake
Champlain to St. John's, leave a force there to protect their rear, and
march on a Montreal defended by no more than forty British regulars.
Then Canada could be used as a bargaining counter in negotiations with
the mother country. Arnold concluded his plan with the modest note:
"If no person appears who will undertake to carry the plan into execution (if thought advisable), I will undertake it, and, with the smiles of
Heaven, answer for the success of it."

The essence of Arnold's plan was speed. But speed was the one
thing it was futile to expect from Congress or, indeed, any deliberative
body. Weeks passed before Congress sent Arnold's proposal on to
Schuyler, leaving the final decision up to him. Arnold meanwhile, after

writing Congress that Governor Carleton of Canada was daily strengthening his positions and taking steps to forestall an invasion, was relieved
of his command at Ticonderoga by the Massachusetts Provincial Congress. At the same time, Schuyler began collecting men and supplies to
launch his own expedition. Lacking, in one historian's phrase, "the fury
of Arnold's energy," and hampered by his general lethargy, Schuyler
made little progress. He was also much concerned about the intentions
of the Iroquois who lived in the Mohawk Valley and were under the
influence of Guy Johnson, nephew of Sir William Johnson, the Indian
agent who of all white men had had the strongest hold on the loyalty
and affection of those warlike tribes. Nevertheless Schuyler did move.
Leaving behind him various requisitions for supplies, he decided to
proceed to Ticonderoga and establish his forward base there. Traveling
north, Schuyler stopped at his comfortable estate near Saratoga. There
he heard the alarming word that the Six Nations were stirring. Guy
Johnson, with Joseph Brant, a Mohawk Indian, as his secretary (Brant's
older sister, Molly, had been Sir William Johnson's mistress), was
reported to be going from tribe to tribe, conferring with his Indian
friends.

The fact was that Guy Johnson had arranged a great powwow in
Montreal, where nearly seventeen hundred Indians assembled to meet
with him, among them chiefs from each Iroquois tribe. Johnson gave
each chief a war belt, and all joined in singing a war song, after which
they were invited to a mock feast to eat "a Bostonian and drink his
blood—an ox having been roasted for the purpose, and a pipe of wine
given to drink." It was very much to the credit of Guy Carleton that,
despite Johnson's bloodthirsty pageant, he kept the Indians in control.
"What is or can be expected from them farther," he wrote Gage, who
wished to turn them loose on the Americans, "than cutting off a few
unfortunate Families, whose Destruction will be but of little Avail
towards a Decision of the present Contest?"

When Schuyler and his party reached the north end of Lake
George, he got a bitter foretaste of the problems that lay ahead of him.
At this spot, one of considerable strategic importance, Schuyler, arriving
at night, found a sentinel who, upon being informed of Schuyler's
presence, left his post "to go awaken the guard, consisting of three men,
in which he had no success." The general went up to a sergeant's guard.
"Here," he wrote Washington, "the sentinel challenged, and suffered
me to come up to him, the whole guard, like the first, in the profoundest
sleep. With a penknife only I could have cut off both guards, and then

have set fire to the block-house destroyed the store, and starved the people here." At Ticonderoga the situation was even more distressing: "Not one earthly thing for offence or defence has been done: the *commanding officer had no orders, he only came to re-enforce the garrison, and he expected the general!*" Schuyler lacked powder, artillery, lead, and provisions. "I have neither boats sufficient, nor any materials prepared for building them. . . . I have . . . not a nail, no pitch, no oakum, and a want of articles indispensably necessary," he wrote Washington.

In no area of life more than the military is it true that "God helps those who help themselves." There was much that was certainly beyond Schuyler's ability to change. The New York Committee of Safety, quite typically, replied to one of his pleas for men by writing, "Our troops can be of no service to you; they have no arms, clothes, blankets, or ammunition; the officers no commissions; our treasury no money; ourselves in debt. It is in vain to complain; we will remove difficulties as fast as we can, and send you soldiers, whenever the men we have raised are entitled to that name."

The writer of the letter had a philosophical bent, but that was small solace to Schuyler. His officers squabbled about seniority, some resigned in a huff over fancied slights, and Samuel Broome withdrew his company from the regiment to which it had been assigned because of a quarrel with another officer. The Connecticut men who made up the great majority of the troops present became increasingly resentful of the fact that most of their officers were New Yorkers. As one Connecticut soldier wrote, "Why all the places of profit should be filled up with men in York Government, I don't know, and our people are obliged to do all the drudgery." Brigadier General David Wooster, in command of the Connecticut troops in New York, expressed to Connecticut's Governor Trumbull his suspicions of the New Yorkers: "I have no faith in their honesty in the least I must therefore think it not only a disgrace to me but a dishonour to my employers that I am subjected to them—You know not Sr. half their tricks."

An army in camp is usually an unhappy army, especially when it is made up of raw recruits. The routines of camp life are monotonous and disheartening; every kind of pettiness, idle rumor, and shallow discontent burgeon. The remedy is campaigning. A well-planned and well-led campaign, if there is any good in the soldiers, is the only proper antidote for the common complaints of barracks and parade ground.

So it was that Schuyler's force declined daily in health and morale. It was late in August, with good weather running out, before Schuyler was ready to move northward with some thirteen hundred men and twenty days' provisions. Ethan Allen's Green Mountain Boys, perhaps annoyed with their leader's flamboyance, had voted him out of his command and voted in his lieutenant, Seth Warner; so Allen turned up without his boys, and put himself at the disposal of Schuyler, who probably found Allen something of a fifth wheel. "I always dreaded his impatience of subordination," Schuyler wrote of Allen; "and it was not until after a solemn promise, made me in the presence of several officers, that he would demean himself properly, that I would permit him to attend the Army. . . ."

The New Yorkers who joined Schuyler were poorly equipped in spite of the best efforts of the Provincial Congress of that colony. One captain, Schuyler wrote, "wants many things, such as shirts, stockings, underclothes, haversacks, and cash, having advanced all himself that has been paid his men as yet."

With his expedition finally ready to move, Schuyler received word from Washington that he was dispatching another expedition under Arnold by way of Maine to march on Quebec—with the intention of diverting Carleton and creating a modest envelopment of the small British force in Canada.

At this point Schuyler was called back to Albany to an Indian parley. During his absence, his command devolved on Richard Montgomery. When Montgomery heard that Carleton was preparing a naval expedition to sweep Lake Champlain and recapture the forts at Ticonderoga and Crown Point, he decided that he must block the British commander before his fleet debouched into the lake. He thus set out at once, leaving behind a request for Schuyler to reinforce him. "The moving without your orders I don't like," Montgomery wrote his chief; "but on the other hand, the prevention of the enemy is of the utmost consequence. . . . Let me entreat you (if you possibly can) to follow us in a whale-boat, leaving someone to bring forward the troops and artillery. It will give the men great confidence in your spirit and activity. How necessary this confidence is to a general, I need not tell you."

Montgomery was delayed by head winds—"a barbarous north wind" as he put it—and Schuyler eventually caught up with him at Isle La Motte on the fourth of September; they moved from there to the Isle-aux-Noix, blocking Carleton's access to the lake. There Schuyler issued a declaration addressed to the Canadians: He came to rescue them from British tyranny, he declared. The Americans would respect the rights of

Canadians and preserve their property. He also came with presents for the Indians. Ethan Allen and John Brown were charged with spreading this message among the population between St. John's and Montreal. Schuyler then advanced to St. John's, which was defended by several hundred British soldiers. While the Americans were making their way through a "close deep swamp" toward the fortifications defending the town, they were attacked by a party of Indians. "But," as Schuyler wrote, "our troops gallantly pressing on them, they soon gave way and left us the ground." The Americans made camp and set up defensive positions, intending to attack the town in the morning. That night, however, Schuyler had a visitor he refused to name, who came to inform him that all the British regulars in Canada were at St. John's, except about fifty left at Montreal plus some one hundred Indians. The informant also said that Carleton's schooners would be ready to sail in a few days. The visitor concluded by advising "that in the situation we were in, he judged it would be imprudent to attack St. Johns, and advised us to send some parties among the inhabitants, and the remainder of the Army to retire to Isle-aux-Noix" and there consider a flanking move on Montreal.

Had Schuyler's informant been in the pay of the British he could hardly have done them a better service. Schuyler was ill, and his illness, plus a native lack of resolution, persuaded him to accept the visitor's advice to retire to Isle-aux-Noix, put booms across the river, and wait for reinforcements. He retreated without taking steps to verify the report of his mysterious nocturnal visitor.

At the Isle-aux-Noix, Schuyler placed his artillery to command the river and waited while 300 more men came in from Connecticut and 400 from New York, giving him command of 1,700 men, two mortars, and five cannon. Meanwhile, Allen and Brown had ranged the country north of St. John's and made contact with an Englishman, James Livingston, who had managed to muster up some Canadians. Livingston's little force, starting off to join Schuyler, got word that Indians were waiting to waylay them and sent word to Schuyler asking for assistance in reaching his camp. Livingston believed this could best be done by cutting off the retreat of the British at St. John's. Schuyler responded by ordering a body of five hundred men under Montgomery to take up positions on the St. John's–Montreal road, in the rear of the British positions. The green troops had gone only a few hundred yards along the river when they panicked and retreated headlong. One shot had been fired, but rumors of an Indian ambush were enough to fill the night with terror for the inexperienced soldiers. Indians were bad enough in the daytime. At night their stealth and skill in close combat were enough to daunt the most experienced campaigners.

Montgomery rallied the demoralized soldiers and persuaded them to set out again. This time, protected by one of Montgomery's boats on the river, the Americans routed a handful of men defending a small house near the British positions. Next morning the officers called for a council of war and decided to attack again if the men were willing—"the Troops should declare whether they were ready to march." They consented and were about to push ahead when word came that a British vessel, armed and ready to sail, was waiting just up the river. Another council of war, another vote, this time for retreat. Eight miles from St. John's, Mongomery landed and made another effort to persuade at least a part of the soldiers to accompany him in an attack on St. John's. In the midst of discussion the alarm was given that British boats were coming and "the Troops were with difficulty restrained from pushing off without their officers." The withdrawal continued to Isle-aux-Noix.

There Schuyler listened to Montgomery's indignant account of events. Ethan Allen, operating largely on his own, came in with word that he had bluffed the Indians into pulling back from their rather halfhearted support of the British regulars, and that many Canadians were waiting only for some real show of American strength to rise in substantial numbers against the British. Moreover, there was still Livingston's little force at Chambly, who had committed themselves by seizing British supply boats and must receive some American support if they were not all to be taken and hanged as traitors.

Schuyler, having made the error of retreating to Isle-aux-Noix, paid a heavy price in the illness of his men in that damp and unhealthy spot. Six hundred men were sick and unfit for duty, while Schuyler himself was so ill that he was unable to leave his bed and was carried back down the lake to Ticonderoga. Nevertheless, Montgomery, having restored some modest degree of morale and order, pressed on, planning a joint attack by the river and by land against St. John's. Reinforcements came in. Seth Warner with a contingent of 170 Green Mountain Boys arrived, as did 100 New Hampshire Rangers and Captain John Lamb with the Independent Company of New York Artillery.

Schuyler's illness was a great piece of good fortune for his command. It removed an ailing and indecisive leader from the scene and replaced him with a healthy, skillful, and energetic one. Montgomery promptly surrounded St. John's and cut it off both from the river and the roads leading to Montreal. Some Iroquois visited Montgomery at St. John's and assured him that the Canadian Indians wished to remain neutral. Montgomery got the impression that the allegiance of the Indians was for sale. He begged the needed cash from Schuyler: "Send me money as fast as possible, my dear General," he wrote, saying that otherwise the Indians would think the Americans were cheapskates.

The ubiquitous Ethan Allen soon became a problem for Montgomery. Allen had recruited some Canadians, and he promised hundreds more. Abandoned by his Green Mountain Boys, he apparently hoped to soar "on the wings of fame" with his Canadians in an attack on Montreal. In one of the most quixotic gestures of the war, Allen with 110 men, only 30 of whom were "English Americans" (the rest were French-Canadians), set out to seize Montreal, a city of more than 5,000 people. John Brown, with a force of some 200 men, was to cross the St. Lawrence above the town in a combined operation. On the night of September 24, Allen crossed the river with his little force, making three trips since he did not have enough canoes to carry all his men over at once.

In Allen's defense, it must be said that his attack was based on the belief that his assault would be supported by inhabitants of the city who were favorable to the American cause. The reverse happened. The small British garrison of some forty soldiers recruited four hundred or five hundred of "a mixed multitude, chiefly Canadians, with a number of English who lived in the Town, and some Indians." Greatly outnumbered and with no help from Brown, Allen, short on canoes, could not escape. He opened fire on the British as they advanced, and when the enemy moved to outflank his hastily occupied position, he sent a detachment of some forty men to protect it. Judging wisdom to be the better part of valor, the detachment simply kept on going. Finally, with only thirty-eight men left, seven of whom were wounded, Allen surrendered.

After he had surrendered his sword, an Indian came running at him with "an incredible swiftness"; in Allen's own rather lurid prose, "his hellish visage . . . beyond all description, snake eyes appear innocent in comparison of his, his features distorted, malice, death, murder, and the wraths of devils and damned spirits are the emblems of his countenance." Rushing up to Allen, the Indian tried to get a shot at him with his musket without hitting the British officer. "I twitched the officer . . . between me and the savage, but he flew around with great fury, trying to single me out to shoot me . . . but this time I was as nimble as he, keeping the officer in such a position that his danger was my defence."

Allen was rescued from this mad dance by a British soldier who drove off the Indian with his bayonet. Allen was then taken as a prisoner to the city, where the British commander ordered him put in irons aboard the *Gaspee.*

So ended in the main the military career of Ethan Allen—on the whole, a good thing for the American cause. He was carried to England under the threat of being hanged as a traitor, then returned to America and exchanged for a British officer in 1778. He turned up at Valley Forge, where Washington, it may be imagined with some misgivings, commissioned him as a colonel, whereupon he returned to the New Hampshire grants and spent the rest of the war harassing New York settlers, secretly negotiating with the British to establish the independent state of Vermont, and causing all sorts of mischief. Captain Alexander Graydon, who met Allen when he was a prisoner in New York during the British occupation of the city, wrote in his *Memoirs,* "I have seldom met a man possessing . . . a stronger mind, or whose mode of expression was more vehement and oratorical. His style was a singular compound of local barbarisms, scriptural phrases and oriental wildness; and although unclassical and sometimes ungrammatical, it was highly animated and forcible. . . ."

However that may be, Allen had been a liability from his first appearance on the scene. His poorly conceived attack on Montreal was a disaster, not simply in itself but because it rejuvenated the defenders of Montreal, who congratulated themselves on having captured the feared and famous Ethan Allen. It put a virtual end to any hope of recruiting Canadians for the American side. Finally, Allen's failure encouraged the Indians, always and understandably concerned with throwing in their lot with a winner, to rally to the British standard.

Montgomery's little army now began to pay a heavy price for the various delays in the campaign. The weather was wet and miserable, with cold, soaking rains causing colds and chills and pneumonia—not to mention a general depression of the spirits of everyone involved. Montgomery wrote, "We have been like half-drowned rats crawling through the swamp." Powder and food were in desperately short supply, and nothing had come forward from Ticonderoga. When Schuyler recovered from his illness and reached Ticonderoga, he found in that post "a scandalous want of subordination and inattention to my orders. . . . If Job had been a General in my situation, his memory had not been so famous for patience." If Schuyler was a weak commander in the field, he was a capable and efficient military administrator, and he was soon able to get a flow of supplies moving up the Lake to St. John's. He was not exaggerating when he noted, "If I had not arrived here, even on the very day I did, as sure as God lives the army would have starved."

When Schuyler tried to commandeer the services of Wooster's Connecticut militia at that fort, they pointed out that they were not enlisted in the Continental Army. When an effort was made to enroll them, they balked, "as the soldiers thought their signing the articles would dissolve their present obligations [which were] for a limited time, to their own Colony, with many disadvantages to both officers and soldiers, and involve them in a service, the end of which was uncertain, and would leave them, perhaps, on no better footing than that of the Regulars."

Finally, ponderous old Wooster arrived in Ticonderoga, and his troops, who had preceded him, consented "with the greatest reluctance" to sail to the support of Montgomery. It had taken all of Wooster's powers of persuasion to prevail on them. Officers and men had argued, with a good deal of acumen as it turned out, that they would be "detained in Canada all winter; that they may be prevented by frost from returning; that they will perish with cold or sickness. . . ."

That was in fact to be the fate of many of them. Frustrating as it must have been to Schuyler to find himself engaged in such an extraordinary debate, one cannot help feeling considerable sympathy for the soldiers. They were willing to do their part for the cause of freedom, to defend their homes and do their best to drive the British out of their colony and, indeed, out of their country. But a rigorous campaign in Canada with winter coming on was another matter. Patriotism did not seem to them to require an inadequately equipped and poorly supplied participation in an expedition that common sense readily indicted. Of the 335 that set out, 51 "sick and sham sick" were left at Ticonderoga.

Supplies were only part of Montgomery's troubles. Equally disheartening was the behavior of his men in camp and on the march. They were impatient of any restraint: "I did consider," Montgomery wrote, "I was at the head of troops who carry the spirit of freedom into the field, and think for themselves." It was a new principle of military operation when soldiers were allowed to vote on matters of tactics. When Montgomery wanted to move his battery of light fieldpieces into range of the British fortifications, "a general dissatisfaction prevailed," with hints of mutiny. "The universal sense of the Army" opposed the general's orders—and prevailed. Much had to do with the narrowness and suspicion of the New Englanders towards any "foreigners."

Montgomery, surrounding the British garrison at St. John's and commanding the river, sent some cannon on shallow-bottomed bateaux down the river to Chambly, which was defended by a force of less than 100 Royal Fusiliers who were guarding a cache of supplies, including 124 barrels of powder, desperately needed by the Americans. A brisk bombardment of their little fort quickly persuaded them to surrender. Montgomery's list of captured materials ended with "Royal Fusiliers, 83. Accoutrements, 83." When Washington received the account of the affray, he wrote to Schuyler: "We laugh. Does Montgomery consider them as inanimates, or as a treasure?"

Montgomery's artillerymen sank the British schooner, which could not maneuver in the narrow river; then, finally prevailing on his soldiers to move the cannon nearer St. John's, Montgomery directed an effective fire that gradually reduced the town to rubble. But the garrison held out, hoping for reinforcements from Carleton. Carleton did, in fact, set out with a motley force of French-Canadians, Indians, and a few regulars, but Seth Warner and his Green Mountain Boys, backed up by a few light cannon, opened such a heavy fire on his boats from ambush that Carleton abandoned the effort. His small force could have afforded little relief to the besieged soldiers at St. John's. Colonel Richard Prescott, who a few weeks earlier, while commanding the forces at Montreal in Carleton's absence, had ordered Ethan Allen put in irons to be transported to England as a traitor, now commanded the force at St. John's. With the arrival of a mortar called "the Old Sow," which lobbed shells into the town with devastating effect, and with the failure of Carleton's effort at relief, Prescott was forced to capitulate on the second of November. Among the British who marched out of the fort was a Major John André. When the British were allowed to keep their reserve supply of clothing, the New Yorkers, shivering in their rags, almost mutinied. "There was no driving into their noodles," Montgomery wrote, "that the clothing belonged to the British."

With St. John's captured after this protracted winter siege, the soldiers—who had had enough of cold, poor food, and the pervasive damp of river and swamp, of colds, grippe, and dysentery—were ready to go home. Montgomery pleaded with them to push on to Montreal, the goal of the whole campaign. It would be folly, he pointed out, to stop with the prize practically in their grasp. Finally, he prevailed upon them to continue by promising that once Montreal had been captured, they could all go home. "Under our Feet was Snow and Ice and Water," wrote a chaplain, "Over our Heads Clouds Snow and rain, before us the mountains appeared all white with Snow and Ice. It was remarkable to See the Americans after almost infinite Fatigues and Hardships marching on at this advanced Season, badly clothed and badly provided for to Montreal, pressing on to new Sieges and new Conquests." And this was certainly the truth of it. Anyone who, on a camping trip, has been overtaken by a cold rain that soaked clothes, bedding, and equipment, and has tried to maintain his morale and that of his party, will perhaps be able to imagine what it meant to endure almost two months of such conditions, with inadequate food and constant danger, several hundred miles away from home.

Carleton, with no troops to defend Montreal, escaped to British vessels in the river, leaving the city to Mongomery, who marched in and formally occupied it without resistance. He promised the residents to respect their religion and to pay a fair price for supplies needed by his soldiers. At the same time, he reorganized his little army, requisitioned warm clothes for them, and settled down to await word of Benedict Arnold's expedition against Quebec.

5

Arnold's March

Benedict Arnold, who had been relieved of the command of Ticonderoga and had seen command of the Canadian expedition go to another man, was not the type to sit on the sidelines. Hurrying to Cambridge, he persuaded Washington of the advantages to be gained by a combined attack on Quebec, in which Schuyler's army, having taken Montreal, would continue up the St. Lawrence to Quebec and there join with an expeditionary force coming up the Kennebec River from the east.

It was fine to seize Montreal, but any amateur strategist could see by looking at a map that Quebec commanded the approach to Montreal, and that there was little hope of holding the lower city without also holding its more northern neighbor. Washington, impressed with Arnold's ardor and with his strategic grasp, dispatched him on a long and arduous route: by sea to the mouth of the Kennebec River, and then up the river by boats. The distance from the mouth of the river to Quebec was about 230 miles. This included numerous portages around falls, several of them between two and six miles, ending in the "great carry" from the Kennebec to the Chaudière River, which emptied into the St. Lawrence four miles above Quebec. Arnold's march to Quebec became one of the great military ventures in history. Taken as an

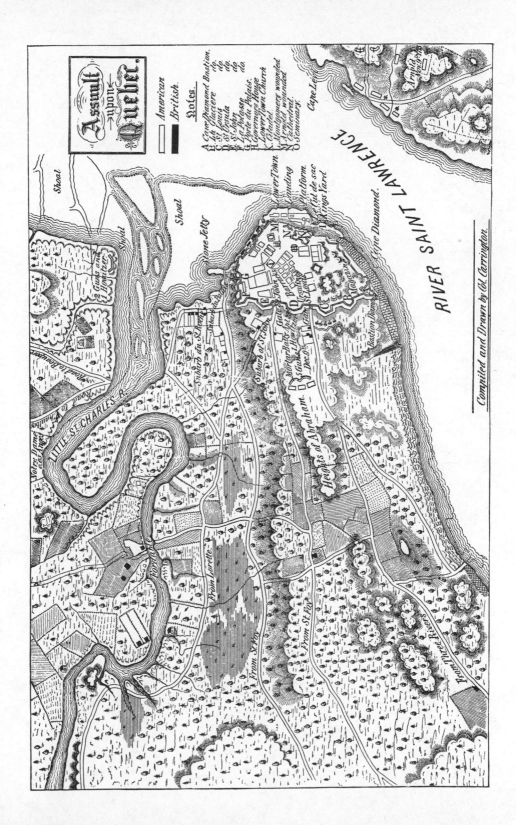

Assault upon Quebec.

American
British

Notes.

A Cape Diamond Bastion.
B la Glaciere.   do.
C St. Louis   do.
D St. Ursula   do.
E St. John   do.
F La Potasse
G Porte du Palais.
H Governor's House
I Lower Town Church
K Citadel
L Montgomery wounded
M Arnold wounded
N Cathedral
O Seminary.

RIVER SAINT LAWRENCE

Compiled and Drawn by Col. Carrington.

achievement of will, the expedition must always arouse the admiration of everyone who admires skill and daring carried to the limits of human endurance.

Washington informed Congress at the end of September that he was sending Arnold to Canada to cooperate with Schuyler's force. To Arnold Washington wrote: "Sir: You are intrusted with a command of the utmost consequences to the interests and liberties of America; upon your conduct and courage, and that of the officers and soldiers detached on this expedition, not only the success of the present enterprise, and your own honor, but the safety and welfare of the whole continent, may depend." Arnold was especially enjoined to see that no soldier under his command performed any act of depredation or violence against any Canadian or Indian they might encounter on their march. His men must also "avoid all disrespect or contempt of the religion of the country," and indeed conduct themselves with "common prudence, policy, and true Christian spirit." An effort might certainly be made at conversion, provided it was done with tact and modesty, remembering that "God alone is the judge of the heart of man, and to him only in this case are they [the Canadians] answerable." In short, Arnold must appear to the Canadians, so far as possible, as a liberating rather than a conquering hero.

In his baggage Arnold carried a large number of printed broadsides inviting the Canadians to join hands in the struggle against Great Britain. "The hand of tyranny has been arrested in its ravages," the declaration read, "and the British arms, which have shone with so much splendor in every part of the globe, are now tarnished with disgrace and disappointment. . . . Come, then, my brethren, unite with us in an indissoluble union; let us run together to the same goal. We have taken up arms in defence of our liberty, our property, our wives, and our children; we are determined to preserve them or die. We look forward with pleasure to that day, not far remote, we hope, when the inhabitants of America shall have one sentiment, and the full enjoyment of the blessings of a free government. . . ."

Knowing of Arnold's unseemly squabble with Ethan Allen over command of the Ticonderoga expedition, Washington also made it clear to Arnold that were he to join forces with Schuyler, he would be under Schuyler's authority in the strictest degree. The little army that Arnold commanded was the first truly intercolonial detachment. The bulk of Arnold's force was made up of eleven companies of musket-bearing infantry from Massachusetts, Connecticut, and Rhode Island, but included were three companies of riflemen: Captain Daniel Morgan's company from Virginia, the company of Captain William Hendricks from Cumberland county in Pennsylvania, and another Pennsylvania company under the command of Captain Matthew Smith.

One of the young riflemen from Pennsylvania, John Joseph Henry, whose mother had made his buckskin leggings and fringed hunting jacket, noted that the principal distinction between the Pennsylvanians and their Yankee companions-in-arms "was in our dialects, our arms and our dress." Each man of the rifle companies carried, in addition to his rifle, a tomahawk and a long knife, usually called a scalping knife. "It was the silly fashion of those time," Henry later recalled, "for riflemen to ape the manners of savages."

The most impressive of the riflemen was Captain Daniel Morgan, a large, handsome man, severe and formal in first encounter "but where he became attached . . . kind and truly affectionate." William Hendricks, captain of one of the Pennsylvania companies, was "tall, of mild and beautiful countenance" with "a genuine spark of heroism." Matthew Smith was the roughest of the lot, "illiterate and outrageously talkative."

The companies left Prospect Hill near Washington's Cambridge headquarters on September 11 and made a rendezvous at Newburyport, from whence they sailed in ten transports to the mouth of Kennebec River, a distance of some 150 miles. When the little flotilla set sail from Newburyport under a pleasant breeze, with drums beating, fifes playing, and colors flying, "many pretty girls stood upon the shore, I suppose, weeping for the departure of their sweethearts," Isaac Senter, the expedition's doctor, noted. At a Maine shipyard the expedition was loaded into small boats for the 355-mile wilderness trek to Quebec. Some 200 flat-bottomed bateaux had been built in a few weeks, each large enough to hold four men with a quantity of supplies, yet light enough to be carried over the numerous portages.

There is perhaps one other introductory fact about the expedition that is worthy of mention. Five or six members of the expedition faithfully kept diaries, and this among men taxed to the utmost day after day is remarkable. The diary is one of the particular achievements of the individualistic Protestant consciousness. It was not simply the pleasure of literate men with time on their hands; it was the crucial record, kept as often by simple men as grand ones, of the state of the individual's soul and the corporal embodiment of that soul, under God's care and judgment. It was a discipline and a kind of ledger sheet, so it was quite natural to pious Abner Stocking to note that "though we were in a thick wilderness, uninhabited by human beings, yet we were as much in the immediate presence of our divine protector as when in the crowded city." The records made by these men constitute the story of Arnold's march.

An officer and seven men were detailed to push ahead of the main party and reconnoiter the Indians' paths and fords at the various points on the river. This advance party was provided with two birchbark canoes and two local guides. The canoes of the advance party were hardly thicker than cardboard—one of the most ingenuous creations of primitive men in any place or time. Each of them carried from five to seven men, their arms and baggage, a barrel of pork, a bag of meal, and 200 weight of bisquit, and yet at a portage one man could carry a canoe for hundreds of yards without undue fatigue. And thus began an epic journey as perilous as Xenephon's *Anabasis,* the "upcountry march" of the Greeks. Arnold's Americans had to push through one of the grimmest forests of the American continent in the cold of late fall and early winter.

The advance party lived largely off the land and lived very well, catching trout, shooting ducks and grouse and deer, astonished at the sight of the huge "moose deer" with his gigantic rack of antlers, passing the abandoned sites of Indian villages and camping grounds, and meeting an occasional frontiersman living alone in the vast woods many miles from the nearest settlement. With one of these they traded some flour for a beaver tail, which when cooked was as rich and sweet as butter. At every portage they blazed a trail for the main party to follow.

The main force followed several days behind the scouts. According to tradition, Aaron Burr, who was Arnold's aide, brought with him an Indian girl, Jacatagua, an "abnaki Queen with golden thighs." There were two other women on the expedition, the wives of soldiers. They cooked and sewed and gave the little army a taste of the amenities that only women can bring and that lightened the burden of the long labor up the waters of the Kennebec. The morale of Isaac Senter, a twenty-two-year-old physician from Rhode Island, reflected that of the army. "We were all in high spirits," he wrote in his journal, "intending to endure with fortitude all the fatigues and hardships that we might meet with in our march to Quebec."

Rowing the heavy bateaux, loaded with soldiers and supplies, against the swift current was backbreaking work. The first day the army, still fresh and energetic, made only seven miles, but they camped that night on the edge of a cornfield and dined "very sumptiously" on the sweet ears of freshly picked corn. From here on, the current grew swifter, and the bateaux frequently ran aground on sandbars and underwater obstacles. On September 27, the army encountered its first portage at Ticonnick Falls, a short carry of a few hundred yards. The soldiers unloaded, transported boats and equipment, loaded, and resumed their laborious way. They made only three miles that day, a foretaste of what was to come.

Rowing soon proved impossible. The only way to make any progress was for soldiers with ropes over their shoulders like draft horses to haul the bateaux against the current. The water was bitterly cold, and the men slipped and stumbled over the bruising rocks, sometimes stepping into sinkholes in which they were totally submerged, or scraping their legs on snags and jagged tree limbs below the surface. At night, "wet and fatigued, as we were, we had to encamp on the cold ground. It was at this time," physician Senter added, poignantly, "that we inclined to think of the comfortable accommodations we had left at home."

The Kennebec at its upper reaches proceeded through deep gorges that rose steeply on both sides of the river. Here the water was so deep and swift that the men could neither row nor haul the bateaux; they were reduced to pulling them along, hand over hand, by means of bushes and fallen limbs along the banks. Some bateaux were smashed against the rocks by the currents and had to be laboriously repaired. Each day illness and injury depleted the little company, and those further down the river were demoralized to encounter bateaux returning, loaded to the gunnels with the sick and disabled.

At Norridgewock Falls, the little force camped at the site of an old Indian village where Father Rales, a Récollet missionary, had established an Indian mission many years before. The simple little church still stood with, to the eyes of the Protestant soldiers, "some curiosities such as crosses, etc." From this spot the French-allied Indians had sailed out to slaughter men and women in the Maine settlements until the colonial militia had wiped out the mission in a counterraid.

Leaving the Kennebec, the boats and supplies were carried over swamps and ridges to the Dead River, which began as a placid stream but soon turned into falls and rapids. The green wood of the bateaux sprang leaks constantly; fortunately, carpenters were part of the expedition, brought along to repair the boats. Water shipped in the rapids spoiled much of the food. The salt was also washed out of the salt fish and the beef, thus removing the preservative, and the bisquits and peas were thoroughly soaked.

Those bateaux in the lead, urged on by the indefatigable Arnold, outran their food supply, and Colonel Christopher Greene's Connecticut division found themselves at nightfall on October 24 with nothing to eat but candles, "which were used for supper, and breakfast next morning, by boiling them in water gruel." The army had been, by this time, a month at the most exhausting of possible labors, with insufficient food, increasing cold, and diminishing progress, often measured in yards rather than miles.

A council of war was called in Arnold's absence (he was at the head of the long column of bateaux strung out over many miles of river). It had snowed during the night, the men were half-frozen, and the provisions when averaged out came to a bare five days' rations. At this juncture a vote was taken. A majority of the men favored returning. Those who decided to continue made arrangements to send ahead a detachment to clear the roads and, so far as possible, the river; to construct bough huts, and, in general, to prepare crude accommodations for the exhausted soldiers of the main body when they were ready to make camp. "The invalids and the timorous" were to return.

But here another critical issue arose. Since the returnees would have by far the easier and quicker voyage down the river, those who were determined to press on wished a disproportionate share of the meager supplies remaining. The returnees, for their part, insisted on an equal division. When Colonel Enos, who was to be in charge of those who were turning back, was appealed to, "he replied that his men were out of his power, and that they had determined to keep their possessed quantity whether they went back or forward." For a time the threat of violence hung over the miserable little army, but, as Isaac Senter noted, "to compel them [the returnees] to a just division we were not in a situation, as being the weakest part." Those who were going on thus took the "small pittance . . . received it, put it on board of our boats, quit the few tents we were in possession of, with all the camp equipage, took each man to his duds on his back, bid them adieu, and away—passed the river, passed over falls and encamped."

The next day, with an estimated 150 miles still to go, the remnant of the army "passed over several rocky mountains and monstrous precipices, to appearance inaccessible; fired with more than Hannibalian enthusiasm, American Alps nor Pyrenees were obstacles." Captain Morgan's riflemen, who somehow carried their bateaux over the rugged terrain, were able to navigate a series of small lakes, while the balance of the army made its way as best it could through marsh and swamp.

Finally, after three days of slogging, half-starved and half-lost, "with as little knowledge of where we were or where we should get to, as if we had been in the unknown interior of Africa, or the deserts of Arabia," as Senter put it, the various contingents, minus those who had simply fallen exhausted to die where they fell, met at the headwaters of the Chaudière River. Arnold, with an advance party, pushed ahead down the Chaudière, into the area called the Caldron.

Their course now lay downhill along the banks of the river, which flowed into the St. Lawrence. But they still suffered wretchedly from the cold and, above all, from hunger. Water and flour was all that was left for them to eat. This mixture was christened "Lillipu." Where they had once been weakened by diarrhea, the men now, on a diet of bread and water, suffered from the binds. "Clean and unclean were forms now little in use," Senter wrote. "In company a poor dog [who had] hitherto lived through all the tribulations, now became a prey for the sustenance of the assassinators. The poor animal was instantly devoured, without leaving any vestige of the sacrifice. Nor did shaving soap, pomatum, and even lip salve, leather of their shoes, cartridge boxes, etc., share any better fate." In this condition the men, like heroes out of a Homeric legend, still marched between twenty and thirty miles a day. One of the soldiers whose wife had accompanied him fell by the trail, unable to go on. After pleading with his companions to carry him with them, his wife stayed back and took care of him as best she could until he died. Then, taking his rifle, she hurried on and caught up with the main body.

Where before all the effort had been to make way against the increasingly heavy current of the Kennebec, it was now to prevent the boats from being smashed to kindling and the men from being drowned in a rush down the swift current. At "a very long rapid," all the boats carrying Arnold and the advance party were overturned and most of the supplies lost. The drenched soldiers reached shore to find that their dousing had been providential, since because of it they had avoided going over a waterfall that would certainly have drowned them all.

At last, with the main body strung out along twenty miles of river, those soldiers trudging in advance, each step a tribulation, saw what was either a mirage or the sweetest of sights—"a vision of horned cattle, four-footed beasts. . . . Upon a higher approach our vision proved real! Exclamations of joy, echoes of gladness resounded from front to rear with a *Te Deum*." A heifer was butchered and each man given a pound of meat; two Canadians arrived in a canoe with corn meal, mutton, and tobacco. A sinner accepted into paradise could have felt no greater exaltation and relief than the remnants of Arnold's tattered legion, at last approaching the end of its incredible odyssey. In Dr. Senter's terse but expressive sentence: "We sat down, eat our rations, blessed our stars, and thought it a luxury." The men's clothes "hung in strings—few of us had any shoes," one wrote, "but moggasons made of raw skins—many of us without hats—and beards long and visages thin and meager. I thought we much resembled the animals which inhabit New Spain, called the Ourang-Outang." Arnold was quite right when he wrote to Schuyler: " . . . in about eight weeks we completed a march of six hundred miles, not to be paralleled in history. . . ." His men, Arnold calculated, had waded some 180 miles hauling their boats behind them, carried them a total of 40 miles at portages, and marched for a week on less than half rations.

The ill and wasted were nursed back to health by the friendly Canadians. The inhabitants of Quebec were dumfounded at the appearance of Arnold and his tattered band. "Surely," a Frenchman wrote, "a miracle must have been wrought in their favor. It is an undertaking above the common race of men, in this debauched age."

At the beginning of the expedition, Arnold had sent out an advance party with instructions to kill Natanis, an Indian chief known to be hostile to the Americans. When Arnold arrived at Sartigan, across the river from Quebec, Natanis came into the camp and greeted the soldiers in a friendly and familiar spirit. It turned out he had shadowed the little army during its terrible journey. "Why did you not speak to your friends?" he was asked. "You would have killed me," Natanis replied. He and a few of his warriors joined Arnold in the assault on Quebec.

With his soldiers "almost naked, bare footed and much fatigued," with little powder and only ten rounds of ammunition per man, Arnold wisely restrained his impatience and waited for Montgomery to join him from Montreal. Arnold's initial efforts to establish contact with Montgomery had been unsuccessful. But eventually word got through, and Montgomery, as daring and energetic as Arnold himself, raced with his three hundred men to Sartigan to make up for the lost time as best he could. He brought artillery plus some warm clothing for Arnold's tattered band. Arnold's men recognized the soldier in the tall, thin, balding Montgomery. One described him as "a genteel polite man . . . Resolute, mild, and of a fine temper and an excellent generall." Another noted that he was "born to command. His easy and affable condescension to both officers and men, while it forbids an improper familiarity, creates love and esteem; and exhibits him the gentleman and the soldier." And Montgomery found Arnold "active intelligent, and enterprising. . . . Indeed," he added, "I must say he has brought with him many pretty young men."

"We propose immediately investing the town and make no doubt in a few days to bring Gov. Carleton to terms," Arnold wrote to Schuyler on November 27. It was a vain boast. Quebec, rising proudly on its plateau above the St. Lawrence, was, if not impregnable, as close to it as a city could be. Colonel Allan Maclean had brought a regiment of Royal Highland Emigrants to the citadel; the governor of the city had mustered five hundred soldiers; three hundred men were pressed into service from ships in the harbor. When the combined forces of Arnold and Montgomery were ready to attack Quebec, Carleton commanded some seventeen hundred men, well equipped and well protected by stout fortifications.

Montgomery and Arnold together commanded fewer than one thousand men. Against such a fortress Montgomery's cannon had little effect. "I propose," Montgomery wrote Schuyler, with the same optimism that characterized Arnold's communications, "amusing Mr. Carleton with a formal attack, erecting batteries, etc., but mean to assault the works, I believe towards the lower town, which is the weakest point. . . . I find Colonel Arnold's corps an exceeding fine one, inured to fatigue. . . . There is a style of discipline among them much superior to what I have been used to see in this campaign." But Montgomery was no fool; he added a soberer note that may have told more of his true feelings than his bolder words: "Fortune often baffles the sanguine expectations of poor mortals. I am not intoxicated with the favours I have received at her hands, but I do think there is a fair prospect of success."

Montgomery and Arnold knew that they did not have a sufficient force to storm the defenses of the city. Yet having come so far with such extravagant hopes and endured such miseries, they could not bear to withdraw. A surprise attack seemed the only possibility. The men were placed in a state of readiness. Perhaps if they moved under cover of darkness and a howling snowstorm, the defenders might be caught off guard and the city occupied. Between four and five o'clock on the morning of January 1, in a violent blizzard, the diminuitive army, hardly more than a reinforced patrol, attacked the most impregnable city in North America.

A night attack offers many obvious advantages, but it requires the most disciplined and seasoned troops. To attack at night in a snow storm, when vision is limited to a few feet, is the severest test that can be given soldiers. Montgomery moved from the southwest against a block-house and picket post some two hundred yards ahead of the "Pot-Ash," a fortified position with several pieces of artillery. At the sight of the ghostly figures of Montgomery's advance party emerging from the darkness, the Canadian guards at the blockhouse fired a few random shots and fled.

With the blockhouse cleared, the Americans, with Montgomery himself in the van, made their painstaking way in single file along a narrow path toward the Pot-Ash battery, clambering over huge lumps of ice and boulders along the riverbank. Montgomery, "having reassem-bled about two hundred men, whom he encouraged alike by his voice and his example, he advanced boldly and rapidly at their head to force the barrier." As Montgomery and his men picked their way through the darkness, several of the Canadians who had taken to their heels at the sight of the feared Americans became emboldened at the delay; return-ing to the Pot-Ash battery, they picked up a slow match, burning near one of the fieldpieces already aimed at the path along which Montgom-ery's soldiers were advancing, and placed it to the touchhole. The range was pointblank; Montgomery and the men closest to him were within forty yards of the cannon when it was fired. Montgomery and two captains, one of them his aide, along with a sergeant and private, were killed instantly. The command devolved to an officer who lacked Montgomery's fanatical determination. The men melted silently back into the storm, leaving Arnold and his detachment to carry the full burden of the attack.

As Arnold's men approached the so-called Palace Gate of Quebec, they heard the chilling sound of cannon fire and the ringing of alarm bells in the city. Arnold, like Montgomery, moved ahead of the main body of his troops. Next came the riflemen, followed by the New Englanders. As John Henry wrote: "Covering the locks of our guns with the lappets of our coats, holding down our heads (for it was impossible to bear up our faces against the imperious storm of snow and wind), we ran along the foot of the hill in single file" toward some abandoned buildings. Here, spread out at wide intervals, they came under heavy fire from the battlements above and saw the first of their casualties fall on the frozen ground, unable to return fire against defenders they could not even see.

As the main body of soldiers were still stumbling forward, half-blinded by the snow, Arnold, who had been wounded in the leg, passed them, an officer on each side half-carrying him, his trousers and boot stained with blood. As he passed, he "called to the troops in a cheering voice . . . urging us forward." The sight of Arnold wounded, the man whose spirit alone had brought them so far and had, at last, propelled them into this mad assault, was enough to dampen the boldest soul. What was extraordinary was that they indeed pressed on, driven by the momentum of their attack. At the first barrier they drove back the defenders. Discovering that their guns would not fire, because the snow lodged in the folds of their coats had been melted by the warmth of their bodies and had dampened the powder in the priming pans, many of the Americans threw away their own useless weapons and picked up muskets that the defenders of the first embrasure had abandoned.

Beyond the first breech, a street ran for several hundred yards to a second line of fortifications at the foot of the hill leading to the upper town. With Montgomery dead and his diversionary attack lost, the men defending the eastern side of the city were quickly redeployed to meet the initial penetration of Arnold's force. The narrow street leading from the first barrier to the second became a trap for the Americans. They could not deploy or find cover except in the houses on both sides of the street. When they rushed the barricade itself, they could not climb it, and those who did manage to struggle to the top faced the direct fire of a cannon loaded with grapeshot. As though this were not enough, the upper floors of the houses beyond the barrier, looking down upon it and down the street up which the Americans were advancing, were filled with soldiers who kept up a steady musket fire. Captain Humphreys ordered an improvised mound piled under the barricade to help mount it, but he was driven back by a "formidable phalanx of bayonets" and by a shower of grapeshot from the cannon, and finally he fell with a bullet in his heart. The riflemen swept the crew from the cannon, and while Captain Daniel Morgan, head of the Virginia riflemen, "stormed and raged," the other officers attempted to find a way through the barrier. Finally Morgan, seeing men falling around him and realizing their advance was blocked, ordered the troops within earshot to take cover in the houses and keep up their fire from there.

At this point, Carleton dispatched a force of two hundred men to seal off the avenue of escape. Several hundred of the attackers, who had not passed the first barrier, saw the flanking movement in time and fled across the ice that covered St. Charles Bay. The Canadian auxiliaries that Arnold had recruited, fearing they would be hanged if they were captured, led the flight. The retreat was, in the words of John Henry, "a dangerous and desperate adventure . . . running two miles across shoal ice, thrown up by the high tides. . . ." Somehow Arnold too escaped with a handful of his men.

By nine o'clock, with the winter sun well up in the sky, the remaining Americans in the city surrendered. The colonials counted some sixty killed or wounded, the majority of these in the rifle companies that had borne the brunt of the attack; some four hundred were captured.

The wounded Arnold was taken to a hospital in the suburb of St. Roche, north of the city. Here a surgeon operated on him and removed the musket ball from his leg. Other wounded men trickled in, bringing the dismal news of the difficulties of the assault and, finally, of the surrender of the main forces under Dearborn and Morgan. Then word came that Carleton had sent a party to attack St. Roche. Invalids and those of the wounded who could still maneuver turned out to man two fieldpieces. The surgeon tried to persuade Arnold to allow himself to be carried to some safe spot, but "he would neither be removed, nor suffer a man from the Hospital to retreat. He ordered his pistols loaded, with a sword on his bed etc., adding that he was determined to kill as many as possible if they came into the room. We were now all soldiers, even so the wounded in their beds were ordered a gun by their side." The artillery fire turned the British back, and the hospital and its dangerously wounded were safe.

So, to all intents and purposes, ended the American effort to seize Canada. It was an astonishingly bold project, and it came within a hairsbreadth of success. In terms of conventional warfare it was more than a little insane, but the Americans were not yet committed to conventional warfare, and this extravagant venture came close enough to victory to startle the world. The measure of its failure can, indeed, be summed up in one word: "Time." At every stage of the operation, a few weeks' time would have certainly made an enormous difference. Time meant, essentially, supplies. Supplies, in turn, depended on the energy and resolution of those charged with providing them. The vacillation of Congress in regard to the invasion of Canada was certainly an inhibiting factor.

John Adams made the bitter charge that John Dickinson was responsible for the ultimate failure of the Canadian campaign. "I have always imputed . . . the loss of Quebec and Montgomery to his unceasing, though finally unavailing efforts against independence. These impeded and paralyzed all our enterprises. . . . If every measure for the service in Canada, from the first projection of it to the final loss of the

Province, had not been opposed and obstinately disputed by the same party, so that we could finally carry no measure but by a bare majority— And every measure was delayed, till it became ineffectual."

If Adams' judgment of Dickinson was too harsh, it is certainly true that a substantial portion of the blame for the failure of the operation must be laid at the door of Congress, that timid and dilatory body. But perhaps Montgomery's goddess of fortune, who so often baffles the most sanguine hopes, must bear a heavy charge as well. When every day counted, it was bad luck that Arnold's initial messages urging Montgomery to meet him at Quebec failed to reach the general at Montreal.

The death of Montgomery, which had about it something of an accident, doomed the attack on the city at its very inception. Knowing that general's courage and resourcefulness, we can assume that he would have had an excellent chance to penetrate the city, or at least to divide and demoralize the defenders, most of whom had very little heart or stomach for their task and looked on the Americans either as prospective friends or as fearsome and frightening figures. It is evident that it would have taken very little impetus for the panic that was initially felt by many of those charged with defending Quebec to have spread throughout the city. That Arnold's men, with their leader wounded, still fought so resourcefully and penetrated the lower city as far as the second barricade, suggests that with either a little luck or the support of Montgomery's force, they might well have swept into the heart of that bastion.

The difference in numbers between the Montgomery-Arnold force and the levies assembled to protect the city is misleading. A soldier counts only if he is willing to fight; his simple existence, however well-equipped and heavily armed he may be, is otherwise of little consequence. The Americans who fought at Quebec were undoubtedly among the best soldiers who ever fought against discouraging odds. They were superbly led; they came to fight. The most notable victories in warfare have, with few exceptions, gone to those armies who forced the "breaks" by their energy and resolution. There are no defenses, however formidable, that are proof against a determined and well-led attack.

It must also be remembered that the invasion of Canada was based on the assumption that the Canadians themselves would welcome the Americans and make common cause with them against the British government, and this calculation had just enough tantalizing truth in it to prove irresistible to the planners of American strategy. The Canadians were, for the most part, sympathetic and ready to help with food and supplies and occasional men, but they were largely lacking in the deep sense of grievance and moral outrage that provided so powerful an incentive to their neighbors to the south. Thus they never rose in any substantial numbers, and never came close to providing the levies of citizen-soldiers that Washington and his staff had dreamed of. They were throughout the Revolution passive observers rather than active participants.

Distressed as Americans were at the news of the defeat and capture of Arnold's force—and above all by the death of Montgomery, which awakened memories of the tragic death of General Wolfe—they were deeply stirred by the daring of the attack. When word of Montgomery's death reached England, he was praised in Parliament by Edmund Burke and Barré and Charles James Fox as a hero. To which North replied that Montgomery was "brave, able, humane, generous; but still only a brave, able, humane and generous Rebel. . . ." Fox had the last word, however. He noted that all the great defenders of liberty had, in their time, been called rebels, and the members of Parliament "even owed the Constitution which enabled them to sit in that House to a rebellion," a reference to the English Civil War of 1640.

The fact is that Arnold's march to Quebec could not have been carried through by any other soldiers in the world. It was an achievement unique to a people whose individualism was so powerful a reality that it enabled them to overcome innumerable practical difficulties with an innate resourcefulness, and beyond that, to support the will to survive and persevere in the face of incredible hardships. Much credit must go, of course, to Arnold. That cold, hard, ambitious man was a superb leader, the type who leads by inspiring emulation, by doing first himself the most arduous and demanding tasks. He was a fanatic, and probably more than slightly mad; most of the Americans captured at Quebec must have felt a guilty sense of relief at being freed at last from that insatiable and demonic spirit. If the British could have seen, beyond the simple and deceptive fact of the American defeat, the remarkable intensity of purpose symbolized by the Canadian invasion, they would perhaps have learned—even better than the Battle of Bunker Hill could have taught them—the eventual outcome of their efforts to reduce the colonies to a "proper degree of subordination."

Arnold, wounded and in command of a vastly reduced force, persisted in his determination to try to capture Quebec. The news of Montgomery's death and the failure of the attack on Quebec stirred the Congress to a fever of activity to try to reinforce Arnold and complete the conquest of Canada. Washington prepared to send three of his own regiments from Boston. A bounty was offered for all those troops who enlisted. The Green Mountain Boys emerged from the woods to resume campaigning, and Congress directed that one thousand Canadians be recruited. An address to the Canadians was drafted, assuring them that they would not be abandoned.

Despite such a commendable bustle of activity, little help reached Arnold. The reason was simple enough: For the moment there was insufficient armament to equip the soldiers who were being recruited at such a surprising rate. The supplies of powder had gradually grown by importation and by local manufacture, but the critical shortage of muskets made it impossible to arm the new recruits. Indeed, many of the muskets already issued were old and were giving out almost as fast as replacements could be manufactured. A Maryland gunsmith offered to make one hundred guns a month if the locks could be provided elsewhere and if he were given a working capital of one thousand dollars. At that rate it would take six months to equip one regiment with muskets. The crucial lack, as always, was money. Although Congress had ordered printed what seemed to its members enormous quantities of money, the presses could not keep up with the demand, nor could the signers of the bills sign them fast enough. "For God's sake," Washington wrote, "hurry the signers of money, that our wants may be supplied. It is a very singular case, that their signing cannot keep pace with our demands."

A heavy blow to plans for securing Canada came from the refusal of the New York regiments at Montreal to re-enlist. A bounty, prompt pay, substantial reinforcements, or a commander of Montgomery's caliber might have prevailed on them to sign on again. John Adams, as we have seen, placed the blame squarely on Congress, where much blame must rest; but certain things, such as the shortage of muskets, were beyond the capacities of that body to rectify, however energetic it might have been. A large and well-equipped army (some estimates run as high as ten thousand men) doubtless could have taken and held Canada. But one must seriously consider that the real problem was that American ambitions clearly outran their capabilities. If Washington could not muster ten thousand men at Boston, what hope was there of collecting, transporting, and supplying a larger number at Montreal and Quebec? The main chance to take Canada was lost in that first campaign, when delay and confusion vitiated the remarkable achievements of Montgomery and Arnold.

6

Clinton Attacks Charles Town

THE dramatic events of Lexington and Concord, along with the spectacular Battle of Bunker Hill two months later, focused attention on military events in the province of Massachusetts; but in Virginia, John Murray, the Earl of Dunmore, always energetic if not always wise, took pains to rally the Tories of Virginia, forming them into companies of irregulars. With Norfolk—a refuge for Loyalists, the majority of whom were British and Scottish merchants involved in the colony's tobacco trade with Great Britain—firmly in Dunmore's grasp, his forces carried out frequent raids against the exposed plantations of the tidewater area.

Dunmore's problem was that he was too ingenious; he could not leave well enough alone. On the seventh of November, 1775, he issued a proclamation declaring martial law and calling on every loyal citizen to support the Crown. In addition, he offered freedom to all slaves belonging to those planters who were in rebellion against the king, if they would join with him in fighting against their masters. By this offer, Dunmore aroused the specter of a Black Insurrection that haunted the dreams of every Virginian. He could have found no issue that would have solidified feeling against him more.

The proclamation was the inauguration of an ambitious scheme to form an alliance of frontier Indians, a group of Loyalists settled near

Pittsburgh, a detachment of British regulars from Detroit, and Virginia slaves. With this mixed force Dunmore intended to lay waste the plantations of rebels throughout the province. However, patriots captured Dunmore's agent, John Conolly, a doctor and soldier of fortune, at Hagerstown, Maryland, and, thus alerted, took steps to prevent the planned uprising.

The interesting thing is that slaves did respond to Dunmore's appeal in sufficient numbers to cause great uneasiness among the patriots. When the delegation to the Virginia Convention replied to Dunmore's proclamation, they included a provision that revolting slaves who returned to their masters within ten days would be pardoned. And Washington, when he heard of Dunmore's proclamation, wrote to Richard Henry Lee. "If . . . that man is not crushed before spring, he will become the most formidable enemy America has; his strength will increase as a snow ball, by rolling; and faster, if some expedient cannot be hit upon to convince the slaves and servants of the impotency of his designs. . . . I do not think forcing his Lordship on shipboard is sufficient; nothing less than depriving him of life or liberty will secure peace to Virginia. . . ."

Like the Massachusetts Provincial Congress, the Virginia Convention applied to Congress for legitimation, requesting that the troops it had raised be paid and supplied by that body. Congress, in turn, encouraged the Virginians "to resist to the utmost the arbitrary government intended to be established therein, by their Governor Lord Dunmore." Virginia thus, appropriately, joined Massachusetts as the second active theater of war, and the assembly dispatched one of the colony's two regiments of infantry to try to oust Dunmore from Norfolk. These troops, although augmented by several hundred volunteers, were easily defeated by Dunmore's larger and more experienced force, the nucleus of which was two companies of British regulars. The commander of the Virginia force, William Woodford, rallied his men below Norfolk on the other side of a creek crossed by the so-called "Great Bridge," which, in turn, was approached by causeways that led through one of those forest swamps common to the area. The British constructed a fortification at the northern end of the bridge and emplaced artillery to command the bridge and its approaches. The Virginians dug in at the southern end of the causeway, where they established an outer work held by some hundred men, with a larger body stationed at the rear.

Dunmore, confident that his little force, stiffened by the regulars under command of Captain Fordyce, could sweep away the "shirtmen," as the Virginians in their hunting shirts were called, ordered an attack supported by brisk cannon fire. The British started across the bridge. As at Breed's Hill, the Americans held their fire until the enemy were within fifty yards of the first breastworks. Then the American musket-men exacted a heavy toll. For the British, "The brave Fordyce exerted himself to keep up their spirits, reminded them of their ancient glory, and waving his hat over his head, encouragingly told them the day was their own." He was killed in the next volley from the breastworks; his lieutenant was wounded and captured, and a number of the British regulars were killed or wounded. The Virginians then counterattacked, drove the remnants of Dunmore's force back across the bridge, and spiked his fieldpieces. Fordyce was buried by the Americans with the honors of war, along with twelve of his soldiers. Seventeen of the enemy were wounded and captured. The American casualties were one man wounded.

The defeat at the Battle of Great Bridge was a serious setback for Dunmore. He decided that he did not have a large enough force to defend Norfolk, and, taking as many Tory families with him as he could find room for on board the ships in the harbor, he abandoned the town to Woodford, who had been joined by several companies of citizen-soldiers from North Carolina. Woodford occupied Norfolk while Dunmore and his fleet lay offshore, crowded and uncomfortable.

Dunmore next requested that supplies be provided him by the town. This Norfolk, under the command of the North Carolina Colonel Robert Howe, supported by Woodford and his Virginians, refused, and Dunmore decided to burn the town. His only warning was the rather ambiguous statement that "it would not be imprudent" if women and children were to leave the town. Thereupon the British ships began the bombardment of Norfolk and sent a landing party to set fire to the warehouses and buildings along the shore. The Virginia riflemen, in addition to fighting off the British landing party, took advantage of Dunmore's actions to set fire to the homes of the more notorious Tories in the town. Apparently the shirtmen of Virginia, instead of attempting to extinguish the fires, were active in plundering and pillaging the burning houses. The fires burned for three days and leveled most of the town.

When news of the burning of Norfolk spread through the colonies, it was, needless to say, without the particular details concerning the role of the militiamen. As for Dunmore's decision to burn the town, it was a singularly wilful and capricious act that caused great indignation and cost the British cause considerable support.

The British ministry had already begun to make plans for a campaign in the South, the purpose being to join forces with the large groups of Loyalists who, North was assured by Governors Tryon and Lord William Campbell, waited only for some indication of British support to rise and annihilate their rebel persecutors. The planning of such an operation was started by William Legge, the Earl of Dartmouth, Secretary of State for the Colonies, and carried forward by his successor, Lord George Germain, when he took over that cabinet post. General Sir Henry Clinton received instructions on January 6, 1776, to command a combined military and naval force for the purpose of besieging Charles Town, [now Charleston], South Carolina. He left Boston several weeks later with two companies of light infantry. He was to be joined off the mouth of the Cape Fear River in North Carolina by a fleet under Sir Peter Parker, sailing from Cork with several regiments commanded by Lord Charles Cornwallis. Clinton's orders were to establish British authority in the colonies of Georgia, North and South Carolina, and Virginia, and then, placing the Loyalists securely in charge, to rejoin Howe "as soon as the navigation of the northern coasts of North America became practicable."

Meanwhile Governor Josiah Martin of North Carolina issued a proclamation in January declaring the colonists to be in "most horrid and unnatural Rebellion" and commissioned the Regulators and Scottish Highlanders to rally to the king's standard. Under the command of Brigadier General Donald Macdonald, a sizable number of Loyalists, some said as many as five thousand, began a march to the seacoast to join forces with Clinton's expedition against Charles Town.

As soon as word of Macdonald's movement spread through the colony, patriot militia converged on the column from every direction. Colonel James Moore and his militia regiment were the first to encounter Macdonald, who called on Moore to surrender in the name of His Majesty, George III. Moore refused and proposed that Macdonald and his men instead take the Association oath swearing to resist the unconstitutional authority of Parliament. Macdonald then turned north, hoping to avoid a fight, but at Moores Creek Bridge he found his way blocked by Colonels Richard Caswell and Alexander Lillington with their North

Carolina militia regiments. Macdonald had the advantage in numbers (some fifteen hundred Loyalists to one thousand patriots), but the Americans had the advantage of the terrain. Caswell at first planned to defend the bridge and built a rough field fortification on Macdonald's side of the creek, but then he wisely withdrew across the bridge, removing the planking as he went. Macdonald's soldiers, coming on the empty fortifications, concluded that the patriots had fled and began to cross the creek on the stringers of the bridge. Caswell's militia held their fire until the advance party of the Loyalists had crossed, and then opened up a withering fire with muskets and cannon. The officer leading the advance was killed instantly, and his demoralized followers jumped from the bridge or were blown off it. Caswell pursued the Highlanders, captured Macdonald, and seized all his supplies.

These were the "melancholly tidings" that greeted Clinton when he arrived off the coast of North Carolina with his little fleet. The Loyalists in South Carolina, he was told, had also been routed and their leaders captured. In the absence of the English fleet, Clinton paraded his two companies on shore and inspected the beauties of the Carolina coastline, blossoming into a rich display of springtime foliage—"hunisuckle," crab apple, "Jessamines, prickle paires" and the shining and splendid magnolias. He noted the "offencive animals," beasts, birds, and serpents, the most notorious being the "wipping snake," which, it was said, could whip a man cruelly and two of which could kill a horse. With nothing but salt beef and salt pork on board his ships, Clinton discovered a delightful variety of edible plants and vegetables, among them "the Cabage tree; which when young Cuts up into wholesome and palatable food; when boiled like artichoak bottom, and when raw, like chestnut."

At Cape Fear, Clinton settled down to wait for the arrival of Sir Peter Parker's fleet and the troops under the command of Cornwallis. It proved to be a long wait—from late February until the thirty-first of May.

Congress, aware of the planned British thrust against Charles Town, looked to the defense of that important city. South Carolina had already mustered six regiments—the First, Second, and Third Foot, Roberts Artillery Regiment, and the First and Second South Carolina Rifles. This force was supplemented by three volunteer artillery companies, seven hundred Charles Town militia—who rivaled the elite corps of Philadelphia light infantry in the splendor of their accouterments—and some two thousand militia recruited from the interior country. A

Continental regiment from Virginia and one from North Carolina were ordered south by Congress to augment the defense of Charles Town and the forts that guarded its seaward approaches.

The entrance to Charles Town Harbor ran past Sullivan's Island to the north and James Island to the south. These were less islands than large areas of land separated from the mainland by rivers or inland waterways. James Island was defended by Fort Johnson, formerly a royal fort mounting twenty large-caliber guns, and by a smaller twelve-gun battery near Charles Town. The fort on Sullivan's Island was not begun until January, when Congress first got wind of the plan to seize Charles Town. Instead of the heavy masonry walls that distinguished a proper fort, Colonel William Moultrie, who undertook to oversee the construction of the works, was forced to use fibrous palmetto logs. Moultrie, who had won his spurs as a militia captain in the Cherokee expedition at the end of the French and Indian War, had been appointed colonel of the Second South Carolina Colonial Regiment in June of 1775.

Moultrie had two parallel walls built of the palmetto logs and had the space between filled with sand. Emplacements were made for twenty-five guns, ranging in caliber from nine- to twenty-five-pounders. The rear of the fort was only seven feet high, and here Moultrie placed six 12-pounders. The northern tip of Sullivan's Island was three miles from the fort itself. Extending farther north was a long, narrow island called Long Island (now Isle of Palms), separated from Sullivan's Island by shallows known as the Breach.

In the interval between the British decision to attack Charles Town and the actual assault, the South Carolina colonists made active efforts not only to raise a patriot militia and suppress Tories, but also to draft and ratify a new constitution. On March 26, a Legislative Council was chosen, and it, with the General Assembly, chose a president and commander in chief, and a vice president. John Rutledge was elected president and Henry Laurens vice president, with William Drayton as chief justice. In Drayton's words: "On this occasion, when a constitutional government, by the free voice of the people, first commenced its operations, a procession was determined on. . . ." The provincial troops and militia of the city were formed two deep along Broad Street opposite St. Michael's Church. The two houses of the legislature then paraded from the State House to the Exchange, led by the sheriff bearing the sword of state. At the Exchange, "amidst the heart-cheering plaudits of the people," the artillery fired thirteen discharges, and the cannon of American ships in the harbor joined in the tumult.

Congress now busily looked for a general to send south to take charge of Charles Town's defense. Washington had dispatched General Charles Lee to New York City in January, 1776, to supervise the construction of defensive works on Manhattan and the adjacent islands (Long Island and Staten Island particularly). On February 17, Congress directed Lee to take over command of the Northern Department from General Philip Schuyler, and then, when the New York delegates in Congress organized strong support for the New York general, reversed itself and ordered Lee south to take command of the Southern Department. Lee soon started for South Carolina, but he proved as dilatory as Clinton. He loitered at Williamsburg for almost a month and then, under heavy pressure from anxious Carolinians, proceeded to Wilmington, North Carolina.

The first ships of Parker's fleet did not reach Cape Fear until April 18; the last did not arrive until six weeks later. By this time Clinton, never a persistent or resolute man, had lost whatever slight enthusiasm he may have had for the venture and tried to persuade Parker to make forays into the Chesapeake Bay, where bases could be established from which Loyalists might be recruited and organized.

Parker, however, was after bigger game. He prevailed on Clinton to persevere in the plan to capture Charles Town. The city would serve as a rallying point for Southern Loyalists, and Clinton could rejoin Howe with his mission accomplished. Suppressing his misgivings, Clinton acquiesced. The British frigates and transports left Cape Fear on May 31, but again bad weather delayed their passage down the coast and across the perilous Five Fathom Hole, the entryway into Charles Town's outer harbor. The fleet dropped anchor on June 7, and Clinton proceeded to make a careful reconnaissance of the waterways surrounding Charles Town.

Lee, meanwhile, had reached Charles Town on the fourth of June, a bare three days before Clinton's force. Twelve hundred soldiers were encamped on Sullivan's Island in palm-leaf-covered huts while work continued on the fort itself. Lee announced that the fort and the island were alike untenable. Fort Sullivan, he declared, "could not hold out half an hour; and that the platform was a slaughtering stage." Since he could not persuade Rutledge to abandon the fort, Lee withdrew a number of the troops and a quantity of powder and began the fortification of Haddrell's Point, across the Cooper River from Charles Town, with forces under the command of Brigadier General Armstrong.

Lee bustled about everywhere, giving orders, cursing loudly, impressing everyone within earshot with his knowledge. "Nor was he wanting in discourses," Chief Justice Drayton noted, dryly, "to inform the public mind as to military matters; or backward, in proceeding on horseback or in boats, directing military works, and ordering such matters to be done, as the particular crisis demanded."

There was certainly much that still urgently needed to be accomplished. Aside from the still unfinished works on Sullivan's Island, little enough had been done in Charles Town itself to put that city in a state of readiness to withstand an attack. Again in Drayton's words, "Fleches were thrown up, at those places where troops might land; and traverses were erected across the streets, which might be exposed to any raking fire of the enemy; and as lead was scarce, the leaden weights from the windows of houses were offered by their owners to be cast into musket balls, for the public service." Everyone turned to—Negroes, militia, and, occasionally, a gentleman—and "laboured with alacrity . . . nor did the rainy or sultry weather give any interruption to their progress." The effects on morale were salutory; the citizens of the city felt themselves able to act in their own defense.

Lee meanwhile fired off a barrage of letters to Moultrie, ordering, wheedling, and admonishing. One such read: "For heaven's sake, sir, as you are in a most important post . . . exert yourself; by exerting yourself, I mean, when you issue any orders, suffer them not to be trifled with: everybody is well persuaded of your spirit and zeal, but they accuse you of being too easy in command; that is, I suppose, too relaxed in discipline, than which, in your situation, give me leave to say, there is not a greter vice. Let your orders be as few as possible but let them be punctually obeyed." All very true, but not taken too kindly by the independent Moultrie. It was typical of Lee that he should arrive at the eleventh hour, disheveled and peremptory, with his staff and his little yapping spaniels, and proceed to criticize everything that had been done so laboriously.

Clinton, after his aquatic reconnaissance, had decided to land a substantial force on Long Island rather than Sullivan's Island. He was assured that his troops could wade the Breach between the two islands at low tide. From Long Island he could, he thought, advance on the land side of the fort while Parker's warships bombarded it from the bay. Therefore on June 16 he landed 2,000 regulars and 500 or 600 seamen—only to discover, to his "unspeakable mortification and disappointment," that the Breach was full of potholes, some as much as seven feet deep, and that his force was, in effect, marooned. Clinton sent a message to Parker informing him of his plight and asking how his troops could be deployed in support of Parker's attack. A reply from Parker, who was doubtless impatient with Clinton's mismanagement and eager to make an undisputed claim to the laurels of victory, suggested that he was confident that his own ships could carry the day unaided, leaving it to Clinton to create whatever diversion might seem useful.

Aside from the useful work done in strengthening the immediate defenses of the city, most of Lee's orders were either impossible to carry out (such as the notion of building a floating bridge from Sullivan's Island to the mainland) or outright dangerous (i.e., his order to Moultrie to launch an attack on Clinton's force on Long Island). What Moultrie did do was establish a post, defended by some eight hundred men, at the northern end of Sullivan's Island, commanding the Breach and the southern end of Long Island. From this point to the fort was a distance of between two and a half and three miles.

This deployment appeared to put the troops in an exposed position, and it was warmly criticized by General Lee. But Moultrie was not alarmed. "For my part," Moultrie wrote, "I never was uneasy on not having a retreat because I never imagined that the enemy could force me to that necessity; I always considered myself as able to defend that post against the enemy. I had upwards of 300 riflemen, under Col. Thompson, of his regiment, Col. Clark with 200 North-Carolina regulars, Col. Horry, with 200 South-carolina, and the Raccoon Company of riflemen, 50 militia at the point of the island between sand hills and myrtle bushes; I had also a small battery with one 18-pounder, and one brass field-piece, a 6-pounder, at the same place, which entirely commanded the landing and could begin fire on them at 7 or 800 yards before they could attempt to land. . . . Col. Thompson had orders that if they could not stand the enemy they were to throw themselves into the fort, by which I should have had upwards of 1000 men in a large strong fort, and General Armstrong in my rear with 1500 men, not more than a mile and a half off, with a small arm of the sea between us, that he could have crossed a body of men in boats to my assistance. I therefore," Moultrie, wise after the event, continued, "felt myself perfectly easy because I never calculated upon Sir Henry Clinton's number to be more than 3000 men. . . ."

As the battle approached, Charles Town had become impressively well fortified. The city's other fort, Fort Johnson, had some 380 defenders and twenty heavy cannon—French 26-pounders and English 18-pounders. In the city itself there were 3,600 soldiers, militia and continentals, with a substantial number of cannon of various calibers. At Haddrell's Point, there were a total of 1,500 men under Armstrong's command.

The British attack on Charles Town was preceded, as all such affairs were in the eighteenth century, by a demand that the city surrender. "Whereas," Clinton's pompous proclamation declared, "a most unprovoked and wicked rebellion that for some time past prevailed. . . . I do most earnestly entreat and exhort[his Majesty's subjects] to return to our common Sovereign, and to the blessings of a free government . . . hereby offering in his Majesty's name, free pardon to all such as shall lay down their arms and submit to the laws."

Admiral Parker, in making plans for the attack on Charles Town, placed heavy reliance on a Negro pilot named Samson, who had brought his fleet through the treacherous Five Fathom Hole into a safe anchorage. The British commander scheduled his naval bombardment of Fort Sullivan for June 23, but adverse winds forced him to wait until the twenty-eighth. It was fortunate for Moultrie that Parker was not delayed any longer, for Lee, indignant with Moultrie's failure to carry out Lee's contradictory orders, had decided to replace him with a more tractable officer. But before Lee could do so, Parker began his assault. Clinton, whose men on Long Island had suffered from the heat, poor rations, and above all the mosquitoes (a British officer called them "a greater plague than there can be in hell itself"), had requested supporting fire from some of Parker's gunships. He had two alternate plans; one, to try a crossing of the Breach, the other, to cross to the mainland and attack Haddrell's Point.

The morning of the twenty-eighth dawned "very sultry with a burning sun; the wind extremely light, and the water consequently smooth." The improvised flag that flew over Fort Sullivan—a white crescent on a blue field with the word Liberty emblazoned across it—hung listlessly instead of "flying defiantly." As Parker's ships, seven frigates and a bombship, the *Thunder,* led by Parker's flagship, the *Bristol* of fifty guns (the others carried twenty-eight), moved into position, anxious crowds collected along the battery in Charles Town to watch the coming engagement. Parker ordered the *Active,* the *Experiment,* and the *Solebay* to form a line, with the *Bristol* in the center, within five hundred yards of the fort. Farther from the fort and echeloned to the southeast, the *Actaeon,* the *Sphynx,* and the *Syren* made up a second line, bringing a total of more than one hundred guns to bear on Moultrie's fort.

When eighteenth-century warships anchored to deliver sustained fire against a land installation, they put out anchors, bow and stern, on cables with springs attached to absorb the recoil of the guns and thereby prevent the anchors from dragging or the planks of the vessel from being sprung. The frigates, moving into position, began this rather laborious process while the bombship *Thunder,* anchored at the extreme limit of its range, was supported by the twenty-two-gun *Friendship.*

These maneuvers took time, and it was eleven in the morning before the first bombs and shells began to fall on Fort Sullivan. The solid shot and the shrapnel plowed into the palmetto logs and the sand, which effectively absorbed their impact and contained the explosion of the cannister. As for the bombs of the *Thunder,* in Moultrie's words, "most of them fell within the fort, but we had a morass in the middle that swallowed them up instantly, and those that fell in the sand in and about the fort were immediately buried so that very few of them bursted amongst us." Indeed, the *Thunder,* in order to reach the fort at all, had to so overcharge its mortars with powder that their recoil shattered the firing beds and "so damaged the ship as to render her unfit for further service."

Clinton, meanwhile, supported by an armed schooner, *Lady William,* and a sloop, embarked some men and light fieldpieces in boats, preliminary to an attempt to cross the Breach. But the Americans under Colonel Thompson opened fire with an 18-pounder from their positions on the northern end of Sullivan's Island, and Clinton turned back—wisely, in the opinion of one of his officers, who wrote that the Americans "would have killed half of us before we could make our landing good." After that brief and abortive effort, Clinton became, with thousands of others, a "quiet spectator" for the rest of the battle.

It became clear early in the engagement that the principal danger to the fort lay in its meager supply of powder. When Moultrie appealed to Lee for more powder, the general, who had never had any confidence in the capacity of the fort to hold out under a British assault, advised Moultrie to withdraw. "If you should unfortunately expend your ammunition without beating off the enemy or driving them on ground," he wrote, "spike your guns and retreat with all order possible: but I know you will be careful not to throw away your ammunition."

Moultrie's request for more ammunition, however, passed into the hands of President Rutledge, who responded in a different spirit: He sent five hundred pounds. "I should think you may be supplied well from Haddrell's," he wrote. "You know our collection is not very great. *Honor* and *Victory,* my good sir, to you, and our worthy countrymen with you." There was a postscript: "Do not make too free with your cannon. Cool and do mischief."

Unwilling to contemplate abandoning the fort and, more especially, deserting Thompson and his contingent on the northern end of the island, Moultrie ordered his gunners to conserve their fire, making every shot count. That he succeeded was confirmed by an officer on the *Experiment* who acknowledged that the batteries in Fort Sullivan were "exceedingly well directed."

At this point, Parker, observing that the fire of his frigates was doing little damage to the fort, ordered the *Syren,* the *Sphynx,* and the *Actaeon* to raise anchor and move to positions in the cove between Haddrell's Point and the southeast or open side of the fort. This was just the maneuver that Lee had feared and that he had repeatedly and fruitlessly warned Moultrie to prepare his defenses for. Now it appeared that Lee's foreboding was about to be realized. Fortunately, whether through the fault of the black pilot Samson or others, the three British vessels got stuck almost immediately on the Middle Ground, a hidden sand bar running across the harbor. The *Sphynx* and the *Syren* struggled free after several hours of desperate effort, but the *Actaeon* remained fast. If there was a decisive point in the engagement, this was it. Soon afterwards the *Bristol,* which had already been struck in the hull by cannonballs a number of times and had many wounded sailors and marines, had one of its cables severed and swung around with its stern to the fort, in which helpless position it received an especially galling fire until the cable was repaired. During the cannonading, barges passed from one ship to another "and to the transports; for the purpose of removing the wounded, and obtaining fresh men, as occasion required."

The principal casualties in the fort came from a British ball that entered an embrasure and carried away half the crew of a gun. Another shell eviscerated a Sergeant M'Daniel, but before the fatally wounded soldier died, he cried out, *"Fight on my brave boys; don't let liberty expire with me to-day."* His words, Judge Drayton tells us in his account of the battle, were passed along the firing platforms and inspired his fellows. Another dramatic incident came when a British ball brought down the flag above the fort. Sergeant William Jasper leapt over the parapets to retrieve it in the face of heavy fire from the frigates and tied it to a palm-tree staff, where it proclaimed that the fort still held out.

Besides clinging jealously to the substantial supply of powder at Haddrell's Point, hoarded against an attack that never came, Lee's only contribution to the battle was to visit the fort; there he aimed a few guns and departed with the comment, "Colonel, I see you are doing very well here. You have no occasion for me, I will go up to town again."

By two o'clock in the afternoon, Moultrie was so concerned about his dwindling supply of powder that he ordered his gunners to cease firing for several hours to conserve what ammunition was left. When the firing from the fort stopped, one of the seamen on the *Bristol* called out, "The Yankees have done fighting." Another voice replied, "By God, we are glad of it, for, we never had such a drubbing in our lives. We had been told the Yankees would not stand two fires; but we never saw better fellows."

When the guns in the fort began firing again, any illusion that the British ships had silenced them was dissipated. The British fire, which had remained heavy, began to slacken at sundown. By nine thirty it had ceased, and under the cover of darkness the British warships slipped their cables and were carried away by the outgoing tide. The *Actaeon,* still stuck on the Middle Ground, remained behind. In Drayton's (and Moultrie's) opinion, only the Americans' lack of powder prevented the British ships from being forced to strike their colors or be pounded to pieces. The wind and tide had been against them; during the day they could not have gotten out of range of the cannons in the fort.

The British fire had been tremendous. The *Bristol* alone expended 15,000 pounds of powder, while Moultrie's total supply, after Lee had withdrawn a substantial portion, was 5,400 pounds. Indeed Drayton calculated that the British warships among them used perhaps 34,000 pounds of powder and 102,000 pounds of ball and shell in a total of 12,000 shots fired. The estimates of British casualties vary considerably, but a total of 225, the greater part of them on board the *Bristol* and the *Experiment,* seems near the mark. There were more than 100 casualties on the *Bristol* alone, of whom 40 were killed. On the *Experiment,* 23 were killed and more than twice as many wounded. Lord William Campbell, the royal governor of South Carolina who fought on the *Bristol* as a volunteer, was badly wounded. Captain Alexander Scott of the *Experiment* lost his right arm, and Sir Peter Parker, besides losing his breeches, suffered a painful shrapnel wound in his posterior.

Lee's comments on the performance of Moultrie's troops were

doubtless more revealing than he intended. "The behaviour of the garrison, both men and officers with Colonel Moultrie," he wrote, "I confess astonished me. It was brave to the last degree. I had no idea that such coolness and intrepidity could be displayed by a collection of raw recruits." What the members of the garrison had done, in effect, was not to run away. The fact was that they had no place to run to. The artillery men had served their guns skillfully, and the infantry had remained under cover. Of the 1,000 or so men in the fort, 12 were killed in the eight-hour battle and 25 wounded. That showed good luck and an admirable instinct for self-preservation. But it seems hardly to have rated Lee's encomium; one wonders what the general expected. Had Lee replaced Moultrie with Colonel Nash, a more compliant officer, he would doubtless not have hesitated to order Nash to abandon the fort early in the engagement, with consequences that would certainly have been disastrous for the Americans.

On the other hand, if the *Actaeon,* the *Syren,* and the *Sphynx* had been able to get into the cove and take Fort Sullivan in the flank and rear, it would perhaps have been impossible for Moultrie's gunners to have held their posts, and the fort might very well have been forced to surrender. On that point at least Lee was on solid ground. Judge Drayton, reviewing the chances of the battle and reflecting upon the opportunities the British lost for securing a victory, decided, not entirely surprisingly, that most of the credit for the American success should go to "that Almighty Power, in whose hands, are the destinies of nations; and whose intentions at that time were, to favour the injured rights and liberties for which America was contending. . . ." Drayton even had a good word for Lee, who, "however disagreeable" his "manners were, and his modes of doing business," had, nonetheless, "taught us to respect ourselves, and to trust to our courage and exertions for our own safety." That was, after all, doing a good deal.

When the sun rose on the morning of the twenty-ninth, Sir Peter Parker's pennant, attached to a jury-rigged main topmast considerably lower than the foremast (the mainmast had been demolished by shot from Fort Sullivan), was hardly visible. "How glorious," Drayton noted, "were the other points of view? The azure colours of the fort, fixed on a sponge-staff, waved gently on the winds—Boats were passing and repassing in safety, from and to, the fort and Charleston—And the hearts of the people were throbbing with gratitude, and the most exhilarating transports!" The *Actaeon* was still stuck on the Middle Ground. Her captain loaded her guns, set her colors flying, and set fire to her to keep her out of American hands. The British had no sooner left her, however, than three boatloads of Americans boarded the ship. Seeing that they could not extinguish her fires, they aimed her guns at the crippled *Bristol* some distance away and fired them, and then stripped her of her ship's bell, her colors, and whatever else their boat could carry away. They had hardly pushed off before the ship blew up with a tremendous explosion, "and the smoke ascending in column, and afterwards expanding around, is said at its first expansion to have forced an appearance, not unlike the majestic stem and umbrella top of the palmetto-tree. This display," Drayton added, "was therefore peculiarly grateful to the pride and feelings of Carolinians," since Fort Sullivan had been constructed of palmetto logs.

The defenders of the fort received as reward for their valor two hogsheads of "excellent Antigua rum," one given by President Rutledge and one by Mr. William Logan, a prominent merchant of Charles Town. To Sergeant Jasper, who had retrieved the fallen flag, Rutledge presented his own sword. Finally, Fort Sullivan was renamed Fort Moultrie in honor of its commander.

Americans interpreted the battle (if it could be called that) as a humiliating setback for the British. The campaign of which the battle was the culmination was a classic example of the difficulties of a combined land and sea operation, as well as of British dilatoriness and arrogance. From the time that Congress got wind of the intended attack on Charles Town until the time Parker's ships opened fire on Fort Sullivan, more than six months elapsed. In that interval, the South Carolina patriots had had ample time to assemble a substantial force and almost complete an excellent fort.

Clinton's failure to ascertain whether the channel between Long Island and Sullivan's Island was fordable was surely a major blunder. The failure of Parker to make a serious effort to coordinate his bombardment with Clinton's movement by land was perhaps the most serious mistake of the whole operation. Of course, a land attack might have failed as well, but the odds were much more in its favor. Certainly Parker's notion that he could simply pound Fort Sullivan into submission was based on a curious combination of arrogance on the one hand and stupidity or inexperience on the other. He was new to the year-old war in America and doubtless brought with him that contempt for the military capacities of the Americans that characterized virtually all British professional military men at the beginning of the conflict. Clinton, who had participated in the carnage at Bunker Hill, knew better, but, reluctant to appear faint-hearted or irresolute, he allowed himself to be persuaded by Parker. As in most military decisions made by British commanders, career considerations were prominent if not paramount. Officers almost invariably approached engagements with an eye to the effect of victory or defeat on their careers. Thus Parker, having not yet had an opportunity to earn laurels for himself in the war, was hungry for glory. Clinton, on the other hand, was wary of possible defeat—and of getting blamed for it.

Efforts by both Clinton and Parker to pin the blame on the other did, in fact, begin at once. Germain and the king exonerated Clinton of blame, but they did it privately, not openly, and made no reply to Parker's public charge that Clinton had failed to support him by a land attack. To which, of course, Clinton responded that Sir Peter had failed to support *him*. But somehow his answer never caught up with Parker's accusation, and the burden of the defeat rested heavily on Clinton's shoulders. When he returned to England the next spring, he was given the Order of the Bath by the king as a kind of consolation prize for having been made the scapegoat. And then, of course, a year later he was given command of the British forces in America, and in that capacity he returned to Charles Town, did the job right, and captured the city very neatly. But meantime, the patriots had three crucial years to consolidate their hold on the Southern states.

Moultrie felt that he received less credit than he was due. (In his opinion, he deserved all the credit, and who could gainsay him?) Most of the credit went to General Lee. Lee, having arrived at the last moment, and then reluctantly, and then having done his best to persuade Moultrie and Rutledge to abandon their laboriously constructed fort, inherited a major part of the plaudits for the victory. He returned to New York, dawdling as usual on the way, with his reputation considerably enhanced. Congress voted him thanks for his splendid victory and advanced him thirty thousand dollars to pay for a handsome plantation in Virginia.

7

Guerrilla Warfare on the Water

THE war in New England continued to be a stalemate. Gage and his army sat in Boston; Washington and his troops ringed the city—and did nothing. There was activity in one area, however: on the sea, where a hit-and-run guerrilla war flared and sputtered, smoked, and burst into flame. It was a tempest in a teapot, confined as it was to the coastal waters of Massachusetts and Rhode Island, but it produced its share of death and destruction, of heroism and folly—and of occasional comedy.

The fact that there was a two-sided naval struggle was in large part due to the inefficiency of the British navy and especially of the commander in American waters, Admiral Samuel Graves. A better led British naval force could easily have mopped up the colonists' paltry attempts to maintain their own navy. But the British efforts were sapped by maladministration, slowness, and bungling. If General Gage was notably inactive in Boston, Admiral Graves did his best to emulate him on the sea. That gentleman reacted so slowly to every emergency (or even the common daily needs of his ships and sailors) that one might conclude his own botton was as encrusted with barnacles as the bottoms of the vessels under his command. Indeed, General Burgoyne, with his ineffable cleverness, entertained himself and presumably Lord Germain with a detailed letter telling what Graves was not doing. Among the damning items in Burgoyne's inventory: "He is not supplying the troops with sheep and oxen . . . He is *not* defending his own flocks and herds, for the enemy has repeatedly and in the most insulting manner plundered his own appropriated islands. He is *not* defending the other islands in the harbour . . . He is *not* employing his ships to keep up communication and intelligence with the servants and friends of the Government."

John Montagu, the Earl of Sandwich, who had been a prominent member of the infamous Dashwood Circle (a group of profligate aristocrats), was now the First Lord of Admiralty, but his only qualification seems to have been a contemptuous and vindictive spirit toward the Americans. In all those qualities needed for the resolute and orderly management of the naval establishment he was, fortunately for the colonial rebels, sadly deficient. The navy, like the army, was weakened by patronage and corruption, by the buying and selling of commissions, and, of course, by the wretched conditions that characterized the life of a sailor in His Majesty's Navy. Any system that depended on the press gang's seizure of men who were hardly to be distinguished from kidnapped slaves must have been cruel and inhuman beyond measure. Little or no care was taken for the health of sailors, who were crowded below decks in what were most commonly foul holds. Deaths from sickness and disease far outnumbered casualties in battle. Scurvy and dysentery were as prevalent as the common cold and made men susceptible to every kind of contagious infection. Sandwich, with simpleminded optimism, insisted that the British navy, which had deteriorated seriously since the end of the French and Indian War, was entirely adequate for the purpose of helping to subdue the cowardly Americans. Indeed, as a gesture of bravado, he proposed to reduce the number of seamen in 1775 to two thousand fewer than those asked for the previous year. Such a First Lord was well served by an admiral as foolish and inefficient as Graves.

One incident reveals several of the major flaws in Graves's character. Graves and his wife lived in Boston, and they needed fodder for their horses and cows. So Graves undertook to mow some of the hay on an island in the bay. He shortly discovered that a Boston Tory, Benjamin Hallowell, owned the island. Graves and his sailors denied Hallowell access to the island and forced him to sell half the hay to Graves. Then, out of pique, Graves still refused to allow Hallowell to go to the island to mow and remove the remaining hay. When the two men met on the street, they exchanged words, and Graves attacked the unarmed

Hallowell with his sword. Hallowell, who was a burly, fearless man, took the admiral's sword away from him and snapped it in two.

In addition to being petty, vindictive, and cowardly, Graves, who had no sons, seems to have devoted more time to trying to obtain offices for his three nephews than in supplying the hungry troops in Boston. In a series of querulous and self-congratulatory letters to Dartmouth and Sandwich, he showed some ingenuity in presenting his failures as triumphs and blaming everyone but himself for the wretched state of the ships and sailors under his command.

Yankee whalers and fishermen soon found that they could raid and harass Graves's fleet with virtual impunity. The Americans first singled out the lighthouses: they burned the Cape Ann Lights on Thatcher's Island, and then, right under the noses and guns of British men-of-war riding in the harbor, "some Rebels in Whaleboats went from Nantasket" and put the torch to the Boston Light. Some three hundred whaleboats were collected in the coves, inlets, and rivers north and south of the city, and these systematically, and without any substantial interference from Graves, carried off the stock and fodder from the numerous islands adjacent to Boston, thereby denying to the besieged British precious supplies of meat as well as vegetables and milk.

Graves sent a working party of Tory carpenters, guarded by marines, to rebuild the Boston lighthouse. The carpenters smuggled rum from Boston, the marines got sodden drunk, and the colonials attacked the island in their ubiquitous whaleboats at dawn—thirty-three boats each carrying some thirteen men. Many of the marines were still, in the words of one of their officers, "in liquor and totally unfit for service." While the carpenters hid in the unfinished lighthouse, the lieutenant in charge of the marines tried to get his men aboard their own boats and out to a schooner anchored nearby before they were captured by the Americans. The lieutenant was wounded, and the schooner, raising anchor, promptly ran aground and was seized by the raiders. The Americans rounded up all the prisoners they could find, set fire to the half-finished lighthouse, and made their escape before the British could intercept them. Their toll: fifty-three British killed or captured, among them the unfortunate officer in charge. The Americans lost one man killed, two "just grazed with balls," and one boat sunk.

In Graves's fleet, illness and desertion worked a constant attrition. The *Boyne*, which had sailed from England with 520 men, was, after six months in American waters, down to 325 fit for service.

One of the principal uses Graves made of his warships was to station them in harbors where their presence would, Graves hoped, intimidate the patriots ashore. The *Scarborough* was, with this purpose, anchored off Portsmouth, New Hampshire, where its captain bargained with the people of the town for fresh supplies of food. In New York, the *Asia* served a similar purpose and enjoyed a similar provisioning arrangement.

The most entertaining of such incidents involved the seafaring town of Bristol, Rhode Island. There a British captain, Sir James Wallace, in charge of a fleet of sixteen vessels, including three men-of-war, lined up his ships in front of the town and sent a barge ashore to demand that the inhabitants supply him with beef and mutton. Wallace also tried to lure some hostages by proposing that "two or three of the principal men or magistrates of the town . . . go on board his ship to hear his proposals." If they refused, he threatened to immediately bombard Bristol. The spokesman for the town replied that it was more proper for the captain to come ashore and make his demands known to the town: "If he would come to the head of the wharf the next morning, he should be treated as a gentleman, and the town would consider of his demands."

Captain Wallace's reply was to begin a bombardment. At this the commander of the Bristol militia, Colonel Potter, requested that hostilities cease until the inhabitants of the town could choose a committee to negotiate with Captain Wallace. When the committee appeared, Wallace declared that he wished two hundred sheep and thirty fat cattle. This was impossible. The farmers had driven off all their stock. There were no more than "a few sheep and some milch cows" left. The bargaining went on for several hours, with offer and counteroffer. Finally, the exasperated captain, hardly a match for the canny Rhode Islanders in this game, declared, "I have one proposal to make: If you will promise to supply me with forty sheep, at or before twelve o'clock, I will assure you that another gun shall not be discharged."

The committee, "seeing themselves reduced to this dreadful dilemma of two evils, reluctantly chose the least, by agreeing to supply them with forty sheep at the time appointed. . . ."

This heroic martial event was promptly commemorated in verse. The captain, having issued his highhanded order and been rebuffed:

> At eight o'clock by signal given,
> Our peaceful atmosphere was riven:
> Women with children in their arms
> With doleful cries ran to the farms.

With all their firing and their skill
They did not any person kill,
Neither was any person hurt
Except the Reverend Parson Burt.

And he was not killed by a ball
As Judged by Jurors one and all,
But being in a sickly state,
He frightened fell, which proved his fate . . .

They fire low, they fire high
The women scream, the children cry,
And all their firing and their racket
Shot off the topmast of a packet!

Even more heroic doings occurred off the coast of Maine. In June of 1775, Ichabod Jones, a Boston Tory, decided to try to get a supply of desperately needed wood for the city at the seaport town of Machias, Maine, where he had connections with other prominent Tories. Admiral Graves assigned Jones an armed schooner, the *Margaretta,* as an escort for two supply ships. Arriving off Machias, Jones began negotiating with the townspeople for a supply of lumber. At first the town agreed, "considering themselves nearly as prisoners of war in the hands of the common enemy," but Jones's arrogance and tactlessness stimulated a plot to seize him and the midshipman commanding the schooner while they were attending church. Jones, warned, took to the woods, where he was captured. The midshipman got back aboard the *Margaretta,* from which he threatened to bombard the town if Jones were not released. The town was obdurate: the midshipman must surrender to the Sons of Liberty. At this point Jones's two sloops which had been intended to transport the timber to Boston, were seized by the Sons of Liberty. When the *Margaretta* sailed too close to the shore, she ran aground and was fired upon by the Americans.

The midshipman got the schooner off and tied up in the harbor. The next morning he tried to make his escape, but some forty colonists armed with "guns, swords, axes, and pitchforks" manned one of Jones's sloops and pursued him. Although the *Margaretta* was well provided with "Swivels, Musguets, Hand Grenades" and was manned by "twenty of the best men" of the warship *Preston,* the colonists overtook her, demanded that she surrender, and then, when that was refused, fired a volley into the *Margaretta* and boarded her. The only mortal wound was suffered by the midshipman. As he lay dying, he was asked why he had refused to strike his colors, and he replied, in the best tradition of the

British Navy, that "he preferred Death before yielding to such a sett of villains."

The capture of the *Margaretta,* though a modest enterprise, may properly be called the first naval engagement of the American Revolution. It infuriated the British, who always considered an attack upon one of their naval vessels, particularly a successful one, as a most grievous insult.

In Machias, emboldened by the capture of the *Margaretta,* the two leaders in that venture—Jeremiah O'Brien and Benjamin Foster—converted Ichabod Jones's lumber sloops into privateers, using primarily the armament of the *Margaretta,* supplemented by whatever other ordnance they could round up. Thus they had in effect their own personal navy, and when two British ships, the *Diligent* and the *Tattama-gouche,* sailed quite innocently into the harbor to take soundings for an improved naval atlas to be called *The Atlantic Neptune,* O'Brien and Foster captured them with all their surveying records.

Other successes crowned the colonists' naval ventures. At Pownalborough, down the Maine coast, where a fleet of transports was collecting food and lumber for Gage's troops at Boston, the local militia captured three sloops and a schooner. Maine, which was then part of Massachusetts, appealed to the Provincial Congress of that colony both for assistance and for recognition of its small navy. The assembly, primarily to free the enterprising sailors of Machias from the danger of being taken as pirates, voted to commission O'Brien and Foster and their ships and to give them all possible support. On O'Brien was bestowed the quite elegant title of "Commander of the Armed Schooner *Diligent,* and of the sloop *Machias-Liberty,* now lying in the Harbour of Machias."

The fledgling American navy grew apace. Rhode Island, whose ports and seacoast towns were, as the episode at Bristol proved, highly vulnerable to British warships, chartered two vessels, one manned by eighty men and equipped with ten four-pounders, fourteen swivels, and ample small arms. The larger of the two ships had hardly been put in service before it captured one of the tenders of Captain Wallace's command ship *Rose.* Connecticut, prompted by the British seizure of some two thousand sheep on Gardiners and Fishers islands, commissioned the *Minerva* and the *Spy* to help protect its shores.

South Carolina, some one thousand miles down the coast, carried out the boldest foray. A sloop manned by enterprising rebels came alongside a British brigantine that was unloading powder at St. Augustine, "and in a hostile and violent manner instantly boarded her with 26 men, some armed with Muskets and Bayonets fixed, and others with Swords and Pistols. . . . and then in an audacious and piratical-like manner, opened the hatches and took out of the said Brigantine, and put on board the said Sloop, one hundred and eleven barrels of Gunpowder belonging to His Majesty. . . ."

Although Washington's authority did not extend to naval operations, the general, from his headquarters in Cambridge, observed with increasing uneasiness the forays of the British navy against the unprotected seacoast towns of New England. For his undersupplied army, the British merchant ships that sailed in and out of Boston harbor were tempting targets. Washington had, to be sure, no authority to establish a continental navy, but he could grant army commissions. He thus signed a commission for Nicholson Broughton of Marblehead and issued him orders that read, "You, being appointed a Captain in the Army of the United Colonies of North America, are hereby directed to take command of a detachment of said Army, and proceed on board the Schooner Hannah. . . ."

The captain's mission was to intercept British supply ships sailing to and from Boston and to send them into the port nearest Cambridge. In addition to their wages, Broughton's crew was to receive a third of the value of all cargoes seized. Broughton immediately captured a large vessel filled with provisions and naval supplies, and in a few weeks he had "taken a Brig from Quebec with Stock, another with Turtle and Fruit from Providence [in the Bahamas] and a third Transport from Bristol with 2200 bbls of Flour."

The experiment was so successful that Washington repeated it numerous times, dispatching a dozen or more of his "army" ships to prey on British supply vessels. But like his army, Washington's embryonic navy presented numerous problems. The sailors in their stubborn individualism were like the soldiers, except, if possible, more so. They resisted any form of discipline, were greedy, contentious, and profane. "The plague, trouble, and vexation I have had with the crews of all the armed vessels," Washington wrote John Hancock, "are inexpressible. I do believe there is not on earth a more disorderly set. Every time they come into port, we hear of nothing but mutinous complaints."

Stephen Hoylan, charged with helping to outfit Washington's navy and finding it difficult to get his fellow townsmen in Salem to do a decent day's work for their wages, burst out in a fit of exasperation: "There is one reason, and I think a Substantial one, why a person born in the same town or neighborhood should not be employed on publick affairs of this nature in that town or neighborhood, it is that the Spirit of equality which reigns thro' this Country, will make him afraid of exerting that authority necessary [to] the expediting of his business, he must shake [every] man by the hand and desire, beg, and pray, do brother, do my friend, do such a thing, whereas a few hearty damns from a person who did not care a damn for them would have a much better effect, this I know by experience."

Yet the little navy was to enjoy one success that counterbalanced all its shortcomings. John Manly, who displayed on the sea those qualities. of leadership demonstrated on land by Benedict Arnold, caught a British supply ship, the *Nancy*, which had become separated from her convoy, boarded her without a struggle, and sailed her into Gloucester. For an army in desperate need of flints for firelocks, the capture of the *Nancy* provided 100,000 flints as well as 2,000 muskets with bayonets and cartridge boxes and, most intriguing of all, a huge 16-inch brass mortar that General Putnam christened "The Congress" and used initially as a punchbowl to celebrate the capture of the *Nancy*.

While Washington was laboriously augmenting his little auxiliary navy, Rhode Island placed before Congress a proposal to establish a continental navy. Congress was mired down in a peculiarly complicated and frustrating debate over what action to take in regard to colonial trade. Those who still clung to the hope of reconciliation with the mother country wished to maintain nonimportation and nonexportation; to abandon it would be, in effect, to abandon the hope (or delusion) that Britain could be forced to change her policy by economic pressures. To those who believed that the colonists had long since passed the Rubicon (a group that included most of the New Englanders), continuing nonimportation and nonexportation seemed the height of folly. Such a policy would further weaken American commerce when supplies and armament of every kind were desperately needed. In the midst of this debate, word reached Congress that two unarmed and unconvoyed brigs had sailed from England "loaded with arms, powder, and other stores, for Quebec." With the colonies in desperate need of military supplies, could such an opportunity be passed up?

The more timid delegates were full of fears and, as John Adams saw it, specious objections. It was represented as the most wild, visionary, mad project that ever had been imagined. It was an infant, taking a wild bull by his horns; and what was more profound and remote, it was said it would ruin the character, and corrupt the morals of all our seamen. It would make them selfish, piratical, mercenary, bent wholly upon plunder." Adams answered the doubters: "Why should not America have a navy? No maritime power near the sea-coast can be safe without it. It is no chimera. The Romans suddenly built one in their Carthaginian war."

After two days of debate, Congress decided to attempt to intercept the ships and sent off dispatches to Washington suggesting that he borrow the navies of Rhode Island and Connecticut and apply to Massachusetts for whatever assistance that colony could provide, all to be done "on the continental risque and pay." Washington at once began to assemble what was, in fact, the nucleus of a Continental navy.

Graves and Gage meanwhile had decided to punish those seaport towns that had been most troublesome by dispatching a British fleet reinforced with soldiers to burn the offending communities. Falmouth, Maine, was marked for such condign punishment, as was bold little Machias. Gloucester, Portsmouth, and Newburyport (for its part in obtaining supplies for Washington's army) were also on Graves's list. Captain Henry Mowat was to command the expedition, which consisted of his ship, the *Canceaux,* with eight guns and forty-five men, and the Halifax, carrying six guns and thirty-four men. His instructions were to "burn, destroy and lay waste."

It was October, 1775, before the ships were ready to sail. Mowat decided to pass up Gloucester for the time being and headed for Falmouth. Anchoring off the town, he sent an officer ashore with a sanctimonious statement to be read to the people of the town, who had remained fractious despite "Britain's long forbearance of the rod of correction, and the merciful and paternal extension of her hands to embrace you, again and again." Instead of gratitude, the colonists had been guilty of "the most unpardonable rebellion, supported by the ambition of a set of designing men." Mowat thus had orders "to execute a just punishment on the Town of Falmouth." The citizens had two hours grace to "remove . . . the human species of the said Town." At the end of that time the town would be set afire. If the "least resistance" was shown, Mowat would, he declared, no longer feel bound by those rules of humanity that now guided his action.

A more insolent document can hardly be imagined. Mowat not only spoke of the colonists as bad children, not only declared his intention of destroying their whole town without distinction between Tory or patriot, but congratulated himself on his humanity.

To the committee that went on board the *Canceaux* to plead with

Mowat to spare the town, he displayed his orders. He demanded that the four cannon that he had observed in the town be delivered to him and went so far as to promise that if the cannon, all arms and ammunition, and some hostages were turned over to him, he would refer the matter of the destruction of the town back to Graves at Boston. The committee replied that the cannon had been sent away. Mowat then offered to extend the deadline for the destruction of the town until the next morning if all small arms were delivered.

During the night the town was not evacuated. Next morning, still stalling for time, the committee tried once more to persuade Mowat to delay his bombardment. It must be said that the citizens of Falmouth seem to have given little or no thought to defending their town. The truth seems to be that there was no trust between the town, which had harbored a disproportionate number of Tories, and the interior farmers who made up the bulk of the local militia. In any event, everyone spent his time carrying off to safety as many of his possessions as possible, instead of preparing for the defense of the town. Finally Mowat, his patience exhausted, loosed on the town a "horrible shower of balls, from three to nine pounds weight, bombs, carcasses, live shells, grape shot and musket balls." Despite the heavy fire few buildings were set ablaze, and men could be seen extinguishing those that were. Finally, Mowat sent a detachment of soldiers ashore to complete the work, and by six at night "Falmouth, with the Blockhouse and battery, the principal wharfs and storehouses, with eleven sail of vessels, at and near this town . . . all laid into ashes, including a fine distillery, four vessels taken, all without the loss of one person, and only two slightly wounded."

The destruction of Falmouth was a capricious and vindictive act that served no important military purpose and did far more to stimulate American bitterness and strengthen the patriot cause than any conceivable advantage that could have accrued to the British. If it was intended to frighten other towns into compliance, it had just the opposite effect. Efforts were made everywhere to augment the defenses of seaport towns, and additional impetus was given to the movement to build up a navy. Considerations of humanity aside, punitive actions against civilians in wartime are both foolish and cowardly; they degrade those who perform them as surely as they punish the guilty and innocent indiscriminately.

Washington's reaction when he heard the news of the destruction of Falmouth may be taken as typical. To him it was "an outrage exceeding in barbarity and cruelty every hostile act practiced among civilized nations." To those of us who live in the twentieth century, Washington's reaction can only seem extreme. We are so accustomed to the ruthless destruction of cities by aerial bombardment and the extermination or mutilation of their inhabitants that the action of Captain Mowat against Falmouth seems by comparison very mild indeed.

The other towns marked for destruction were spared. Mowat's ships had suffered damage from the firing of their own guns since much of the ammunition had proved faulty, winter was approaching, and the weather was considered too treacherous for further operations.

Congress, even before it received word of the destruction of Falmouth, had resolved to establish the nucleus of a navy. It ordered the construction and outfitting of first four vessels and then eight, the largest to be a ship of twenty-four guns. The commander of the little fleet was to be Ezek Hopkins of Rhode Island. John Paul Jones was a lieutenant on the flagship and had the honor of raising the union flag. The ships with their full complement of officers and men were ready to sail by the first of the year, 1776, but they remained icebound until the middle of February. Then Hopkins sailed to the Bahamas, where at Nassau he seized some naval ordnance and supplies. It was not what could be called a glorious start, but at least America had something that could be called a navy.

8

Dorchester Heights

Having created a naval branch of the army, Washington did his best to discern the intentions of Gage in Boston. "Unless the ministerial troops in Boston are waiting for reinforcements, I cannot devise what they are staying in there for," he wrote Congress.

On the tenth of October, Gage left for England to give an accounting to Lord North, and responsibility for governing the city devolved on Howe. But the change in command brought no change in the actions or, more properly, inactions of the British. They seemed, if not content, at least resigned to remaining cooped up in Boston, of no earthly use to anyone, consuming large quantities of supplies provided at great cost by the home government. Washington was "unable upon any principle whatever to account for their silence, unless it be to lull us into a fatal security. . . . If this be the drift, they deceive themselves, for if possible, it has increased my vigilance, and induced me to fortify all our avenues to our camps, to guard us against any approaches upon the ice."

Impatient with the British inaction, Washington consulted his generals about the practicality of an attack on Boston by the Continental Army. Twice he asked them whether it was possible to "make a successful attack upon the Troops in Boston, by means of Boats co-operated by an attempt upon their lines at Roxbury," and twice they advised unanimously against it. It is hard to believe that Washington, shrewd judge of military capabilities that he was, could have thought that his raw and undisciplined troops could have stormed Boston, which had been made virtually impregnable by the British. Perhaps he only wished to encourage his general officers to think in terms of offensive rather than defensive action.

When Washington fortified Plowed Hill in front of his lines, the British began a heavy bombardment from Bunker Hill and from ships in the harbor, but with little effect. The Americans learned to make light of British cannonading, and often competed with each other to catch the cannonballs while they were still rolling, a practice frowned on by their officers since the men sometimes misjudged and were wounded or killed.

Aside from this exchange, the only other military engagement during the siege was Clinton's attack on Lechmere Point, across the Back Bay. On November 9, 1775, he made an amphibious assault with three hundred light infantry, catching a handful of defenders by surprise and carrying off forty-five head of cattle. The only result was that Washington ordered the Point so strongly fortified that further raids were clearly impractical, and the Point itself was effectively denied the British in the event they should decide to launch an attack from the city.

Washington, despite his keen disappointment over the number of enlistments in the new establishment, gave constant attention to his fortifications. The equipment he most lacked was artillery. He conceived the daring notion of sending Henry Knox, his civilian artillery expert, to Fort Ticonderoga to somehow drag the cannon some three hundred miles to Boston for use in the siege. It was a formidable undertaking, to say the least, but Knox proved equal to it. The cannon were loaded on sleds, or "slays" as Knox called them, and dragged up and down hill along the road from Ticonderoga. Knox got them across frozen lakes by drilling holes in the ice across which the pieces were to pass. One of the heaviest cannon crashed through and had to be hauled out at vast trouble. Finally, in the middle of January, Knox at last reached Boston.

Having the cannon, with Knox to direct their fire, was an opportunity too tempting for Washington to pass up. The British had failed out of carelessness or lethargy to fortify Dorchester Heights, which, as Lieutenant Samuel Webb, an American officer, wrote in his Journal, "commands the south part of the town and is at least 600 yards within their outer lines on the Neck near Roxbury. A strong battery erected on this point would enable us to cut off the communication between the town and their outworks on the Neck, at the same time annoy the ships and the town." Howe apparently felt that it would be impossible for the Americans to fortify the commanding ground at Dorchester before he could rally out and sweep them aside.

Howe, having ample intelligence about Washington's plan to seize Dorchester, satisfied himself with sending a company of grenadiers and light infantry to "destroy the houses and every kind of cover whatever upon that peninsula, which was executed, and six of the enemy's guard made prisoners." But that was as far as he went. He may, indeed, have left the point undefended in hopes that the Americans, by attempting to occupy it, would give him a chance to avenge the disaster at Bunker Hill. He let it be known, in any event, that he would attack at once if the continentals dared to try to establish themselves there. "This is what we wish for," Lieutenant Webb wrote, "trusting (through the assistance of Heaven) this would be a means of rescuing from their hands our capital and many of our friends."

Nevertheless, Washington decided to gamble and try to fortify Dorchester Heights. Since the winter-frozen ground was too hard to dig in, Washington ordered the construction of portable timber frames that could be carried onto the hill, assembled, and packed with hay. Barrels were also collected and filled with earth and rocks to form a further barricade. Then, on the night of March 2, Washington opened a heavy diversionary bombardment of Boston Neck. Knox, starting from scratch, had produced a highly efficient corps of artillerymen. His achievement was the more remarkable since the colonials did not have enough powder to do much cannonading. The British officers were therefore startled when the American bombardment began. As a British officer wrote to Lord Bute: "Their shells were thrown in an excellent direction. . . . Our lines were raked from the new battery they had made and tho' we returned shot and shell, I am very, very sorry to say with not quite so much judgment."

As soon as it was dark, an advance party of some 800 men moved out to take up defensive positions on Dorchester Heights. After them came the carts with entrenching tools, and then the main body under General John Thomas, consisting of 1,200 men with more than 300 carts loaded with pressed hay, fascines, barrels, and rocks. In the words of the Reverend William Gordon, "every one knew his place and business." The constant cannonading from the Continental artillery covered the noise of parties erecting fortifications. Even the wind favored the Americans by carrying the sounds of their work inland. By ten o'clock at night, the Americans had erected two forts capable of defending them from small arms' fire and from grapeshot. At three in the morning, fresh work parties relieved those who had been busy all night. The night itself was mild, with a bright moon that aided the soldiers in their work, but with, at the same time, a low-hanging mist that shrouded them against the observation of the British. Again the colonials were at their best—digging. When morning light revealed the strength and extent of their defenses, a British army engineer expressed his astonishment. Such works, in his opinion, could not have been built by less than 15,000 or 20,000 men. Another officer reported that the dawn of March 4 revealed "two posts upon the highest hills of Dorchester peninsula, that appeared more like majick than the work of human beings."

The fortifications on Dorchester Heights had appeared, in the words of still another British officer, "with an expedition equal to that of the genii belonging to Alladdin's wonder lamp," and Howe wrote to Lord Dartmouth that the American fortifications must "have been the employment of at least 13,000 men." His reaction, as he looked across at the hill, teeming with soldiers strengthening the fortifications, was that he must attack at once before the defenses became impregnable and Boston, in consequence, too exposed to hold. While the British prepared for a re-enactment of Bunker Hill, the Americans strengthened their position until it was far more formidable than the works on Breed's Hill had ever been.

The fortifications on Dorchester Heights were by and large completed on the fourth of March, and the colonials anticipated an attack by the British on the fifth, the anniversary of the Boston Massacre. The Reverend Mr. Gordon reported that Washington said to a group of soldiers, "Remember it is the fifth of March, and avenge the death of your brethern." That at least was the report that ran through the camp, "which added fresh fuel to the martial fire before kindled."

Howe began to plot his attack immediately. Plans were hastily drawn for the assault, and troops were told off to carry them out. A Bostonian with rebel sympathies, watching the soldiers embark in boats under the cover of darkness, noted "that they looked in general pale and dejected, and said to one another that it would be another Bunker's Hill or worse." A violent storm came up during the evening, which churned the waters of the harbor to such a froth that it was soon clear no boats could cross. It was a reprieve for Howe and his men. Washington, anticipating an attack by Howe, had made plans for a counterattack.

General Sullivan wrote of the plan to John Adams some days after the seizure of Dorchester: "We were to land our Boats on the North of Boston, and carry the Town, sword in hand. I was appointed to command the first Division, and General Green the Second. . . . The attack was to have been made with 4,000 we not having Boats to carry more. Our Boats were prepared, and men Paraded by them ready to Embark, and all seemed to be in longing Expectation for the Signal. . . ."

Howe must certainly have been aware of Washington's intention to make an amphibious assault on the city. Archibald Robertson, a young British engineer, spent much of the day of March 5 trying to get an audience with Howe to tell him that he thought the colonial defenses were virtually impregnable, and that an attack upon them by the modest force available to Howe could only be a disaster. Although he did not get to see Howe, he expressed his misgivings to a number of officers, among them his immediate superior, Captain John Montresor. The latter, coming apparently from a council of war, told Robertson at seven in the evening that the officers present "had advised the going off altogether"—the evacuation of the city, rather than an attack—and that "the General said it was his own Sentiments from the first, but thought the honour of the Troops Concerned." Robertson went back to his quarters and wrote, "so it is agreed immediately to Embark everything."

It thus seems evident from Robertson's diary that the decision not to attack had been made before the storm blew up, and that the "Hurrycane" simply provided a face-saving excuse for calling off the assault. It is, of course, possible that without the storm Howe would have attacked, but that is hard to believe. Had Howe done so, it seems as certain as anything can ever be that his troops would have been driven back and much more than decimated. If, at the same time, the American counterattack on Boston had succeeded, the British would have suffered a defeat that might have ended the war then and there. What is perhaps more likely is that the British attack on Dorchester Heights would have failed with great loss of life, and that this defeat would have been to a degree mitigated by the failure of the American counterattack, since such an operation is always subject to unforeseen risks and hazards. Even such a result would have been a disaster for the British, who would, in any event, have had to evacuate the city almost immediately.

The fact was that Howe had been completely outmaneuvered. Boston, of course, should never have been occupied to begin with. No military purpose had been served. Between five and ten thousand British soldiers had been immobilized for more than a year—almost half the entire British army in North America—when they would certainly have been put to better use in a dozen other places. The colonials had been given great encouragement by Bunker Hill; precious time had been given Washington to form the nucleus of an army. Congress had been allowed ample opportunity to get itself together and to begin the laborious task of supplying an army and developing the agencies and instruments of self-government. The whole continent had been permitted time enough to ponder the idea of independence. Almost any disposition of British troops would have been preferable to sitting in Boston for more than sixteen months.

The fortification of Dorchester Heights was carried out in a manner that contrasted dramatically with the hasty defense of Breed's Hill eight months earlier. With enormous effort and remarkable persistence, Washington had created an army, and within that army, perhaps most notably, the beginning of a staff, a group of officers upon whom he could depend to plan and carry out his orders with reasonable efficiency.

At any rate, Washington's occupation of Dorchester made Boston untenable for Howe and his troops. The unhappy general had, therefore, to write to the Earl of Dartmouth and inform him of his intention of evacuating the city, a necessity imposed on him by his own dereliction in not securing Dorchester Heights. He tried, not unnaturally, to make it sound as though it were somehow Dartmouth's fault or Admiral Graves's, "My Lord," he wrote, "It is with great regret I am obliged to inform your lordship that after all my struggles to supply the army with provisions from the Southern provinces and the West Indies . . . and after an anxious expectation of more transports to convey the troops, stores, civil officers, inhabitants, and effects, the enemy by taking possession of and fortifying the commanding heights on Dorchester Neck, in order to force the ships, by their cannon, to quit the harbor, has reduced me to the necessity either of exposing the army to the greatest distresses by remaining in Boston, or of withdrawing from it under such straitened circumstances."

When the inhabitants of Boston, Whig and Tory alike, heard that Howe planned to evacuate the city, they came to plead with him not to burn it. Howe, quite shrewdly, proposed a bargain, if the Americans would not interfere with his evacuation of the city, he would promise not to burn it on his departure. This word was sent to Washington, and by tacit agreement the British were permitted to withdraw unmolested.

The loading of the ships was a major undertaking. Tories and their families, and as much of their personal belongings as they could take with them, had to be provided for, though crudely enough. The wealthy Benjamin Hallowell had to sleep in a crowded cabin where "men, women, and children; parents, masters and mistresses, obliged to pig together on the floor, there being no berths." Howe ordered that "Household Furniture and other useless Luggage, brought to the docks, which could not be shipped, should be thrown overboard," and the harbor was reported filled with handsome desks, cabinets, and sofas. The city was also stripped of whatever goods remained in its stores that might be of use to Washington's army. Any supplies that could not be carried away were burned or otherwise destroyed. Although Howe issued strict orders against plundering the abandoned houses, much pillaging went on. John Andrews, who had assumed responsibility for six houses of friends in the days before the British sailed away, "underwent more fatigue and perplexity than I did through the whole siege; for I was obliged to take my rounds all day, without cessation, and scarce ever failed at finding depredation made upon some one or the other of them, that I was finally necessitated to procure men at the extravagant rate of two dollar a day to sleep in the several houses and stores for a fortnight before the military plunderers went off—for so sure as they were left alone one night, so sure they were plundered."

As the British prepared to depart, Washington, assuming that Howe would set sail for New York and determined, if possible, to be there to intercept him, began to send off units of his army to begin the long march south, meanwhile keeping a wary eye on the British lest Howe, at the last moment, should try to catch the Americans off guard and retrieve the situation. Howe, his men and equipment loaded, lingered on, inexplicably, until Washington, by fortifying Foster's Hill on the Dorchester Neck, brought his artillery to bear on the docks and wharves and gave a final impetus to the British departure. The British soldiers at Charlestown left some mementoes behind. When the American soldiers approached, they noticed sentinels apparently still standing at their posts. Closer inspection revealed "the Centinels to be images dressed in the Soldiers Habit with Laced Hatts and for a Gorget an Horse Shoe will Paper Ruffles their Pieces Shouldred fixed Bayonets with this inscription wrote on the Breat (viz) welcome Brother Jonathan"—a touch of humor and of affection by common soldiers who had perhaps come to envy and admire their enemy.

Timothy Newell, a selectman of Boston, wrote in his journal on Sunday, March 17: "Thus was this unhappy distressed town through a manifest interposition of divine providence relieved from a set of men whose unparalled wickedness, profanity, debauchery and cruelty is inexpressible." The boys of the town, freed of their long confinement, raced off to spread the word that it was empty of British at last.

Some 125 vessels loaded with almost 9,000 men and officers, more than 1,100 Loyalists, and almost 1,000 women and children of the soldiers, made their way out of Boston harbor, covering the water for miles around with their sails.

Washington had expected Howe to head for New York, which from its accessibility and the effectiveness of its defense—as well as from the number and ardor of its Tories and its central location between the northern and southern colonies—would have provided an ideal base of operations for the British army, and which of course, in time, it did. But Howe sailed instead to Halifax, where he unloaded his Loyalist passengers, refitted his ships, and laid in fresh supplies. Meanwhile Washington and his army, anticipating Howe's movement to New York, headed for that city posthaste.

9

Patriots and Tories

THE year that intervened between Lexington and Concord and Washington's arrival with his army in New York was one in which the American patriots worked hard to put their house in order. This meant, primarily, suppressing—or neutralizing the influence of—the Tories and of the royal governors.

John Adams estimated that at the outbreak of the war, one-third of the colonists were warm patriots, one-third clung to their allegiance to the Crown (usually at great personal cost), and one-third were neutral, took no sides, and simply wished to be left alone.

A careful analysis of the patriot and loyalist parties was written by David Ramsay, delegate to the Continental Congress and historian of the Revolution, who had the advantage of living through the events he subsequently described. Ramsay pointed out:

> The revolution had its enemies, as well as its friends, in every period of the war. Country, religion, local policy, as well as private views, operated in disposing inhabitants to take different sides. The New-England provinces being mostly settled by one sort of people, were nearly of one sentiment. The influence of British office holders in Boston, together with the connections which they had formed by marriages, had attracted sundry influential characters in that capital to the British interest, but these were as dust in the balance, when

compared to the numerous independent Whig yeomanry of the country.

The same and other causes produced a large number in New York, who were attached to royal government. That city had been the headquarters of the British army in America, and many intermarriages, and other connections, had been made between British officers and some of their first families. . . . The governors thereof had long been in the habit of indulging their favourites with extravagant grants of land. This had introduced the distinction of landlord and tenant. There was therefore in New York an aristocratic party, respectable for numbers, wealth and influence, which had much to fear from independence. The city was also divided into parties by the influence of two ancient and numerous families, the Livingstones and Delanceys. These having long accustomed to oppose each other at elections, could rarely be brought to unite in any political measures. In this controversy, one almost universally took part with America, the other with Great Britain.

Ramsay went on to note that the Scotch-Irish in America "with a few exceptions, were attached to independence. They had fled from oppression in their native country, and could not brook the idea that it should follow them." Scots, on the other hand, were inclined to support Great Britain. At the same time, Ramsay pointed out, some of the most outstanding members of Congress and officers in the army were natives of Scotland.

As for the Germans, many of them were, in Ramsay's words, "determined Whigs." But with the Germans there was often a language barrier. "Such of them as resided in the interior country, were, from their not understanding the English language, far behind most of the other inhabitants in a knowledge of the merits of the dispute. Their disaffection was rather passive than active."

Ramsay emphasized that the majority of Tories in the Southern states were found on the frontier. Their grievances against tidewater plantation owners alienated them from the patriot cause. "Religion," Ramsay continued, "also divided the inhabitants of America. . . . The Quakers, with a few exceptions, were averse to independence. In Pennsylvania they were numerous, and had power in their hands. Revolutions in government are rarely patronized by any body of men, who foresee that a diminution of their own importance is likely to result from the change. Quakers from religious principles were averse to war, and therefore could not be friendly to a revolution, which could only be affected by the sword."

In addition to religion, nationality, family, and sectional antagonisms,

> . . . the age and temperament of individuals had often an influence in
> fixing their political character. Old men were seldom warm Whigs;
> they could not relish the great changes which were daily taking place;
> attached to ancient forms and habits, they could not readily accommodate themselves to new systems. Few of the very rich were active in
> forwarding the Revolution. This was remarkably the case in the
> eastern and middle States; but the reverse took place in the southern
> extreme of the confederacy. There were in no part of America more
> determined Whigs than the opulent slaveholders in Virginia, the
> Carolinas, and Georgia.
>   The active and spirited part of the community, who felt themselves possessed of talents that would raise them to eminence in a free
> government, longed for the establishment of independent constitutions: but those who were in possession or expectation of royal
> favour, or of promotion from Great Britain, wished the connection
> between the Parent State and the Colonies might be preserved.

There were, Ramsay went on to point out, Tories or Loyalists in
every colony. Their story was on the whole a tragic one. Those whose
loyalty or neutrality was based on religious principles and who were
identifiable as members of sects living in more or less homogeneous
communities had the easiest time of it. It was natural that the more
conspicuous or active an individual Tory was, the more he suffered
from the resentment and hostility of patriots, or Whigs, as the patriots
were frequently called. Besides those Tories whose official position
required them to support the Crown, there were many who did so out
of principle and conviction. They often showed great personal courage
as well as persistence in the face of harassment and persecution.

The Tories, like the patriots, were moved by a variety of motives
and had very different degrees of ardor for their cause. Those who
were quite irreconcilable at the outbreak of the Revolution left for
Canada or Great Britain and lived the unhappy lives of political refugees, incapable of truly finding a new home or of returning to their old.
In some instances, Tories joined the British army or, especially in the
South, formed bands of Tory irregulars. But these were, relatively, only
a handful. Most Tories kept their opinions to themselves and weathered
the storm as best they could. Many of them were individuals respected
and liked in their own communities. In such cases, their courage in
making the decision to oppose the majority of their friends and neigh-

bors, not to mention in many instances members of their own family, and their persistence in the face of public pressure, usually won for them a grudging respect, and public opinion protected them from open persecution.

Under the protection of the British army, the Boston Tories grew so bold in their efforts to "disunite and embarrass" the cause of liberty that James Warren anxiously asked John Adams if the time had not come for the patriots to take more aggressive action "before the Tories can compleate their efforts. . . . They are more assiduous than Satan was with our first Parents, and equal to him in deceit and Falsehood, and with many find Success. No stone is left unturned to effect their purposes."

It is clear enough why the Tories asserted themselves in all the colonies. They never had any doubts about what the outcome of the struggle would be once the mother country overcame her weak and vacillating policy towards the colonies and acted with resolution to bring the demogogues and agitators to book. Then the Tories would be vindicated, their fortunes restored, and their tormenters punished. Like the British ministry, the Tories constantly assured themselves that the resistance to Great Britain had been stirred up by a handful of ambitious intriguers. The mass of the people were docile and loyal, devoted to His Majesty George the Third, and totally indifferent to fine points of constitutional theory.

The Tories were as confident as the British that even if worst came to worst and war broke out, the mere sight of battle-seasoned British regulars would be enough to overawe the colonists. Perhaps, indeed, a short war might be the better course. Once thoroughly beaten and humiliated, the agitators and demogogues would hardly dare to trouble their betters again. Then there would be an end to mobbing, to tarring and feathering, to nonimportation agreements and insolent inquisitions. Dr. Samuel Peters, a Tory minister of Boston, wrote in this vein to a friend in Connecticut. "I am in high spirits. Six regiments are now coming from England and sundry men of war. So soon as they come, hanging work will go on, and destruction will first attend the seaport towns."

As the preparations for armed warfare went on at an accelerating pace and the Tories, confident that British power must prevail, became more and more active, the attention of the patriots was directed increasingly toward them. They became the primary enemy; Parliament and the British ministers, three thousand miles away, seemed a less immediate menace than the patriots' Tory neighbors. Thus we find in the letters and statements of the patriots a growing concern with the Tories.

The Tories in turn looked to the royal officials for protection and encouragement. Of all Crown officials, the royal governors had the most exposed and vulnerable positions. But one by one the royal governors gave up the effort to represent the authority of the Crown. Governor John Wentworth of New Hampshire, one of the most popular and successful of all the royal governors, retired to Boston in the fall of 1775, to the protection of Gage's army. Governor William Tryon, having been transferred from North Carolina to New York, found that his days were numbered in that colony. Congress had received word from England that Tryon intended to organize the Loyalists. The Congress in Philadelphia thereupon voted to recommend to the various provincial congresses "to arrest all persons who might endanger the liberties of Americans." Hearing of plans to arrest him, Tyron took refuge on a British man-of-war in New York Harbor and made it his headquarters for almost a year. In New Jersey, however, Governor William Franklin, the illegitimate son of Benjamin, remained a stubborn and outspoken Tory. He not only refused to relinquish his post, but also constantly denounced the patriots as traitors and rebels. For more than a year he brazened it out before he was finally arrested and formally deposed.

The proprietary governor of Pennsylvania, John Penn, grandson of the founder, William, was caught between the supporters of the proprietors, most of whom were patriots, and the more conservative elements in the colony. As a result, John Penn lay low. The Pennsylvania assembly was inclined toward support of the Crown, but the presence of the Continental Congress in Philadelphia plainly inhibited the Tories and strengthened the hands of the more radical colonists. John Dickinson's own vacillation weakened his standing with the friends of liberty and eventually made it possible for the most ardent patriots to take control. Without real leadership from Dickinson, the moderate party never established itself in a colony that was, in many ways, second only to New York in conservative and loyalist sentiment.

Delaware, which shared John Penn as governor, followed much the same course as Maryland, simply ignoring the governor and his agents and placing power in a state convention organized and dominated by Caesar Rodney.

In Maryland, another proprietary governor, Robert Eden, appointed by Lord Baltimore, found his authority gradually eroded. The Marylanders had been among the most zealous in the cause of liberty. When Eden prorogued the assembly in a dispute over taxes, Maryland's Provincial Convention simply took over the assembly's functions. The convention even prevailed on Eden to supply it with arms and ammunition, on the grounds that there was an impending slave insurrection. In June, 1775, the convention issued a "Declaration and Pledge" calling for resistance to Great Britain and setting up a Council of Safety and Committees of Observation.

In Virginia, Governor Dunmore had been embroiled with the House of Burgesses and with his particular bête noîre, Patrick Henry, since his arrival in the colony. Persistent in his efforts to maintain the authority of the Crown, Dunmore was finally frightened out of the colony by the report that a company of riflemen from the frontier region were on their way to arrest him. At first he found asylum on board a British naval vessel, the *Fowey,* where he ordered the Burgesses to meet with him. Finally, to resolve the deadlock and leave the field open for the Convention, the Burgesses adjourned in June, 1775. Dunmore meanwhile scraped together a small force of British soldiers and marines and occupied Norfolk, the seaport of Virginia. From this vantage point he was industrious in his efforts to recruit Loyalists, to encourage resistance to the convention, and, finally, to bring on the most dreaded event of all, an uprising of slaves against their masters.

Josiah Martin, Tryon's successor as governor of North Carolina, had won over the "Regulators," the frontier group that had taken up arms under Hermon Husband to protest their exploitation by an Assembly dominated by seacoast representatives. The Battle of Alamanace in 1771, in which Tryon, strongly supported by the colony's establishment, had routed the Regulators, had left the frontiersmen deeply alienated. Martin took advantage of their bitterness to tie them to the Crown, persuading them that they had better hope for justice from that source than from their own assembly.

The situation in South Carolina was similar. Here, too, the frontier settlements had deep grievances that the Charles Town aristocrats had ridiculed or ignored. Put in overly simple terms, when the ruling class in the Carolina colonies subscribed overwhelmingly to the patriot cause, the lower class, concentrated largely on the frontier, turned to the Crown. The Southern frontier thus became, outside of certain counties in the province of New York, the only region in colonial America that could be properly called a Tory stronghold.

Despite the loyalist sympathies of the frontier, North Carolina's Governor Martin could not hold out against the patriot party. A Provincial Congress was organized, which then turned itself into an Assembly. It was promptly prorogued by the governor—and just as promptly reverted to a Congress again. Martin, threatened by the more militant Whigs, finally took refuge first in Wilmington, North Carolina, and then, like several of his fellow governors, on board a British warship. From there he wrote to both Gage and Dartmouth assuring them that North Carolina was basically loyal and that with help from England the patriots might be easily routed and the colony made secure for the Crown.

The new governor of South Carolina, Arthur Campbell, who arrived in June of 1775, was soon at swords' points with the old assembly as well as with the Provincial Congress that had been called to give effect to the injunctions of the Continental Congress. The assembly greeted him with words of classic ambiguity: "We readily profess our loyal attachment to our sovereign, his crown and dignity: and, trusting the event to Providence, we prefer death to slavery." Having, at the news of Lexington and Concord, seized the arms in the public magazine at Charles Town, the patriot leaders dispatched a vessel to Florida to collect more powder and followed the path taken by South Carolina's sister colonies: they enlisted troops, suspended the royal courts, enforced the Association, and suppressed the local Tories. When the patriots learned of a plan by Campbell to secure British troops and, with the help of the Regulators, take firm possession of the colony for the Crown, the Council of Safety seized the Charles Town fort and prepared to arrest the governor. He wisely retired to a British ship in the harbor; when the colonists fired on it, it raised anchor and sailed off. For a time, it appeared as though the Regulators might take up arms without waiting for British support and plunge the colony into civil war, but an uneasy truce was arranged. By tacit agreement, the less fervent frontier was exempted from the busy attentions of the various patriot committees that had taken over the government of the colony.

Sir James Wright, the able and conciliatory governor of Georgia, the most recently settled of the colonies, managed perhaps better than any other royal governor to preserve good relations with the inhabitants of his colony and to put the damper on patriotic agitation. Georgia sent no delegates to the First Continental Congress, and it was not until well into the Second Congress that Georgia was fully represented. But slowly, the now familiar pattern emerged. Committees were formed, the Association was subscribed to by a majority of the colonists, and a

Provincial Congress gradually filled up. By the fall of 1775, Georgia was securely in the patriot camp.

What is most striking is how most of the colonies, radical or conservative, all took virtually the same line, some sooner and some later, but with no significant deviation. The agencies of what was, in effect, a revolutionary government developed with remarkable uniformity and with a surprising lack of friction and confusion.

Among the conclusions to be drawn from these facts are these: While the leadership in each colony was important, especially as it affected the promptness with which the people of a particular colony supported their New England cousins, of far greater significance was the fact that the resistance to Britain was a widespread and deep-rooted popular movement. Indeed, nothing could bear more striking testimony to its "popular" nature—a profound protest of the people against a position of dependence and subordination—than the common forms that the resistance took in every colony. And this despite the many differences among the colonies—differences in religion, in politics, in social structure and stratification, and in historical development. In the words of one historian: "In not a single colony did a royal governor keep his authority: in none was there a loyalist party resisting by the old legal forms the coming of the new. The old Assemblies and Councils quietly disappeared: those governors who had not yet fled remained only on sufferance and were presently to go. And in their places the solid men of the new politics had control of each colony."

Of far more consequence than the retreat or ousting of the colonial governors was the suppression of the Tories. This unpleasant duty, if we may properly call it that, was carried on primarily on the local level by Committees of Safety and Committees of Observation. Here neighbor was pitted against neighbor, friend against friend, and, not infrequently, father against son.

The treatment of Tories varied greatly, of course. A good deal of the time of the Committees of Public Safety was expended on such matters as that which occupied the committee of Bucks County, Pennsylvania. They summoned before them Thomas Meredith and Thomas Smith. Meredith was accused by Benjamin Hair, John Hair, and John Harry of having "spoken injuriously of the distressed people of the town of Boston, and disrespectfully of the Measures prosecuting for the redress of American Grievances." He was required to recant and signed a statement declaring, "I do hereby declare, that I am heartily sorry for what I have done, voluntarily renouncing my former principles, and promise for the future to render my Conduct unexceptionable to my Countrymen, by strictly adhering to the measures of the Congress."

Thomas Smith proved more obdurate. In the words of the committee's report, he was charged with having "uttered expressions to the following purport, viz: That the Measures of Congress had already enslaved America and done more damage than all of the Acts of Parliament ever intended to lay upon us, so that the whole was nothing but a Scheme of a parcel of hot-headed Presbyterians and he believed that the Devil was at the Bottom of the whole; that the taking up Arms was the most scandalous thing a man could be guilty of, and more heinous than a hundred offences against the moral law, etc., etc., etc." Since Smith refused to recant, he was to be "considered as an enemy to the Rights of British America," and all persons were enjoined to "break off every kind of dealing with him until he shall made proper satisfaction to this Committee for his misconduct."

A Loyalist lady reported to a friend "the most shocking cruelty" practiced on an old tidesman (that is, customs inspector) named Malcolm, who, despite a determined defense, was seized by a mob, stripped naked on a bitter January night, tarred and feathered, dragged about in a cart "with thousands attending," and then beaten and whipped. But the stubborn old man, when his tormentors ordered him to curse the king, cried out instead, "Curse all traitors!" Even with a rope around his neck and the threat of hanging, he dared them to do their worst, "for God was above the Devil."

Another who was dismayed at the behavior of some of the more zealous patriots was Philadelphian Alexander Graydon, normally a sympathizer with the colonial cause. Graydon was particularly outraged by the treatment given Dr. Kearsley. Dr. Kearsley, a prominent physician and Tory of Philadelphia, was not content simply to stand on his principles. He took every opportunity to express his colorful and venomous contempt for those who, in his view, were traitors to their king. As a consequence Dr. Kearsley was captured by militia—he put up a desperate struggle in the course of which he was wounded in the hand by a bayonet—and placed in a cart to be drawn about the city "amidst a multitude of boys and idlers." Graydon was at the coffeehouse when the procession passed by. The doctor, "foaming with rage and indignation, without his hat, his wig disheveled and bloody from his wounded hand, stood up in the cart and called for a bowl of punch," which he drained off at one long swallow. Graydon confessed himself shocked at the spectacle of "a largely respected citizen so cruelly vilified." He announced to any one who would listen that if he had been a magistrate he would have "at every hazard . . . interposed my authority in suppression of the outrage. . . ." If such behavior was the measure of a true patriot, Graydon reflected, "I wanted nerves for a revolutionist." Yet in the next breath, he noted that "the conduct of the populace was marked by a lenity which peculiarly distinguished the cradle of our republicanism. Tar and feather had been dispensed with, and excepting the injury he had received in his hand, no sort of violence was offered by the mob to their victim."

There were, of course, those who wished to see all Tories hanged. Joseph Hawley, the mentor of James Otis and Samuel Adams, asked Elbridge Gerry how America could survive: "Did any State ever subsist, without exterminating traitors?" he wrote. "It is amazingly wonderful that, having no capital punishment for our intestine enemies, we have not been utterly ruined before now." He compared Tories to vermin who "Crawl among the Roots of Vegetables endeavoring to secret themselves . . . or in Sheep's Cloathing secretly watching for prey to gratify their voratious Appetites."

The persecution of the Tories was mitigated by the fact that many patriot leaders had close friends among the Loyalists. Also, since the Tory-patriot split was often a split between the young and the old, there were many instances where fathers remained loyal to the Crown while their sons took up the patriot cause. John Dickinson's wife and his mother, for example, were of Tory sympathies. Gouverneur Morris's mother was also a staunch Loyalist. She implored her son to keep out of politics—to which he grandly replied: "What may be the event of the present war, it is not in men to determine. Great revolutions of empire are seldom achieved without much human calamity; but the worst which can happen is to fall on the last bleak mountain of America, and he who dies there, in defence of the injured rights of mankind, is happier than his conqueror, more beloved of mankind, more applauded by his own heart."

John Randolph of Virginia, a Tory, and Thomas Jefferson were, and remained, close friends. Writing to Jefferson while sailing to exile in England, Randolph said, "Tho we *may politically* differ in sentiments, yet I see no reason, why *privately* we may not cherish the same esteem for each other, which formerly, I believe, subsisted between us. . . . We both of us seem to be steering opposite Courses; the success of either lies in the womb of Time. But whether it falls to my share or not, be assured that I wish you all Health & Happiness."

John Jay and Peter Van Schaack, both New Yorkers, had been the closest of friends. When Van Schaack's Tory sympathies finally forced him to retreat to England, Jay retained his affection for his friend. "Be assured," he wrote Schaack, "that John Jay did not cease to be a friend to Peter Van Schaack. No one can serve two masters. Either Britain was right and America was wrong, or America right and Britain wrong. They who thought Britain were bound to support her. . . . To such of them as have behaved with humanity I wish every species of prosperity that may consist with the good of my country. You see how naturally I slide into the habit of writing as freely as I used to speak to you. . . . My best wishes always attend you, and be assured that, notwithstanding many political changes, I remain, dear Peter. Your affectionate friend and servant, John Jay."

One of John Adams' closest companions had been his college friend, Jonathan Sewall. One day, in the months following the passage of the Coercive Acts, the two lawyers, on circuit together with the courts, took a walk on the hills above Casco Bay while Sewall tried to turn Adams from his support of the patriot cause. "Great Britain is determined on her system," he told Adams; "her power [is] irresistible and it will certainly be destructive to you, and all those who . . . persevere in opposition to her designs."

"I know that Great Britain is determined in her system, and that very determination determined me on mine." Adams replied. "I have passed the Rubicon; swim or sink, live or die, survive or perish with my country—that is my unalterable determination." This farewell, Adams told Sewall, "is the sharpest thorn on which I ever set my foot." Many feet trod such thorns, deeply penetrating, deeply wounding thorns. Many decent, brave, and honest men were Tories, men of quite as much faith and conscience as their patriot adversaries. It was one thing to nourish bitter feelings toward Tories as a group, Tories in general, Tories as an abstraction of wickedness; it was quite another matter when the Tory was a brother, a son, a dear friend, or a father. One knew them then in all their vulnerability and their humanity as friends and companions, as kin, bound together by many of the most precious acts and associations of our common life. It is this that makes civil war, which in a substantial measure the Revolution was, the bitterest of all conflicts. The drama and the tragedy of the Tories, which must inevitably be blurred and obscured by the fact that this is, essentially, the story of the patriots, nonetheless serves to remind us that while the accounts of past events as recorded in our history books may seem vivid, colorful, poignant, or dramatic, we can never really recapture the heartbreaking sadness, the wrenching emotions, the daily and hourly ebb and flow of feelings, of fears and doubts and hopes, which are such a familiar part of the lives of all of us and which in times of crisis are raised to a much higher level of intensity. This being the case, the very least a historian can do is take with the utmost seriousness those emotions that the actors in the history he is recording quite evidently felt.

There were, in fact, as many kinds of Tories as there were patriots. The impoverished Carolina frontier Loyalist and the wealthy Tory merchant of Boston or New York had nothing in common except their attitude toward the Crown. There were Tories who loved America, who loved their patriot friends yet considered themselves the true defenders of liberty; Tories whose allegiance to the Crown was a painful decision, reached in prayer and anguish of spirit. Such Tories, if they could afford to, often migrated to Canada or England, sometimes to avoid persecution, sometimes to relieve their friends of the embarrassment of their continued presence. Others, filled with bitterness and animosity, gave whatever comfort and support they could to British authority, civil and military, operated as spies, nursed their hatred, and waited for the day when they would have the upper hand once more.

The feelings of those Tories who retired to England are well illustrated by the case of Samuel Curwen of Massachusetts, who wrote a Salem friend deploring "the dissipation, self-forgetfulness and vicious indulgences of every kind which characterize" London. "The temptations are too great for that degree of philosophy and religion ordinarily possessed by the bulk of mankind. The unbounded riches of many afford the means of every species of luxury, which (thank God) our part of America is ignorant; and the example of the wealthy and great is contagious." At the same time, Curwen wrote to a Tory friend recently arrived in England, "I congratulate you on your retreat from the land of oppression and tyranny; for, surely, greater never appeared since the days of Nimrod. I sincerely wish well to my native country, and am of opinion that the happiness of it depends on restraining the violences and outrages of profligate and unprincipled men, who run riot against all the laws of justice, truth and religion."

Once in England, the Tories waited impatiently for the success of British arms to make it possible for them to return triumphantly to their native land. They waited to see their enemies humiliated, to see all the "artful and designing men" who had been the agents of their misery brought to justice. "None here," Jonathan Sewall wrote his rebel friend, John Foxcroft, "entertains the penumbra of a doubt how the game will end. . . . I would like to take one peep at my house, but I suppose I should not know it again. . . . Every dog they say has his day, and I doubt not I shall have mine. Ah, my old friend, could you form a just idea of the immense wealth and power of the British nation, you would tremble at the foolish audacity of your pigmy states. . . . I feel for the miseries hastening on my countrymen, but they must thank their own folly. God bless and carry you safe through!"

We can get a picture of the plight of the Tories who stayed in America from a Tory letter written in the fall of 1775: "Taciturnity is the greatest Safety we have and we are obliged to observe it, daily contrivances are hatching to bring us under greater subjection and to alienate the minds of loyall Subjects. When perswasions faile they have recourse to menaces by which means weak Capacitys are overcome. The advantage they have is great, every avenue to truth is stop'd and nothing is printed but what is in their favour."

Many Americans were neither patriot nor Tory, but found themselves victims of divided loyalties. Some favored resistance to British encroachments on American freedoms but could not stomach the idea of a declaration of American independence. Such divided feelings afflicted families as well as individuals, such as the influential and highly respected Allen family of Philadelphia, whose head was William Allen, chief justice of the colony. Three of the four sons of William Allen, all prominent and able men, had pledged themselves to fight for the rights of America, but they had made it known that if independence were declared they would cast their lot with the British. John, the eldest son, was a member of one of the revolutionary committees in the city of Philadelphia at the time of Lexington and Concord. Andrew was an officer in the First Philadelphia Troop City Cavalry, a member of the Committee of Safety, and a delegate, in 1775, to the Second Continential Congress. William, the youngest son, had served in Canada as lieutenant colonel of a Pennsylvania regiment. When the Declaration of Independence was passed, all of the Allen sons with the exception of James resigned their respective posts and went over to the British. William, in fact, raised a corps known as the Pennsylvania Loyalists and commanded them until the end of the war.

James Allen had written in his diary as early as July, 1775, "The

Congress is now sitting here & have just published their Declaration & address to the inhabitants of Great Britain. Hitherto our arms have been successful; but God knows what will be the event of this war, as there seems to be a thorough determination on both sides to prosecute it. Many thinking people believe America has seen its best days, & should it even be victorous, peace & order will with difficulty be restored. . . . These reflections are in the mouth of all thinking people. We however keep up our spirits & gloomy as things appear, prefer our situation to a mean acquiescence. It is a great & glorious cause. The Eyes of Europe are upon us; if we fail, Liberty no longer continues an inhabitant of this Globe; for England is running fast to slavery. The King is as despotic as any prince in Europe; the only difference is the mode; & a venal parliament are as bad as a standing army."

But as the months passed and James Allen observed more and more instances of confusion and disorder, particularly among what he thought of as the lower class of people, his doubts grew. He joined the militia in the fall of 1775 as a private, and wrote in his diary, "My inducement principally to join them is; that a man is suspect who does not; & I chuse to have a Musket on my shoulders, to be on a part with them; & I believe discreet people mixing with them, may keep them in order. . . . With all my zeal for the great cause we are engaged in, I frequently cry out—Dreadful times!"

By March, 1776, he had a still more sober entry. "The plot thickens; peace is scarcely thought of—independency predominant. Thinking people uneasy, irresolute & inactive. The Mobility triumphant. . . . I love the Cause of liberty; but cannot heartily join in the prosecution of measures totally foreign to the original plan of Resistance. The madness of the multitude is but one degree better than submission to the Tea-Act."

In May, when Congress recommended to the state that they establish "new forms of government," James Allen was deeply disturbed. The radicals and independents would take new heart from the measure. "My feelings of indignation were strong," he wrote, "but it was necessary to be mute. . . . Peace is at a great distance, & this will probably be a terrible Summer. . . . I am obnoxious to the independents; having openly declared my adversion to their principles & had one or two disputes at the coffee-house with them." A month later, having done his best to oppose the spirit of independence and found "the Tide . . . too strong," Allen set off with his family for Northampton County, determined to play no further role in the political life of his state.

As events turned out, he was given little choice in the matter. As remote as Northampton was, he soon felt the pressure of local patriots. He must declare himself for independence or be considered a traitor to the cause. Rumor had it that the local Committee of Safety had made out a list of two hundred persons believed to be disloyal, who were to be seized and sent to North Carolina for the duration of the war. The Allen brothers heard that they were on the list, and in December, 1776, against their brother James's advice, they went to Trenton and placed themselves in the protection of General Howe.

Their action threw further suspicion on James Allen, who was finally brought under guard to Philadelphia to be examined as to his views and actions. Allen reiterated his devotion to the cause of liberty—and his abhorrence of independence. "I drew a picture," he wrote, "of the state of the province, the military persecutions, the invasions of private property, imprisonments & abuses, that fell to the share of those whose consciences would not let them join in the present measures." It took a good deal of courage on Allen's part to speak so boldly, but his interrogators, several of whom were personal friends, took his criticisms in good part. Allen "pledged my honor verbally not to say or do anything injurious to the present cause of America. So," he wrote, "we parted amicably & as we had began, with great politeness on both sides."

Nonetheless, he soon afterward had a most unpleasant experience when militia stopped his carriage with his wife and children in it and slashed it with their bayonets until the party was rescued by a friend. There was no question by now of where Allen's own feelings lay, and it was equally clear that there was a large element of class feeling in his view of the course that the revolution had taken. "The Province of Pennsylvania," he wrote, " . . . may be divided into two classes of men, viz. Those that plunder and those that are plundered. No justice has been administered, no crimes punished for 9 months. All Power is in the hands of the associators, who are under no subordination to their officers. . . . To oppress one's countrymen is a love of Liberty. Private friendships are broken off, & the most insignificant now lord it with impunity & without discretion over the most respectable characters." Allen occupied himself as best he could, "gardening, planting etc." but he missed his brothers behind the British lines. "There are few families," he wrote, "who live on terms of purer love & friendship than ours; which is owing not only to natural affection, but the conviction of each others integrity and disinterestedness.

"Our assembly have at length in their wisdom prepared a test act obliging all to vow allegiance to their state & abjure the King; the penalty is being in effect outlawed, unable to sue or be sued or travel out of their county. But it is as little regarded as the rest of their Laws; They are indeed a wretched set. This convulsion has indeed brought all the dregs to the Top. . . . Melancholy as the state of this wretched Country is, to one not embarked in the present pursuit; yet I keep up my spirits, & stand my ground amongst the Whigs, with whom it is my lot to associate in this quarter."

Other families were far more deeply divided than the Allens. The Tilghman family of Maryland and Pennsylvania was one such family. James Tilghman had served as attorney general of Pennsylvania. He remained loyal to the Crown, but three of his sons allied themselves with the patriot cause (although the youngest son, Philemon, went to England at the age of fifteen and served in the British navy). The eldest son, Tench, became an aide to Washington. Tench and his brothers maintained close relations with their Tory father, who never hesitated to speak in the most contemptuous terms of Congress and of the army in which his sons served.

Six months after Congress had declared the colonies to be independent of Great Britain, Tench Tilghman wrote his father, "I know we do not agree in political sentiments, quite, but that, I am convinced, does not abate, in the least, that ardent affection that I have for you, and makes me happy, far happier than any other title when I call myself, your most dutiful son." Trying to cajole his father into taking an active political role among the conservative Pennsylvania patriots, Tench Tilghman wrote, "I saw plainly how Matters would go, and that our provincial Affairs, for want of able pilots, would end in distraction—I do not think it yet too late to over set this Cabal . . . but it can only be done by Men of Sense and Rank stepping forth determined to give opposition to the power at present hanging over with undoubted intent to first subjugate and then Rule with a Rod of Iron." If the natural leaders in the state had not hung back so long, Tench Tilghman felt, the radicals would not have been able to take matters into their own hands.

But Tench Tilghman continued to argue the American cause with his father. The elder Tilghman had done all he reasonably could to express his loyalty to the British Crown, "not by acting, but by speaking your sentiments moderately and in such a manner, that even those of a different opinion have not blamed you," young Tilghman wrote. "A Majority of the people upon this Continent are determined to support the independency of America. Things being thus circumstanced, it is no more derogatory to your honour and Conscience to take an Oath of fidelity to the form of Government under which you live, than it is for a Member of any representative Body to take an Oath which he had opposed in the House. He takes it because the Majority think it right." And a month later, again urging his father to sign the test oath, he wrote, "to see you at peace with and conforming to what is now the establishment of this Country would give me a greater pleasure than anything I have experienced in a Contest, in which I have faithfully laboured. . . ."

The arguments were in vain. The senior Tilghman remained loyal in his sentiments, to the distress and embarrassment of his son, who was acutely conscious of the awkwardness of his situation: he was an aide of Washington's with a Tory father. But Tench's situation, as he himself knew, was far from exceptional.

There were among the Tories many moderate men and women who loved both the mother country and liberty and who clung tenaciously to the hope of reconciliation. Most of these were dismayed by the thoughtless, boasting spirit of their countrymen, who seemed to believe that Great Britain could be vanquished by bluff and bravado. Samuel Shepard of Virginia was such a man, and he committed his misgivings to his diary in the spring of 1776. Riding in a coach from New Canton to his home in Buckingham County, Virginia, after a seven-year absence in England, he felt "a dreadful pain at the heart because of the primitive land I had returned to, returned to forever as it might be. The snow had almost left the trees, the mud piled high on our wheels, and for conversation I could hear nothing more than the latest declarations of the leaders of the rebellion, so wild and childish and yet brave that I was both ashamed and proud. I tried a few reasonable words on the part of Britain, arguing for peace. My companion looked at me angrily. I said no more, understanding in that bitter look that he was no longer of sound mind on this subject but subject to constant alarms and ill humors."

In the tavern at the town of Buckingham, Shepard met eight of his old friends. After an exchange of warm greeting, "there was talk of the rebellion to which I said nothing but looked at the exalted faces around me." One of the company, noticing Shepard's silence, asked if he disagreed with the sentiments that were being expressed. Shepard replied, mildly enough, that he acknowledged "the great sins of the British to the colonies but expressing a belief that there was enough spirit of agreement between the contestants to discover a way to peace, quoting the words I had heard from leaders in Oxford and London: that the King was not all of the Kingdom, but a sadly biased man and the friends of the colonies were the ones to listen to, not the obeisant followers of the sad monarch." Shepard was encouraged to continue in this vein. "In my best manner, calm and judicious, I opened the subject, stating both sides as well as I could without ill temper or prejudice." For a few moments he had the illusion that his audience was with him, silent and attentive.

When he had finished describing the possibilities and advantages of peace, his host and another man left the room, red-faced and angry. In a few minutes they were back with a sheriff to accuse Shepard of "treasonable acts and speech." "I was thoroughly awakened from my childish faith in reason," Shepard wrote. Startled and furious at this betrayal by friends, he drew his sword to defend himself, backing into a corner as he did so. At once he was the object of "bedlamite execration." Realizing the hopelessness of his position, Shepard surrendered his sword to the sheriff and then spoke his mind to the gathering. "Men," he said, "are not fit to govern themselves until they grow up and can't do it in their infancy." When he had cleared himself of the charges against him he would, he warned them, challenge each of his tormentors to a duel. He then turned his back on them to another storm of hoots and catcalls.

Shepard was confined in a cold and dank jail, but his jailer proved an amiable enough man, bringing him firewood and then coming to entertain him, "sitting beside the fire with his fiddle, showing me such good nature that I, musing over my welcome to Buckingham, listened with some pleasure." In addition to the music, the jailer had some sound advice. "You will learn not to think aloud in this place, for we are going to have a hard time and we can't have treasonable talk to weaken our cause. . . . You are most fortunate in not having old man Pat Henry here at the tavern, he would have addressed the people and you would have been treated badly." The next day Shepard was released with admonitions from the justices and drove home, "hating my position, met like a foreign thief after seven years absence. . . ."

He arrived unexpectedly, a prodigal father, to find "the boys grown to man, my wife changed, her beauty deepened as though a sculptor had cut the lines of her face again making them more decisive and mature." Feeling like an old man, Shepard took his fiddle into the drawing room and played a tune he had learned in Seville from a street musician, his family "applauding the song and not my playing which is not good now that my wrist is getting stiff. The place is beautiful," he added. "The fields. The mountain. My own trees. The foxes barking in the ravine. The moon a great pearl. The slaves happy and comfortable. My family well." But when Shepard told of his reception at Buckingham, there were embarrassed looks and "unhearty indignation." "I had come home to a nest of rebels," he added, with a dry humor. "Let me thank God for a safe return and a happy one—it is a happy one. Men's opinions will not kill me or even, I vow to God, spoil my temper. I pray He will be kind to all our peoples and give to me more humility. Amen."

In the poignance of Shepard's diary entry, so vivid and so moving, the tragedy of every civil war or revolution is brought powerfully home. One is reminded of the passage in Thucydides' narrative of the Corcyrean rebellion where words changed their meaning and moderation became cowardliness or treason. Shepard kept both his principles and his temper. His sons went off to fight for the rebels. He loved them and his wife and his fertile acres and his slaves; he played his fiddle, read the classics, and survived. His diary demonstrates that a single item, a tiny bit of datum, can reveal more of the inner spirit of an epoch than a vast accumulation of facts. Among all the extraordinary treasures of source material that have survived from the Revolutionary period, Shepard's excerpt sparkles like a particularly precious gem. It is not simply that Shepard has a prose style of great clarity and force that under different circumstances might have made him a literary figure of consequence. It is also that he offers us such a moving picture of a wise and humane man caught in a revolutionary situation. Shepard was "radical" enough, he simply recoiled, as many of us would have, from the "implications" of revolution. He thus provides a contrast to James Allen, who, we suspect, recoiled from traveling the full route to independence because he was afraid that the lower social orders would use the occasion to seize power from Allen's own class. If we can keep Shepard's diary entry in mind throughout the events that follow, we will inevitably have a keener sense of the human tragedy of the Revolution.

The diary also reminds us that at a certain time of life one becomes particularly reluctant to shoot another person, even for the best of principles. We see principles come and go and men become more savage in their name than beasts of the jungle. We discover that small personal decencies have become dearer to us than the most resounding principles; it is then that we are spoiled for revolution.

10

Common Sense

Wɪᴛʜ the suppression of the Tories, the ousting of royal governors, and the establishment of independent governing bodies in the various colonies, talk of independence grew. Letters and editorials appeared more and more frequently in newspapers arguing the case for a statement by Congress declaring the colonies to be independent. In the newspapers and among poets and ballad writers—and perhaps above all in the army—the sentiment for independence far outran the cautious statements of public bodies. General Nathanael Greene of Rhode Island was emphatic on the subject: "George the Third's last speech has shut the door of hope for reconciliation. . . . We must submit unconditionally, or defend ourselves. . . . We are now driven to the necessity of making a declaration of independence."

Newspapers talked openly of the advantages of independence, and Philip Freneau, a young poet, touched a responsive chord with many Americans when he wrote:

> Too long our patient country wears her chains,
> Too long our wealth all-grasping Britain drains:
> Why still a handmaid to that distant land?
> Why still subservient to their proud command? . . .
> Fallen on disastrous times, they scorn our plea:-
> 'Tis our own efforts that must make us free. . . .

In a more belligerent mood, Freneau wrote of "pirates sent out by command of the king/ To plunder and murder, but never to swing." And he added:

> From the scoundrel, Lord North, who would bind us in chains.
> From a dunce of a king who was born without brains . . .
> From an island that bullies, and hectors, and swears.
> I send up to heaven my wishes and prayers
> That we, disunited, may freemen be still,
> And Britain go on—to be damned, If she will:

Through all the vicissitudes of colonial resistance to the enactments of Parliament, Americans had clung, in a stubborn and touching spirit, to the conviction that the king himself was a wise and benevolent figure who would eventually prevail upon his wicked ministers to cease their persecution of the colonists. Bit by bit this image of the king was eroded by events. The illusion became increasingly difficult to preserve. In November, Jefferson wrote to his friend John Randolph, "It is an immense misfortune to the whole Empire, to have a King of such a disposition at such a time. We are told, and everything proves it true, that he is the bitterest enemy we have. . . . To undo his Empire, he has but one more truth to learn: that, after Colonies have drawn the sword, there is but one more step they can take. That step is now pressed upon us, by the measures adopted, as if they were afraid we would not take it."

Jefferson assured Randolph there was not "in the British Empire a man who more cordially loves a union with Great Britain than I do." But he would rather die than accept "a connection on such terms as the British propose, and in this I think I speak the sentiments of America. We want neither inducement nor power, to declare and assert a separation. It is will alone which is wanting, and that is growing apace under the fostering hand of our king. . . ."

The time was ripe for a squint-eyed English stay-maker with a large, pockmarked nose to occupy the center of the stage—Thomas Paine. Paine's radical views had recently brought him to America and to Philadelphia with a letter of introduction from Benjamin Franklin. Paine found a congenial hangout at Aitken's bookstore, where patriot literature was sold and where the works of authors like the Scots political thinkers James Burgh and Adam Ferguson could be found, along with other writers favorable to the cause of liberty. It was here that Paine met Dr. Benjamin Rush, who, like many other young professional men—doctors, lawyers, and college professors—was a staunch radical. They found themselves instantly congenial. Rush, who was Philadelphia's most progressive physician, was struck by the boldness and eloquence of the Englishman. "His conversation," he wrote later, "became at once interesting. I asked him to visit me, which he did a few days afterwards. Our subjects of conversation were political." In Paine, Rush found a strong advocate of American independence, who considered "the measure as necessary as bringing the war to a speedy and successful issue."

Rush had been preparing an essay on the necessity of independence, but he was not sure the time was yet ripe for such a revolutionary statement. It might cause a reaction in favor of Crown and Parliament, and beyond that seriously impair the practice of a young doctor who numbered among his patients many of the more conservative burghers of the city. Rush mentioned the project; perhaps Paine would be the man to undertake it. He had no roots in America, as Rush did. If things got too hot for Paine in conservative Philadelphia, he could easily depart for the more congenial soil of New England. As Rush put it, "My profession and connections . . . tied me to Philadelphia where a great majority of the citizens and some of my friends were hostile to a separation of our country from Great Britain." He had his wife and children to think of, as well as himself.

Paine was delighted with the proposal and set to work at once. As each chapter was finished he brought it by to read to Rush, who was charmed by the force and vigor of the language and the boldness of the sentiments. One sentence in particular, which did not survive in the final version, stuck in his mind: "Nothing can be conceived of more absurd than three millions of people flocking to the American shore every time a vessel arrives from England, to know what portion of liberty they shall enjoy."

That Rush should have encouraged Paine to write the pamphlet that Paine entitled *Common Sense* was one of the happiest accidents in American history. Paine was a largely self-educated, working-class Englishman, a Quaker by birth and a freethinker by instinct, who had had an impoverished and unhappy childhood and been apprenticed as a corset-maker at the age of thirteen. He had served on a British warship at the end of the Seven Years' War and had been, successively, a stay-maker, tax collector, schoolteacher, tobacconist, and grocer. He had failed in each vocation or had abandoned it, as he abandoned his wife, but all the time he had read history and political theory with the avidity of a starving man. Things had seemed desperately wrong to him in England, and he had searched the books to try to find out why, and what might be done to change things for the better. He could not believe that God had intended that the rich should grind down the poor; or, as Sir Algernon Sidney had put it, that some were born with saddles on their backs and others were born booted and spurred to ride them.

Paine's angry eloquence had impressed his fellows in the tax-collector's office, and they had chosen him as their agent in an effort to get higher salaries from Parliament. All Paine had gotten for his trouble was dismissal from his position as tax collector and bankruptcy. But he had attracted the attention of Benjamin Franklin, who had abetted his plan to start his life anew in America by providing letters of introduction that commended him as an "ingenious worthy young man." So, at the age of thirty-seven, Paine had set out for the province of Pennsylvania to try his fortune in the New World.

Common Sense was written for the common man. It came out of Thomas Paine's own guts—out of the bitter years of poverty, the soured dreams, and the dreams that persisted in spite of disappointment and failure. It flowed from Paine's anger and frustration with a complacent and self-congratulatory society that turned its back on misery and injustice, while complaining of the insolence and radicalism of the lower classes. It is passion that gives power to language, and Paine's passion flowed into the sentences he wrote. Government and society were often confused, he told his readers. Actually they were quite different things. "Society is promoted by our wants and government by our wickedness; the former promotes our happiness *positively* by uniting our affections, the latter *negatively* by restraining our vices. . . . The first is a patron, the last a punisher." That was the way, in any event, in which Thomas Paine had experienced government, as the punisher, as that aspect of society that preserved for the few their privileges against the needs of the many.

"Society in every state is a blessing, but government, even in its best state, is but a necessary evil; in its worst state an intolerable one. . . . Government, like dress, is the badge of lost innocence; the palaces of kings are built upon the ruins of the powers of paradise." If men were willing simply to obey the promptings of their consciences there would be no need for government. But that was not the case. Paine accepted the Lockean argument that man, in order to have greater security for his property, surrenders part of it along with part of his freedom. "*Wherefore,* security being the true design and end of government, it unanswerably follows that whatever *form* thereof appears most likely to ensure it to us, with the least expense and greatest benefit, is preferable to all others. . . ."

But there was another distinction, Paine wrote, "for which no truly natural or religious reason can be assigned, and that is the distinction of men into *kings* and *subjects*. Male and female are the distinctions of nature, good and bad the distinctions of heaven; but how a race of men came into the world so exalted above the rest, and distinguished like some new species, is worth inquiring into, and whether they are the means of happiness or of misery to mankind." In early times "there were no kings; in consequences of which there were no wars; it is the pride of kings which throws mankind into confusion."

Moreover, the "evil of monarchy" brought with it hereditary succession, "and as the first is a degradation and lessening of ourselves, so the second . . . is an insult and imposition on posterity. For all men being originally equals, no *one* by *birth* could have a right to set up his own family in perpetual preference to all others forever. . . . One of the strongest natural proofs of the folly of hereditary right in kings, is that nature disapproves it, otherwise she would not so frequently turn it into ridicule by giving mankind an *ass for a lion*."

The fact was that England was closer to a republic than to a monarchy, for what it most prided itself on—its constitution and its elected Parliament—were the very things least compatible with kingship in its classic form. Indeed, it could be said that "in England a king hath little more to do than to make more and give away places, which in plain terms is to impoverish the nation and set it altogether by the ears. A pretty business indeed for a man to be allowed eight hundred thousand sterling a year for, and worshipped into the bargain! Of more worth is one honest man to society, and in the sight of God, than all the crowned ruffians that ever lived. . . ."

The opening of *Common Sense,* with its attack on the institution of kingship, was certainly one of the most radical statements Americans had ever heard. In Freudian terms, it was the supreme act of patricide, the ultimate destruction of the notion of the father-king. These opening passages were full of Utopian enthusiasm, of brilliant rhetoric—as well of as bad politics and social theory. It is untrue, for example, that only kings cause wars. But these passages in *Common Sense* touched the deepest chords in many of those who read it, whatever their nationality, because it reawakened one of the most beguiling dreams of the race, the dream of primal innocence. Was not government, like dress, simply the mark of lost innocence?

There was much of Paine's Quaker hostility to authority, and of his belief in the voice of conscience, in the opening pages of his tract. There was also much of the new spirit of romanticism, whose most eloquent

expositor had been the French philosopher Jean Jacques Rousseau.
And there was much old English radicalism that went back to the Civil
War of the seventeenth century. There were elements of Locke and of
the Glorious Revolution of 1688. Above all, there was Paine's own
anguish and suffering. What Paine said so compellingly—what overrode the demagogic tone, the flawed logic, the shaky politics—was that
nothing in nature or in Scripture indicated that some people were
destined to be *kings* and others *subjects,* or that some people were, by
birth, superior to their fellows, intended by God himself to enjoy greater
privileges, indeed *all* the privileges, while others, "subjects," were to
endure lives of perpetual deprivation.

To have begun with this dramatic attack on the institution of
kingship was a stroke of genius. On the surface, it might have seemed to
have little to do with the conflict over the authority of Parliament. And
yet it had everything to do with it, because the king was the agency in
which the colonists had placed all their hopes. It was the king who
symbolized the power, the majesty, the inviolability of Great Britain and
its empire. The Crown was the umbilical cord that still bound the
colonies to the mother country. The king must, therefore, be destroyed,
with all his majesty stripped from him in a few deadly phrases, the
vanity of his pretensions laid bare with a surgeon's scalpel. And once the
king had been ritually killed, the colonies might at last become independent and fatherless. The first part of *Common Sense* proclaimed an end
to subordination and dependence based on birth or rank and, of course,
an end to dependence of Americans on Great Britain, Parliament,
ministers, or king, without distinction.

Having cleared the ground, Paine went on to speak in more conventional terms (but in no less striking language) of the nature of the
conflict. "The sun," he wrote, "never shined on a cause of greater worth.
'Tis not the affair of a city, a country, a province, or a kingdom, but of a
continent—of at least one-eighth part of the habitable globe. 'Tis not the
concern of a day, a year, or an age; posterity are virtually involved in the
contest, and will be more or less affected even to the end of time by the
proceedings now. Now is the seedtime of continental union, faith, and
honor. . . . By referring the matter from argument to arms, a new era
for politics is struck—a new method of thinking has arisen. All plans,
proposals, etc. prior to the nineteenth of April, i.e., to the commence-
ment of hostilities, are like the almanacks of the last year; which though
proper then, are superseded and useless now."

Paine then reviewed and rebutted those arguments designed to
prove that America reaped substantial commercial and economic bene-

fits as part of the British Empire. This was hard going, and perhaps the least convincing portion of the pamphlet, but Paine was bound at least to attempt it. As part of Great Britain, America had been—and could expect in the future to be—drawn into all the military ventures of the mother country. Europe, ruled by kings and sunk deep in iniquity, was in a constant turmoil that was fed by pride and ambition. An America dependent on Great Britain must be embroiled in bloody and expensive conflicts that would curtail its trade and leach its resources. "Everything that is right or reasonable pleads for separation. The blood of the slain, the weeping voice of nature cries, '*Tis time to part.*' Even the distance at which the Almighty hath placed England and America is a strong and natural proof that the authority of the one over the other was never the design of heaven. . . . It is repugnant to reason, to the universal order of things, to all examples from former ages, to suppose that this continent can long remain subject to any external power. . . . The utmost stretch of human wisdom cannot, at this time, compass a plan, short of separation, which can promise the continent even a year's security. Reconciliation is *now* a fallacious dress. Nature has deserted the connection, and art cannot supply her place."

The fact was that the colonies had grown too large and their affairs too complicated to make it practical any longer to preserve the connection with Great Britain. "To be always running three or four thousand miles with a tale or a petition," Paine wrote, "waiting four or five months for an answer, which, when obtained, requires five or six more to explain it in, will in a few years be looked upon as folly and childishness. There was a time when it was proper, and there is a proper time for it to cease."

The tract closed with a final blast at the idea that things might still be patched up. "Ye that tell us of harmony and reconciliation, can ye restore to us the time that is past? Can ye give to prostitution its former innocence? Neither can ye reconcile Britain and America. The last cord is broken. . . . There are injuries which nature cannot forgive. . . . As well the lover forgive the ravisher of his mistress, as the continent forgive the murderers of Britain."

"O ye that love mankind!" Paine continued. "Ye that dare oppose not only the tyranny but the tyrant, stand forth! Every spot of the old world is overrun with oppression. Freedom hath been hunted round the globe. Asia and Africa have long expelled her. Europe regards her like a stranger, and England hath given her warning to depart. O receive the fugitive, and prepare in time an asylum for mankind!"

Thomas Paine was not a wise or learned man. His enemies said that he was often dirty, that he drank too much, and that he was not scrupulous about financial matters. He was no match as a political theorist for an Edmund Burke or, in America, for John Adams and a dozen others. But all the passion of a flawed and damaged life cried from the lower depths with a power beyond learning, beyond discreet and logical analysis and argument, and that passion touched hundreds of thousands of hearts. A newly articulated vision gains much of its power from the fact that it is *in time*. It is a response, not to abstract formulations, but to the particular agonies and confusions of the historical moment. It is like the voice of a medium through whom pour all the resentments and all the aspirations of the voiceless. No scholar, no graduate of Harvard, or Yale, or the College of New Jersey at Princeton, however radical his politics, could have written *Common Sense*. Their class, their backgrounds, their education had made them too conventional in their language, too academic, too logical, to speak with such power or touch such common chords.

To say that it was the most successful political pamphlet in history is to do it insufficient credit. *Common Sense* belongs in a category all its own. Published in Philadelphia on January 9, 1776, it was republished everywhere; all through the colonies from Charles Town, South Carolina, to Salem, Massachusetts. It crossed the ocean and was translated into German, French, and Dutch. It was even published in London, with most of the treasonable strictures against the Crown omitted. Paine himself estimated that within three months it had sold more that 120,-000 copies; and copies were passed from hand to hand until they became stained and ragged. A conservative estimate would be that a million Americans read it, or almost half the population of the colonies. Moses Coit Tyler, the great literary historian, wrote, "It brushes away the tangles and cobwebs of technical debate, and flashes common sense upon the situation." One could agree with the first part of Tyler's assessment, while rejecting the second. Paine's essay had little to do with the practical, the factual, the common sensical, as that term is generally used; it spoke first to common *feeling,* common *emotions,* common *dreams,* and only secondarily to "common sense."

"I beg leave to let you know that I have read *Common Sense,*" Joseph Hawley, one of the senior radicals from Massachusetts, wrote to Elbridge Gerry, "and that every sentiment has sunk into my well-prepared heart." Washington himself noted that *"Common Sense* is working a powerful change in the minds of men."* He stopped toasting the king at official meals. While John Adams deplored Paine's superficial and naive political theorizing, he recognized the power of the tract and welcomed its effect in solidifying sentiment for independence. When it appeared in Philadelphia, he immediately sent a copy to his wife, Abigail, and to a number of friends and relatives. Deacon Palmer, thanking him, wrote, "I believe no pages was ever more rapturously read, nor more generally approved. People speak of it in rapturous praise." To Joseph Ward it was "a glorious performance," and Abigail Adams, charmed at the writer's sentiments, wondered how "an honest heart, one who wishes the welfare of his country and the happiness of posterity, can hesitate one moment at adopting them." William Tudor, Abigail's cousin, observed that the "doctrine it holds up is calculated for the climate of N. England, and though some timid *piddling* souls shrink at the idea," a hundred times more "wish for a declaration of independence from the Crown."

Paine was not known in the colonies, and, in fact, his name was not put on the pamphlet's title page. For months rumors circulated about the authorship. The unsigned pamphlet was attributed by some to John Adams, but Adams was well aware that he could not have equaled the strength and brevity of the author's style, "nor his elegant simplicity, nor his piercing pathos." "Poor and despicable" as was some of the thinking on political matters beyond the author's competence, it was, on the whole, "a very meritorious production." The author, if but "very ignorant of the science of government," was "a keen writer." *Common Sense* was credited not only to John Adams, but also to half a dozen other likely candidates, including John's cousin, Sam. Franklin was mentioned as the author, and so was Richard Henry Lee.

Not all readers, of course, were as enthusiastic as Joseph Ward and William Tudor. The Tories were indignant or furious, according to their natures, and many moderate patriots, especially those who interested themselves in political theory, thought it a mischievous work that would encourage false notions of government, as indeed it did. Colonel Landon Carter, a member of the Virginia aristocracy and a strong patriot, was one. In his view *Common Sense* "is quite scandalous and disgraces the American cause much. . . ." When a friend praised it, Carter replied testily that "it was as rascally and nonsensical as possible," Carter recognized the true radicalism of Paine's pamphlet. It was "a sophisticated attempt to throw all men out of principles," a leveling, egalitarian document, fitter for the radicals of New England than the sober republican principles of Virginia. The author, in Carter's view, "advances new and dangerous doctrines to the peace and happiness of every society."

Common Sense was especially welcome in New England, where, indeed, it provoked a flood of letters, petitions, and addresses to Congress urging the delegates to declare independence. "This is *the time* for declaring independence," one such correspondent wrote, "we never have had such a favorable moment before, and 'tis not likely we shall have such another if we neglect this." The ordinary people of Massachusetts, James Warren wrote John Adams, "can't account for the hesitancy they observe" in Congress. They wonder why "the dictates of common sense have not had the same influence upon the enlarged minds of their superiors that they feel on their own." The answer in part, of course, was that the radicalism of *Common Sense,* which seemed to hint at the abolition of all government, made the more conservative delegates unwilling to cast off the last mooring that bound them all to certainty and security. Warren, on the other hand, believed that "people are as they should be, the harvest is mature. I can't describe the sighing after independence," he added. "It is universal. Nothing remains of that prudence, moderation or timidity with which we have so long been plagued and embarrassed."

The authorship of *Common Sense* was uniformly attributed by the British to Samuel Adams. Ambrose Sarie, a British officer stationed in New York, found it "a most flagitious Performance, replete with Sophistry, Impudence & Falsehood; but unhappily calculated to work upon the Fury of the Times, and induce the full avowal of the Spirit of Indpendence in the warm and inconsiderate. His attempt to justify Rebellion by the Bible is infamous beyond Expression. That Religion, which Renders Men bad Subjects and bad Citizens, can never be of GOD, who instituted Civil Government that all things might be done decently, and in order. He is not the author of Confusion, but of Peace."

11

Toward Independence:
The Virginia Resolves

As the spring of 1776 wore on, Congress inched closer and closer to that final, irrevocable act of rebellion, a declaration of independence. Many were loath to cut off all hope of reconciliation with Britain. But these laggards were given a spur by the daring declarations passed by the Virginia Provincial Congress, the so-called Virginia Resolves.

The New Englanders in Congress were under pressure from their constitutents to declare independence. The delegates, nevertheless, remained determined to move slowly enough to bring the other colonies with them and grew touchy and irritable at the constant criticism. Adams wrote to Joseph Warren in Boston, "Why don't Your Honors of the General Court, if you are so unanimous in this, give positive instructions to your own delegates to promote independency? . . . The Southern colonies say you are afraid." Word from the South was that they spoke there of nothing "but *Common Sense* and independency."

No one wished for a declaration of independence more than Adams, but he reminded Warren that it was necessary to do more than simply declare independency. It was also essential to create a stable and orderly government. "Such mighty revolutions," he wrote, "make a deep impression on the minds of men, and set many violent passions at work. Hope, fear, joy, sorrow, love, hatred, malice, envy, revenge, jealousy, ambition, avarice, resentment, gratitude, and every other passion, feeling, sentiment, principle, and imagination were never in more lively exercise than they are now from Florida to Canada inclusively." Considering the problems faced by Congress, Adams, impatient as he had often been, did "not at all wonder that so much reluctance has been shown to the measure of independency. All great changes are irksome to the human mind, especially those which are attended with great dangers and uncertain effects. No man living can foresee the consequences of such a measure and therefore I think it ought not to have been undertaken until the design of Providence by a series of great events had so plainly marked out the necessity of it that he that runs might read."

Most of the delegates shared Adams' view that "there must be a decency, and respect and veneration introduced for persons in authority, of every rank, or we are undone. In a popular government, this is the only way of supporting order, and in our circumstances, as our people have been so long without any government at all, it is more necessary than in any other." It was this kind of problem that the author of *Common Sense,* with his romantic indictment of all authority and good order, had no inkling of. Hence the "dangerous" consequences of his essay.

A major stumbling block hindering a declaration of independence was the fact that the Pennsylvania and New York delegates were bound by the instructions of their respective assemblies to oppose any move for independence. As early as March, 1776, John Adams had thought of a clever stratagem—he drew up a resolution recommending that those colonies "who have limited the powers of their delegates to this Congress, by any express instructions that they repeal or suspend those instructions for a certain time," in order that the delegates might have an opportunity "without any unnecessary obstruction or embarrassment, to concern, direct and order such further measures as may seem to them necessary for the defense and preservation, support and establishment of right and liberty in these colonies." But Adams' clever gambit failed. The Pennsylvania delegates continued to take the lead in opposing even a debate on the subject.

Richard Henry Lee joined John and Samuel Adams in devising another strategy for bringing Pennsylvania and New York into line. On the tenth of May, Lee proposed that "it be recommended to the respective assemblies and conventions of the United Colonies, where no government sufficient to the exigencies of their affairs hath been hitherto established, to adopt such government as shall, in the opinion of the representatives of the people, best conduce to the happiness and safety of their constitutents in particular, and America in general." John Adams seconded the motion and it passed with little debate.

On the surface the resolution seemed innocuous enough. But it was followed by a second resolution that put some teeth in the first one. A committee was appointed to prepare a preamble to the first motion. It was not an accident that John Rutledge, John Adams, and Lee were chosen to make up the committee. Five days later they reported to Congress a preamble much stronger than the resolution itself; it stated, bluntly enough, that since the king had, in effect, excluded "the inhabitants of the United Colonies from the protection of his Crown" and waged a ruthless war upon them, it was necessary that "the exercise of every kind of authority under the said Crown should be totally suppressed, and all the powers of government exerted under the authority of the people of the colonies."

As soon as the preamble had been read, James Duane of New York was up to oppose both preamble and resolution alike. "I do protest against this piece of mechanism, this preamble, for the fabrication of independence," he declared. "Congress ought not to determine a point of this sort about instituting governments. What is it to Congress how justice is administered? You have no right to pass the resolution any more than Parliament has. . . . Why all this haste? Why all this urging? Why all this driving? I shall take the liberty of informing my constituents that I have not been guilty of a breach of trust," he declared, flushed and angry.

But Duane sensed that he had been outmaneuvered. The Massachusetts-Virginia axis had doubtless assured themselves of sufficient votes to carry both resolution and preamble. John Adams answered Duane. The preamble was more than a machine for manufacturing independence; it was the fact of independence. But there must be more: "We must have it with more formality," he declared. Thomas McKean of Pennsylvania supported Adams: I think, he said, "we shall lose our liberties, properties, and lives too, if we do not take this step." Samuel Adams backed up McKean. Duane's argument was not that he opposed the preamble but simply that he had not the authority, under his instructions, to vote for it. Adams reminded the delegates that it was the king who had cast out the colonies, not the colonies who had rejected the king.

James Wilson, a florid, nearsighted young Scotsman—like McKean a delegate from Pennsylvania—vehemently opposed the new resolution, basing his resistance on the principle that "all government originates from the people. We are the servants of the people, sent here to act under a delegated authority. If we exceed it, voluntarily, we deserve neither excuse or justification. Some have been put under restraint by their constituents; they cannot vote without transgressing this line." He, like Duane, was under binding instruction from the assembly of his province, which had "done much and asked little from Congress." "In this Province if that preamble passes," he declared dramatically, "there will be an immediate dissolution of every kind of authority; the people will be instantly in a state of nature. Why then precipitate this measure? Before we are prepared to build the new house, why should we pull down the old one?"

The argument was a persuasive but dangerous one. If delegates waited until the states and Congress itself had built "the new house"— that is to say, framed new constitutions—they might wait a very long time indeed. Beyond that, it was the old chicken-and-the-egg problem. Should not a declaration of independence precede the establishment of new forms of government and new sources of legitimacy? Wilson's remarks showed where the anxiety of the moderate Pennsylvanians lay: They did not wish to surrender power to the more radical elements in the colony. More specifically, the Quaker ruling class did not wish to be pushed off the stage it had held for so long by an alliance of former proprietary interests, merchants, Philadelphia artisans, and western radicals.

Wilson's plea prevailed for a time. The Continental Congress agreed to delay the final vote on the preamble until a new Pennsylvania Assembly had had an opportunity to meet. This Assembly upheld by a margin of two votes the "deadly instructions" not to allow its delegates to Congress to vote for independence. This angered the Pennsylvania radicals, who prepared to call a convention to supersede the Assembly. One of the Pennsylvania conservatives wrote gloomily, "A Convention chosen by the People, will consist of the most fiery independents: they will have the whole Executive and legislative authority in their hands. . . . I am determined to oppose them vehemently in assembly, for if they prevail there; all may bid adieu to our old happy constitution and peace." Congress, as soon as it received word of the actionl or inaction, of the Pennsylvania Assembly, passed the preamble over the objections of New York and Pennsylvania.

The Philadelphia patriots meanwhile called a meeting in the State

House yard. There the resolve of Congress was read, and "the people, in testimony of their warmest approbation, gave three cheers." A series of resolutions were passed, most of them unanimously, condemning the stand of the assembly as having "a dangerous tendency to withdraw this province from that happy union with the other Colonies, which we consider both our glory and our protection."

The resolution and preamble represented another laborious if large step toward a straightforward declaration of independence. As such it was very nearly the culmination of a campaign that the Massachusetts and Virginia delegates had waged for more than a year, a campaign full of inconclusive skirmishes and defeats, but a campaign in which the leaders had seldom slackened their efforts. In the course of their efforts, every wile and stratagem consistent with honesty had been employed by men who had learned political tactics in two different but perhaps equally demanding schools: the Virginia county parish and the New England town meeting.

With this victory, the time at last seemed ripe. To John Adams, it was "an epocha, a decisive event."

As soon as the preamble had passed, Richard Henry Lee hurried off to Williamsburg with the intention of prevailing upon the Virginia convention, which was sitting there, to declare independence and to instruct its delegates in Congress to press for a similar declaration. He wrote to John Adams that news of the passage of the resolve had been created with general rejoicing. "The British flag on the capitol was immediately struck, and the Continental hoisted in its room. The troops were drawn out, and we had a discharge of artillery and small arms."

There was no doubt of the implications of the resolve and preamble in John Adams' mind. He wrote his wife Abigail: "Great Britain has at last driven America to the last step, a complete separation from her; a total absolute independence, not only of her Parliament, but of her Crown, for such is the amount of the resolve of the 15th. . . . I have reasons to believe that no colony, which shall assume a government under the people, will give it up. There is something very unnatural and odious in a government a thousand leagues off. A whole government of our own choice, managed by persons whom we love, revere, and can confide in, has charms in it, for which men will fight. . . ." John Adams also wrote exultantly to James Warren: "This Day the Congress has passed the most important Resolution that ever was taken in America." Adams, and many others of a like mind, were determined to see the resolve and preamble as, in effect, a statement of independence. The

Rubicon had, at long last, been crossed. But further action was needed. "There remains, however," Adams reminded Warren, "a great deal of work to be done besides the Defence of the Country. A Confederation must now be pursued with all the Address, Assiduity, Prudence, Caution, and yet Fortitude and Perseverance, which those who think it necessary are possessed of. It is the most intricate, the most important, the most dangerous and delicate business of all. It will require Time. We must be patient."

Virginia delegate Carter Braxton sent the resolve and preamble to his uncle, Landon Carter. Braxton wrote that once the two motions had been passed, the Maryland delegates had withdrawn "and gave us," Braxton wrote, "to understand they should not return nor deem our further Resolutions obligatory, until they had transmitted an Acct. of their Proceedings to their Convention and had their Instructions how to act . . . upon this alarming occasion. This event is awaited with impatience. . . ." There were rumors that the Pennsylvania delegates might follow suit. "What will be the consequence," Braxton wrote, "God only knows." To Braxton it was evident that "the wise Men of the East and some from the South" were not going to wait very long in pushing for a further, more final, declaration—that "their favourite plan" was independence.

Braxton confirmed his uncle's suspicions that the New England Colonies had no interest in reconciliation. "Two of the New England Colonies," he wrote—meaning Connecticut and Rhode Island—"enjoy a Government purely democratical the Nature and Principle of which both civil and religious are so totally incompatible with Monarchy, that they have ever lived in a restless state under it." The other two, Massachusetts and New Hampshire, were little better. "The best opportunity in the World now being offered them to throw off all subjection and embrace their darling Democracy, they are determined to accept it. . . . Upon reviewing the secret movements of Man and things I am convinced [nevertheless] the Assertion of independence is far off." There were so many sharp disputes and divisions among the colonies just over land and boundaries that the chances of the radical whigs "Lugging us into independence" were, he mistakenly assured his uncle, very slim. Were such drastic action to be taken, "the Continent would be torn to pieces by Intestine Wars and Convulsions. Previous to Independence all disputes must be healed and Harmony prevail."

Massachusetts delegate Elbridge Gerry took a very different view of matters. As he wrote James Warren on May 20: "It appears to me that the eyes of every unbeliever are now open; that all are sensible of the perfidy of Great Britain, and are convinced that there is no medium between unqualified submission and actual independency. The Colonies are determined on the latter. A final declaration is approaching with great rapidity." John Adams was equally optimistic. He wrote the same day: "Every Post and every Day rolls in upon Us, independence like a Torrent." The delegates from Georgia appeared that very day "with unlimited Powers and these Gentlemen themselves are very firm." South Carolina was "firm enough" and North Carolina had repealed its instructions against "Confederation and Independence." "A Multitude of Letters from Virginia, all . . . breathe same Spirit." So already there were four southern colonies to match the four northern ones. It was only the five middle colonies that were "not yet quite so ripe; but they were," Adams said, "very near it." New York, it was predicted, would change its instructions within the week. It was hoped the Pennsylvania Assembly would finally do likewise. New Jersey would fall into line, and "the Delaware Government," in Adams' words, "generally is of the same opinion with the best Americans, very orthodox in their Faith and very exemplary in their Practice." That left Maryland, "so eccentric a Colony—sometimes so hot, sometimes so cold; now so high, then so low" that no one knew what to make of it. "When they get agoing," Adams added, "I expect some wild extravagant Flight or other from it. To be sure they must go beyond every body else when they begin to go."

By the end of May, the radicals felt that all their labor, their maneuvers, their patience was about to come to fulfillment. But there were still obstacles and perplexities. Word from Maryland indicated that colony was still obdurate: "They repeat and enforce their former instructions—declare that they have not lost sight of a reconciliation with Great Britain. . . ." New York also hung back. John Adams tried to reassure himself and a constituent, Benjamin Kent, who had written that a declaration of independence was long overdue. "Some people," he answered Kent, "must have time to look around them; before, behind, on the right hand, and on the left; then to think, and, after all this, to resolve." Others see "at one intuitive glance into the past and future, and judge with precision at once. . . . You cannot make thirteen clocks strike precisely alike at the same second." But this, in fact, was what the Adamses and the Virginians, including Richard Henry Lee, had to do.

Meanwhile the Pennsylvania *Journal* was emphatic in denouncing "the false light of reconciliation. There is no such thing. 'Tis gone! 'Tis past! The grave hath parted us—and death, in the persons of the slain, hath cut the thread of life between Britain and America. . . . Be not deceived. It is not a little that is at stake. Reconciliation will not now go down, even if it were offered. 'Tis a dangerous question, for the eyes of all men begin to open." There were two questions facing America, the writer stated. "The first and great question, and that which involved every other in it, and from which every other will flow is *happiness.*" Could America be happy under the government of Great Britain? And the second question was: "Can she be happy under a government of our own?" The second question was as readily answered as the first. "As happy as she pleases; she hath a blank sheet to write upon. Put it not off too long."

Under the pressure created by the meeting in the State House yard, the Pennsylvania Assembly at last gave way on the fifth of June and appointed a committee to bring in new instructions for their delegates to Congress. Two days later Richard Henry Lee read a crucial resolution from the Virginia convention, urging Congress to "declare that these United Colonies are, and of right ought to be, free and independent states . . . and that all political connection between them and the state of Britain is, and ought to be, totally dissolved." The Virginia resolution was read aloud outside of the Philadelphia State House to an enthusiastic audience, after which there were fireworks "and other demonstrations of joy." The Virginia resolution marked indeed a definite turning point in the campaign to extract a statement from Congress supporting independence.

When the new instructions to the Pennsylvania delegates became public knowledge, it was clear that they were anything but bold; they simply permitted the delegates "to concur with the other delegates in Congress. . . in adopting such . . . measures as shall be judged necessary for promoting the liberty, safety and interests of America." The Pennsylvania delegates were thereby placed on the spot. They had opposed any formal statement of independence on the grounds that their instructions forbade them to consider independence. They had now been, on the other hand, instructed to vote for independence. But they continued to hang back.

The debates in Congress grew more bitter. The opponents of independence, fighting for time, exhausted their ingenuity in advancing arguments describing the dangers and disadvantages of separation from Great Britain. They were answered by the indefatigable John

Adams. Could not the delegates see, Adams insisted, that the people were strongly for independence? "The voice of the representatives," he declared, "is not always consonant with the voice of the people, and . . . It would be vain to wait either weeks or months for perfect unanimity, since it was impossible that all men should ever become of one sentiment on any question." But arguments were in vain. The Adams-Lee board of strategy decided that still more time was needed for the middle colonies to "ripen." The question was postponed until the first of July. The delay was a severe strain on the radical leaders. John Adams wrote to his friend William Cushing: "Objects of the most stupendous magnitude and measure in which the lives and liberties of millions yet unborn are intimately interested, are now before us. We are in the midst of a Revolution, the most complete, unexpected, and remarkable of any in the history of nations."

All that could be retrieved for the moment was the appointment of a five-man committee to frame a declaration in conformity with the Virginia resolution "That these United Colonies are, and of right ought to be, free and independent states." The members of the committee were Thomas Jefferson, John Adams, Benjamin Franklin, Roger Sherman, and Robert Livingston, Jefferson to be chairman. Jefferson, at thirty-three was one of the youngest members of Congress, a tall, slender young man with light coloring, coppery hair, and a sharp-featured face, careless in his dress, charming and gracious in manner, but with a kind of ultimate reserve or aloofness. He was, through his mother who was a Randolph, connected with one of the oldest and most powerful families in Virginia. In the debates of Congress he said little, although it was clear that he was an ardent patriot. He was not a skillful or effective speaker, but he thought clearly and wrote well. The committee, apparently without discussion, designated Jefferson as the drafter of the statement that was to explain and justify the action of the Americans in declaring independence.

Why Jefferson? Robert Livingston, a member of the powerful and conservative Livingston clan in New York, was opposed to independence and was not, in fact, to vote for it. He had been placed on the committee primarily for the purpose of trying to reconcile New York to independence. He was not a serious candidate for drafter. Roger Sherman, self-educated, a former shoemaker and classic New England Jack-of-all-trades who had been successively (and sometimes simultaneously) county surveyor, lawyer, treasurer of Yale College, publisher of almanacs, and amateur astrologer, was a man, as John Adams put it, as "honest as an angel and as firm in the cause of American independence as Mount Atlas." But he was no master of prose. His style of writing was devoid of eloquence or elegance, as blunt and knotty and forthright as the man himself.

Franklin was one of the most famous literary figures of the day on either side of the Atlantic. Adams had already won so general a reputation as a political writer that many people credited him with having written *Common Sense*. Jefferson certainly had demonstrated his skill as a writer in an essay entitled, "A Summary View of the Rights of the British Colonists."

But why Jefferson? Either Adams or Franklin would seem to have been the natural choice. Both were senior to Jefferson in years, experience, and public renown. Both had somewhat more than the normal quota of vanity and ambition (something that Adams was quite ready to admit on his own account and on Franklin's as well). It is hard to believe they would have so casually assigned the writing of the declaration to the young Virginian if they had suspected how important that document was to become. The fact of independence was the important thing. A "declaration" was almost an afterthought. The drafting of it would provide a little more time to bring reluctant delegates into line. Certainly some formal statement was appropriate, in fact necessary, but it need not be elaborate; a simple listing of the steps by which the colonists had been forced, as they saw it, to declare themselves independent of the mother county would do.

Franklin was notoriously lazy and inclined to be facetious; Adams was busy politicking around the clock to line up votes. The chore thus fell to Jefferson as the junior member of the committee (if we except Livingston, whose sentiments disqualified him) with demonstrated competence as a writer. Adams and Franklin could hardly have anticipated the subsequent fame of the declaration; if it had been the kind of straightforward, routine document that everyone assumed it would be, it never would have achieved such fame. This was Jefferson's opportunity; and his genius, as his contemporaries might have put it, proved adequate to the task.

Adams, in later years, took credit for persuading Jefferson to write the declaration (which was the next best thing he could do, having passed up that dazzling chance for immortality). Jefferson was the right man for the job. Adams told him: "Reason first—You are a Virginian, and a Virginian ought to appear at the head of this business. Reason second—I am obnoxious, suspected, and unpopular. You are very much otherwise. Reason third—You can write ten times better than I can." The last reason is the most suspect. Adams wrote very well and knew it. In any event the chore fell to Jefferson, largely by default.

12

The Declaration of Independence

THOMAS Jefferson set to work on the declaration in his lodgings—a comfortable brick house at the southwest corner of Market and Seventh streets where he had rented the second-floor parrlor and bedroom. He wrote on a writing desk of his own design in his small neat hand. As he wrote, he enunciated no new principles of government or political theory. Everything he had to say was drawn from familiar sources—from Locke most clearly, from Montesquieu, and from a dozen other political and moral philosophers. For his opening sentences, Jefferson turned to the Virginia Bill of Rights, drafted by George Mason, one of the most able and respected of that colony's patriots. It is not too much to say that, as the original of the declaration and as the basis of the first ten amendments of the Federal Constitution, the far less well-known Virginia Bill of Rights is one of the most influential documents ever written, entirely worthy of a place beside the Magna Carta and the Declaration of Independence itself.

The Virginia document had begun with the statement: "That all men are by nature equally free and independent, and have certain inherent rights, of which, when they enter into a state of society, they cannot by any compact deprive or divest their posterity; namely, the enjoyment of life and liberty, with the means of acquiring and possessing property, and pursuing and obtaining happiness and safety."

The paragraph was almost pure Locke, taken from his *Second Treatise on Government,* where the Englishman had sketched out the basis of human society as a contract or compact that man, leaving "a state of nature," had entered into to procure greater security for himself and his possessions. The natural and inherent rights of man Locke had listed as the right to "life, liberty and property." When Locke wrote his *Treatise,* Englishmen were struggling to establish beyond question that the king could not arbitrarily seize the property of his subjects through taxation or, indeed, by any other means. Taxes could only be levied by a Parliament in which the people were represented—no taxation without representation. The security of property was thus one of the most essential and basic of all rights.

To the famous Lockean trinity of life, liberty, and property, Mason had added happiness—"pursuing and obtaining happiness and safety." ("Safety" was rather an anticlimax after "happiness," and might, in any event, be properly subsumed under "life.") Of course the notion of "happiness" was by no means new either. But political theorists had described it not as a right, but as the proper aim of good government— "the happiness of the governed."

The change was significant and very American. And in a sense, it was a very "modern" one. It was also a peculiarly *Virginia* one. It would never have occurred to a New Englander to have proposed that "happiness" was a *right* coequal with life and liberty. A devout Christian was not placed in the world to pursue happiness but to serve God and further His Kingdom on earth, and this mission, while it might partake of joy, had very little to do with happiness. Nor would the kings and potentates, the powers and principalities of this world have thought of including "happiness" among the rights of a people or even among the possibilities, except for a select and fortunate few. The great mass of people were doomed to labor by the sweat of their brows, tirelessly and ceaselessly, simply in order to survive. They might have their crude and simple pleasures in animal rut or drunken revelry, but they would not, surely, expect happiness. That spoke of a certain spaciousness of life, of at least some intermittent freedom from care and toil, based on a degree of economic security and well-being.

We cannot know how many of these thoughts entered Jefferson's conscious or subconscious mind when he sat down to compose the declaration, but he took the trouble to explain that his sources were "the harmonizing sentiments of the day, whether expressed in conversation, in letters, in printed essays, or in the elementary books of public right. . . ." But conscious or unconscious, they were there. It was certainly no accident that he altered the Lockean trinity; and where Mason had *added* "happiness" to the trinity, Jefferson, perhaps out of some stylistic desire for a more balanced and harmonious sentence, *dropped* "property" and replaced it with "happiness." The dropping of "property," it might be argued, was more significant than the adding of "happiness," for in the latter instance, Mason had already preceded him. In purely logical terms, or in regard to history or political theory in general, "property" makes much more sense than "happiness." Few people would seriously contend (1) that happiness is a "right" in any real sense, the equivalent of life or property; (2) that it should be "pursued"; or (3) that if pursued, it can be caught. The happiness of the governed may be the proper aim of government, but at best that happiness can only be assured in a negative way, by preventing, or abstaining from, persecution, injustice or any arbitrary acts; by protecting the citizen's life, liberty, and property so that he is free to seek his own happiness if and as he wishes. If a man's life, liberty, and property are respected and to a reasonable degree protected, it may be presumed that he has some expectation of being happy.

Not to put too fine a point on it, Jefferson did say "the pursuit of happiness"; and if we were to substitute "the opportunity" (not nearly so pleasing a word) for "pursuit" (an active, seeking word), there would, after all, not be much to boggle at other than to reiterate that the original trinity—life, liberty, and property—made more sense logically, historically, and practically. But life is not necessarily guided by any of these eminently worthy principles. Parliament had attempted to take property in the form of taxes from Americans without their consent. In the revolutionary agitation there were innumerable evocations of the "right of property" as a paramount right that the British were trampling underfoot. Jefferson himself was a great property owner. There were thus entirely valid reasons for preserving "property" as a basic right. Yet it was an inspiration on Jefferson's part to replace it with "pursuit of happiness." Unsatisfactory as the phrase was from a logical or even a philosophical point of view, it was *psychologically* right, because it embedded in the opening sentences of the declaration that comparatively new and certainly splendid and luminous idea that a life of weary toil— meager, grim, laborious, anxious, and ultimately tragic—was not the only possible destiny of "the people," the great mass of whom had, theoretically, been created "equal." That "equality," aside from answering the purpose of political philosophers, might mean that in the opportunity for happiness there was, or might be, or should be, equality as well.

And that was the most revolutionary part of the Declaration of Independence, which, aside from that one felicitious if misleading phrase, contained few notions that were not political commonplaces in 1776. But the document, or its author, made no claim to originality. Jefferson had not set out to proclaim new principles, but to assert familiar ones that all fair and honest men must acknowledge to be true.

George Mason, in the third article of the Virginia Bill of Rights, reviewed the reasons for establishing governments ("for the common benefit, protection, and security of the people"). It followed that when governments no longer performed these functions, they no longer had the right to claim the allegiance of their subjects ("that when any government shall be found inadequate or contrary to these purposes, the majority of the community hath the right to reform, alter or abolish it"). By shortening and condensing Mason's first three articles, Jefferson skillfully combined the notions of equality, rights, the nature of government, and the obligation of the governed to resist or "abolish" any government that failed of its duties. In Jefferson's version, these ideals were expressed with a force and energy lacking in Mason's original: "We hold these truths to be self-evident, that all men are created equal, that they are endowed by their Creator with certain unalienable rights, that among these are life, liberty, and the pursuit of happiness."

All public papers should be as brief and simply stated as possible. Would-be writers of an imperishable document should make it no longer than a schoolboy or schoolgirl of average intelligence can memorize. Jefferson edited Mason's three articles down from approximately 170 words to 86, almost exactly half. Stylistically the gain was very substantial. Since the words would not, in any event, bear sustained critical scrutiny, little if anything was lost in logic or coherence.

After a week or so of work, most of it directed to filling out and refining the lengthy inventory of grievances, Jefferson copied off a rough draft and took it to Franklin and Adams for their comments and suggestions. Adams, in his usual methodical way, made a copy of it. The suggested changes were scratched in by Jefferson's hand on the rough draft; there was a total of forty-eight changes altogether, some identified as Franklin's or Adams', others as Jefferson's own emendations or those of friends who may have read it or of Congress itself. In the original, Jefferson had written, "We hold these truths to be sacred and undeniable." For "sacred and undeniable," "self-evident" was substituted, which hardly improved the logic. A better case could probably be made for the proposition that the equality of all men was "sacred" than for the proposition that it was "self-evident." Jefferson had written "created free & independent," but "independent," which had appeared in Mason's document, was crossed out.

Adams liked the draft, felt its force and trenchancy, and had only two or three minor suggestions for improving it. Franklin proposed more changes, but he softened his criticisms with the story of a hatter who was opening a shop and wished to have a striking sign painted to advertise his wares. He thus proposed to the painter the picture of a hat with the words: "John Thompson, Hatter, makes and sells hats for ready money." One friend declared "Hatter" superfluous and it was discarded. Someone else said the word "makes" was unnecessary because people didn't care who made the hats as long as they were reasonable in price and of good quality. Still another pointed out that "ready money" was not needed because no one would expect to buy a hat on credit. "John Thompson sells hats" was left. But another busybody argued that "sells" was beside the point; no one gave hats away. And as for "hats," there was already a picture of a hat and that was quite sufficient.

Whether the story comforted Jefferson we do not know, but it has been of inestimable value to uncounted newspaper editors and, more recently, teachers of journalism in instructing neophyte reporters to avoid verbosity.

Before Jefferson's draft of the declaration could be submitted to Congress, the delegates had, of course, to agree to a resolution stating that the United Colonies "were and of right ought to be independent." The date set to take up the debate once more was the first of July. Before he hurried off to the State House on the first, John Adams wrote a friend: "This morning is assigned for the greatest debate of all. A declaration, that these colonies are free and independent states, has been reported by a committee appointed some weeks ago for that purpose, and this day or tomorrow is to determine its fate. May Heaven prosper the newborn republic and make it more glorious than any former republics have been!"

When the resolution on independence was placed once more before the delegates, John Dickinson rose to oppose it, speaking with, as

Adams said, "ardent zeal" at "great length," and with "all his eloquence" but with "politeness and candor." It was more for the record than in hopes of defeating the motion. Indeed, within the limits of his rather narrowly circumscribed situation in the colony, Dickinson had done his discreet best to reconcile the more adamant opponents of independence to the eventuality.

John Adams replied, going painstakingly over familiar ground, emphasizing the legal and constitutional arguments, the measures of the ministers and Parliament against colonial liberties, the successive steps of the deepening crisis, the aggressive military actions of the British, and the advantages to be gained by declaring independence immediately.

Before the question was put, the New Jersey delegates arrived. Their new instructions authorized them to vote for independence but did not make such a vote mandatory. The delegates wished to have the arguments in favor of independence summarized. South Carolina's Edward Rutledge came up to Adams, laughing, and announced that he must undertake the chore. "Nobody will speak but you on this subject, Mr. Adams. You have all the topics so ready that you must satisfy the gentlemen from New Jersey." Adams protested that he was not an actor or a gladiator to be summoned to perform for every new audience. He would be embarrassed to repeat himself. But Dr. John Witherspoon, one of the New Jersey delegates, joined in the request, and Adams gave in and recapitulated as briefly as possible his main arguments. Another New Jersey delegate, Richard Stockton, later wrote his son that "the man to whom the country is most indebted for the great measure of independency is Mr. John Adams of Boston. I call him the Atlas of American independence. He it was who sustained the debate, and by the force of his reasoning demonstrated not only the justice but the expediency of the measure."

Following Adams' speech, a hasty canvass showed only nine states firm for independence, that is, nine states in which a majority of the delegates supported the resolution. Maryland had come along in "a general and unanimous vote." And New Jersey. But there was one defection, South Carolina, where Edward Rutledge used all his influence to keep that colony's delegates from supporting independence. Delaware's delegation was split evenly, with one delegate, Caesar Rodney, who was known to be a friend of independence, absent at his home where his wife was sick. Thomas McKean, one of the proindependence delegates from Delaware, sent off a messenger on a ninety-mile trip to urge Rodney to dash back to Philadelphia by the following morning. The New Yorkers, still claiming that their instructions obliged them to oppose independence, abstained. Pennsylvania, its delegates no longer bound by their instructions, opposed independence by a vote of four to three. Rumor had it that the New York assembly had voted to free its delegates Richard Henry Lee persuaded Rutledge to promise that he and his fellow Carolinians would drop their opposition if Pennsylvania and Delaware came in.

Pennsylvania, it was clear, was the crucial colony. James Wilson had swung over to independence. Franklin of course supported it, and so did James Morton. John Dickinson still held out on the negative side, as did fellow Philadelphian Robert Morris and two other lesser known Pennsylvanians. Finally, a compromise was worked out. Morris and Dickinson would not take their seats officially, thus canceling out two of the negative votes. Franklin, Wilson, and Morton might then carry the colony, three votes to two, for independence.

After all these bargainings and maneuvers it seemed that Congress would at last, pressed and cajoled, vote with great reluctance to declare the colonies "free and independent" when the delegates met the next day. But John Adams, weary from a day of feverish politicking and chagrined that his oratory had failed of its purpose, wrote to Samuel Chase that the "great debate" that was to have terminated in a unanimous vote had been, instead, "an idle dispence of time." He was confident that with the hoped-for arrival of Rodney next day, the resolution would pass "perhaps almost with unanimity." But, he added with characteristic realism. "If you imagine that I expect this declaration will ward off calamities from this country, you are much mistaken. A bloody conflict we are destined to endure. This has been my opinion from the beginning. . . . If you imagine that I flatter myself with happiness and halcyon days after a separation from Great Britain, you are mistaken again. I do not expect that our new government will be as quiet as I could wish, nor that happy harmony, confidence and affection between the colonies that every good American ought to study, labor and pray for, will come for a long time. But freedom is a counterbalance for poverty, discord and war, and more. It is your hard lot and mine to be called into life at such a time. Yet," he added, "even these times have their pleasures."

The session of July 2 opened to the accompaniment of squalls of rain and a perceptible tension in the handsome room where the delegates gathered. Everything waited on the arrival of Rodney, who, word had it, was on his way. The morning was spent in routine business, and just as the delegates reassembled after a leisurely lunch, Rodney dashed up on horseback, muddy and soaked to the skin, his small round face with its livid cancer sore showing the marks of an exhausting ride. That brought Delaware to the side of independence. South Carolina followed. Pennsylvania added its vote as expected. Only New York held out; its delegates abstained. Twelve for independence, none opposed.

John Adams, who had worked as long and hard as any man in Congress for this day, sat down on the third of July to write to his beloved Abigail. "Yesterday the greatest question was decided which ever was decided in America, and a greater, perhaps, never was nor will be decided among men." Reflecting on all that had happened since the passage of the Stamp Act more than a decade earlier, he was amazed "at the suddenness as well as the greatness of this Revolution!" It seemed to him that Britain had been "filled with folly, and America with wisdom; at least this is my judgment. Time must determine. It is the will of Heaven that the two countries should be sundered forever. . . ."

The years ahead would not be easy, he wrote, but "the furnace of affliction" produces refinements, "in states as well as individuals and the new governments we are assuming in every part will require a purification from our vices, and an augmentation of our virtures." Had a resolution of independence been made earlier, there would have been many advantages, among them a treaty with France, but the delay had given time "for the whole people maturely to consider the great question of independence, and to ripen their judgment, dissipate their fears, and allure their hopes, by discussing it in newspapers and pamphlets, by debating it in assemblies, conventions, committees of safety and inspection, in town and county meetings, as well as in private conversations, so that the whole people, in every colony of the thirteen, have now adopted it as their own act. This will cement the union and avoid those heats, and perhaps convulsions, which might have been occasioned by such a declaration six months ago."

Adams predicted that July 2 would in the future be celebrated. It would be marked down as a holiday, "the most memorable epoch in the history of America" if not of mankind. He was sure, he wrote Abigail, "that it will be celebrated by succeeding generations as the great anniversary festival." It should be commemorated by "a solemn act of devotion to God Almighty. . . . It ought to be solemnized with pomp and parade, with shows, games, sports, guns, bells, bonfires and illuminations, from one end of the continent to the other, from this time forward forevermore."

After the passage of the resolution declaring the colonies independent, the delegates proceeded to debate the draft of the declaration submitted by Jefferson. Franklin, always reserved in public discussion, said nothing, and Jefferson felt it inappropriate for him to defend his own handiwork. It thus fell to Adams, as a member of the committee, to support the declaration on the floor of Congress. In the "abuses and usurpations" section, Jefferson had listed the sending of "Scotch and other foreign mercenaries." The Scotch were deleted here as not being, in the strict sense, foreign mercenaries; the phrase had, in any event, a tendency to insult many patriotic Americans of Scottish antecedents.

The most striking of all the charges leveled against the king by Jefferson was that he had "waged cruel war against human nature itself, violating its most sacred rights of life & liberty in the persons of a distant people who never offended him, captivating & carrying them into slavery in another hemisphere, or to incur miserable death in their transportation hither. The piractical warfare, the opprobrium of *infidel* powers, is the warfare of the *CHRISTIAN* king of Great Britain, determined to keep open a market where MEN should be bought & sold. He had prostituted his negative [veto power] for suppressing every legislative attempt to prohibit or to restrain this execrable commerce, and that his assemblage of horrors might want no fact of distinguished die, he is now exciting those very people to rise in arms among us, and to purchase that liberty of which *he* has deprived them by destroying those people upon whom he also obtruded them; thus paying off former crimes committed against the *liberties* of one people, with crimes which he urges them to commit against the *lives* of another."

This effort to indict George III for the misery of slavery was surely one of the most exaggerated efforts in the history of political rhetoric. Allowing everything possible for the heat and passion of the moment, the charges were nonetheless so manifestly absurd that it is hard to imagine, from this perspective in time, how a rational man could have composed such a turgid and flamboyantly written tirade. Although the charge that the king had aided and abetted, indeed had ruthlessly foisted slavery upon the defenseless Americans was only one of many "abuses and usurpations," the passage on slavery took up more than a fourth of that entire portion of the declaration devoted to specific grievances.

It should not take a trained psychologist to discern in this mistaken indictment the strength of Jefferson's feelings about slavery. What we cannot bear to face ourselves, we are most prone to blame on others. Jefferson's fear and horror are only too clearly manifest in these sentences. Perhaps the whole intolerable burden of slavery could be transferred from the slaveholders of America to the shoulders of the king of England, and thus the paradox of a people claiming their rights as free men while holding other human beings as slaves might be obscured or somehow palliated. At least it was worth the effort. Far-fetched as it was, we can hardly blame Jefferson for trying.

But Congress would not buy a denunciation of slavery for a moment. Those delegates who were opposed to slavery felt the passage smelled of hypocrisy—not Jefferson's, but Congress's. Those who were disposed to defend the institution felt personally impugned by Jefferson's attack on it. In short it upset nearly everyone, making them either embarrassed, uncomfortable, indignant, or guilty; some of the delegates felt all of those unpleasant emotions. A few of the Northern delegates seemed inclined to swallow it, and Jefferson was certainly not the only Southerner whose deepest feelings were reflected in it; but South Carolina and Georgia, whose prosperity was even more dependent on slavery than their neighboring colonies, Virginia and North Carolina, were adamant. The whole portion was dropped in the name of unanimity and, one would hope, of decency.

Some harsh words directed at the English people were deleted. The sentence, "We must endeavor to forget our former love for them [the people of Great Britain]" was dropped, properly, I think; but it is interesting that it was included in the draft. And then perhaps the most poignant phrase in the whole document: "We might have been a great & free people together; but a community of grandeur & freedom it seems is below their dignity."

In that one sentence was condensed all the anguish of the separation, the suffering and the bitter regret, the sense of rejection and humiliation. It was an unsuppressible cry that welled up from the heart of Jefferson and spoke to thousands upon thousands of other hearts, cast out by the beloved parent into a dangerous and difficult world. Worse, not only cast out but cruelly chastized.

For just that reason—that it was a *cri de coeur*—it had no place in a state document. It was the lament of the rejected lover over what might have been if stubborness and vanity had not been, as they so often are in this world, stronger than trust and love.

Finally, on July 4, having much improved Jefferson's draft, all of the delegates present, except John Dickinson, approved it, and President John Hancock and Secretary Charles Thomson signed it. It was early August before the engrossed copy was ready to be signed by the delegates themselves. By then, the composition of Congress had changed: some delegates who had voted for independence had left Philadelphia; others, who had voted against it, had been replaced. Those who had been absent during the debates and the voting but who arrived in time to sign became, by that single act, immortal. As "Signers" they were assured a permanent place in history; whereas those unfortunates who had voted for independence and had approved the declaration but who left Philadelphia before the signing got considerably less credit from posterity than they deserved.

It has been said that the capitalization and punctuation of the first printing of the Declaration of Independence followed "neither previous copies, nor reason, nor the custom of any ages known to man." It was printed in great haste on the night of the fourth by John Dunlap. This was the first official copy, and it was attached to a page in the rough Journal of Congress. Since New York had still not voted for independence, it was called, somewhat ambiguously, "A Declaration by the Representatives of the United States in General Congress Assembled."

Congress directed that copies be sent to the assemblies or conventions of the various states, and to the army. A copy was given to the Committee of Safety in Philadelphia, but it was the eighth before it was read by John Nixon, commander of the Philadelphia city guard, to a large crowd in the State House yard, a crowd that, according to a Tory observer, contained "very few respectable people." The declaration was read from a circular platform used by David Rittenhouse for astronomical observations. As Nixon finished reading the document, the air rang with cheers and huzzas. The bells of the city were set to ringing far into the night. On July 9 the Declaration of Independence was read to the troops at New York, and there was general rejoicing. Lieutenant Isaac Bangs and "the whole Choir of our Officers," as he put it, expressed their delight in a common mode: they all "went to a Publick House, to testify our joy at the happy news of independence. We spent the afternoon merily in playing at bowles for wine. . . ." The following day the declaration was read at a public meeting on the common, and afterward the handsome gilt-over-lead statue of George III was "pulled down by the Populace." The gold leaf was scraped off; and four thousand pounds of lead were melted down to make "Musquet balls for the use of the Yankies, when," as Lieutenant Bangs wrote, "it is hoped that the Emanations of the Leaden George will make as deep impressions in the Bodies of some of his read Coated & Torie Subjects, & that they will do the same execution in poisoning & destroying them, as the superabundant Emanations of the Folly & pretended Goodness of the real George have made upon their Minds, which have effectually poisoned & destroyed their Souls. . . ."

In Boston a great crowd gathered at the State House, and after hearing the declaration and realizing what a wicked villain George III was, the citizens took down the King's Arms from over the State House door and burned them in King Street.

On the nineteenth of July word reached Congress that the New York assembly had fallen in line, and instructions went to the engraver to head the engrossed document "The Unanimous Declaration . . ." At the end of July, a child in East Windsor, Connecticut, was baptized Independence.

PART VI

Washington in New York

A͏FTER more than a year of sitting outside Boston, Washington's army was about to learn how to march. As soon as he was convinced that the British were sailing away from Boston, Washington started the greater part of his troops on the 220-mile trek to New York, leaving five regiments in Boston under the command of Artemas Ward. Washington used the march from Boston to New York as an extended training exercise. A lengthy march is more important in forming an army than months of close-order drill. The army that arrived in New York City during the first weeks of April was a much better army than the one that left Boston. Many of the bad habits acquired in the tedious months of camp life at Cambridge had been rooted out. The men were tougher and more confident, the officers more sure of themselves.

The army moved in columns of divisions, three men abreast or—where the roads permitted—four. An advance party under a deputy quartermaster moved ahead to select sites for the various units to make camp. Since there was no prospect of encountering the British, the security precautions were simpler than if the army had been in an approach march preparatory to engaging the enemy in battle. A troop of dragoons or mounted light horse rode some 800 yards ahead of an infantry company, which in turn preceded its parent brigade by 200 yards, with the main body of the army 300 yards in the rear. Behind the infantry divisions came the baggage train, the wagons with tents, hospital supplies, and such food as there was, along with much of Knox's heavy artillery. The rear guard was extended in much the same manner as the advance guard, spaced out with several hundred yards between elements, the last unit in the line of march being, again, a detachment of dragoons.

The troops were burdened not only with their muskets, but also with other gear. A heavy iron cooking pot was issued for every six men, along with a tent. The six men constituted a "mess"; they received a common ration and cooked it in their pot. On the march, the men of a mess took turns lugging the pot, which was a not inconsiderable burden. Muskets were carried as the men wished, provided that, for safety's sake, the muzzles were elevated. In the rain, the musket was carried at "secure," with the muzzle pointed downwards, a foot or so from the ground; it was held by the left hand with the lock under the arm and was thus protected, to a degree, against the rain. The march was started by a "ruff" on a drum in the lead elements, which was then passed on down the line by drummers in other units. If the leading echelons moved too fast, the drums of the rear battalion gave "three long runs," which were passed up the column as a signal to slow the pace. When the rear had closed up, they sounded "a common march," which again was passed up the line.

At the end of a day, when the troops reached their bivouac areas, they came upon a series of stakes that had been planted along a line by the advance party to mark the location of each row of tents. As the units arrived, they planted their guidons or colors at the successive stakes and secured and pitched their tents in rows extending back from the guidons in parallel lines, the officers' tents at the rear. Latrines were dug and guards were posted around the camp, more to intercept would-be deserters than to halt marauders. Soldiers scrounged for firewood, and soon each mess was busy over a campfire preparing its evening meal and cooking a ration to eat on the next day's march. The journey from Boston to New York consumed about twelve days.

Washington, having supervised the initial stages of the march, hurried on ahead of his army and arrived in New York on April 13. He was convinced that the city should be defended against the landing by Howe that he anticipated. "It is the Place that we must use every Endeavour to keep from them," he wrote to William Alexander, claimant to the earldom of Stirling and Charles Lee's successor as commander in New York. "For should they get that Town, and the Command of the North River, they can stop the Intercourse between the northern and southern Colonies, upon which depends the Safety of America." However, Washington well realized that the defense of the city against seaborne attack presented almost insurmountable problems. The city itself covered only about a square mile on the southern tip of Manhattan island. Charles Lee, who had been sent ahead by Washington to survey the area with a view to planning its defense, wrote his superior that it was accessible from so many different directions that it could not be defended indefinitely against a determined attack. The best that could be done was to charge the British as much as possible for seizing it.

Washington had to consider both the strategic and the psychological cost of abandoning the city to Howe. It seemed clear to him that whatever the price, everything possible must be done to defend it. Lee had laid out an elaborate plan for fortifications and had begun work on them before he was ordered south to take charge of the defense of Charles Town against an anticipated attack by Clinton's forces. After Washington arrived, all the able-bodied men of the city were put to work digging and hauling in a great rush to throw up substantial earthworks before Howe's arrival, which was expected daily. As soon as the troops from Boston arrived, they joined in.

For the country boys who arrived in New York, that large, bustling city of some twenty thousand souls was a great metropolis, full of novel sights and sounds, of dangerous and intriguing pleasures. The foremost of these was the notorious Holy Ground, the section of the city given over to prostitutes. Whenever they could get leave from their garrison duties, the soldiers and officers hurried off, eagerly or sheepishly, to the Holy Ground—the more moral or more cautious to stare, mouths agape, the bolder to find their way to the arms of a whore or lady of pleasure appropriate to their taste, their class, and their pocketbook.

Pious Lieutenant Isaac Bangs, Harvard 1771 and an officer in the Massachusetts line, was among those who came to stare. "When I visited them at first," he wrote, "I thought nothing could exceed them for imprudence and immodesty; but I found the more I was acquainted with them the more they excelled in their Brutality. To mention the Particulars of their Behaviour would so pollute the Paper I write upon that I must excuse myself." Bangs went, he declared, only out of curiosity. It seemed strange, he said, "that any Man can so divest himself of Manhood as to desire an intimate Connexion with these worse than brutal Creatures." Yet despite warnings, some officers and soldiers had been so indiscreet as to seek their favors, "till the Fatal Disorder seized them & convinced them of their Error." According to one account, forty men in one regiment had caught the dreaded "French disease" from the New York prostitutes. "Unless there is some care taken of these horrid wretches by the Genl.," Bangs concluded, "he will soon have his Army greatly impaired, for they not only destroy Man by Sickness, but they sometimes inhumanly Murther them; for since Monday last two Men were found inhumanly Murthered & concealed, besides one who was castrated in a barbarous Manner." Indignant soldiers responded by tearing down the houses "where the Men were thus treated. . . . This, together with the common Riots incident to such Places, made our Men a little more Cautious how they ventured to prophane Holy Ground with their Presence."

Bangs, a good Congregationalist, also attended a Church of England service, but the satisfaction he got from an excellent sermon "was greatly allayed by the Pedantick behaviour of the Priest, the Irreverent behaviour of the People & the foolish parrade of Ceremonies."

Soon the army was almost too busy digging defenses for dalliance at the Holy Ground. Across the East River was the western end of Long Island, with the town of Brooklyn and, looming one hundred feet above the town, Brooklyn Heights. Here "a post or entrenched encampment" for three thousand men was begun on a knuckle of land between Wallabout Bay and Gowanus Bay. Gowanus Creek, running through tideland marshes, formed a natural line of defense, and entrenchments were built from the north end of the creek to Wallabout Bay, a distance of about a mile and a half. At the northern end of the line on Wallabout Bay, a redoubt containing five guns was constructed. Along the line of entrenchments were interspersed other redoubts—from the first, Fort Putnam, to Fort Greene, the Oblong Redoubt, and Fort Box. Anchoring the southern flank was Fort Stirling, with eight fieldpieces. At Red Hook, a large wart projecting far out into the river opposite Governors Island, Fort Defiance was erected to command boats passing up the river; it was armed with four 18-pounders, with the forward edge of the earthworks protected by a ditch. The earthworks were, in fact, constructed quite simply out of the soil thrown up out of the ditch. Sharpened stakes were then driven into the ditch to block easy passage by attackers. Trees were cut and placed with their butt ends toward the entrenchments and their tops pointing toward the enemy, their branches intertangled and interlaced. Thus attackers would find themselves increasingly impeded as they advanced, having to fight their way through the abatis of stout limbs.

William Alexander, or Lord Stirling, as he preferred to be called, had made a good start in preparing the defenses of the city. Stirling was a large, robust man with a fresh, ruddy complexion; he was fond of drinking and conviviality but, in the opinion of his officers, was "as brave a man as ever lived." Like Greene and Knox, he was an assiduous reader of military history and manuals of tactics.

Throughout May and into June, the fortifications that had been started were completed and strengthened and new works begun at strategic points on Manhattan. Among these were Fort Washington (on what is now called Washington Heights) and Fort Constitution (now the Riverdale section of the Bronx). Fort Washington was situated on a heavily wooded plateau at the northern tip of Manhattan. This promontory was 230 feet high and a mile long. Cliffs rose directly from the Hudson to the plain that was commanded by the fort. North of Fort Washington, just across the Harlem River where it meets the Hudson, was Fort Constitution. Across the Hudson in New Jersey, Fort Lee—named for General Charles Lee—was constructed so that its guns and those of Fort Washington commanded the Hudson.

The construction of such works was striking evidence of the resourcefulness and energy of the Americans and contradicted in the most emphatic way the British charge that they were lazy. Whatever else might be said about the slothfulness and lack of discipline of the American soldiers, everyone was in agreement that they were most ingenious and industrious diggers. When British Lieutenant Frederick Mackenzie landed in Manhattan, he noted, "The works which the Rebels have made at different times in and near New York are really astonishing for their number and extent. The shore of the Island, from Hellgate on the East River, quite round, by the town, up to Bloomingdale on the North River, an extent of near 14 miles, is fortified at almost every accessible part. . . . The works . . . must have cost them an immensity of labour. . . . The parapets are high and very thick, with numerous traverses, & other works to prevent Enfilading and the effects of Shells. The narrow part of the top of the Embrasures are covered with strong planks and Sods, to prevent the men at the Guns from being exposed to the fire from the Men of war's tops."

In June and July militia arrived in substantial numbers to supplement the nucleus of Washington's Continental Army, and recruiting took a new lease on life as the scene of the war shifted south and new resources of men and material were drawn upon. The so-called Flying Camp, intended to function as a highly mobile strategic reserve, was formed of Delaware, Maryland, and Pennsylvania militia enlisted for six months under the command of Hugh Mercer. Washington was authorized by Congress to raise ten thousand of these troops, whose name suggested much more dash and efficiency than the corps ever displayed. When Washington asked for two thousand of the Flying Camp to assist in the defense of New York, Mercer had difficulty rounding up even that modest number. Then they turned out to be a poorly trained and ill-disciplined lot.

By June 3, 1776, there were theoretically 28,500 men under Washington's command, but of this impressive number no more than 18,000 were present and fit for duty. Still, this was almost double the number that Washington had commanded at the siege of Boston and constituted, for that day, a substantial army. General John Sullivan, who after the British evacuation of Boston had led a relief force to support the invasion of Canada, returned from that abortive venture with what was left of his command. With the addition of Sullivan's depleted brigade, Washington divided the army into five divisions, including this time John Morin Scott's four regiments from New York and four Massachusetts regiments under James Clinton. Clinton had served as a militia officer with his brother, George, at the end of the French and Indian War and had been in command of a regiment of New York soldiers with Montgomery in the invasion of Canada. John Morin Scott, one of the leaders of the New York Sons of Liberty, was a brigadier general with political ambitions. John Fellows commanded four more Massachusetts regiments; these three brigades—Fellows', Clinton's, and Scott's—made up Israel Putnam's division. The second division was composed of George Clinton's five New York regiments and Thomas Mifflin's brigade of two Pennsylvania, two Massachusetts, and one Rhode Island regiment. Mifflin, a Quaker by birth, had been one of the more radical members of the generally conservative Pennsylvania delegation to the First Continental Congress. A friend and political ally of Joseph Reed and one of the youngest field-grade officers, he had won Washington's confidence as an aide-de-camp at Cambridge and had been appointed quartermaster general a few months later. This second division was under the command of General William Heath.

Joseph Spencer commanded the third division. Spencer, one of the oldest officers in the Continental Army, was the Connecticut brigadier who had gone home in a huff when Congress gave Israel Putnam a higher rank. He had been cajoled into resuming a command, and he was appointed major general after he had taken charge of the third division at New York. Under Spencer was Samuel Parsons' brigade, made up of four regiments from Connecticut and one from Massachusetts, and seven Connecticut regiments under James Wadsworth. Parsons was a Connecticut lawyer, a graduate of Harvard, nephew of one of the governors of the colony and a major in the New London militia. He had been in the expedition that captured Ticonderoga and had impressed Washington by his management of his troops at the siege of Boston.

John Sullivan, back from Canada, commanded the fourth division. The Canadian interlude had done little to enhance his reputation. A congressional investigating committee made up of Benjamin Franklin, Samuel Chase, and Charles Carroll had made the tortuous journey to Montreal to report to Congress on the state of that enterprise. They found the soldiers under General David Wooster "thoroughly disorganized, half-starved, and visited by the scourge of the small-pox." Sullivan, a member of the committee wrote, "is active, spirited and zealously attached to the cause. He has his little wants and foibles. The latter are manifested in his little tincture of vanity which now and then leads him into embarrassments. His wants are common to us all. He wants experience to move on a large scale; for the limited and contracted knowledge which any of us have in military matters stands in very little stead, and is quickly overbalanced by sound judgment and some acquaintance with men and books, especially when accompanied by an enterprising genius, which I must do General Sullivan the justice to say, I think he possesses."

Lord Stirling commanded the most oddly assorted brigade of all— one regiment from Maryland, one from Delaware, a Pennsylvania rifle regiment, a Pennsylvania musketry battalion, and three corps of Pennsylvania militia. Alexander MacDougall, the man who had entertained forty-five patriotic ladies in the prison to which he had been sentenced for disrespect to the New York assembly, commanded the other brigade of Sullivan's division, made up of two regiments from New York, one from Connecticut, and one of ordnance men.

The fifth division was Nathaniel Greene's, composed of John Nixon's brigade (consisting of three Massachusetts regiments, two from Rhode Island, and one from Pennsylvania), Nathaniel Heard's brigade of five New Jersey regiments, and Oliver Wolcott's brigade of twelve regiments of Connecticut militia, plus Nathaniel Woodhull's two regiments of Long Island militia. John Nixon, who was forty-nine years old, had enlisted at the age of eighteen in Sir William Pepperell's regiment that had taken part in the siege of Louisburg. He had also been present at Concord with a militia company from Sudbury and had been wounded at Bunker Hill. Oliver Wolcott, a year older than Nixon, had been one of the most brilliant graduates of Yale College, a volunteer in the Canadian expedition of 1747, a prominent patriot in his hometown of Litchfield, Connecticut, sheriff, judge of the court of probate, and colonel of militia. In July of 1776 he was, in effect, on leave from his appointment as a delegate to the Continental Congress.

On June 18, the Provincial Congress of New York gave a handsome entertainment for General Washington and his staff and the commanding officers of the regiments stationed around the city. After a series of toasts drunk "with the greatest pleasure and decency," according to an eyewitness, two black musicians who played the drum and fife were brought in with "little Phil of the Guard" to sing a new patriotic song, which ended with the stirring verses:

> Let spirit and union dispel party strife,
> While struggling for freedom and empire and
> life;
> Ungenerous sentiments nobly disdain
> Fir'd with the idea of such a campaign.
> Then wreaths shall be twined of fading renown,
> Our brows to encircle and actions to crown;
> And the clarion immortal, of sonorous fame,
> Shall transmit to all ages, this glorious campaign.

The party was hardly over before a "conspiracy" aimed, it was rumored, at the abduction or assassination of Washington was uncovered. The plot to deliver New York and Washington, dead or alive, to the British was hatched in a network of taverns throughout the city. One plotter was the landlord of the Highlander, at the corner of Beaver Street and Broadway. Another was the publican of the Robin Hood. Among the ringleaders seems to have been a man named Corble, whose tavern was not far from Washington's headquarters.

The mastermind of the plot was Governor Tryon, who, from a British warship in the harbor, directed his agents in the city. The most important of these was David Matthews, the Tory mayor of New York. Even the Tory historian of New York, Thomas Jones, described Matthews as "a person low in estimation as a lawyer, profligate, abandoned, dissipated, indigent, extravagant, and luxurious, over head and ears in debt, with a large family as extravagant and voluptuous as himself. . . ." It was to Matthews that Tryon sent money to bribe soldiers and purchase arms. Contact with Tryon was maintained through a "mulatto-colored negro, dressed in blue clothes." Among the corrupted soldiers were Thomas Hickey, one of Washington's guards; Greene, a drummer; and Johnson, a fifer. Hickey was an Irishman who had deserted from the British army and was presumably a key figure in the plan to seize or assassinate Washington.

The plot was apparently discovered when a waiter in the Sergeant's Arms tavern came to a city official and told of a conspiracy, naming Gilbert Forbes, a gunsmith, as one of the disaffected. At the same time an anonymous woman seems to have gotten word to Washington that his life was in danger. Armed with the information from the waiter, a party of patriots captured Gilbert Forbes in his bed at two in the morning, and a number of incriminating documents were found in his room. Forbes himself confessed and implicated others.

Among Forbes's papers was a letter from a fellow Tory that read, "Our cause thrives most wonderfully and providentially hereabouts. We have great hopes that the tyranny of our cruel task-masters will soon be ended. The little finger of these despots is heavier than the loins of the most arbitrary ministry. . . . The people groan under their oppressions, and comparing their present misery with their former happiness and tranquility, long to throw off the yoke. They plunder our barns, enter our houses, and forcibly take from us what we sweated and toiled for; giving us nothing in return but their paltry paper. If we are to be slaves, let us be so to the lion, and not to the lousy dirty vermin of New England." Over two hundred colonials had already pledged themselves, the letter stated, to oppose by whatever means were necessary the tyranny of Congress and its myrmidons. "We are well supplied with arms, which every man keeps hid, to use when occasion permits." Other letters concerned shipments of guns and powder. In one letter the writer observed, "We now meet frequently at each others houses, drink the King to our marrow-bones, and confusion to the congress. . . ."

A committee appointed by New York's Provincial Congress took testimony regarding this "most wicked and dangerous conspiracy . . . against the liberties of America." Among the members of the committee or "court" were Alexander MacDougall and Peter Livingston. They met on June 23 to examine a number of witnesses. They heard from several tavern keepers as well as from William Cooper, a soldier. Cooper testified that he had heard one James Clayford inform a group of conspirators that a young woman named Mary Gibbons "was thoroughly in their interest." Mary Gibbons, according to Clayford, was a New Jersey girl "of whom General Washington was very fond" and whom he "maintained . . . very genteelly at a house near Mr. Skinner's—at the North River; that he came there very often late at night in disguise. . . ." Mary Gibbons, who was also mistress to Clayford, reportedly told Clayford everything that Washington confided to her, and in addition smuggled out military dispatches, which were copied and sent to Tryon. Clayford told his Tory friends that he believed Washington could easily be captured since Mary Gibbons had offered to assist in the scheme, but the plan was abandoned as too hazardous. Another witness, William Savage, a frequenter of the Sergeant's Arms, corroborated the testimony of Cooper. He had heard the plan to kidnap Washington proposed and dismissed as "a mad scheme."

At this point Peter Livingston called a recess in the hearings to allow the members of the committee to consult with Washington "as he is some way affected by the last witnesses to apprize him of it, and consult with him. . . ." The committee thereupon adjourned until the third of July. "During this interval," the minutes of the court read, "the committee had many conferences on the subject with General Washington, and many other officers." In addition, a cavalry company was sent to Jamaica, Long Island, to seize a group of some twenty conspirators, who put up a determined fight before a number were wounded and the rest surrendered. It was only at this point that the mayor, David Matthews, was implicated and placed in jail.

In the meantime, Thomas Hickey, the member of Washington's guard, was tried by a court-martial, which "found him guilty of mutiny and sedition, and treacherous correspondence with the enemy, and sentenced him to be hanged." On the morning of the twenty-eighth of June, all the officers and men of the four brigades in Manhattan assembled under arms and marched to a field near Bowery Lane. There twenty men from each brigade with fixed bayonets constituted the guard, and in the presence of some twenty-thousand people, Thomas Hickey was hanged by the neck.

When the committee reconvened, the first witness was James Clayford. The charge against him was that "in privacy and covenant with Mary Gibbons, you feloniously and secretly copied writings of the commander in chief, which were afterwards sent to be communicated to the foes of America; that you in your heart conceived and proposed a plan to seize on the person of General Washington, and carry him a prisoner to the mercenary army." A witness testified that Clayford "used frequently to boast of his amours with Mrs. Gibbons; that he proposed with this woman's assistance to seize General Washington's person and carry him off; that he frequently brought papers and letters of the General's to the society, which were copied and sent away."

Clayford heatedly denied the charges, insisting that he had only said that such a thing might be done and had never had any intention of carrying out the act. It was the court's opinion, however, that Clayford was guilty as charged, and they instructed him "to prepare for that death you deserve, and to which you are condemned by the authority of your country." At this Clayford lost his composure and "was then very abusive, calling the court tyrants and murderers, but the guard hurried him away."

When the Tory mayor David Matthews was brought before the committee-court, he treated the members contemptuously and declared boldly enough, "I scorn your mercy, and am ready to suffer for my King and country. . . ." He indignantly rejected the suggestion of the committee, which was plainly unhappy at having to deal with such a prominent prisoner, that he confess and express contrition. The committee recommended that he be executed for treason, and the Provincial Congress upheld its finding. But before the day appointed for his execution arrived, the execution was postponed, and he was sent to Connecticut to be kept imprisoned "till further orders."

The fact is that evidence of a conspiracy against Washington was unsubstantial. Clearly there were a number of Tories in New York and its environs who were eager to do whatever they could to advance the cause of what they considered to be their country—England. Hickey, who was actually in jail for counterfeiting when his disloyalty was revealed, had been, as a guard, dangerously close to Washington's person, but it seems hardly likely that he would have made an attempt to capture or kill Washington without much more extensive support than he in fact had. It is evident that, to a considerable degree, the unhappy man was chosen as an example to the disaffected in and out of the army.

What will be more striking to the reader are the statements by witnesses that Washington was involved in a liaison with a woman of Mary Gibbons' character. The action of the committee in adjourning the hearings was testimony that the members believed the statements of the witnesses were serious enough to require "many conferences on the subject with General Washington." We have, of course, no notion of what Washington said to the committee. We can assume that he did not take any action to hush up the inquiry as it related to Clayford. Clayford was called to the stand and there once more was charged by witnesses with having been involved with Mary Gibbons. Nothing more was said directly of Washington's own relation with the woman, but the statement was repeated that she had been instrumental in securing papers of Washington's that Clayford had boasted of possessing and of having copied. It seems reasonable to assume that Washington could have prevailed upon the committee to drop its investigation of Clayford if he had tried to do so. Thomas Hickey had been hung for mutiny and treason, and public attention was focused on the so-called conspiracy. In addition, Howe was on his way to Long Island, and the city of New York was in imminent danger of attack. In such circumstances it would, one assumes, have been a relatively simple matter to drop the whole affair. By the same token it would be thoroughly in character for Washington to put no impediment in the way of the committee's completing its investigation. Their deliberations were, after all, secret, and there was no reason to believe that they would ever be made public (it is, in fact, notable that the minutes of the committee were not destroyed; such would have been the safer course). I have been unable to find out what happened to Clayford; was he, in fact, executed, or was he sent with the rest of the Tories to Connecticut?

The final word on the matter of Washington's relationship with Mrs. Gibbons may well be taken from the introduction to an 1865 edition of the minutes of the trial of the conspirators: "Respecting the charge against the morality of Washington—often asserted by his contemporaries—whether true or not, and we should be loathe to believe it, it must be recollected, that at that day a laxness of social virtue was not visited with so severe a censure as it is in our own time—and that some of the prominent men of the age were not proof against temptation, we know from the confessions of Hamilton and the intrigues of Burr."

Nevertheless, some strange inconsistencies and questions remain. Assuming that Washington was not above such liaisons, would he have found time in the hectic days of June, when his army was frantically constructing defenses on Long Island and Manhattan, to have stolen away for such trysts? If he had, would he have come in disguise, with his pockets full of letters and dispatches that Mary Gibbons could have copied? When would such documents have been copied? Could Washington have been ninny enough to confide strategic plans to a woman like Mary Gibbons? On the other hand, the whole case against James

Clayford rested on the charge that, as Mary Gibbons' lover, he had prevailed on her to betray Washington and had boasted of persuading her to be an accomplice in the kidnapping of the general. If the story of Washington's involvement with Mary Gibbons was false, then Clayford's story was false and he was not guilty of obtaining official secrets or plotting to carry Washington off. In this case he had only to say so and, presumably, produce Mary Gibbons to corroborate his defense. It is, in any event, a most puzzling episode.

While Washington's army worked on the fortifications of New York, General Howe set out from Halifax on the tenth of June with a fleet of 127 vessels. Sailing on a fast frigate, the *Greyhound*, he arrived off New York a week before the main body of his fleet. He was as yet uncertain of the strength of the force that he would have under his command for the purpose of seizing and occupying New York City. The British also had in mind the capture of Newport and the neutralization of Rhode Island, and they were in the process of dispatching a strong force to Canada to secure that province beyond any hopes of American conquest, and from Canada to launch an attack down the line of the Hudson. In this disposition, it was not clear to Howe the extent of his own army and, following from that uncertainty, the best strategy to pursue. Governor Tryon came aboard the *Greyhound* promptly for a consultation. Howe abandoned his initial plan to land his force at Gravesend when a reconnaissance revealed a high, densely wooded ridge that would have afforded an ideal defensive line for the Americans. He decided wisely to wait for reinforcements from the fleet under the command of his brother, Admiral Lord Richard Howe, which he knew was on the way from England, and, hopefully, from Sir Peter Parker's fleet with Henry Clinton's soldiers, returning from their attack on Charles Town.

"As I must esteem an impression upon the enemy's principal force collected in this quarter, to be the first object of my attention, I shall hold it steadily in view," he wrote Germain. Canada, Rhode Island, and a projected southern campaign were all of secondary importance.

So General Howe waited for his own troops to arrive, along with those being carried across the Atlantic by Admiral Lord Howe. The admiral's fleet met intense head winds and then dead calm, and the general's fleet coming from Nova Scotia arrived first, on the thirtieth of June. Three days later the British troops disembarked on Staten Island.

On board Admiral Howe's flagship, his secretary, a priggish young Englishman named Ambrose Serle, kept a diary in which he recorded at considerable length his impressions of America and Americans. Serle, snob though he was, was not without redeeming features. He was a devoted family man who missed his "dear wife" and daughters intensely. He was a pious Christian, a member of the Church of England who went regularly to church and was well informed on all points of modern doctrine. He was an amateur scholar who read widely in Greek, Latin, Hebrew, French, and German. He was unfailingly loyal to his commander in chief, Lord Howe, although he thought him much too sympathetic toward the Americans. He was unwavering in devotion to his king—"the most enlightened of monarchs"—and to his country, which he considered the wisest and most enlightened nation in the world and, indeed, in all recorded history. However biased the opinions expressed in it, Serle's diary, which has been preserved, affords us a matchless view of the Revolution as seen from British eyes.

Admiral Lord Howe's fleet finally appeared off Sandy Hook on Friday, July 12. Serle recorded that "nothing could exceed the joy that appeared throughout the Fleet and Army upon our Arrival. We were saluted by all the Ships of War in the Harbour, by the Cheers of the Sailors all along the Ships, and by those of the Soldiers on the Shore. A finer Scene could not be exhibited, both of country, Ships, and men, all heightened by one of the brightest Days that can be imagined."

Howe brought with him nearly 150 transports loaded with troops. "The Rebels," Serle wrote, "(as we perceived by the Glasses) flocked out of their lurking Holes to see a picture, by no means agreeable to them." The same day the *Phoenix,* a man-of-war of forty guns, sailed along with the smaller *Rose* through the Narrows between Long Island and Staten Island. The batteries so painstakingly mounted along the New York shore and at Paulus Hook in New Jersey opened fire. The British ships replied with heavy broadsides. It was the city's first taste of battle, and the women in New York were terrified by the bombardment. As Washington wrote, "The shrieks and cries of the poor creatures, running every way with their children, were truly distressing, and I fear they will have an unhappy effect on the ears and minds of our young and inexperienced soldiery."

Most daunting was the fact that the American batteries, which were supposed to prevent the British fleet from sailing up the Hudson River and taking the American positions in the rear, proved completely inadequate to their purpose. The *Phoenix* and the *Rose* sailed arrogantly by, hardly scratched by the colonial gunners. Having penetrated forty miles up the river, they sailed back six days later and anchored off the Narrows. Perhaps the most alarming development, however, was the news that General Greene, in command of the positions on Long Island, was on the fifteenth of August "confined to his bed with a raging fever." Sullivan was assigned to take over his command.

With Admiral Lord Howe's flagship anchored in New York's Lower Bay, Admiral Shuldham, who had replaced the unhappy Graves as naval chief in American waters, came on board to welcome Howe. General Howe joined his brother and informed him of passage by Congress of the Declaration of Independence "with several other Articles of Intelligence, that proclaim the Villainy & Madness of these deluded People," as Serle put it in his journal. Ambrose Serle's reaction to the news of the Declaration of Independence was characteristic of most of his countrymen: "A more impudent, false and atrocious Proclamation was never fabricated by the Hands of Man." Serle noted shrewdly, "Hitherto, they had thrown all the Blame and Insult upon the Parliament and ministry: Now, they have the Audacity to calumniate the King and People of Great Britain. 'Tis impossible to read this Paper, without Horror at the daring Hypocrisy of these Men, who call GOD to witness the uprightness of their Proceedings by which they attempt to justify themselves."

Next morning the captains of the fleet waited on the admiral on his flagship *Eagle* and learned from him that the Americans had been driven out of Canada in inglorious retreat, and that Burgoyne "is coming down to Albany with the Army under his Command, together with 1000 Indians."

From the *Eagle,* Howe and his officers had "a distinct View of the rebel's encampments, of the Town of New York, and of the Hudson's River for a considerable Space beyond the Town." They estimated the rebel garrison at thirty thousand men, "but," in Serle's words, "from the Mode of raising them, no great matters are to be expected, especially when their loose Discipline is considered."

The arrival of Admiral Howe was followed by a small but significant comedy. The admiral sent an emissary under a flag of truce to negotiate the release of a prisoner of war. Seeing the boat approach the city, Henry Knox and Joseph Reed dropped down the river in a barge to receive the message. A captain in the British boat rose and bowed:

"I have a letter, sir, from Lord Howe to Mr. Washington."

"Sir," Colonel Reed replied, "we have no person in our army with that address."

"Sir," replied the officer, "will you look at the address?" He handed Reed a letter that read: "*George Washington,* Esq., New York, Howe."

"No, sir." Reed answered. "I cannot receive that letter."

"I am very sorry," said the officer, "and so will be Lord Howe, that any error in the superscription should prevent the letter from being received by General Washington."

"Why, sir. I must obey orders."

"Oh yes, sir, you must obey orders, to be sure."

At this point, letters from British prisoners to their friends and families were turned over to the British, and with a final flurry of bows and salutes, the two boats drew apart. The oarsmen had hardly rowed a half dozen strokes when the British put about and the officer in charge called: "By what particular title does Mr. Washington chuse to be addressed?"

"You are sensible, sir, of the rank of General Washington in our army?" Reed asked.

"Yes, sir, we are. I am sure my Lord Howe will lament exceedingly this affair, as the letter is quite of a civil nature, and not a military one."

"Upon which," Knox wrote his adored wife, Lucy, telling her of the incident, "we bowed and parted in the most genteel terms imaginable."

This comic interlude was followed by another similar session, this time at Washington's headquarters. Here Howe's adjutant general, Colonel Paterson, tried all his wit to persuade Washington to accept a letter simply directed to "George Washington, Esq., etc., etc." "In the course of his talk," Knox wrote, "every other word was, 'May it please your Excellency,' 'If your Excellency so pleases.'" All Washington's formal titles were, Paterson insisted, included in the et ceteras. Lord Howe, he informed Washington, had come with great powers to make peace—if possible.

"Yes," Washington replied, "powers to pardon. But he came to the wrong place with his pardons; the Americans had not offended, therefore they needed no pardon."

This enterprising reply clearly confused the colonel. There was more inconclusive talk, much of it about the amiable dispositions of the two Howes, ending with Paterson's query: "Has your Excellency no particular commands which you would please to honour me to Lord and General Howe?"

"Nothing, sir," Washington replied with his famous dignity, "but my particular compliments to both."

It was Colonel Paterson's first meeting with a rebel leader—with, in this instance, the rebel leader, the commander of what professed to be an army that every Englishman knew to be but little better than a half-organized mob. To encounter a figure of such power and presence was disconcerting to say the least. Paterson, expecting to find a crude provincial playing at soldiers, a man who could be awed or beguiled into compliance with Lord Howe's wishes, found the matter turned about. It was he who was awed. The officers of Washington's staff, observing the Englishman's confusion, were filled with pride and quiet satisfaction. They knew their general was a great man, and now they could see in the British officer's demeanor evidence that he knew it too and found that knowledge troubling and perplexing. "General Washington was very handsomely dressed," the delighted Knox wrote his wife, "and made a most elegant appearance. Colonel Paterson appeared awe-struck, as if he was before something supernatural. Indeed I don't wonder at it. He was before a very great man indeed." Washington and his staff joined Howe's emissary in a cold collation—cold meats, jellied fish, cheese, bread, fruit, and cake—but Paterson seemed preoccupied and excused himself before the wine was served; the Howes would be waiting for him on board the *Eagle*. And so he hurried off to convey to his masters his impressions of the rebel chieftain whom they did not deign to call "General."

That first meeting between a British staff officer and the general of the ragged, poorly trained, and ill-equipped Continental Army was one of the most dramatic events of the war, more significant in some ways than the battle for New York that followed it. If Paterson had any wit at all, he had wit enough to discern that, in Knox's words, "he was before a very great man indeed." A cause that could command the services of such a man was not a cause to be taken lightly. Behind Paterson was such an array of military might as to strike fear into the heart of the boldest soldier, an immense mustering of the resources of the greatest military and naval power in the world. In front of him stood, in a manner of speaking, one man. Events would prove that one man equal to all the weight that the British government could bring to bear against him.

To Ambrose Serle, who had not seen Washington and heard at second hand of his refusal to accept Howe's letter, he was "a little paltry Colonel of Militia at the Head of a Banditti of Rebels" who refused to treat "with the Representatives of his lawful Sovereign, because 'tis impossible for him to give all the Titles which the poor Creature requires." Rebellion hardened the heart "against every sound Principle of Religion and Duty."

While the Howes made plans for the investment of New York, American newspapers were brought aboard the British ships by visitors, and rebel rhetoric caused much amusement among the officers. In one paper the editor had written, "Be assured, the Sun, moon & Stars shall fall, the Ocean cease to roll, and all nature change its Course, before a few English, Scotch & German *slaves* shall conquer this vast Country." Quoting this, a British officer added. "There are several other Paragraphs in the Paper equally full of Nonsense, Madness & Fury."

A parade of Loyalists visited the British ships. Governor John Wentworth and his son dined with Lord Howe, and he and others brought a stream of reports of varying degrees of reliability concerning the mood and the military dispositions of the rebels. The Loyalists and the British served to reinforce each others' prejudices. When Governor Tryon, Oliver De Lancey, and a number of other New York Tories dined on board the *Eagle,* they assured their attentive listeners that the people of New York were already "weary of their new masters the mob" and had decided that the British government was, after all, "more lenient & less arbitrary than that of a Congress." One Tory refugee reported that "great Sickness & mortality prevailed in the Rebel Camp; that the Town was perfectly contagious through Filth, and the Rebels both in it and in the Camp covered only with Rags & Vermin. . . ." And Serle, taking note of the Tory account, wrote, "Our Army now consists of about 24,000 men, in a most remarkable State of good Health & in high Spirits. On the other Hand, the Rebels are sickly & die very fast."

The sailors and naval officers, as is the case in all modern warfare, had a far more pleasant time on board ship than the soldiers camped on Staten Island. There the relentless heat of a New York summer, quite beyond anything the British were accustomed to, was interspersed with heavy rains. Serle commented quite accurately on the "hard unpleasant Life" of a soldier "which is passed in a little paltry Tent which will neither keep out Wind, or Rain, or Vermin," and who "seems to have little other Solace on this dusty Island than the Association of multitudes in the same Condition." "The Ship is a House or a Palace compared with the Accommodations of the military," he added.

Young Lord Rawdon, in command of the Fifth Foot, had a cruder observation that was, in its own way, as revealing as Serle's supercilious comments. Stationed on Staten Island, he wrote: "The fair nymphs of this isle are in wonderful tribulation, as the fresh meat our men have got here had made them as riotous as satyrs. A girl cannot step into the bushes to pluck a rose without running the most imminent risk of being ravished, and they are so little accustomed to these vigorous methods that they don't bear them with the proper resignation, and of consequence we have most entertaining courts-martial everyday."

Walking on Staten Island with the chaplain of the *Eagle*, Serle and his companion came on a little encampment of New York Tories "who had just escaped out of Long Island from the Tyranny of those insolent Demagogues, who, under pretences of superior Liberty, are imposing on all about them the worst of Bondage. It excited one's sympathy to see their poor meagre Faces, and to hear their Complaints of being hunted for their Lives like Game into the Woods and Swamps, only because they would not renounce their allegiance to their King and affection for their Country."

As for the Americans in general, Serle wrote, "The People appear to be remarkably slothful in all their Concerns, excepting by Starts, when they equal any Men. I impute this almost entirely to the Climate, which in Summer occasions a Langour of the Body & Spirits, and in the Winter shocks their enervated Frames too much by the contrary Extreme." "How happy," Serle added, "might the People live, if they knew their own Blessings, or were properly sensible of the Advantages of that mild and just Government, which they are endeavoring to extirpate among them, and under which they so long have lived happy and safe."

Serle had a simple enough explanation for the Revolution. "It may be safely asserted," he wrote in his journal, "that Debts to English Merchants, Smuggling, and the total Relaxation of Government have laid the Foundation of all the present Rebellion in this Country." In another entry, he noted. "One cannot help observing how, in all multitudes, one or two busy men prepare the way & lead on every Measure, while the rest gape almost at every thing, and follow the Sheep with the Bell."

When Admiral Howe gently pointed out to Serle, who was his secretary, that Serle's theory that only the rabble and a few demagogues constituted the opposition to Parliament and the Crown "failed to take into account the Fact that almost all the People of Parts & Spirit were in the Rebellion," Serle met this argument in characteristic fashion. "If this be true," he wrote in his journal, "it is another very cogent argument that, as we must regain Possession of this Country by the Sword, by the Sword only can we expect to keep it."

2

The Battle of Long Island

THROUGH the summer months of 1776, Washington's army waited suspensefully while the elements of Howe's army assembled and the impending battle drew near. The Americans nervously strengthened their fortifications, looking out uneasily as they did so on one of the most formidable fleets ever gathered. Rumors circulated endlessly, many of them clearly products of American anxieties. Brigadier General Daniel Roberdeau of Pennsylvania told Washington that a postrider had informed him that General Howe proposed to withdraw his fleet and army and settle "the present dispute on any terms asked by Washington. . . ." There was another rumor that England and France were formally at war. Washington, afraid such stories would prove demoralizing, issued an order rebuking gossipmongers.

All during July and into August, the British force on Staten Island, far from withdrawing, grew in numbers. Henry Clinton, turned back at Charles Town, arrived with General Lord Charles Cornwallis's soldiers and Sir Peter Parker's fleet of nine warships, thirty transports, and 2,500 men. On August 12, Commodore Hotham sailed into New York's increasingly crowded harbor with six men-of-war and twenty-eight transports carrying 2,600 of the guards, the finest soldiers in the British army, and 8,000 mercenaries from the German principalities.

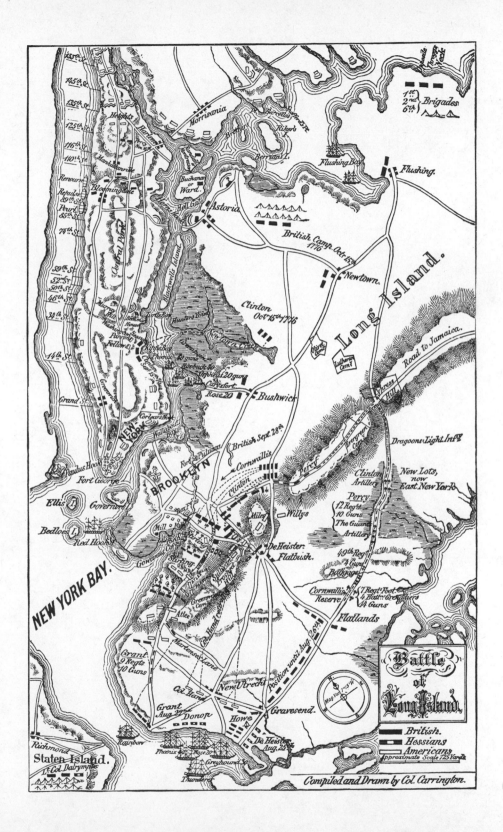

These mercenaries were soon known to the Americans by the generic term Hessians, though they were not only from Hesse, but also from other small German principalities—Brunswick, Ansbach, Waldeck, and Anhalt-Zerbst.

All together, it was a formidable and well-generaled force. Howe now had under his command twenty-seven regiments of infantry, four battalions of light infantry, four of grenadiers, two of guards, three brigades of artillery, one regiment of mounted light dragoons, and 8,000 Hessians. The total force under Howe's command numbered nearly 32,000 of the best-trained and best-equipped soldiers in the world, supported by dozens of warships and almost 500 transports and supply vessels. General Philipp von Heister, the commander of the Hessians, was a skilled professional soldier. Howe, Clinton, Lord Percy, and Cornwallis were among the most experienced officers in the British army.

The long lull was marked by numerous incidents. When British Lieutenant Blennerhassett and a detachment of men tried to cut off an American boat near the New Jersey shore to capture the crew, colonial soldiers opened fire on them and killed the lieutenant—which to young Serle, the diary keeper, was an example of the "unmanly and infamous kind of War" the rebels waged. "An uncommon Spirit of Murder & Cruelty seems to actuate them in all their Proceedings."

General Howe decided that Brooklyn Heights on Long Island was the key to the American defensive works around New York. From the modest summit of the Heights, the city itself would be under Howe's guns. Howe therefore determined to remove his troops from Staten Island, land them on Long Island, and advance on the American defenses from the south and east. As the British prepared to land at Gravesend Bay, Ambrose Serle comforted himself with the thought that "we strove as far as Decency and Honor would permit, or Humanity itself demand, to avert all Bloodshed and to promote an Accommodation."

On the morning of the twenty-second of August, Howe began to debark his troops on Long Island. It was the kind of maneuver in which the British were at their best—a complicated operation, requiring the close cooperation of military and naval units, careful staffwork, and the meticulous carrying out of orders by all echelons. The soldiers were carried ashore in seventy-five flatboats, eleven bateaux, and two galleys, all these landing craft built expressly for the purpose. Each transport was sailed sharply up to the point where it was to load its soldiers in the line of waiting boats. By twelve o'clock, fifteen thousand men with their arms and supplies had been landed "without mishap or delay" at Gravesend Bay, south of Brooklyn Heights. The night before, there had been a violent storm, but the morning dawned bright and clear. The landing made a splendid sight. The vessels of the fleet whitened the water with their sails spread to dry, catching the sun; the hills and fields, green and shining, exhibited, Ambrose Serle thought, "one of the finest & most picturesque Scenes that the Imagination can fancy or the Eye behold."

Philip Fithian, a chaplain with the New Jersey militia, heard the American warning guns that signaled the landing: "Crack! Crack! An alarm from Red-Hook. Crack! Crack! Crack! The alarm repeated from Cobble-Hill. Orders are given for the drums to beat to arms. . . . I equipt myself for an action with my gun, canteen, blanket, and with the regiment entered [Fort-Box] and waited for further orders."

With Howe's attack on Long Island, the Revolution entered an entirely new phase. First of all, it signaled a realization on the part of the British government that the American resistance could only be crushed by a major military campaign. The notion that a few thousand soldiers in Boston and elsewhere could intimidate and overawe the Americans had been abandoned and a campaign planned, the extent and serious-ness of which was demonstrated by the forest of ships' masts crowding New York waters. For the first time, the Americans would be forced, unless they chose simply to retreat indefinitely and allow the British to occupy large areas of the country, to meet a trained military force in conventional warfare, in all those elaborate maneuvers that were such a severe test of the best-disciplined troops. The Americans—inadequately armed, supported, and equipped, and led by officer-civilians with the sketchiest of military qualifications—would have to give some account of themselves or abandon the field. Where before they had chosen their own ground and fought indifferently or well in situations most favora-ble to their particular skills and style of life, the Americans must now meet the enemy on his own terms. It was a task so formidable that no one who was not already a zealous partisan of the colonial cause, now the cause of independence, would have given it even the remotest chance of success.

As the British landed, the American outposts, showing no signs of panic, retreated slowly, driving off the cattle and burning hayricks to prevent the hay from falling into the hands of the British commissary.

Apple trees were heavy with fruit, and British soldiers and those sailors who could steal away from their boats "regaled themselves with the fine apples," as "merry as in a Holiday." Serle attributed the fortitude of the American pickets to "their Numbers, which were indeed very great." In the "cool clear & pleasant morning" Serle followed much of the action through a spyglass from the poop deck of the *Eagle*. To him it appeared that the rebels fled at the first serious encounter, and he praised the British and Hessian soldiers "for their Spirit & Intrepidity" in attacking what he insisted was a more numerous enemy, adding, "in one thing only they failed—they could not run as fast as their Foes, many of whom were ready to run over each other. This 'tis presumed will be their last, as 'tis their first effort to fight us upon plain Ground. . . . The wretches burnt & destroyed Houses & Barns as they retired, and those especially whose Proprietors they believed were attached to G. Britain. Ignoble warfare becoming only such ignoble Minds!" A Hessian officer, Captain Bardeleben, advancing with his regiment toward Flatbush, observed "the fiendish rage" of the Americans who "had left destruction everywhere . . . burned houses, tall corn in the fields in ashes, roads covered with dead cattle. . . . broken chests, chairs, mirrors with gilded frames, porcelain, and many other beautiful things were all over the ground."

With General Greene still ill with a fever, General John Sullivan was in overall command of the Long Island defenses. Lord Stirling commanded the American right, nearest Gravesend Bay where the British had landed. Under him was Colonel Edward Hand, formerly a surgeon's mate in the Eighteenth Royal Irish Regiment, who had settled in Pennsylvania and now served in the American army. It was Hand's men who were so industrious in burning hayricks, crops, and other things of possible use to the British. They were so busy, in fact, that Hand neglected to inform higher headquarters of British movement. This was unfortunate, for the British almost immediately gave away the drift of their tactical thinking. Moving eastward, Cornwallis with four battalions of grenadiers, Colonel Carl Emil Kurt von Donop's corps of Hessians, and ten battalions of light infantry advanced unopposed to Flatbush in an effort to find out whether the pass through the range of hills facing the American position was defended. A stout redoubt and entrenchments barred his way, and Cornwallis's division came to constitute the center of the British line that stretched along the hills to Gravesend Bay. But this easterly move indicated that the British were thinking of enveloping the American fortifications by marching around the American left.

The ridge of hills on which the American defenses stood had four passes, through which ran roads perpendicular to the main American defensive positions on Brooklyn Heights. These roads appeared to be the principal avenues of approach to the Heights. The most direct road ran along the bay, cutting through the hills just back of Red Lion. This was the section of the American lines under the command of Lord Stirling. The second road was that whose passage had been tried by Cornwallis. Cornwallis's troops were now astride it, facing the ridge and the pass beyond. The third road, starting at the same point as the second, ran through the same pass and then, just beyond Flatbush, branched off to the right (or north). The fourth road, starting also at Flatbush, ran off more sharply to the right through a pass opening toward the village of Bedford. A fifth road, which started at Gravesend and ran parallel to the American positions on the ridge (the center hill of which was named Prospect Hill), then veered to the left to cross through the northernmost pass, intersecting a road from Jamaica that ran down the ridgeline toward the positions on Brooklyn Heights and in doing so cut in behind the advanced positions on Prospect Hill. It was this road that was to become the key to the American defensive positions.

The initial British dispositions appeared to indicate an intention to drive through the passes. Colonel Grant on the British left (the American right) faced Stirling in the strip of land between the bay on the west and road number one on the east. (Grant was distinguished by his contempt for American soldiers, acquired during the French and Indian War. They were, in his view, of no military use except as beasts of burden.) Cornwallis took his position in the center, while Clinton pushed north through the marshy land around New Lots, later East New York, to a position just south of the Jamaica Road.

When Washington received a full tally on the British units landed at Gravesend on August 22, he dispatched six regiments to reinforce the garrison on Brooklyn Heights and ordered General Heath, stationed at the north end of Manhattan Island, to be ready to send several regiments from his command if they should be needed.

General Sullivan's report to Washington on the events of the twenty-second read as follows: "This afternoon the enemy formed, and attempted to pass the road by Bedford [this was Cornwallis's probe]. A smart fire ensued between them and the riflemen. The officer sent off for a reinforcement which I ordered immediately. A number of musketry came up to the assistance of the riflemen, whose fire, with that of the field pieces, caused a retreat of the enemy. I have ordered a party out for prisoners to-night. We have driven them a mile from their former station. These things argue well for us, and I hope are so many preludes to a general victory."

Washington read the dispatch with irritation. Sullivan did not seem to be able to write a military dispatch without making it sound like a harangue. Its tone of vapid self-confidence, and its author's evident inability to grasp the situation adequately or to convey to his commander in chief any real picture of the enemy's disposition, convinced Washington that Sullivan must be relieved; and having reached that difficult decision, he did so at once, giving the command to Israel Putnam, with Sullivan serving under him.

Washington's choice of commander was again not wholly wise. It would not be unfair to say that Putnam had developed a Bunker Hill mentality. In his mind's eye, he saw the British advancing in waves, mowed down by American musket fire. It might indeed be doubted whether Putnam had ever been a convert to Washington's new-model army; he still envisioned embattled farmers fighting Indian-fashion from behind trees and stumps. He took command on the twenty-fourth, and proved much more energetic than Sullivan as he dashed hither and yon, encouraging the troops and giving orders; but it was, in large part, activity lacking in purpose. He had some eight thousand men under his command to face a force almost twice as large.

On the twenty-third, a brief skirmish had taken place in the British center near Bedford Pass. There Hand's Pennsylvanians attacked one of the Hessian outposts and drove Von Donop's men out of several positions before a German counterattack forced them to retreat. This was the only significant action between the British landing on August 22 and the twenty-sixth, when Howe launched his attack on the American positions.

Meanwhile, Putnam was little improvement over Sullivan. Washington was soon almost as dissatisfied with the reports that reached him of the behavior of the troops under Putnam's command as he had been with Sullivan. He instructed Putnam rather sharply to stop the "scattering, unmeaning and wasteful firing, which prevents the possibility of distinguishing between a real and false alarm, which prevents deserters from approaching our lines, and must continue so long as every soldier conceives himself at liberty to fire when, and at what he pleases. . . . The distinction between a well regulated army and a mob, is the good order and discipline of the former, and the licentiousness and disorderly behavior of the latter. . . ."

A good account of the battle—and of much of the entire war—is provided by Private Joseph Martin of the Connecticut line. Martin wrote and published his account of the war many years after it was over, but his memory remained fresh and sharp, and his descriptions of the Revolution's battles remain one of the most vigorous and amusing eyewitness records that we possess. As Martin remembered it, he had been ordered on a work detail, but before his group had begun their chores a sergeant major hurried up and announced that the enemy had landed in large force on Long Island and the regiment had been ordered to move at once from Manhattan to support the positions around Brooklyn Heights. "Although this was not unexpected to me," Private Martin noted, "yet it gave me a rather disagreable feeling, as I was pretty well assured I should have to snuff a little gunpowder." Going to his quarters to pack his clothes, he could see the distant puffs of smoke from the artillery pieces, but the wind carried the sound away. The end of training was over and now fighting was to begin. "The horrors of battle there presented themselves to my mind in all their hideousness. I must come to it now, thought I—well, I will endeavor to do my duty as well as I am able and leave the event with Providence."

As the men of Martin's regiment marched off, they passed "several casks of sea-bread, made . . . of canel and peas-meal, nearly hard enough for musket flints, the casks were unheaded, and each man was allowed to take as many as he could as he marched by." As Martin reached the cask, the regiment halted briefly and he quickly "improved the opportunity thus offered me, as every good soldier should upon all important occasions, to get as many of the biscuits as I possibly could. . . . I filled my bosom, and took as many as I could hold in my hand, a dozen or more in all, and when we arrived at the ferry-stairs I stowed them away in my knapsack."

Martin's regiment was loaded on boats for the hasty trip across the East River, and once across they climbed the cliff to the Heights. There they saw for the first time one of the most devastating sights of warfare for green soldiers—the wounded being evacuated, "some with broken legs and some with broken heads." "The sight of these," Martin noted, "a little daunted me and made me think of home." The men rested and gnawed at their biscuits, which were, Martin said, "hard enough to break the teeth of a rat." When one of his fellow soldiers complained of not having any water, his officer pointed to Martin and said, "Look at that man; he is not thirsty, I will warrant it." The seventeen-year-old Martin "felt a little elevated to be stiled a man." As the soldiers rested and ate, they could see numerous skirmishes between British and American soldiers below them.

At least one officer in Martin's unit lost his poise. Either frightened or intoxicated, or perhaps a bit of both, "he ran round among the men of his company snivelling and blubbering, praying each one if had aught against him, or if he had injured any one, that they would forgive him, declaring at the same time that he, from his heart forgave them if they had offended him. . . . A fine soldier you are, I thought, a fine officer, an exemplary man for young soldiers! I would have then suffered anything short of death rather than have made such an exhibition of myself; but, as the poet says,

> Fear does things so like a witch
> 'Tis hard to distinguish which is which."

John Morin Scott summed up the American dilemma quite accurately. "You may judge of our situation," he wrote John Jay, "[we are] subject to almost incessant rains, without baggage or tents and almost without victuals or drink, and in some parts of the line the men are standing up to their middles in water. The enemy were evidently incircling us from water to water with intent to hem us in upon a small neck of land."

By the evening of August 26, the American dispositions were as follows. On the American left at Bedford Pass was Colonel Samuel Wyllys with his Connecticut Continentals, and the Connecticut State Regiment under the command of Lieutenant Colonel Solomon Wills. Colonel Samuel Miles, with 400 Pennsylvania riflemen, was charged with patrolling the area between Bedford Pass and Jamaica Pass on the extreme American left. The American right, under the overall command of Lord Stirling, was anchored at Gowanus Bay and straddled the Gowanus Road, running north toward Brooklyn Heights. Colonel Hand's First Pennsylvanians to the number of 200 were supported by Colonel Sam Atlee's Pennsylvania batallion, for a total of some 550.

In the center of the American positions, at the Flatbush Pass, were 1000 Americans with four artillery pieces—Rhode Island, Connecticut, and Massachusetts continentals crowded behind hastily constructed defenses.

The American positions consisted of a heavily fortified main line of resistance on Brooklyn Heights, with a forward defense line along the high ground in front of the Heights.

Howe's carefully worked out plan of attack called for a feint against the first line of defense. This feint was to be directed against Stirling's positions on the American right. Meanwhile, Clinton was to move far to the American left, slipping through Jamaica Pass and coming down on the American forward lines from the rear.

Near midnight, August 26–27, some of Hand's men surprised and fired on British soldiers in a watermelon patch near the Red Lion Inn. Soon afterward Hand's men were relieved by Major Edward Burd's Pennsylvania battalion. They had hardly taken up their positions when they were attacked by Grant's advance guard, moving up the Gowanus Road.

When word of the British movement reached Putnam at 3:00 A.M., he ordered Stirling to move with two regiments to block Grant's advance. Stirling, with Colonel William Smallwood's Maryland battalion and Colonel John Haslet's Delaware battalion, moved out promptly and took up a defensive position.

On the other end of the American forward lines, the main British effort was getting under way. A little after nine o'clock at night Clinton, with an advance detachment of the light dragoons, two battalions of light infantry, and fourteen pieces of artillery, moved through New Lots toward the point on Cypress Hills where the Flushing and Jamaica roads intersected. A few hundred yards from this intersection, a narrow causeway and Shoemaker's Bridge crossed the marshy ground between Cypress Hills and Evergreen Cemetery. The causeway and bridge were too narrow to allow for the passage of more than a single column. Clinton, moving slowly and cautiously and in complete silence, with his scouts well in advance of the main body, reached the causeway at three in the morning. Even the most rudimentary American defensive works would have delayed his progress for hours, but Sullivan, in command of the division on Prospect Hill behind Bedford Pass, had neglected to block the road, and Clinton passed over the bridge without incident. Behind Clinton came Lord Hugh Percy with the main army—the guards, the second, third, and fifth brigades, and ten fieldpieces. The only sign of the colonials was a small American patrol that was captured without a fight. The pass was occupied along with the heights on either side, and the troops were given time to eat and rest.

The British were now in possession of the high ground along the ridgeline and astride the Jamaica Road. The Battle of Long Island was, for all intents and purposes, decided. A considerable amount of fighting remained, but the Americans, by failing to secure their left flank at its most vulnerable point, had exposed themselves in such a way that only an extraordinary effort could have retrieved the situation. Perhaps reasoning from the British attack on Bunker Hill, the Americans assumed that the enemy was incapable of any more sophisticated tactic than a frontal assault. Sullivan had been active reconnoitering the positions he had been charged with defending, but he had little sensitivity to the terrain. Even a thin line of pickets would have given him sufficient warning to make proper dispositions to protect his left flank.

During Clinton's encircling movement, the Hessian von Heister had made diversionary maneuvers against the Flatbush Pass, just south of Prospect Hill, where Sullivan had his headquarters. This strategy worked as intended. Colonel Samuel Miles, who was defending the Bedford Road, and Colonel Samuel Wyllys, who was deployed on the other side of it, were quite unaware that the main British army was, for all practical purposes, in their rear.

The one man who suspected the truth was Colonel Miles. Miles, having, according to his own report, done his best to convince General Sullivan that the British could be expected to attack down the Jamaica Road, moved his regiment in that direction with the intention of blocking the road. This meant moving through Colonel Wyllys's position, and Wyllys, insisting that his continental commission outranked Miles's state commission, ordered him back to defend the Flatbush Road. Miles finally persuaded Wyllys to permit him to double back in an effort to block the Jamaica Road near the point where it intersected the Flatbush Road, thereby remaining available if an attack was launched against Wyllys' regiment, Wyllys reluctantly consented, and Miles immediately set off through the woods to try to intercept the movement he was convinced had already been started. After a scrambling march of a half hour he came to the Jamaica Road, and "to my great mortification," he wrote, "I saw the main body of the enemy in full march between me and our lines, and the baggage guard just coming into the road."

General Sullivan, in command of the troops on Prospect Hill facing Flatbush and uneasy about the security of the Bedford Road, set out to reconnoiter with a "picket of four hundred men." His expedition promptly ended in disaster. When he ran into Clinton's main force, Sullivan surrendered meekly enough. It was an odd enterprise at best, and it is difficult to see what Sullivan expected to accomplish by this reconnaissance in force. He himself does not tell us, other than to mention his concern for the road. Nor can he escape the primary blame for his failure, before he was superseded by Putnam, to block the Jamaica Road. By the same token, it is hard to be too severe on Putnam. An officer taking over a well-established position is not apt to be very concerned about the integrity of his defenses. He assumes that, having been prepared in good time and by officers who know their business, they are in good order; more pressing matters occupy his attention. But of course while it is important to be fair to Putnam, it is nonetheless a fact that a first-rate officer with an instinct for proper tactical deployment would have satisfied himself at once that his flanks were properly secured. It is difficult to imagine that General Greene would have left the Jamaica Road undefended.

Meanwhile, on the American right, Stirling came up to reinforce Major Burd against Grant's advance. As he moved forward, Stirling picked up a portion of Huntington's Connecticut Continentals and Colonel Atlee's Pennsylvania Musketry Battalion under command of Samuel Parsons. Atlee's men occupied the high ground at the southern end of the ridgeline and, with Stirling's troops, contained Grant's force until late morning. Atlee had positioned his men skillfully, deploying them so that their fire would enfilade Grant's troops in any frontal assault on Stirling. Grant, observing Atlee's movement, turned his men sharply to the right, trying to turn Atlee's flank and drive him back. Stirling responded by ordering two Delaware companies to support Atlee and to try to block Grant's flanking maneuver. The disposition was initially successful. Grant attacked Atlee's position twice and was thrown back each time with a loss of more than sixty officers and men.

Grant then turned to assault Stirling. Still Atlee, with the auxiliaries that Stirling had sent to support him and two artillery pieces, brought enough fire to bear from the high ground on Grant's right to delay the attack on the American positions for several hours. Casualties mounted, but with no substantial gain for the British. Things were at a standoff, or, more properly speaking, the British were kept at bay by a resourceful and energetic American defense. In the words of one American soldier, "Our men stood it amazingly well, not even one showed a disposition to shrink. Our orders were not to fire till the enemy came within 50 yards of us; but when they perceived we stood their fire so coolly and resolutely, they declined coming any nearer, though treble our number. . . . Our men fought with more than Roman valor."

The sound of firing from the northeast in the direction of Flatbush grew brisker during the morning, and by eleven o'clock, the devastating effect of the main British drive down the Jamaica Road was felt in Stirling's rear. Howe, Clinton, Percy, and Cornwallis, having rested their men, had resumed their advance about eight-thirty, still without having been discovered by the main body of Americans; debouching from the ridge, the light infantry and light dragoons seized the road that ran to Flatbush and took Wyllys's company in the rear. A detachment of guards with three pieces of artillery joined in, and, pushing the demoralized remnants of Miles's and Wyllys's regiments ahead of them, the combined British force cleared Prospect Hill. The low ground between the Prospect Hill line and Brooklyn Heights itself was, in effect, a corridor, an extension of the Jamaica Road, that also served the fateful purpose of providing access behind the American defensive system protecting the approaches to Brooklyn Heights. It was like a lance thrust into the back of Stirling, whose troops had fought so well against Grant. Now, with the British pouring down on them in vastly greater numbers and Grant's force in front of them, they were between the anvil and the hammer. As soon as this British force under Clinton opened fire from Stirling's left rear, Von Heister, whose Hessians had to this point simply carried out diversionary maneuvers in front of Prospect Hill, ordered his German riflemen to advance in an open skirmish line, using only the bayonet.

Von Heister's movement was hardly needed to complete the rout of the Americans. Almost surrounded and badly outnumbered, they fled when they could, hid where they could find a hiding place, or surrendered when they could not avoid it. Stirling, having retreated in good order as far as he could go, gave instructions to his men to make their escape individually as best they could. Some fled across a marsh on the right of the American lines, from which they approached the right of the Brooklyn Heights fortifications and so got within the American lines. But the tide was coming in, and others soon found that line of retreat barred. Stirling, with 400 men of Smallwood's Maryland battalion, made a valiant effort to seize and hold the Flushing Road and thus keep open a critical line of retreat, but Cornwallis was there ahead of him in superior numbers. Then Stirling, having attempted to move to the left to gain the refuge of an advance position in the Brooklyn Heights fortifications, and having been blocked by a force of Cornwallis's grenadiers, turned back to his right to Prospect Hill, where he ran directly into Von Heister's advancing Hessians. There, with all avenues of escape sealed, having fought with skill and valor, he surrendered to the German general.

The more mobile Hessian units were organized into commando groups and sent to scour the woods for rebel prisoners. The Hessians were, for the most part, large men, and with their high shakos they made a formidable sight. They also had a reputation for bloodthirstiness and brutality. "The prisoners were thoroughly beaten," the Hessian officer, Captain Bardeleben, noted, "and knelt and begged for mercy." On the other hand, when General Von Heister offered several of the captured American officers wine to toast King George, "One of these officers . . . who was a schoolmaster, would not accept his glass for the toast to the king. He was first encouraged to drink and then he was threatened with death if he persisted in his traitorous attitude toward the king. All the threats accomplished nothing. He answered with firmness: he was a schoolmaster and it was his duty in his position to instruct his pupils that they should never favor the king of England. He would sacrifice his own life and give up everything before he would change his opinion." Bardeleben was struck by the wretched clothing and equipment of the rebels. "They carried . . . with them a cloth sack," he noted, "in which they put their food; next to it they have a large powder horn. Others have nothing more than their wretched peasant's garb and their weapons. Most of the officers are not clothed any better than the regular soldiers."

Thus ended the Battle of Long Island. The American losses were 1,079 prisoners (among them three American generals, Sullivan, Stirling, and Woodhull), including 67 wounded men and officers. American casualties—both dead and wounded—were roughly 970 men and officers. Stirling's brigade accounted for half the total of American casualties, and the Maryland battalion for one-fourth.

The more accurately tabulated British losses were very light in comparison: five officers killed and 21 wounded or missing; 58 noncommissioned officers and men killed, and 316 enlisted men wounded or missing.

In conventional terms, it was a serious defeat for Washington. Aside from the large bag of more than a thousand prisoners, the Americans lost more than twice as many in killed and wounded as the British, and they had been driven from the field. But a closer look revealed, paradoxically, some grounds for encouragement. For one thing the Battle of Long Island was the first large-scale battle of the

Revolution. The episode at Lexington and Concord was a guerrilla action that proved primarily that Americans were willing to fire at British soldiers from the cover of walls and buildings, and that they could direct such fire with considerable accuracy. Bunker Hill proved that Americans could improvise field fortifications with astonishing rapidity and defend them with tenacity. The actions at Ticonderoga, St. John's, Montreal, Quebec, and Fort Moultrie were unique, more of a demonstration of American initiative and endurance than of fighting skill. They were sneak attacks, sieges, defenses involving at the most a few thousand men.

The Battle of Long Island, however, was a classic set piece, essentially a battle of maneuver between what were, for that day, large armies—9,000 Americans and 15,000 British and Hessians. In the battle the American soldiers proved that they could preserve their discipline and morale in the most difficult and demanding of military exercises—maneuvers in the field under heavy enemy fire. Here more was involved than simple courage or the effective use of armament. For a squad, platoon, company, regiment, battalion, brigade, or division to respond to commands to advance, change position, retreat, regroup, or deploy to the left or right is very demanding. It is often not done very well by experienced soldiers in practice maneuvers. If we then add the factors present in real battles—fear, anxiety, and confusion—we begin to get a notion of the difficulty of doing anything on the field of battle (except running for one's life) that has any substantial chance of success.

The Battle of Long Island tested Americans severely in this phase of modern warfare. And in the face of enormous odds, the American soldiers, the noncommissioned officers, the company-grade officers (the lieutenants and captains), and the field-grade officers (from majors on up to colonels) had conducted themselves, for the most part, in exemplary fashion. They did, much more frequently than many of their superiors had dared to hope, what they were told to do, and did it on the whole reasonably well. That is all that can ever be expected of soldiers. They advanced, chose their positions with a keen eye to the nature of the terrain, and in several instances defended them valiantly. When told to shift their positions to support another unit or to protect their flank, they did so, generally under enemy fire, with courage and dispatch.

There was one ultimate and disastrous failure (which was certainly not of the soldiers' doing), and that was, of course, the inexcusable failure of Sullivan, and to a lesser degree Putnam, to fortify, or at least have heavily patrolled, the Jamaica Road. It was this error that undid everything—the tedious weeks of preparation, the bravery and enterprise of many soldiers and men, the tenacious (one is tempted to say brilliant) defense of the American right by Stirling's brigade.

In a sentence: The American soldiers and their officers acquitted themselves with honor at the Battle of Long Island; through the incompetence of their general officers (Stirling of course excepted), a large number of them were killed, wounded, or delivered into the hands of their enemies. The colonial soldiers had passed a fateful test. If the British army in August, 1776, had been equipped with computers and trained computer analysts, they would, at that point, have had enough information to feed into the computer to produce a "print-out" that would have made clear to the British that their hopes of reducing Americans to a proper degree of subordination were, in that splendid word so favored by our ancestors, "chimerical." But the British had no computers, and if they had had they would, it seems probable, have paid no attention to them.

3

The Evacuation of Brooklyn

WHILE the historian can linger over the Battle of Long Island, discussing its strategies and its implications, Washington had to do his desperate best to retrieve the situation. He must have had mixed feelings about the outcome. He was doubtless furious at the failure to block the Jamaica Road, but beyond that he must have felt a vast relief. The worst that could have happened—that the Americans would throw down their arms and the army disintegrate—had not happened. If a battle had to be lost, it was infinitely better that it be lost through the stupidity or inexperience of the generals than through the cowardice and indiscipline of the common soldiers. One may always hope to find better generals, or hope that the existing ones may learn something, but it is not easy to find a new army braver than the old one. And of course it must be said that in war, where at certain echelons (among the noncommissioned officers, for instance) experience is essential, in generals, where one would assume experience would be of the essence, it seems to count for relatively little. Few great generals have failed to display their genius from the first moment they took the field, experience only augmenting their natural gifts. And few, on the other hand, of the merely competent have, through experience, become great. One of the best measures of an efficient army is the speed with which it gets rid of

745

the inefficient or blundering leader—and the infrequency with which it ever gives him a command to begin with.

It was not conceivable that Sullivan's and Putnam's ill-equipped force would defeat the British or even long delay them; what was essential was that the army survive. Washington, at least at this stage of things, was far less concerned with being outmaneuvered than with his army being outfought. He could give the British two-thirds of the American colonies and triumph in the end if he could preserve his army more or less intact.

Nevertheless, the American losses had certainly been excessive: between those captured and wounded Washington had lost somewhat more than half of those engaged and almost a quarter of his entire command. Further, he now inherited the consequences of his decision to defend Brooklyn Heights. His much-diminished and demoralized force was cut off from the island of Manhattan by the East River and by the ships of the British fleet, as well as from the Jersey shore and from the mainland north of Long Island. Either Washington would have to watch as his army was slowly whittled away—his fortifications sapped by engineers and smashed by the fire of British artillery and ships' cannons, and the remnants of his army at last captured—or he would somehow have to extricate his men.

Knowing Washington, we can imagine that retreat was a bitter dose for him to swallow. He must more than once have turned back to the possibility of defending Brooklyn Heights against the full force of a British assault. But Washington knew that there was little chance that Howe would repeat the tragic error of Bunker Hill. Time was on the side of the British commander; he had no reason to rush things. The prize seemed within his grasp whenever he wanted to take it.

Washington realized that he had no real alternative to extricating, as best he could, that portion of his army now marooned on Brooklyn Heights. But he kept his own counsel, giving everyone the impression that he intended to reinforce the garrison there and defend the position to the bitter end. Orders were dispatched to collect all the small boats that could be found for the purpose of carrying reinforcements across the river. Heath and other commanders of divisions stationed on the northern tip of Manhattan were directed to keep men in readiness to march to the lower end of Manhattan Island for embarkation to Long Island. The soldiers in Brooklyn were encouraged by reports that reinforcements were on the way.

Washington had himself ferried across the East River and personally took command on the Heights, directing the strengthening of defenses, visiting the guard posts and the men at the breastworks, his powerful presence putting fresh courage in the troops as nothing else could have done. By noon of August 28, General Mifflin had made his way across from New York with the Pennsylvania regiments of Colonel John Shea and Colonel Robert Magaw and with John Glover's "Marble-head Amphibians," expert seamen from the Massachusetts fishing center. The new arrivals brought the garrison to the number of nine thousand and strengthened the impression that Washington intended to defend the Heights.

At this point the weather intervened. A heavy, at times torrential, downpour fell all afternoon, preventing any further British attacks. Of course it also made life miserable for the American troops, filling the trenches, soaking the men—who were for the most part without tents or covering other than their blankets—making it impossible to cook and extremely difficult to keep powder dry. Washington seemed never to sleep or rest. Patient, insistent, indefatigable, he was everywhere through the long afternoon and evening. As on many other occasions, he demonstrated how essential an element physical stamina is in the make-up of a commanding officer. A group of soldiers, drenched to the skin, struggling disconsolately in the mud to prevent an embrasure from collapsing, had only to look up and see the general, so splendidly self-possessed, so outwardly confident, to at once feel a fresh hope and assurance and bend more cheerfully to their work.

The day following the battle, August 28, Joseph Martin and his companions-in-arms had "a considerable tight scratch" with the British when they went foraging for food. Heading for a field of corn, they encountered a party of British on a similar mission. A brisk fire fight followed, with the British first being driven back, then returning to the fray reinforced and the Americans following suit until finally the British were driven from the field. That evening Martin and the other soldiers were ordered to parade and discharge their pieces. It was to be an exercise in massed fire, but, Martin noted, "we made blundering work of it; it was more like running fire than firing by divisions. However, we got our muskets as empty as our stomachs." The soldiers' muskets, it turned out, were more readily loaded than their stomachs.

All through the night of the twenty-eighth the heavy storm continued, and Washington and his staff made the sentry rounds "with periodic exactness." The next day rain was intermittent, and the British pushed the construction of their own works from which to begin the preliminary bombardment of the American lines. Washington, continuing to give every indication of an intention to engage the British in a major defensive action, quietly developed his plans for a stealthy escape. Washington's overall strategy now was to avoid another major confrontation, choose his own ground, keep open his lines of retreat, school his army (especially his officers) in the painfully learned lessons of war, and, above all, keep his army in existence. It was this last that was to prove the most essential and formidable task.

That evening Washington held a council of war and asked his generals for their endorsement of his plans for an immediate withdrawal from the Heights. While Washington, acting under instructions from Congress, was scrupulous in calling councils of war, it would be a mistake to assume that these were democratic sessions in which majority rule carried the day, or that Washington simply carried out the decisions thus arrived at. Even a democratic army is not very democratic. Washington was not only the military commander in chief, he was the moral and spiritual commander of his troops and his staff. At the Long Island council of war there was no question of who commanded the army. Washington put forth his proposal and spoke briefly and convincingly in defense of it, and it was "unanimously agreed in the affirmative."

Washington had, in fact, already put his plan into operation, having ordered the boats for the evacuation hours before the council met: "to impress every kind of craft . . . that could be kept afloat, and had either oars or sails . . . and to have them all in the East River by dark." The action was typical of Washington's decisiveness. By dark, the oddly-assorted little flotilla was at the foot of Brooklyn Heights. At eight o'clock, the Americans in the fortifications were ordered under arms as though preliminary to making an assault upon the British lines, some six hundred yards away. Glover's Marblehead men were assigned to the boats to act as sailors. While Mifflin with his three fresh regiments guarded the defenses, the main body of Americans filed down to the shore and began to embark.

Secrecy was so well preserved that no hint of the planned evacuation leaked out. The operation suffered one major snafu, however. Washington, posted at the steps leading up from the beach, sent his aide-de-camp, Colonel Scammell, to hurry the remaining units along. Scammell, passing down the line, by mistake gave the command to General Mifflin, in charge of the covering force, to withdraw his men. Mifflin, in turn, passed on the word to General Hand, who formed his regiment and then stopped to collect his camp equipment. When Mifflin rode up and asked the reason for the delay, Hand told him the men had stopped to collect their equipment. "Damn your pots and kettles!" Mifflin burst out. "I wish the devil had them! March on!"

Hand had hardly started his men when Washington's figure appeared out of the darkness. As soon as Washington saw Hand, he asked him why he had abandoned his post. "I did not abandon it, sir, I marched by order of my immediate commanding officer."

"That's impossible!"

"I trust that if I can secure General Mifflin's word that he ordered me to withdraw, that will clear me, sir, of any imputation of cowardice."

"Of course, I should not blame you if you can prove you acted under orders."

At that point Mifflin rode up. Why were the troops not on the move? Washington, furious, stepped out of the darkness: "Good God! General Mifflin," he said to that startled officer, "I am afraid you have ruined us by so unseasonably withdrawing the troops from the lines."

Mifflin replied with equal heat: "I did it by your order."

"That, sir, is impossible."

"By God, I did. Did Scammell act as aide-de-camp for the day, or did he not?"

"Yes, he did."

"Then I had orders through him."

"Well, I gave no such orders. Colonel Scammell misunderstood."

"Things were in such a state of confusion at the ferry," Washington declared, "that unless Hand's men could resume their posts before the British discovered that they had been abandoned, there would undoubtedly be the devil to pay."

The matter was straightened out, and Hand's men, grumbling, took their station in the line once more. The episode demonstrated very clearly how easy it is for orders to go astray in the midst of any military maneuver, however simple.

Most of the Americans had hardly slept for three nights, and they stumbled exhausted into the boats; many of them were asleep before they reached the New York shore. The night was stormy, the channel rough, the boats of varying degrees of seaworthiness. The wind that whipped foam off the waves into the faces of the men was too strong to allow the Marblehead men to set the sails, so the boats had to be rowed back and forth across the dangerous channel with muffled oars. At midnight, the wind at last died down; the tide, which had been running strongly to the sea, turned, and the water grew calm. The evacuation, in consequence, was much speeded; each boat could carry a much larger human cargo.

The entire movement was carried out with amazing dispatch and efficiency. Before dawn, Mifflin's covering force was withdrawn under the providential cover of a thick fog, and Washington himself boarded the last boat to leave Long Island. The movement had lacked the elegance and precision of the British landing on Long Island, but it was a difficult maneuver, carried out with remarkable speed and secrecy, without a trace of panic and with close-march discipline on land and water. It was a credit to the general and to the men under his command, perhaps above all to the nameless crews who navigated the channel through the long night, bending to their oars without rest. The Italian historian Carlo Botta wrote of the operation: "Whoever will attend to all the details of this retreat will easily believe that no military operation was ever conducted by great captains with more ability and prudence, or under more favorable auspices."

Given the state of security, or of military intelligence, or more specifically the ubiquitousness of the New York Tories, no movement of such a scale could long have been kept wholly secret. Howe was awakened and informed of the evacuation well before dawn, indeed before Mifflin's covering force had made its way to the shore.

Historians have criticized Howe for not ordering an immediate attack that, had it been carried out, would perhaps have netted Washington. This assumes first that Howe had complete information about the extent of Washington's withdrawal, rather than initial rumors that had to be confirmed before any sensible action could be planned; and second that he had only to press a button, so to speak, to start an assault by British troops.

It must be kept in mind in all discussions of military engagements that there is, even in the best-trained and best-managed armies, an inevitable gap between the time that a decision is made and an order based on that decision is written and distributed (often by messenger even in the present day of instant communication) and then acted upon. Officers have to be roused from sleep, drink, cards, amours, or whatever their ingenuity may have suggested as a way of escaping the endless boredom of army life even in the field. The men themselves have to be mustered, the missing accounted for, equipment checked, additional ammunition secured, rations distributed, and a thousand things made ready. Unless troops are already on the alert and prepared to move instantly—unless, in other words, all these things have been attended to in consequence of "preliminary" orders—an interval of some two hours intervenes between the issuing of an order and its being carried out, and this in an experienced and well-trained army.

Howe, as an experienced soldier, knew all this very well. Moreover, he had no possible way of knowing that Washington still lingered on the Long Island shore, overseeing the embarkation of the final units. So here at least we cannot charge Howe with dilatoriness. If anything he had been too successful. On all accounts his army had done well; his strategy had been good and its execution virtually flawless. As the British heard the story, the cowardly Americans fled so precipitantly that they drowned each other in their mad scramble for safety. Some, according to diarist Serle, were "half distracted with the Fright." "A little Spirit & Perseverance," he added, "would soon bring this Country to Reason or Subjection. And though I am an utter Enemy to all Tyranny, I am persuaded that absolute Submission would be eventually the interest of this People, because it would take the Power out of improper Hands, and prevent the Land from becoming . . . a Field of Blood, perhaps for ages."

If the Americans during the Battle of Long Island destroyed property suspected of belonging to Tories, the Hessians took ample vengeance. After the evacuation of Brooklyn Heights, Serle, in company with Lord Dunmore, walked over a substantial part of the battlefield. "It is impossible to express the Devastations, which the Hessians have made," he wrote, "upon the Houses & Country Seats of some of Rebels. All their Furniture, Glasses, Windows, and the very Hangings of the Rooms are demolished or defaced. This with the Filth deposited in them, make the houses so offensive that it is a Penance to go into them." The Hessians were especially disposed to use excrement to defile buildings, although the custom was not limited to them. "Add to all this," Serle wrote, "putrid dead Bodies are lying in the Fields about the Country, as the Army has hardly had Time to bury them."

Serle reflected the opinion of the British staff when he noted that "the Rebels . . . must be pushed warmly & unremittingly" so that they "may not have Time to recover from their Panic." "No dependence," he continued, "is to be placed upon the Generosity of their Tempers, which has never appeared even among each other . . . and . . . no impression is to be made upon them otherwise than by Fear and an apprehension of Superiority. They have a Tartness of Temper, without Firmness, and an ardent Warmth of Soul, not animated, however, by true Courage. . . . The Rebels behaved very ill as men; and their officers, to make them fight, were obliged to push them on with their Swords. . . ." Another sharp chastisement, Serle judged, would be the end of their pitiful army.

With all his scorn for the rebels, Serle might have read some portent in the very composition of the American army. It was, he wrote "the strangest that ever was collected: Old men of 60, Boys of 14, and Blacks of all ages, and ragged for the most part, compose the motley Crew. . . ." A Tory observer wrote of "the infamous desertions, the shameless ravages, and seditious speeches and mutinous behavior which prevail throughout the army," more like "highwaymen and robbers" than real soldiers.

Serle was correct in part. Washington's army had serious discipline problems. An order issued by Washington on September 4 that fell into British hands gave an unflattering if doubtless accurate picture of the condition of the American army. After urging that daily reports of troop strength be made to his headquarters, Washington exhorted his regimental commanders "not to suffer the men of your Corps to straggle from their quarters, or be absent from the Camp without leave and even then, but a few at a time. Your own reputation, the safety of the Army, and the good of the Cause, depends, under God, upon our vigilance. . . . To prevent straggling, let your Rolls be called over three times a day, and the delinquents punished. I have one more thing to urge, and that is, that every attempt of the men to plunder houses, orchards, Gardens, etc. be discouraged; not only for the preservation of the property, and sake of good order, but for the prevention of those fatal consequences which usually follow such diabolical practices. In short, Sir, at a time when everything is at stake, it behoves every man to exert himself."

While Washington and his staff were bemoaning the inefficiency and lack of discipline of the American soldiers, Hugh Percy, writing to his father, the Duke of Northumberland, on the first of September declared, "I think I may venture to assert, that they [the Americans] will never again stand before us in the Field. Every Thing seems to be over with Them, & I flatter myself now that this Campaign will put a total End to the War."

A Scots officer, Sir James Murray, concurred in this low estimate of the continental army's fighting potential. After the Battle of Long Island he wrote of the Americans as "the poorest mean spirited scoundrels that ever . . . pretended to the dignity of Rebellion. . . . If they ever do face us again, the flow of spirits and conscious superiority of our men, with the contrary feeling under which they undoubtedly labour will speedily decide the fate of our 'Western Empire.'"

Kip's Bay

AFTER Washington had brought his army from Brooklyn Heights to Manhattan, he was faced with the problem of what his next move should be. Many of his men were ill, and the army's morale had been shaken by the defeat at Long Island. "The militia," Washington wrote Congress, perhaps a little ungratefully, for some had certainly given a good account of themselves, "are dismayed, intractable, and impatient to return home. Great numbers have gone off, in some instances by whole regiments. . . . with the deepest concern I am obliged to confess my want of confidence with the generality of the troops." The fault had been more with the officers than the men. But Washington, of course, could not admit weaknesses in that quarter without damaging the reputations of officers he could not do without, and without badly alarming Congress.

The situation, bad as it was, was not as bad as Washington's gloomy dispatches to Congress suggested. In spite of the heavy losses on Long Island and a toll of sick, the number of men present for duty on September 2 was slightly under 20,000. To be sure, there might better have been 50,000 to oppose the splendidly equipped and trained British force of some 30,000 men, but if Washington had more American

754

troops he could not have found food or weapons for them, or more important, officers to command them.

Given a brief respite by the Howe brothers, Washington once more reorganized his command "in order that they might act with union and firmness," this time into three divisions. The first was under General Putnam, who, if he had not distinguished himself in any way at the recent battle, had at least had the wit or luck not to be captured. Putnam and his men were assigned to whatever defense might be made of New York City. With Greene still ill, the second or center division was placed under the command of General Joseph Spencer, with instructions to be ready to march to Harlem at the north end of Manhattan Island to prevent an enemy landing there. General Heath, in command of the third division, was ordered to the vicinity of King's Bridge, to protect the line of retreat from Manhattan.

Putnam soon urged Washington to concentrate all his forces on one single objective—blocking the North or Hudson River to Admiral Howe's fleet and his brother's army. To effect this, Putnam proposed the further fortification of Mount Washington, Harlem Heights, and the opposite Jersey shore. Putnam was aware that this gave New York City to the British, but Putnam added, "What are ten or twenty towns to the grand object. If Howe gets to Albany, our northwestern army must quit Ticonderoga or fall a sacrifice." Two days later General Greene, almost recovered, joined Putnam in urging the evacuation of New York, but Washington was reluctant to abandon the city without at least the pretense of a fight; he knew it would go down hard with Congress, especially the delegates from the middle colonies.

While Washington was regrouping his forces and making new tactical dispositions, the British pushed ahead energetically, completing the occupation of the western end of Long Island, especially the towns facing Manhattan Island across the East River and those islands—Governors, Ward's, and Randall's—that dot the river and harbor. British ships also ventured up the river as far as Wallabout Bay and Newtown Inlet.

As the British consolidated their gains, the captured American generals Stirling and Sullivan dined with Admiral Howe (Sullivan, flattered to be in the company of such a famous man, was most loquacious) and were treated to a lecture by the priggish young Serle "in which," as he later wrote, "I labored to convince them of their Error, how the People in America had been duped by artful insinuations. . . ." It was, Serle insisted, by "the insidious Arts wch designing men had employed" that the Americans had been so sadly misled, "that such men, whoever they were, were not only Foes to Great Britain, but to America chiefly, and to all Humanity itself. . . ." These innocent bumpkins, Serle implied, had never had matters properly explained to them before: "They seemed to feel a good Deal, and came down vastly in their Style & Air, which at first was rather lofty & warm." If he could only talk to the rebels singly he could soon, he felt confident, convince them all of their folly.

To the Howe brothers it seemed an excellent time to try again to negotiate a peace. They had failed before in their efforts to enter into "peace discussions" with Washington—primarily because they would not address Washington as "General." Now, the Howes reasoned, the success of British arms on Long Island might have improved the chances of finding both Washington and Congress in a tractable mood. Perhaps sensing that the captured New Hampshire general, John Sullivan, was somewhat overawed by the might of British arms, the Howes decided to employ him as an emissary to Congress. Consequently, he was packed off to Philadelphia. Congress received the defeated Sullivan rather coolly, and after four days of debate over whether to pay any attention to the Howes' advances, it appointed Benjamin Franklin, Edward Rutledge, and John Adams to confer with the Howes at the general's headquarters on Staten Island. They were to go as a committee representing "the free and independent states of America."

By giving the committee such a provenance, Congress hoped to make it impossible for Howe to receive it without thereby appearing to acknowledge officially the independence of America. Moreover, sending the committee might delay the attack on New York, give evidence of the American desire for peace, and, finally, place the onus of renewing the conflict on the British. Thus on the ninth of September the committee set off for Perth Amboy on the New Jersey shore, from where they were ferried over to Howe's headquarters two days later.

Lord Howe met the Americans at the landing, and there was a ceremonious exchange of courtesies. The admiral was famous for his graciousness, charm, and good humor. His friendship for Americans was well known, as was his reluctance to accept his present command. The Americans had been warned to be on guard against his persuasiveness, and Adams, for one, was not seduced. Despite Howe's praise of Massachusetts Bay, Adams could not help but notice that the admiral seemed to have a poor grasp of the real issues in the conflict. Howe declared "that such was his gratitude and affection to [America] . . . that he felt for America as for a brother, and, if America should fall, he should feel and lament it like the loss of a brother." Franklin, Adams noted, with "a bow, a smile and all that *naïveté* which . . . is often observed in his writings, replied, 'My Lord, we will do our utmost endeavors to save your lordship that mortification.'"

The beginning was not a promising one. Howe could not deal with the committee as representatives of Congress; that idea, he thought, might "easily be thrown out of the question at present, for that if matters should be so settled that the King's government should be re-established, the Congress would of course cease to exist, and if they meant such an accommodation, they must see how unnecessary and useless it was to stand upon that form which they knew they were to give up upon the restoration of legal government."

He assured the Americans that it was not their money the British wanted, it was "her commerce, her strength, her men. . . ." At this Franklin produced what was by now a rather familiar joke of his: "Ay, my Lord, we have a considerable manufactory of men"—a reference to how prolific the Americans were.

Howe ignored the lame witticism. "Is there no way," he asked, "of treading back this step of Independency, and opening the door to a full discussion?"

No, Franklin replied. The British had undertaken to punish the Americans for wishing to protect their English liberties, and "all former attachment was *obliterated*. . . . America could not return again to the domination of Great Britain." The issue must thus, apparently, rest on force. Adams supported Franklin, and Rutledge went so far as to argue that an independent America would, in fact, be of more advantage to the former mother country than a group of reluctant and unhappy colonies.

Howe dismissed this notion. He had no authority to even discuss the matter of independence. "Well, my Lord," Franklin said after a brief pause, "as America is to expect nothing but upon total unconditional submission . . ." Here Howe interrupted. No, he had not meant to suggest that. "Great Britain did not require unconditional submission . . . he thought that what he had already said to them proved the contrary. . . ." But Franklin plowed on, "as your Lordship has no proposition to make us, give me leave to ask whether, if we should make propositions to Great Britain . . . you would receive and transmit them."

He had no authority, Lord Howe told the members of the committee, to negotiate with Congress or with Americans in any character except that of English subjects. Indeed all he had to offer, it seemed, were assurances that the king and Parliament "were very favorably inclined toward redressing the grievances and reforming the administration of the American colonies."

This was not even the proverbial half a loaf. The committee, after a brief consultation, informed the admiral that they had no authority to confer with him "or to treat or converse with him" except as members of Congress. The admiral could be sure, Adams remarked, that "America would never treat in any other character than as independent states." The colonies had gone through a "complete revolution"; they were practical enough to know that the British could never govern them again except through force of arms. There was nothing more to be said. Howe expressed his regrets; the Americans bowed and withdrew.

When Franklin, Adams, and Rutledge departed, Serle noted in his journal, ". . . now, nothing remains but to fight it out against a Set of the most determined Hypocrites & Demagogues, compiled of the Refuse of the Colonies, that ever were permitted by Providence to be the Scourge of a Country."

Admiral Howe, a warm friend to the cause of liberty, also professed to be disenchanted with its actual proponents, or those who proclaimed themselves such. Instead of a grateful and contrite people who welcomed his generous and conciliatory, if vague, offers, he found a body of truculent and wary people, and he seems to have soon come to agree with his young secretary that "the Leaders of the Faction [were] for the most part, men of low or of suspicious Character."

The negotiation with the representatives of Congress had at least the effect of delaying General Howe's pursuit of Washington's demoralized army. One of the severest critics of Howe's dilatoriness was Sir George Collier, the commander of the British frigate *Rainbow,* who wrote sarcastically about the "generous, merciful, *forbearing*" British who seemed determined to "take no unfair *advantages*." "For many succeeding days," Collier said, "did our brave veterans, consisting of twenty-two thousand men, stand on the banks of East River, like Moses on Mount Pisgah, looking at their promised land, a little more than half a mile distant."

Howe and a succession of British commanders have been too harshly criticized for procrastination, failure to press advantages, and an inability to finish off a beaten and demoralized enemy. In their defense—Howe's and his successors'—it must be said that they were, in a manner of speaking, the victims of their own professionalism. They were trained to fight a particular kind of war, a war in which professional soldiers were deployed like chessmen in elaborate moves and countermoves. Hurried and hasty movements were as inappropriate to the campaigns that made up such wars as they would be in a chess match.

Furthermore, in a conventional European conflict the people of the rival nations were never active participants. They were passive observers or, often, unhappy victims of war. It made little difference to them by which monarch they were ruled, what officials taxed them, or who oppressed them; there was little to choose between one authority and another; all were repressive or indifferent.

Now, however, the people of America were very much involved. The American Revolution was the first "people's movement" of modern times, the first instance in which a substantial number of quite ordinary people had attempted to assert some degree of control over their own lives and fortunes.

It is thus hardly surprising that the British government and its army, the agent of its policy in America, could not make much sense of what was going on. They had no experience, no categories, no antecedents, no analogies to guide them. Underlying whatever errors the British commanders might have made—and these were very seldom tactical errors (in this respect the British more than justified their awesome reputation)—was a basic inability to take the war or the rebel army seriously. Why, Howe must have asked himself, pursue unrelentingly an opponent of demonstrated incompetence whose miserable army was, by all accounts, disintegrating? Why subject officers and men to rigors not encountered in any properly run war simply for the sake of harassing a wretched and demoralized enemy who, in the next serious engagement, would most certainly be demolished?

Further, despite the charge of needless delay from the captain of the *Rainbow,* General Howe did not in fact let the time pass idly. Some eighty flatbottomed boats were collected to use in an assault landing on Manhattan, and preparations went ahead for an amphibious operation. Meanwhile, the British batteries fired from time to time on American batteries, which returned the fire, and snipers from the American lines kept a sharp lookout for any target that presented itself on Long Island.

The American position was, in fact, extremely vulnerable. British ships controlled the Hudson and the East River as well. The British could land at almost any point on Manhattan and establish a beachhead before American soldiers could be collected in sufficient numbers to oppose them. The elaborate earthworks dug so recently only covered certain parts of the Manhattan shoreline and were all but useless if the British struck elsewhere. Besides, Washington feared having any large part of his force pinned down in defensive works. He must keep his troops reasonably mobile—and he must prepare Congress for a withdrawal from the city of New York itself. He did this in a series of dispatches that gave strategic instruction to the delegates. "It is now obvious," Washington wrote Congress, "that they, [the British army] mean to enclose us on the Island of New York, by taking post in my rear, while the shipping secures the front, and thus oblige us to fight them on their own terms, or surrender at discretion. . . ."

And in another letter, written September 8, he declared, "On our side, the war should be defensive: it has been called a war of posts; we should on all occasions avoid a general action, and never be drawn into a necessity to put anything to risk. Persuaded that it would be presumptuous to draw out our young troops into open ground against their superiors in numbers and discipline, I have never spared the spade and pickaxe. . . . I am sensible that a retreating army is encircled with difficulties; that declining an engagement subjects a general to reproach: but when the fate of America may be at stake on the issue, we should protract the war, if possible. That the enemy mean to winter in New York, there can be no doubt; that they can drive us out, is equally clear: nothing seems to remain, but to determine the time of their taking possession."

Congress responded to Washington's dispatch of September 8 by giving him carte blanche. It hastened to inform him that "it was by no means the sense" of that body "that the army or any part of it should remain in that city a moment longer than he shall think it proper for the public service that troops be continued there." Washington's epistolary campaign had been a shrewd one.

Such an aura of sanctity has surrounded Washington that it has been considered almost treasonous to suggest that he might have had such a common human trait as shrewdness, but it is certainly the case that Washington managed Congress with great skill. He gave a much worse account of the capacities, training, and courage of his troops than their certainly considerable shortcomings justified. He thereby kept Congress in such a state of anxiety and apprehension that it strained every nerve to try to comply with an unending but legitimate series of requests for men and supplies.

Moreover, Washington, by continually denigrating the quality of his soldiers, took out a kind of disaster insurance. No one was surprised when such poor soldierly material did poorly in battle. When they did well, most of the credit accrued to the general himself for having accomplished so much with so little. This was not dishonesty but rather common prudence. Generals and legislators mix no better than oil and water. Congress was incapable, despite the best of intentions, of understanding the real complexity of Washington's task. He had, therefore, to put it into terms that they could more readily grasp. The lack of training and discipline among the soldiers was something they could comprehend.

Having waited to move more than two weeks after the Battle of Long Island, Howe now determined to move swiftly and in strength. His strategy, like all good strategy, was simple. He would land on Manhattan, scoop up all the American soldiers who might be in the city or defending its fortifications, then make a strong movement against Washington's positions on the northern end of the island, meanwhile sending a strong force around Washington's left flank at Astoria to cut off his retreat. Once more Howe urged upon his soldiers "an entire dependence upon their bayoncts, with which they will ever command the success which their bravery so well deserves."

On the thirteenth of September, four or five British frigates sailed up the East River. These were supplemented the next day by six more men-of-war. Word followed that 3,000 or 4,000 British soldiers had been carried from Long Island to Montressor's Island in the East River under the protection of the British ships. On Sunday, September 15, three British warships sailed up the Hudson, effectively cutting off escape in that quarter. Leaving Putnam with 4,000 men to cover the American retreat from the lower part of the island, Washington established his headquarters at Harlem Heights, where he anticipated the British would center their main attack once they had landed.

Private Joseph Martin, whom we first encountered in a relief force at Brooklyn Heights, was stationed with his regiment along the East River on the American left when the British frigates *Phoenix, Roebuck,* and *Rose* made their way up the East River to a point abreast of Kip's Bay. Half of Martin's regiment was dispatched on what, in Martin's judgment, was a thoroughly pointless mission to "man something called 'lines,' although they were nothing more than a ditch dug along the bank of the river." The next night it was Martin's turn. "We arrived at the lines about dark, and were ordered to leave our packs in a copse wood, under a guard, and go into the lines without them. . . ." It was the kind of senseless order in which every army abounds and the burden of which invariably falls on the common soldier. "What was the cause of this piece of *wise* policy," Martin wrote sarcastically, "I never knew; but I knew the effects of it, which was that I never saw my knapsack from that day to this; nor did any of the rest of our party, unless they came across them by accident during our retreat." All along this hastily constructed "line," sentries passed the word during the night that "all is well," to which the British sailors on the frigates, scarcely a hundred yards away, called back, "We will alter your tune before to-morrow night." And, Martin noted, "they were as good as their word for once."

At dawn, Martin and his fellows saw the British warships, anchored with springs upon their cables, cleared for action and within musket shot of the line of American defenders. "They appeared to be very busy on shipboard," Martin later wrote, "but we lay still and showed our good breeding by not interfering with them, as they were strangers and we knew not but they were bashful withal."

While the British warships prepared to bombard the American defenses, British troops boarded flatbottomed boats that would ferry them across the East River from Brooklyn. It was an awesome sight for Martin to watch the British boats form up in a solid phalanx on the Long Island side of the river, packed together until they looked "like a large clover field in full bloom," to use Martin's own metaphor. As Martin waited in the silent morning, he stepped into an abandoned warehouse nearby. The floor was strewn with papers, and he was poking idly through them "when all of a sudden there came such a peal of thunder from the British shipping that I made a frog's leap for the ditch, and lay as still as I possibly could, and began to consider which part of my carcass was to go first." A heavy cannonading began both from the American shore batteries and from the British warships anchored in both the East River and the Hudson.

Here occurred again one of those splendid eighteenth-century set pieces of war—made possible by the nature of the terrain and the style of fighting—so dear to the hearts of military men. "The whole Scene," Serle wrote, "was awful & grand; I might say, beautiful, but for the melancholy Seriousness which must attend every Circumstance, where the Lives of Men, even the basest Malefactors, are at Stake. The Hills, the Woods, the River, the Town, the Ships, the Pillars of Smoke, all heightened by a most clear & delightful morning, furnished the finest Landscape that either art and nature combined could draw, or imagination conceive."

Serle estimated that seventy large cannon from the ships concentrated their fire on the landing zone until the American defenders, terrified by the "horrid din," abandoned their positions and fled for their lives. Washington, riding from his headquarters at Harlem Heights toward the beach where the British advance units were already landing, found to his "surprise and mortification" that the troops who had been stationed there, and the reserves as well, were "retreating with the utmost precipitation . . . flying in every direction and in the utmost confusion, notwithstanding the efforts of their generals to form them. I used every means in my power," Washington wrote after the battle, "to rally and get them in order, but my attempts were fruitless and ineffectual, and on the appearance of a small party of the enemy, not more than sixty or seventy in number, their disorder increased, and they ran away without firing a shot." Such was the "battle" of Kip's Bay.

Washington with his sword drawn and on horseback, attempting to check the "disgraceful and dastardly" flight, was a conspicuous target for the advancing British. He seemed almost beside himself with fury and despair, and quite heedless of his own safety. For a moment, General Greene, accompanying Washington, had the impression that the general was determined to ride upon the enemy alone and invite a swarm of enemy bullets. Washington's aides were all terrified that he might be shot or captured by the British, but they were unable to restrain him until Washington, seeing that nothing could be done to retrieve the situation, finally yielded to General Greene's pleadings and withdrew.

No one ever again saw Washington so near an act of despair. George Weedon, an officer from Virginia, wrote to a friend, John Page, that Washington was so enraged that he struck several officers who were running from the field, threw his hat on the ground, and exclaimed, "Good God, have I got such troops as these!"

Ambrose Serle used the same word that Washington had—"dastardly"—to describe the behavior of the Americans. "The Ground where our People landed," he noted, "was far from being advantageous; the Tide rapid; the Current unequal; the Shore shallow; and themselves obliged to march up on the Ground where these Poltroons had been at work to entrench themselves for several months. . . . Thus this Town and its Environs, wch these blustering Gentlemen had taken such wonderful Pains to fortify, were given up in two or three Hours without any Defence, or the least appearance of a manly Resistance."

Joseph Martin had a somewhat different account. He and his

fellows had kept the line until the British were almost abreast of them, and then their officers, "seeing we could make no resistance, and no orders coming from any superior officer, and that we must soon be entirely exposed to the rake of their guns, gave the order to leave the lines." In retreating, the soldiers had to cross a large open area, and there the British, in Martin's words, "gave it to us in prime order, the grape shot and language flew merrily, which served to quicken our motions." In other words, Martin and those about him ran for their lives.

Benjamin Trumbull, a chaplain with the First Connecticut Regiment, gave a vivid description of the cannonade, "which," as he later wrote, "soon levelled [our lines] almost with the ground in some places, and buried our men who were in the lines almost under sand and sods of earth, and made such a dust and smoke that there was no possibility of firing on the enemy to any advantage, and then not without the utmost hazard." The British frigates were anchored so close to the shore that marines on the round tops were able to fire swivel guns loaded with grapeshot down on the American positions. Without orders, confused, deafened and demoralized by the volume of British fire, the Americans took to their heels. General Wyllys and three of his colonels were captured, and some 150 men were either killed or taken prisoner.

The fault, in Parson Trumbull's opinion, was the failure of the officers to form some proper plan of defense. "The men were blamed for retreating and even flying in these circumstances," he noted, "but I imagine the fault was principally in the general officers in not disposing of things so as to give the men a rational prospect of defence and a safe retreat should they engage the enemy."

The analysis was a shrewd and fair one, and Trumbull added, equally wisely, " . . . it is probable many lives were saved and much [loss] to the army prevented, in their coming off as they did, tho' it was not honourable. It is admirable that so few men are lost."

From one perspective, that of Washington and his staff (as well as of Serle and the British command), the soldiers who fled at Kip's Bay were a cowardly rabble who panicked and ran for their lives. From another, they were frightened but practical men who made their own quite sensible estimate of the military situation and decided it was better to "run away and live to fight another day."

Out of range of the British cannon, Joseph Martin paused to catch his breath. Units were so scattered that he recognized only one of his friends among the rather sheepish-looking soldiers who began to search for their fellows. With this friend and a hometown companion encountered on the way, Martin went looking for refreshment. He found it in a house by the roadside, "in which were two women and some small children, all crying most bitterly; we asked the women if they had any spirits in the house; they placed a bottle of rum upon the table and bid us help ourselves. We each of us drank a glass and, bidding them good bye, betook ourselves to the highway again."

One does not have to look far for the reason why the American soldiers fled in disorder from their positions. In virtually every engagement they performed well in the face of enemy musket fire and badly in the face of heavy bombardment. The most demoralizing experience for the untrained soldier is heavy artillery fire (or, in modern warfare, aerial bombardment). The comparative remoteness of the enemy, the sense that, safely beyond range of your own weapons, he can strike at you with impunity, and that your only defense is to lie still and pray that a random ball will not destroy you—this is the most severe test of morale. The very chanciness of artillery fire is one of its most demoralizing features. Strangely, it is easier, in psychological terms, to cope with an enemy who is aiming his fire directly at you than with the impersonality of massed fire that seeks its victims quite at random. Added to this is the "horrid din" that, when unfamiliar, is doubly terrifying. So is the smoke, dust, and flying debris that fill the air and make contact difficult between men and their officers. The battlefield terrors of isolation and abandonment are particularly keen under heavy shelling. It was not, as everyone seems to have immediately concluded, that the Americans were cowards; many of the men who fled so precipitously from Kip's Bay on the fifteenth of September had three weeks earlier fought with courage and persistence in the Battle of Long Island.

As soon as Washington had regained control of himself, he returned to Harlem Heights to prepare for a British attack on the defensive position hastily built there. He dispatched reconnoitering parties and gave particular attention to putting the men and officers under his command in a state of mind to stand fast against the enemy.

Howe meanwhile had come ashore with his men at Kip's Bay. He formed his lines north of the bay, sending the Fifth British Brigade and Colonel Von Donop's Hessians southward to take possession of the city itself. Frederick Mackenzie, an officer in the Royal Welsh Fusiliers, urged Howe to cut the waist of the island with troops and thus seal off any Americans who might be lingering at the southern end of the island. "But as he is slow," Mackenzie noted in his diary, "and not inclined to attend to whatever may be considered as advice, and seemed more intent upon looking out for comfortable quarters for himself, than preventing the retreat of those who might be in the town, upon my urging the matter with some earnestness . . . he grew angry, and said I hurried him, and that he would place the brigade as he thought proper." This turned out to be in the houses and barns along the road to New York, with his own headquarters in Mr. Elliott's comfortable mansion.

The flight of the American defenders at Kip's Bay imperiled General Putnam's division, which was on the southern tip of Manhattan. Colonel Von Donop's Hessians drove directly toward the city, and Putnam, abandoning "heavy cannon and a large quantity of provisions, camp kettles, tents, and other essentials to the enemy," escaped by moving north up the west side of Manhattan, skirting what is now Central Park. The main British force also advanced north, marching on a parallel route east of present-day Central Park. The two forces could not see or hear each other because of the dense woods between them.

Putnam's escape might have been frustrated had flanking parties of Howe's troops been actively searching for the Americans. But Howe, as was so often the case, dallied, and Putnam escaped. The reason for the delay, the story goes, was that Howe and his staff, unaware that there were Americans in the vicinity, stopped, as Private Martin had done, to get some refreshment. Fortune brought them to the home of Robert Murray, a Quaker and a stout patriot. Mrs. Murray, an attractive and vivacious lady, "treated them with cake and wine, and they were induced to tarry two hours or more." The incident may have saved Putnam's division. The Reverend James Thacher, the indefatigable diarist, noted, "It has since become almost a common saying among our officers that Mrs. Murray saved this part of the American army." It was Lieutenant Mackenzie's estimate that about seventy Americans were killed and two hundred taken prisoner in the desultory fighting that followed the British landing.

The British were greeted as liberators by the Tories who had waited anxiously for their coming. "Nothing," Serle noted, "could equal the Expressions of Joy, shewn by the Inhabitants. . . . They even carried some [of the] British officers upon their Shoulders about the Streets and behaved in all respects, women as well as Men, like overjoyed Bedlamites." One exultant woman pulled the "Rebel Standard" from the fort, and another raised the British flag after trampling on the American one with a volley of lively curses. Serle, observing the scene, was strengthened in his conviction that the great majority of New Yorkers, if not Americans generally, were loyal subjects of His Majesty, bullied into resisting his wise and benevolent rule by a handful of ambitious demagogues. "They have felt so much of real Tyranny, since the New England & other Rebels came among them," Serle wrote "that they are at a Loss now to enjoy their Release."

5

Turnabout: Harlem Heights

DURING the long afternoon following the debacle at Kip's Bay, scattered groups of Americans from all over Manhattan Island made their way north, occasionally fired on by British scouting parties, meeting up with other units, trudging through the midday heat, hungry, frightened, and exhausted. Private Joseph Martin and his friends joined two successive groups of militiamen who, when fired upon by the British, abandoned everything they carried and took to their heels. Martin reported, "The ground was literally covered with arms, knapsacks, staves, coats, hats, and old oil flasks"—the latter used to carry stolen wine.

Martin himself was forced to hide in a bog to escape capture; a British patrol came so close he could see the buttons on their coats. When the soldiers passed on, he pressed forward until he came to a small stream where a number of tired and thirsty soldiers had stopped to get a drink of water. One man who had lain down to drink did not get up. "He will kill himself with drinking," a soldier said with a laugh. Another reached over to touch the man. His body was as chill as the water; the man was dead.

As Martin approached Harlem, he encountered more and more soldiers moving in the same direction. Finally he passed through some hastily constructed lines, and at last he joined his own regiment. The positions on Harlem Heights were the rallying point for the Americans who had fled at Kip's Bay, for Putnam's rear guard, and for every company or detachment that could find its way north. "The men were confused," Martin wrote, "being without officers to command them. I do not recollect of seeing a commissioned officer from the time I left the lines on the banks of the East River in the morning until I met with . . . one in the evening. How could the men fight without officers?" Many of the men had not eaten for two days and had had little sleep. The commissary eventually found some beef somewhere. When Martin arrived, men were broiling the meat on small sticks Indian style around bonfires. The meat was "black as a coal on the outside and as raw on the inside as if it had not been near the fire." However, Martin wrote, "I asked no question but fell to and helped myself to a feast of this raw beef without bread or salt."

Washington placed Nathanael Greene's division of 3,300 men along the southern rim of Harlem Heights. Putnam's division, consisting of some 2,500 men, was a half mile to the rear, and Spencer's division, the largest with 4,200 men, was dug in another half-mile back. Washington quickly put the demoralized soldiers to work strengthening the fortifications as they straggled in. Fall was in the air, the nights were growing cold, and on the evening of September 15 a bitter rain began to fall. Many of the men had, like Martin, abandoned their packs and were without blankets, tents, or cooking utensils. It was a thoroughly uncomfortable night for most of the troops, waiting somewhat apprehensively for the appearance of the British. "We are now encamped with the main body of the army upon the Heights of Harlem," Washington wrote that night to Congress, "where I should hope the enemy would meet with a retreat in case of an attack, if the generality of our troops would behave with tolerable bravery; but experience, to my great affliction, has convinced me that this is a matter to be wished, rather than expected."

On the morning of September 16, Washington sent Lieutenant Colonel Thomas Knowlton on a reconnaissance with 150 Connecticut rangers. Knowlton's little force crossed at Hollow Way, a gully south of today's West 125th Street, and advanced up Vandewater's Heights. At dawn the Americans ran into two light infantry battalions and part of the famous "Black Watch," the Forty-second Scottish Highlanders. The Americans held their ground, firing volley after volley at the redcoats.

Washington, hearing the sound of firing to his front, rode forward to the advance posts and then dispatched his aide, Colonel Joseph Reed, to make contact with Knowlton. Reed returned shortly to report that Knowlton's men were holding off a substantial British force. He advised sending reinforcements and volunteered to lead them. Washington consented. At this point Knowlton, with the Black Watch threatening the flanks of his small force, ordered a withdrawal. As the Americans began to pull back in good order, Reed saw the advance guard of the enemy in open view and heard them sound their bugles "in the most insulting manner . . . as is usual after a fox chase." It was a calculated gesture of contempt for the cowardly American rabble that was supposed to take to its heels at the appearance of the British. "I never felt such a sensation before," Reed wrote, "it seemed to crown our disgrace."

Those Americans who understood the bugle flourish shared Reed's anger. Reed, recruiting Lieutenant Colonel Archibald Army and 150 volunteers from John Nixon's brigade, led a counterattack. The British advance force at this point was perhaps a regiment in strength. Reed's plan was to send one regiment directly at them to hold their attention while he maneuvered with a larger force, consisting of three rifle companies of General George Weedon's Third Virginia Regiment, to take them in the rear.

For a time the fighting was brisk but inconclusive. Washington dispatched the rest of Nixon's brigade, some eight hundred men. The plan for enveloping the British failed when the poorly disciplined but eager troops rushed toward the firing despite Colonel Reed's efforts to control them. "Finding there was no stopping them," Reed later wrote, "I went with them the new way—and in a few minutes our brave fellows mounted up the rocks and attacked them; then they ran in turn." A halloo went up from the Americans. There went the famous British heroes, scrambling for their lives. For almost a mile and a half the Americans had the exhilarating experience of driving the British before them like cattle. This was the kind of fighting they relished. No lying in a ditch waiting for a cannonball to crush them, but firing and moving, seeking cover, reloading, and singling out a redcoated figure to bring down with a well-aimed shot.

For a time it seemed as though all the fleeing British were in danger of being killed or captured. Some made a stand about noon in a buckwheat field near present-day West 120th Street, between Broadway and Riverside Drive. At that point, reinforcements finally arrived in the form of a company of Hessian jaegers with two 3-pound cannon. These guns fired some sixty rounds between them, helping to hold off the Americans and save the light infantry from being wiped out. With the ammunition for their fieldpieces exhausted and the Americans still pressing, the British once more withdrew, turning on their pursuers a final time at Jones's Farm. By this time the British units, heavily reinforced, numbered some five thousand men. Afraid that his soldiers would outrun their own support and find themselves surrounded by a much larger body of British, Washington ordered the Americans back to their own lines, and at two in the afternoon the fighting ended.

The Americans had suffered substantial losses, among them Colonel Knowlton of Connecticut, who, dying in Reed's arms, had been concerned only about the bravery of his men. Despite the difficulty Reed had had in controlling the troops under his command, it was plain that the soldiers were vastly heartened by the number of senior officers who voluntarily had joined in the attack to provide both leadership and example. "I suppose many persons will think it was rash for so many officers of our rank to go into such an action," Colonel Reed wrote, "but it was really to animate the troops who were quite dispirited and would not go into danger unless their officers led the way."

The British lost almost one hundred men killed and wounded, but the battle was far more important than the number of casualties on either side indicated. The Americans had met the British in open battle and put them to flight. "If I only had a pair of pistols," General James Clinton, one of the American officers who attacked that day as a volunteer, wrote, "I am sure I would at least have shot a puppy of an officer I found slinking off in the heat of the action." Young Tench Tilghman, writing to his Tory father, spoke with pride of the fact that the Maryland and Virginia regiments fought "with the greatest bravery." A British soldier taken prisoner told his American captors that the British "expected our men would have run away as they did the day before, but that they were never more surprised than to see us advancing to attack them." The American General Weedon, who a few hours before had written gloomily to John Page about the fighting qualities of his soldiers, now declared that the British "got cursedly thrashed."

Praise for the soldiers' bravery was in sharp contrast to the lamentations over their cowardice at Kip's Bay the day before. The soldiers were essentially the same at both engagements; only the circumstances and the leadership were different. Further, it was a priceless discovery that British soldiers and officers were human after all; that they could panic and run just like ordinary mortals. "The men," Colonel Reed noted, "have recovered their spirits and feel a confidence which before they had quite lost." Perhaps even more important, the officers had recovered confidence in their men. It was not, Reed was quick to point out, an engagement that would inhibit the enemy in any significant way, but it was tonic to the American spirit.

The significance of the warm skirmish on September 16 was not lost on the British. Lieutenant Mackenzie of the Royal Welch Fusiliers noted that "it was an unfortunate business, and gave the General a good deal of concern, and nothing was intended or gained by it. . . ." A young officer from a British ship in the river, having witnessed the engagement, returned to his vessel and swore gloomily that the rebels would fight and it would take years to subdue them.

Spirit alone, however, was not sufficient. "Alas," Reed observed, "our situation here must soon be a very distressing one if we do not receive much relief in the articles of stores, provision, forage, etc. The demands of a large army are very great and we are in a very doubtful condition on this head." In addition, after the Harlem Heights engagement, Washington issued a sharp reprimand to those officers who had acted without, or beyond, or in direct contradiction to their orders. "The loss of the enemy yesterday would undoubtedly have been much greater," he declared, "if the orders of the commander-in-chief had not in some instances been contradicted by inferior officers, who however well they may mean, ought not to presume to direct."

The spirit of insubordination or independence was exemplified by an incident involving Private Joseph Martin, who, while returning alone from a night of guard duty, came to a rail gate just ahead of General Putnam, who was on horseback. The general "bawled out, 'Soldier, let down those bars.'" Martin, seeing that the general was still a way off, removed one and slipped through, ignoring Putnam's order, whereupon the general "in a dreadful passion" drew his pistol, shouted his favorite epithet, "Curse ye!," and threatened to shoot Martin, who took refuge discreetly in the bushes. "I verily believe the old fellow would have shot me or endeavored to have done it if he could have got within reach of me," Martin observed.

While Washington's army regrouped on Harlem Heights, a destructive fire broke out in New York to the south. Before the retreat from the city, there had been a warm discussion among the members of Washington's staff centering on whether to burn New York and thus deny it to the British as a headquarters. The official decision had been not to burn the city. Nevertheless around midnight on September 20, "a most dreadful fire broke out in New York, in three different places in the South, and windward part of the town." The wind spread the flames so rapidly that nothing could be done by the British troops to check the fire's progress until almost a quarter of the city had been burned down.

The British assumed, not unnaturally, that it was an act of sabotage by the rebels, and diarist Ambrose Serle stated it as a fact that "some Rebels, who lurked about the Town, set it on Fire; and some of them were caught with Matches and Fire-balls about them. One Man, detected in the Fact, was knocked down by a Grenadier & thrown into the Flames for his Reward. Another, who was found cutting off the Handles of the Water-Buckets to prevent their Use, was first hung up by the Neck til he was dead and afterwards by the Heels upon a Sign-Post by the Sailors. Many others were seized, on account of Combustibles found upon them and secured; and, but for the officers, most of them would have been killed by the enraged Populace & Soldiery."

"It is almost impossible," Lieutenant Mackenzie wrote, "to conceive a scene of more horror and distress than the above. The sick, the aged, women and children half naked were seen going they knew not where . . . in several instances driven a second and even a third time by the devouring element. . . . The terror was increased by the horrid noise of the burning and falling houses. . . . The confused voices of so many men, the shrieks and cries of the women and children, the seeing the fire break out unexpectedly in places at a distance, which manifested a design of totally destroying the city . . . made this one of the most tremendous and affecting scenes I ever beheld."

The rumor was that New Englanders, who hated New Yorkers and Tories, had conceived the plot to set the town afire. But if the fire was the result of arson, it was a consequence of individual initiative rather than official policy. Whatever its origin, it served the American cause well; Howe was seriously inconvenienced, many of his supplies were consumed by the fire, and his attention, for the moment at least, was distracted from applying pressure on Washington's army. Washington's own terse comment was, "Providence, or some good honest fellow, has done more for us than we were disposed to do for ourselves."

If Howe was discomforted by the fire in New York, Washington was enduring even graver setbacks. The situation on Harlem Heights deteriorated day by day as soldiers whose terms of enlistment were up left for home. The Americans had shown that with effective leadership they would fight, but every time there was a lull in the fighting they demonstrated anew that they were restless, impatient, and ill-equipped by temperament for the tedious routines of camp life. Joseph Reed, serving as adjutant general to Washington, wrote to his wife suggesting that Washington's principal aim was to hang on through the fall of 1776 in hopes of rebuilding his army during the winter. "We are still here in a posture somewhat awkward," he noted; "we think (at least I do) that we cannot stay here and yet we do not know how to go—so that we may be properly said to be between hawk and buzzard. . . . Our comfort is that the season is far advanced, and if a sacrifice of us can save the cause of America there will be time to collect another army before spring and the country be preserved." Looking about him, Reed was "lost in wonder and surprise" at how few of those who had talked in earlier days so grandiosely about "death and honour" were still around. "Your noisy Sons of Liberty," he added, "I find are the quietest on the field. . . . An engagement or even an expectation of one gives a wonderful insight into the characters of men . . . but we are young soldiers."

Two nights after the great fire, an event occurred that, while decidedly minor in the annals of the war, eventually took a prominent place in the imagination of the patriots. Nathan Hale, a young officer from Connecticut and captain of the Nineteenth Continental Regiment, volunteered to serve as a spy to collect intelligence about British troop movements. He was captured by the British on Long Island and identified by his Tory cousin, Samuel Hale. Nathan Hale had in his possession sketches of the British positions and readily confessed his mission. General Howe interrogated him and passed him on to the provost marshal. He was tried and hanged, as Howe's orderly book notes, at eleven o'clock on September 22 in front of the Artillery Park, which was near present-day Grand Central Station.

Undoubtedly British indignation over the fire had something to do with the summary fashion in which Hale was executed. Lieutenant Mackenzie, who was present, was much impressed by the courage with which the young American officer met his death by hanging. He noted in his diary: "He was about 24 years of age, and had been educated at the College of Newhaven in Connecticut. He behaved with great composure and resolution, saying he thought it the duty of every good officer to obey any orders given him by his Commander in Chief; and desired the spectators to be at all times prepared to meet death in whatever shape it might appear."

The *Essex Journal* of February 13, 1777, reported that Hale had declared before his death that "if he had ten thousand lives, he would lay them down, if called to it, in defence of his injured bleeding country." An American officer, William Hull, recorded in his memoirs a conversation with a British officer a few days after Hale's execution. The officer, who came into the American lines under a flag of truce, brought the word of Hale's execution and told Hull of the calm and dignified manner in which the young officer had faced his death. Hale's words, as recalled by the British officer, had been, "I only regret that I have but one life to lose for my country."

News of Hale's death spread quickly through the American army, and an anonymous ballad writer composed a long, sentimental song celebrating his courage:

> The guards of the camp, on that dark, dreary
> night,
> Had a murderous will, had a murderous will.
> They took him and bore him afar from the shore
> To a hut on the hill, to a hut on the hill.
>
> No mother was there, not a friend who could
> cheer,
> In that little stone cell, in that little stone cell.
> But he trusted in love, from his father above.
> In his heart all was well; in his heart all was well.
> . . . .
> The faith of a martyr, the tragedy shewed,
> As he trod the last stage, as he trod the last stage.
> And Britons will shudder at gallant Hale's blood,
> As his words do presage, as his words do presage.
>
> "Thou pale king of terror, thou life's gloomy foe,
> Go frighten the slave, go frighten the slave,
> Tell tyrants, to you their allegiance they owe
> No fears for the brave, no fears for the brave."

After the sharp skirmish at Harlem Heights, General Howe took his time deciding on his next move. Washington meanwhile had to face problems more severe than armed combat—the gradual disintegration of his army. Reed's tally on the third of October showed 25,735 men on the rolls, but 8,075 of them were either sick or on furlough. Eleven thousand men were needed to complete the regiments, most of which were woefully under strength. An army in New Jersey, made up primarily of militia and the flying camp, consisted of 6,548 officers and men stationed along a line from the Amboys to Newark and Fort Constitution.

In addition to the problem of attrition because of illness, furloughs, expiring enlistments, and desertions, discipline remained a serious problem. Joseph Reed wrote to his wife that he was planning to resign his commission since it seemed impossible to produce the proper discipline or degree of subordination between the officers and the men under their command. "Either no discipline can be established," he wrote, "or he who attempts it must become odious and detestable, a position which no one will choose."

The real problem, as Reed's letter hints, was less with the men than with their officers. "Could our *officers* be brought to a proper sense of their duty and dignity and the weight of the army," Colonel Smallwood of the Maryland Line wrote to the Council of Safety in his home state, "the enemy might be checked in their course." Smallwood was convinced that the British for all their pomp and arrogance "are as much afraid and cautious of us, as we can be any of us of them. *Their officers alone give the superiority.*"

Again it was in staffwork that Washington suffered most severely. He could give orders, but unless he personally supervised their execution, they would often be changed or ignored. General Knox wrote in a similar vein to his brother: "The General is as worthy a man as breathes, but he cannot do every thing nor be everywhere. He wants good assistants. There is a radical evil in our army—the lack of officers. . . . The bulk of the officers in the army are a parcel of ignorant, stupid men, who might make tolerable soldiers, but are bad officers. . . ." Knox was convinced that until Congress offered sufficient incentives for the development of a first-rate officer corps, "it is ten to one" the Americans would be beaten until they were "heartily tired of it." "We ought to have academies," he concluded, "in which the whole theory of the art of war shall be taught, and every other encouragement possible given to draw persons into the army that may give a lustre to our arms. As the army now stands, it is only a receptacle for ragamuffins."

Washington, near despair himself, wrote a long letter to John Hancock as president of Congress, detailing the mountain of problems that weighed him down. "We are now, as it were, upon the even of another dissolution of our Army." "The present temper and situation of the troops," added to the problems of supply, convinced Washington "beyond the possibility of doubt, that unless some speedy, and effectual measures are adopted by Congress, our cause will be lost."

What Congress must understand was that appeals to patriotism were not sufficient to form an effective army. It was true that men would when "irriteated, and the passions inflamed . . . fly hastely and chearfully to Arms; but after the first emotions are over, to expect, among such People, as compose the bulk of the Army, that they are influenced by any other principles than those of Interest, is to look for what never did, and I fear never will happen; the Congress will deceive themselves therefore if they expect it. . . ."

"It becomes evidently clear then," Washington continued, "that as this Contest is not likely to be the Work of a day; as the War must be carried on systematically, and to do it, you must have good Officers, there are, in my Judgment, no other possible means to obtain them but by establishing your Army upon a permanent footing; and giving your Officers good pay; this will induce Gentlemen and men of Character to engage. . . ."

The same principle applied to the enlisted men. They had been encouraged to think that a reconciliation would be effected and that the war would be over in a short time. They had thus been enlisted for brief periods, they were poorly paid and inadequately clothed and fed, and they were constantly tempted by the easier terms of militia service, so that the Continental Army had to compete continually with the particular states for soldiers. It was Washington's opinion that a good bounty should be offered immediately, with the promise of "at least 100, or 150 Acres of Land and a suit of Cloathes and Blanket" to each noncommissioned officer and soldier in order to get them to enlist for the duration of the war. For, Washington added, "however high the Men's pay may appear, it is barely sufficient in the present scarcity and dearness of all kinds of goods, to keep them in Cloathes, much less afford support to their Families."

Washington had a special word to say on the subject of state militias. Congress, in its constant effort to cut financial corners, was inclined to place too much confidence in the militia, who were, after all, supported by the individual states. "To place any dependence upon Militia, is, assuredly, resting upon a broken staff," Washington wrote. "Men just dragged from the tender Scenes of domestick life, unaccustomed to the din of Arms, totally unacquainted with every kind of Military skill, which being followed by a want of confidence in themselves, when opposed to Troops regularly trained, disciplined, and appointed, superior in knowledge, and superior in Arms, makes them timid and ready to fly from their own shadows. . . . Men accustomed to unbounded freedom, and no control, cannot brook the Restraint which is indispensably necessary to the good order and Government of an Army; without which, licentiousness, and every kind of disorder triumphantly reign."

While Washington perhaps overstated the case against the militia, it is understandable that he did so, for Congress had to be weaned from its reliance on them. As auxiliary troops, they could often be counted on to fight well, especially in defense of their homes, but it was certainly true that no reliable military force could be fashioned from them.

Congress had anticipated Washington's letter by resolving that eighty-eight battalions be enlisted "as soon as possible to serve during the present war." Each state was called upon to furnish its quota, Massachusetts and Virginia fifteen each, and little Delaware, one. Those who enlisted were to get a bounty of twenty dollars. But if not too little, Congress's action was too late. More than half of the members of Washington's army were at the end of their period of enlistment. Howe, who was well aware of the situation, issued a statement pledging that he would guarantee "the blessing of peace and secure enjoyment of their liberties and properties, as well as a free and general pardon," if the troops refused to re-enlist. Some did desert to the British, and others were insubordinate and mutinous.

From Joseph Martin we get a vivid picture of the hardships endured by the average soldier, and some notion of why it was difficult to persuade them to re-enlist or even to remain until the term of their enlistment had expired. "It now began to be cool weather, especially the nights," he wrote. "To have to lie as I did almost every night (for our duty required it) on the cold and often wet ground without a blanket and with nothing but thin summer clothing was tedious. I have often while upon guard lain on one side until the upper side smarted with cold, then turned that side down to the place warmed by my body, and let the other side take its turn at smarting, while the one on the ground warmd. Thus, alternately turning for four or six hours till called upon to go on sentry . . . and when relieved of a tour of two long hours at that business and returned to the guard again, have had to go through the operation of freezing and thawing for four or six hours more. In the morning the ground was white as snow with hoar frost. Or perhaps it would rain all night like a flood; all that could be done in that case was to lie down (if one could lie down), take our musket in our arms and place the lock between our thighs and 'weather it out!'"

6

White Plains

Washington had shown his amazing resourcefulness in getting his army safely across the East River from Brooklyn, and then again in taking the advantageous high ground of Harlem to fortify. But the British, moving not fast but inexorably, would not let him rest. Soon he was to have once more to extricate his army from a potential trap and once more to improvise a line of defense, testing again his own stamina and that of his army.

In the days immediately following the skirmish at Harlem Heights, there were frequent raids and forays by British and American parties; cannon and musket fire were exchanged constantly. The Americans attempted to seize Montressor's Island at the mouth of the Harlem River, but the British, alerted, beat them back with heavy losses. A detachment of Howe's Fifty-seventh Regiment captured a redoubt near Paulus Hook when the Americans abandoned it without a fight and retired to the well-fortified positions at Bergen in New Jersey. A stream of American deserters came into the British lines, bearing, as deserters will, a substantial amount of information, most of it wrong. A servant of Joseph Alsop, one of the New York delegates to the Continental Congress, came over to the British with a report that the delegates were "in great confusion, and much dissatisfied with each other." He had, he solemnly declared, met nearly four thousand Southerners on their way home from the army. "The Country in general," he told the British, "are tired of the war, and wish that things were returned into their former Channel."

Lieutenant Mackenzie, recording all this in his journal, added, "By the most authentic accounts which we receive of the State of their Army in this neighbourhood, it is extremely sickly, and many desert; so that the numbers of the Militia of the Northern Colonies who are daily coming in, are scarcely sufficient to make up their losses by death and desertion."

Where enemy soldiers were within shouting distances of each other, the exchanges were usually verbal, though snipers exchanged fire occasionally and the German jaegers, or riflemen, took pains to demonstrate their marksmanship when the occasion offered. Joseph Martin watched a British sharpshooter on an island in the East River shooting ineffectually at Americans along the New York shore. One of the guards in the American line asked permission from his officer to return the fire, although the distance was a half-mile or so. The officer gave his consent, and the soldier "rested his old six-feet barrel across a fence and sent an express at him. The man dropped," Martin noted, "but as we then thought it was only to amuse us, we took no further notice of it but passed on. In the morning . . . we saw the brick-colored coat still lying in the same position we had left it in the evening before. It was a long distance to hit a single man with a musket."

Howe, anxious to avoid a direct attack on the American positions at Harlem Heights, prepared to probe the flanks of the American lines in New Jersey and across the East River. Lieutenant Mackenzie was aware of a considerable bustle of preparation in Howe's staff and throughout the army. Cartridges were being made in large numbers, coal was collected to keep the soldiers warm during the winter, forage was collected for horses. Mackenzie anticipated an effort to cut off Washington's army at King's Bridge, although there were rumors of an attack on Philadelphia. "From the discontent which prevails in the Rebel Army and among the people in general," he wrote, "and the dangerous situation in which they will find themselves as soon as General Burgoyne makes any progress through the Country towards Albany, it is highly probable that, if the intended plan [of Howe's] is crowned with moderate success, we shall have very little more trouble with the Rebel Army, and that they will never make another stand of any consequence."

On the ninth of October, six days' rations were issued to the British troops, and conjecture ran rife. Vessels of all sizes were collected, "great numbers of Sloops, Schooners, Pothangers, and other small craft," and the tedious and exacting job of embarking a large army and all its equipment began. The discipline of the army was indicated by the preservation of secrecy as to its objective. "The Commander in Chief," Mackenzie noted approvingly, "seems to have considered every thing with great attention, and to have made every previous arrangement, and provided every means for ensuring success to the Army; and as his plan is to be put in execution by troops of known bravery, and zealous in the cause of their Country, the most brilliant success . . . may be expected."

This was what the British were best at. An army cannot fight unless it is equipped properly and, even more important, placed, by one means or another, on the field of battle. It is here that logistics becomes as important as the fighting qualities and the leadership of the soldiers and officers themselves. Logistics is the domain of staff officers and their subordinates, the most complete professionals in any army. Dashing young gentlemen, buying and selling commissions, leading their men into battle with courage and panache, might come and go, win plaudits and medals for their derring-do, fall in battle, or, after a campaign or two, return to England to sit in Parliament or manage their estates. But the largely anonymous staff officers who fed and bedded them, who provided them with guns and ammunition and got them where they were directed to go, were for the most part career men who, if they frequently lined their own pockets, knew their jobs and did them with a shrewd mixture of quiet efficiency and cautious graft.

On the twelfth of October, Howe started to move a major part of his army from Long Island around the tip of Manhattan and up the Hudson, hoping to get above Washington's positions and take him in the rear. In addition Howe loaded the guards, the light infantry, and Von Donop's Hessians on frigates and carried them to Throgs Neck on Long Island Sound, some ten miles east of the main American lines. This movement was delayed for several days by the difficulty that the transports and warships had in getting through the dangerous Hell Gate into Long Island Sound. Howe's intention evidently was a double envelopment.

Once landed on Throgs Neck, the British found that the Neck was separated from the mainland at high tide, and that the mainland was fortified and defended at this point by Hand's American Rifles and by additional regiments under Prescott and Graham. In addition, the Americans had two light artillery pieces trained on the causeway to the Neck. It was clear that it would be an expensive move to attack there, and Howe, bringing up further reinforcements, had the troops under his immediate command transferred to Pell's Point farther north along the shoreline on October 18.

Washington, alarmed at the prospect of being surrounded, began his own withdrawal from Harlem Heights, moving north up the island past Fort Washington and then across King's Bridge, which was covered by Fort Independence. When General Greene, who was in command at Fort Lee on the New Jersey side of the Hudson, heard of Howe's landing at Throgs Neck, he requested permission from Washington to cross the river with three brigades and move into Westchester to oppose Howe. Washington gave permission and at the same time held a council of war. The question was whether, considering all circumstances, Fort Washington should be abandoned. It was decided to hold the fort "as long as possible."

When Howe abandoned Throgs Neck and set sail for Pell's Point, Colonel John Glover hurried to take up positions across Howe's line of advance. Glover had some 750 men. Putting a portion of his small force behind a stone wall directly in front of the advancing British, he placed Joseph Read's Massachusetts regiment behind another wall that ran perpendicular to the first one. Glover then began a series of maneuvers with the remainder of his force that were designed to lure the British into an attack on the walls. Firing and withdrawing, Glover enticed the British forward, and then, fifty yards from the main wall, he ordered the decoys to flee. The British gave a shout of triumph and started forward. When they were thirty yards away, Read's men rose up from behind their wall and fired an enfilade volley that drove the British back in disorder. When the main body came up, Glover estimated the British force at some four thousand soldiers, supported by seven artillery pieces. The British came on in full battle array, flags flying and drums and fifes playing. When they were within fifty yards, Glover's men rose up from behind their barricade and fired almost pointblank at the enemy. After seven rounds, Glover again dropped back. This time, when the British rushed forward, Colonel Shepherd's men "behind a fine double stone wall . . . rose up and fired by divisions," the colonel keeping them at it until they had fired some seventeen rounds and caused the British to fall back several times.

There was no question of a few hundred Americans being able to

seriously contest the field against four thousand British, but they continued to harass the redcoats with artillery and musket fire until dark.
Then Glover led his men some three miles to Dobbs Ferry, where, as
Joseph Martin reported, they made camp "after fighting all day without
victuals or drink, laying as a picket all night, the heavens over us and the
earth under us, which was all we had, having left our baggage at the old
encampment. . . ." The Americans counted eight killed and thirteen
wounded, the British considerably more. The engagement was a minor
one, but it was valuable in reminding Howe that the Americans, under
the proper circumstances, could fight doggedly and well.

With Howe's movement on his left fully developed, Washington
could simply have crossed the Hudson River into New Jersey and
undertaken to defend a line along the river (or he could have hurried
north, intent on escaping Howe's encirclement). But it was never Washington's intention to escape battle. His overall strategy involved avoiding
wherever possible large-scale engagements that required battlefield
maneuvers of the traditional kind. He wished to create a series of
situations where Howe must attack him on ground of Washington's own
choosing and in carefully prepared defensive positions.

Still uncertain of Howe's intentions, Washington left nothing to
chance. He had built a bridge of boats over the Bronx River to connect
him with Greene's force in Westchester; and reluctantly pulling out of
his almost impregnable positions at Harlem Heights, he constructed a
succession of strongpoints along the Bronx River to block any move on
Howe's part to cross the river before Washington had extricated his
army from Manhattan.

The precaution was typical of Washington. It is true that 90 per
cent of the precautions taken by a commanding officer against enemy
actions are unnecessary—in the sense that the enemy does not in fact
attack the prepared position. But on the remaining 10 per cent rests the
safety of the whole army. It is also true that the failure of the enemy to
attack a strong defensive position is due, in most instances, to the very
fact that it is well fortified.

By the twentieth of October, Washington had his withdrawal well
under way. The heavy cannon and mortars, the more cumbersome
camp equipment, and most of the men were moving northward, their
retreat covered by a rear guard. In addition to the line of fortifications
along the Bronx River, Washington, who had already established a
depot of critically needed supplies at White Plains, ordered General
Heath to prepare defensive positions there, selecting the ground him-

self. General Heath's division made a night march and reached White Plains on October 22. He established his divisional headquarters at Chatterton Hill, a piece of high ground that lent itself readily to defense, and set about digging other works at Valentine's Hill and other spots around White Plains. General Sullivan's division arrived the next night, and that of Lord Stirling (who, like Sullivan, had been exchanged by the British for a prisoner held by Washington and had resumed his command) soon after. Washington moved his headquarters to White Plains the same day; General Lee, back from Charles Town, was drawn in from his post at King's Bridge, and the Americans utilized the time allowed them by Howe's slow and careful advance to extend and augment the breastworks that spread in a semicircle around White Plains, taking advantage of every fold and declivity in the terrain.

The bulk of Washington's army was safely out of Manhattan; but it was by no means in first-class fighting trim. The men were woefully short of even the simplest comforts of the field—blankets, tents, and warm clothes—and were perpetually hungry. Joseph Martin was in the regiment at Valentine's Hill, where, he wrote, "we continued some days, keeping up the old system of starving." He begged a sheep's head from army butchers who were slaughtering it for, as Martin put it with a touch of bitterness, "the 'gentlemen officers,'" and this was his main ration for several days. Scouring the woods for food, Martin found a chestnut tree and stuffed himself with raw chestnuts. When he got back to camp, his sergeant ordered him to get ready for a two-day scouting expedition. This was the last straw. Filled with chestnuts that lay on his stomach like rocks, Martin protested that he was sick and could not go on patrol.

All right then, the sergeant replied, go to the doctor, and if he says you are sick, you will be excused. Martin saw the surgeon's mate nearby, trying to cook his supper over a small smoky fire, "blowing the fire and scratching his eyes. We both stepped up to him and he felt my pulse, at the same time very demurely shutting his eyes, while I was laughing in his face. After a minute's consultation with his medical talisman, he very gravely told the sergeant that I was unfit for duty, having a high fever upon [me]. I was as well as he was," Martin added; "all the medicine I needed was a bellyful of victuals."

As the sergeant turned away, Martin stopped him. He would go on the patrol after all. "I only felt a little cross," he noted, "and did not know how just then to vent my spleen in any other way. I had much rather go on an expedition than stay in camp, as I stood some chance while in the country to get something to eat."

The episode suggests both a lack of the most rudimentary skill on the part of those men charged with attending to the health of the Continental Army, and a disposition on the part of those men, well aware of the physical condition of the soldiers, to be lenient in how they defined sickness. It indeed helps to explain why such a large portion of the Continental Army was constantly listed as sick. Certainly there was much genuine illness—flu, crippling diarrhea, pneumonia, and ailments of varying degrees of seriousness resulting from the unsanitary conditions of camp life. Inadequately fed and with little protection from the elements, many soldiers were in a state of chronic ill-health, suffering from malnutrition and exposure. So they frequently went on sick call. Nonetheless, when the enemy approached they took up their muskets and fought as best they could.

When Washington had shifted his headquarters to White Plains, Martin and his fellows had been routed out in the middle of the night. Since there were only three men of his mess present for duty, they had among them to carry the mess's cooking utensils ("at that time," Martin observed, "the most useless things in the army"). The pots were made of heavy cast iron. "I was so beat out before morning with hunger and fatigue," Martin wrote, "that I could hardly move one foot before the other. I told my messmates that I *could not* carry our kettle any further. They said they *would* not carry it any further." What good was a kettle with nothing to put in it? He set the kettle down in the road "and one of the others gave it a shove with his foot and it rolled down against the fence, and that was the last I ever saw of it." When the trio got to White Plains, they found "our mess was not the only one that was rid of our iron bondage."

While Washington improvised his defenses at White Plains, Howe established his army two miles beyond New Rochelle. There Howe waited for General Von Heister and his Hessians to join up; and then, in command of a splendid army, he advanced, step by cautious step, until on the twenty-eighth, a week after he had launched his maneuver, he came within a mile of the village of White Plains, which consisted of little more than a courthouse and a scattering of homes. Howe had taken six days to cover thirty miles. Since the success of his strategy depended primarily on cutting off Washington's line of retreat, Howe's dilatoriness defeated his project far more decisively than Washington could possibly have done. At the same time, it should be said in Howe's defense that the terrain over which he had to advance was broken and difficult. He had expected substantial help from a regiment of cavalry in running detachments of Americans to ground and reconnoitering the way ahead; but after the initial shock of encountering mounted men, the Americans, especially the riflemen, responded to Washington's offer of a reward of one hundred dollars for the soldier who could bring in an armed rider and his horse. The harassment of the cavalry by sharp-shooters, and the network of stone fences across their way, rendered the cavalry thoroughly ineffective.

A large part of Howe's problem was that the Bronx River, which protected Washington's left flank better than a dozen regiments could have done, was not fordable until White Plains. The most notable incident of the British advance was a raid ordered by Lord Stirling against the Queen's Rangers, a Loyalist corps under the notorious Major Robert Rogers, famous for his exploits in the French and Indian Wars. Rogers' corps was part of Howe's advance contingent. Colonel John Haslet crossed the Bronx River with a raiding party made up of some of his Delaware continentals, caught Rogers and his men by surprise, captured thirty-six, killed almost as many others, and brought back sixty muskets. It was an especially sweet victory against the hated Tories, and to it was added a minor victory by Colonel Hand's regiment over the Hessian jaegers near Mamaroneck.

The defensive positions that Washington chose at White Plains were well selected. His left was protected by very rough terrain, his right by a sharp bend in the Bronx River. A series of earthworks provided a succession of defensive positions, and the road network connecting with the Hudson River at Dobbs Ferry to the south and Tarrytown to the north was well covered. Chatterton Hill secured the southern flank of Washington's defenses, separated as it was by the better part of a mile from the main positions around White Plains. It was defended by Haslet's regiment, supported by General McDougall's brigade—both of them tested in combat.

The defense was still being perfected when the British approached. On the twenty-seventh of October, Washington ordered a reconnaissance by those generals not on duty. While the officers were discussing defensive arrangements, a messenger, his horse lathered and out of breath, galloped up to Washington. "The British are on the camp, Sir." Washington turned to his generals: "Gentlemen, we have now other business than reconnoitering," and galloped off for his headquarters, the other officers following.

At Washington's headquarters, Reed informed the general that the advance guards had all been forced in and that the American forces were at their posts in order of battle. The advancing British, in two

columns, turned to their left, hoping to take the main American posi-
tions in the flank. This brought them against Chatterton Hill. The
British force was made up of the Second British Brigade, Von Donop's
Hessian grenadiers, the Lossberg Regiment, and Colonel Johann Rall's
Hessians—a force of some four thousand, nearly a third of Howe's
army.

The initial phases of the defense of Chatterton Hill were discouraging. The British began with a heavy cannonading. The first volley
wounded a militiaman in the thigh, and the sight of the gaping wound
and the blood, plus the groans of the soldier, sent the other soldiers
flying. Colonel Haslet and his officers rallied them and brought them
back to their positions. Haslet's request for artillery at first produced
only one gun, which Haslet himself was helping to drag forward when it
was struck by a British cannonball that shattered the carriage and set a
wad of packing on fire. The artillerymen thereupon fled, except for one
man who remained to put out the blaze.

As the British attack developed, some twenty light horse wheeled
off to make a dash against Heath's division on the American right, but a
rattle of artillery fire turned them back, and the main attack pressed
down through a steep draw toward the Bronx River, there hardly more
than a rivulet. Heath, watching the advance, saw the British moving
slowly through the flaming autumn trees and heavy brush. "The sun
shone bright, their arms glittered," he noted, adding, "perhaps troops
never were shewn to more advantage than these now appeared." Then
the two British and Hessian columns halted, and the soldiers sat down in
position to eat.

When the advance resumed, the left column forded the river and
moved to the left under the cover of Chatterton Hill, their column now
a line of skirmishers. They then turned and moved up Chatterton Hill
in good order while the British cannonade of the hilltop, which had
covered their advance, was lifted. The American artillery, now in place
on Chatterton Hill, went into action. Alexander Hamilton directed the
fire of two light artillery pieces with especially good effect. Colonel
William Smallwood's regiment, supported by Colonel Rudolph Ritz-
ema's, made forays down the hill that slowed the British attack.

For a few moments, it appeared as though the British attack had
been halted. Joseph Martin, his regiment coming up in support of
Haslet's regiment and forming behind a stone wall, could see the British
constructing some sort of bridge over the Bronx River to carry their
artillery and wagons across. A hundred yards in front of the stone wall

where Martin crouched and lower down the hill was an apple orchard. Beyond the orchard, the ground fell off sharply. Here a line of British and Hessian troops would advance until they could see the Americans behind the stone wall, fire, retreat into defilade to load their muskets, then once more move up the hill to fire and fall back. The Americans in turn would fire on the British and Hessians "as soon as they showed themselves above the level ground, or . . . to aim at the flashes of their guns."

This exchange of fire went on until the Hessian Colonel Rall, by a sudden movement to the left, turned the American flank. Martin's unit suddenly found itself in danger of being surrounded by Rall's advance on the other side of the hill. "We fell back a little distance," Martin noted, "and made a stand, detached parties engaging in almost every direction." As the British advance continued, the Americans, seeing themselves heavily outnumbered, "moved off . . . in a great body, neither running nor observing the best order." When the British and Hessians, their long lines moving inexorably forward, reached the summit of the hill, they dressed their line, swung to the right, and began to dig entrenchments overlooking the main American positions.

When the Americans took stock of their losses at the end of the day, the tally was a mixed one. Some 130 Continental soldiers and officers had been killed and wounded, among the latter Colonel Smallwood, who had fought bravely on this as on other occasions. The British had lost approximately 230 men and officers, but they had gained the high ground on the American right, forcing an extensive realignment of the American defensive positions. That Washington's troops had, on the whole, fought with resolution and skill was indicated by the casualty lists, the American no less than the British. Had Smallwood been promptly reinforced, the outcome of the battle might have been different, but to have supported the defender of Chatterton Hill adequately would have seriously weakened the main American positions in the center, and this Washington was understandably reluctant to do.

During the night, the British brought up artillery on Chatterton Hill and, as Joseph Martin put it, "entertained us with their music all evening." The Americans hastily dug makeshift entrenchments, then found that water soon seeped in to shoe-top level—"which," Martin wrote, "caused many of us to take violent colds by being exposed on the wet ground after a profuse perspiration." Martin got a severe cold and was "sent back to the baggage to get well again, if I could, for it was left to my own exertions to do it and no other assistance was afforded me. . . . I had the canopy of heaven for my hospital and the ground for my hammock." Martin found some dry leaves and made a kind of bed to curl up in. Chilled and miserable, without food or water, he alternatively burned and shivered. In the evening, one of his fellows brought him some half-boiled "hog-flesh" and stolen turnips. "He did all he could do," Martin wrote. "He gave me the best he had to give, and had to steal to do that, poor fellow. Necessity drove him to do it to satisfy the cravings of his own hunger as well as to assist a fellow sufferer."

The twenty-ninth saw a lull in the battle as Howe once more waited for reinforcements, this time Lord Percy with the third brigade and two battalions of the fourth brigade. The Americans meanwhile drew back to higher ground where defensive positions had already been prepared, and with the left at White Plains as the axis, pivoted around until their defensive line, which had initially run roughly north and south, ran almost due east and west. The next day, when Howe planned to attack, the rain and wind were so heavy that he suspended his assault for another twenty-four hours. Meanwhile Washington moved his army some five miles to the north to an eminence called North Castle Heights and prepared for Howe's renewed attack. Reconnoitering the new position, Howe decided that it was virtually impregnable, and after lingering near White Plains for several days, he encamped his army at Dobbs Ferry on the east bank of the Hudson. Here British ships, having broken the blockade of the Hudson at Fort Washington, could supply his troops. Once more Washington had fought well against a determined and well-planned British attack, and had survived.

7

The Struggle for Fort Washington

WASHINGTON and the major portion of his army were secure in their earthwork-defended high ground north of White Plains. But he had left a portion of his army behind on Manhattan, the garrison of Fort Washington. The question that now presented itself to Washington was whether or not to defend the fort that bore his name. The decision was a crucial one. Fort Washington was, besides West Point, the strongest fortification in American hands. It commanded, or was intended to command, the lower Hudson. The fort proper was the center of extensive American positions that included four other strongpoints. To abandon it without a fight would be to concede to the British the control of the Hudson. To defend it, however, isolated as it now was, would be to risk the capture of the defenders and, even more important, the seizure by the British of all the desperately needed ordnance that it contained.

Washington vacillated. General Nathanael Greene, whose opinion Washington respected, stubbornly insisted that the fort could be held indefinitely against British attack. Greene then returned to Manhattan and recaptured Fort Independence, scarcely a mile north of Fort Washington, which had been abandoned, as part of the retreat to White Plains. Greene thereby recaptured much of the shot, shell and spears that had been left behind, plus five tons of bar iron along with other

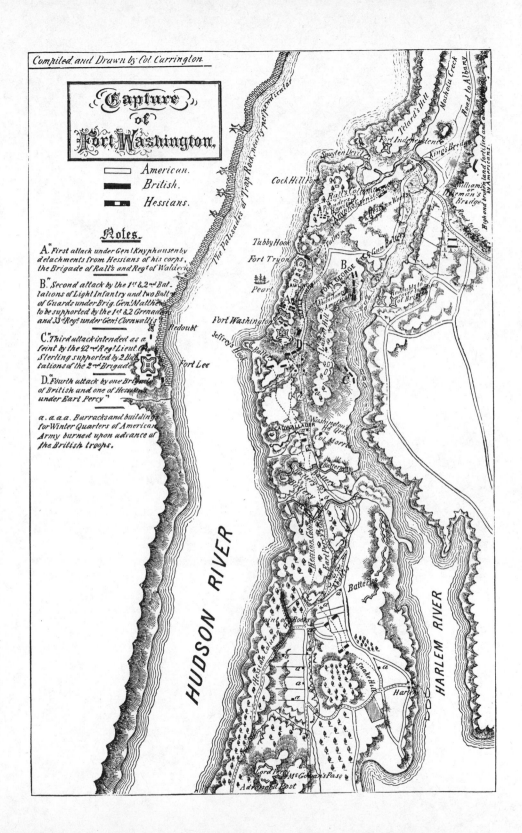

Compiled and Drawn by Col. Currington.

Capture
of
Fort Washington.

☐ American.
▬ British.
▬◻ Hessians.

Notes.

A.* "First attack under Gen! Knyphausen by detachments from Hessians of his corps, the Brigade of Rall's and Reg! of Waldeck.

B.* "Second attack by the 1st & 2nd Battalions of Light Infantry and two Batt! of Guards under Brig. Gen! Matthew, to be supported by the 1st & 2 Grenadiers and 33d Reg! under Gen! Cornwallis."

C.* "Third attack intended as a feint by the 42nd Reg! Lieut. Col. Sterling supported by 2 Battalions of the 2nd Brigade.

D.* "Fourth attack by one Brigade of British and one of Hessians under Earl Percy."

a. a. a. a. Barracks and buildings for Winter Quarters of American Army burned upon advance of the British troops.

HUDSON RIVER

HARLEM RIVER

THE STRUGGLE FOR FORT WASHINGTON / 791

valuable supplies. Washington was gratified at this news, but he wrote Greene advising him to evacuate Fort Washington. However, Washington gave Greene authority to decide whether to fight or evacuate. "If we cannot prevent vessels passing up [the Hudson] and the enemy are possessed of the surrounding country, what valuable purpose can it answer," Washington asked, "to hold a post from which the expected benefit cannot be had? I am therefore inclined to think it will not be prudent to hazard the men and stores at Mount Washington, but as you are on the spot, leave it to you to give such orders as to evacuating Mount Washington as you judge best. . . ."

Greene was ordinarily a sound soldier. Anticipating that Howe might move into New Jersey, he made careful calculations as to the best lines of defense that Washington would find there. He even estimated the quantities of supplies that should be collected at each point to provide for Washington's army, retreating and fighting as it went. However, Greene persisted in thinking that Fort Washington gave an advantage to the Americans. "I cannot conceive the garrison to be in any great danger," he wrote Washington, "the men can be brought off at any time"—presumably by boat across the Hudson. It would, in Greene's opinion, be December before the British could lay siege to the fortification.

Leaving the final decision on the defense of the fort to Greene, Washington began to move his army across the Hudson at Peekskill. Again, he did most of the demanding staffwork involved in the amphibious crossing himself, supervising the tedious and difficult maneuver personally, leaving nothing to chance or to the inexperience of his staff. He instructed his general officers, as enlistments were soon to expire and much of the army would be leaving for home in a few days, to collect equipment and what few tents there were—"tents to be repaired against another season, intrenching tools to be collected or placed where General Lee should direct."

Washington's orders reached down to the lowest echelons, and included the smallest details: " . . . no officer of any rank to meddle with a wagon or cart appropriated for any other regiment or public use; that no discharged men be allowed to carry away arms, camp kettles, utensils, or any other public stores; recruiting officers so detailed, to proceed with their duty; no boys or old men to be enlisted, and if so, to be returned on the hands of the officer, with no allowance for any expense he may be at."

By the fourteenth of November, all of the troops destined to make up Washington's army in New Jersey had crossed the Hudson, and Washington had joined General Greene at his headquarters at Fort Lee. Left behind was General Heath with his division, with orders to defend the passes through the "highlands" north of Manhattan. Left behind also was Private Joseph Martin. A number of sick and wounded soldiers were sent to Norwalk in Connecticut to assist in recruiting, and Martin, still shaky from what was apparently an attack of influenza, was sent with them as a nurse, responsible for seven or eight sick soldiers "who were," he wrote, "(at least, soon after their arrival there) as well in health as I was. All they wanted was a cook and something for a cook to exercise his functions upon."

Washington established his own headquarters at Hackensack, some nine miles from Fort Lee, and waited to see what action the British might take against Fort Washington. The garrison there had recently been reinforced by some of the Flying Camp and numbered almost three thousand. Why Washington left such a sizable force to be besieged by the British is not clear. Evidently he was reassured by Greene's confidence that the garrison could be brought off across the river if their position became untenable. He may also have anticipated another Bunker Hill, where the Americans, in positions much stronger than those at Charlestown, could presumably inflict crippling casualties upon the attackers. Beyond all this, he had abandoned enough fortified positions; somewhere his soldiers must stand their ground. "I propose to stay in the neighborhood a few days," he wrote Congress; "in which time I expect the design of the enemy will be more disclosed, and their incursions made in this quarter, or their investiture of Fort Washington if they are intended."

Fort Washington had been hastily constructed and was, in the words of Alexander Graydon, "without a ditch of any consequence and with no exterior defenses that could entitle it to the name of a fortress in any degree capable of sustaining a siege." More serious, there was no well in the fort, and all water had to be windlassed up from the Hudson, a hundred yards below. Worse—and this Washington had no way of knowing—a traitor, William Demont, an ensign in Colonel Magaw's Fifth Pennsylvania Regiment, had taken detailed plans of the fort to the British lines. Demont reported that the Americans had been ordered to defend Fort Washington "to the last extremity, having therein two months provisions, many cannon and plenty of ammunition." Howe was convinced, partly by Demont's testimony, that "the importance of this post . . . made the possession of it absolutely necessary."

Washington, for his part, expected Howe to cross the Hudson into New Jersey without stopping for a major assault on Fort Washington. Like Washington, Lieutenant Mackenzie assumed that Howe would send a major part of his army into the South or "penetrate into Jersey and endeavor to enlarge the quarters of the army in a province abounding with provisions, fuel and other necessary supplies." The extension of the area of British occupation into New Jersey would, moreover, "give the Loyalists an opportunity of declaring themselves, and circumscribe the resources of the enemy." Both Washington and Lieutenant Mackenzie were right—Howe did plan to march into New Jersey. But not before attacking Fort Washington.

Commander on the scene at Fort Washington was General Robert Magaw. Magaw distributed the main body of his three thousand troops between the fort proper and the field fortifications supporting it, "the lines being," in Washington's words, "all to the southward." On the east side of the Washington redoubt there were no organized defensive positions, since the fort had been built to command the river and was thus oriented to the west. Not only were the earthworks skimpy on that side, there were no properly prepared and defended advance positions to the north with the exception of a modest work called Cock Hill Fort. All this information, which was carried to the British by Demont, strengthened Howe's determination to overwhelm the fort. The crucial information here was not the plan of the redoubt itself, but the disposition of the troops charged with defending the approaches to it. With the information provided by Demont, Howe directed General Wilhelm Von Knyphausen and his Hessians to attack Fort Washington from the north and east. On November 2, Von Knyphausen with six Hessian battalions crossed the Harlem River and camped just north of Fort Washington.

With preparations for the attack completed, Howe sent an officer under a flag of truce to the fort to demand that Magaw surrender or have his men "put to the sword." Magaw declared that he was determined to defend his post, adding as a response to Howe's bloodthirsty-sounding ultimatum, "I think it rather a mistake, than a settled purpose of General Howe to act a part so unworthy of himself and the British nation." Putnam and Greene, receiving word from Magaw of Howe's threat, crossed the river and inspected the American positions there. When Washington heard of the impending attack, he started across the Hudson to assure himself that proper dispositions had been made to withstand the British assault. Halfway over the river, he encountered Greene and Putnam "Just returning from thence, and they informed me," Washington wrote, "that the troops were in high spirits and would make a good defense, and it being late at night, I returned."

The attack on the fort was planned and carried out with boldness and imagination. A British frigate was stationed to cover the march of the Hessians and to flank the American forward positions. Some thirty shallow-draft transports then sailed up the Hudson under the cover of darkness and undetected entered Spuyten Duyvil, the narrow waterway between the northern tip of Manhattan and the Bronx. From there it was a short distance to King's Bridge, where they disembarked in the rear of the American defenses.

When the Hessian attack began, Colonel Rall's regiment easily outflanked Cock Hill Fort, one of the hastily constructed fortifications north of Fort Washington, giving no quarter to those Americans who tried to surrender. General Knyphausen meanwhile moved down the ridgeline that ran from King's Bridge on Rall's left, taking substantial losses as he went from Americans fighting in the woods at his front and flanks. The two forces, Rall's and Knyphausen's, joined in front of an earthwork guarding the northern approach to the main redoubt at Fort Washington. From this point to the main American positions, the Hessians had to cross a deep ravine. The soldiers were forced, as one of them told it, "to creep along up the rocks . . . obliged to drag ourselves by the beech-tree bushes up the height. . . . At last, however, we got about on the top of the hill where there were trees and great stones. We had a hard time of it there together. Because they had now had no idea of yielding, Col. Rall gave the word of command, thus: 'All that are my grenadiers, march forwards!' All the drummers struck up the march. The hautboy-players blew. At once all that were yet alive shouted, 'Hurrah!' Immediately all were mingled together, Americans and Hessians. There was no more firing, but all ran forward pell-mell upon the fortress." Philipp Waldeck, a German regimental chaplain, noted that during the Hessian advance the British batteries on higher ground gradually silenced the American artillery in a barrage lasting some forty-five minutes. It was primarily this covering fire that enabled the Hessians and Waldeckers to climb the cliffs below the fort and drive in the outer lines of defenders.

While the Hessians were attacking the fort from the north, Lord Percy began what was at first intended as a feint against the old positions at Harlem Heights, still held by an American regiment commanded by Colonel John Cadwalader. Percy's force then covered the southern approaches to Fort Washington. At this moment British Generals Matthews and Cornwallis landed their units from transports in the Harlem River. This force met heavy fire from Americans on Laurel Hill but nevertheless advanced, driving the Americans back on the Fort Washington redoubts. Howe now ordered Colonel Sterling to land a half mile to the south of the fort with two more battalions. This landing was also strongly resisted by the Americans. Nevertheless the British effected the landing in spite of the brisk fire, and the Americans retreated in such disorder that 170 were cut off by Sterling's men and taken prisoners.

The British were now able to converge on Fort Washington from three directions. The forces of Cornwallis and Matthews moved down Laurel Hill, driving the Americans from this commanding ridgeline and clearing the way for Sterling's battalions to cross the hill and join forces with them. Cadwalader, meanwhile, was forced to withdraw from Harlem Heights in considerable haste as Percy pressed up from the south. Those Americans who had not been killed or captured now found themselves hemmed into Fort Washington's main redoubt, almost three thousand men crowded into space built to contain no more than one thousand defenders.

The final act of the drama came suddenly. General Magaw, hoping that he might escape across the river that night with the greater part of his force, asked for a five-hour parley. The British consented to no more than half an hour. Magaw thereupon surrendered the fort and its defenders to the British. The bag consisted of almost three thousand soldiers and officers, 161 cannon, 400,000 cartridges, and of course the weapons of the soldiers themselves.

The losses for the Americans were staggering, although the killed and wounded amounted to no more than 130. The British lost 128 in killed, wounded and missing, and the Hessians, 326. From the casualties inflicted by the Americans, it is clear that they gave a good account of themselves in the actual fighting. It is also clear that they were seriously outmaneuvered. Once again they were poorly led. Their initial dispositions were weak, and no effective reserve was employed to reinforce those points in the American lines that had to bear the main attacks of the British and Hessians. If the Americans had been officered well enough for the men to be able, without retreating, to sustain casualties in proportion to their numbers, the British and Hessians might well have suffered too heavily to persist in their attack.

Monday-morning generaling, like Monday-morning quarterbacking, is a tempting exercise. Fort Washington was not in any way essential to Washington. Its value was as an embarrassment and an inconvenience to Howe. Greene's opinion that it could be defended was bad judgment; Washington's acceptance of that judgment was an example of the kind of indecision that he occasionally showed. Washington's inexperience with defending large fortifications, plus the memory of Bunker Hill, were surely partly to blame for the defeat. So was British expertise, a combination of good planning and good execution. Howe once more displayed his skill as a master of conventional warfare, and the British and Hessian forces put on a striking demonstration of the capabilities of troops well trained and well led.

Washington's vacillation about the defense of Fort Washington was undoubtedly related to the fact that Howe had on numerous occasions, most lately indeed at White Plains, shown a marked reluctance to attack strong defensive positions. At any rate, Washington knew he had made a bad mistake and said so in a letter to his brother. "What addes to my mortification is, that this post after the last ships went past it, was held contrary to my wishes and opinions, as I conceived it to be a hazardous one. . . . I did not care to give an absolute order for withdrawing the garrison till I could get round and see the situation of things, and then it became too late, as the fort was invested. . . . I have given as my opinion to General Greene, under whose care it was, that it would be best to evacuate the place: but as the order was discretionary, and his opinion differed from mine, it unhappily was delayed too long to my great grief."

One of the most destructive consequences of the loss of Fort Washington was the erosion of confidence in Washington's leadership. Even Washington's closest and heretofore most loyal officers had misgivings about his competence. Joseph Reed, the adjutant general, with whom Washington had shared so many of his doubts and fears, wrote to General Charles Lee "most earnestly wishing" that he was at "the principal scene of action." "I do not mean to flatter, nor praise you at the expense of any other, but I confess I do think that it is entirely owing to you that this army, and the liberties of America so far as they are dependent on it are not totally cut off. You have decision, a quality often wanting in minds otherwise valuable." Reed implied that other staff officers shared his feelings. "But General," Reed continued, "an indecisive mind is one of the greatest misfortunes that can befall an army— how often have I lamented it in this campaign."

Reed's letter is significant because it indicates the beginning of a general disenchantment with Washington among some members of his staff and certain of his general officers. This dissatisfaction, so plainly expressed by Reed, found its center in the mercurial Lee, and Lee was quick to respond to Reed. It was certainly true, he wrote, that indecision in war "is a much greater disqualification than stupidity or even want of personal courage . . . eternal defeat and miscarriage must attend the man of the best of parts cursed with indecision." He had remained at Peekskill, he declared, because "part of the troops were so ill-furnished with shoes and stockings, blankets, etc. that they must inevitably perish in this wretched weather. Part of 'em are to be dismissed on Saturday next and this part is the best accoutred for service." In addition, Lee had learned that a detachment of Robert Rogers' Loyalist corps along with some British troops were nearby and might be seized by a quick raid. As soon as the "business . . . of Rogers and Co." was over, Lee assured Reed, he would "then fly to you—for to confess a truth I really think our Chief will do better with me than without me."

Greene himself wrote to Henry Knox of the loss of Fort Washington: "I feel mad, vexed, sick and sorry. . . . This is a most terrible event: its consequences are justly to be dreaded." Washington, reporting the disaster to Congress, noted, "The loss of such a number of officers and men, many of whom have been trained with more than common attention, will I fear be severely felt. But when that of the arms and accoutrements is added, much more so, and must be a farther incentive to procure as considerable a supply as possible for the new troops, as soon as it can be done." The loss of the fort was of little consequence; the loss of the men and equipment was a staggering blow to the American cause. Washington's sadly depleted little army, growing smaller by the day, could ill afford to lose almost a fourth of its number as well as a half-dozen of its ablest officers killed or wounded.

The day after the surrender of Fort Washington, Howe completed the humiliation of the Americans by sending Cornwallis across the Hudson with six thousand men to seize Fort Lee, the evacuation of which had started several days before. One of the British officers wrote a friend that Cornwallis had come on Fort Lee so swiftly that "the pots were left boiling on the fire and the tables spread for dinner of some of their officers. In the fort they found 12 men, who were all dead drunk." Cornwallis, moving toward the Hackensack River to cut off the retreat of Washington's fleeing Americans, encountered a rebel detachment on its way from Newark to reinforce Fort Lee and scattered it. The principal coup was several thousand cattle captured in the meadows near Hackensack; they had been driven north from Pennsylvania to supply Washington's army and the American posts in New Jersey. The loss of this fresh meat plus two thousand barrels of corn left behind in Fort Lee was another disaster for the undernourished American soldiers.

"You see, my dear sir," one British officer wrote in a letter, "that I have not been mistaken in my judgment of this people. The southern people will no more fight than the Yankees. The fact is that their army is broken all to pieces, and the spirits of their leaders and their abettors is also broken. However, I think one may venture to pronounce that it is well nigh over with them."

Another British officer, one of the captors of Fort Lee, noted, "On the appearance of our troops, the rebels fled like scared rabbits. . . . They have left some poor pork, a few greasy proclamations, and some of that scoundrel Common Sense man's letters, which we can read at our leisure, now that we have got one of the 'impregnable redoubts' of Mr. Washington's to quarter in."

The Americans fell back to Hackensack, and Washington once more began the desperate labor of trying to pull his army into some sort of order. Lieutenant Mackenzie expressed a general view of the American army when he wrote after the battles at White Plains and Fort Washington: "The Rebel Army must suffer greatly as soon as the severe weather sets in for want of proper Clothing, of which they are now in the greatest need. It is a fact that many of the Rebels who were killed in the late affairs, were without shoes or Stockings, & Several were observed to have only linen drawers on with a Rifle or Hunting shirt, without any proper shirt or Waistcoat. . . . Under all the disadvantages of want of confidence, Clothing and good winter quarters, and constantly harassed by a victorious and incensed Army, it will be astonishing if they keep together 'till Christmas."

New York was now entirely in British hands, while Washington retreated as fast as his depleted army could move across New Jersey. Ambrose Serle, the indefatigable diarist, gloried in the capture of New York City. His pleasure in the warm welcome afforded the British soldiers who marched into New York was tempered, however, by the realization that many rebel sympathizers remained in the city. He discovered that "there were many pretended Friends in N. York, who are ready enough to do any Mischief. If they dared: Some of them have secretly injured or stolen the English horses brought over for the Use of the Army, and do communicate all they can to the Enemy. The People in general form the most impudent, base & hypocritical Characters, that can be met with out of Crete or Greece." They could, he added, perhaps best be compared "to some of our upstart, ill-bred Tradesmen, who have Meanness enough to be ostentatious or wrangle about any thing, but capable of shewing the Spirit or using the Language of Gentlemen in nothing."

Serle noted and recorded everything—and understood nothing. Naturally kind and generous in his personal relationships, he became the center in New York of a coterie of Tories, some of them New Yorkers, many refugees from other colonies. He was especially drawn to Anglican divines loyal to the Crown, and young Charles Inglis, senior curate of Trinity Church, was a frequent companion in Serle's walks about the city and its environs. Henry White, a member of the New York Council, also became a close friend and confidant. White explained to Serle that the public affairs of New York were "governed by a Set of illiterate Assembly-men, who for the most part were Farmers, and absolutely dependent, for their Seats of Power, on men, if possible, more ignorant and arrogant than themselves. . . ." In the "new Constitution of Things" the Crown should bestow all offices, and elections should be done away with as tending to excite the people and provide opportunities for demogogues. Evidently these two humane and liberal men never stopped to consider that in their plans for the future government of the defeated colonies, they were advocating a system of complete political repression. Indeed, if such a point had been made to them, they would have rejected the charge with indignation.

When Joseph Galloway, a refugee from Pennsylvania, arrived in New York, he struck a responsive chord at once in Ambrose Serle. "His opinion with all others I have seen," Serle wrote, "is, that the Power of the Rebellion is pretty well broken, and that though 'tis probable, that the Colonies may make some further Efforts; those Efforts will only be feeble and ineffectual."

Galloway and Serle together developed a scheme designed to end the rebellion promptly and without further bloodshed. They would frame an appeal, to be endorsed by Lord Howe and addressed to the colonial governors, urging the colonial assemblies to publicly reject the authority of Congress, "to profess . . . a dutiful allegiance to His Majesty, and a Hatred of all Rebellions & treasonable Conspiracies. . . ." Such action would give "a convincing proof of Loyalty & attachment to the King & Constitution" and, by undermining the power of Congress, would bring the rebellion to a speedy conclusion. "Hereditary Honors,"

Serle and Galloway agreed, " . . . shd. be introduced in order to counter-act all levelling ideas, and, in short, that a liberal arrangement shd. take Place, wch might combine all the several Branches of the Empire into one whole." This conversation, Serle noted complacently, "was carried on by great Friendliness and mutual Confidence in the Uprightness of each other's Intentions, and the true & solid Regard we both of us have for the common Good of the whole Community or Empire."

Serle is most valuable because he enables us to see quite vividly the strange, illusory world of the Tories through the eyes of an Englishman, entirely sympathetic and representing, in himself, emotions and reac-tions typical of a majority of his countrymen. Serle was a veritable collecting station for rumors, most of which concerned some striking triumph of British arms. Where an actual engagement had taken place, the reports, without exception, greatly exaggerated the American losses.

The New York Tories, as we see them so vividly in Serle's diary, were both irritating and pathetic. They formed a closed company who fed each other's fantasies. Living in relative comfort and surrounded by the reassuring power and splendor of the British army of occupation, they persisted in the assurance that they would be vindicated. They would have been less than human if they had not longed for revenge against their enemies, waited impatiently for the day of reckoning, criticized the dilatoriness of Howe and his generals, and told each other endless tales, many of them certainly true, of the sickness, demoraliza-tion, jealousies, and cowardice of the rebels. Washington's dwindling ragamuffin army was a joke; another month, another campaign, another severe winter, another Loyalist uprising, and all would be in ruins.

It was exhilarating for the Tories to meet Admiral Lord Howe, General Sir William Howe, Sir Henry Clinton, Lord Percy, and dozens of other lesser luminaries of the British aristocracy who made up the officer corps. To move even on the fringes of such exalted company was to be reassured about the final outcome. Every new Tory who appeared to swell the little group of exiles found a ready audience for his tales of patriot impotence, for his assurances that the great body of Americans were sick of the war and sick of their leaders and only waiting for the right moment to rise up and declare their loyalty to king and Parliament.

So unanimous was that chorus that it is small wonder the British believed it, and it is hard to doubt that there was some truth in the tales.

If the rather shaky structure of patriot authority had collapsed, if Washington's army, which was the symbol of that authority, had disintegrated, as it seemed time after time on the verge of doing, the very considerable numbers of Loyalists in New York, Pennsylvania, and the southern colonies might have gained sufficient courage to have risen against their tormenters and turned the Revolution into a genuine civil war.

8

Howe Invades New Jersey

Sɪʀ William Howe, encouraged by the capture of Fort Washington, pushed ahead with his plans to invade New Jersey. He was assured that the region swarmed with Tories who would flock to his support. Washington's army was there, and just possibly Howe might be able to catch Washington's force, engage it in a major battle, and defeat it.

Not that such a battle would end the war. If many officers in Howe's force believed that one more determined campaign would bring colonial resistance to an end, Howe himself was under no such delusion. He saw that a far greater British effort than any made so far would be needed. Writing the Secretary for State for the American Colonies, Lord George Germain, Howe requested sufficient reinforcements to bring his army up to fifty thousand men. Ten thousand of these, according to Howe's plan, would be stationed at Newport with its excellent harbor. From there they could penetrate, almost at will, into New England and particularly into Massachusetts, the heart of the rebellion. Twenty thousand men should be stationed in New York, of whom seventeen thousand would constitute an army of maneuver that could roll up New Jersey and Delaware and strike as far south as Philadelphia if necessary, as well as command the Hudson and maintain contact with British forces moving down from Canada. Another ten thousand men would be used in an extensive campaign in the South, which, it was hoped, would attract substantial Loyalist support.

The plan, which was carried out in bits and pieces but never on the scale that Howe envisioned, is an interesting one because it demonstrates very vividly the real difficulty of the British task. There were, after all, thirteen colonies, now states, each a potential center of resistance and each able, if necessary, to give aid to its neighbors. By proposing the plan, Howe was, in effect, conceding that the Revolution could not be suppressed simply by defeating Washington's army. It was plain, in any case, that Washington was determined to avoid the kind of large-scale engagement that Howe sought that might result in the capture or destruction of Washington's army. Howe and Washington might play cat and mouse forever. As long as Washington could fall back and in doing so draw on fresh supplies of manpower, no conclusion, Howe realized, could be reached.

Howe's plan brought home to the British cabinet more sharply than any event since the evacuation of Boston the true dimensions of the task they had undertaken. The general scheme was not new to the cabinet, but Howe's estimate of the number of troops required to effect the desired result was a severe blow nonetheless.

While waiting for the cabinet to act, Howe put in motion two parts of his plan. First he embarked three thousand men under General Clinton for Newport, Rhode Island. The principal consequence of Clinton's expedition was to delay the departure from Rhode Island of General Benjamin Lincoln with six thousand Massachusetts men recruited to fill up the gaps in Washington's army left by the expiration of enlistments.

Howe's second move was to send General Cornwallis and a force of 4,000 men into the interior of New Jersey. Cornwallis, having taken Fort Lee, turned his attention to Washington's remnant of an army. And remnant it was. Washington had left General Lee at North Castle Heights with 7,500 men, and Lee, forever dilatory, only crossed the Hudson to join Washington several weeks later. North of Lee, at Peekskill on the Hudson, Washington had left General Heath and his division, which on November 24 was reported as numbering 4,016 men. Washington's own army counted only 5,400 men fit for duty, and by December 1, returns by company and regiment showed a mere 4,334 men, of whom more than 1,000 were sick or absent.

Besides the desperate state of Washington's army, these figures suggest two things: one, the ravages of sickness and disease, worse enemies by far than the British; and inferentially, the wretched conditions of service in the Continental Army, where survival in garrison or camp was more doubtful than in the most severe battles. Under such conditions, it is little wonder that those whose enlistments were up were determined to return home. As Captain Ebenezer Huntington put it, ". . . the persuasion of a Cisaro would not any more effect their tarrying than the Niagara Falls would the kindling of a fire. . . ."

With so small a force, Washington had no hope of doing any more than delaying Cornwallis's penetration of New Jersey. Knowing that the area between the Hackensack and the Passaic rivers was a potential trap, Washington wisely withdrew across the Passaic not far ahead of Cornwallis's advance guard, which tried to prevent the destruction of the bridge. After a sharp fire fight, the Americans succeeded in demolishing it, and Cornwallis, without boats or pontoons in his baggage, was stymied for the moment.

Having crossed the river, Washington moved southwest along its right bank to Newark and then on the twenty-ninth of November, two days later, to New Brunswick on the south side of the Raritan. Cornwallis, boasting that he would catch Washington as a hunter does a fox, crossed the Passaic and came up with Washington at the Raritan—again almost in time to trap the American army, now shrunk to some 3,400 men. The German jaegers who made up the advance guard opened fire on the American rear guard, which was destroying the bridge over the Raritan, and drove them off before the work could be completed. But Cornwallis, who had pressed his men near the limit of their endurance on a forced march of twenty miles in the rain and over bad roads, had to rest his troops. Once more Washington narrowly escaped.

Washington was convinced by Cornwallis's activity that the British intended to push on and take the key city of Philadelphia at once. But there was little that Washington could do. His small army shrank continuously, neither General Lee nor General Heath showed up with his reinforcements, and the troops Washington did have were in dreadful shape. A New Jersey Tory assured Ambrose Serle that he had seen "about 2000 Rebels who had been picked up in Maryland for their Army, almost naked and the poorest Wretches that can be conceived, and that they stripped the Country as they went, not excepting the nasty Coverings of Negroes, of all the Blankets they could find."

One of the most unusual soldiers in the army that made its way by one narrow escape after another across New Jersey was Thomas Paine of the Pennsylvania Flying Camp. Paine's *Common Sense* had crystallized

American feeling against British authority in the symbolic person of the king and in favor of independence as no single other essay or address had. Now, serving as a volunteer assistant aide-de-camp to General Greene, Paine wrote the first of his "crisis papers," which was printed in the *Pennsylvania Journal* on December 19 and distributed to the soldiers in Washington's command. The essay opened with words that were like a bugle call. "These are the times that try men's souls," Paine wrote. "The Summer soldier and the sunshine patriot will, in this crisis, shrink from the service of his country; but he that stands by it now, deserves the love and thanks of man and woman. Tyranny, like hell, is not easily conquered; yet we have this consolation with us, that the harder the conflict the more glorious the triumph; what we obtain too cheap we esteem too lightly. . . . Heaven knows how to put a proper price on its goods; and it would be strange indeed if so celestial an article as Freedom should not be highly rated. . . . I have as little superstition in me as any man living, but my secret opinion has ever been, and still is, that God Almighty will not give up a people to military destruction, or leave them unsupportedly to perish, who have so earnestly and repeatedly sought to avoid the calamities of war by every decent method which wisdom could invent." Paine also had a word for George III, who, Paine said, had no more right to look to Heaven for support of his cause than "a common murderer, a highwayman or a house-breaker."

After tracing the painful story of the retreat from Fort Lee, in which he had participated, Paine, doubtless aware that some members of Congress were beginning to question Washington's leadership, ended his essay with warm praise of the general. "There is a natural firmness in some minds which cannot be unlocked by trifles, but which, when unlocked discovers a cabinet of fortitude; and I reckon it among those kind of public blessings which we do not immediately see, that God hath blessed [Washington] with uninterrupted health, and given him a mind that can even flourish upon care."

Meanwhile news that the British had taken New Brunswick caused a near panic in Philadelphia. Shops were closed up, schools dismissed, and "the streets filled with people fleeing to the country with their household possessions." Congress, to provide a good example, continued its sessions at the State House.

Leaving a small force at Princeton to delay his pursuers, Washington made for Trenton and the Delaware River, which he hoped to cross. Once at the Delaware, Washington rounded up all the boats he could from Philadelphia and along the river for seventy miles above the city.

He had left two brigades of one Delaware and five Virginia regiments under the command of Lord Stirling at Princeton. Having moved his supplies and baggage across the Delaware, Washington informed Congress that he intended to march back to Princeton in hopes of joining forces with General Lee. Advancing toward Princeton, Washington met Stirling, who had been forced out of Princeton by the arrival of Cornwallis's vastly superior force, and the Americans again fell back to Trenton and crossed the river on December 8. Cornwallis, usually expeditious in his movements, waited at Princeton for seventeen hours, thus giving Washington precious time to cross the river. But it still seemed that nothing could stop the progress of the British toward Philadelphia. That at least was the conclusion of Congress, and that body departed with almost indecent haste for Baltimore.

Again the British had arrived at the instant that the last elements of the American army had crossed a river barrier. Once over the river, Washington deployed his army along the Delaware from Burlington to Coryell's Fairy, a distance of almost fifty miles. Against such an overextended defense, Howe and Cornwallis would have had little difficulty making a crossing and seizing Philadelphia. Instead, Howe held Cornwallis on the northern bank of the Delaware and announced that his troops would go into winter quarters, "the weather having become too severe to keep the field." The campaign in New Jersey was at an end, at least for the moment.

Howe's decision was, of course, a reprieve for Washington. His principal task was now to try to find Lee and his force and to drum up still more reinforcements. He had sent orders to General Schuyler on the twenty-sixth of November to send all the Jersey and Pennsylvania troops in the Northern Department to Pennsylvania, but this force was nowhere in sight. Washington's frame of mind is indicated by a letter to his brother Lund, which, after describing the condition of the army, ends: "A large part of the Jerseys have given every proof of disaffection that they can do, and this part of Pennsylvania are equally inimical. In short, your imagination can scarce extend to a situation more distressing than mine. Our only dependence is now upon the speedy enlistment of a new army. If this fails, I think the game will be pretty well up, as, from disaffection and want of spirit and fortitude, the inhabitants, instead of resistance, are offering submission and taking protection from Gen. Howe in Jersey."

Howe visited Cornwallis's headquarters and expressed much pleasure in that officer's initiative. "I cannot too much commend Lord

Cornwallis' good service during this campaign," he wrote; "and particu-larly the ability and conduct he displayed in the pursuit of the enemy from Fort Lee to Trenton, a distance exceeding 80 miles, in which he was well supported by the ardor of his troops, who cheerfully quitted their tents and heavy baggage, as impediments to their march." Having bestowed this accolade on Cornwallis, Howe retired to his comfortable headquarters—and an obliging mistress—in New York.

The forces in New Jersey, made up of both British and Hessian troops, established their winter encampments in several villages that formed a line running roughly north and south, including Bordentown, New Brunswick, and Trenton, right across the Delaware from Washing-ton's headquarters. The third Waldeck regiment and Von Lossberg's Hessian regiment were stationed in Elizabethtown, where the Waldeck chaplain was impressed by "the fine taste of the people here. The inside of the houses the decorations of the rooms, and the fine carpets which are fitted for all the rooms and corridors showed us that the Americans do not lack, at least in this province, artists and fine pieces of good workmanship. I believe that these fine woodwork articles surpass all others I have seen." The chaplain, a Lutheran minister, preached on Sunday in the "English church." "Our officers," he noted, "invited the women of the community to our service; the latter brought along many other inhabitants of the area. Many of these people had longed to go to church because since last summer they had had neither a preacher or divine service. . . . We celebrated the holy birth of Christ in the peace we had so long desired."

So the British and the Hessians, snug and comfortable in houses abandoned by the rebels or requisitioned by the army, or simply moving in with hospitable Tory families, settled down for the winter.

As soon as Washington learned that Howe had returned to New York and that the British and Hessians had gone into winter quarters, he began to make plans for an attack upon one of the British encamp-ments. He was emboldened by the arrival of the reinforcements he had asked of General Schuyler. Led by General Horatio Gates and Colonel Benedict Arnold, three regiments from Ticonderoga arrived in Wash-ington's Delaware River encampments. Gates, a British-born Virginian with whom Washington had served during the French and Indian War, was a tireless self-promoter, more interested in his own career than in fighting for Independence. But at least he did bring his troops, bor-rowed from the Northern Department, to Washington's aid as ordered, which is more than could be said for General Lee, who was still missing.

On December 14, Washington wrote to Governor Trumbull of Connecticut: "The troops that came down from Ticonderoga with Arnold and Gates, may in conjunction with my present force, and that under General Lee, enable us to attempt a stroke upon the forces of the enemy who lay a good deal scattered, and to all appearances in a state of security. A lucky blow in this quarter would be fatal to them, and would most certainly raise the spirits of the people which are quite sunk by our late misfortunes."

But Lee, despite the exhortations of Reed and Washington, lingered on in a comfortable mansion at Peekskill, where he had established his headquarters. There he lavished on his pack of yapping little dogs more attention than he did on his cold and hungry troops. Hinting at various plans for expeditions against the enemy, he came very close to insubordination. To remain at Peekskill when Washington so desperately needed every man who could carry a musket was hardly the part of a bold and resolute soldier. When Lee finally did begin his march to meet Washington, he was as slow in his movements as he had been in obeying the general's instructions to join him. Instead of heading for the Trenton area, across from which Washington had established his headquarters, he went to Morristown, from where he wrote Washington stating that since "I am assured you are very strong, I should imagine we can make a better impression by hanging on [the British] rear . . . It will annoy, distract and weaken 'em." When Washington got this curious message, he replied immediately urging Lee to "join me with all your whole force with all possible expedition." Washington's situation was "directly opposite to what you suppose it to be." Every available soldier was needed.

Knowing the seriousness of Washington's position, Lee still delayed, and on December 13 at Basking Ridge, just a few miles from Morristown, he wrote to Horatio Gates criticizing his commanding general for the loss of Fort Washington. *"Entre nous,"* he added, "a certain great man is most damnably deficient." Lee then enumerated for Gates his own problems: "I have neither guides Cavalry Medicines Money Shoes or Stockings . . . Tories are in my front rear and on my flanks . . . in short unless something which I do not expect turns up We are lost."

Reviewing Lee's actions and statements, it is hard not to conclude that he wished at all costs to avoid joining Washington's depleted army, and there are certainly grounds for strong suspicion that Lee, believing Washington's situation hopeless and the general himself incompetent, was waiting only for the destruction of that army and the death or capture of Washington to become himself commander in chief, a position that Congress must, he felt, inevitably bestow on him.

But a different fate was in store for Lee. Before another letter from Washington could reach Basking Ridge, Lee was captured by a cavalry reconnaissance of the Queen's Light Dragoons. The officer in charge of the main British force had placed a young subaltern, Banastre Tarleton, in command of an advance party of six troopers. The little detachment headed for Morristown, where it was rumored General Lee had his headquarters. The British were told by friendly Tories that Lee was only a few miles away at White's Tavern. Tarleton's men, pressing forward, caught two American sentries by surprise. "The dread of instant death," Tarleton later wrote, "obliged these fellows to inform me . . . of the situation of General Lee. They told us he was about a mile off, that his guard was not very large and that he was about half a mile in the rear of his army."

Armed with this information and some more specific intelligence extracted from a captured American courier who, indeed, pointed out the tavern in which Lee was staying, the British rushed the building. Lee had spent the morning squabbling with officers of the Connecticut light horse, ridiculing their old-fashioned wigs and speaking contemptuously of their troops. It was ten o'clock in the morning before the general and his staff sat down to a delayed breakfast, the general without his wig and still wearing his dressing gown. Captain Wilkinson, a member of Lee's staff, was gazing out the window when, to his stupefaction, he saw British mounted dragoons galloping down the driveway. "Here, Sir," Wilkinson cried, "are the British cavalry."

"Where?" the startled Lee asked.

The answer came in the form of shots fired by the British cavalrymen. "Where is the guard?—damn the guard, why don't they fire?" Lee said. Then, turning to Wilkinson. "Do, Sir, see what has become of the guard."

Meanwhile Tarleton, ordering his men to fire into the building, called out that he knew Lee was within and, in Tarleton's own words, "that if he would surrender himself, he and his attendants should be safe, but if my summons was not complied with immediately, the house should be burnt and every person without exception should be put to the sword." At this point Tarleton discovered that Lee was attempting to escape with his staff through the back door. In the fight that followed, the staff officers were killed or wounded and Lee himself captured. It was a brilliant and daring action by the British. They, of course, were delighted to have captured one of the highest-ranking officers of the American army and especially the Irish-born Lee, a turncoat and traitor in British eyes. For the Americans it was a blessing in disguise that they did not readily penetrate. They believed Lee's capture a terrible misfortune, hardly less of a blow than the loss of Forts Washington and Lee.

Washington, who had put up so patiently with Lee's intransigence and disobedience, confined himself to one brief observation: "It was by his own folly and imprudence, and without a view to effect any good that he was taken." General Sullivan, who succeeded Lee, at least knew how to obey orders. Sullivan marched to the Delaware, crossed the river at Phillipsburg, and came down to join Washington at last.

9

Trenton

WHILE the British and Hessians luxuriated in cozy winter quarters, Washington's army, camped in the open on the western bank of the Delaware River, kept warm and fed as best it could. Despite the desperately ragged shape of his suffering troops, Washington plotted one of the most daring strikes against the enemy of this—or any—war.

Washington also did a multitude of jobs to get his force into some semblance of fighting trim. Congress had fled from Philadelphia to Baltimore at the near approach of British troops, but before its departure it had passed a very useful act: *"Resolved:* that until Congress shall otherwise order, General Washington be possessed of full power to order and direct all things relative to the department and to the operations of the war." In short, Congress gave Washington dictatorial powers. Washington replied to the Congress, assuring the members that he would not misuse his new powers. "Instead of thinking myself freed from all *civil* obligations, I shall constantly bear in mind that, as the sword was the last resort for the preservation of our liberty, so it ought to be the first thing laid aside when those liberties are finally established. . . . I shall instantly set about making the most necessary reforms of the army." In the same vein, Washington wrote Congress on December 20, "I can only say that desperate diseases require desperate remedies; and I with truth declare that I have no lust after power, but I wish with as much fervency as any man upon this wide-extended continent for an opportunity of turning the sword into the ploughshare." Washington was always aware that history provided many examples of generals going on to be military dictators. He wanted to be certain that Congress did not suspect him of any such aim.

The powers Congress bestowed upon Washington before parting from Philadelphia provided the general with an opportunity he was not slow to use. In addition to requisitioning all the militia he could summon as well as all arms and able-bodied patriots willing to bear them, he fired off requests for more soldiers and more money to every provincial assembly within range and offered commissions to "any good officers" who were able "to raise men upon continental pay and establishment." He ordered the recruiting of three battalions of artillery, and he directed Major Sheldon of Connecticut, his only officer with cavalry experience, to collect a battalion of six troops of horse and furnished him with fourteen thousand dollars to carry out his assignment. Washington also issued an order "requiring all able bodied men in [Philadelphia], not conscientiously scrupulous about bearing arms, to report in the State House yard the next day with their arms and equipments." All who had arms "which they can not or do not mean to employ in the defense of America" were ordered to turn them over to an agent of the army who would pay for them; the order continued, "those who are convicted of secreting any arms or accoutrements will be severely punished."

But Washington was not content to sit and wait for arms and enlistments to come in. It is a striking indication of his aggressive temperament that when he heard that the British were repairing and rebuilding bridges below Trenton, his first thought was how he might make use of them to harass his pursuers. He divided the river-line defenses into three divisions. Light earthworks were to be built opposite ferries and places where easy crossings might be made by the British. In addition, guard posts were established at intervals, and contact was maintained among these by constant patrolling. Rendezvous areas were designated in case of an attempted crossing at a weakly held point. Three days' rations were to be kept on hand at all times, and the boats in the hands of the Americans were to be kept ready for use. The artillery was distributed to cover the points most likely to receive an enemy attack.

Howe had excellent intelligence from Tory spies. They gave him

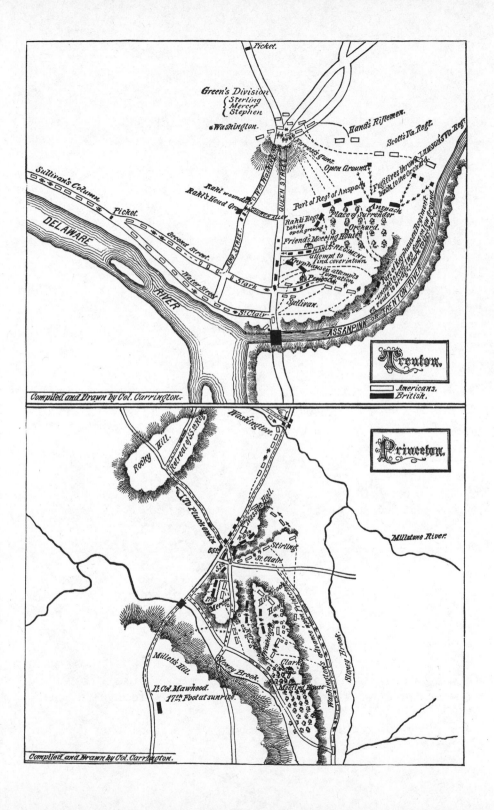

Picket.

Green's Division
Sterling
Mercer
Stephen

Washington.

Hand's Riflemen.

Scott's Va. Regt.

Forrest's guns.

Open Ground.

Lawson's Va. Regt.

Rahl wounded.
Rahl's Head Qrs.

Fugitives thrown
back to the Orchard.

Part of Regt. of Anspach

Anspach

Rahl's Regt.
taking
open ground

Place of Surrender

Orchard

Friends' Meeting House

RAHL REGIMENT
Attempt to
reform and
cover town

Knyphausen's
attempts
formation
Prospect.

Part of Knyphausen Regiment
unable to hold two guns on low ground
en route to bridge, and drove back by St. Clair.

Stark

Sullivan

St. Clair

SULLIVAN'S COLUMN

Picket.

DELAWARE

Second Street.

Water Street.

RIVER

ASSANPINK or TRENTON RIVER

Trenton.

Americans.
British.

Compiled and Drawn by Col. Carrington.

Washington.

Rocky Hill.

Retreat of 55 Regts.

Princeton.

Millstone River.

Ld. Pluckemin.

Nassau Hall.

Stirling

65th

St. Clair.

55th

Mercer

High school

Hand

Princeton Avenue

Washington's Advance on Princeton

Stony Brook.

Miller's Hill.

Stony Brook.

Clark

Meeting House.

Lt. Col. Mawhood.
17th Foot at sunrise.

Compiled and Drawn by Col. Carrington.

with surprising accuracy the number of Washington's troops, their location, what defensive positions they occupied, the number of pieces of artillery attached to each unit, and a Tory's perception of the state of the men's morale. It could be argued, indeed, that Howe was a victim of the accuracy of his intelligence sources. Every report confirmed the picture of an army depleted in numbers, wretchedly clothed and equipped, near the end of its period of enlistment, and powerless to take any aggressive action. If Howe had had no intelligence at all, he might have been better off. Then, as a well-trained soldier, he would have insisted on those precautions—ceaseless patrolling, round-the-clock guard duty, and so forth—that any army must take when on campaign against a resolute and resourceful enemy.

Washington also had good intelligence, which told him that the enemy forces were divided up in small units all over New Jersey. His best spy was one Pomeroy, who on this, as on a number of other occasions, proved to have excellent eyes and ears. Pomeroy reported to Joseph Reed in Bristol, south of Trenton, and Reed in turn wrote to Washington. "Pomeroy, whom I sent by your order to go to Amboy, and on through the Jerseys, and round about Princeton to you, returned to Burlington yesterday." In Burlington County, Pomeroy found the Hessians "scattered through the farmers' houses, eight, ten, twelve and fifteen in a house, and rambling over the whole country."

Washington had already decided to undertake a raid in force. The only question to be decided was its objective. But of 10,000 men carried on the rolls of Washington's own army, only about 4,700 were fit for duty. However, he had some 1,200 men from the Northern Department under Gates, Cadwalader's Pennsylvania militia in the number of 1,800 men, and Sullivan's division with 3,000. The total of effectives was nearly 9,000. On December 23, Washington sent word to Reed that he planned to launch an attack against Trenton on Christmas night, striking the Hessian garrison one hour before dawn on the twenty-sixth. "For Heaven's sake," Washington wrote, "keep this to yourself, as the discovery of it may prove fatal to us; our numbers, sorry am I to say, being less than I had any conception of; but necessity, dire necessity, will, nay must, justify the attack." Washington's instructions to Reed at Bristol directed him to attack as many of the nearby British posts as he could, since "the more we can attack at the same instant, the more confusion we shall spread, and the greater good will result from it."

Perhaps the principal "necessity" that Washington felt was that on December 31 the terms of most of the enlisted men in Washington's army would expire. After January 1, no more than two thousand soldiers would remain—plus, of course, those who might be persuaded to re-enlist. Washington was also convinced that as soon as the Delaware was frozen over solidly, Howe would resume his campaign against Philadelphia. Better to strike Howe's force suddenly than wait for Howe to take the initiative.

Washington's soldiers were issued three days' cooked cold rations. These and their blankets and muskets were all they were to carry. Every precaution was taken to see that no one crossed the river without the express permission of an officer. The success of the raid depended, as Washington wrote Reed, on complete surprise. Spying and informing were so common that only the barrier of the river, which could be closely guarded, prevented deserters or Tories from passing over to the British and Hessians with word that the Americans were preparing to launch some kind of an offensive movement.

Washington, with that flair for the dramatic that he occasionally showed, issued the password for December 25: "Victory or Death."

The garrison at Trenton consisted of the Hessian regiments of Von Lossberg, Knyphausen, and Rall, along with fifty chasseurs and twenty light dragoons—a force of almost fifteen hundred men with six pieces of artillery, two placed in front of Colonel Rall's headquarters. Trenton itself was protected by no fortifications or defensive works of any kind. Rall had rebuffed several attempts to persuade him to fortify the town. He was reported to have said to an engineer officer sent by Von Donop at Bordentown (whose own security was imperiled by Rall's cavalier attitude), " . . . only let them come on! We'll meet them with the bayonet." Rall was a hell-for-leather officer who reportedly had asked for the most advanced post as the position of honor.

Rall's officers took a more serious view of the matter than their commander. Those in the Von Lossberg regiment drew up a letter to General Von Heister, urging that Trenton be properly fortified. But to take the simplest precautions seemed to Rall to be little better than cowardice. Yet despite Washington's precautions rumors persisted that the Americans intended to make an attack. General Thomas Leslie, who was in command at Princeton, sent word to Rall that Washington was preparing to cross the Delaware.

Then, on December 25, a company of Virginians made an attack on the guards at the north end of Trenton, wounded six Germans, and quickly withdrew. The Virginians had been dispatched by Adam Stephen, a fellow officer with Washington in the French and Indian War.

Stephen's action was typical of his mercurial and insubordinate nature. When word of the foray reached Washington, he turned on Stephen in a rage. "You, sir," he declared, "may have ruined all my plans by putting them on guard."

Instead of being alarmed by this bold incursion, Rall chose to consider it the rumored attack and, as such, evidence that the British were unduly concerned about American intentions. "These country clowns cannot whip us," he is reported to have said. Certainly if the Americans had been planning an attack in any force, they would not have dispatched a small raiding party to alert the enemy. Rall's only response was to reinforce the guard post on the Pennington Road west of Trenton to a total of some twenty-five men. Christmas night in Trenton was devoted to revelry, to drinking and singing by both officers and men. The next day, a bitterly cold winter morning, those who tumbled out of their quarters for the usual morning formation at eight o'clock were sleepy and soon returned to bed to continue their interrupted sleep.

Washington ordered General Samuel Griffin, with a small force of militia, to create a diversion against Von Donop's force at Bordentown. General James Ewing, with a brigade of five hundred men, was assigned the task of crossing the river just below Trenton and cutting off communication with Bordentown to the south. Cadwalader was to carry his men over the river at Bristol, south of Bordentown, and be prepared to attack Von Donop's regiment if the opportunity presented itself. Washington took personal command of the left wing of the American army, comprised of the divisions under Greene and Sullivan, some 2,400 men, that would cross nine miles above Trenton at McKonkey's Ferry. General Putnam, stationed at Philadelphia, had instructions to come over the river with 1,000 men to help Cadwalader roll up the left bank of the Delaware.

The men, poorly clothed and in consequence half-frozen, started out on the twenty-fifth in a violent storm. Thomas Rodney, a captain in the Delaware militia, wrote that it was "as severe a night as I ever saw—the frost was sharp, the current difficult to stem, the ice increasing, the wind high and at eleven it began to snow." Greene's and Sullivan's divisions formed up under the cover of the high ground behind McKonkey's Ferry. Several days of mild weather had broken up the ice that had formed on the river, but the hard freeze was beginning to thicken a new skin of ice on the Delaware sheathing the boats, the oars, and the oarlocks in an icy coating and impeding the movement across the river.

At Bristol Cadwalader found it impossible to get his artillery across and, after a half-hearted effort, withdrew, assuming that Washington would cancel the attack on Trenton because of the weather.

Included in the force under Washington's command were both veterans of Bunker Hill and raw recruits. John Stark, who had had his hours of glory at the rail fence below Bunker Hill, was in that benumbed company. John Glover, whose Marblehead amphibians had done such a heroic job in the evacuation of Long Island, was there, along with William Washington, the general's nephew. Young James Monroe, still a Princeton undergraduate, commanded a rifle company. In the tattered, footsore band were, in addition to the most experienced and able American generals, John Marshall, a first lieutenant of the Fifteenth Virginia regiment, Alexander Hamilton, commanding a battery of Knox's artillery, and Aaron Burr, a veteran of Arnold's march to Quebec.

Each phase of the attack had its own hardships that bore cruelly on the soldiers. First there was the long wait, hour after tedious hour, while the army assembled at the point of embarkation and the boats were brought down the river. Soldiers are used to waiting, but the biting wind and falling temperature left the men stamping their feet on the crisp snow and huddling in their blankets, trying to preserve some spark of warmth. The river crossing itself was laborious and dangerous; the men crouched down together for what warmth they might accumulate, but they were lashed by wind and a spray that froze on their blankets, on the muskets they clutched in numb hands, on their eyebrows and hair. The snow, when it began to fall, brought a slight rise in the temperature, but it cut visibility to a few feet and made it extremely difficult to maintain contact between units and even among men in the same unit.

The crossing was the most difficult phase of the attack. The boats used were freshwater freighters, cargo boats that normally carried iron, grain or whiskey. They were some sixty feet in length and eight feet wide, on the average, with a shallow draft of slightly more than two feet. They were pointed at both ends, propelled downstream by oars and upstream by poles. A single boat could hold one of Washington's depleted regiments. On the night of December 25, the boats were manned by Glover's amphibians.

The Delaware at McKonkey's Ferry was about 300 yards wide and chock-full this night of large slabs of ice that were borne on the swift current. "The floating ice in the river," Colonel Knox wrote, "made the labor almost incredible." But "perseverance accomplished what at first seemed impossible," and 187 pieces of artillery under the direction of Colonel Knox were ferried across. As snow and later sleet fell, the artillery came to be of paramount importance. Few men would be able to keep their powder dry. It was much easier to fire a cannon than a musket in wet weather.

Complex military movements are seldom completed on schedule. It was Washington's intention to be over the Delaware by midnight and to be in position to attack Trenton at dawn. But it was three o'clock in the morning before the artillery had crossed, and it was four, only some two hours until daybreak, before the soldiers were formed up on the east bank of the Delaware, ready to begin the final approach to Trenton. The Americans could not expect to be ready to attack at dawn, and the chances of the Hessian garrison discovering them were thereby greatly increased. But it was too late, by the same token, to turn back. The three-hour delay filled Washington with anxiety. He despaired "of surprising the town, as I well knew we could not reach it before day was fairly broke. But," he added, in a letter informing Congress of the action, "as I was certain there was no making a retreat without being discovered and harassed on repassing the river, I determined to push on at all events." So Washington went ahead, ordering Stirling's brigade, which had been the first to cross, to move off toward the town of Pennington. From there Stirling's men were to move down the Pennington Road to Trenton, roughly parallel to the River Road and converging with it at Trenton.

Washington was disheartened to hear that Cadwalader had turned back and that Putnam had abandoned the attempt to cross the Delaware below Bristol. It was actually fortunate, however, in view of the three-hour delay, that the two divisions to the south had not had the tenacity to persevere in the face of the storm. Had they managed to get over the river and to attack the Hessians at Burlington and Bordentown, they might have alerted the garrison at Trenton and thus have destroyed any hope of surprise in that quarter.

The main part of the army picked up the road to Trenton a mile and a half from the ferry at a tiny village called Bear Tavern. It was three miles from there to the town of Birmingham. There Sullivan sent word to Washington that in spite of all efforts to keep the firing pans dry, the arms of the men were wet and would not fire. "Tell your General," Washington told the messenger who brought this word, "to use the bayonet and penetrate into the town. The town must be taken. I am resolved to take it."

818 / A NEW AGE NOW BEGINS

At Birmingham the force led by Washington himself split off from Greene's division, branching to the left and moving cross-country to the Scotch Road, which joined the Pennington Road four miles from the outskirts of Trenton. It is a formidable task at best to move even a well-trained and well-staffed army at night under such weather conditions over unfamiliar terrain. To find the right route, to avoid false turns, interminable delays, and the loss of contact at some critical juncture requires both skill and luck. It requires, above all, careful and detailed planning, and this was the greater part of Washington's genius. It was not remarkable that the army found itself three hours late; what was remarkable was that under the worst possible conditions Washington had managed to get it across the river and, having passed that formidable barrier, was able to march on to Trenton. What made the achievement all the more remarkable was that it had to be conducted as silently as possible and with a minimum of light. For a time, some light was allowed. Artillery pieces, which were at the head of the long columns of men, had torches "stuck in the exhalters [which] sparkled and blazed in the storm all night . . ." and served as beacons to draw the little army forward on its laborious march. But at Birmingham Washington ordered even these lights extinguished, and from then until the first light of dawn the army marched in darkness.

Shortly after dawn, Washington halted the column and rode down the long line of shivering men exhorting and encouraging them. "Soldiers," he repeated, as he rode along, "keep by your officers. For God's sake, keep by your officers." Elisha Bostwick of the Seventh Connecticut Regiment remembered that the words were spoken "in a deep and solemn voice."

From McKonkey's Ferry to Trenton was a distance of at least nine miles. Stirling, whose division had to advance to the Pennington Road, added thereby another two or three miles to his march. In daylight, under normal conditions, an average unit may be expected to cover some three miles an hour. Cold, exhausted, half-blinded by sleet and snow and chilled to the bone, stumbling on frozen, often bloody feet over the rutted, uneven roads, Washington's army managed to cover the nine miles in something less than four hours. Some of the men, at the end of their resources, fell out and tried to find some shelter from the storm. Lieutenant Joshua Orne dropped into a ditch and was soon almost covered with snow; fortunately, someone in the rear of the column saw him and dragged him to his feet. Two privates who were not so fortunate froze to death where they fell.

The officer in command of the Hessian sentries, Lieutenant Andreas Wiederhold, had drawn in his pickets just after dawn because of the severity of the weather. They were huddled in a hut that served as a guardhouse. A spy had identified the hut for Washington on a map, and as Washington, peering through the snow and mist, sighted the hut, Wiederhold stepped to the door to look out. What he saw was Americans less than fifty yards away. He called out, "Der Feind! Heraus!" The guard tumbled out and, seeing that it was heavily outnumbered, fired and fell back. Three minutes later Sullivan's division hit the enemy outpost at the south end of Trenton. [The axis of the town ran almost due north and south.] The Hessian sentries and the guard that supported them did not panic. They withdrew, calling the alarm and firing as they went; but the north wind blew rain and sleet in their faces, and they could hardly see the misty shapes of the advancing Americans. Washington, with the forward elements, noted that "from their motions, they seemed undetermined how to act." They were trained to fight in formations as rigidly prescribed as the steps of the minuet, to respond to orders like well-trained automatons. On this morning, orders were random and confused; with men mixed helter-skelter from various regiments, with many officers cut off from their men, the reassuring formations could not be formed. Meantime, Rall, hearing the firing, came to the window of his headquarters in his nightshirt and called out to an officer in the yard, "What's the matter?" When Rall was dressed, Wiederhold reported to him that a large force of Americans seemed to be attacking the town and to have sealed off all avenues of escape.

Beginning at Front Street, by the river, King Street and Queen Street ran north, parallel to each other, to the Princeton Road, which veered off to the right, and the Pennington Road, which turned left (and northwest). As the advance units of Greene's division drove in the sentries on the Pennington Road at the north end of town, General Hugh Mercer's brigade filed off to the right of their line of march and took positions west of King Street, slightly behind Rall's own headquarters, to block egress from that side of town. The regiments under the command of Greene crossed the northern terminus of King Street, Queen Street, and another long parallel street, Quaker Lane, and deployed to close off the east side of the town. Stirling meanwhile placed his force at the point where the Pennington-Princeton road juncture intersected with King and Queen streets.

The dispositions of the eighteen artillery pieces ferried across the river with such labor was important. Four pieces were to be at the head of each column and three at the head of each division. two pieces with each of the reserves. This allocation had been only roughly observed. As the fighting began Henry Knox, in his first close infantry combat, thought "the hurry, fright and confusion of the enemy was not unlike that which will be when the last trump shall sound." Knox's cannon were placed in position at the head of King and Queen streets to command both those thoroughfares.

Captain Hamilton, seeing several of the Hessian cannon being wheeled into position by artillery horses, directed the fire of his brass six-pounders toward them and saw two horses drop on one gun and three on another; they thrashed about in the bloody snow. Eight members of the Hessian gun crew were wounded or killed, but the survivors still managed to fire six rounds from one cannon before they were overrun by Americans led by Captain William Washington and Lieutenant James Monroe. The fighting swirled through the town, often hand-to-hand, as the Americans pursued the Hessians with bayonets and clubbed muskets.

At the south of the town, Sullivan's force blocked the bridge. One of Sullivan's artillery sergeants described the action in these words: "We had our cannon placed before a bridge. . . . The enemy came on in solid columns . . . then by given signal, we all fired together. . . . The enemy retreated. . . . Our whole artillery was again discharged at them—they retreated again and formed. . . . We loaded with cannister shot and let them come nearer. We fired altogether again and such destruction it made, you cannot conceive—the bridge looked red as blood, with their killed and wounded and their red coats. The enemy beat a retreat. . . ."

Glover's brigade, which had performed such notable services in carrying the army across the Delaware, was in the van of Sullivan's division and drove directly into the southern edge of the town. Here they caught the soldiers of Rall's regiment trying to escape to the east. Greene's men had by this time taken up their positions, and the Hessians were caught between the crossfire of Glover's men in their rear and Greene's regiments in front of them. One large group of Hessians, quartered at the southern end of the town, fled toward the Assunpink Creek bridge and the road to Bordentown. The bridge across the Assunpink Creek was still open, and through this gap a few hundred fleeing Hessians instinctively found their way, like water through the hole in a dike. But these were virtually the only ones to escape. Glover started to pursue the Hessians and then, thinking better of it, put his two guns in position on high ground south of the creek, closing off this last avenue of escape. Knyphausen's men, retreating in some semblance of order, found Glover's men covering the bridge and turned right along the riverbank, where Arthur St. Clair's brigade trapped them in a bog with their backs to the creek. Glover's artillery began to fire on them from the opposite shore. At this point most of the men of Knyphausen's regiment threw down their arms and surrendered, a few making their escape across the creek.

The Americans by now had possession of the center of the town, but Colonel Rall, advised by a junior officer that the Americans could be driven out by a determined assault, rallied a portion of his own regiment and led them back toward the town. Knox, who had taken charge of several abandoned Hessian guns, had them trained on an orchard where Rall's regiment had taken refuge. As soon as the Hessians reappeared, Knox opened fire with grape and cannister with devastating results. Rall himself was mortally wounded, and his men turned and fled. "The poor fellows," Knox wrote his wife, "after they were formed on the plain saw themselves completely surrounded, the only recourse left was to force their way through numbers unknown to them. . . . They did not relish the idea of forcing, and were obliged to surrender upon the spot, with all their artillery, six brass pieces, army colors etc. . . ." "Providence," Knox added, quite accurately, "seems to have smiled upon every part of this enterprise. It must give sensible pleasure to every friend of the rights of man."

As Washington was directing that cannon be aimed at a group of Hessians collecting in a field beyond the town, an officer rode up to him to announce, "Sir, they have struck."

"Struck?"

"Yes. Their colors are down!"

Washington wiped off his field glasses, looked at the brightly colored figures standing out so sharply in the snow-covered field, and replied, "So they are." As he moved through town to make contact with Sullivan's division, another horseman brought word that Knyphausen's Hessians bogged down in the marsh southeast of the town had also surrendered. Washington's famous reserve cracked; he gave an exultant cry; "This is a glorious day for our country." When the Hessians were herded together, there seemed to be too many to count. Finally there was a rough tally: 920. The Americans, astonishingly, had no dead, except of course the frozen on the march, and only a few wounded, among them James Monroe and William Washington. William Washington and Monroe had been leading the charge against the Hessian cannon in King Street when both had been wounded by musket balls.

One of the victorious Americans gave a brief resume of the battle: "Hessian population of Trenton at 8 A.M., 1,408 men and 39 officers; Hessian population at 9 A.M.,—0. The difference is accounted for thus:—Hessians killed 22; wounded 84; taken prisoner, including the wounded, 918; fled 507. Officers killed or captured: one colonel [Rall their commander, who was killed], two lieutenant-colonels, three majors, four captains, eight lieutenants."

Washington thought seriously of pursuing the fleeing Hessians and trying to scoop up the Hessian regiments in Bordentown and Burlington. Since Cadwalader and Putnam had faltered, he would try to repair their failures by pushing down the east bank of the Delaware. He called a council of war to discuss the plan, but his weary officers knew that the men were near the limit of their endurance. They could not be counted upon to go farther. Some had already ferreted out the Hessian brandy supplies and were drunk, and others had fallen asleep in the nearest shelter. A group of ingenious soldiers had found a barrel of whiskey and a barrel of sugar in an abandoned cellar. They poured the contents into a rain barrel, stirred the punch, so the story went, with a fence rail, and drank the potion out of their shoes—which indicated that there were at least some pieces of footwear in the army without holes.

Washington was nevertheless tempted to continue until his staff pointed out that a delay of even a few days might make it difficult if not impossible to get back across the Delaware. Cornwallis could be counted upon to be down like a wolf on the fold as soon as word of the disaster at Trenton reached him. So, reluctantly, Washington acceded. The tipsy were sobered up as best as they could be, the sleeping were roused out of their warm beds, and the army began its march back to the boats at McKonkey's Ferry, carrying with it almost a thousand Hessians, six brass artillery pieces, a thousand muskets, and as much supplies as could be loaded into available wagons. The captured regimental flags of Rall's, Knyphausen's, Von Lossberg's, and the Anspach regiments snapped gaily in the chill air.

The march back to McKonkey's ferry took place under conditions far less severe than those of the preceeding night and morning, but it was, nonetheless, an ordeal for the weary men and their officers. The best evidence of the bitterness of the weather was to be found in the fact that a number of the soldiers and officers who made that dreadful march never fully recovered their health. Stirling himself was invalided for weeks, and rheumatic and respiratory diseases haunted many others. Once more Glover's amphibians ferried the exhausted soldiers across the Delaware, Washington waiting at the ferry until the last contingent of soldiers was loaded into the broad-beamed boats.

On the way back across the river, the boats became so encrusted with ice that they became almost unmanageable, and Glover's boatmen began stamping on the planking to break the ice loose. In the boats carrying the Hessian prisoners, they were instructed to join in, "and they all set to jumping at once with their cues flying up and down." In such fashion was the ice jarred loose, to the entertainment of the American soldiers who observed the scene.

On the twenty-seventh, unaware that Washington had returned over the Delaware, Cadwalader crossed over from Bristol with eighteen hundred men (the river was so far frozen that the soldiers had to walk the last hundred yards to the Jersey shore on the ice) and moved on Bordentown, where he expected to find Von Donop and his Hessians. But Von Donop, on hearing of Rall's death and the capture of the garrison at Trenton, had felt himself too vulnerable to remain in Bordentown. He departed posthaste, leaving most of his stores as well as his sick and wounded behind. Generals Ewing and Mifflin followed Cadwalader with five hundred and eight hundred men respectively, but the Hessians had already abandoned their posts at Mount Holly and Black Horse and were headed for the comparative safety of Amboy. When the Hessians at Elizabethtown heard the news of Trenton, the Waldeck regiment's chaplain wrote: "Our pleasure in Elizabethtown is over. One can no longer go to sleep without thinking this night is the last of your freedom. Previously we had been accustomed to undressing every night for bed. Now, however, it is just the opposite. We go to bed completely clothed, for we are to be ready for battle."

Though unpursued, the British and Hessians everywhere took alarm. It was almost as though they had been frightened by the ghost of an army. So unthinkable, so sudden, and so devastating had Washington's attack been that the British, from feeling utter contempt for his ragged legions, now imagined them everywhere, magically transported now to this spot, now to that.

The captured Hessians were paraded through Philadelphia as a practical demonstration of the fact that they were human after all.

"From the general to the common soldier," Thomas Rudney noted, they "curse and imprecate the war, and swear they were sent here to be slaughtered."

The attack on Trenton reminds us of several important facts. Perhaps the most important was simply Washington's physical stamina. Where any ordinary man would have long since come to the end of his rope both emotionally and physically, Washington was still completely in command of himself and of his army. In terms of endurance, it was one of the most remarkable performances by a general in all military history. For weeks, without rest or respite, he had carried on under the most discouraging and exhausting circumstances, scraped together an army, planned strategy, and attended to those myriad details upon which the success of the simplest military operation largely rests. He did much the greater part of the work that a trained professional staff performed for his counterpart, General Howe. By an act of his will, he drove a pathetic remnant of an army through the most desperate venture of the war and on to the most dazzling victory. By doing so, he saved his army, or what was left of it; he discomfited his domestic enemies, or at least those who had lost confidence in him and wished to see him replaced by General Lee; and thus undoubtedly he saved himself and, in saving himself, saved the army of which he had become, increasingly, the embodiment.

Of Washington's entire plan, it can be said that it was too complicated and extended over too large an area, where, events were to prove, effective liaison was almost impossible. Fortunately the storm, which so impeded the movement of his own army, turned back the less determined Cadwalader, who could not imagine any more than the Hessians at Trenton that a general would march out in such cruel weather. Washington was thereby saved from the possible effects of his too-ambitious strategy.

In addition to the storm and the failure of Cadwalader and Ewing to get across the river the night of December 25–26, there was the raid of the Virginians, which, instead of alerting Rall, had convinced him that the rumor of a large-scale attack was based on this small party and had thus further increased his complacency. Also, if Washington had arrived earlier, he might have encountered the Hessians being called out for reveille. As it was, they had answered that formation and had returned to bed. But as it is often and truly said, aggressive leadership "forces the breaks." Washington succeeded in large part because he did what no British or Hessians thought he could possibly do. He drew his wretched, disintegrating little army together and counterattacked the enemy under the most exacting conditions. Thus he made his own luck, and nothing can dim the luster of his generalship in this critical hour. The capture of the Hessians at Trenton took its place at once alongside the great military feats in history.

One thing more should be kept in mind. The Battle of Trenton was, pre-eminently, an artillery action. Without the artillery, which at every juncture performed crucial service, it is extremely doubtful that the Americans could have overwhelmed the Hessians. Indeed, there is every reason to believe otherwise. Although American artillery had played a relatively minor part in earlier engagements, Washington understood its utility in an operation such as that against Trenton and was determined to get it across the river and into action, though he himself could hardly have foreseen how effectively it would be used. Throughout the tortuous hours of that long night, with precious time slipping away, he must have been tempted more than once to leave the cannon behind or to take only a portion of the artillery pieces with him. Yet at all hazards he took the cannon, and the cannon in turn took Trenton.

Congress, to its credit, had acted to confirm and augment the powers it had granted to Washington on the twelfth of December by resolving on the twenty-seventh, even before word had reached Baltimore of Washington's success at Trenton, to give him very broad authority for a period of six months, specifically: "Full, ample and complete powers to raise and collect together, in the most speedy and effectual manner, from any and all of the United States sixteen battalions of infantry in addition to those already voted by Congress; to appoint officers ... to raise officers and equip three thousand light horse, three regiments of artillery and a corps of engineers, and to establish their pay;—to apply to any of the States for such aid of the militia as he shall judge necessary ... to displace and appoint all officers under the rank of Brigadier-general, and to fill up all vacancies in every other department of the American army; to take, where ever he may be, what ever he may want for the use of the army, if the inhabitants will not sell it, allowing a reasonable price for the same, and to arrest and confine persons who refuse to take the continental currency, or are otherwise disaffected to the American cause."

The delegates were greatly heartened by the news from Trenton and quite readily suppressed any misgivings they may have felt in granting such extraordinary powers to Washington. "Most sincerely do we rejoice," the resolution of that body read, "in your Excellency's success at Trenton, as we conceive it will have the most important publick consequences, and because we think it will do justice, in some degree, to a character we admire, and which we have long wished to appear in the world, with that brilliancy that success always obtains, and which the members of Congress know you deserve."

The ubiquitous balladeer produced a patriotic song to mark the victory. "On Christmas day in seventy-six," it began, "Our ragged troops with bayonets fixed/ For Trenton marched away. . . . In silent march we passed the night/ Each soldier panting for the fight,/ Though quite benumbed with frost. . . .

> Twelve hundred servile miscreants,
> With all their colors, guns and tents,
>   Were trophies of the day.
> The frolic o'er, the bright canteen
> In centre, front and rear was seen
>   Driving fatigue away.
> Now, brothers of the patriot bands,
> Let's sing deliverance from the hands
>   Of arbitrary sway.
> And as our life is but a span,
> Let's touch the tankard while we can,
>   In memory of that day."

The results of Trenton were, in truth, incalculable. The battle was like a stone dropped in a pond, waves spreading out farther and farther. Lord Stirling wrote to Governor Livingston of New Jersey: "The effect is amazing: the enemy have deserted Borden-Town, Black Horse, Burlington, and Mount Holly, and are fled to South Amboy. We are now in possession of all those places and the spirit of that part of the country is aroused." Benjamin Rush, the army doctor with a detachment at Crossides, wrote: "There is no soil so dear to a soldier as that which is marked with the footsteps of a flying enemy. Everything looks well. Our army increases daily." A most important consequence of the victory was that a substantial portion of the soldiers who intended to return home when their enlistments ended on the first of the new year were persuaded to re-enlist, while hundreds of others who had been reluctant to join a lost cause now were proud to go with a winner.

Across the sea, the politicians who had brought all this about, and who certainly understood very little of what was going on, demanded the heads of those responsible. The Landgrave of Hesse-Cassel, who had sold his subjects as mercenaries, was furious at the news of their defeat and was determined to punish and humiliate officers and men alike. He would, he declared, never restore their colors to those regiments that had lost them until they captured an equal number of rebel standards. He wrote a cruel letter to Knyphausen, stating that he could not hold up his head "until his troops had smothered the remembrance of this wretched affair in a crowd of famous deeds."

In Britain, Lord Germain declared, "All our hopes were blasted by the unhappy affair at Trenton"; and Burke, writing an account of the battle for the *Annual Register,* noted, "It has excited not less astonishment in the British and auxiliary quarters than it has done joy in those of the Americans. The Hessians will be no longer terrible and the spirits of the Americans will rise amazingly." It was Burke who made a characteristically penetrating analysis of the Hessian defeat: "From the vast superiority which they perceived in themselves in army actions, the 'Hessians' had held the Americans in too great contempt, both as men and as soldiers. . . ."

An Englishman who crossed through the American lines reported that "volunteer companies are collecting in every county on the continent and in a few months the rascals will be stronger than ever. Even the parsons, some of them, have turned out as volunteers and pulpit drums or thunder, which you please to call it, summoning all to arms in this cursed babble. Damn them all."

10

Princeton

WASHINGTON had little time to savor his victory at Trenton. There was every reason to believe that General Cornwallis would be pressed by his commander, General Howe, to strike some decisive blow that might counteract the effect of Trenton on popular opinion. It would be ironic if that dazzling success set in motion a British winter offensive that completed the destruction of Washington's army, which through sickness, desertion, and above all the expiration of enlistments seemed well on its way to dissolution.

To maintain the semblance of an army, Washington's first step was to try to prolong the periods of enlistment, if only for a few weeks. Six weeks would get the army through the period of rebuilding with men who had enlisted for several years or for the duration of the war. Even an extension of two weeks would enable Washington to meet a renewed offensive on the part of the British. Washington thus made a personal appeal directly to his soliders. He would guarantee a bounty of ten dollars to each man who would re-enlist for six weeks; and since no money was presently available (Robert Morris, the financier, was busy trying to raise the necessary funds in Philadelphia), Washington would pledge his own private resources to fulfill the promise.

The individual American regiments were turned out on parade, and Washington exhorted them in the name of liberty and love of country to hang on for another six weeks. To men who had been anticipating for months an end of their miseries and discomforts, to these place-bound men, most of whom had never been more than a few miles from home before, six weeks seemed a long time. Washington explained the strategic situation to them, one regiment at a time. In order to reap the benefits of the victory at Trenton, it was necessary to keep an army in the field. The moment was a critical one, and their services were needed more than ever. "In the most affectionate manner," one soldier recalled, "he entreated us to stay. The drums beat for volunteers, but not a man turned out. The soldiers, worn down from fatigue and privations, had their hearts fixed on home and the comforts of the domestic circle. . . . The General wheeling his horse about—rode through in front of the regiment, and addressing us again said: 'My brave fellows, you have done all that I have ever asked you to do, and more than could be expected; but your country is at stake, your wives, your houses and all that you hold dear. . . . The present is emphatically the crisis, which is to decide your destiny.'"

The drums beat a second time. There was a long, painful pause, and then a murmuring and a stirring in the ranks. Finally a few stepped forth, "and their example was immediately followed by nearly all who were fit for duty in the regiment. . . ."

The ritual was repeated a dozen times: Washington's appeal reinforced by the pleas of the other general officers and their subordinates. Finally some three thousand men consented to remain, and these, with the Flying Camp and such militia units as had been rounded up, gave Washington about four thousand effectives. Washington checked the status of the troops he had left in Morristown, New Jersey, when he had retreated with the bulk of the army to the Delaware. From Morristown, where Colonel De Hart commanded three regiments, Washington got the welcome news that the men there would remain for two more weeks after the end of their term of enlistment. Generals William Maxwell and Alexander MacDougall, also at Morristown, were directed by Washington "to collect as large a body of militia as possible, and assure them that nothing is wanting but for them to lend a hand and drive the enemy from the whole province of New Jersey."

Washington by this time had determined to recross the Delaware and carry the warfare to the enemy while he still had the semblance of an army to command. He notified General Maxwell on the twenty-eighth of December that he was "about to enter the Jerseys with a considerable force immediately, for the purpose of attempting a recovery of that country from the enemy. . . ." Maxwell, he hoped, would do everything he could to harass the British and create a diversion. On December 30, Washington once again crossed the Delaware and occupied Trenton.

Cornwallis, who had been about to depart for England at the time of the Battle of Trenton, instead returned to New Brunswick and assumed command of the division there. Hearing that Washington had re-established himself at Trenton, Cornwallis set out by way of Princeton to drive him back over the Delaware or, more to be hoped, to pin Washington's army against the river and destroy it. Washington, for his part, instead of falling back before his larger and better-equipped foe, ordered Generals Mifflin and Cadwalader to move up from Bordentown and Crosswicks—to reinforce him, bringing his total force to some five thousand men. He then deployed his forces along the east bank of the Assunpink, across the bridge that Sullivan had closed to the fleeing Hessians a few days earlier. The troops were placed in successive lines to offer support to forward positions and to permit a maximum of flexibility in shifting units to those points that might come under heaviest pressure from enemy attack. General De Fermoy's brigade established an advance position a mile or so beyond Trenton on the Princeton Road with two pieces of artillery. De Fermoy, in turn, sent out Colonel Edward Hand with his riflemen to a point well ahead of his own lines.

Cornwallis had under his command, as he started south from Princeton, some seven thousand soldiers, including the Waldeckers and Von Donop's Hessians who had decamped from Bordentown with such celerity on the twenty-seventh. Cornwallis left behind in Princeton three companies of light dragoons and three regiments of infantry. At Maidenhead, approximately halfway from Princeton to Trenton, Cornwallis, with the advance guard, encountered Hand's riflemen, who withdrew slowly in a classic delaying action, picking up reinforcements and forcing Cornwallis to bring up another regiment with artillery support to push ahead. At this point General Greene came up with the better part of a brigade. The intention was to so delay Cornwallis that he could not reach Trenton before nightfall.

It was in fact almost dark when Cornwallis finally pushed back the American advance guard and reached Trenton, but he nonetheless sent skirmishers along the river to test the American defenses and search out possible fords. He also brought up artillery and opened fire on the American positions across Assunpink Creek. These probing actions gave clear evidence that the Americans were in strong positions ready to oppose any attempted crossing of the river. With the light rapidly fading, Cornwallis pushed down Queen Street to the Assunpink Bridge, but American fire was so heavy there that he pulled back and prepared to make camp for the night, sending back to Princeton for the light dragoons and two infantry regiments. General Leslie, who had been at Maidenhead, was also ordered to join Cornwallis for an attack shortly after dawn. Sir William Erskine is reported to have urged Cornwallis to launch a night attack against the Americans, declaring, "My Lord, if you trust those people tonight, you will see nothing of them in the morning." But even Erskine could hardly have guessed where, in fact, the missing Americans were to show up.

The British and American camps were within a mile of each other, with forward pickets, of course, much closer. Campfires were lighted on both sides of the creek as the temperature dropped sharply and the ground froze. Cornwallis, confident that his forces were strong enough to scatter the American army, made plans to attack the next day.

Washington's dilemma was how to avoid a battle with a superior adversary without at the same time undertaking another of those extended retreats that were so demoralizing to his men and so disheartening to patriots in general. He realized that he was perilously close to being a victim of his own success in Trenton. If, in the face of the expectations aroused by the Trenton victory, he withdrew without a fight, there would be widespread criticism and disappointment. Cornwallis might then pursue him and force an engagement under highly unfavorable conditions or, what was more likely and equally undesirable, cross the Delaware unopposed and seize Philadelphia, which had been stripped of defenders to augment Washington's army on the Assunpink. Washington had rallied his army and prevailed on many soldiers to stay on for a few more weeks on the grounds that they were desperately needed to oppose the British. If he failed to use them now, there would be no keeping them.

The solution was as ingenious as the assault on Trenton. It seemed clear that Cornwallis, fired by the desire to avenge the Trenton fiasco, was busy collecting his resources for an all-out attack. Washington's scheme was to slip away from Cornwallis's army during the night and, by a forced march, make an attack on Cornwallis's base of supplies at New Brunswick. A reconnaissance party brought back word that the old Quaker Road to the east of the Assunpink was free of British troops. Colonel Von Donop had, in fact, urged Cornwallis to send a division by the same road to take Washington's army in the rear and close off his line of retreat to the south, but Cornwallis had ignored the advice. Now Washington made preparations to move his army as quickly and as stealthily as possible from the front of the British camp. A hastily summoned council of war endorsed the plan. The army's baggage was ordered back to Burlington, and a small detail of men was assigned to keep the campfires burning and give the illusion that all was normal in the American lines.

Before the Americans moved out of their lines on the Assunpink, the wheels of the cannon were wrapped in rags to muffle their turning, and the horses' hoofs were likewise padded. The march began at one in the morning, and once more men whose shoes were worn and split or whose cracked and chilblained feet were bound in cloths left traces of blood on the snow. Nevertheless, the march discipline was excellent; the men moved off quickly and silently and covered precious miles while the British slumbered.

In the abandoned camp, the tenders of the campfires and the pickets played out their little drama convincingly, calling out the sentry challenges and feeding the flames. Another party was noisily busy digging fieldworks near the bridge, where they were likely to be observed. Just before morning, the little band of actors abandoned the stage and moved off to join Washington's main force. By dawn, Washington's army had reached Stony Brook, a few miles southeast of Princeton. Here he re-formed his columns and detached General Hugh Mercer with instructions to destroy the bridges across the stream, thereby delaying pursuit by Cornwallis when he discovered that the fox had escaped his trap, while at the same time protecting the left flank of the main army, moving on to New Brunswick, against any foray from the British forces that remained in Princeton.

Mercer, with some four hundred men, was almost at the Princeton-Trenton Road when he encountered the Seventeenth British Foot headed for Trenton to reinforce Cornwallis. The British had already sighted the Americans, and a race began between Mercer and the British officer, Lieutenant Colonel Charles Mawhood, to take the high ground commanding the road just north of the creek. Mercer reached it first, and from there he advanced to a rail fence that crossed the top of the hill and opened fire on the British. Mawhood's soldiers fired a volley in return and charged with their bayonets while the Americans were still reloading. Mercer's men fell back in considerable disorder until their officers rallied them in a nearby orchard.

Washington, as soon as he heard the firing on his left, hurried reinforcements to Mercer, including several cannon, but again the men of the Seventeenth Foot, placing their reliance on their bayonets, charged so resolutely that several American companies reeled back, and the British pressed on in an effort to capture the American artillery. Washington, taking in the situation and determined to check the retreat of the men, rode his horse through the fleeing militia directly into the face of the advancing British. One soldier, running for the cover of a patch of woods, looked up to see Washington riding toward him. The general brandished his sword and called, "Parade with us, my brave fellows. There is but a handful of the enemy, and we will have them directly." As at Kip's Bay, Washington displayed a reckless desperation quite different from bravery though certainly containing it. The demoralized men, seeing their general so dangerously exposed to enemy fire, rallied, and officers hurried Washington out of the direct line of fire.

As Mawhood and his men topped the hill, driving Mercer's troops ahead of them, it dawned on the astonished English colonel that he had engaged the entire American army. From the hill he could see that Washington's force had wheeled left and was approaching Princeton. The Fifty-fifth Regiment was prepared to march off after the Seventeenth for Trenton, and it attempted to come to Mawhood's assistance. But Colonel Hand, who had been with the contingent of troops that Washington had initially dispatched to support Mercer, observing the British plight, pushed between Mawhood's regiment and Princeton, turning the British officer's left flank and preventing him from making contact with the Fifty-fifth. That regiment soon had its own hands too full to worry about Mawhood. General Stirling and General St. Clair were advancing with almost two brigades. Finding himself cut off from Princeton and heavily outnumbered. Mawhood abandoned his cannon, got his men over Stony Brook, and made for Trenton.

The British Fifty-fifth Regiment meanwhile established itself on a point of high ground just south of Nassau Hall at the College of New Jersey, where the men were protected by a ravine. While the American artillery opened a sharp fire on the British positions, several regiments skirted the hill and entered the main street in front of the college. The British, in danger of being surrounded, took refuge in Nassau Hall. Captain Alexander Hamilton placed his cannon to command the hall; and when the British refused the demand that they surrender, Hamilton gave the order to fire. The first shot crashed through the Prayer Hall and, it was said, through a portrait of George II, obliterating the head (it was later replaced by a portrait of Washington, commissioned by the trustees and painted by Charles Willson Peale). The next shot struck the cornice of the building and ricocheted, killing an officer's horse. An anonymous narrator of the Battle of Princeton tells of seeing a British soldier "shot with an Iron Gun rammer in Stead of bullet. Which entered under his chin and came out again at his nose near his eyes one end of it, and the other end lapt round his thigh. . . ." The British had had enough; a white flag was thrust from a window, and some two hundred redcoats surrendered. The rest, made up of the Fortieth and the remnants of the Fifty-fifth, fled to New Brunswick or Kingston.

The British killed and wounded numbered 100, and 230 in all were captured, among them 14 officers. More precious than any count of prisoners was a large store of blankets. The battle over, a group of soldiers poured into a nearby house, and its owner noted that "though they were both hungry and thirsty some of them were laughin out right, others smileing, and not a man among them but showed joy in his countenance."

The American losses were far less than the British, but Washington lost officers he could ill afford to lose, among them General Mercer, killed trying to rally his men, and Colonel Haslet, who had emerged as one of his steadiest, most reliable officers. A disproportionate number of officers had been killed in the early stages of the action when they had risked their lives, as Washington did, to rally their men.

Washington had no time to tally his gains and losses. His men, who had had no food or rest for many hours, fell asleep wherever they stopped. Word came that Cornwallis and his troops were rushing up from Trenton "In a most infernal sweat—running, puffing, and blowing and swearing at being so outwitted." Not only had Cornwallis's hope of a pleasant interlude in England been destroyed, he had been made a fool of in the bargain—first Rall and his Hessians, and now Cornwallis and his Britishers. The hungry and exhausted colonials had to be prodded up once again to stagger a few more weary miles to Kingston. There Washington consulted with his general officers about the plan to attack New Brunswick. They were strongly of the opinion that further offensive action was quite beyond the physical resources of the men. The army would do well enough to escape its pursuers, hot on the trail. Reluctantly Washington concurred. New Brunswick, with its store of supplies and seventy thousand pounds in British army pay chests, would be a splendid prize, but one's luck could only be pushed so far.

As Washington's army, burdened with the spoils of war, marched out of town—or it would be perhaps better to say staggered, both from drink and exhaustion—Cornwallis's advance party reached Stony Brook, where a party of Americans were hard at work destroying the bridge. Cornwallis, concerned for his base of supplies at New Brunswick and not sure that Washington had not in fact dispatched a raiding expedition with the town as its objective, pushed through Princeton to Kingston without stopping; from there he took the right-hand road to New Brunswick with his main body, meanwhile sending a detachment of horse along the Millstone River in pursuit of Washington. Again the Americans got over a river one jump ahead of their pursuers. Captain Rodney, with a detachment of carpenters covered by riflemen, broke up the bridge, and the British horsemen turned back. That night the colonial army made camp at Somerset Court House, some fifteen miles from Princeton. They had begun a tiring night march of sixteen miles almost twenty-four hours before; they had fought a battle and then marched another fifteen miles without food except for what they could scrounge in the brief interval at Princeton. Now they made camp without their baggage, which was miles away. But victory is a soldier's best tonic, and Rodney reported that the men, although "extremely fatigued . . . are in good health and high spirits."

At Somerset Court House, 150 of the British prisoners captured at Princeton simply marched off with twenty wagons loaded with linen and clothing. The New Jersey militia who had been detailed to guard them were afraid to fire, and the rest of the soldiers were too weary to go in pursuit.

When Cornwallis reached New Brunswick, he found that the refugees from the Fifty-fifth and Fortieth regiments had spread terror through the town, and that the officer in command had already ordered that all baggage and military stores be removed along with the seventy-thousand-pound payroll. Angered and embarrassed, Cornwallis insisted Washington's strike had been a desperate blow. If Washington tried another similar movement, Cornwallis vowed, "the march alone will destroy his army."

The British had launched their campaign in New Jersey partly because the area was supposed to be crawling with Tories who would help the British cause. This mass of Tories did not appear. In fact, the people of New Jersey had been thoroughly alienated by the pillaging of the British and Hessian troops. The Hessians had the reputation for being the most thorough and the most ruthless of requisitioners, seizing whatever they wished and destroying much out of a spirit of simple wantonness. Most provoking was the sight of women camp followers, dressed in finery stolen quite indiscriminately from patriot and Tory ladies alike. To see these jades flaunting themselves in front of decent people was obnoxious to Americans of all political persuasions.

Looting and destruction of property in New Jersey certainly were not confined to the Hessians. At Princeton, one eyewitness reported, "British soldiers not only Burnt up all the fire wood that the Inhabitants had Provided for Winter, but Stript Shops, out Houses and Some Dwelling houses of the boards that Covered them, and all the loose boards and Timbers That the Joiners and Carpenters had in Store to work up, they Burnt with all their Fences and Garden Inclosures with in the Town & After sent their Carriages and Drew away the Farmers Fences adjoining within a mile, and laid all in Common. They also cut down Apple trees and other fruit bearing trees and burnt them." In addition they burned several mills and farmhouses in the countryside around Princeton. The soldiers simply took from anyone they encountered whatever they wished, the hats off their heads, the coats off their backs, their horses, sheep, and hogs, and burned what they could not carry off. When one of a party of Hessian soldiers snatched the hat off the head of a peace-loving Quaker, "he (though but a Smal man and between Fifty and Sixty Years of age) laid hold of their Champion and Struck up his heels and threw him on the Ground and clapt his foot on his Sword and Prevented his drawing it, And took his Hat again from him Upon that the three other Platoons Drew their Swords, and he was obliged to Yield up a very good Hat. . . ."

The British and Hessian soldiers, our same informant tells us, "go out late in the night and Steal and Kill Sheep and cattle even Milch Cows and skin them, and leave their skins and hides and take away the meat. . . . To give a Particular account of Every Robery and outrage comitted by the Hessians and Regulars in and within five miles of Princeton . . . would fill a Vollum therefore I have Mentioned a few particulars out of a Multitude and most of those that I have given an Account of are Quakers a People that never bore Arms against them which they Knew well. . . ."

There was, of course, the dismal list of atrocities that are an inevitable consequence of the passions and lusts set loose by war. Wounded prisoners were, on more than one occasion, "barbarously mangled or put to death." Prisoners were confined in filthy makeshift prisons, where they died of malnutrition and disease. Especially offensive to a pious people was the fact that "place of worship, ministers and other religious persons of some particular Protestant denominations . . . have been treated with the most rancorous hatred, and at the same time with the highest contempt."

Washington's recrossing of the Delaware, his challenge to Cornwallis and his skillful evasion of the British general—culminating in the success at Princeton—were part and parcel of his seizure of Trenton on the morning of December 26. He had, by his two brilliant maneuvers, changed the entire complexion of the war. It was his supreme moment as a general. Frederick the Great of Prussia declared, "The achievements of Washington and his little band of compatriots between the 25th of December and the 4th of January, a space of 10 days, were the most brilliant of any recorded in the annals of military achievements." Botta, the Italian historian who wrote of the American Revolution in the early decades of the nineteenth century, expressed in eloquent if in somewhat inflated prose the general reaction of all friends to the American cause: "Achievements so astonishing acquired an immense glory for the Captain General of the United States. All nations shared the surprise of the Americans. All equally admired and applauded the prudence, the constancy and the noble intrepidity of General Washington. An unanimous voice proclaimed him the saviour of his country; all extolled him, as equal to the most celebrated commanders of antiquity."

The distinguished Prussian general-historian Friedrick Wilheim von Bülow, in his book *The Spirit of the Modern System of War,* published in England in 1809, wrote: "The maneuvers of the American general at Trenton and Princeton were masterpieces. They may be deemed models for the conduct of a general supporting a defensive war against a superior enemy. . . ."

One British officer, Colonel William Harcourt, in the aftermath of Washington's drive through New Jersey, made a shrewd analysis of rebel strength. In the first place, the British were constantly deluding themselves with the hope of a major uprising of Loyalists. Harcourt had not "yet met with ten, I believe I have said two, disinterested friends to the supremacy of Great Britain. . . ." Moreover, the British superiority in men and arms was frittered away in futile pursuits that accomplished nothing. Finally, the fact was that while the Americans "seemed to be ignorant of the precision and order, and even of the principles, by which large bodies are moved, yet they possess some of the requisites for making good troops, such as extreme cunning, great industry in moving ground and felling of wood, activity and a spirit of enterprise upon any advantage. . . . Though it was once the fashion of this army to treat them in the most contemptible light, they are now become a formidable enemy." Even so, Harcourt was confident that "provided affairs continue quiet in Europe, and the expected reinforcements arrive in good time, we shall soon bring this business to a happy conclusion."

11

The Continental Congress

WHILE the battles were fought and armies marched and counter-marched, while Washington with one desperate expedient after another kept his ragged army in being, the Congress kept on meeting and doing the absolutely essential task of supplying Washington as best it could with money, armament, and supplies. The Congress did not do a very efficient job of it; it was hamstrung in a dozen different ways from exerting the necessary degree of authority over the member states to do the job. But the members tried, some of them with heroic tenacity, to give Washington what he needed. In the meanwhile the Congress kept itself in being month after difficult month, becoming a symbol, second only to the Continental Army, that such a thing as the United States, a free and sovereign nation, existed.

The Congress's great creative period, of course, was prior to July 4, 1776. As a forum for the leading political figures from each colony, as an enunciator of constitutional principles, as the voice of those American colonists who were determined to be free, it was one of the most impressive legislative bodies in history. After July, 1776, Congress became a group of men without clear authority, without defined powers, without even a constitution to give them some degree of legitimacy, baffled and frustrated at every turn, their requests for money and supplies often simply ignored by their client states, at whose pleasure Congress existed. Whatever shreds of authority Congress might have drawn about itself were often denounced as a reckless lust for power. The Tories of course rejected its authority out of hand and constantly abused it as "more despotic and tyrannical than the Egyptian pharaoh."

Congress's members were divided into factions that almost invariably bickered and fought with each other during the course of the war. Not only were there frictions and animosities among the delegates from various states, but also particular state delegations were often sharply divided. This was generally no accident, since different factions among the patriots of a single state were usually represented in the choice of the various delegates themselves. Thus Sam Adams and John Hancock of Massachusetts were frequently on opposite sides of issues. Adams suspected Hancock of attempting to discredit him by spreading the rumor that Adams had tried to discredit Washington. James Warren, strongly anti-Hancock, wrote John Adams from Boston mockingly: "The Great Man [Hancock] Tarried here till after Election, and then went off with the Pomp and retinue of an Eastern prince."

Henry Laurens and Christopher Gadsden were, with John Rutledge, the leading patriots in the state of South Carolina, yet Gadsden and Laurens were constantly at loggerheads. The language of their charges and countercharges could be rough. When Laurens heard that Gadsden had accused him of being an intriguer, Laurens replied angrily that Gadsden, "according to his custom, stabb'd me in conversations and private letters" rather than speaking directly to him; he had learned of Gadsden's "discourteous, injurious attempts" only by accident.

Nor did Congress meet under ideal circumstances. Philadelphia was the home of Congress except on those occasions when its members were forced by the ebb and flow of military campaigns to decamp to York or Lancaster, Pennsylvania, or Baltimore. Philadelphia had a large number of Tories, and even after the avowed Tories were driven out, there remained fellow-traveling Tory sympathizers not bold enough to publicly declare their allegiance to George III. These were men and women who, in their hearts, hoped for an American defeat and a return to the authority of Great Britain. While these lukewarmers, from their very disposition, did not openly oppose Congress or impede the cause, they gave it little or no support unless coerced into doing so, and they created an atmosphere that was debilitating to the patriots.

The members of Congress, like the soldiers in Washington's army, lived far from their homes and families—though under conditions far less arduous than those endured by the men and officers of the Continental Army. Certainly they suffered that common general ailment, homesickness, quite as acutely. They traveled long distances in inclement weather over wretched roads to Philadelphia or wherever Congress happened to be meeting, and they, like the soldiers of the states they represented, were often inadequately supported, both in their own salaries and expenses and in the money and provisions they requisitioned for the Continental Army. They worked long hours, had to waste a vast amount of time on the most trivial details, and suffered, like ordinary mortals, from the humid heat of Philadelphia in the summer and the damp and frigid winds in winter.

The diversions of the delegates were, for the most part, very modest indeed. The splendid dinners and handsome parties that had characterized the meetings of the First Continental Congress existed only in fond memories. Samuel Holton, a Massachusetts delegate, recorded in his diary: "Attended Congress. Toward night I walked out with a number of gentlemen of Congress about a mile to a farmhouse. The people was kind, we eat Cherries and drank whiskey." This was, to be sure, while Congress was in exile at York; Philadelphia offered more sophisticated pleasures, but these were cramped by wartime austerity and diminished as the conflict dragged on. Nathaniel Peabody wrote: "A Number of Us Generally attend from one to two hours in the morning before we can make a Congress, and then are obliged to *set* till Near *Sunset* before we adjourn, and by the time we have dined and done a Little Committee business it is honnest bed time. . . ." Cornelius Harnett wrote to Thomas Burke, begging his fellow North Carolinian to hurry to Philadelphia. "For God's sake come on to relieve me in Nov., but at the furthest the very beginning of December. . . . I acknowledge it is cruel in me to wish you to return; you have already suffered more in your private Concerns than any man who has been in the Delegation for some time past. But you have this Consolation: that, should you fail of receiving your reward in this world, you will no doubt be singing Hallelujahs in the next to all Eternity. Tho' I acknowledge your Voice is not very well Calculated for that business. . . ."

Congress had its contentious and difficult members as well as its long-winded ones (its "six-deep Orators," as Henry Laurens put it). Titus Hosmer wrote Governor Trumbull of Connecticut, "The idleness and captiousness of some gentlemen, maugre the wishes and endeavors of an honest and industrious majority, in my apprehension, threaten the worst consequences. . . . Nine States make a Congress, some States have delegates so very negligent, so much immersed in the pursuit of pleasure or business, that it is very rare we can make a Congress before near eleven o'clock . . . and those who occasion the delay are callous to admonition and reproof. . . . When we are assembled several gentlemen have such a knack at starting questions of order, raising debates upon critical, captious, and trifling amendments, protracting them by long speeches, by postponing, calling for the previous question, and other arts that . . . precious time is lost, and the public business left undone."

Hosmer's fellow Connecticut delegate, Andrew Adams, had many of the same criticisms. "There are here," he wrote, "as in most other Assemblys some very Sensable Speakers, and some very loud Talkers. . . ." But even without the "loud Talkers," a house uniformly "composed of very able and sensable Gentlemen" would have had difficulty enough, since they belonged "to different states, whose Laws, Manners, Genious and Inhabitants and indeed almost every thing else are very different."

There was so much logrolling among delegates that Cyrus Griffin, an irascible Virginian, wrote to Jefferson, "Congress exhibit not more than two or three Members actuated by Patriotism . . . Congress are at present a Government of *Men*. It would astonish you to think how all affairs proceed upon the interested Principle: Members prostituting their votes in expectation of mutual assistance upon favorite Points." While many of the charges against Congress were undoubtedly true, since it was made up of men and not archangels, Griffin's tirade smacks more than a little of self-righteousness.

With all this carping, the delegates still accomplished much. They provided, however inadequately, for Washington's army, and this primary task was the principal excuse for their existing at all, the mortar that held them together, and their best claim to the gratitude of their countrymen. The Board of War and Ordnance, for example, was charged with "keeping an accurate roster" of "all officers of the land forces of the United Colonies, with their rank and the dates of their respective commissions; and also regular accounts of the state and disposition of the troops in the respective colonies," as well as "exact accounts of all the artillery, arms, ammunition and warlike stores belonging to the United Colonies . . . and . . . the immediate care of all such . . . warlike stores." It was also responsible for "the raising, fitting out, and distpatching [of] all such land forces as may be ordered for the service of the United Colonies; for the care of prisoners of war and the handling and filing of all correspondence dealing directly with the waging of war against Great Britain." To carry on this vast labor the board was to have a secretary and one or more clerks appointed by Congress.

Congress also established the rudiments of a foreign service by dispatching a series of amateur diplomats to Europe and directing their activities through the Committee of Secret Correspondence, which functioned rather like a state department. Then, as now, the operation of this state department was not always smooth. In the field of diplomacy the Southerners, with some exceptions, supported the suspicious and contentious Arthur Lee of the Virginia Lees, while the New Englanders backed the clumsy and inept ambassador to France, Silas Deane of Connecticut. First the Southerners sent Arthur Lee to France to check on Deane, then Northerners sent Benjamin Franklin to check on Lee, and finally John Adams was dispatched to protect the interests of New England. And so it went.

The Congress also created a navy through the Marine Committee and equipped it and directed its operations. The members developed an awkward and complicated process of judicial review by Congressional commissioners for cases in which the courts of no particular state were competent and for cases involving disputes between states, and thus they laid the foundation for the Supreme Court. Perhaps most notably of all, they worked out a procedure of admitting new states to their precarious union on the basis of equality with the original states, the first time in history that an existing government had shown such generosity in enlarging its jurisdiction. Finally, in addition to doing, in practical fact, everything that needed to be done and that there was nobody else to do, they survived and continued, through all the vicissitudes of the war, to exercise an authority, however feeble, that preserved both the symbol and the fact of American unity. They even hammered out a constitution—the Articles of Confederation—which, while it was not adopted until near the end of the war and was never adequate to the exigencies of the time, nevertheless marked a clear advance in the notion of a confederated government that could draw together thirteen disparate political entities called states.

Viewed in this light, the Congress's accomplishments were remarkable. Out of their own membership, which fluctuated constantly during the war as weary veterans left and were replaced by novices, the members of Congress, in effect, carried on all the functions of a modern government. They made up the legislative, executive, and judicial departments. Among themselves they performed a host of functions if not well at least adequately.

Soon after the passage of the resolution on independence on the second of July, 1776, the delegates took up the question of a constitution. A committee had been appointed on the eleventh of June to draft a constitution in anticipation of a vote in Congress declaring for independence. John Dickinson, reconciled to independence, was the principal author of the Articles of Confederation, and his small-state predilections became evident as the attention of the delegates focused on Article Seventeen: "In determining questions, each colony shall have one vote." This was the single most important constitutional issue faced by the delegates. It divided the states into two groups that cut across sectional lines—the large states and the small ones. The large states had accepted earlier the principle of equal representation, but they had done so only under the heaviest pressure, and they were plainly dissatisfied with the bargain. Franklin, from a large state, put the matter most bluntly: "Let the smaller colonies have equal money and men, and then have an equal vote. . . . If they have an equal vote without bearing equal burdens, a confederation upon such an iniquitous base will never last long."

Dr. John Witherspoon, president of the College at Princeton and a representative of the small state of New Jersey, replied: "Is it not plausible that the small states will be oppressed by the great ones?" As befitted a professor, Witherspoon went on to recall the Spartans' oppression of the Helots, and Rome's oppression of the states subordinate to it. Part of the problem was that if the simple principle of equal representation was abandoned, on what grounds were the respective states to be represented—on size, population, wealth, or a combination of all three? The prosperous and populous states such as Massachusetts and Pennsylvania wished representation to be by a combination of population and wealth. The South wished to count its slave population twice by such terms, once as property and once as population. Article Eleven of the proposed confederation provided that contributions to defray the cost of carrying on the war should be levied on each colony, "in proportion to the number of inhabitants of every age, sex and quality." That clearly included blacks. If they were to be counted as "inhabitants" for purposes of assessing contributions, they should certainly be counted for purposes of representation.

Roger Sherman of Connecticut suggested a bizarre compromise. The vote should be both by individual colonies and by proportion of inhabitants on every issue, a majority of both required for the passage of a law. The somewhat cynical political mind of John Adams supported the big-state solution—and then went on to the problem of how America was to be governed after a constitution was written. Adams argued that "reason, justice and equity" never could be counted on, but only self-interest. It thus followed that the interests within Congress "should be the mathematical representative of the interests without doors." The argument that the states were in some way like individuals was "mere sound." It had some validity under the authority of Great Britain and some present reality, but the real question was what America would be "when our bargain shall be made"—when a constitution was adopted. "The confederacy," he insisted, "is to make us one individual only, it is to form us, like separate parcels of metal, into one common mass. We shall no longer retain our separate individuality, but become a single individual," at least in all questions that came before the confederacy.

The debate revealed, besides the division between small-state men and large-state men, a difference in basic philosphy between those delegates who felt that the individual states should retain their essential sovereignty and simply join in a loose union for certain common purposes, and those who felt they were engaged in creating a single nation in which the states would be subordinate. It was a most difficult problem. "You love to pick a political bone," John Adams wrote to Abigail, recounting the debate, "so I will throw it to you."

Another crucial question was whether Congress should "have authority to limit the dimensions of each colony." Virginia claimed a western boundary reaching to the Pacific Ocean. If Congress recognized Virginia's claim, that state would eventually overshadow all its neighbors. Each state had its quota of industrious land speculators. Usually their speculations were based upon the claims of their own state to extensive holdings in the west. Connecticut, for example, claimed what came to be called the Western Reserve, a large area in Ohio and the upper third of Pennsylvania. New York land speculators claimed what later became the state of Vermont. Member of Congress and prominent patriots in every state were actively engaged in land speculation. Washington himself was a member of a company established to speculate in Western lands, and so were Franklin, Patrick Henry, and numerous others. These men, good patriots though they were, constituted a lobby, or rather a series of lobbies, each one of which attempted to protect his own particular land venture.

The delegates were soon forced to put aside the Articles of Confederation in order to take up more urgent matters. The difficulty of raising money and supplies was demoralizing to Congress, as were, of course, the defeats or "strategic withdrawals" of Washington and the Continental Army. When Congress, alarmed by Howe's thrust into New Jersey, departed for Baltimore, leaving most authority in Washington's hands, Congressional morale reached a new low. The euphoria produced by Trenton was rapidly dissipated. In February, 1777, when the number of delegates present had shrunk to a mere twenty-two, William Hooper wrote a despondent letter to Robert Morris, lamenting the thinness of representation. "New York, Delaware, Maryland may almost as well desert the cause as so lamely support it. . . . There will be a time," Hooper concluded, "& I hope it is not at a great distance when the distinction of whig & Tory will be lost & resolve itself into the common appellation of *Citizens of the Independent States,* all political grudges will die away & harmony & happiness cement the whole."

12

The States Make Constitutions

As the Revolution progressed, virtually all the states drew up their own constitutions. This flurry of constitution-making was one of the most remarkable political episodes in history. It demonstrated as nothing else could the degree of political sophistication that had developed in the American colonies in the years of crisis prior to the outbreak of hostilities. Every colony had become a hothouse of political ideas in the stormy decade from 1765 to 1775, from the Stamp Act to Lexington and Concord.

The writing of these constitutions also produced remarkable results. In them the leading patriot politicians worked out many of the principles of constitutional government that would eventually find their way into the Federal Constitution.

The fever of constitution-writing was given impetus, as were so many things in the Revolutionary era, by John Adams. It began in 1775, when two delegates to the Continental Congress from North Carolina, William Hooper and John Penn, were about to return to their home state and prevail upon the North Carolina provincial assembly to undertake to draft a constitution. Their colleagues at home had instructed them to bring along "every hint [they] could collect concerning government," and they, in turn, having heard John Adams "dialate" on the proper principles of government, urged the New Englander to write down his thoughts for their guidance. Adams responded enthusiastically. He "concluded to borrow a little time from his sleep" and made two copies of his *Thoughts on Government,* one for each of the Carolinians. George Wythe, dean of the Virginia bar and Thomas Jefferson's teacher, saw William Hooper's copy and asked for one for himself and then one for Jonathan Sergeant of New Jersey. Richard Henry Lee then requested one, and Adams, flattered though he was, felt he had done all the secretarial work he was capable of for the moment and borrowed Wythe's copy, giving Lee permission to publish it in a "very incorrect, and not truly printed edition." Crude as it was, it might at least serve to "mark out a path and put men up on thinking."

The *Thoughts* were prefaced by the observation that "since the blessings of society depend entirely on . . . constitutions of government, there can be no employment more agreeable to a benevolent mind than a research after the best." Some writers had argued that the particular form of a government made little difference if the government was well administered. This in Adams' view was manifestly absurd. "Nothing is more certain," he wrote, "from the history of nations and the nature of man, than that some forms of government are better fitted for being well administered than others." The principal end of government was the happiness of the governed, and "all sober inquiries after truth, ancient and modern, pagan and Christian" agreed that happiness was found only in virtue. Thus that government was best which most effectively stimulated the virtue of its citizens and suppressed their vices.

Every government must, moreover, rest on some principle or passion in the minds of the people. Typically this "passion" had been fear, Adams said, or the "honor of a few," but in framing governments for the American states, "the noblest principles and most generous affections in our nature" must be called forth to create "the noblest and most generous models of government." It was also evident to anyone who read the great political scientists—Locke, Milton, Hooker, Harrington, and Sidney, among others—that "there is no good government but what is republican . . . because the very definition of a republic is 'an empire of laws, and not of men.'" Men are secured in their rights to life, liberty, and property by clear and fair laws, falling equally on all, wisely and justly administered.

Among republics there was a wide variety, Adams continued, and it was necessary to choose the best. A republic must have a representative assembly chosen by the owners of real property (i.e., land) or by electors otherwise qualified. The assembly should be "in miniature an exact portrait of the people at large. It should feel reason and act like them. . . . Equal interest among the people should have equal interests in it." But there could not be simply one popular legislative body—"a people cannot be long free nor ever happy," Adams wrote, "whose government is in one assembly," for a "single assembly is liable to all the vices, follies, and frailties of an individual; subject to fits of humor, starts of passion, flights of enthusiasm, partialities, or prejudice, and consequently productive of hasty results and absurd judgments."

Adams' concern about the tendency of a single or unicameral legislature to be carried away by emotion or popular prejudice was an article of political faith for virtually all the statesmen of the Revolutionary generation. It reached back to Rome and Greece for its antecedents; to Thucydides, Polybius, Plato, and Aristotle. The history of ancient times was understood to demonstrate the dangers of unchecked democracy, the placing all power directly in the hands of a simple majority of the people. In all such cases, it was argued, the majority had, by their emotional reactions, produced a degree of political instability verging on anarchy. In such instances the rights of the minority were ruthlessly trampled on—and this, in turn, had resulted in the rise of a dictator or tyrant whose principal attraction was that he promised to restore order. A single unchecked legislature, Adams declared, will lust after power and, after a time, "not hesitate to vote itself perpetual." A one-house legislature was, moreover, unable to perform the executive functions of government "for want of two essential properties, secrecy and dispatch." It was even less able to perform judicial functions; "it is too numerous, too slow, and too little skilled in the laws."

The legislative branch should therefore consist of two houses, with the second, or council, chosen from the first, and the two together electing by joint ballot a governor. Governors and the two legislatures were each to have, in effect, a veto upon the actions of the others. All elections should be annual, for "where annual elections end, there slavery begins." Yearly elections, Adams pointed out, would teach politicians "the great political virtues of humility, patience and moderation, without which every man in power becomes a ravenous beast of prey." "A constitution founded on these principles," Adams wrote a friend, inspires the people "with a conscious dignity becoming freemen; a general emulation takes place which causes good humor, sociability, good manners, and good morals to be general." Such a government, animated by high ideals of freedom and the general good, "makes the common people brave and enterprising," and the opportunity to advance themselves in the world makes them "sober, industrious and frugal."

"You and I, my dear friend," Adams wrote at the end of his *Thoughts on Government,* "have been sent into life at a time when the greatest lawmakers of antiquity would have wished to live. How few of the human race have ever enjoyed an opportunity of making an election of government, more than of air, soil or climate, for themselves or their children! When, before the present epocha, had three millions of people full power and a fair opportunity to form and establish the wisest and happiest government that human wisdom can contrive?" This almost ecstatic ending of Adams' treatise gives us a notion of the sense of challenge and excitement that many of the Revolutionary statesmen felt at the prospect of having the chance, unique in history, to establish government on correct constitutional principles.

When the *Thoughts* appeared in print, Adams sent a copy to Patrick Henry. Virginia was already at work on a constitution, and George Mason was busy writing its bill of rights. Henry wrote Adams: "I am not without hopes it [the *Thoughts*] may produce good here where there is among most of our opulent families a strong bias to aristocracy . . . Go on, my dear friend, to assail the strongholds of tyranny."

Virginia did not, of course, have to rely on John Adams for the proper theoretical lumber out of which to fashion its constitution. There were, first of all, the colonial governments. Along with the royal governor exercising the executive function, all of the colonies except Pennsylvania had had royal councils that functioned much in the manner of an upper house—in American terms, a senate. The lower houses, or assemblies, in the colonies were already popularly elected. There was, moreover, the generally admired English system, with its executive, legislative, and judicial branches. The problem was how to translate the positive aspects of the British government and the colonial governments themselves into free, "republican" governments.

Adams was encouraged to hear both that Virginia was well advanced in forming a constitution and that Patrick Henry was actively involved. Adams considered Henry a "masterly . . . builder," who could be counted upon to keep at bay "the dons, the bashaws, the grandees, the patricians, the sachems, the nabobs, call them by what names you will." These fine gentlemen and aristocrats might "sigh and groan, and fret and sometimes stamp and foam and curse, but all in vain." It was the will of the great body of the people and their leaders in every state "that a more equal liberty than has prevailed in other parts of the earth must be established in America." The "insolent domination" of "a few, a very few, opulent, monopolizing families" would "be brought down nearer to the confines of reason and moderation. . . ."

The Virginia conservatives, led by Edmund Pendleton and Carter Braxton, did in fact urge moderation. Patrick Henry, helping to lead the democratic forces, wrote to Richard Henry Lee: "Moderation . . . hath nearly brought on us final ruin. And to see those, who have so fatally advised us, still guiding, or at least sharing, our public counsels, alarms me." To John Adams he wrote, "my most esteemed republican form has many and powerful enemies."

In practical fact, George Mason had much more to do with the Virginia constitution than Patrick Henry, which may have been for the best. Henry was viewed with open suspicion by the more conservative planters of the tidewater. To such men as Carter Braxton he was a radical, imbued with the heretical notions of Thomas Paine and much too sympathetic to the "leveling tendencies" of New England. George Mason, however, was widely respected for his levelheaded wisdom, and the Virginia constitutional convention was dominated by men like Mason and Archibald Cary. James Madison, who had not long before been graduated from the College at Princeton, was also a delegate. "In Convention debate," Edmund Randolph said, "his lips were never unsealed except to some members who happened to sit near him; and he who had once partaken of the rich banquet of his remarks, did not fail to wish to sit daily within reach of his conversation."

The Virginia constitution began with a recapitulation of the bill of rights, modeled directly on the English Bill of Rights of 1689. After stating that "all men are by nature equally free and independent," the bill of rights of the Virginia Convention declared "that all power is vested in, and consequently derived from, the people. . . ." This sentence was not accepted without heated debate. Thomas Ludwell Lee wrote to his brother Richard Henry Lee, "A certain set of aristocrats— for we have such monsters here—finding that their miserable system cannot be reared on such foundations, have to this time kept us so at bay on the first line, which declares all men to be born free and independent. A number of absurd or unmeaning alterations have been proposed."

Also affirmed was the principle that the legislative and executive powers of the state should be separate from the judiciary. Elections must be free, and "all men having sufficient evidence of permanent common interest with an attachment to the community" had the right to vote and could not be taxed or deprived of their property "for publick uses, without their own consent." "The permanent common interest" meant, as the Virginia constitution defined it, fifty acres of improved land or one hundred acres of unimproved land. When land could be purchased for a few dollars an acre and everyone aspired to own land, such a limitation of the franchise affected relatively few Virginians. It expressed the view of the framers of the Virginia constitution that in order to vote responsibly, an inhabitant of the state should have a stake in the society, as represented by the ownership of land.

The Virginia bill of rights, in its eighth article, covered the rights of the individual in law, and since these remain the basis of our legal rights today, it is appropriate to quote the article in full: "That in all capital or criminal prosecutions a man hath a right to demand the cause and nature of his accusation, to be confronted with the accusers and witnesses, to call for evidence in his favour, and to a speedy trial by an impartial jury of his vicinage, without whose unanimous consent he cannot be found guilty; nor can he be compelled to give evidence against himself; that no man be deprived of his liberty, except by the law of the land or the judgment of his peers."

The subsequent articles prohibited excessive bail or fines, "cruel and unusual punishments," and the issuing of "general warrants whereby an officer or messenger may be commanded to search suspected places without evidence of a fact committed, or to seize any person or persons not named, or whose offense is not particularly described and supported by evidence. . . ." Further articles guaranteed freedom of the press, "one of the great bulwarks of liberty" and trial by jury, which should be "held sacred"; and stated that "standing armies in time of peace should be avoided as dangerous to liberty; and . . . in all cases the military should be under strict subordination to, and governed by, the civil power."

The fifteenth article declared that "no free government, or the blessings of liberty can be preserved by any people, but by a firm adherence to justice, moderation, temperance, frugality and virtue, and by frequent recurrence to fundamental principles," and, finally, that since faith and conscience could not be coerced, "all men are equally entitled to the free exercise of religion . . . and that it is the mutual duty of all to practice Christian forbearance, love, and charity towards each other."

The actual body of the Virginia constitution began by listing

George III's "misrule . . . by which . . . the government of this country, as formerly exercised under the crown of Great Britain, is TOTALLY DISSOLVED." The legislative, executive, and judicial branches of the new government were to be "separate and distinct," and the legislature was to be composed of two distinct branches, one the House of Delegates, consisting of two representatives chosen from each county, the other to be called the "Senate." For the purpose of electing senators, the counties of the state were to be divided into twenty-four districts, each of which would elect one senator. The delegates were to be elected annually and the senators for three-year terms. All laws were to originate in the House of Delegates and to be approved or rejected by the Senate with the exception of money bills, "which in no instance shall be altered by the Senate, but wholly approved or rejected." Readers familiar with the Federal Constitution will recognize that the powers allocated to the "House" and "Senate" of the General Assembly of Virginia were very similar to those later adopted by the delegates to the Federal Convention and incorporated in the United States Constitution.

In the matter of the election and the powers of the chief executive officer of the state, or governor, the Virginians' suspicion of executive authority as represented for them by the king of England—and even more by his surrogates in the American colonies, the royal governors— led to a weak executive. The governor was to be chosen annually by joint ballot of both houses. He could not serve more than three successive years, and he was then ineligible for re-election until he had been out of office for four years. His salary was to be "adequate, but moderate," and he could do little without the concurrence of a kind of cabinet, to be called a privy council and to be chosen by the legislature from among its own members or from "the people at large."

The "Houses of Assembly" had the right to appoint judges to the various courts of the state as well as to select the attorney general. The determination of the framers of the Virginia constitution to keep church and state separate is indicated by the provision that "all ministers of the Gospel of every denomination, [shall] be incapable of being elected members of either House . . . or the privy Council."

The final paragraph of the Virginia constitution states that the delegates to the convention that had framed the document should also choose the governor and privy council and whatever other officers were needed to run the affairs of the state. There was no mention of any process of ratification. The times were too pressing for such niceties; a government was needed whatever its deficiencies or however uncertain its legitimacy. On May 15, 1775, the Virginia Convention had voted unanimously to undertake to draft a new constitution, and six weeks later it was unanimously adopted. The following day the Virginia troops paraded in honor of the new constitution, and the Continental flag was flown over the capitol.

The striking fact about the Virginia constitution is that it was widely imitated by the other states. Hastily constructed as it was, it proved an influential model. Rhode Island and Connecticut, which had had the most liberal colonial charters and had from the beginning elected their own governors, found that they could get by very well by simply changing the preambles to their charters and deleting all mention of the British Crown. Other states, however, quickly realized that with independence their old charters were void and that they badly needed new governments based on new constitutions. In New Jersey, for example, a large majority of the members of the Provincial Congress were determined to establish a bona fide state constitution. Despite messages from some New Jersey towns opposing the drafting of a constitution as making a reconciliation with Great Britain more difficult, the Provincial Congress decided by a vote of fifty-four to three to press on with the task.

In North Carolina, the ever-present menace of the Tories produced strong early sentiment for independence and for a state constitution. When the constitutional convention met in November, 1775, it was divided between conservatives and radicals. As a conservative delegate, Samuel Johnston, wrote glumly, "Everyone who has the least pretensions to be a gentleman is borne down per ignobile vulgus—a set of men without reading, experience, or principles to govern them." The constitution that emerged was a compromise between the moderates and the radicals.

On one point at least the radicals had their way. The most powerless executive of all was that provided for in the constitution of North Carolina. The governor had to be at least thirty years old, to have lived in the state for five years, and to own property worth at least one thousand pounds; and he was no more than a figurehead. "What powers, sir," one of William Hooper's constituents asked, "were conferred upon the Governor?" "Power," Hooper replied, "to sign a receipt for his salary." Any adult freeman resident in the state for one year could vote for members of the lower house, while anyone possessing fifty acres could vote for a senator.

In South Carolina there was strong sentiment against declaring independence, and the Charles Town Committee of Safety was split between radical and conservative patriots, with Henry Laurens holding the balance. When word reached South Carolina that Congress had begun in the winter of 1776 to discuss the question of independence, Laurens, a wealthy conservative landowner, compared himself to a child turned out of his father's house. The word "independence," he wrote, "cuts me deep—has caused tears to trickle down my cheeks." John Rutledge also wept at the news, but the resistance of South Carolina patriots to independence was virtually ended by the news that Parliament had authorized the confiscation of the property of Americans as rebels. This spurred the drafting of a "plan of government" that fell far short of a formal constitution. At least some of those who voted for it considered it an interim measure, designed to last only until the colonies returned to the fold. It is perhaps worth pointing out that in the Revolutionary legislature of South Carolina, which finally drafted the constitution of that state, there were 144 members from the plantation counties of the tidewater region and 40 from the uplands, although three-fourths of the population lived in the latter area.

While Georgia did not produce a formal constitution for several years, that state's Provincial Congress did enact a set of "Rules and Regulations" that served the purpose for a time. A president and commander in chief was elected by the congress for six months. Subject only to the advice of the Council of Safety, the president exercised all the executive powers, while the legislative functions were retained by the Provincial Congress.

Maryland, which was securely in the hands of a planter aristocracy, adopted one of the most conservative constitutions, one in which the upper house was elected indirectly by an electoral college. Led by Matthew Tilghman, the very model of the "bashaw" against whom John Adams had inveighed in his letter to Patrick Henry, the delegates fought off all efforts to liberalize the document. The House of Delegates was to be elected annually, but the senators, fifteen in number, were chosen for five-year terms by electors.

The principal figures in the framing of the New York constitution were John Jay, Gouverneur Morris, and Robert Livingston. They were all young lawyers; Jay, the oldest, was thirty-two. He belonged to an old Huguenot family that had come to America in 1686 and had married into the Knickerbocker family. Livingston had been at King's College (now Columbia) with Jay, and he was also a member of one of the most prominent and powerful families in the state. Gouverneur Morris was

only twenty-four, a New York aristocrat like his friends Jay and Livingston. All three were basically conservative in their outlook, all three were
scholars. Morris was the most exotic of the lot, the most articulate in
debate, given to the flamboyant gesture, and very much of a gallant. Jay
wrote to John Rutledge (the two had been allies in the Second Continental Congress, fighting unsuccessfully against the radicals) in July, 1776:
"We have a government, you know, to form; and God only knows what
it will resemble. Our politicians, like guests at a feast, are perplexed and
undetermined which dish to prefer."

New York was under such heavy military pressure from Howe that
the beleaguered assembly did not get around to debating a draft of the
constitution until March, 1777. There is some obscurity surrounding
the adoption of the New York constitution; the initial draft was apparently written by Jay. His son recalled years after the event that his father
had told of working on the constitution. In the son's words, "Upon
reflecting on the character and feelings of the Convention he thought it
prudent to omit in the draft several provisions that appeared to him
improvements, and afterwards to propose them separately as amendments. . . . It is probable that the Convention was ultra-democratic, for I
have heard him observe that another turn of the winch would have
cracked the cord."

It seems most improbable that the convention was "ultra-democratic," because the document that they approved was certainly not. It
was conservative in the sense that it followed closely on John Adams'
notion of a proper balance between the various branches of the government; and while the other state constitutions had shown a distrust of
executive power, the New York constitution was distinguished by the
fact that it provided for the direct popular election of the governor and
came closer to giving him powers adequate to his office than any other
constitution. Both senate and assembly were directly elected, the assembly annually, the senate quadrennially. Proportional representation was
set in the assembly; the state was divided in four large districts, each
sending six senators. Only freeholders could vote for members of the
assembly, and they must have property of the value of twenty pounds.

The constitution was finally adopted in April, 1777, by a vote of
thirty-two to one, with only a third of the convention still in attendance.
Since Georgia had passed its constitution on the fifth of February, 1777,
New York was the last of the thirteen states to adopt a formal frame of
government. The time from the framing of New Hampshire's rather

nugatory constitution, adopted on January 5, 1776, to that of New York covered a period of some sixteen months.

The Pennsylvania constitution is a fascinating document. It was the high-water mark of the democratic idealism expressed most typically in Thomas Paine's *Common Sense*. Despite its awkwardness and impracticality, it had about it a spaciousness of spirit that did credit to its framers. For whatever combination of reasons—and the principal one was undoubtedly that the stubborn resistance of the conservatives to independence had destroyed their power in the state and had removed them from the arena of local politics at least for the moment—Pennsylvania came up with the most original, one might safely say bizarre, constitution of all the thirteen states, as well as (by no means coincidentally) the most democratic one. Pennsylvania had freed itself with considerable difficulty from the control of the Quaker oligarchy, whose domination of the assembly had blocked all efforts by the patriots to place that colony in the forefront of resistance to parliamentary taxation. Now, with that power finally broken, the more radical patriots turned their attention to framing a constitution that would place power securely in their own hands. A week after John Nixon had read the Declaration of Independence to the assembled citizens of Philadelphia, the Pennsylvania Constitutional Convention gathered in the State House.

The western Pennsylvanians, who had long felt themselves inadequately represented in the assembly, lent a sympathetic ear to some of the more radical political theorists of Philadelphia. The "bawling Dr. Young," a kind of peripatetic revolutionist whose practice it was to travel about and try to win over members of constitutional conventions in various states to his radical doctrines, seems to have exerted considerable influence. Timothy Matlack was another stout democrat. He was abetted by James Cannon, a Scotsman and teacher of mathematics at the College of Philadelphia, who declared that all learning was an "artificial constraint on human understanding," and that the uninstructed intelligence was the best. A number of the delegates were described as "honest well meaning Country men . . . intirely unacquainted with such matters," men "hardly equal to the Task to form a new plan of government"; an unsympathetic conservative dismissed them as "numsculs." Thomas Smith, who had been a strong supporter of the proprietary party in the colony, and was himself a delegate, wrote, " . . . not a sixth part of us ever read a word on the subject [of government] but I believe we might have at least prevented ourselves from being ridiculous in the eyes of the world were it not for a few enthusiastic members who are totally unacquainted with the principles of government. It is not only that their notions are original," he added, "but that they would go to the devil for popularity."

The preamble of the Pennsylvania document is a revealing one. The king of England was carrying "with unabated vengeance, a most cruel and unjust war . . . employing therein not only the troops of Great Britain, but foreign mercenaries, savages and slaves, for the avowed purpose of reducing [the colonies] to a total and abject submission to the despotic domination of the British Parliament." The colonies were thus relieved of their former allegiance and now must "as free and independent States" form "permanent and proper forms of government . . . derived from and founded on the authority of the people only. . . ."

The representatives "of the freemen of Pennsylvania" had met, "confessing the goodness of the great Governour of the universe (who alone knows to what degree of earthly happiness mankind may attain by perfecting the arts of government) permitting the people of this State, by common consent, and without violence, deliberately to form for themselves such just rules as they shall think best for governing their future society." It was their intention, the delegates declared, "to establish such original principles of government as will best promote the general happiness of the people of this State and their posterity, and provide for future improvements, without partiality for or prejudice against any particular class, sect, or denomination of men whatever. . . ."

The prefacing "Declaration of Rights" was modeled on that of Virginia, but with several interesting additions. One, out of deference to the Quakers, stated that no man could be forced to bear arms "if he will pay such equivalent." Another stated the right of people to emigrate from one state to another "or to form a new State in vacant countries . . . whenever they think that thereby they may promote their own happiness." The clause advanced the interests of the land speculators, of which there were a number in Pennsylvania, and joined their interests with those of settlers who might wish to move west.

In the main body of the constitution were provisions for a single legislative body, popularly elected, with the supreme executive power lodged in a president and a council. The most radical or advanced part of the Pennsylvania constitution was contained in the next article, which quaranteed the vote to "every freeman of the full age of 21 years, having resided in this State for the space of one whole year . . . and paid public taxes during that time . . . Provided always, that sons of freeholders of the age of 21 years shall be entitled to vote although they have not paid taxes." This was the farthest toward universal white manhood suffrage that any state except New Hampshire was willing to go. Members of the House of Representatives were to be persons "most noted for wisdom and virtue," the constitution declared hopefully, and none could serve for more than four years in seven.

There was a further democratic impulse behind the statement that the doors of the House of Representatives should always "remain open for the admission of all persons who behave decently," and in the provision that the "votes and proceedings of the General Assembly shall be printed weekly during their sitting, with the yeas and nays, on any question. . . ."

The *Pennsylvania Evening Post* spoke out engagingly for annual elections. "A poor man," a writer for the *Post* observed, "has rarely the honor of speaking to a gentleman on any terms, and never with familiarity but for a few weeks before the election. How many poor men, common men, and mechanics, have been made happy . . . by a shake of the hand, a pleasing smile, and a little familiar chat with gentlemen who have not for these seven years past condescended to look at them. . . . Thus the right of annual elections will ever oblige gentlemen to speak to you once a year, who would despise you forever, were it not that you can bestow something upon them."

To prevent those hasty and ill-considered actions so feared by political philosophers and to which single-branch legislatures were thought to be particularly prone, the Pennsylvania constitution provided that "all bills of a public nature" must be "printed for the consideration of the people" before they are voted on and "shall not be passed into laws until the next session of assembly. . . ."

Like the governor of Virginia, the president of Pennsylvania was carefully hedged about with restraints on his power. He could do little without the concurrence of his council, and he could be easily impeached for acting in defiance of the constitution or for malfeasance in office. The judges of the state supreme court were to be appointed for seven years only, at the end of which time they might be appointed for an additional term. Thus were combined the principle of judicial independence on the one hand and the accountability of justices to the people on the other.

One of the most enlightened provisions of the Pennsylvania constitution was the article that forbade keeping a debtor in prison "after delivering up . . . all his estate real and personal for the use of his creditors. . . ." The debtors laws that left a man to rot in jail until all his debts were paid were cruel survivals of a harsher age.

Another reform designed to lessen the necessity of "visible punishments of long duration" and of "sanguinary punishments" provided that "convicted criminals should be punished by hard labour . . . for the benefit of the public, or for reparation of injuries done to private persons. . . ."

The radical idealists who drafted the constitution were anxious, as reformers always are, to legislate sin and corruption out of existence. They thus provided that any voter who received "any gift or reward for his vote in meat, drink, monies or otherwise, shall forfeit his right to elect for that time. . . ." This presumably rules out the political barbecue. By the same token, any aspiring politician who resorted to such common but debased methods of attracting votes would be "thereby rendered incapable to serve" at least for "the ensuing year," which was plainly a practical compromise with the well-known inclination of those seeking public office to blandish the electors.

The problem of what to do about remunerating public and elected officers was clearly a puzzling one to the democratic reformers. It was clear that men should not seek public office because of monetary considerations. However, to refuse to attach stipends to offices would undoubtedly create a tendency to abandon the field to those candidates who could afford to serve without pay. Again a compromise seemed called for. "As every freeman to preserve his independence (if without a sufficient estate) ought to have some profession, calling, trade or farm whereby he may honestly subsist," the Pennsylvania article in question read, there should be no need "nor use in establishing offices of profit, the usual effects of which are dependence and servility unbecoming freemen" and "faction, contention, corruption and disorder among the people. . . ." However, if any man was "called into public service to the prejudice of his private affairs," he had a right to reasonable compensation. Nonetheless, when an office became so lucrative that people actually applied for it, "the profits ought to be lessened by the Legislature."

The provisions regarding the period of residency required for citizenship and public education were notably liberal: Foreigners of good character could hold land in the state, and after a year's residence would be entitled to all the rights of a natural-born subject of the state. The legislature should, moreover, undertake to establish schools in each county, "for the convenient instruction of youth, with such salaries to the masters paid by the public as may enable them to instruct youth at low prices: And all useful learning shall be duly encouraged and promoted in one or more universities."

Perhaps the most eccentric feature of this Utopian document was the so-called Council of Censors, elected every seven years, "whose duty it shall be to enquire whether the Constitution had been preserved inviolate in every part. . . ." The council, copied from ancient Rome, was directed to recommend to the legislature the repeal of "such laws as appear to [the Censors] to have been enacted contrary to the principles of the Constitution" and to call a convention to amend the constitution when, in their judgment, amendments were necessary.

From the first, the Pennsylvania constitution had its critics. The idea of a unicameral legislature offended John Adams. "No country ever will be long happy, or ever entirely safe and free, which is thus governed," he wrote a friend, and he wrote to Abigail, "We live in an age of political experiments. Among many that will fail, some, I hope, will succeed. But Pennsylvania will be divided and weakened, and rendered much less vigorous in the cause by the wretched ideas of government which prevail in the minds of many people in it."

The opposition to the constitution, led by John Dickinson and Robert Morris, was so bitter and determined that efforts to organize the new government were frustrated for almost four months—until a threat by Congress to take over administration of the state finally broke the conservative resistance. After the democratic idealism of the Pennsylvania radicals has been given full credit, the fact remains that their doctrinaire insistence on features that were sure to alienate many of their fellow citizens resulted in the state's being wracked with dissension for almost ten years and diminished the effectiveness of its rule in the war itself.

What is perhaps most astonishing of all is not that the constitutions were framed—obviously something had to be done to provide legitimate governments—but that they survived in a number of instances for fifty years or more and in that time worked reasonably well. Most important of all, the state constitutions were an indispensable preliminary to the formation of the United States Constitution. There is hardly a single idea or article contained in the Federal Constitution that was not first proposed or assayed in a state constitution, with the important exception of the role of the Supreme Court. We often are inclined to think of our national constitution as something that, in some miraculous way, sprang fully formed from the brains of the men who met at the Philadelphia State House in the summer of 1787. Virtually all of the leading figures in the Federal Convention had served their apprenticeships in the constitutional conventions of their own states. They had thought through and fought through principles that, in most cases, they were eager to apply to a national constitution. Indeed, if we were to trace the ideas most warmly espoused by various delegates to the Federal Convention, we would find that these were for the most part ideas that the same men had championed, successfully or unsuccessfully, in their own state conventions.

It has been truly said that the state constitutions, like the Federal Constitution, were the work of a prosperous aristocracy in the South and of an upper-class professional and business elite in the middle states and New England. Most of these men had profound reservations about what they thought of as "democracy"—the direct and unlimited rule of the majority. They believed that all men were stained by original sin and if allowed free rein would behave in a greedy, selfish, and ultimately destructive way. Yet in state after state the more liberal spirits prevailed. In Virginia, "the Bashaws, the grandees, the patricians" were put down, their plans overthrown. In New York, it seemed many years after the event that the "ultra-democrats" had prevailed. While all the constitutions were basically conservative in the sense that they were based on a conservative view of human nature, all of them contained a large measure of that radical idealism, outspoken for its own day, that had informed the patriot cause from its inception; the new consciousness was everywhere evident. It is thus insipid for us today to indict the constitutions framed in those months for being conservative or undemocratic; to most of those people who had held in their hands the agencies and instruments of power, they seemed shockingly radical, and if we cannot recapture at least some of that perspective—the perspective from which the Edmund Randolphs, the Carter Braxtons, and their counterparts in other states viewed the new frames of government—we cannot understand them at all or appreciate the fact that by and large they represented a new vision of the terms under which members of human societies might live together.

If we take Pennsylvania as a classic case, we might recall that from the beginning of the period of resistance to the power of Parliament to tax the colonies, there were leading men in Pennsylvania who rejected outright any argument that proposed a limitation on the authority of Parliament, and who viewed any resistance as little short of treason. By the time of the First Continental Congress, these men had, by and large, withdrawn in sullen resentment and frustration from the political scene. The leadership of the state was in the hands of men like Joseph Galloway, less conservative and traditional, but only slightly. On this "ideological level" were grouped Galloway's allies and supporters. After Galloway's failure to block the nonimportation agreements and to prevail upon the delegates to take a moderate line, he and his followers dropped out. At this point John Dickinson and Robert Morris, as the next rank or level of moderate politicians, assumed leadership. Their stubborn resistance to independence lost them their influence and their control over the political affairs of the state. They, in turn, gave way, albeit briefly as it turned out, to the George Bryans, James Cannons, and Timothy Matlacks.

While the process described went further in Pennsylvania than in any other colony, a process roughly similar went on in all the colonies or states. Layers of conservative leadership were, in a manner of speaking, stripped away by successive crises until at last the more radical or resolute patriots in each state held the reins of government. At the same time there was an important counterweight to the radicals. In most states the need to preserve unity in the face of the enemy had the effect of disposing the radical leaders to compromise with the moderate and conservative patriots. Such men, powerful, experienced, wealthy, could not simply be tossed aside. Their support was vital to the revolutionary cause. The moderates and conservatives for their part were brought to accept constitutions that, in many instances, were a good deal more radical (or republican) than they would have wished. The pressure of an invading army and their desire to preserve unity in the patriot ranks disposed them to compromise. The unhappy condition of Pennsylvania, virtually immobilized by the bitter political divisions that were the consequence of its "radical" constitution, served as a sobering example of the dangers of pushing doctrinaire views too far and riding roughshod over the sentiments of many staunch patriots in the process.

13

England, 1776

THROUGH most of the Revolution, large majorities in both the House of Commons and the House of Lords supported measures aimed at defeating America and bringing the rebellious colonies to heel. Yet it is important to keep in mind that America had, all through the revolutionary crisis, eloquent and courageous English friends who resolutely opposed the measures taken by Parliament against the colonies.

One of those most loyal to the American cause was Augustus Fitzroy, Duke of Grafton, who while prime minister had unsuccessfully urged the repeal of the tea duty. After trying to push the North government in the direction of conciliation, he went over to the opposition in the fall of 1775, declaring in Parliament that he had "concurred when he could not approve," in the hope that a strong and united Parliament would be more disposed to an "amicable adjustment with the colonies than a fractious and divided one." He then recommended that all acts relating to America that had been passed since 1767 be repealed. Henry Conway followed Grafton and, like him, fought in vain from the opposition bench for a more liberal policy.

Charles James Fox was also pro-American. Only twenty-seven years old in 1776, a volatile and dissipated young man, he had been dismissed from a relatively minor government position as a commissioner of the

Treasury by Lord North for insubordination. At once Fox became an ally of Edmund Burke as one of the most brilliant exponents of the American cause in Parliament.

It was the historian William Lecky's judgment that opinion in England as a whole was, in 1775 and 1776, much more evenly divided than it was in Parliament. The problem was that a large majority of the "most powerful and most intelligent classes" supported the government. Sir Charles Pratt, Earl of Camden, wrote in February, 1775, "I am grieved to observe that the landed interest is almost altogether anti-American, though the common people hold the war in abhorrence, and the merchants and tradesmen, for obvious reasons, are likewise against it." The Church of England establishment was also vigorously anti-American, and the bishops who sat in the House of Lords supported all coercive measures. The two great universities of Oxford and Cambridge were strongholds of anti-American sentiment, and most of the influential lawyers and judges were similarly disposed. Horace Walpole declared in 1776, "The Court have now at their devotion the three great bodies of the clergy, army, and law"—in other words, the principal organs of the established order.

There was also strong support of the government in literary circles. Dr. Samuel Johnson was caustically anti-American to the distress of his biographer James Boswell, and Edward Gibbon, the historian of Rome's decline and fall, was one of Lord North's most loyal adherents in Parliament.

The greatest support for the Americans came from the Dissenting and Nonconforming Protestants, those bodies that, like the Quakers and Methodists, had a marginal position in British life and had themselves done battle, in some instances for a century or more, against the guardians of the old order. Richard Price, a Presbyterian minister, wrote an *Essay on Liberty* in 1775 that strongly espoused the colonial cause, and in two years the pamphlet passed through eight editions.

The Reverend John Wesley, the founder of Methodism and the most popular evangelical preacher of the day, also took up the American cause. He wrote Lord Dartmouth a rather overblown account of the suffering and discontent in England that was occasioned by the Coercive Acts and the colonial resistance: "I aver," Wesley wrote, "that in every part of England where I have been (and I have been east, west, north and south within these two years) trade in general is exceedingly decayed, and thousands of people are quite unemployed. . . . The bulk of the people in every city, town and village where I've been, do not so much aim at the Ministry . . . but at the King himself. He is the object of their anger, contempt and malice. They heartily despise his Majesty and hate him with a perfect hatred. They wish to imbue their hands in his blood, they are full of the spirit of murder and rebellion . . . It is as much as ever I can do, to keep this plague from infecting my own friends . . . Never did the recruiting parties meet with such ill success in every part of this Kingdom as at present, so invincible is the dislike of all ranks of people to the American service. The inhabitants of Bandon, Youghall, Birr, and other towns have entered into a resolution not to suffer any among them to enlist for the purpose of enslaving their American brethren. . . ." Those who had been drafted as replacements for regiments in America swore "they will never draw a trigger against the Americans, among whom they have all relations. . . ."

Wesley called North's attention to the disproportion between the British and American losses at Lexington and Concord. "You see, my lord," he continued, "whatever has been affirmed, these men will not be frightened, and it seems they will not be conquered as easily as was at first imagined. They will probably dispute every inch of ground, and, if they die, die with sword in hand. . . . They are as strong men as you; they are as valiant as you if not abundantly more valiant, for they are one and all enthusiasts, enthusiasts for liberty . . . We know men animated with this spirit, will leap into a fire, or rush into a cannon's mouth." Lord North, Wesley said, had been fed a constant stream of misinformation on which he had based his policy. He had been told that the colonies were "divided among themselves," but such divisions, Wesley warned were superficial—"my lord, they are terribly united."

Wesley went on to enumerate the practical advantages that the colonists would enjoy in a prolonged war: the sense that they were fighting for their homes and families; easier access to supplies than the British, who would have to transport theirs over the ocean; the possibility that the Americans would seek and get substantial foreign aid—that France and Spain might take the opportunity to settle old scores with Great Britain. Perhaps most dangerous of all, there was "the general disposition of the people" of England to consider. They, Wesley assured North, "are exasperated almost to madness . . . ripe for open rebellion." It seemed to Wesley that the judgment of God Himself might be on England for its "shocking impiety," for its luxury and its indifference to the claims of truth and justice.

Wesley was by no means alone in his gloomy prophecies about the effects of British policy. Catharine Macaulay, a lady historian who corresponded with Mercy Otis Warren and John Adams, wrote an "address to the People of England, Scotland Ireland" on the American crisis. "If a civil war commences between Great Britain and her Colonies," she wrote, "either the Mother Country, by one great exertion may ruin herself and America, or the Americans, by a lingering contest, will gain an independency. . . ." And England will become "an easy prey to the courts of France and Spain, who, you may depend upon it, will fall upon you as soon as they see you fairly engaged in a war with your Colonists." The address ended with an appeal to Britons to rouse themselves "from that state of guilty dissipation in which you have too long remained, and in which, if you longer continue, you are lost forever."

Wesley's analysis of the state of mind of the common people of Great Britain was echoed by a number of more or less impartial observers. The exotic Frenchman Beaumarchais, jeweler, musician, playwright, and confidant of the king of France, wrote to that monarch in September, 1775, to inform him that "England is in such a crisis, such a state of disorder within and without, that it would be almost on the point of ruin if her neighbors and rivals were themselves in a state to occupy themselves seriously about her." The philosopher David Hume, in most other matters a Tory, joined in denouncing British policy toward the colonies. The effort to make Americans into loyal and obedient subjects by force of arms, Hume declared could lead to nothing but "disaster and ruin."

Public opinion is, of course, notoriously volatile. The attitudes of many Britishers toward the Americans certainly contained a measure of ambivalence and often shifted according to the fortunes of war. In August of 1775, Edmund Burke, the most steadfast friend of America in Parliament, wrote to Rockingham, "I am satisfied that within a few years there had been a great change on the national character. We seem no longer that eager, inquisitive, zealous, fiery people which we have been formerly. . . . No man commands the measures which have been pursued, or expects any good from those which are in preparation, but it is a cold, languid opinion, like what men discover in affairs that do not concern them. . . ." And a month later Burke wrote, "The real fact is that the generality of the people of England are now led away by the misrepresentations and arts of the Ministry, the Court and their abettors, so that the violent measures towards America are fairly adopted and countenanced by a majority of individuals of all ranks, professions, or occupations in this country"—exclusive, of course, of those nonpeople, the laboring classes of Great Britain, the vast majority of the population who were without a voice in the halls of Parliament.

Pitt, when his health permitted, remained a strong advocate of the Americans. He had persuaded his eldest son to withdraw from the army rather than be sent to fight in America. There was a dramatic scene in Parliament when Kenneth Howard, Earl of Effingham, also resigned his commission. Lord Effingham, who had served for nine years in the army and had the rank of captain in the Twenty-second Regiment, declared the Americans "have come to you with fair arguments, you have refused to hear them; they have made the most respectful remonstrances, you answer them with bills of pains and penalties; they know they ought to be free, you tell them they shall be slaves. . . . In this dreadful moment, a set of men more wise and moderate than the rest exert themselves to bring us all to reason. They state their claims and their grievances; nay, if anything can be proved by law and history, they prove them. . . . Ever since I was of an age to have any ambition at all, my highest has been to serve my country in a military capacity. . . . It is not small sacrifice a man makes, who gives up his profession. . . ."

The City of London, led by Lord Mayor John Wilkes, voted thanks to Effingham for resigning his commission and then addressed a letter to the king, denouncing the ministerial policy toward America as a tyranny that ran counter to the very principles that underlay his own throne. After the Battle of Bunker Hill, Charles Lennox, Duke of Richmond, declared that "he did not think that the Americans were in rebellion, but that they were resisting acts of the most unexampled cruelty and oppression." John Horne Tooke, the political radical, raised a subscription for the widows and children of Americans who had been wounded or killed at Lexington and accused the British soldiers who were at Lexington of murder.

Popular opinion in Britain swung sharply in favor of the war, however, as the year 1776 progressed. English morale, which had sunk so low after the news of the Battle of Bunker Hill, revived with General Howe's successes on Long Island and in New York. The Declaration of Independence, which seemed to those British who troubled to read it to be a piece of windy bombast, apparently removed all hope of reconciliation. The people of a nation at war can be readily mustered in support, especially if the war goes well; the deepest sentiments of loyalty and nationalistic zeal are commonly roused. The friends of America were, for a time, virtually silenced, and many of the Rockinghamites, finding themselves defeated by great majorities in Parliament, stayed away. For the first time since the beginning of the trouble with the colonies in 1765, it could be said that the majority of Englishmen of all but the lowest classes supported the government. The effects of American raids on British commerce caused widespread hardships and increased the bitterness towards the rebels. Sir George Savile, a staunch Whig, writing to Rockingham in January, 1777, declared: "We are not only patriots out of place, but patriots out of the opinion of the public. The reputed successes, hollow as I think them, and the more ruinous if they are real, have fixed or converted ninety-nine in one hundred. The cause wears itself away by degrees from a question of right and wrong between subjects, to a war between us and a foreign nation, in which justice is never heard, because love of one's country, which is a more favourite virtue, is on the other side. I see marks of this everywhere and in all ranks."

Burke lamented this unreasoning swing in popular opinion. He wrote to Fox in the spring of 1777 that "the popular humor" was worse than it had ever been before in regard to America. Bristol, which was Burke's own constituency, had just voted the freedom of the city to the vindictive Earl of Sandwich, First Lord of the Admiralty. In Liverpool, Burke noted, "they are literally almost ruined by this American war, but they love it as they suffer from it." "The Tories," he added, "do universally think their power and consequence involved in the success of this American business."

Burke's warnings that Britain was pursuing a hopeless course and could never extract a revenue from America fell on deaf ears, as did his argument that practical considerations rather than philosophical principles should guide British policy. One of the things that troubled Burke most was that dissent was suppressed on the ground that it constituted treason. In the process, traditional principles of British liberty were discredited, and the Tory party, indifferent to ancient rights and freedoms, was so strengthened that hopes of ever overturning it seemed infinitely remote. Just the fact that the Americans presented themselves as champions of British liberties served to discredit those liberties in England. The Duke of Richmond was convinced that Parliament, an increasingly pliant tool of Lord North and the king, might perfectly well establish a new despotism.

The Whigs were stigmatized as un-British, a treacherous faction that put their own notions of justice above the interests of their country. Fox, the brilliant and energetic orator, was especially susceptible to this charge. Convinced that the seats of power would be forever shut to him,

Fox was merciless in his castigation of the ministry. Indeed, his inclination to exult over American victories and British defeats greatly reduced his influence. He described (though not in public) the news of Howe's success on Long Island as "the terrible news from Long Island." In Parliament, he predicted the entry into the war of France and Spain and did so as though he looked forward to the event as punishment to the British.

The more isolated the Whigs became, the more feverish and extreme their rhetoric seemed to grow. Speeches praising Washington and Franklin were made in the House of Commons, Sir Gilbert Elliot, a moderate Tory, complained bitterly about "the parricide joy of some in the losses of their country. . . . They don't disguise it. A patriotic Duke told me some weeks ago that some ships had been lost off the coast of North America in a storm. He said 1,000 British sailors were drowned—not one escaped—with joy sparkling in his eyes. . . . in the House of Commons it is not unusual [for Whigs] to speak of the Provincials as 'our army.'"

By running so persistently in the face of popular feeling, the Whigs, in the opinion of many, simply strengthened the government. Such, in any event, was Sir Gilbert Elliot's view. The North ministry, he believed, had made errors that would have brought it down had it not been for the relentless attacks of the Whigs. "It was the wish of Great Britain to recover America. Government aimed at least at this object, which the Opposition rejected." That the Whigs were often intemperate is certainly true, but it is equally true that they were right in rejecting the notion that Great Britain could "recover America" except at the price of virtually destroying that country and bringing on a revolution at home. And since they were convinced that the policy of the government was not merely a hopeless but also a disastrous one, it is not to be wondered that they grew increasingly bitter.

It was evident to the Whigs that the king more and more was taking the direction of affairs into his own hands. Nothing of importance was done without his orders or his concurrence, and it was rumored that even speeches in Parliament were outlined by him and assigned to Tory orators. This development appeared to the Whigs, not unnaturally, as a frightening accretion of royal power. As Lecky puts it: "It was not merely that he claimed a commanding voice in every kind of appointment. The details of military management, the whole course and character of the war . . . were prescribed by him; and ministers . . . were prepared to act simply as his agents, even in direct opposition to their own judgments."

A case in point was Lord Barrington, the minister of war, who had stated as early as 1774 that the colonies could not be coerced into obedience to Great Britain, but who remained as a reluctant servant of the king until the end of 1778. "Every means of distressing America," the king wrote, "must meet with my concurrence." George III's correspondence tells the tale of his constant chivvying and exhorting of an often vacillating and dispirited North. The king bombarded North with letters when he could not confer with him in person, and he brought further pressure to bear through a close friend of North's, John Robinson, a minor official in the Treasury. George III wrote North soon after the news of Trenton: "The accounts from America are most comfortable. The surprise and want of spirit in the Hessian officers as well as the soldiers at Trenton is not much to their credit, and will undoubtedly rather elate the rebels, who till then were in a state of the greatest despondency. . . . but I am certain by a letter I have seen from Lord Cornwallis that the rebels will soon have sufficient reason to fall into the former dejection. . . ." The king believed that a firm hand was all that was needed to bring the Americans around. The Indians should be used for their ability to terrorize; any inclination to leniency or mercy should be sternly suppressed. Fear was the only agency that could be counted on to bring the colonists to a more tractable mood.

Against the determination of the king, all the arguments and invective of the Whigs was unavailing. In Lecky's words: "A party [the Whigs], small indeed in numbers, but powerful from its traditions, its connections, and its abilities, had identified itself completely with the cause of the insurgents, opposed and embarrassed the Government in every effort to augment its forces and to subsidise allies, openly rejoiced in the victories of the Americans, and exerted all its eloquence to justify and to encourage them." But for all the Whigs' energy and passionate resistance to what they saw as fatal policies, the king and the North ministry went blindly ahead with the war. It might even be argued that the Whigs, by their tenacity and aggressiveness, kept North and his party constantly on the defensive and more preoccupied with exculpating themselves than with seeking a resolution of the American conflict. By this line it could be maintained that ultimately they did a disservice to the American cause and prolonged the war by confusing that issue with party politics in England. But this is a tendentious and precarious argument. It was most important that the genuine moral outrage that the Whigs felt toward the efforts of the government to beat the Americans into submission be openly and eloquently expressed. By doing so, the Whigs kept open both the hope of reconciliation and the possibility of reform in British society itself.

Although the Whigs did not prevent the disastrous policy of the government or manage to terminate the war at any of those half-dozen points at which its futility was plain enough to any sensible man, they nonetheless performed an essential function by constantly enunciating (and thereby keeping alive) the great principles of British constitutional liberty. They did this with courage and resolution, often in the face of heavy pressure from their colleagues and constant imputations concerning their loyalty. I believe that they thereby saved Britain from a social revolution more ferocious and destructive than the French Revolution, because they preserved that faint but persistent hope among the commonalty of England that justice might finally be done them, that principles might ultimately become practice.

No matter how heedless, insensate, materialistic, selfish, unjust, and greedy a society may be, if there can be found in it a few clear and powerful voices that speak out unafraid against its corruptions, the spirit and the hope of reform can persist. The Whigs, unsuccessful as they were, stood as proof to the Americans that their sacrifices were in a great cause; that they were fighting for more than selfish ends; that they had brothers of the same faith in their former homeland. These matters are not quantifiable, they cannot be fed into computers and reduced to columns of statistics, to charts and diagrams; but they are, perhaps for that very reason, the quintessence of the drama of history, as everyone who has felt them vibrate in his own heart knows.